THE 43rd LIGHT INFANTRY
IN MESOPOTAMIA AND
NORTH RUSSIA

COLONEL E. A. E. LETHBRIDGE, C.M.G., D.S.O.

HISTORY *of the* 43rd *and* 52nd (Oxfordshire and Buckinghamshire) LIGHT INFANTRY *in the* GREAT WAR, 1914-1919

VOLUME I

THE 43rd LIGHT INFANTRY IN MESOPOTAMIA AND NORTH RUSSIA

By

CAPTAIN J. E. H. NEVILLE, M.C.
(Late 43rd Light Infantry)

Ὦ ξεῖν', ἀγγείλον Λακεδαιμονίοις ὅτι τῇδε
Κείμεθα τοῖς κείνων ῥήμασι πειθόμενοι.

Epitaph on those who fell at Thermopylae.   SIMONIDES.

To England, stranger, let thy tidings fly
That here, obedient to her words, we lie.

The Naval & Military Press Ltd

Reproduced by kind permission of the Central Library,
Royal Military Academy, Sandhurst

Published by
The Naval & Military Press Ltd
Unit 10, Ridgewood Industrial Park,
Uckfield, East Sussex,
TN22 5QE England
Tel: +44 (0) 1825 749494
Fax: +44 (0) 1825 765701
www.naval-military-press.com
www.military-genealogy.com

© The Naval & Military Press Ltd 2008

In reprinting in facsimile from the original, any imperfections are inevitably reproduced and the quality may fall short of modern type and cartographic standards.

Printed and bound by Lightning Source

TO
THE OFFICERS
WARRANT OFFICERS, NON-COMMISSIONED OFFICERS
BUGLERS AND PRIVATES
WHO HAD THE HONOUR TO SERVE IN THE
43RD LIGHT INFANTRY
DURING THE WAR 1914 TO 1919
AND TO THOSE NOW SERVING
THIS BOOK IS
DEDICATED

AUTHOR'S PREFACE

THIS volume gives the story of the 43rd's service in Mesopotamia and North Russia during the war 1914-1919; and is a harbinger of that of the 52nd now being written by a pre-eminently competent hand.

Histories have already appeared covering the service of the 1st/4th and 2nd/4th Battalions; the 1st/1st and 2nd/1st Buckinghamshire and the 7th Battalions.

When the author volunteered to compile this story he was fully aware that he could not please everybody. He set himself a standard; and in this story of the 43rd in the Mesopotamia Campaign he has tried to include every relevant detail. There may be those who will think that this book contains much matter that never concerned the 43rd. To them it should be pointed out that every cause has an effect; and to make history intelligible it is as necessary to trace the causes as to describe the effects. The student of history soon realizes how fine are the threads on which hang great destinies. The Government primarily controls war by defining the policy to be pursued, and the Services carry out its dictates. Therefore the policy, which in the Mesopotamia Campaign was by no means constant, should be recorded. Furthermore, extraneous influences bore on the operations and these have been shortly sketched.

In the accounts of the operations themselves it has often been necessary to detail minutely the actions of troops other than the Regiment; for the reason that originally the operations in Mesopotamia were on a very small scale compared with those in France. There there were no night marches over unmapped terrain, and the only uncovered flank soon lay on the Belgian coast. In Mesopotamia co-operation between forces, widely separated, figured largely; and the success or failure of an operation depended upon the actions of other troops and formations.

Finally the author's plea for political and military detail lies in his desire that the story of the 43rd in Mesopotamia and North Russia shall be fit for the student rather than the dilettante; and that any who reads it shall be able to comprehend the diversities of the two campaigns from every standpoint: that it shall, in fact, be fit to be referred to by present and future generations of the Regiment.

It will be seen that this book contains a host of footnotes and references to authorities. These were found necessary directly the typescript was sent round for criticism to those who served in Mesopotamia. The author soon found that he had to be prepared to substantiate practically every sentence by a footnote as proof that he was not a slave to his imagination. A very great historian has said that he who writes history without using his imagination should confine his activities to rhymes for Christmas crackers; yet the blunt and prosaic critics refused to allow any artistic embellishments. They were undoubtedly right.

Many references might well have been omitted before going to print, but as they may help the real student of the campaigns they have been included *in toto*. For the abbreviations of the authorities used in the footnotes the reader is requested to refer to the bibliography on page xxiv.

The author wishes to record his grateful thanks to the following who, by their criticisms, corrections and co-operation, have contributed to the accuracy of the story of the 43rd in Mesopotamia during the war of 1914-1918:—

Major-General H. R. Davies, C.B., chairman of the history committee, who read the manuscript, typescript and proofs, and whose suggestions and advice have been followed throughout; Major-General L. H. R. Pope-Hennessy, C.B., D.S.O.; Brigadier F. H. Stapleton, C.M.G.; Colonel E. A. E. Lethbridge, C.M.G., D.S.O.; Lieutenant-Colonel J. J. Powell; Lieutenant-Colonel G. E. Whittall, M.C.; Major W. E. T. Morland, D.S.O., M.C.; Major C. F. Henley; Major G. Naylor, M.C.; Major H. E. F. Smyth, M.C.; Captain W. Rance; Captain H. W. Bleeze; and Captain C. M. Banks.

The author is also indebted to Colonel Lethbridge for the loan of his memoirs; to Lieutenant-Colonel R. Stephens for his diaries and photographs of the early phases of the campaign; to Major Henley for his diary of the Qurna *Regatta* and march into captivity; to Major Morland for his copies of panoramas and bird's-eye views from Kut al Amara; to Major Naylor for his diaries of the whole campaign, including the Battles of Es Sinn and Ctesiphon, the siege of Kut and march into captivity; to Captain H. T. Birch Reynardson, C.M.G., for the loan of his collection of photographs and for permission to use his book, *Mesopotamia 1914-1915*; to Captain Sir John S. P. Mellor, Bart., for his account of the Battle of Ctesiphon and the Turkish attack on the Fort on Christmas Eve 1915; to Lieutenant T. P. Williams for his diary of the period when the 43rd was on the line of communications; to Major C. Fitzgerald, Lieutenant L. J. Rock, ex-Serjeants Bull and Ponting, and ex-Private Brinkman for their collections of photographs; to Captain Banks for panoramas, etc., of the Euphrates front; and to Captain J. W. Meade and Lieutenants D. S. Northcote and D. A. T. Wilmot.

It has been found possible to include only a small percentage of photographs so kindly lent. In making the difficult choice the committee decided to reproduce, as far as possible, those which have not already appeared in the Regimental *Chronicles* and *Journals*.

The Secretary of the Permanent Committee on Geographical Names of the Royal Geographical Society gave most valuable help in elucidating the approximate position and the correct spelling of many, though not all, of the villages mentioned phonetically in the various records of the march into captivity.

The thanks of the Regiment are also due to His Majesty's Stationery Office and the Imperial War Museum for permission to reproduce maps and certain photographs; and to Major N. V. L. Rybot, D.S.O., who has graciously allowed the reproduction of certain of his excellent panoramic and humorous sketches made during the siege of Kut al Amara.

The author would like to acknowledge the patient and tireless efforts of Captain F. M. Roberts, M.C., and his staff at the Depot, and ex-Regimental Serjeant-Major Love, D.C.M., and ex-Quartermaster-Serjeant Burbidge, D.C.M., who largely contributed to what accuracy attaches to the lists of prisoners in Appendix XI; and also the special help that Mr. Seager, of Gale & Polden, Ltd., has given the committee.

For criticism of the North Russian Campaign of 1919 the author is indebted to Lieutenant-Colonel C. S. Baines, D.S.O.; to Major H. E. F. Smyth, M.C.; to Major G. Naylor, M.C., and for the loan of his photographs, maps and orders; to Major P. Booth; Captain D. C. Colvill, M.C.; and to Captain L. W. Giles, M.C., and Captain H. J. King, Royal Warwickshire Regiment, who lent photographs.

And lastly the author takes this opportunity of thanking the most patient collaborator of all, his wife who, during his leisure hours of the past five years and more, has cheerfully endured first the silence while he was immersed in two, three or more tomes simultaneously; then the disorder of extracts and manuscripts strewn over her parlour; the dreary reading and correction of the manuscripts; the exasperating tap-tap of the typewriter at every available opportunity; the revision of the typed copies; and the reading and correction of the proofs. To her goodwill and unfailing encouragement the completion of this book is in no small measure due.

J. E. H. NEVILLE.

CONTENTS

CHAP.		PAGE
I.	BRITISH RELATIONS WITH TURKEY BEFORE THE WAR	1

German influence—The Baghdad Railway—Anglo-Russian Agreement of 1907—Results of the Turkish Revolution of 1908—The Turco-German Alliance—Turkey's strategical position—The Balkan wars—British interests in Anglo-Persian Oilfields.

| II. | THE ARMY IN INDIA BEFORE THE WAR | 4 |

Inadequacy of all equipment in 1914—Deficiency of munitions—Protection of Anglo-Persian Oilfields.

| III. | THE TURKS IN MESOPOTAMIA | 7 |

British interests in Mesopotamia before the war—Origin of British connection with the Persian Gulf—The Turkish Army—Dispositions of army corps—Turkish troops in Mesopotamia on the declaration of war—The Turkish and British policy from August to November 1914—Turkish mobilization—The *Goeben* and *Breslau*—Anti-British demonstrations in Basra—Anglo-Persian Oil Company requests protection—6th (Poona) Division earmarked for service in Mesopotamia—German intrigues—Proclamation of *Jehad*—Turco-German fleet bombards Russian ports—Declaration of war.

| IV. | GREAT BRITAIN DECLARES WAR | 13 |

Contrast in India—Mobilization of 6th (Poona) Division—Its composition—The 16th Brigade sails—General Delamain's instructions—The 43rd ordered to prepare for embarkation.

| V. | MESOPOTAMIA | 16 |

Extent — Geography — Rivers — Floods — Resources — Roads — Seasons — Diseases—Population—The tribes.

| VI. | OPENING OPERATIONS | 19 |

Arrival of 18th Brigade and Lieutenant-General Sir Arthur Barrett—The action at Saihan—Mirage—The action at Sahil—Capture of Basra—Future policy.

| VII. | THE 43RD TAKES THE FIELD | 22 |

Order of battle—Arrival at Maqil—Christmas with the 43rd—The 43rd reaches Qurna—Reconnaissance of Muzaibila—Fortification of Muzaira'a—Reconnaissance of Ruta—Turkish strength in January 1915—Basra threatened—Floods—Arab raid on Muzaira'a—Turkish threat on Ahwaz.

| VIII. | ON THE DEFENSIVE | 36 |

The pipe-line breached—Floods rise—*Bellum* brigade initiated—The 43rd flooded out of Muzaira'a—General situation—Affairs at Shaiba and Ahwaz—Reinforcements ordered.

CHAP.		PAGE
IX.	THE 43RD AT QURNA, MARCH 1915	40
	Flies and floods—*Bellum* parades—Euphrates Blockade Force—The Shaiba front—Sir John Nixon takes command—Battle of Shaiba—April 1915—The 43rd at Qurna—Turkish retreat from Shaiba—The 43rd on the Euphrates blockade—Policy in Mesopotamia defined—General Nixon advises offensive —Operations near Ahwaz—Dunlop's force advances towards Amara.	
X.	PRELIMINARIES TO THE ADVANCE TO AMARA	51
	Success of *bellum* brigade—Decision to attack Turkish position in *bellums*— *Bellum* practice—Preparations for attack—The Turkish position—The plan —The Qurna Regatta, 30th May—The 43rd's casualties—Attack on Abu Aran—Turkish retreat—Pursuit—Capture of Amara—The 43rd in Amara— Despatches.	
XI.	JUNE AND JULY IN AMARA	66
	Torrid heat—Casualties—Medical arrangements inadequate—Operations on Tigris and Euphrates—Arrival of Dunlop's force at Amara—Reconnaissance of Ali Gharbi by party of 43rd—Turkish threat from Nasiriya— Operations on the Euphrates—Capture of Nasiriya.	
XII.	POLITICAL AND MILITARY ASPECTS OF AN ADVANCE TO KUT AL AMARA	72
	Threat to oilfields and pipe-line—British Government agrees to capture of Kut—The advance to Kut al Amara—Turkish strength—Orders to advance—Heat and dust—Second line transport—Capture of Shaikh Saad—Turks hold Es Sinn—The 6th Division halts at Sannaiyat— Townshend's plan—Feint march on the right bank—The 18th Brigade advances—The 17th Brigade concentrates—The night march—The battle of Kut al Amara or Es Sinn—The 43rd attacks—Success—The 43rd's casualties—The final attack—Incidents of the battle—The night after the battle—The plight of the wounded—General Nixon's despatch.	
XIII.	RESULTS OF THE BATTLE	92
	Turkish retreat—Pursuit—The 43rd clears the battlefield—Turks evade pursuit—The 43rd rejoins at Aziziya—General Nixon's memorandum— Sir Beauchamp Duff warns the Viceroy—Memorandum by General Staff— Cabinet authorizes advance on Baghdad—Concentration at Aziziya— Townshend's estimate of Turkish strength—The advance to Ctesiphon— Capture of Zor—Townshend's preparations.	
XIV.	THE TURKISH POSITION AT CTESIPHON	104
	The plan—Order of battle of the 43rd—The approach march—The battle of Ctesiphon—Attack by " R " and " S " Companies under Captain Wynter— Lieutenant-Colonel Lethbridge's experiences—The 43rd's casualties—The aftermath of the battle—Turkish counter-attack—Plight of the wounded.	
XV.	THE RETREAT FROM CTESIPHON	122
	Townshend's *communiqué*—The 43rd reaches Lajj—Advance of enemy forces—Retreat continued—Affair at Umm at Tubul—The 17th Brigade acts as rear-guard and 43rd as rear party—Lieutenant Heawood's description—The 43rd reaches Kut.	
XVI.	POLITICAL AND MILITARY ASPECTS, DECEMBER, 1915	132
	Townshend's reasons for standing at Kut—The Turks invest Kut— Turkish attack on the 10th—The 43rd in the Fort—The Turks attack the Fort—The 43rd's defence—Casualties—Relief preparations—Nixon's problems—Transport difficulties—Aylmer commands relief expedition— Details of the 43rd outside Kut—Draft from England.	

CHAP.		PAGE
XVII.	JANUARY WITH THE RELIEF FORCE	148

Aylmer's difficulties—Townshend urges relief—The action at Shaikh Saad—Turks retreat—The action of Wadi and first attack on Hanna—General Nixon hands over command—Political and military aspect—The draft for the 43rd—Its experiences—January in Kut—Floods—Townshend finds supplies of food—His *communiqué* to the garrison.

XVIII.	FEBRUARY WITH THE RELIEF FORCE	167

February in Kut—The siege becomes passive—Townshend decides to issue horseflesh.

XIX.	MARCH WITH THE RELIEF FORCE	176

The Turkish position on the right bank—Aylmer decides to attack Dujaila—The approach march—Dujaila reported unoccupied—Attack postponed—Turks reinforce—Attack fails—Aylmer withdraws—Causes of failure—Gorringe supersedes Aylmer—Rest and training—March in Kut—Townshend's *communiqué*—Rations reduced—Floods.

XX.	SECOND ATTACK ON HANNA	191

Strength of 43rd—First attack on Sannaiyat, 6th April—2nd/43rd wiped out—Its casualties—Second attack on Sannaiyat—Capture of Bait Isa—Turkish counter-attack—Floods—Third attack on Sannaiyat fails—*Julnar* attempts to run the blockade—Last days in Kut—Negotiations for surrender—The 43rd marches to Shumran—Casualties during the siege—Honours and awards.

XXI.	THE 43RD IN CAPTIVITY	223

Officers separated from men—Mortality in the 43rd—The marching out state—The march into captivity—Brutality of Arab escort—The prisoners reach Baghdad—The train journey to Samarra—The march to Tikrit—Sharqat—Mosul—Terrible sufferings—The march to Ras al 'Ain—The train journey to Islahiya—The journey to Mamoura and march to Baghche—The 43rd prisoners detailed for work on railway at Airan—Ravages of disease—Treatment at Afiun Qarahisar and Angora—News reaches England—The Parliamentary Report—The Regimental Care Committee—Statistics of parcels—The journey of the officers into captivity—Echelon A and B—Yozgad—Secret communication with England—Colonel Lethbridge's summary of the Turks' characteristics.

XXII.	REORGANIZATION AND PREPARATION	250

The 43rd at Sandy Ridge—Shortage of rations—Sickness and disease—The 43rd detached—The toll of disease—Training—Drafts—Lieutenant-Colonel Pope-Hennessy assumes command—Specialists—Maude succeeds Gorringe—Maude becomes Commander-in-Chief—Policy—Organization of the Tigris defences—The 43rd moves into forward section—Maude's offensive in December 1916—The 43rd takes over a section of the blockhouse line—Maude ordered to defeat the Turks—The regimental school at Dujaila.

XXIII.	THE OFFENSIVE	268

Fourth attack on Sannaiyat—Fifth—The passage of the Tigris—Capture of Kut—Turks escape annihilation—Pursuit—Attenuation of communications—Halt—Pursuit restarted—Capture of Baghdad, March 11th.

XXIV.	OPERATIONS FOR THE PROTECTION OF BAGHDAD	272

Co-operation with the Russians—Operations on three fronts—Heavy fighting.

CHAP.		PAGE
XXV.	MARCH TO JULY WITH THE 43RD	275

Redistribution of the Tigris Defences—The 43rd dismantles the light railway—The line of communications—The 43rd moves to Aziziya—Weather conditions—Yilderim—The Russians retreat—Mesopotamia reinforced—Improvements in communications—The Mesopotamia Commission—Defection of the Russians—The 43rd attempts to capture Turkish agent—Sickness in the 43rd—The 43rd moves to Hinaidi—Turks defeated at Ramadi—Death of Sir Stanley Maude—Appreciation—General Marshall assumes command—Birth of Bolshevism—Russian armies disintegrate—Dunsterforce—Withdrawal of 7th Division to Egypt.

XXVI.	THE 43RD JOINS THE 50TH BRIGADE ON THE EUPHRATES	284

Capture of Khan Abu Rayan—The 43rd patrols towards Hit—Capture of Hit—The country—The Turks hold Khan Baghdadi—Concentration of supplies—The enemy's strength—The 11th Cavalry Brigade arrives—Enemy's dispositions—General Brooking's plan—The battle of Khan Baghdadi—Rout of the Turks—Pursuit—Capture of Haditha and Ana—Turkish losses—The 43rd withdraws to Sahiliya—Summer operations—Reconnaissances—The 43rd raids enemy cavalry—The beginning of the end—The battle of Sharqat—The Turkish armistice—The German armistice—Demobilization—The cadre leaves for England—Arrives at Aldershot.

XXVII.	ORIGIN OF THE EXPEDITION TO NORTH RUSSIA	303

The Russian revolution—Its effect—The Bolshevik party—Germany overruns the Ukraine—The Treaty of Brest-Litovsk—British and Allied forces occupy Murmansk and Archangel—Summary of British and German aims in Russia—Garrison troops' exhaustion—Plight of Europe after the Armistice—The situation in Russia in April 1919—The 43rd detailed for active service—Lack of men of the Regiment—The 43rd is brought up to establishment—Moves to Crowborough—Inspected by General Rawlinson—Sails for Archangel—List of officers—The outward journey—Murmansk—The White Sea—Archangel—The 43rd disembarks—Russian welcome—General Ironside—The *honourable tea*—Parade of the 1st Battalion Slavo-British Legion—The 43rd is ordered to leave Archangel.

XXVIII.	APPRECIATION OF THE SITUATION	320

Bolshevik strength—the Country—Communications—Supply and Transport—Front to be handed over to Admiral Koltchak—The plan of campaign—The 43rd leaves Archangel—The journey upstream—The 43rd reaches Osinova—Leaves for the Vaga front—"A" Company's march from Ust Vaga to Mala Bereznik—The position at Mala Bereznik—Patrol work—Mosquitoes—Regimental headquarters come up to Seltso—The bloodsucking clegs—"A" Company at Seltso.

XXIX.	GENERAL SITUATION	334

Transport difficulties—Communications—Situation elsewhere—Plan of the 43rd's raid—"A" Company's role—The raid of 26/27 June—Advance to Ignatovskaya—Bolshevik resistance—The commanding officer's gallantry—Casualties—Plight of the wounded—Afterthoughts—"A" Company detailed for second raid—The advance through the forest—The attack—Casualties.

XXX.	THE MUTINY OF THE SLAVO-BRITISH LEGION	350

Description of the position—Mutiny of the Slavo-British Legion—A prisoner returns to our lines—The Bolshevik internecine battle—Life at Nijni Kitsa—Flies, mosquitoes, clegs and monotony—Rations—Health—Mutinies elsewhere—General situation—Press campaign at home—Government defines its policy—General Ironside's difficulties—"D" Company withdrawn from Vaga Column to Konetzbor—General headquarters return to Archangel—Vaga Column under Dvina Force's orders.

CHAP.		PAGE
XXXI.	AUGUST ON THE VAGA COLUMN	359

Signs of offensive—Withdrawal of Russians from Vaga Column—Heavy kits sent downstream—The attack by Dvina Force—The Vaga Column ordered to co-operate—Weather breaks—Vaga Column's attack postponed and later cancelled—Patrolling—Two platoons of "C" Company withdrawn to Seletskoe—"A" Company takes over Koslovo in addition to Nijni Kitsa—Departure of the 60-pounder—Russian desertions—Withdrawal postponed—Plan of withdrawal—Captain Wyld's visit—General situation—Demonstrations on the Vaga Column—Bolsheviks bombard Mala Bereznik.

XXXII.	SEPTEMBER ON THE VAGA	365

Bolsheviks attack Mala Bereznik—"B" Company's counter-attack—Patrol actions—Communications cut—The garrison at Ust Vaga—Bolsheviks surround "C" Company at Ust Vaga—"C" Company's desperate fight—Major Northcote counter-attacks—Disperses Bolsheviks—Bolshevik plan frustrated—Reinforcements sent up—All Russians leave—Withdrawal postponed—Kits sent downstream—Bolsheviks bombard Mala Bereznik—Forest tracks trapped with bombs—Withdrawal again postponed—Frost—"C" Company reach Koslovo—Bolsheviks threaten Koslovo—Bombardment of Mala Bereznik—Enemy sighted from Nijni Kitsa—Bolsheviks surrender—The officer's story—Condition of his troops—Withdrawal ordered for the 15th—Cancelled—Reordered.

XXXIII.	THE WITHDRAWAL OF THE VAGA COLUMN	375

The 43rd evacuates positions—Ust Vaga handed over to Russians—The march to Bereznik—The 43rd embarks—The 43rd leaves Bereznik—Journey downstream—The 43rd reaches Archangel—Disembarks at Bakharitsa—Concentration of the 43rd—Surplus officers embark on the 25th—43rd on the 26th—Convoy sails on the 27th—Rough passage—Arrival at Liverpool—Reception—Disbandment—Rewards and decorations.

INDEX		447

APPENDICES

APPENDIX		PAGE
I.	Composition of Force "D" on the 1st December 1914	387
II.	Reorganization of Force "D" as on the 1st April 1915	390
III.	Composition on the 14th November 1915 of Major-General C. V. F. Townshend's Column Advancing on Baghdad	392
IV.	Order of Battle at Ctesiphon	394
V.	Casualties at Ctesiphon and on the Retreat from Ctesiphon. Compiled from the Official List	395
VI.	Order of Battle of the Force, under Major-General C. V. F. Townshend, besieged in Kut	397
VII.	Reorganization of Tigris Corps, 15th January 1916	399
VIII.	Order of Battle and Distribution of the British Forces in Mesopotamia on the 27th February (excluding the Garrison of Kut al Amara)	401
IX.	Casualties at the First Battle of Sannaiyat, 6th April 1916	404
X.	Casualties in the Siege of Kut	407
XI.	Statistics of the Casualties among the Rank and File Prisoners of War	410
	List of Those who Died, with Presumed Place and Cause of Death	410
	Lists of Reservists or Attached Men who Died or are Presumed to have Died in Captivity	416
	Known Survivors of the 43rd	418
	Possible Survivors of the 43rd	420
	Survivors of Attached	420
	Probable and Known Survivors of the Reservists	420
XII.	Order of Battle at Khan Baghdadi, 26th March 1918	421
XIII.	Roll of Officers commanding the 43rd Light Infantry, 1914-1919	423
XIV.	Records of Services	424
XV.	Records of Services of Attached Officers	439
XVI.	Summary of Officer Casualties in Mesopotamia	442
XVII.	Order of Battle, "A" Company, North Russia	443
XVIII.	Casualties of the Vaga Column	444

ILLUSTRATIONS

PLATE.		
I.	Colonel E. A. E. Lethbridge, C.M.G., D.S.O.	*Frontispiece*

FACING PAGE

II.	43rd Camp at Maqil, December 1914—The first day at Qurna, guarding Arab Suspects—Reconnaissance of Ruta, "R" Company in Action, 20th January 1915	24
III.	Raising the Road to Muzaira'a—Pontoon Bridge between Qurna and Muzaira'a—Inside No. 3 Redoubt, Muzaira'a—Flooded Date Garden, Qurna, April 1915—Building Reed Huts	40
IV.	Mudlarking, April 1915—Lieutenants Powell, Courtis and Whittall—Floods at Qurna, looking towards the Kilns—"Q" Company practising in Bellums—Parading for the Dress Rehearsal of the Regatta—The Regatta Rehearsal	53
V.	Preparing for Embarkation, 30th May 1915—The Attack on Norfolk Hill	58
VI.	Armoured Machine Gun Bellum—Mountain Gun Bellum stuck during the Attack—Major Hyde, Captains Morland and Stephens and Lieutenant Powell on Abu Aran Island—Turkish Prisoners—Captain Startin, R.A.M.C., and Colonel Donaghan, R.A.M.C., on Norfolk Hill	62
VII.	Officers' Mess, Ezra's Tomb, 3rd June 1915—The Great Arch of Chosroes at Ctesiphon	116
VIII.	Kut al Amara from the Air, February 1916—Major L. J. Carter, D.S.O.	168
IX.	Aeroplane Photograph and Key Map of the Turkish position at Sannaiyat	193
X.	Group of Prisoners at Kastamuni	223
XI.	Major-General L. H. R. Pope-Hennessy, C.B., D.S.O.	256
XII.	Brigadier F. H. Stapleton, C.M.G.	272
XIII.	Lieutenant-Colonel G. E. Whittall, M.C.	282
XIV.	On the March to Falluja—Hit from the Euphrates	288

PLATE		FACING PAGE
XV.	Turkish Officers, Prisoners and Transport captured at Khan Baghdadi ...	293
XVI.	Group of Officers, Southampton ...	299
XVII.	Going through the White Sea—Archangel, from the Sabornaya Quay ...	314
XVIII.	Refuelling on way upstream—Canadian Village, Mala Bereznik—Road Post, Mala Bereznik—Trenches in the Bolshevik forward position—Taken during the Raid on Ignatovskaya: No. 3 Platoon advancing from the captured Bolshevik forward position—Lieutenant Tamplin and Captain Watson, intelligence officers of the Vaga Column, interrogating Bolshevik prisoners ...	329
XIX.	Aeroplane Photograph of the Bolshevik forward position	336
XX.	Patrol of the Transport Section on the Chamovo Trail—Koslovo Village—Captain Peck crossing the Footbridge from Koslovo to Gunner Lines—The Vaga River from Nijni Kitsa—Group of Officers at Nijni Kitsa ...	350
XXI.	No. 4 Post, Nijni Kitsa, looking towards the Brown Patch—Serjeant Bristow—Mudborough Road, Nijni Kitsa—Bolshevik Prisoners, captured 13th September 1919—Going Downstream ...	370

	PAGE
Birdseye View looking towards Kut ...	150
Panorama from Kut looking towards the Fort ...	164
Panorama from Kut looking towards Es Sinn ...	186
Kut Frescoes, No. X ...	213

MAPS

MESOPOTAMIA

NO.			
1.	LOWER MESOPOTAMIA	facing page	1
2.	MUZAIRA'A AND QURNA	page	42
3.	QURNA	facing page	64
4.	THE BATTLE OF KUT	,, ,,	88
5.	THE BATTLE OF CTESIPHON	,, ,,	120
6.	THE AFFAIR OF UMM AT TUBUL	page	126
7.	THE TIGRIS FROM KUT TO BAGHDAD	,,	130
8.	THE ACTION OF SHAIKH SAAD	,,	152
9.	THE ACTION OF THE WADI	,,	154
10.	THE FIRST ATTACK ON HANNA, 21ST JANUARY 1916	,,	158
11.	THE ATTACK ON DUJAILA REDOUBT	facing page	182
12.	HANNA AND SANNAIYAT: OPERATIONS BETWEEN 10TH MARCH AND END OF APRIL, 1916	page	206
13.	THE DEFENCE OF KUT AL AMARA	facing page	216
14.	THE FORT AT KUT	page	218
15.	OPERATIONS ON THE TIGRIS, 13TH DECEMBER 1916 TO 25TH FEBRUARY 1917	facing page	270
16.	AREA NORTH OF BAGHDAD	,, ,,	274
17.	THE ACTION OF KHAN BAGHDADI	,, ,,	296
18.	OPERATIONS ON THE EUPHRATES LINE	page	300
19.	THE MIDDLE EAST	facing page	302

NORTH RUSSIA

20.	NORTH AND CENTRAL RUSSIA	page	321
21.	THE ARCHANGEL FRONT	,,	322
22.	THE VAGA FROM SELTSO TO MAKSIMOVSKAYA	,,	338
23.	BOLSHEVIK DEFENCES AT IGNATOVSKAYA	,,	340
24.	BOLSHEVIK FORWARD POSITION NEAR MALA BEREZNIK	facing page	348
25.	MALA BEREZNIK	,, ,,	366
26.	NIJNI KITSA AND DEFENCES	page	376
27.	DVINA AND VAGA FRONT	facing page	384

FOREWORD

THOUGH I feel sure that the pages which follow were a labour of love to Captain Neville, they must have entailed an immense amount of research and other work. He begins with the work of the 43rd in fields of action as far apart as Mesopotamia and North Russia, and when the volume to follow with the history of the 52nd has been compiled by another writer we shall have laid before us a full account of the place the two Regiments took in the Great War. I feel sure that it will be the one sentiment of all his comrades, that we all owe him such a debt of gratitude as will be hard, if not impossible, to repay.

J. HANBURY WILLIAMS, *Major-General,*
Colonel, Oxfordshire and Buckinghamshire Light Infantry.

HENRY III TOWER,
WINDSOR CASTLE.
September, 1937.

BIBLIOGRAPHY

The Oxfordshire and Buckinghamshire Light Infantry Chronicles: Vol. XXIII, 1914; Vol. XXIV, 1914-15; Vol. XXV, 1915-16; Vol. XXVI, 1916-17; Vol. XXVII, 1917-18; Vol. XXVIII, 1919-20; Vol. XXXV, 1927; Vol. XXXVI, 1928. (Referred to as Chronicles.)

Regimental War Diary.

Official History of the War: Mesopotamia Campaign, Vols. I-IV. (Referred to as Official History.)

My Campaign in Mesopotamia, by Major-General Sir Charles V. F. Townshend, K.C.B., D.S.O.

In Kut and Captivity, by Major E. W. C. Sandes, M.C., R.E.

The Long Road to Baghdad, by Edmund Candler, Vols. I and II.

Mesopotamia, 1914-15, by Captain H. T. Birch Reynardson, 43rd Light Infantry. (Referred to as Birch Reynardson.)

La Campagne de l'Irak, by Commandant M. Moukbil Bey.

Following the Drum, by Sir John Fortescue, K.C.V.O.

Behind the Scenes in Many Wars, by Lieutenant-General Sir George MacMunn, K.C.B., K.C.S.I., D.S.O.

Bengal Lancer, by Major F. Yeats-Brown.

The Road to En-Dor, by E. H. Jones.

Loyalties: Mesopotamia, 1914-17, by Sir Arnold Wilson, K.C.I.E.

War Letters of a Light Infantryman.

Bolos and Barishniyas, by Captain Singleton-Gates.

My War Memories, Vol. II, by General von Ludendorff.

Manuscripts:

    Colonel E. A. E. Lethbridge's Memoirs.
    R.S.M. Love's Roll of Prisoners at Airan.
    R.S.M. Love's Ration Roll at Airan.
    Lieutenant-Colonel R. Stephens's Diary.
    Major Henley's Diary.
    Major Naylor's Diary.
    Lieutenant Williams's Diary.

MAP No. 1.

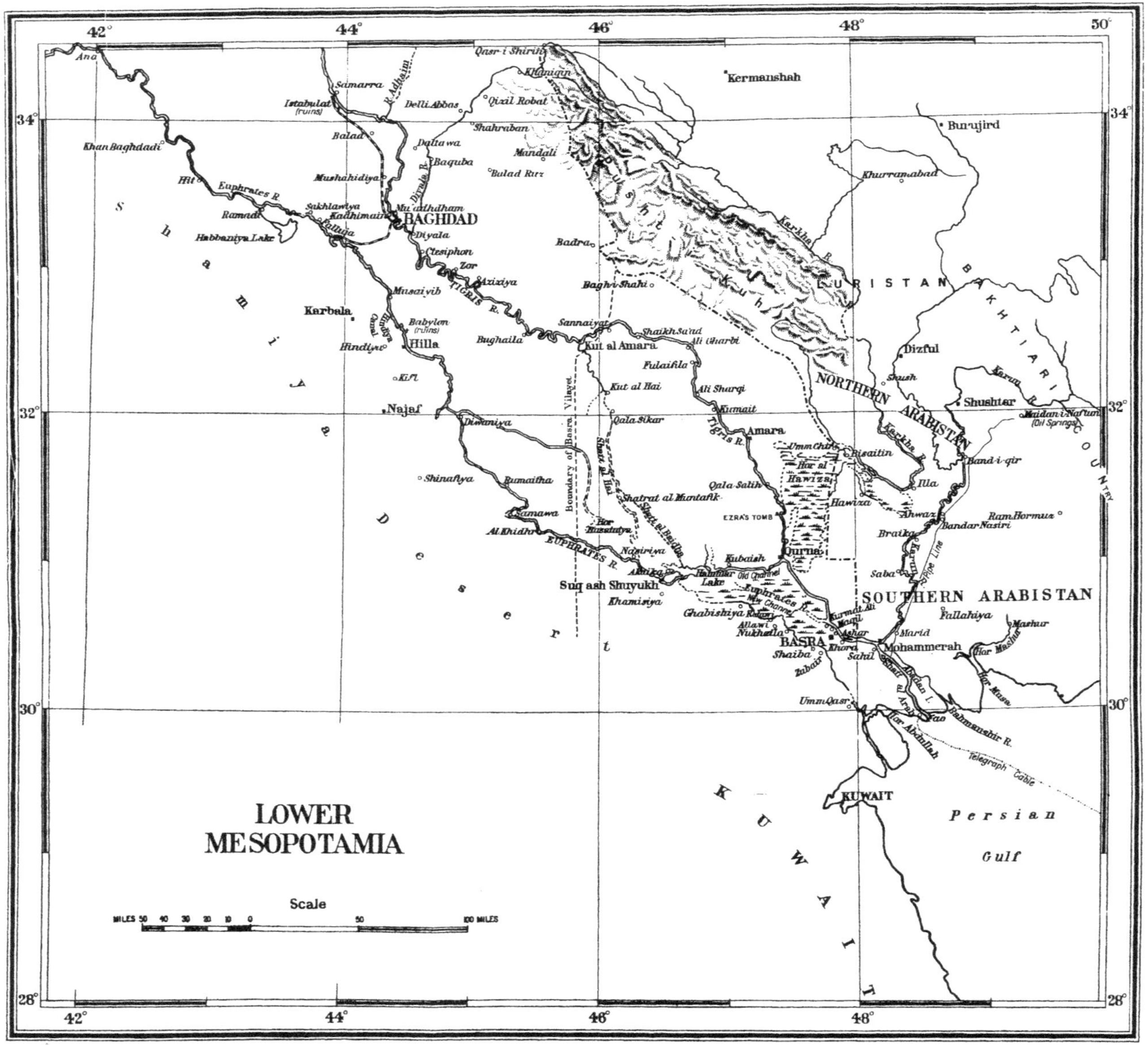
LOWER
MESOPOTAMIA
Scale
MILES 50 40 30 20 10 0 50 100 MILES
BAGHDAD
BASRA
Kermanshah
Burujird
Khurramabad
Dizful
Shushtar
Karbala
Najaf
Hilla
Kut al Amara
Amara
Qurna
Mohammerah
KUWAIT
Persian
Gulf
SOUTHERN ARABISTAN
NORTHERN ARABISTAN
LURISTAN
BAKHTIARI COUNTRY
Shamiya Desert
KUWAIT
Pusht i Kuh
Euphrates R.
EUPHRATES R.
TIGRIS R.
Tigris R.
Karkha R.
Karun
Diyala R.
Shatt al Hai
Shatt al Arab
Boundary of Basra Vilayet
Samarra
Istabulat (ruins)
Balad
Khan Baghdadi
Hit
Ramadi
Habbaniya Lake
Falluja
Kadhimain
Mu'adhdham
Ctesiphon
Aziziya
Sannaiyat
Babylon (ruins)
Kifl
Diwaniya
Samawa
Nasiriya
Suq ash Shuyukh
Hammar Lake
Ezra's Tomb
Qasr i Shirin
Khaniqin
Mandali
Badra
Ahwaz
Fao
Telegraph Cable
Pipe Line
Maidan i Naftun (Oil Springs)
Ana
42°
44°
46°
48°
50°
34°
32°
30°
28°

43rd LIGHT INFANTRY

CHAPTER I.

British Relations with Turkey before the War.

German influence—The Baghdad Railway—Anglo-Russian Agreement of 1907—Results of the Turkish Revolution of 1908—The Turco-German Alliance—Turkey's strategical position—The Balkan wars—British interests in Anglo-Persian Oilfields.

(*See Maps facing pages* 1 *and* 302.)

Until the latter part of the nineteenth century, England had been on friendly terms with Turkey. " England had backed Turkey to the verge of war in 1878," against Russia, " and during the Crimean War, England had supported her in arms."[1] But Gladstone's policy of supporting the cause of the Armenians and other Christian races in subjugation to Turkey put an end to these friendly relations.

Now Germany, for many years before the war, had cultivated Turkey's friendship as a means whereby to strike at British power and commercial prosperity in the East.[2] For forty years German diplomacy worked to foment trouble " between England and Russia in regard to Turkey, Persia and India, or to create discord between Turkey and Great Britain in regard to Egypt, Arabia, Mesopotamia, and the Persian Gulf."[2] There is no doubt but that Germany visualized an empire spreading from the North Sea to the Persian Gulf, with her allies, Austria, Bulgaria and Turkey, as mere dependencies. With this intent German banks were quick to finance Turkey, and especially her railways. The British concessions for the Euphrates railway, obtained in 1857, lapsed on the change of sentiment towards Turkey; and German interests were predominant in the Anatolian and Baghdad railways. The Germans obtained two concessions in 1893 and 1899, and finally the all-important Baghdad Railway Convention was signed on the 5th March 1903.[3]

Russia's attack on Afghan troops in 1885 had nearly resulted in war with England, but with the intervening years a better understanding between the two countries had grown and culminated in the Anglo-Russian agreement of 1907. This agreement helped England in her relations with Turkey and

[1] *Foundations of Reform*, by the *Times* military correspondent.
[2] *Official History*, Vol. I, p. 22.   [3] *Ibid.*, Vol. I, p. 23.

Germany, but Turkey and Persia never trusted Russia. For sixty years Russia had been straining for an outlet to the sea, and Turkey had appeared to supply the best means of attaining it.

The Turkish revolution of 1908 revived many of the old feelings of friendship for England among the Young Turks; but this was short-lived, for England distrusted the closer relations with their co-religionists in Egypt, Persia and India which the new form of government sought to foster by means of the Pan-Islamic and Pan-Turanian Movements. On the other hand, German influence increased in inverse ratio. Germany lent Turkey money and sold her warships which England and France had refused.[4] Moreover, disturbances in the provinces of Baghdad and Basra which the Turkish authorities made no efforts to control were aimed at British prestige in Mesopotamia and the Persian Gulf. The Turco-German alliance, thus effected, was a masterly piece of strategy on Germany's part. " Magnificently placed astride three continents, inveterately hostile to Russia, whose overwhelming numbers lay upon the soul of the German strategist like a nightmare, embittered with England on account of the loss of Cyprus and Egypt, and capable of serving as a weapon against Russia, Austria or England at will, the warlike Empire of Othman appealed to the soldier-heart of a military State."[5] And at the same time its strategical position threatened Great Britain's communications with India and Australia. As one result of this alliance German officers were sent to train the Turkish Army in modern methods, under Marshal von der Goltz; but so unsuccessful were the Turkish arms in the war against Italy in 1911 in Tripoli, and the Balkan States in 1912-13, that there was a great revulsion of feeling, and Germany incurred a considerable loss of prestige. Here was a heaven-sent chance to break with one stroke the web which Germany had woven round Turkey so assiduously for close on fifty years, but the opportunity of frustrating finally Germany's influence was allowed to slip.

Meanwhile, the proposed Baghdad railway received considerable attention in England. Its possible influence on our prestige not only in the Persian Gulf but also in our Musalman dominions was not altogether overlooked. Agreements[6] were reached with regard to British and Indian interests in Mesopotamia and navigation rights on the Tigris and Euphrates; and the political *status quo* on the shores and waters of the Persian Gulf was recognized definitely. These agreements were awaiting ratification when war broke out.

But beyond these agreements, England had no influence over Turkey, thanks to the masterly diplomacy of the German Ambassador, Baron Marschall von Bieberstein.[7] Before the war, the British Government had obtained

[4] *Ibid.*, Vol. I, p. 38.
[5] *Ibid.*, Vol. I, p. 37.
[6] *Ibid.*, Vol. I, pp. 21, 42.
[7] *Ibid.*, Vol. I, p. 38.

a predominant interest in the Anglo-Persian Oilfield at Maidan-i-Naftun,[8] as a strategical supply for the needs of the Navy, yet the Government complacently allowed the Germans to establish preponderating influence over Turkey. Baghdad became an ideal centre for German propaganda in Persia and Afghanistan, and for undermining thereby British prestige—nay, even dominion—in India and the East. Germany without Musalman possessions was safe in instigating sedition among England's Musalman subjects, and when war broke out our moral authority in the Persian Gulf demanded attention. There was always the possibility of Turkey, the head of the Musalman religion, declaring a *Jehad*, or holy war, which would strike at the very foundations of England's grip on India.

---

[8] See Map No. 1, facing p. 1.

CHAPTER II.

The Army in India before the War.

Inadequacy of all equipment in 1914—Deficiency of munitions—Protection of Anglo-Persian Oilfields.

(See Map facing page 1.)

In 1914 the total strength of the army in India was 76,000 British and 159,000 Indians. A year earlier " only six divisions and six cavalry brigades were fully equipped,"[1] and plans had been made for the movement of only five divisions and four cavalry brigades. Also it was known that the whole field army could not be concentrated on the Frontier for months after the outbreak of war. By 1914 war with Afghanistan or internal rebellion had become the chief dangers. Russia had ceased to be a menace and mutual relations had much improved.

On the outbreak of war, the field army consisted of " seven and one-third divisions, five cavalry brigades, and certain army troops."[2] It was well equipped only for war on the Frontier, and " was not well found for an expedition overseas."[3] There were clothing and boots sufficient for only six divisions and six cavalry brigades; motor transport had not arrived from home, and there was no reserve of short magazine Lee-Enfield rifles; only material for four million rounds of small arms ammunition could be manufactured; there were only four aeroplanes in India; wireless equipment was non-existent, and telephones were insufficient.[3] British regiments were dependent upon home reserves for reinforcement,[4] while the Indian Army reserve amounted to only 33,000 and was inefficient. The reserve of British officers for the Indian Army numbered forty; and the shortage of medical officers, although well known by the authorities for many years, had not been made good. This shortage amounted to three to four hundred medical officers and two hundred assistant surgeons, and the Army Bearer Corps numbered no more than one hundred men.[5]

---

[1] *Official History*, Vol. I, p. 59.　　[2] *Ibid.*, Vol. I, p. 62.

[3] Sir Beauchamp Duff's evidence before Mesopotamia Commission. *Official History*, p. 63.

[4] The establishment of British regiments in India provided for a ten per cent. reinforcement.

[5] *Official History*, Vol. I, p. 67.

Government was caught unprepared. The possibility that the whole of the Empire might be embroiled simultaneously in military operations had never been conceived, and for multifarious reasons[6] India was unable to expand her army and supply the deficiencies in munitions and equipment without help from England.

It is interesting to note that India's annual manufacture of rifles was only nine thousand, of shells twenty-four thousand, of field artillery guns a few and of small arms ammunition fifty-two million rounds. Moreover, on the outbreak of war the Army in India was still using Mark VI small arms ammunition; the new Mark VII ammunition had not yet been issued. Machine guns and heavy artillery were not made. Any expansion in the production of munitions had to be supplied from home where there was soon a shortage. This improvidence applied to practically all military equipment. For instance: transport was so short that on the dispatch of the 3rd and 7th Indian Divisions Quetta was denuded of A.T. carts, and two thousand camels were borrowed from the Khan of Kelat to carry on essential duties. At the outbreak of war India's air pilots were sent home, and the replacement of them was supplied by the Dominions.

Though the co-operation of the Army in India in a major war in Europe had been mooted in 1912 when the General Staff at the War Office realized the likelihood of war with Germany, and though the Government in India had promised two divisions and one cavalry brigade in that event, yet little was done to equip the troops with the necessaries of modern war. For instance: when the 3rd and 7th Indian Divisions sailed for France in 1914 the shortage of field batteries was such that India had practically to be denuded in order to equip these divisions with three field brigades each, with the result that when the 6th Division went to Mesopotamia it had only one field brigade and two mountain batteries as its complement of artillery.

At the same time, an arrangement was made whereby the General Staff in India was made responsible for the Persian Gulf and a portion of Arabia while the General Staff at home was responsible for the rest of Arabia and Mesopotamia, but there was no prearranged plan for operations in Mesopotamia[7] beyond the occupation of Basra. On the outbreak of war the General Staff at home was far too busy to co-ordinate plans of operations, and was fundamentally opposed to the detachment of any but the minimum force for subsidiary purposes, as the principles of war demanded the maximum concentration of all available forces at the decisive point in Western Europe. The policy in the East, therefore, was to protect the Suez Canal from the Arabs, the Anglo-Persian Oilfields from the Turks, maintain our authority in the Persian Gulf and guard against the proclamation of a *Jehad* and the

---

[6] *Ibid.*, Vol. I, pp. 64-65.   [7] *Ibid.*, Vol. I, p. 70.

possible rising of the Musalmans in Afghanistan, the North-West Frontier, and even in India itself.

This History is only concerned with that part of the policy which originally related to the Anglo-Persian Oilfields in Mesopotamia, for the protection of which one division was sent, though Sir O'Moore Creagh, Commander-in-Chief before the war, had advised that three divisions would be required to occupy Basra, one of them being kept in reserve in India.[8]

---

[8] Sir O'Moore Creagh's evidence before the Mesopotamia Commission. *Official History*, Vol. I, p. 73.

CHAPTER III.

THE TURKS IN MESOPOTAMIA.

BRITISH INTERESTS IN MESOPOTAMIA BEFORE THE WAR—ORIGIN OF BRITISH CONNECTION WITH THE PERSIAN GULF—THE TURKISH ARMY—DISPOSITIONS OF ARMY CORPS—TURKISH TROOPS IN MESOPOTAMIA ON THE DECLARATION OF WAR—THE TURKISH AND BRITISH POLICY FROM AUGUST TO NOVEMBER 1914—TURKISH MOBILIZATION—THE " GOEBEN " AND " BRESLAU "—ANTI-BRITISH DEMONSTRATIONS IN BASRA—ANGLO-PERSIAN OIL COMPANY REQUESTS PROTECTION—6TH (POONA) DIVISION EARMARKED FOR SERVICE IN MESOPOTAMIA—GERMAN INTRIGUES—PROCLAMATION OF " JEHAD "—TURCO-GERMAN FLEET BOMBARDS RUSSIAN PORTS—DECLARATION OF WAR.

(See Maps facing pages 1 and 302.)

MESOPOTAMIA was divided into three *vilayets*, Mosul, Baghdad, and Basra, and administered by *Valis* or Governors, who were the political representatives of the Ottoman Government, but had no control over the *zaptiehs*, the military police responsible for law and order. The *Valis* were responsible for the collection of taxes, and these they farmed out with the consequent bribery and corruption. The country was honeycombed with agents and spies, who reported direct to Constantinople, where the power of the Central Government was supreme.[1]

After the unsuccessful wars against Italy and the Balkan States, Arab discontent in Mesopotamia became very prevalent, coupled with disaffection in Kurdistan; the rivers from Baghdad to the Persian Gulf became unsafe and a general rising of the Arabs was feared.[2] At this time, too, much was heard of the Pan-Islamic Movement which aimed at uniting all Musalman races under the leadership of the Sultan, the Khalifa liberating them from foreign control. This movement affected Persia, Afghanistan and India, but the Arab of Mesopotamia knew the Turks too well to trust its motives.[2] The Persians disliked the Turks and would probably have been definitely pro-British, had they not had an inveterate hatred of Russia, our ally. Therefore, the tendency of Persia leant towards the Turks at the outbreak of war, with the result that Persia became a centre for the dissemination of anti-British propaganda.[3] The Shaikh of Mohammerah, however, was definitely pro-British. The Arab State of Kuwait,[4] south of Basra and bordering the north-west coast of the Persian Gulf, was also pro-British. South-east of

---

[1] *Official History*, Vol. I, p. 17.
[2] *Ibid.*, Vol. I, p. 19.
[3] *Ibid.*, Vol. I, pp. 24-25.
[4] See Map No. 1, facing p. 1.

Kuwait lies Al Hasa,[5] from which the Turks had been ejected by Ibn Saud, Emir of Nejd, in 1913. He espoused the cause of Great Britain in 1914, but Ibn Raschid, the Wahabi chief of Hail,[5] together with the Shaikhs of the Muntafik and Bani Lam tribes, north of Amara, took up arms for Turkey.

The Bedouins were hostile to the Turks, but in the war many fought against us, though their co-operation was never dependable; nor could they be relied upon not to turn against the Turks when the tide of war flowed against them. In fact, they harassed both British and Turk indiscriminately when the prospect of loot appeared to be good, and they mutilated the dead or wounded with impartiality. The marsh Arabs on both banks of the Tigris and lower Euphrates had a bad reputation.[6]

II.—British Interests in Mesopotamia before the War.

British association with Mesopotamia was well over two hundred years old when the war broke out. As far back as 1639 the East India Company traded with Basra; in 1775 the defence of Basra against the Persians was in the hands of Englishmen. "By the end of the seventeenth and throughout the eighteenth century, the Company's ships navigated the Euphrates and Tigris,"[7] and during the first part of the nineteenth century British ships plied regularly on the waterways. In 1841 Captain Lynch founded his line of ships which were allowed to navigate the rivers under the British flag. Periodical protests against these rights of navigation occurred in 1864 and 1883, but on two occasions were confirmed by the Ottoman Government.

In the Shatt al Arab the only effective policing of the river and estuary was carried out by His Majesty's ships, and it was due to the British that the channels had been buoyed and periodically surveyed[8] at very considerable cost, and therefore that navigation had been possible with a consequent expansion of trade to the mutual advantage of the Turks and Persians, as well as the British.

Now the British connection with the Persian Gulf was still older, dating from 1622, "when under an agreement with the Shah of Persia, the East India Company undertook to ' keep two men-of-war constantly to defend the Gulf,' and at the same time despatched a fleet to aid the Persians in expelling the Portuguese. . . . This undertaking to patrol the Gulf became a permanent obligation which has been fulfilled for three centuries."[8]

III.—The Turkish Army.

The numbers of the Turkish Army that fought in the war have not been computed accurately. When war broke out the Army was still suffering

---

[5] See Map No. 19, facing p. 302.
[7] Ibid., Vol. I, p. 43.
[6] Official History, Vol. I, pp. 14-15.
[8] Ibid., Vol. I, p. 45.

from the disorganization caused by the unsuccessful campaigns of 1911 against the Italians in Tripoli and the Balkan Wars of 1912-13. Many new formations were raised during the war to replace those captured or annihilated; " desertions were rife, and disease was constant and often of an epidemic nature, causing sudden and considerable reductions; casualties were frequently not reported; and fraudulent returns were not unknown."[9]

The organization of the Turkish Army into four Inspections was effected in 1911 by von der Goltz. The first Army Inspection at Constantinople consisted of the first five army corps of one cavalry brigade and three infantry divisions each; the second occupied the Kurdistan area with the IX, X and XI Army Corps; the third in Syria and Cilicia had the VI and VIII Army Corps; the fourth was responsible for Mesopotamia with the XII and XIII Army Corps. " During the course of the war seventy divisions in all were raised, though there were never this number in being at the same time."[10] The cavalry regiments were organized in four field squadrons with one depot squadron, and the artillery consisted of regiments of two or three battalions, each of three four-gun batteries. But the Turks in 1914 were still deficient in guns, a great number having been captured in the Balkan Wars. Infantry regiments consisted of three battalions of four companies each, and were armed with Mauser rifles of two different patterns, for the supply of which they had to rely upon Germany. Most infantry regiments had machine-gun companies. The air service hardly existed, and the " medical organization, though complete on paper, was actually insufficient and inefficient."[11] In Mesopotamia there were no modern land defences, and the only warship was the gunboat *Marmariss*.

The mobilization on the 3rd August proceeded slowly but without enthusiasm; and the methods of requisitioning were such as to cause great discomfort, starvation, and financial ruin to thousands of Ottoman subjects. But by the end of October the Turkish Army was as ready as it ever could hope to be. On the 28th, just before war was declared, the latest information about the enemy forces was that the " two regular divisions of the XIIth (Mosul) Corps had moved westward, and the 37th Division of the XIIIth (Baghdad) Corps had been reported at Mosul moving towards Erzerum, and there were left at Baghdad fourteen guns of the 37th Artillery, thirteen model battalions, five hundred men of the 114th Infantry and nine thousand reservists, of whom four thousand were without rifles."[12] Therefore there was left in Mesopotamia only the 38th Regular Division, of which " 4,700 rifles, 18 guns, and 3 machine guns were concentrated in the vicinity of Basra."[13]

[9] *Ibid.*, Vol. I, p. 26.
[11] *Ibid.*, Vol. I, p. 30.
[13] *Ibid.*, Vol. I, p. 100.
[10] *Ibid.*, Vol. I, p. 29.
[12] *Ibid.*, Vol. I, pp. 103-104.

IV.—THE TURKISH AND BRITISH POLICY FROM AUGUST TO NOVEMBER 1914.

According to Djemal Pasha, the Turkish Minister of Marine, the Turco-German Alliance was signed on the 2nd August 1914, but in spite of entreaties from Germany the Turks did not declare war, preferring in true Oriental fashion to mobilize their Army under the cover of neutrality, for the general sentiment in Turkey was pro-British rather than pro-German. But this alliance was not known in England, and it was explained to Sir Louis Mallet, the British Ambassador at Constantinople, that the mobilization on the 3rd August was entirely precautionary. It was in fact effected by the agency of the German military mission in Turkey.[14]

On the outbreak of war we retained the two dreadnoughts which were building for Turkey, for our own needs. This action was used by the Germans as a handle wherewith to lever the Turks, until they, in turn, broke the laws of neutrality by harbouring the crews of the two German warships, the *Goeben* and *Breslau*. All through August Anglo-Turkish relations were exceedingly strained, for " there was a continuous stream of German officers and men into the country for the Turkish army, navy, and munition factories, and of arms and ammunition."[15] Also it was reported that Turkish and German agents had been dispatched to foment trouble in Arabia, India, Egypt, Persia and Afghanistan. On the 12th and 14th August news reached the Indian Government that the XIII Corps was being mobilized in Baghdad and that martial law had been proclaimed, and this at the time when the Indian field army was being prepared to answer England's call. British rights of domicile had been violated and Turkish officials had been openly pro-German. Adding to these disquieting tidings came the news that " the *Vali* of Basra had notified British merchants that he might commandeer all supplies of coal and oil "[16]; that the oil company's settlement at Abadan was fearful of a Turkish attack, and requested the protection of a British warship; that Musalmans were anti-British and that agitators might be sent from Basra to rouse India. As a result of this, orders were issued on the 25th August to the naval commander-in-chief to send H.M. Ships *Odin* and *Lawrence* to the Shatt al Arab.

Meanwhile Turkish troops were streaming south by the Tigris and Euphrates, and the Admiralty urged the necessity of sending troops to protect the oil works at Abadan. But to do so might have meant a collision with the Turks, and this the British and Indian Governments were determined to avoid for many reasons, the most important being the effect on the Indian Musalmans of a declaration of war on the head of their creed. But, at the same time, the Shaikhs of Mohammerah and Kuwait and Ibn Saud, all

---

[14] *Ibid.*, Vol. I, p. 76. [15] *Ibid.*, Vol. I, p. 77.
[16] *Ibid.*, Vol. I, p. 78.

friendly to Great Britain, were isolated and liable to be seduced from their alliance either by Turkish propaganda or force of arms.

On the 16th September the sloop *Odin* arrived at Mohammerah; whereupon the *Vali* of Basra protested against the violation of neutrality. The answer to this was that the Turks had harboured the *Goeben* and *Breslau*. On the 26th General Barrow, the Military Secretary at the India Office, wrote an appreciation of the situation,[17] and came to the conclusion that one brigade of the 6th Division, two mountain batteries, and two companies of sappers, to be known as Force " D," would be sufficient to protect the oil works at Abadan. Such action " would checkmate Turkish intrigues, and demonstrate our ability to strike; encourage the Arabs to rally to us, and confirm the Shaikhs of Mohammerah and Kuwait in their friendly attitude; would safeguard Egypt . . . and would effectually protect oil installations at Abadan."[18]

This appreciation was seen by Lord Crewe and Lord Kitchener, and a telegram was sent to the Viceroy on the 26th instructing him to hold the 6th Division—previously earmarked for France—in readiness and, should the Cabinet so decide, to ship the brigade of the 6th Division with its artillery and sappers at once as if bound for Egypt.

On the same day news was received that thirty-two secret agents, including German officers, were on their way to preach a *Jehad* in Baluchistan, Afghanistan, and India, and on the 27th the Turks closed the Dardanelles. But still there was no declaration of war. All through October telegrams passed from India to England and England to India, and every day the intention of the Turks became more patent and their attitude more hostile. On the 2nd October the situation was so critical that the Government decided to take precautionary measures by sending Force " D," the brigade of the 6th Division, to the Shatt al Arab, at the same time warning the Viceroy that no hostile action was to be taken against the Turks without orders. The force was, in fact, to protect the oil tanks and pipe and British interests in Persia, and cover the landing of reinforcements in case of war with Turkey. As the pipe-line[19] extended for over one hundred miles into Arabistan, Brigadier-General Delamain's 16th Brigade[20]—earmarked for the operation— was obviously not strong enough, and therefore it was proposed that the rest of the 6th (Poona) Division should be held in readiness to reinforce it. Above all, the Musalmans in India were to be prevented from supposing that we intended to attack Turkey. Eventually, Bahrein was substituted for Abadan as the destination of Force " D," as this was a British protectorate and its

[17] *Ibid.*, Vol. I, p. 86.   [18] *Ibid.*, Vol. I, p. 88.
[19] The friendly Shaikh of Mohammerah was responsible for patrolling this, but expected help from Great Britain in the event of a Turkish attack.
[20] For telegraphic instructions see *Official History*, Vol. I, p. 92.

occupation could not arouse Turkish suspicions of an immediate attack. This force was to sail from India about the 15th. But for the rest of the month reports came in that the Germans and Austrians were trying to involve Turkey in the war; that German officers of the military mission had taken up commands and appointments in the field army; that mines, destined for Basra, had reached Baghdad; that the banks of the Shatt al Arab were being fortified; that preparations were being made to block the channel; and that reinforcements continued to stream down the Tigris. Then on the 29th October " the Germans took the law into their own hands," and the *Goeben* and *Breslau*, together with some Turkish destroyers, bombarded Russian ports on the Black Sea.[21] This was an act of war on our ally, and on the 5th November Great Britain formally declared war on Turkey. Turkey was ready, having had thirteen weeks in which to mobilize her Army.[22]

---

[21] *Official History*, Vol. I, p. 98.
[22] The sequence of events was as follows :—
    30th October ... Allied ambassadors demanded their passports.
    31st October ... Admiralty and India Office issued " war " telegrams.
    5th November ... A state of war with Turkey was proclaimed in London.

CHAPTER IV.

Great Britain Declares War.

Contrast in India—Mobilization of 6th (Poona) Division—Its composition—The 16th Brigade sails—General Delamain's instructions—The 43rd ordered to prepare for embarkation.

(See Map facing page 1.)

On the 4th August 1914 Great Britain declared war on Germany. The banks and Stock Exchange were closed; a moratorium was declared. A pall fell upon the nation, numbed and unaware of the meaning of modern war. But this pall was soon lifted; proclamations called for recruits, bands paraded the country, the anthems of all the Allies were sung, and meetings were held to entice the manhood of the nation to take up arms and fight.

But how did this explosion affect the East? In Ahmednagar the 43rd's " world did not shake, and even for a little while we wondered what all the noise had been about; there was no sudden paralysis of business—no rush on the banks—no panic—no fear of imminent starvation—no roar of troop trains through the night."[1] There was, of course, much speculative talk about the help that the Army in India could and was to give to the Army in Europe. Rumours flew round the messes and generally proved true. Secrecy was not one of the characteristics of the Simla offices. For instance, the divisions to be mobilized for service in France were known before orders to mobilize were issued. In Ahmednagar the Regiment was kept fully informed of its destination by bazaar stories which invariably proved correct. The first outward indication of the war was provided by a party of German prisoners who were housed in the old infantry lines and were treated with the utmost leniency. With permission to come and go where they wished, they soon abused their privileges. The issue of the war was to them a foregone conclusion, and with their innate arrogance they broadcast their opinions round the bazaars, with the result that the native mind, so receptive of impressions of the moment, became rather restive. The authorities decided that their stories of an imminent German victory were to be stopped. The prisoners were therefore properly interned, a wire fence was erected round the lines, and a guard of British troops set over them.[2]

On the 6th September the 6th (Poona) Division was ordered to mobilize

---

[1] Birch Reynardson, p. 2. [2] Colonel Lethbridge's Memoirs.

as part of Force "A," destined for service in France.[3] This division consisted of the 16th (Poona) Brigade—2nd Dorsetshire Regiment, 104th (Wellesley's) Rifles, 20th Punjabis, 117th Mahrattas; the 17th (Ahmednagar) Brigade—43rd Light Infantry, 103rd Mahratta Light Infantry, 119th Infantry and 130th Baluchis[4]; and the 18th (Belgaum) Brigade—2nd Norfolk Regiment, 7th Rajputs, 120th Infantry, and the 110th Mahrattas. Mobilization in the Regiment went forward " smoothly as if by clockwork " amid peaceful surroundings. One of the results of mobilization was that the Regiment was found to be short of officers. The 52nd, fully employed, could not produce officer reinforcements; and the 3rd Battalion became the feeder of the 52nd. The deficiency was made good by promotion from the ranks. Though this was not unprecedented in the Regiment—for example, Abraham Shaw in the Peninsular War and George Garland in the Indian Mutiny, both of whom became adjutants of the 43rd—yet never had the 43rd to absorb so many from the ranks. Of those promoted from the 43rd, only R.S.M. Mason was commissioned to the Regiment, and he too rose to be acting adjutant to Lieutenant-Colonel Lethbridge after the Battle of Ctesiphon. The Regiment also received Second Lieutenants G. Naylor (from serjeant, Somerset Light Infantry), D. Murphy (from lance-corporal, Yorkshire Regiment), R. C. Loverock (from colour-serjeant, Durham Light Infantry) and F. Brown (from the 14th Hussars).

Those who had never known war itched to be actively employed. Once mobilized, speculation on the Regiment's destination became the topic of conversation : soldiering became a serious business of " long route marches, field days, tactical exercises, lectures,"[5] and minute inspection of all equipment, added to which work of divers sorts was carried out by night. But none of these things compensated for the Regiment's inactivity when it was known that the 52nd was fighting for its life. Orders to move at eight hours' notice came at odd intervals, only to be countermanded by cancelling wires; and hounds met as usual on the Khanbagh road. In the early days of August the 43rd had been earmarked for France; then rumour had it that Egypt or Aqaba was to be its destination. But as the days passed into months, it had become increasingly obvious that the Regiment was to serve in Mesopotamia.

In the meantime, the 16th Brigade, under Brigadier-General Delamain, C.B., D.S.O., had received orders on the 4th October to be in readiness to go overseas on the 10th, with the 22nd Company, Sappers and Miners, and 1st Indian Mountain Artillery Brigade (23rd and 30th Mountain Batteries)

---

[3] *Official History*, Vol. I, p. 99.
[4] The 130th Baluchis were left behind at Bombay when the brigade embarked, and their place was taken by the 22nd Punjabis who joined the brigade at Maqil.
[5] Birch Reynardson, p. 3.

and certain medical supply and transport units.⁶ General Delamain's instructions included plans for the

- (i) Protection of British interests at the head of the Persian Gulf, that is the trade monopolized by British merchants and river steamers which had for many years been recognized and welcomed by the Turkish Government;
- (ii) The support of Mohammerah on the Karun River by co-operation with the Shaikhs of Mohammerah and Kuwait, the capture of Fao at the mouth of the Shatt al Arab, the occupation of the oil works at Abadan, and careful reconnaissance of Umm Qasr at the head of the Hor Abdulla as a likely base for the whole 6th Division;
- (iii) Operations in the event of war with Turkey in Mesopotamia by the occupation of Basra.

At the same time, General Delamain was warned "to avoid hostilities with the Turks and friction with the Arabs,"⁶ and, should the occupation of Abadan be ordered, he was advised to advance up the Hor Bahmanshir, to the east of the Shatt al Arab and in Persian territory, though he was not provided with launches of sufficiently light draught to enable him to obey his instructions. Force "D," the 16th Brigade, left Bombay on the 16th October with part of Force "A" and Force "B" bound for France and East Africa respectively. On the 19th the convoys parted company and Force "D" headed for Bahrein Island, which was reached on the 23rd. Here the 16th Brigade remained until war broke out,⁷ practising disembarkation from ships' boats. On the same day the 43rd was ordered to be ready to embark at short notice.

⁶ *Official History*, Vol. I, p. 99.
⁷ On the 31st October General Delamain received from India the news of the Turkish attack on Odessa; the following day he received the India Office's "war" telegram, stating that war had broken out with Turkey.

CHAPTER V.

MESOPOTAMIA.

EXTENT — GEOGRAPHY — RIVERS — FLOODS — RESOURCES — ROADS — SEASONS — DISEASES —POPULATION—THE TRIBES.

(See Maps facing pages 1 and 302.)

" THE boundaries of Mesopotamia are on the north the Armenian plateau and Kurdistan; on the east Persia; on the west the Arabian tableland and the Syrian desert; on the south the Persian Gulf and the deserts of North-Eastern Arabia."[1] Through the centre of this area flow the two great rivers, the Tigris on the east and the Euphrates on the west, which unite at Kurmat Ali, five and three-quarter miles above Basra, and thereafter flow into the Persian Gulf in one stream known as the Shatt al Arab. " This is a fine river, about one and a half miles wide at the mouth, narrowing at Basra, sixty-two miles upstream, to about six hundred yards,"[1] and navigable by any vessel which can negotiate the bar at the mouth.

Forty-five miles upstream the Karun river joins the Shatt al Arab at Mohammerah, and provides the principal communication with Northern Arabistan and the Persian oilfields.

The Euphrates has two channels, the old meeting the Tigris at Qurna and the new at Kurmat Ali. Both these channels are very difficult to navigate, especially in the flood season; and thirty-five miles west of Qurna the river flows through the Hammar Lake, which is so shallow that only vessels of three-foot draught can navigate it; also the channel runs through great swamps from Qurna to the lake and beyond it for seven miles. From Musaiyib, above Hilla, to Falluja where the course runs nearest to the Tigris the depth averages six and a half feet at its lowest. In 1914 the Euphrates was navigable by boats of three-foot draught from the Hammar Lake to Falluja, due west of Baghdad. Above Falluja only flat-bottomed boats, called *shakturs*, could be certain of navigation.

The Tigris is the main communication with Baghdad. In the flood season from mid-November to May the channel from Basra to Baghdad is not less than thirteen feet deep, but in the low-water season it drops to five

---

[1] *Official History*, Vol. I, p. 1.

GENERAL DESCRIPTION

feet between Ezra's Tomb and Qala Salih. Above Baghdad the river is only navigable by small steamers as far as Samarra. The country contained by the two great rivers is the ancient Babylonian plain which, though fertile, was never exploited, thanks to Turkish misrule which neither attempted a system of water conservancy nor means of preventing the inundation of the countryside from broken banks in the flood season. These inundations consequently cause large areas of swamp and marsh, sometimes from twenty to fifty miles in length, though not necessarily adjacent to the river banks. The dry belts of ground between the river and marshes are intersected by many creeks which sometimes require to be bridged.

Though the annual rainfall is only six and a half inches between October and April, yet heavy storms turn the sandy loam soil into a glue which precludes all military movement. The best season of the year comes between March and May when the temperature is tolerable; but at this time the floods are highest owing to the melting of the snows, and military operations are therefore rendered difficult. Only date palms exist, contiguous to the river; therefore fuel and building material have to be imported from abroad, and there is no stone for road making. In 1914 there were hardly any roads south of Baghdad; though tracks across the desert were well defined, they soon became " heavy under artillery and transport traffic."[2]

The hottest season comes between June and September, but cools in November; and from December to February it is decidedly cold. In the spring sandstorms and high winds are prevalent. Added to these extremes of climate, " Mesopotamia is a hotbed of ravaging diseases. Plague, smallpox, cholera, malaria, dysentery, and typhus, if not actually endemic, are all prevalent."[3]

Buildings are made of sun-dried brick without any sort of sanitation or ventilation, and were found unsuitable for military occupation. The principal products of the country are " dates, rice, barley and wheat, wool, and goats' hair, hides and skins "[4]; grain and meat were available but impossible of collection, and grazing for horses, though extant in places, could not be relied upon. The population of two and a half millions consists of Armenians and Kurds in the north, and Arabs comprise the greater part in the plains, with a sprinkling of Persians, Jews, Christians of different sects, Circassians, etc., in the towns. The Arabs, being masters of intrigue, treachery and blackmail, were undependable either as friends or foes, and were only subject to the administration of the tribal shaikhs. Of these the Shaikhs of Mohammerah and Kuwait were definitely friendly to the British, as was also Ibn Saud, the Emir of Nejd, in Southern Arabia. Basra is the best port, but in

[2] *Ibid.*, Vol. I, p. 6. [3] *Ibid.*, Vol. I, p. 8.
[4] *Ibid.*, Vol. I, p. 9.

1914 it was wholly devoid of wharves and quays, so that all unloading from ocean-going steamers had to be effected in midstream into primitive native boats; nor had it any resources capable of assisting its development to meet the increased traffic.

From this short account of the country it can be gathered that " all military problems therein, whether strategical, tactical or administrative, are affected by local conditions to an extent rarely met with in any theatre of war. Nearly all the conditions combine to create difficulties; there is little to alleviate them, and most may be ascribed either to a lack of water or a surfeit of it. Far away from the rivers want of water makes operations impossible, while near them the excess of water is almost as great a source of trouble."[5]

---

[5] Field Notes, General Staff, India, p. 10

CHAPTER VI.

Opening Operations.[1]

Arrival of 18th Brigade and Lieutenant-General Sir Arthur Barrett—The action at Saihan—Mirage—The action at Sahil—Capture of Basra—Future policy.

(See Map facing page 1.)

On the 31st October the news of the Turco-German attack on undefended Russian ports was received in the Persian Gulf, and operations were opened without delay. H.M.S. *Espiègle*, from Mohammerah, promptly dealt with the guns which threatened the oil works at Abadan, and H.M.S. *Odin* was ordered to await the arrival of the expedition at the bar of the Shatt al Arab. All steam tugs and launches were collected and armed, and ordered to co-operate with the 16th Brigade in clearing the river as far as Shamshamiya, an island in the river about five miles above Mohammerah, there to await reinforcements.

On the 2nd November Major Radcliffe, 2nd Dorsetshire Regiment, was sent to Kuwait to get into touch with the friendly shaikh while the convoy was assembling off the bar. On the 5th Major Radcliffe returned with the information that Fao Fort, at the mouth of the Shatt al Arab, was in ruins, but that the place was held by four hundred Turks with seven or eight old guns. On the 6th landing operations were begun. When our ships started sweeping for mines the Turks opened fire with four Krupp field guns; but by 10.45 H.M.S. *Odin* had silenced them from the close range of 1,700 yards. As she approached the shore heavy rifle fire was opened on her by three hundred Turks entrenched on the river bank, but these were likewise silenced by shrapnel. The landing party consisted of three companies of the 2nd Dorsetshire Regiment, the 20th Punjabis, 117th Mahrattas and 100 Marines, all under Lieutenant-Colonel Rosher of the Dorsetshire Regiment. This party required four relays of boats, thus emphasizing from the positive inception of operations that shortage which was not made good until disaster stared the Staff in the face. The troops landed without any opposition, and immediately occupied the important telegraph station at Fao, which was garrisoned by a company of the 117th while the rest of the force proceeded to capture the fort with little difficulty.

[1] See Map No. 1, facing p. 1.

The next day the force proceeded sixteen miles upstream and on the 9th and 10th occupied Sanniya, two and a half miles above the oil works at Abadan. On the 11th the Turks attacked at 5.30 a.m., but were driven off with great ease, reliable information of the attack having been received from the Shaikh of Mohammerah. Two days later the arrival of transports was reported, and on the 14th Lieutenant-General Sir Arthur Barrett, commanding the 6th (Poona) Division, took over command of operations. With him he had brought

6th Divisional Headquarters;
10th Brigade, R.F.A. (63rd, 76th and 82nd Batteries);
18th Infantry Brigade (2nd Norfolk Regiment, 7th Rajputs, 110th Mahratta Light Infantry, and 120th Rajputana Infantry), under the command of Major-General C. I. Fry;
Divisional Ammunition Column and certain hospitals;
Two squadrons, 33rd Cavalry;
17th Company, Sappers and Miners;
No. 3 Wireless Troop;
34th Divisional Signal Company (less 17th Brigade Section);
48th Pioneers;
10th and 12th Mule Corps;
Jaipur Imperial Service Transport Corps;
1,200 Camels, supply, ordnance, veterinary units, etc.[2]

General Barrett's objective was to be Basra if he considered his force strong enough to capture that place. In the disembarkation of the troops on the same day the shortage of tugs and lighters was so great that only the Sappers and 63rd Field Battery could be landed, and in this disembarkation the difficulties were greatly increased by the state of the ground, sodden by recent rain.

However, the following morning General Delamain carried out a reconnaissance in force to the north, and in a pretty action drove the Turks from their position at Saihan, thus ensuring the safe disembarkation of the reinforcements. Added to the viscous conditions underfoot, the troops experienced yet another of the disabilities of the country, namely, that mirage which was " to cause our troops endless trouble in the months to come."[3] Nothing is immune from the distortion of mirage: animals appear as men, infantry seem to be mounted, trees become hillocks, villages forts with towering walls, and often a string of camels miles distant appear to be walking close at hand and suspended in the firmament.

In order to influence the local Arabs and protect the Shaikh of Mohammerah who was threatened by a Turkish attack, General Barrett advanced on

[2] *Official History*, Vol. I, p. 113. [3] *Ibid.*, Vol. I, p. 117.

the 17th towards Sahil. The ensuing engagement, in which the Turks were driven from their positions, proved the superiority of the British and Indian troops despite the difficulties of mud, mirage, rain and sandstorm which effectively combined to render a hot pursuit and annihilation of the enemy a physical impossibility. But this action had been so successful and so demoralizing to the Turks that they evacuated their next position; and on the 20th the Shaikh of Mohammerah sent information to the effect that the Turks had also evacuated Basra and were retiring on Amara. " Till then General Barrett had not realized the decisive nature of his victory of the 17th."[4]

On the 22nd a detachment of the 18th Brigade under Major-General C. I. Fry occupied Basra and took over the guards on shore from the naval party which had arrived the previous day. Meanwhile the main force marched overland and reached the outskirts of Basra at noon, and saved the town from being looted and burnt by the Arabs.

On the 23rd General Barrett's force made a ceremonial entry into the town, the Union Jack was hoisted on one of the principal buildings, and the immediate objective was attained. Thereafter for many days the troops were fully employed in clearing up the age-old ordure round their camp and billets, in landing stores from the ships in midstream, and in reconnaissances of neighbouring villages, while the sappers and pioneers concentrated on making jetties, roads and bridges; and also on the improvement of the sanitation of the area which under Turkish rule had been disregarded. Drinking water for the troops was only available from midstream, and this " had to be fetched from the centre of the river and then chlorinated before use."[5] The disembarkation of stores, equipment and transport was necessarily very slow owing to the shortage of suitable craft for the purpose, and, more especially, the non-existence of quays at which the big ships could berth.

Meanwhile General Barrett had no inkling of the future policy or action to be taken by his force. But as the outcome of an extensive interchange of telegrams, in which an immediate advance on Baghdad was suggested, he was ordered to advance only as far as Qurna so as to consolidate his position at Basra and influence the Arab tribes on whose friendliness and co-operation the success or failure of the expedition so much depended. The deciding factors in this policy had been the lack of suitable craft, of which General Barrett " had only three steamers and four iron lighters available for navigation above Qurna,"[6] and the undisclosed attitude of some of the tribes. Up till this time only the Shaikhs of Mohammerah and Kuwait had shown a friendly hand; nothing had been heard from Ibn Saud and the Muntafik Shaikh, Ajaimi, was a doubtful quantity, inclined, if anything, towards hostility.

[4] *Ibid.*, Vol. I, p. 127.   [5] *Ibid.*, Vol. I, p. 132.   [6] *Ibid.*, Vol. I, p. 138.

CHAPTER VII.

THE 43RD TAKES THE FIELD.

ORDER OF BATTLE—ARRIVAL AT MAQIL—CHRISTMAS WITH THE 43RD—THE 43RD REACHES QURNA—RECONNAISSANCE OF MUZAIBILA—FORTIFICATION OF MUZAIRA'A—RECONNAISSANCE OF RUTA—TURKISH STRENGTH IN JANUARY 1915—BASRA THREATENED—FLOODS—ARAB RAID ON MUZAIRA'A—TURKISH THREAT ON AHWAZ.

(See Maps facing pages 1 and 64, and on page 42.)

MEANWHILE, in Ahmednagar, the same question is reiterated, " Where are we going ? " Rumour treads on the heel of rumour amid a forced semblance of peace. The young unblooded officers and men of the Regiment are still straining at the leash of patience, heedless of the quiet warnings of the veterans that war is a sad pastime. And then one cool evening at the beginning of November, Lieutenant Courtis " with furious toots of the horn came tearing down the moonlit road, stopped in front of the Club with a screech of brakes, and almost threw his machine into the arms of a gaping syce."[1] From table to table the news spread round, " The Brigade will proceed on active service " on Tuesday, the 17th November. At last the news was official, and the Regiment was to be relieved by a Territorial battalion from England. The following day another wire came ordering the Regiment to stand by and await further orders. Meanwhile " the luckless Territorials," the 1st/4th Dorsetshire Regiment, " were dumped down at the railway station " early on the morning of the 16th. By the 17th the Regiment was ready packed for active service, except for the orderly room typewriter, and still no time for departure had been ordered. Lieutenant-Colonel Lethbridge, therefore, ordered a route march; at 8.30 a.m. the Regiment " might have been seen plodding its way down the white dusty road "[2] to Khanbagh. At 10.30 a message from brigade headquarters intimated that the 43rd would entrain at 5 p.m. Arriving back in barracks soon after twelve, the Regiment was ready to move off punctually at 3.30 p.m., and " as it swung out on to the road to the railway station, the band struck up the regimental march."[3] The departure " was certainly not impressive : there were no flagged streets, nor enthusiastic crowds " as the gallant 43rd marched away, 875 strong with 25 officers, to the strains of " Tipperary," leaving behind the comfort of can-

---
[1] Birch Reynardson, p. 4.   [2] *Ibid.*, p. 6.
[3] *Ibid.*, p. 7.

tonments, barracks, bungalows, mess and polo ground which perhaps had not been quite fully appreciated in the piping times of peace. Behind, unmoved and dispassionate, lay the known, ahead lay the unknown.

Arriving at the station at 5.30 p.m., it was found that the troop train had broken down, and the Regiment was ordered to bivouac behind the station. The ground so allotted by the staff proved to be the town refuse ground, mephitic almost beyond endurance, but the 43rd made the best of a bad smell and stood its ground till 1.30 a.m., when the train came in and bore the Regiment off to Bombay, which was reached late that night, the 18th November, after a journey in which the arrangements for feeding the troops were conspicuously poor, an earnest of the future campaign.

The Regiment was ordered to march from Victoria Sidings to Alexandra Dock at 8 a.m. As the staff had omitted to provide any transport, bullock-carts had to be collected from the streets of Bombay by Lieutenant Whittall of the Regiment. The embarkation on the British India ship *Thongwa*, however, proceeded without a hitch, in spite of very cramped quarters and a " detachment of Imperial Service Transport with their complement of squealing, kicking, country-bred ponies and equally obstreperous mules."[4] And so, after one last rush to the shops for necessaries and a last taste of the fleshpots of Bombay, the Regiment sailed at 6.35 a.m. on the 20th November, cheered by a solitary couple, an ex-colour-serjeant of the Regiment and his daughter, who stood on the lock gates as the *Thongwa* passed through.

Those who went on service were :—

Lieutenant-Colonel E. A. E. Lethbridge, D.S.O., commanding.
Major A. C. Hyde, senior major.
Captain Hon. J. C. W. S. Foljambe, adjutant.
Captain T. E. Ivey, quartermaster.

" P " Company.[5]	" Q " Company.[5]
Captain C. F. Henley.	Major L. J. Carter.
Captain R. R. M. Brooke.	Captain W. E. T. Morland.
Lieutenant K. Horan.	Lieutenant F. M. Davenport.
Second Lieutenant A. E. Mason.	Lieutenant J. H. Courtis (machine gun officer).
Second Lieutenant D. Murphy.	Second Lieutenant R. C. Loverock.

[4] *Ibid.*, p. 10.
[5] The 43rd had but lately changed from the old eight- to the new four-company organization; and so as to avoid confusion the double companies were lettered " S," " P," " Q," " R," after the insignia borne on the Roman standards—*Senatus Populusque Romanus*. It was a pity that the 2nd/43rd reverted to the " A," " B," " C," " D " lettering, and that " S," " P," " Q." " R " were not revived after the war.

"R" Company.[5]	"S" Company.[5]
Captain F. H. Stapleton.	Captain C. E. Forrest, D.S.O.
Captain R. Stephens.	Captain R. V. Simpson.
Lieutenant G. E. Whittall (transport officer).	Lieutenant J. J. Powell (signalling officer).
Lieutenant H. T. Birch Reynardson.	Lieutenant F. C. W. Wynter.
	Second Lieutenant G. Naylor.
Lieutenant J. S. Kearsley.	Second Lieutenant F. Brown.

Captain J. Startin, R.A.M.C., medical officer.

On the 26th the Regiment awoke to find itself one of a fleet of many others, heading for Fao and the bar of the Shatt al Arab, which was crossed the following morning at 9 a.m., with "much bumping and churning of the screws." Steaming upstream past the Abadan oil works, with the decks crowded with eager eyes to see the new yet incredibly ancient land, the *Thongwa* eventually anchored ten miles below Mohammerah. But eager eyes were soon satisfied with the impenetrable, apparently interminable and altogether monotonous belt of date-palms on each bank. And here the Regiment stayed until the 3rd December, when a move was made upstream past the picturesque river frontage of Basra, the port of Sinbad the Sailor, with its clusters of native *bellums* and *mashufs,* to a point three miles above the town consisting of "a date plantation, a wharf, and two tin huts of European pattern,"[6] called Maqil, which was reached on the 5th at 10 a.m. Two hours later the disembarkation began, the Regiment being towed ashore by companies in a launch and lighter. The first three days were spent in unloading the ship of its multifarious burden of stores, animals, fodder, ammunition, fuel, equipment and food for British and Indian troops. In this work the crane on the wharf at Maqil—the intended terminus of the Baghdad-Basra railway—proved invaluable, and thanks were proffered by all ranks to the Germans whose kind foresight had installed it for their benefit and ease.

The camp was pitched in a clearing of the date plantations. No sooner was the unloading completed than fatigue parties opened up the restricted view, bridged the creeks, made roads in all directions in true light infantry style, and altered and improved the outpost positions.[7]

Meanwhile, further operations were being undertaken towards Qurna[8] to the north and Shaiba to the west of Basra. On the 3rd December a force, under Lieutenant-Colonel Frazer of the 110th Mahratta Light Infantry, consisting of a section of the 82nd Battery, R.F.A., half the 17th Company,

---

[5] See Note 5, p. 23. [6] Birch Reynardson, p. 25.
[7] For composition of Force "D" on the 1st December 1914, see Appendix I.
[8] See Map No. 3, facing p. 64.

Captain R. Stephens.   C.S.M. Shilcock.

1. 43rd Camp at Maqil, December 1914.
2. The first day at Qurna, guarding Arab Suspects.
3. Reconnaissance of Ruta, " R " Company in Action, 20th January 1915.

CAPTURE OF QURNA

Sappers and Miners, one company of the Norfolk Regiment, the 104th Rifles and 110th Mahratta Light Infantry, proceeded upstream and landed on the 4th December on the left bank north of the Shwaiyib river, under the protection of the guns of H.M. Ships *Espiègle, Lawrence* and *Odin*. Advancing north-west, the force quickly drove the Turks out of the village of Muzaira'a, capturing sixty prisoners and two 9-pounder field guns; then wheeling left through the date plantations, the troops lined the left bank of the Tigris opposite the Turkish position at Qurna. Here it was found impossible to cross the river to the attack of Qurna, and therefore Lieutenant-Colonel Frazer decided to retire to the Shwaiyib landing-point and await reinforcements. Accordingly General Fry, commanding the 18th Brigade, was ordered to take up the remainder of the 2nd Norfolk Regiment, the 7th Rajputs, half the 120th Rajputana Infantry, four guns of the 76th Battery, R.F.A., and assume command of the operations. By the time General Fry arrived at the front it was known that the Turks had reoccupied Muzaira'a and that the enemy numbered about 3,000. With the addition of the 30th Mountain Battery General Fry opened operations on the 7th December, capturing Muzaira'a once again in fine style together with one hundred and thirty prisoners and three field guns and inflicting heavy casualties on the enemy on both banks of the Tigris.

Bivouacking that night in Muzaira'a, part of the force moved out on the 8th to reconnoitre for a crossing. A suitable position was found north of the date plantation, and here the 17th Sappers and Miners succeeded in constructing a flying bridge for the passage of the 110th. Meanwhile the 104th Rifles, moving still farther north to protect the right flank of the 110th, were able to effect a crossing in two *mahailas* above One Tree Hill; then turning south, joined the 110th without opposition. By nightfall the two battalions were safely in bivouac on the right bank above Qurna, while the left bank was held at the flying bridge by the 2nd Norfolk Regiment. The Turks in Qurna, caught in a hopeless trap, surrendered unconditionally on the 9th to General Fry. Besides Subhi Bey, the *Vali* of Basra and commander of the enemy forces, there were captured 45 officers, 989 men, two field guns and two mountain guns.[9] This highly successful operation closed the first phase of the campaign, for the objective had been gained; the pipeline had been secured, and the Arabs, both friendly and potentially hostile, had had an opportunity of witnessing Britain's power by land and water.

On the river the co-operation and the support of the Royal Navy had been fearless and invaluable. During the two attacks on Muzaira'a the guns of the sloops *Odin, Espiègle* and *Lawrence*, and of the armed tugs *Miner, Shaitan* and *Lewis Pelly* had not only shelled the Turkish trenches with

---

[9] *Official History*, pp. 146-151.

lyddite, but also from exposed positions in midstream had neutralized the enemy artillery in the neighbourhood of Qurna, and had protected the troops' left flank. These operations set the seal to a wholly admirable partnership between the Navy and Army which was destined to survive throughout the campaign as a model of that perfection which, unfortunately, was not always attained in other theatres of war.

Meanwhile, the 43rd at Maqil had been improving its camp and communications, and experiencing some of the climatic conditions of wind, rain, mud, and cold for which it was inadequately equipped. Stealthy and generally fruitless visits to Basra to try persuasion on the stony hearted Supply and Transport with a view to hams[10] for the men's Christmas dinners and shooting trips up the new channel of the Euphrates helped to fill the Regiment's spare time. Christmas came and with it a very welcome consignment of plum puddings sent out by Lady Willingdon, but there was no turkey in the officers' mess in spite of the purchase at a high price and presentation of a live female of the species. Being a shrewd bird " Elizabeth " had so insinuated herself into the affections of the donor and the mess serjeant by her " endearing qualities " that her life was spared " to share the vicissitudes of war." Impartial with her favours she slept on or under each officer's camp-bed in turn, and at meal-times was always on parade in the mess tent pecking flies or dozing among the papers in the corner. " At last, one day, she fell ill : her legs swelled, and we thought it was gout; but when she died, mourned by all ranks, the doctor who conducted a *post-mortem* examination gave it as his opinion that death was due to three dozen gramophone needles, four regimental buttons and two trouser ditto, all found in the deceased's possession at the end."[11]

A few days later when the 43rd was beginning to wonder why it had been sent from India to this cold, cheerless land, the Regiment was roused at 5.30 a.m., ordered to stack kits at 7 and parade in full marching order at 8 a.m. for embarkation in the *Blosse Lynch*, bound for Qurna.[12] The journey was uninteresting in the extreme, and not till the evening did the steamer round the bend, disclosing Qurna, the supposed site of the Garden of Eden, " on its peninsula between the two rivers, the blue, leisurely Old Euphrates and the racing, tawny Tigris."[13]

Disembarking at Camp Tigris, a mile above Qurna, the 43rd plodded through the slush and mud of the dripping date plantation to the camp site in the desert. Thereafter, the 43rd was detailed to man the trenches on the western face where there was a gap in the defences, and was warned to expect a night attack. On arrival the trenches proved to be non-existent, and so the best use was made of entrenching tools. Having scraped what cover it could,

---

[10] Birch Reynardson, p. 55.
[11] *Ibid.*, p. 55.
[12] See Map No. 3.
[13] Birch Reynardson, p. 58.

the Regiment waited through the cold night for the attack which never materialized. The reason for this sudden upheaval of the Regiment from its peaceful surroundings at Maqil was that news had reached Sir Arthur Barrett on the 23rd December from the G.O.C. Egypt that the IV Turkish Army Corps was reported to be moving from Syria on Aqaba or Basra. This information was confirmed a few days later by news that reinforcements were moving to Baghdad from Constantinople, and that the XII (Mosul) Corps, consisting of the Arab and Kurd 35th and 36th Divisions of a nominal strength of 25,000 men and 72 old guns, had left Aleppo for Baghdad.

The Government policy of an advance to Nasiriya, which had been suggested in order to block the approaches from Baghdad via the Euphrates or Shatt al Hai and to protect the Muntafik Arabs whose co-operation was canvassed, was necessarily shelved in view of the probable counter-offensive by the Turks,[14] and General Barrett was also compelled to drop his own plan of an advance on Amara by which he hoped to persuade the Arabs to desert the Turks. Moreover, towards the end of December the Turks from Amara under Djavid Pasha moved south towards Ezra's Tomb, on the Tigris above Qurna, to support the Arabs in the neighbourhood who were becoming daily more hostile. Also General Barrett was told that no more troops could be sent to Mesopotamia.

Thus early in the campaign it is possible to trace the change in the objective to be attained by the expedition. Now that the safety of the oil works at Abadan and the pipe-line to Maidan-i-Naftun was practically assured, the policy seems to have veered round towards the accomplishment of alliances with the Arab tribesmen as the objective of the campaign.

On the 1st January 1915 the 43rd less " R " Company, the 103rd and 7th Rajputs, some cavalry, guns and sappers, all under the command of Brigadier-General W. H. Dobbie, commanding the 17th Brigade, moved northwards out of Qurna to reconnoitre the Turkish position at Muzaibila on the right bank, while H.M.S. *Espiègle* and the *Blosse Lynch* with two field guns protected the right flank of the force. Crossing the Barbukh Creek the advance guard brushed aside some Arab opposition and reached Muzaibila, whence a Turkish camp at Sakrikiya, estimated to hold 1,200 men, was easily discernible. On sighting the British force the Turks moved out and occupied trenches on both banks of the Tigris covered by two unfordable creeks. Meanwhile the further progress of the ships to within gun range of the Turks was prevented by two lighters sunk in the fairway below Ruta. This obstruction successfully precluded an attack on the Turks, and therefore General Dobbie withdrew the force without interference from the enemy.

The 43rd spent the early days of January in improving the perimeter of the camp, and the nights in dealing with Arab snipers, who had gradually

[14] *Official History*, pp. 154-156.

become more numerous and accurate. " Regularly every evening at about 4.30 straggling bands could be seen collecting on the edge of the marshes north-west of camp. When the crowd was assembled," Lieutenant Birch Reynardson wrote, " it would start drifting towards us, halting every now and then and working itself up into a state of apparent frenzy, shouting, stamping, and dancing, retreating a few hundred yards and then advancing again."[15] Waving green, white and black banners, the " Salvation Army meetings," as the 43rd nicknamed these fanatical demonstrations, would then melt into the mists, and snipe at the camp with persistent fury all through the night. Eventually the ardour of these enthusiastic demonstrators had to be damped by shrapnel from a section of field guns.

The weather was now more than unpleasant for the Regiment clothed in cotton drill. Pelting rain and cold winds followed one another with no alleviation until the 2nd, when a boat arrived containing the Regiment's tents. On the night of the 6th there was a particularly large Salvation Army Meeting accompanied by chanting of *Allah Illahi* in weird and uncanny cadences. The garrison stood to arms in the trenches; there was a boom, and a star-shell zoomed into the air high over the desert, disclosing the Arabs, banners and all, in a dazzling light. Three rounds of rapid fire from the perimeter crashed into the silence, answered by the drone of Martinis and the fizz of Mausers. But the Arabs did not stay long, and the rest of the night was quiet.

The routine of the Regiment now became one of digging by day and dealing with Arab parties at night. Qurna was gradually being fortified to hold a brigade, but this was no easy matter, as water was struck two feet below the surface. Nevertheless, the subalterns of the 43rd dug out stalls for the chargers under the direction of Captain Morland, who by his energy and ideas was splendid in keeping his brother-officers fully employed and consequently contented. Qurna itself was a filthy little village at the junction of the Tigris and Old Euphrates, boasting a few brick houses on the Tigris front and many vile-stinking mud stews and reed houses amid a tangle of horrible lanes. The eastern and southern sides of the village were flanked by the two rivers, the western by a canal creek running into the Old Euphrates, but the northern front faced the open desert. On the northern and western fronts a broad bank of earth, standing well above the water level, was converted into trenches and breastworks. The earth was hard and needed no revetting—and some well-found solid brick-kilns, built into the bank, were easily turned into observation and machine-gun posts.

Early in January General Barrett had asked for seven more river steamers and four gunboats,[16] and once more had stressed his need of aeroplanes, as the rising of the water round Qurna, the obstruction in the Tigris

[15] Birch Reynardson, pp. 61-65. [16] *Official History*, p. 158.

below Ruta, the difficulties of navigating the Hammar Lake,[17] and the hostility of the Arabs rendered reconnaissances almost impossible. The river ships were allowed, but aircraft refused, as the War Office was unable to spare any from the other theatres of war.

It was now known that several battalions and guns, under Sulaiman Askari Bey, had reinforced the enemy at Ezra's Tomb; and it was reported that the guns were under German officers; also that Ajaimi was assembling Arab tribesmen at Nasiriya and that a *Jehad* was being preached. As the result of this information General Barrett increased the Qurna garrison to "two squadrons of cavalry, four batteries of field and mountain artillery, two companies of sappers and miners, and two brigades of infantry, with half a battalion of pioneers"; and to meet this threat from the north a plan was evolved to make similar field fortifications opposite Qurna across the Tigris facing north and running east as far as Muzaira'a and thence bending back to meet the Shatt al Arab below the junction of the Old Euphrates.

The 43rd was suddenly detailed for this work, and crossed the river at 8 a.m. on the 10th in the *Blosse Lynch*. All day was spent moving animals, kits, tents, and stores two miles east to a point north of the palm belt outside Muzaira'a village. As there were no transport carts available, every single article of the Regiment's equipment had to be man-handled by fatigue parties across the shadeless desert. In such wise was "Elizabeth," the turkey, borne in her cage by her attendant, who was also carrying his rifle and equipment, 130 rounds of ammunition, kit-bag and dixie, to the strains of "We are but little children weak."

The 43rd having been fully employed all day without a chance of constructing a perimeter, lucky it was that the enemy left the tired troops alone that night. The following day a new site for camp was chosen under cover of the date plantation. As this had been previously occupied by the Turks all manner of indescribable filth had to be cleared away before a camp could be pitched; and at the same time a perimeter defence had to be constructed. By the 17th five self-contained redoubts, capable of holding one company in each, had been built in a semi-circle beyond the camp perimeter, protected by barbed-wire entanglements and land mines, and supplied with searchlights. These redoubts with wing trenches and communication trenches, gun emplacements on the flanks[18] and wire fences from the Tigris to the Shatt al Arab, gradually became a formidable fortification.[19] But in spite of ideal weather, cool nights and warm sun by day, two of the many plagues of the

---

[17] See Map No. 1, facing p. 1.

[18] The obvious position for the guns was about 600 yards in rear. As Captain Stephens pertinently remarks in his diary, "If any subaltern had so placed artillery in his schemes in 'D' examination (for promotion) he would have been failed."

[19] See Map No. 2, p. 42.

country quickly asserted themselves: flies and pariah-dogs. The cause was not far to seek: the position had been held by the Turks and was therefore filthy; and they had buried their dead just below the surface. The corpses were therefore reburied, but the plague of pariahs persisted. Accordingly Lieutenant-Colonel Lethbridge ordered a parade of all marksmen, and war was waged against the " big, shaggy, red-eyed, mangy " packs of dogs which slunk about the desert in search of shallow graves.[20]

By the last week in January the Regiment was comfortably ensconced in the gardens and date plantation, the while the floods, little realized at the time, began to encroach relentlessly upon its fortifications and camping-ground. The routine of digging, building, and wiring was varied by intervals for sport among the snipe of the marshes of the Shwaiyib River and pig in the open desert. " The tactics," said Lieutenant Birch Reynardson, " were to ride out early in the morning, when the pig came out on to the desert, and to get between them and the marshes: then the fun began. They . . . would always try to turn back. Anything in the way they charged most gallantly."[21] They also proved excellent eating, and a variety in the diet sheet.

Meanwhile, the diplomatic and political situation in Mesopotamia and India was constantly changing. A Russian victory over the Turks in the Caucasus at this time had merely increased the uneasiness of the Persians, whose neutrality had been violated by both sides. Hostile propaganda was reported to be affecting Persia, and news was also received that Swedish officers of the Persian gendarmerie were intriguing against the British.[22] Though the Russian success might be expected to attract Turkish reinforcements elsewhere, yet the increase in Turkish numbers in Mesopotamia was quite sufficient to threaten the British position. The effect of the *Jehad* in India, both on the North-West Frontier and in the Punjab, was causing such uneasiness that it was considered unsafe to send more troops out of the country.[23] Furthermore, Sir Percy Cox, the political officer in Mesopotamia, reported on the 15th January that some of the Arab shaikhs had abandoned their overtures to us and had joined the Turks; that the *Jehad* was having its effect at Basra, Amara and in Arabistan; and that the Shaikh of Mohammerah was becoming disquieted. As a remedy for the unsatisfactory situation he urged strongly that an advance should be made to Nasiriya and Amara. This suggestion was, however, refused on account of the supply of ships and troops which was insufficient to ensure success.

By the 18th January the Turkish and Arab activity in the neighbourhood of Qurna had much increased. From a position on the sandhills, south of

[20] Birch Reynardson, pp. 67-68.
[21] *Ibid.*, p. 69.
[22] *Official History*, Vol. I, p. 159.
[23] *Ibid.*, Vol. I, p. 160.

Ruta Creek, the enemy had been carrying out nightly reconnaissances up to our trenches, and Arabs, by sniping and raiding, had become a nuisance. General Barrett therefore considered that a strong demonstration should be sufficient to deter Arab activities and also prevent the Turks from creeping farther south towards our position. The force was to consist of two squadrons 33rd Cavalry, 63rd Battery, R.F.A., two sections 76th Battery, R.F.A., and 30th Mountain Battery, 17th Company, Sappers and Miners, the 17th Brigade, the 2nd Norfolk Regiment from the 18th Brigade at Basra, and half the Rajputs; and the *Espiègle, Miner* and *Mejidieh*[24] were to co-operate on the Tigris.

On the 19th General Barrett came up to Muzaira'a. Later Lieutenant-Colonel Lethbridge held a conference of all officers and explained the operations for the following day. The objective was to be the low ridge of sandhills a thousand yards long, south of Ruta Creek, which the Turks had lately occupied and from which they had fired on our patrols.

On the 20th January it was pitch dark and very cold when the 43rd paraded north-east of camp at 4.45 a.m. The advance guard, consisting of two squadrons 33rd Cavalry and "P" Company (Captain Henley's) and "Q" Company (Major Carter's) of the 43rd under Major Hyde, moved off, followed at 5.15 a.m. by the rest of the 43rd in artillery formation with the 103rd on its left. Behind marched the 22nd Punjabis and 119th Infantry with the Norfolk Regiment in reserve.[25]

As soon as the advance guard came under rifle fire from the direction of Halla village[26] at 6.45 a.m., the cavalry withdrew to the flanks and the first line deployed from platoons into extended order, and "S" Company advanced to join "P" and "Q" Companies, with "R" Company in support. "As the long lines went forward, the sun burst up above the eastern horizon with its usual wonderful suddenness, turning the dark desert into a sheet of gold." The colonel could now see what was happening. " A few hundred yards away," wrote Lieutenant Birch Reynardson, " the sandhills stretched across our front, lined not with Turks but with our own men." The Turks had not waited, but after firing one glorious volley had disappeared into the darkness. The ridge of sandhills was immediately occupied by the 43rd with the 103rd on its left and the 22nd Punjabis from the second line filling a gap in the centre. Meanwhile the guns came up to a covered position and opened fire on the Turkish camp behind Ruta Creek at 7.30 a.m.

" At 7.55 the Turkish guns began to reply, at first with common shell," most of which were duds, " and then shrapnel." They had the range to a nicety, but the shrapnel, bursting too high, luckily did very little damage."[25]

[24] Armed with two 18-pounder guns mounted on her top deck in the bows.
[25] *Chronicle*, 1914-15, p. 64.
[26] A burnt village about three miles short of Ruta.

They then switched on to the Regiment lying in the open desert, but luckily again did no damage. During the hour and a half of artillery bombardment the *Espiègle* and *Mejidieh* had been doing great execution with four-inch lyddite on the six Turkish guns, which were practically silenced by 10.45 a.m., while the *Miner* shelled the village of Abu Aran on the right bank, and engaged parties of Arabs and cavalry with great success. At 9 a.m. the 43rd and 103rd were ordered to advance in order to test the practicability of the marshes up to Ruta Creek and reconnoitre the dispositions of the enemy trenches beyond it. "R" and "S" Companies advanced with "P" and "Q" in support. Almost immediately the troops sank knee-deep in the mud and progress became very difficult; added to which the Regiment and 103rd came under enfilade fire from the right bank.[27] But though the Regiment pressed on to within a thousand yards of the enemy position without encountering stiff opposition, the enfilade fire was worrying the 103rd on the left. General Barrett, at this stage, felt much inclined to advance to Ruta village, destroy the enemy's camp and capture his guns, but he was deterred by the absence of materials wherewith to bridge the Ruta Creek. Meanwhile the 43rd formed a line and opened fire at long range on parties of Arabs seen streaming away from the position behind the creek, while the field and ships' guns shelled Ruta village and the *mahailas* in the creek with evident success, for the village was soon seen to be on fire.

At 11.30 a.m. when the operations seemed to be progressing quite favourably and all the enemy's guns, except one, were silent, the 43rd was ordered to retire, much to its disappointment. Encouraged by intermittent artillery and rifle fire from the snipers across the river, the 43rd ploughed its way back through the reeds and clinging mud to the sandhills, beyond which companies were re-formed and marched back to camp at Muzaira'a, having had fourteen men wounded.[28] The withdrawal was successfully covered by the second line and the ships, though the 103rd on the river bank had some difficulty in extricating themselves under the snipers' fire. But it so happened that the Turks were also preparing to retire, and the whole force was allowed to reach Muzaira'a by 2.15 p.m. without molestation, and with the loss of seven killed and fifty-one wounded.[29] Subsequently General Barrett complimented the 43rd on the part it had played in this affair.

The enemy's strength was estimated at five thousand, and prisoners reported that the Turkish losses amounted to two to three hundred killed and many wounded, including their commander, Sulaiman Askari Bey, who had been severely wounded by shrapnel. Reports also stated that the Turks were

[27] War Diary. Twelve men of the 43rd were wounded at this time.
[28] The regimental stretcher-bearers had to carry the wounded over the six miles to camp as the field ambulance failed to appear.
[29] *Official History*, p. 164. Birch Reynardson, pp. 85-87. *Chronicle*, 1914-15, p. 64.

disorganized, that the Arabs had quitted the field, and that gun ammunition had failed. The Turks themselves could not understand why such a successful attack had been stopped at the point of victory, and attributed it to the fact that they had inflicted severe casualties on the British lines; and this story they disseminated among the Arabs as useful propaganda. However, the reconnaissance had the desired effect of stopping the Turks in their southerly encroachment and also of reducing the sniping at our lines by night.

On the 19th information was received giving the enemy's numbers[30] in Lower Mesopotamia as twenty battalions of about six hundred men each. These consisted of five battalions of the 35th Division, nine of the remnants of the 38th Division which had fought at Sahil and Qurna, and six of Turks under Sulaiman Askari Bey. These forces were disposed in three separate bodies—one at Amara, another at Ezra's Tomb, and the third detailed for an attack on Basra from the west. By the 26th January a Turkish cavalry regiment and an infantry battalion, together with a large number of Arabs of the Bani Lam and Bani Turuf at the call of the *Jehad*, were reported to be moving eastward towards Ahwaz on the oil pipe-line. At the same time it was reported that the Muntafik Shaikh, Ajaimi, with fifteen thousand Arabs had joined a force of two thousand Turks and five guns destined to carry out the westward attack on Basra; and it was presumed that the thirteen battalions at Ezra's Tomb would co-operate by an attack on Qurna. This information, which foreshadowed a concerted attack on Basra from three directions, caused General Barrett to ask the Indian Government for reinforcements.

In answer to his request the Indian Government speedily arranged for the dispatch of the 12th Brigade (2nd Royal West Kent Regiment, 4th Rajputs, 44th Merwara Infantry and the 90th Punjabis) under Major-General K. Davison, C.B., by the 1st February. Towards the end of January the 43rd was duly impressed by the arrival at Muzaira'a of a section of 4-inch guns,[31] of an ancient type, drawn by a team of sixteen oxen. These "cow-guns," of early breech-loading pattern, and the four 5-inch "cow-guns" of the 86th Battery, R.G.A., which arrived early in April, were destined to be the heaviest guns with Force "D" until 1916.

Meanwhile the floods in the desert were gradually but perceptibly encroaching on the position, assisted by torrential but spasmodic rain from above, which converted the area into slimy and viscous mud. Nevertheless, the work of fortification continued without interruption or excitement until the evening of the 29th when Lieutenant-Colonel Lethbridge sent for all officers and warned them of an expected attack at 10 a.m. which was interpreted as meaning 10 p.m. The Regiment stood to arms through a blighting

[30] *Official History*, Vol. I, p. 165.   [31] Belonging to the 104th Battery, R.G.A.

cold night. Lieutenant Birch Reynardson, who with Lieutenant Whittall and No. 10 Platoon had reinforced the trenches on the northern front, wrote that "at 1.30 a.m."—the 30th January—"we were awakened by the sounds of heavy firing from our rear, and as we had no parados to our trenches, this was distinctly a nuisance. . . . It was all over by 2 a.m. At daylight, we picked up five killed and eight wounded Turks—including an officer—between No. 1 Redoubt and the eastern face of the perimeter. . . . The casualties on our side were eight wounded, and three horses and one camel killed." Later—and too late—a squadron of the 33rd Cavalry took up the pursuit of the rest of the enemy, numbered at two hundred according to the wounded Turkish officer, and came up with a party of stragglers. The cavalry managed to kill six and wound several others with the loss of one jemadar killed and three sowars wounded.

After this raid by the Turks there were nightly alarms for the next few days due to the spotting of large bodies of Arabs moving towards the Shwaiyib River. As a result two companies of the 2nd Norfolk Regiment and the 20th Punjabis were ordered across from Qurna to strengthen the garrison. At this time, the 43rd held No. 3 Redoubt with a whole company, and 3A trenches with a platoon, in the outer defences; one company and three platoons held the camp perimeter, and one company rested in tents within the date gardens, so that every sixth night was spent in bed.[32]

In the meantime the news from Ahwaz was disturbing. The *Jehad* was undermining the power of the Shaikh of Mohammerah. The assurances from Tehran that the lives and property of Europeans would be protected and any Turkish advance opposed by the Persians had to be viewed with suspicion considering that German agents were known to be intriguing among the Persians and Bakhtiaris. To counter this danger, Lord Crewe, Secretary of State for India, suggested that a small force should be dispatched to Ahwaz forthwith to encourage the Bakhtiaris and Arabs. This suggestion was rejected by the Indian Government, who objected to the dissipation of Force " D " for the protection of the oilfields and pipe-line, as in their opinion the protection of Basra was of paramount importance. At the same time the British Government was requested to supply sufficient reinforcements to constitute two divisions in Mesopotamia.

On the 30th Qurna reported that the Turks seemed likely to advance south from Ruta, and news came in that the enemy had been encountered seven miles west of Shaiba, and that large bodies had left Nasiriya to attack Basra. In spite of this concerted movement on Basra, General Barrett dispatched the 7th Rajputs from Qurna to Ahwaz. This movement of the Rajputs once again emphasized—if emphasis were needed—the complete in-

[32] *Chronicle,* 1914-15, p. 68.

adequacy of the river craft at the disposal of the unfortunate general officer commanding; and, at last, the Indian Government were galvanized into requisitioning the seven river steamers which had already been requested.

Towards the end of January the Viceroy, Lord Hardinge, sailed from India to see for himself the local conditions in Mesopotamia, reaching Basra on the 4th February. The situation appeared to be as follows: " The Turks had five thousand troops with seventeen guns opposite Qurna-Muzaira'a, two thousand about Nasiriya, and seven hundred with two guns moving towards Ahwaz."[33] The remainder, about four thousand, were probably at Amara or moving towards the Euphrates; further reinforcements of six divisions were reported to be concentrating at Baghdad; the Arabs appeared to be increasingly hostile on all fronts and the *Jehad* was affecting not only the Lower Euphrates and Arabistan areas, but also Basra itself. It was then that Lord Hardinge considered it necessary to push the Turks farther away in order to ensure the safety of Basra. At this time the 12th Brigade and 16th Cavalry were on their way; and "S" Battery, R.H.A., and the 7th Lancers were under orders to leave India for Basra.[34]

On the 2nd February the whole of the 43rd was on outpost duty in expectation of an attack which did not materialize. Nevertheless, Arab activity increased considerably, coinciding with the projected visit of the Viceroy on the 6th. On the 5th a monster Salvation Army Meeting in front of Qurna, attended by thousands of Arabs and flags, was dispersed by the *Miner's* six-pounder and machine-gun fire at close range.[35] All was quiet when the Viceroy arrived on the 6th. Captain Stephens, with Lieutenants Powell and Mason, formed a guard of honour on the pier, while the Regiment paraded at 3 p.m. in No. 3 Redoubt. The Viceroy, after inspecting the Regiment and the defences, left at 5 p.m. for Qurna where he stayed the following day. About a month later Lord Hardinge in a memorandum to the Home Government advised the occupation of Amara and Nasiriya in order to safeguard our oil interests in Persian Arabistan and facilitate the administration of Basra. Before leaving on the 8th February, Lord Hardinge told General Barrett that, as it was impossible to send any more troops to Mesopotamia, the Government did not contemplate any big advance. The possibility of an advance on Baghdad was never even discussed. To meet the situation General Barrett informed the Viceroy that he intended to hold the outpost positions Qurna—Muzaira'a—Shwaiyib with three brigades and to concentrate one brigade at Basra, with a cavalry brigade at Shaiba as a movable column capable of supporting any threatened spot; and that he would not require more infantry unless the 7th Rajputs required reinforcing at Ahwaz.[36]

[33] *Official History*, Vol. I, p. 170.
[35] Birch Reynardson, p. 91.
[34] *Ibid.*, Vol. I, p. 170.
[36] *Official History*, Vol. I, pp. 171-173.

CHAPTER VIII.

ON THE DEFENSIVE.

THE PIPE-LINE BREACHED—FLOODS RISE—" BELLUM " BRIGADE INITIATED—THE 43RD FLOODED OUT OF MUZAIRA'A—GENERAL SITUATION—AFFAIRS AT SHAIBA AND AHWAZ—REINFORCEMENTS ORDERED.

(*See Maps facing pages 1 and 64, and on page 42.*)

No sooner had Lord Hardinge returned to India than the situation altered completely and assumed a critical aspect. The Bawi who inhabit the country east of the Karun rose, plundered the oil-stores and breached the pipe-line: the tribes disregarded the orders of the Shaikh of Mohammerah; news came in that the *Vali* of Pusht-i-Kuh, to the north-west of the oilfield, had joined the Turks, and that 2,500 Turkish troops were on their way to Ahwaz. To check this threat and the effect of the *Jehad* on the authority of the Shaikh of Mohammerah, a force consisting of the 4th Rajputs, some cavalry, guns and sappers, was detached and sent up the Karun river to Ahwaz.[1]

Meanwhile, at Qurna and Muzaira'a the floods were steadily rising. As the result of the inundations each infantry battalion was ordered to organize a fleet of four *bellums* manned by a crew of eight men so as to facilitate reconnaissances of the marshes and control of the neighbouring Arabs. Captain Morland[2] was appointed to command the *bellum* brigade with Lieutenant Birch Reynardson in charge of the regimental boats. Each company supplied one crew with shovels for paddles, and morning and afternoon the regimental fleet gyrated on the face of the waters, soldiers turned sailors, under the patient eye of the experts.

The Regiment now had to fight the inexorable advance of the flood, the worst for thirty years as it proved. Day and night the sappers and fatigue parties, carrying hods of dry earth from the desert, laboured to keep the road to the pontoon bridge and Qurna above water-level, until it became a causeway carefully revetted at the sides. Gangs of marsh Arabs, many of them doubtless undesirable characters to have within the defences, were bribed by high wages to participate in the herculean task and made heavy weather of light loads in Oriental fashion. Very soon movement became a matter of wading, likely to develop into swimming. On the night of the 16th

---

[1] *Official History*, Vol. I, p. 174.
[2] Captain Morland was originally put in charge of the regimental boats, with Serjeant Arlett as his immediate subordinate.

"the river bank broke in twenty-two places, and the water among the trees rose nine inches, completely isolating No. 4 Redoubt," which was consequently abandoned, wrote Lieutenant Powell.[3] All available men were hastily detailed to make a *bund* to stop the incursion, but it was impossible to build it fast enough.

The water from the Shwaiyib now extended to the north of Muzaira'a, necessitating the withdrawal of the force. On the 19th the Royal West Kent Regiment and 90th Punjabis of the 12th Brigade were ordered to cross the river to Qurna, whence two battalions were withdrawn to Basra; and during the next few days the cavalry and guns departed for drier quarters. To add to the intense discomfort of the troops, the heavens opened and torrential rain fell night after night, so that only an ark was lacking to produce the picture from Genesis. On the 25th water entered East trenches and was prevented from flooding No. 3 Redoubt by a *bund* built across its front. The following day water seeped into the 43rd camp. On the 27th "P" and "Q" Companies under Major Hyde crossed over to Qurna and took over Forts Peebles and Frazer, man-handling all the carts across the bridge. The next day Headquarters and "R" and "S" Companies arrived, and the Regiment was allotted half the perimeter, to be held by one and a half companies in conjunction with the 103rd. Meanwhile the luckless 22nd Punjabis were detailed to hold the bridgehead at Muzaira'a, and were bidden to enclose themselves within walls of mud on the site of their camp. The evacuation of Muzaira'a signified the destruction by the hand of man or the elements of all the careful and hard work which had been done over a period of two months. This was sufficiently disheartening to all ranks.

The floods in the New Euphrates valley were creating great difficulties in the supply of the western outpost at Shaiba, north-west of which Ajaimi was known to be concentrating. On the 19th he was reported to be within fifteen miles of Shaiba with fifteen hundred Turks and six guns, in addition to about three thousand Arabs. The movable column under General Delamain was consequently ordered to move out of Basra and attack him. Against a gale of wind, driving sand and grit before it, the column trudged through thick mud and water to Shaiba. Arrived, it was reported that the enemy had been greatly reinforced at Nukhaila, and General Delamain, after vainly trying to tempt the Turks to attack him, was forced to return to Basra under indescribably bad conditions.[4]

The general situation in Mesopotamia by the end of February was very obscure. The Turkish screen which extended from Nukhaila in the west to the Karkha river, north-west of Ahwaz, was composed of the 35th Division and gendarmerie, but what troops were shielded behind it was not known. As many as seven divisions were reckoned to be either in or on their way

[3] *Chronicle*, 1914-15, p. 69. [4] *Official History*, Vol. I, p. 176.

to Mesopotamia. Nasiriya and Nukhaila were reported to be supplied with troops sent down the Shatt al Hai, and our cavalry patrols were daily encountering more opposition on their reconnaissances from Shaiba. Consequently on the 24th General Barrett ordered General Delamain to reinforce Shaiba with the 16th Brigade, less the 117th Mahrattas at Kurmat Ali, and the 6th Cavalry Brigade.[5]

On the east the situation was even more disturbing. Arab cavalry was daily becoming more active to the north-west of Ahwaz, and Turkish forces amounting to four thousand with fourteen guns and fifteen thousand Arabs were concentrating on the Karkha river, preparatory to an advance through Bakhtiari territory to attack Basra in the rear. At the same time, H.M.S. *Espiègle* reported that the tribes of Southern Arabistan, east of the Shatt al Arab and Karun river, were so menacing that small garrisons were placed at Abadan and Marid, on the Karun. The situation, however, in front of the Regiment at Qurna was quite normal.[6]

Meanwhile the General Staff in India realized that the position might become critical at any moment, and decided to increase the force to two divisions, in spite of threats of serious internal trouble, mutiny, and rebellion in the Punjab. But divided as General Barrett's little force was into four main detachments without adequate transport either by river or land, it was not inconceivable that each body might be defeated in detail. Ships, both transport and hospital, and gunboats were insufficient to maintain or relieve the needs of the force in its present state of dispersal. An increase, therefore, of troops without a greater proportion of ships was only likely to cause extreme embarrassment and immobility.

Then on the 3rd March two actions were fought on the extreme flanks of the force. In retiring after a demonstration in front of Nukhaila the 16th and 33rd Cavalry, with two sections of "S" Troop, R.H.A., were seriously engaged by nearly two thousand enemy cavalry when light was failing. At one moment the enemy practically enveloped the little force and the gunners had to protect themselves with their revolvers. At the critical moment, however, the infantry supporting force under Lieutenant-Colonel Rosher of the Dorsetshire Regiment, at length able to discriminate between friend and foe, opened a devastating fire from guns, rifles and machine guns on the Arab horsemen, who, completely taken by surprise, made off with all speed.[7]

A similar action was fought north-west of Ahwaz. In this case General Robinson, in command, had received information that the Turks at Ghadir were due to be joined by the Bani Lam and Bani Turuf tribes, and he therefore decided to shell the Turks before the union of the two forces. At dawn the force reached the point within range of the Turks, and the guns opened fire. The result was instantaneous; as if some supernatural hand had stirred

[5] *Ibid.*, Vol. I, p. 178. [6] *Ibid.*, Vol. I, p. 179. [7] *Ibid.*, Vol. I, pp. 181-182.

a hornets' nest. Large bodies of Arabs rushed out of the camp and proceeded with a startling celerity to envelop both flanks of the force which with the greatest difficulty averted a serious disaster, and retired back to its perimeter having lost one 18-pounder gun and part of a mountain gun besides 62 killed and 127 wounded.[8]

In this action 9166 Lance-Corporal R. Parkes, of the 43rd, was in charge of the orderlies of No. 1 Field Ambulance. For his conspicuous gallantry in attending to the wounded in the open under heavy shell and rifle fire, and in protecting them with his own rifle fire from the assaults of the enemy, he was awarded the *Distinguished Conduct Medal* in June.[9]

These two actions on the east and west forced the issue of reinforcements upon the British and Indian Governments, as the political situation in Arabistan and the neighbourhood of the oil pipe-line was exceedingly disquieting, the Shaikh of Mohammerah having lost control of all but one of his tribes.[10] At this point, the British Government stepped in and gave the Indian Government on the 5th March definite orders to send reinforcements, and at the same time relieved the Indian Government of responsibility for the consequences in India. The 33rd Brigade—1st/4th Hampshire Regiment, 11th Rajputs, and 66th and 67th Punjabis—under Major-General Gorringe, and the 1st/5th Hampshire Howitzer Battery from India and the 30th Brigade from Egypt were consequently ordered to Mesopotamia. Also the War Office agreed to send out two aeroplanes, leaving the Indian Government to find the pilots; but it is significant to note that no arrangements were made for the supply of river transport, the importance of which Sir Arthur Barrett once more reiterated at the end of February.[11]

---

[8] *Ibid.*, Vol. I, pp. 183-185.
[10] *Official History*, Vol. I, p. 187.
[9] *Chronicle*, 1914-15, p. 114.
[11] *Ibid.*, Vol. I, p. 186.

CHAPTER IX.

I.—THE 43RD AT QURNA, MARCH 1915.

FLIES AND FLOODS—" BELLUM " PARADES—EUPHRATES BLOCKADE FORCE—THE SHAIBA FRONT—SIR JOHN NIXON TAKES COMMAND—BATTLE OF SHAIBA—APRIL 1915—THE 43RD AT QURNA—TURKISH RETREAT FROM SHAIBA—THE 43RD ON THE EUPHRATES BLOCKADE—POLICY IN MESOPOTAMIA DEFINED—GENERAL NIXON ADVISES OFFENSIVE—OPERATIONS NEAR AHWAZ—DUNLOP'S FORCE ADVANCES TOWARDS AMARA.

(*See Maps facing pages* 1, 64 *and* 302, *and on page* 42.)

At the beginning of March the Regiment at Qurna experienced the first of the hot weather that was to come, and the sultry stillness and steaming heat became very oppressive. The Regiment's quarters, infested with fleas and sand-flies, were at the northern end of the village among the " date palms, on a bit of ground intersected in all directions by irrigation ditches, brimful and odoriferous, the breeding ground of clouds of mosquitoes. As we could walk hardly five yards in any direction without meeting one of these ditches, the pitching of tents was a matter of difficulty, and, in addition, the palms, too precious to be felled, had also to be avoided."[1]

Qurna had altered considerably since the 43rd left for Muzaira'a early in January. Camp Tigris was inundated, but Fort Snipe on the Tigris bank, a thousand yards north of the perimeter, was still held. Still farther north, Norfolk Hill and behind it One Tower Hill and Gun Hill still protruded through the floods, but, save these, there were no landmarks; all was one vast expanse of water. Within the perimeter an encircling causeway and transverse roads had been constructed, giving access to the trenches facing the marshes and the strong points, called Forts Winsloe, Frazer, Observation Post, and Forts Peebles and Fry. Within the causeway on the northern and " western sides of the perimeter lay an expanse of horrid bog which gradually became a stagnant lake, forming a lagoon . . . and on the scarcely solid core of this lagoon, surrounded by stagnant water and moated with many ditches " sat the garrison, " while the waters rose, heat increased and mosquitoes multiplied." As a man in the Regiment shrewdly remarked, " If

---
[1] Birch Reynardson, p. 104.

1. Raising the Road to Muzaira'a.
2. Pontoon Bridge between Qurna and Muzaira'a.
3. Inside No. 3 Redoubt, Muzaira'a.
4. Flooded Date Garden, Qurna, April 1915.
5. Building Reed Huts.

Qurna was the Garden of Eden, it wouldn't take no blinking fiery sword to keep me out of it."[2] The defences at Qurna were roughly square in shape, bounded on the east by the Tigris and by the Euphrates on the south. The brick-kilns on the western *bund* were converted into strong points between the forts. These last were situated thus: Fort Lanyan on the Euphrates front; Fort Peebles on the Euphrates at the southern end of the western *bund*; Fort Frazer at the north-western corner; Fort Winsloe at the north-eastern corner on the Tigris; and Fort Fry at the south-eastern corner of Qurna itself at the confluence of the Euphrates and Tigris. The 17th Brigade was disposed as follows: the 43rd's front extended from Fort Lanyan round the *bund* to a point half-way between Forts Frazer and Winsloe. At this point the 119th Infantry took on the remainder of the northern face and joined hands with the 43rd on the Euphrates front. The 103rd permanently garrisoned Fort Snipe, which had been constructed within the perimeter of the erstwhile Camp Tigris. A section of 4-inch guns and the ships' guns were the only artillery available. Cut off from all intercourse with the rest of the division, the garrison seemed likely to become stale from enforced inactivity and monotony. But this the elements and Arabs did not allow. On the 6th March Lieutenant Powell with No. 16 Platoon of "S" Company embarked on the *Miner* to participate in a punitive expedition against a village up the Shwaiyib, the inhabitants of which had been stealing tools from Muzaira'a. But on reaching the Arab village it was found that the birds had flown, except for three old women sitting in a *mashuf*. Thereupon the village was burned down and the party returned to camp.

Meanwhile the persistent encroachment of the waters kept the Regiment more than busy; seepage was constantly undermining the foundations of its defences; the Regiment became plumbers and plumbed for three months. As counter-attractions the *bellum* brigade put in constant practice; Arabs had to be carefully watched, as thieves stole Captain Morland's *mashuf* and the officers' motor-boat from under the nose of a sentry on the 9th; and to keep the 43rd diverted from monotony the Turkish guns occasionally tried to shell the camp and to blow up the bridge across the river with floating mines, and snipers sniped at night.

The weather, too, proved extremely variable all through March. Abnormal heat gave way to pelting rain, and a sandstorm with a " strong south wind produced an atmosphere like a London fog,"[3] to be followed by torrential rain which inundated the only parts of the camp hitherto untouched by the floods.

On the 13th Lieutenant J. S. Kearsley of " R " Company went down to Basra, returning on the 31st with trench mortars.

[2] *Ibid.*, p. 106.   [3] *Chronicle*, 1914-15, p. 77.

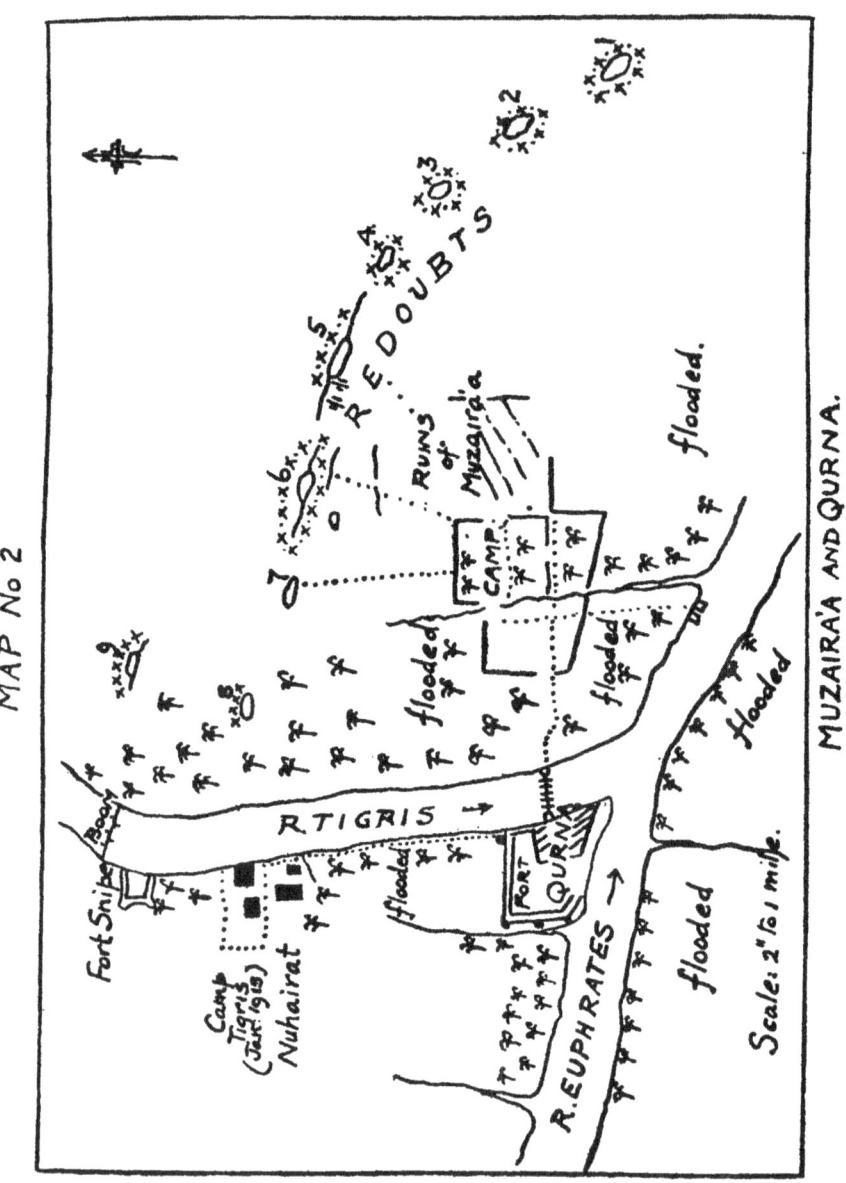

II.—March 1915. The Rest of the Mesopotamian Front.

March was quiet elsewhere, the British remaining on the defensive and preparing for the threatened attack on both flanks. The Turkish left wing in the neighbourhood of Ghadir[4] consisted of about a cavalry regiment, nine battalions with eight guns, and Arabs. But their inactivity was discouraging to the tribesmen whose enthusiasm for the *Jehad* was diminishing. On the other hand, the enemy right wing at Nukhaila was waxing in strength, and it was evident that an attack on Shaiba was intended with simultaneous demonstrations at Qurna and Ahwaz at an early date. In order to harass the concentration on the left flank, the Euphrates Blockade Force, consisting of two detachments of British and Indian infantry with sappers and gunners, was organized to man the stern-wheelers *Shushan* and *Muzaffari*, the paddle-steamer *Salimi*, and the tug *Sumana*. The *Shushan* carried two 3-pounders and the *Salimi* one 18-pounder; and in a 200-ton barge a 5-inch gun was mounted. This force did considerable execution by bombarding the Turkish position and supply *mahailas* at Nukhaila, Allawi and Ghabishiya; and established a complete blockade of the enemy's communications, which was only broken by the necessity for returning to Kurmat Ali for rations and ammunition. The moral effects of this blockade added to the difficulties of the enemy concentration, and also discouraged the Arabs. Elsewhere in Southern Arabia and along the eastern Persian Gulf German agents were active in their efforts to stir up the tribes round Shiraz and Bushire, and were so successful that General Barrett gave the Consul at Bushire leave to draw on any reinforcement arriving in the Gulf if he considered the situation critical.[5] It is significant that up till now the rear and communication of Force " D " had never been absolutely secure, a fact which continually militated against the concentration of the whole British forces.[5]

On the 31st March General Barrett received information that the main Turkish force had left Nasiriyah,[6] and April opened with a hostile reconnaissance of the position at Shaiba by cavalry and infantry.

III.—April 1915. Shaiba Front.

On the 3rd April the enemy was reported south of Zubair, which is south-south-east of Shaiba; and when informed that the enemy had completed his concentration on the 6th General Barrett expected an attack within ten days.

Meanwhile on the Ahwaz front the weak cavalry outposts had been driven in by the enemy on the 31st March and again on the 6th April. But to meet these attacks there were now two divisions in the country, the 33rd

---

[4] *Official History*, Vol. I, p. 190.   [5] *Ibid.*, Vol. I, p. 192.
[6] *Ibid.*, Vol. I, p. 193.

Brigade of the 12th Division with the 1st/5th Hampshire Howitzer Battery and 12th Company, Sappers and Miners, having arrived already, while the 30th Brigade—consisting of the 24th Punjabis, 76th Punjabis and 2nd/7th Gurkhas—reached Basra from Egypt on the 6th April. Command of the two divisions was given to Sir John Nixon, K.C.B., who arrived with his Corps Staff on the 9th, and took over from Lieutenant-General Sir Arthur Barrett, K.C.B., K.C.V.O., who returned to India on the eve of a critical battle, a sick but successful man. With the departure of Sir Arthur Barrett and the appointment of Sir John Nixon in his stead that forward policy was initiated which culminated in the Battle of Ctesiphon. In his orders[7] from Army Headquarters, India, of the 24th March General Nixon was told to "secure the safety of the oilfields, pipe-line and refineries," and to submit a plan "for the effective occupation of the Basra *vilayet*," which extended almost to Kut al Amara, and "for a subsequent advance on Baghdad." He was also required to give an opinion on the advisability of using a regiment of Imperial Service cavalry to guard the pipe-line and a report on (i) the quantity of animal transport required; (ii) a light railway; (iii) armoured cars and mechanical transport; (iv) aircraft; (v) the adequacy of the ships on the way to Mesopotamia, namely, two Nile gunboats, seven Irrawaddy paddle-boats, two flats, two motor-boats, four tugs, four steam launches, two steam cutters and two horse-boats. At long last there was to be some increase in water transport, but still only on a scale unlikely to satisfy the full needs of one division, though there were now two divisions in the country. And here, in General Nixon's orders, for the first time there appears a definite change in policy by a possible advance to Baghdad. When, later, the Mesopotamia Commission took the evidence of Sir Beauchamp Duff, Commander-in-Chief in India, and General Nixon, it was proved that the occupation of the Basra *vilayet* signified an advance to Nasiriya and Amara, and that General Nixon understood that he was to abandon the defensive and assume the offensive.

Hardly had General Nixon assumed command when Major-General Fry, commanding the force of two brigades at Shaiba,[8] reported that the Turks were advancing.[9] Now Shaiba lay eleven miles west of Basra and practically isolated therefrom by nine miles of floods. The garrison consisted of the 6th Cavalry Brigade with "S" Battery, R.H.A., 63rd and 76th Batteries, R.F.A., and 23rd Mountain Battery, the 16th Brigade, 18th Brigade less 7th Rajputs, 48th Pioneers, and two companies of Sappers and Miners. These occupied a semi-circular perimeter backed by the floods, with piquets out in front.

[7] *Ibid.*, p. 194.
[8] For composition see *Official History*, Vol. I, p. 197.
[9] For description of Battle of Shaiba see *Official History*, Vol. I, pp. 199-216; Birch Reynardson, pp. 121-130; and Lieutenant Powell's diary, *Chronicle*, 1914-15, p. 81.

The expected attacks were made on the 12th at 5 a.m. by Turks on the southern and western faces and Arabs on the north; but neither made any impression all day, and a night attack was also repulsed after some stiff fighting. The following day a sortie by cavalry and infantry cleared the enemy from the north, and then swinging round drove the enemy from the low mounds on the west. By the evening of the 13th General Melliss, V.C., who had taken over from General Fry, determined to pursue the advantage, and on the 14th the whole garrison, except the 48th Pioneers and 104th Rifles, advanced against the Turkish position east of Barjisiya Wood. All through a burning day the British crept forward, fighting every foot to reach the well-sited enemy trenches, until it seemed likely that darkness would force a withdrawal. But at the crucial moment the 16th and 18th Brigades stormed the enemy positions and the Turks took to their heels, harassed by their Arab allies, who, immediately changing sides, took upon themselves the mantle of our cavalry and treacherously and mercilessly hung on to their retreat.

How decisive this action at Shaiba was, was not realized at the time. The order to withdraw was given at 6 p.m., and the weary, thirsty troops with all their wounded returned to camp at 8.30 unmolested. The casualties amounted to 1,062, of whom 161 were killed. The enemy casualties in the three days' fighting were estimated at 6,000, and, in addition, 18 officers and 724 other ranks were taken prisoners. Sulaiman Askari Bey, who, though not recovered from his wound, was present in command, shot himself at the close of the battle, cursing the Arabs for their treachery and consequent miscarriage of his plans.

In Basra itself the population congregated round the Zubair Gate during the battle, suitably prepared with offerings wherewith to temper the vengeance of the Turks whom they expected to recapture the town.[10]

IV.—APRIL 1915. WITH THE 43RD.

The first week of April was spent in *bellum* practice, mud-larking, and hut building at which the 43rd was becoming quite expert under Lieutenant Davenport. The Turks, meanwhile, had occupied One Tower Hill and Norfolk Hill on the right bank and One Tree Hill on the left. From One Tower Hill they carried out ineffective shoots on H.M.S. *Espiègle*, Fort Snipe and Qurna. But on the 11th the enemy activity increased, and the camp was shelled all day and far into the night. From this it appeared that the enemy had mounted guns on Gun Hill behind the Barbukh creek as well as on One Tower Hill. The bombardment started again on both sides early on the 12th, the enemy plastering the north face and Fort Winsloe.

---

[10] *Chronicle*, 1914-15, pp. 78-83, and for composition of Force "D" see Appendix II. Birch Reynardson, p. 130.

At the same time, two thousand Bani Lam Arabs from Amara assembled among the trees beyond the creek on the west face. At 7.45 a.m. they started the usual "sing-song performance," but Lieutenant Courtis turned a machine gun on to them as they crossed the Euphrates and successfully moderated their incantations. At about 9 a.m. the bombardment started again; not long before a floating mine hit the centre of the bridge and blew it sky-high, and desultory rifle fire broke out from the Bani Lam Arabs across the creek. Meanwhile another great prayer-meeting and sing-song was being held by the Arabs on the south bank of the Euphrates. "We can see them all marching round and round a green flag," wrote Lieutenant Birch Reynardson at 9 a.m. "Then they all jump together and let off a scream—most entertaining." At 10.30 a.m. H.M.S. *Odin* moved up the Euphrates and shelled One Tower Hill and the Arabs opposite the west face. This shook them so much that at 2 p.m. they cleared out of their positions and punted across the open marsh past the west face at about 1,200 yards' range. Here was a glorious target which was not missed either by the 43rd machine gun or the 4-inch guns which sprayed them with shrapnel. Two hours later more Arabs began to withdraw, and were similarly treated with obvious success; and on this occasion the Turkish guns were distinctly seen to speed their parting allies after our guns had ceased to fire. As an attack was expected the whole Regiment stood to arms through the night, but the enemy never came.

The 13th was quiet, though the distant gun fire of the battle at Shaiba was easily heard. Not till 5.30 p.m. was there any disturbance, when the Turks again shelled the camp, narrowly missing the officers' mess cow. Casualties to date from the enemy shelling amounted to only two men wounded. On the 14th the Turks bombarded the camp periodically and managed to hit the Observation Tower, ninety feet high,[11] without doing serious damage; and rumours of an attack by the Bani Lam kept the Regiment awake at night on the 15th. These scares and half-hearted demonstrations were parts of the plan to create a diversion at Qurna while the main Turkish attack was launched against Shaiba. But no sooner did the news of the result at Shaiba filter through than enemy activity ceased suddenly, and there was peace again on the waters.

It was on the 15th that the Euphrates Blockade Force gave news of the decisive results of the Shaiba battle. Steaming towards Nukhaila, the flotilla encountered many of the enemy attempting to escape in boats, and these "they pursued ... destroying eight and capturing four large *mahailas*."[12] Two days later the flotilla reconnoitred Ghabishiya, which was found to be deserted. On the same day General Nixon sent orders to the flotilla to

[11] *Chronicle*, 1914-15, p. 71, and *Official History*, Vol. I, p. 242.
[12] *Official History*, Vol. I, p. 219.

blockade the main Euphrates channel at Suq ash Shuyukh, and to engage the routed enemy troops there and at Khamisiya. As a reinforcement to the flotilla, "Q" (Major Carter's) Company of the 43rd with Captain Startin, the medical officer, embarked at 3.30 a.m. on the 18th on the *Malamir,* together with a company of the 103rd. But as the enemy was now retiring from Khamisiya to Nasiriya by land, the flotilla was unable to interfere with him. Accordingly the force was ordered to reconnoitre the approaches of the New Euphrates to Hammar Lake and Suq ash Shuyukh. In the meantime on the 21st a message indicated that the east end of the lake was held by three Hotchkiss guns, and Lieutenant Naylor and twenty-five men of "S" Company were sent off in H.M.S. *Lewis Pelly* to investigate, but returned the following day without having found any traces of the enemy. "Q" Company returned on the night of the 25th, having had a welcome change and amusing experiences; and "S" (Captain Forrest's) Company embarked in their place for Hammar Lake in the *Malamir* the following day. Though these reconnaissances with the Euphrates Blockade Force appeared to the troops to accomplish precisely nothing, they helped General Nixon to decide that it was impossible to pursue the beaten enemy and engage him at Nasiriya, owing to the shortage of land transport and of craft of suitable draught to cross the Hammar Lake and negotiate the deceptive channels of the Old and New Euphrates. An offensive from Qurna to press our advantage was impossible for the same reasons. Therefore General Nixon decided to make his counter-offensive from Ahwaz, and was strengthened in his decision by an urgent request from the Admiralty to repair the broken pipe-line, as the oil supply was becoming serious.

On the 19th General Nixon asked India for another cavalry brigade and more pioneers, but these were refused owing to internal unrest on the North-West Frontier. The forces in the country at this time consisted of two divisions, but it is imperative to note that these two divisions were remarkably deficient in ancillary and auxiliary units. They were short of field artillery, pioneers, field ambulances, signalling units, and transport of all kinds. The artillery and pioneers were shunted from front to front as and when their services were required, and two simultaneous operations were almost impossible to carry out owing to lack of transport. " The divisional signal unit for the 12th Division was formed by transfers of personnel and equipment from regimental units."[13]

We will now leave the 6th Cavalry Brigade, the 30th Brigade and divisional troops on their way to Ahwaz by land and river, and return to Qurna. Here heavy rain and rising floods were endangering the very existence of the 43rd's island home and two pumps, driven by oil engines, were installed to keep the water down within the perimeter. By the 23rd the river

[13] *Ibid.,* Vol. I, p. 224.

and floods had risen two feet higher than the camp and were only restrained by *bunds*, necessitating constant vigilance and hard work. The next day Major-General Townshend, who had taken over command of the 6th Division on the 22nd, arrived to inspect the position and report upon the possibility of an offensive up the Tigris. This visit, added to the secret arrival and disposal of the 1st/5th Hampshire Howitzer Battery on the 28th in Fort Frazer on the north-west corner of the perimeter, betokened an offensive at an early date. On the 29th General Townshend inspected the 43rd, and on the 30th the howitzers were taken up to Nuhairat, between Qurna and Fort Snipe. But these were mere preliminaries to the amphibious war which the 43rd was destined to carry out with conspicuous success within a month.

On the 19th Captain F. H. Stapleton was appointed D.A.Q.M.G. to the 6th Division and the command of " R " Company devolved on Captain R. R. M. Brooke.

V.—The Political Aspect.

It will be remembered that General Nixon had been instructed to prepare a plan for the occupation of the Basra *vilayet* which included Amara and Nasiriya.[14] A copy of these instructions was sent to the India Office, but in the meantime Lord Crewe wired to India that the Government would " not sanction at this moment any advance beyond present theatre of operations " —presumably Shaiba—Qurna—Ahwaz. Yet in the very next sentence he stated : " We must confine ourselves to defence of Basra *vilayet* and oil interests in Arabistan. If it is possible to advance to Amara with view to establishing an outpost which will control tribesmen between there and Karun and so contribute to the security of the pipe-line, I should be prepared to accept such a proposal provided it is supported by you, but I deprecate any plan involving undue extension and possible demands for reinforcements. . . . We must play a safe game in Mesopotamia."[15]

General Nixon was later accused of being too ambitious in his plan for accomplishing the British Government's policy of occupation of the Basra *vilayet*. But having a beaten and disheartened enemy in front of him he was naturally reluctant to allow the Turks time to reorganize and reinforce their fighting troops, and he was convinced that the occupation of Amara was necessary to ensure the safety of the oilfield and pipe-line. On the 23rd May the British Government gave their permission for this advance to Amara on the condition that General Nixon gave an assurance that he would not require reinforcements to effect it, and that he was satisfied that he could concentrate a sufficient force at Amara to withstand any attack from Baghdad in the summer months.[16] On the 25th May General Nixon wired to India asking

[14] *Ibid.*, Vol. I, p. 194. [15] *Ibid.*, Vol. I, p. 235.
[16] *Ibid.*, Vol. I, p. 237.

whether the occupation of Amara and Nasiriya was to be effected or not, because his original instructions from Army Headquarters in India disagreed with Lord Crewe's telegram of the 23rd. He pointed out that he could not guarantee that the enemy would not send superior forces to Baghdad; that " the enemy had been strengthening their position on the Tigris about Ruta "[17]; that if an advance were not made to Nasiriya it would be necessary to adopt a defensive attitude at Basra, as the powerful western Arabs would not be content to remain peaceful. Therefore, he urged an advance on Nasiriya as soon as transport should be available from the Tigris, and while the water was still deep enough for ships to navigate the Hammar Lake. Finally, he asserted that he could not protect the oilfields without occupying Amara; but were his attack on Amara successful he could withdraw troops from Ahwaz to garrison the Euphrates or Tigris fronts. On the 27th May the Indian Government instructed him to " expel the Turks from the Lower Tigris below Amara "[18] and thereafter submit a plan for the occupation of the Basra *vilayet*.[19] At last the Government policy was defined, and the general could act. On the same day Mr. Austen Chamberlain took over the India Office from Lord Crewe, and on the 1st June the Viceroy wired requesting that the British Government should not tie the general's hands with precise orders which it might not be possible to obey, and suggesting—in fact—that he should be trusted to do the right thing.

VI.—MAY 1915. OPERATIONS NEAR AHWAZ.

Meanwhile the operations from Ahwaz during May were entirely successful. As soon as the reinforcements were seen in Arabistan, the Bawi and Bani Turuf became more friendly. The difficulty of supply over the desert was so great that General Gorringe was forced to adopt the system of establishing depots for food, fuel and fodder. Despite foul weather ten days' supply was amassed by the 3rd May at Ali Ibn Husain, and a reconnaissance proved that the Turks had retired to the right bank of the Karkha. Three days later the cavalry and 30th Brigade advanced to Illa, and by the 13th the force had crossed the swollen river in the teeth of a raging gale.

On the 16th punitive measures were taken against the Arabs of Khafajiya, who had treacherously mutilated our wounded on the 3rd March. As a result a hundred Arab dead were counted and a thousand sheep and cattle captured. During these operations the troops suffered great discomfort from

[17] *Ibid.*, Vol. I, p. 238. [18] *Ibid.*, Vol. I, p. 239.
[19] The extent of the Basra *vilayet* was probably not fully understood at this time by all parties concerned. Topographically its effective occupation entailed the capture of Kut al Amara as well as Nasiriya. In point of fact the Government did not visualize an advance beyond Amara : a discrepancy in an important detail which caused considerable confusion.

heat, dysentery and brackish water, and it was found that the medical units were insufficient to deal with the cases of sickness; omen of the future. However, a column under Colonel Dunlop struggled on towards Amara early in June, while the remainder were withdrawn weary and stale to Basra after seven weeks in the shadeless, monotonous desert wherein the only diversion from fighting came in the form of grit-laden, suffocating sandstorms. But the object was achieved, for now the safety of the right flank was assured, and the pipe-line mended. The stage was set for a similar advance up the Tigris to Amara.[20]

---

[20] *Official History*, Vol. I, pp. 224-234, and Birch Reynardson, pp. 159-162.

CHAPTER X.

I.—Preliminaries to the Advance to Amara.

Success of "bellum" Brigade—Decision to attack Turkish position in "bellums"—"Bellum" practice—Preparations for attack—The Turkish position—The plan—The Qurna Regatta, 30th May—The 43rd's casualties—Attack on Abu Aran—Turkish retreat—Pursuit—Capture of Amara—The 43rd in Amara—Despatches.

(See Maps facing pages 1 and 64, and on page 42.)

May in Qurna ushered in amphibious warfare for the 43rd. Whereas the Regiment had been on the defensive all through April, immediate offensive action against any body of the enemy was now adopted. As any failure to attack was invariably assumed by the Arabs to be due to weakness, it was henceforth imperative to influence the waverers. On the 18th April[1] each regiment of the 17th Brigade was ordered to train two hundred men to punt and paddle *bellums*. For this purpose *bellums* were bought, hired and stolen from Basra, and the 43rd, with its nucleus of trained crews, soon produced a fleet. Serjeant Arlett of the 43rd, son of the boat-keeper at Henley and a waterman from his youth up, became the instructor in punting to the whole brigade.

On the 4th May Lieutenants Birch Reynardson and Kearsley with fifty rifles of "R" Company and 300 rounds per man embarked on the *Salimi*, armed with one 18-pounder gun and machine guns from the 4th Hampshire Regiment. Captain Brooke went aboard H.M.S. *Espiègle* on the 5th as military adviser. The party was to co-operate with the Shaikh of Medina in a punitive expedition against the Shaikh of Haffa (who had been in the habit of looting the Basra—Shaiba convoys), and was to give moral and physical support, if necessary.

The flotilla started at 7.30 a.m., led by H.M.S. *Odin* and H.M.S. *Espiègle,* and followed by the *Salimi,* the *Sumana* with twenty-five men of the 22nd Punjabis and two 3-pounder guns, and the *Mahsoudi* with another twenty-five men of the 22nd Punjabis. "We steamed up the Euphrates for about two hours," wrote Lieutenant Birch Reynardson, "until, on rounding a bend, we came in sight of Medina, where we found the Shaikh and his army of about 1,500 cut-throats waiting for us."[2] A small proportion of these braves, dressed in a strange motley of garments, were sitting in *mashufs*.

---

[1] *Official History*, Vol. I, p. 244.   [2] *Chronicle*, 1914-15, p. 84.

The rest of the army was still on the river bank, congregated round many multi-coloured flags—including the Turkish Star and Crescent—and jabbering to their hearts' content. As soon as H.M.S. *Odin* anchored, the shaikh boarded the flagship for a conference. It was arranged that the shaikh should ascend the Haffa creek and surround the recalcitrant village with his army, then the *Mahsoudi* was to appear and wreak punishment. After much palaver Medina gave the order to move. This was the signal for an uproar among his followers, " words of command, bellowings of religious ecstasy, shouting, singing, and much brandishing of rifles." Then suddenly there was silence, and the whole fleet shot out into the stream and paddled off.

In the meantime Lieutenant Birch Reynardson's party and Captain Brooke had been transferred to the *Sumana*, and after a suitable lapse of time the steamers set off for their objective. But on reaching the village, two miles up the creek, the Arabs were found sitting in the sun holding one of their numerous prayer-meetings. They had considered it too hazardous a task to surround the village, and had come to the conclusion that it was far wiser to give the enemy a chance to escape if he were so minded. Having warned the enemy that the British warships were on the way, the shaikh had suspended all operations to give the enemy time to decamp. The arrival of the *Mahsoudi*, however, inspired the Arabs to new fervour, and with blood-curdling yells they advanced to the attack the while they discharged their Martinis into the air. It was hardly surprising that the sole occupants of the village were a few decrepit old women. The attack, therefore, was bloodless and successful, and soon the village was a fiery furnace, from which the gallant victors returned laden with spoil. But there were no signs of the stolen rifles and ammunition rather naturally. This affair proved how little reliance could be placed upon Arab co-operation. Fickle, feckless and faint-hearted when most their services were required, the Arabs were useless as allies, and it was decided that where punishment was needed British troops should henceforth administer it.

Accordingly the *bellum* brigade was given the next punitive task on the 8th May. Parading at 6.30 a.m. at Fort Peebles, the eight crews from each of the 43rd, 22nd Punjabis and 103rd Mahratta Light Infantry, twenty-four boats in all, under Captain Morland, 43rd, were made fast to three towing ropes from the *Salimi*, in which were the colonel, Headquarters and " S " (Captain Forrest's) Company. After half an hour's steaming the boats, in two of which Lieutenant Courtis had mounted machine guns, were cast off near a village on the south bank of the Euphrates. Lieutenant Birch Reynardson was given orders to make straight for the village and, if held up by fire, he was to give H.M.S. *Odin* and H.M.S. *Espiègle* the enemy's position, when they would open fire. However, he was given definite orders not to fire on the Arabs until they fired on him, as the shaikh had promised to deliver

1. Mudlarking, April 1915.
2. Lieutenants Powell, Courtis and Whittall.
3. Floods at Qurna, looking towards the Kilns.
4. "Q" Company practising in Bellums.
5. Parading for the Dress Rehearsal of the Regatta (Captains Forrest and Morland in the foreground).
6. The Regatta Rehearsal (Colonel Climo, Commanding 17th Brigade, standing, Captain Morland with flag).

up his rifles. Moving ahead in his *mashuf* with Turner poling and Jackson in the bows ready to open fire, and followed by the little flotilla, Lieutenant Birch Reynardson reconnoitred and found the channel to the village. " On suddenly coming round a bend in the channel," he wrote, " I found the village full of people in a state of great excitement. Several of the men were armed, and got as far as putting up their rifles and covering us; so I shouted back to the boats behind to cover all the armed Arabs. As soon as the latter saw that we meant business, and that I was not alone, many threw down their guns and others made off, wading or swimming." Had he not been tied by his orders, Lieutenant Birch Reynardson might have prevented many from escaping. " We got through the village as quickly as possible, and coming out on the marshes on the far side, found a whole line of *mahailas* . . . drawn up by the edge of the village." Many *mashufs* escaped, but one *mahaila* which " tried to get away, was stopped at once by a group from the machine guns." Now—but too late—the order against firing was cancelled, because there was no sign of the shaikh redeeming his promise. As this village had supplied snipers and raiding parties against the Shaiba convoys, " we were ordered at 11.30 to burn and loot the village, and to collect any Arabs that we could. It was quite extraordinary how difficult it was to make the good, orderly, civilized British soldier play the Hun, and burn and smash things." The " loot consisted of two cows (one of which died in transit), three sheep, some chickens, carpets, Arab clothes, brass ornaments and pots, and three rather nice chests."[3] In this little affair the *bellum* brigade made such a satisfactory and valuable début that " it was considered possible that with further practice it would be fit for a more important rôle in the near future."[4]

In the meantime, while General Gorringe was operating in Arabistan, General Nixon had ordered General Townshend to report on the practicability of using *bellums* in an advance up the Tigris to Amara. That *bellums* could be so used the operations of the 8th May abundantly proved. General Townshend therefore turned to the task of reconnoitring the best route by which to attack the Turkish positions at Ruta, and accordingly ordered a reconnaissance of the Al Huwair creek,[5] to the west of Qurna, on the 9th May. For this Lieutenant Davenport and thirty men of the 43rd embarked on board H.M.S. *Shushan*, armed with two naval 3-pounders and three Maxim machine guns. When about six miles up the creek the *Shushan* encountered marsh Arabs hidden in the reeds, which, standing six feet high, provided cover for an attack from all sides at close range. " Realizing that the reeds rendered this route impracticable for an advance and that further

[3] *Ibid.*, 1914-15, p. 86.
[4] Birch Reynardson, p. 139.
[5] *Official History*, Vol. I, p. 245.

reconnaissance was useless and dangerous,"[6] Lieutenant-Commander Cookson, R.N., in command, determined to turn his ship about, and was severely wounded in the process. Meanwhile Lieutenant " Davenport took command of all the [Maxim] guns, and kept up a heavy fire until they were out of range," and to do so " he kept shifting his guns from side to side and from one deck to another."[7] In this affair Lance-Corporal Gardiner and Private Tappin of the 43rd were slightly wounded.

In Qurna, meanwhile, the howitzers started to register on the Turkish positions on Norfolk Hill, One Tower Hill, and One Tree Hill on the 9th and 10th May, and on the 11th General Nixon issued instructions for an advance from Qurna to drive the enemy from Pear Drop Bend above Ruta and for the subsequent capture of Amara. The following day General Townshend submitted his plan for a frontal attack, covered by land and river artillery, while a detachment on the east bank of the Tigris executed an enveloping movement on One Tree Hill. This plan was accepted by General Nixon, and henceforth all was bustle and preparation for the operations. On the same day Paddler No. 3 (known as P3—one of seven Irrawaddy coolie-boats from Burma) arrived with the 119th Infantry and Brigade Signal Section from Shaiba, thus reuniting the regiments of the 17th Brigade; and Generals Nixon, Kemball (the Chief of Staff), Townshend and Delamain arrived later on a tour of inspection. Qurna had now become the hub of operations after a depressing period of military inactivity. Each regiment was to have eighty *bellums,* of which thirty-two were to be armed with machine-gun shields across the bows. These were carefully and quickly supplied by the sappers at Basra, together with "rafts for mountain and machine guns, barges for heavy guns and *mahailas* for hospital purposes."[8] On the 13th General Nixon inspected the 43rd and 103rd in the morning, and told the officers that the 6th Division was to advance to Amara and that the 17th Brigade had been given the post of honour.[9] " He said that if he could not do it with us, he could not do it at all,"[9] wrote Lieutenant Powell in his diary.

The weather by now was becoming extremely hot—the thermometer always being above 100—and all parades were accordingly finished by 9 a.m. so as to keep the men out of the noonday sun. Parades consisted of *bellum* practice, as every man had to be trained to paddle and pole this craft, and a method also had to be evolved for advancing at close range under fire. In this Captain Morland gave a demonstration to the general officer commanding and commanding officer. " He turned all the men out of the *bellum* and

[6] *Ibid.,* Vol. I, p. 245.
[7] Lieutenant Powell's diary, *Chronicle,* 1914-15, p. 87.
[8] *Official History,* Vol. I, p. 246.
[9] *Chronicle,* 1914-15, p. 88.

made them push it through the reeds broadside on."[10] The operations on the Tigris were to have taken place on the 21st, but it was soon found that they required far greater organization and attention to details than had been at first supposed.

As the preparations progressed it was decided that " each *bellum* was to carry ten men, two to pole, eight to fight, with their equipment, reserve ammunition, water, two picks, two shovels, thirty feet of rope and caulking materials, two spare poles, and four paddles." Moreover, the crews of each *bellum* had to be carefully weighed so that the draught should not exceed eighteen inches. As there were rafts to be built, caulked and distributed to the gunners and machine-gun sections, reconnaissances of the marsh to buoy the shallow water and continuous practice of crews to be carried out, it was found impossible to restrict work to the early cool hours, with the result that several men collapsed with heat-stroke, and fever became a menace. These casualties entailed more work for the hale, for crews had to be changed and trained all over again. Then, it was suddenly decided that each regiment should have twelve double-*bellums*, joined by spars and armoured.[11]

On the 19th May the enemy became active from the sandhills where he was evidently mounting guns, and during the ensuing week sniping at night increased considerably.[12] Two days later General Dobbie, who had broken his leg on the way out, was invalided to India. Colonel Climo, 24th Punjabis, was appointed to the command of the 17th Brigade on the 23rd. All through those feverish preparations *bellum* practice was being carried out and it is not surprising that many were at first fearful of the issue of the experiment, for once afloat it was argued that officers would have very little control over the individual crews. We read of these practices: " Matters were somewhat confused at first, but once out on the open marsh, things went better " when " R " Company was taken out on the 24th; again, " Q," " S " and " P " Companies out at practice in " the morning " of the 25th " and did not do so badly." But gradually the 43rd adapted itself like true light infantry to the task imposed, and boat practice progressed well amid the welter of other work.

The distance across the floods to be covered by the attacking *bellums* on the right bank from Qurna to the first enemy position on Norfolk Hill was three thousand five hundred yards; beyond lay One Tower Hill fifteen hundred yards away, and beyond again, two thousand yards north-west, lay Shrapnel Hill and Gun Hill. Four thousand yards beyond Gun Hill lay the main Turkish positions of Abu Aran and Muzaibila. On the left bank there were two enemy positions, on One Tree Hill and at Ruta. Three regiments —43rd, 103rd and 119th—were to attack the enemy positions on the right

[10] *Ibid.*, 1914-15, p. 89.   [11] Birch Reynardson, p. 144.
[12] *Official History*, Vol. I, p. 248.

bank, while the 22nd Punjabis from Muzaira'a were to envelop One Tree Hill. " When it is remembered that the whole of this distance "—over four miles from Qurna to Gun Hill—" was without any cover from fire and with only rather uncertain cover from view, that theoretically the crowded boats would be under shrapnel fire for the whole of their journey and close-range rifle fire from each position for at least five hundred yards before the crews could disembark and wade through mud to the assault, it may be said that the pessimists had some reason for their misgivings."[13]

The enemy numbers opposed to the 17th Brigade were estimated at three battalions of regulars, one of gendarmerie and an unknown number of Arabs, with ten guns distributed as follows: one on One Tower Hill, two on Gun Hill, four at Abu Aran and two at Ruta, with one on the flank in the marshes of the Al Huwair creek.

Success, it seemed, had to depend largely on the superiority of the British artillery and the co-operation of the Royal Navy with heavy guns, though it was known that the services of the Navy might be greatly restricted by the presence of mines in the channels.

On the evening of the 28th a dress rehearsal for the *Regatta,* as the impending operation was called, was held in full view of the Turks. Moving out from the perimeter at Qurna in three columns, the *bellums* and rafts deployed into two lines (the 43rd and 103rd in the front line and half the 119th in the second) at Fort Snipe whence the attack was to be launched on the 31st. On the left flank the remainder of the 119th was posted, and a half-company of the 43rd escorted the 30th Mountain Battery, echeloned on the right flank.[14] All went well. The front line of each regiment consisted of armoured *bellums,* with machine-gun rafts on the outer flank. It was soon found that the armoured *bellums* were difficult to propel through the reeds, as a result of which the shields were adjusted the next day to rectify this disability. During the rehearsal signal communication with Headquarters on board H.M.S. *Espiègle* was maintained by heliograph, from platforms made regimentally, which stood six feet high in the marsh. The apparatus was then worked by a signaller sitting in a *bellum*. During the whole of the long rehearsal—only twenty-six hundred yards from Norfolk Hill—the Turks crowded on their positions and watched the performance, but luckily did not try to interfere in any way.

The 29th was an exceedingly busy day for all and especially for the chief *bellum* expert, Captain Morland of the 43rd, of whom Lieutenant Birch Reynardson wrote, " Morland is working all day, and doing everyone's job, and is never out of temper."[15] Final issues were made of " caulking materials, red lead, canvas, nails, and wooden pegs to plug bullet holes in the boats.

---

[13] Birch Reynardson, p. 141.   [14] *Official History,* Vol. I, p. 249.
[15] *Chronicle,* 1914-15, p. 91.

THE PLAN

Also shovels, picks, sandbags, baling tins, and tins to hold drinking water." On the same day the 16th Brigade arrived; the whole river front was lined with "barges and boats of every description, and the stream full of R.N. Ships."[16]

On the 30th Lieutenant-Colonel Lethbridge issued his orders.[17] The 43rd was to start at 5 a.m., rendezvous at 5.30 and advance at 5.45 a.m. with the objectives of Norfolk Hill and then One Tower Hill, while the 103rd on the left attacked Gun Hill. The 22nd Punjabis were to attack One Tree Hill on the left flank, and, after capture, concentrate enfilade fire on Norfolk and One Tower Hills to help the Regiment's advance. Meanwhile H.M. Ships *Comet* and *Shushan* were to bombard the enemy on the sandhills opposite Muzaira'a and up the Al Huwair creek. After the capture of One Tower Hill H.M. Ships *Shaitan* and *Sumana* were to sweep for mines to allow of the fleet proceeding to the bombardment of Abu Aran. The artillery[18] to cover the advance by fire on the objectives was to consist of the 1st/5th Hampshire Howitzer Battery at Nuhairat; two 4-inch guns and two 5-inch guns from the 104th and 86th Heavy Batteries respectively, firing from Qurna; while the same number of heavy guns plus one 18-pounder, all mounted in barges, were to co-operate from the river. Added to which, there were available in the river the following of H.M. Ships:—

Espiègle, with six 4-inch, four 3-pounder and two Maxim guns.
Odin, with four 4-inch, two 3-pounder and two Maxim guns.
Clio, with six 4-inch, four 3-pounder and three Maxim guns.
Lawrence, with four 4-inch and four 6-pounder guns.
Shaitan, with one 12-pounder and one Maxim guns.
Sumana, with one 12-pounder and one Maxim guns.
Miner, with one 12-pounder, one 3-pounder and one Maxim guns.

And three naval 4.7-inch guns mounted in horse-boats. For immediate close support the 17th Brigade had the four guns of the 30th Mountain Battery, mounted on rafts.

From this it will be seen that the attacking troops had a great preponderance of artillery. Moreover, two aeroplanes had already arrived in the country and were ready to take part in the operations. By 5 p.m. the Regiment's kits and all equipment were packed on board P2 under Ivey, the quartermaster.

"That night every man slept on the mud opposite his boat, ready to embark without confusion in the dark hours of the morning. It was a steamy night without a breath of wind; warm mist hung above the creek, and clouds

[16] *Ibid.*, p. 92.
[17] For General Townshend's operation order see *Official History*, Vol. I, p. 250.
[18] *Official History*, Vol. I, p. 251.

of mosquitoes quivered over each sleeping form,"[19] while out in midstream the unfortunate 16th Brigade sweltered on the crowded decks of the transports.

II.—THE QURNA " REGATTA."[20]

At 4 a.m. Captain Morland and Lieutenant Birch Reynardson pushed off in a *mashuf* to mark the line of advance across the floods with flags like a point-to-point course—red on the right and white on the left—to ensure that the boats escaped the shallow patches. At 4.30 a.m. each company paraded and embarked in its sixteen *bellums*; " Q " Company (Captain Morland *vice* Major Carter, sick) in the front line in armoured *bellums*; " R " Company (Captain Brooke) in support; "S" Company (Captain Forrest) in reserve; Nos. 1 and 2 Platoons, " P " Company (Captain Simpson and Lieutenant Horan) in armoured *bellums* as escort to the mountain battery; Headquarters and two platoons of " P " Company (Captain Henley) in reserve with " S " Company.

At 5 a.m. the bombardment of the Turkish position started, while the attacking troops threaded their way through the darkness in line ahead towards the rendezvous marked by a large red flag, where the companies formed line abreast. By 5.30 a.m. the three regiments had reached their positions to the west of Nuhairat village without interference, and were ready to move in the following formation :—[21]

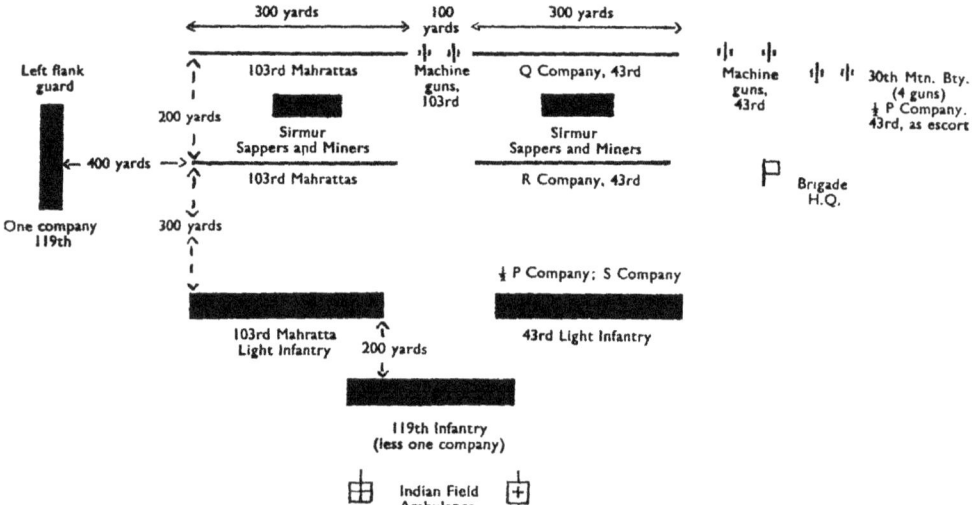

[19] Birch Reynardson, p. 147.
[21] *Official History*, Vol. I, p. 253.

[20] See Map No. 3, facing p. 64.

PREPARING FOR EMBARKATION, 30th MAY 1915.

THE ATTACK ON NORFOLK HILL.

Meanwhile the bombardment of Norfolk and Gun Hills provided " a sight ' magnificently terrible.' Lyddite and shrapnel were falling with such rapidity that it seemed as if the earth were on fire. The dust and smoke hung like a huge cloud over [Norfolk] island and as the columns shot up the place resembled the crater of a volcano."[22]

As the attacking lines moved off the guns lifted from Norfolk Hill and concentrated on Tower and Gun Hills, while the mountain battery in close support took on Norfolk Hill with shrapnel to cover the Regiment's advance.

By 5.45 a.m. the 43rd and 103rd were on the move, and not till 6 a.m. was rifle fire heard from the left bank where the 22nd Punjabis were attacking One Tree Hill. However, at 6.30 a.m. the Regiment came under heavy rifle fire from Norfolk Hill and erratic artillery fire from Tower and Gun Hills, but pushing forward on the flank the 43rd machine-gun section with three guns was able to give covering fire by 7 a.m. At 7.10 the Colonel ordered Captain Brooke with "R" Company to pass through the armoured *bellums* of the leading company[23] and assault Norfolk Hill, " as the armour plating was impeding the advance by catching in the reeds."[24] Under machine and mountain-gun covering fire "R" Company advanced while the enemy rifle fire whipped and cracked round the unarmoured *bellums*. At this point Captain Brooke ordered Captain Stephens to strike his flag and shouted to the men to sit down in their boats while he continued to expose himself. When within two hundred yards of Norfolk Hill Captain Stephens heard that Captain Brooke had been hit. Taking command, he pushed on and when still some distance from his objective he saw Major Hyde[25] charging up the hill alone firing his revolver as he went. Close on his heels by now Captain Stephens and " R " Company leapt from their boats, waded waist-deep through the last hundred yards of mud and water and charging up the slope captured Norfolk Hill by 7.30 a.m.

In the final assault Corporal Pursglove, one of the best shots in the Regiment, spotted two white men beating a hasty retreat towards a boat. Promptly opening fire, he killed them both : they proved to be German officers.

Captain Stephens goes on to say in his diary : " Some of the enemy came out of their trenches and held their hands up; others stayed in their trenches and our men bayoneted and shot a few as they came out . . . most of the enemy were stark naked on account of the heat and their wounds were ghastly. They tried to kiss the men's feet and begged for mercy. . . . The

---

[22] Lieutenant Naylor's diary.
[23] "Q" Company.
[24] *Chronicle*, 1914-15, p. 95.
[25] Lieutenant Naylor in his diary says : ' A Turk was taking aim at him with his rifle, and Hyde very deliberately fixed his pince-nez and then raising his revolver shot the man dead."

dead were a ghastly sight, the big guns having made an awful mess of them and blown limbs off."

Meanwhile Captain Brooke, mortally wounded by a bullet just over the heart, had collapsed into the arms of C.S.M. Shilcock. He only lived about five minutes; twice during that time he asked if the hill had been captured and when told that it had said " That's good " and died quietly without pain. Later he was buried by Lieutenant Kearsley at the foot of Norfolk Hill. But for this loss the casualties in " R " Company up to this time were extremely light, amounting to three men only,[26] namely, Private Butler severely and Privates Rutland and Iremonger slightly wounded.

The Turkish trenches on Norfolk Hill, well sited and provided with overhead cover in places, contained seventy-five dead Arabs as the result of the bombardment; and in addition one officer and sixty wounded and unwounded Arabs were taken prisoners.[27] It was while the Regiment was reorganizing that the officer commanding the field ambulance, Colonel Donaghan, appeared on Norfolk Hill to establish his dressing station. He was the only man in the force suitably dressed that day, for he was wearing khaki trousers lately cut down by nail scissors to shorts; a pair of hospital bandages, soaked in Condy's fluid, as puttees; a pair of dancing-pumps; a shirt with a spine pad; a large topi with a puggaree hanging down his back; and above all a large khaki-covered umbrella.

Having collected his men and prisoners, Captain Stephens took up a position behind the hill until the commanding officer arrived to order two platoons forward. Leaving Lieutenant Kearsley with Nos. 10 and 12 Platoons on Norfolk Hill, Captain Stephens embarked with Nos. 9 and 11 Platoons and joined up with the two platoons of " P " Company under Captain Henley to cover the attack on the second objective, One Tower Hill. To do this the four platoons had to attack a small hill within two hundred yards of One Tower Hill. However, as they advanced under the covering fire of the 30th Mountain Battery and the howitzers and guns at Qurna the Turks hoisted the white flag and the hill and twenty prisoners were captured without loss. Meanwhile H.M. Ships *Espiègle* and *Clio* also advanced and anchored off Norfolk Hill to add their contributions, supported by the *Odin, Lawrence* and *Miner*. One Tower Hill was now subjected to such a concentrated fire (the 22nd Punjabis who had captured One Tree Hill at 6.30 were also helping with machine-gun fire) that it was easily captured by 9 a.m.[28] by " S " Company supported by the 119th, with the loss of Captain Henley of " P "

---

[26] *Official History*, Vol. I, p. 255, and Birch Reynardson, p. 149, agree to five men; C.S.M. Shilcock in *Chronicle*, 1914-15, p. 100, the War Diary and Captain Stephens say three were wounded.

[27] War Diary has: 53 dead, 25 prisoners, 6 wounded.

[28] *Official History*, Vol. I, p. 255, has 9 a.m.; *Chronicle*, 1914-15, p. 95, has 8 a.m.

Company, wounded in the thigh, and Serjeant Armitt of " R," wounded in the arm.[29] On this position the 43rd captured a 16-pounder field gun (the crew of which had been wiped out by a shell from H.M.S. *Odin*), one Turkish officer and ninety Arabs, of whom four were wounded.[30] Two platoons of " S " Company were left to consolidate this hill.

Meanwhile the 103rd and 119th, making a sweep to the westward, were advancing on Shrapnel and Gun Hills so as to attack the Turkish right flanks. In this advance the troops were much handicapped by the great height of the reeds, but the artillery support was so devastating and concentrated that the enemy hoisted a white flag at about 11 a.m. and the two hills were captured soon after 11.30 a.m., together with two 16-pounder field guns, one Turkish officer and one hundred and thirty-two Arab soldiers, as well as a considerable quantity of shells, rifles and ammunition. On Gun Hill the reason for the immunity of the infantry from any artillery fire during their slow advance was soon discovered; the Turks had dug in their guns so deep that close-range targets could not be engaged.

Thus by noon the first objectives had been most successfully captured and consolidated, but such were the terrific heat and glare off the water that General Townshend decided to stop further operations for the day.

In the course of the consolidation of One Tower Hill the Regiment found a dug-out on a small island near by, in which were discovered an officer and five men sitting beside a switch-board with cables which disappeared into the marsh. These were quickly disconnected by Lieutenant Powell, and later when dragged up were found to lead to twenty-four large mines hidden in the river and marshes. Lucky it was for all that the operator forgot to press the key which was ready to his hand.[31]

At 4 p.m. General Townshend issued his orders for the next day's attack on the enemy crescent-shaped position between Abu Aran and Muzaibila. In these the 17th Brigade was to make an enveloping attack to the west starting from Gun Hill at 5.45 a.m., while the 16th Brigade under cover of the naval bombardment was to make a frontal attack along the Abu Aran ridge towards Muzaibila.

The afternoon was spent by the 43rd on the shadeless One Tower Hill, in a sweltering heat of 112 degrees, in clearing up the position and removing the armour from the *bellums*. Even when night came the conditions improved not one whit, for the Regiment bivouacked in a steamy haze from

[29] Casualties are misleading. *Official History*, p. 255, has 1 officer and 2 men; *Chronicle*, 1914-15, p. 100, has 1 officer and 1 man; Birch Reynardson, p. 149, has 1 officer and 10 men; War Diary has Captain Henley and Serjeant Armitt.

[30] War Diary has 75 prisoners and 1 officer, of whom 26 were wounded; 4 dead.

[31] Birch Reynardson, p. 150. *Official History*, Vol. I, p. 256, gives a slightly different account. Colonel Lethbridge understood that damp terminals were the cause of failure.

which arose myriads of mosquitoes to torment it. With the Regiment were the 22nd Punjabis, who had crossed the river; Gun Hill was held by the 103rd; and the 119th occupied Alloa, to the east of Gun Hill on the Tigris bank. The Regiment's disposition was as follows: " S " Company on Tower Hill; " Q " Company and Nos. 10 and 11 Platoons of " R " Company, brought up from Norfolk Hill, on the hill to the west of Tower Hill; one platoon of " R " Company on Shrapnel Hill, and one in rear of Tower Hill; " P " Company on two small hills, north-west of Tower Hill. Captain R. V. Simpson assumed command of " P " Company, *vice* Captain Henley, wounded.

Early the following morning the 17th Brigade took to their *bellums* for the last time, and set out to attack Abu Aran from the west. At 5 a.m. the bombardment was opened by the Navy and river section with 5-inch, 4.7-inch and 4-inch guns until the sandy objective disappeared in smoke and dust. Under cover of the artillery fire the 43rd pressed their way through the tall obstructing reeds without any molestation from Abu Aran or Muzaibila. No sound came until 7 a.m. when an aeroplane, passing north-east over Abu Aran, was heavily fired on by the enemy. Then, just as the Regiment was approaching its objective, the aeroplane circled back towards H.M.S. *Espiègle* and dropped a message. As a result the guns suddenly ceased fire at 8.15 a.m. Half an hour later the 43rd landed on the west side of Abu Aran to find the birds had flown. Lieutenant Davenport with a platoon of " Q " Company immediately advanced to the north end of the island in the hope of catching some of the retreating enemy. But there was nothing to be found except the debris of a hurried flight.[32]

At 9.15 a.m. a message from divisional headquarters arrived with the news that the enemy was in full retreat upstream. General Townshend, therefore, gave orders for an immediate pursuit, and for this purpose he selected the 17th Brigade for the honour of leading the advance. By 11 a.m. the naval flotilla had anchored off Abu Aran, and steps were immediately taken to clear the obstruction below Ruta. This was accomplished by 2 p.m. and the *Shaitan* and *Sumana* steamed off in pursuit of the enemy's ships whose smoke could be seen to the north. An hour later H.M. Ships *Espiègle* —with General Townshend on board—*Clio* and *Odin* passed the obstruction and took up the pursuit.

In the meantime the 16th Brigade had arrived at Abu Aran at 10 a.m. As the 17th Brigade had been given the post of honour this entailed the disembarkation of the 16th Brigade and re-embarkation of the 17th Brigade. All day the 43rd had been grilled upon the spit of Abu Aran until relieved

---

[32] Birch Reynardson, p. 151. *Chronicle*, 1914-15, p. 97. *Official History*, Vol. I, p. 258.

1. Armoured Machine Gun Bellum.
2. Mountain Gun Bellum stuck during the Attack.
3. Major Hyde, Captains Morland and Stephens and Lieutenant Powell on Abu Aran Island.
4. Turkish Prisoners.
5. Captain Startin, R.A.M.C., and Colonel Donaghan, R.A.M.C., on Norfolk Hill.

in the evening by the 16th Brigade to whom the *bellums* were handed over. Embarking on P2, the 43rd found its new quarters no more comfortable than the heat and glare of the shadeless sand-spit. Crammed like sardines on the iron decks under a single awning, the 43rd moved off up-river at 5 a.m. on the 2nd June, making for Ezra's Tomb. " There was not a breath of wind and the thermometer stood at about 114 degrees in the shade."[33] During the journey all ranks tried to clear some of the mud from their arms and equipment after two days of amphibious warfare, but so cramped were their quarters and so great the heat that reorganization was well-nigh impossible. At 1.45 p.m. Ezra's Tomb hove in sight, lying on the right bank like " a huge balloon suspended above a haze of green "[34] in the mirage. Actually the blue balloon was the graceful dome of the tomb. Here General Townshend had left H.M.S. *Odin* and his senior general staff officer to collect his troops before he himself pushed on in pursuit with the rest of the naval flotilla.

At 3.30 p.m. " R " and " S " Companies disembarked and occupied, together with regimental headquarters, the caravanserai built round the tomb. Soon after landing Lieutenant Powell discovered that the telegraph line had been left intact by the enemy, so precipitate had been his flight; and he soon got into communication with Basra. By the evening the whole brigade had been landed and the transports sent back to bring up the 16th Brigade from Abu Aran. The 43rd and 22nd Punjabis shared the area round Ezra's Tomb while the 103rd and 119th camped on the opposite bank.

Meanwhile a marvellous epic of daring impertinence was being enacted upstream by the naval flotilla. As has been said, the Navy took up the immediate pursuit on the 1st June, and soon overtook many lighters and *mahailas* full of troops and stores which had been cast off by the fleeing Turkish boats, *Mosul* and *Marmariss*. At 8 p.m. the flotilla was forced to anchor above Ezra's Tomb, having in the course of the day accounted for the *Bulbul* (which had been sunk by the *Shaitan's* gun fire), about " two hundred Turkish soldiers, three field guns and a large quantity of stores."[35]

At 2 a.m. on the 2nd by the light of the moon H.M. Ships *Espiègle, Clio, Comet, Miner, Shaitan* and *Sumana* pressed the pursuit. The *Marmariss* was soon overtaken, aground and abandoned, and later the steamer *Mosul* with a lighter and seven *mahailas* surrendered. But here H.M. Ships *Espiègle* and *Clio* were compelled to stop owing to difficult navigation. Transferring to H.M.S. *Comet*, General Townshend continued the advance until 7 p.m., by which time the flotilla was six miles above Qala Salih. Early on the 3rd the flotilla started off again. Steaming on ahead, Lieutenant Singleton in the *Shaitan* reached Amara alone and single-handed proceeded to capture

[33] Birch Reynardson, p. 154.   [34] *Ibid.*, p. 154.
[35] *Official History*, Vol. I, p. 259.

eleven officers and two hundred and fifty men, besides scaring away another two thousand. Meanwhile the rest of the flotilla made all speed to the *Shaitan's* support, and landing at 2.15 p.m. General Townshend accepted the surrender of the town. But as his total strength amounted to only forty-one men, namely, twenty-five sailors, four marines and twelve soldiers, his position was obviously precarious if the enemy came to realize his weakness. Accordingly he sent down messages ordering the immediate dispatch of reinforcements, the first of which, the 2nd Norfolk Regiment from the general reserve of the 18th Brigade, arrived in the nick of time at 6.30 a.m. on the 4th.[36]

Thus it was that the 17th Brigade was denied its post of honour through the vagaries of fortune, and the 43rd had the mortification of watching the 16th Brigade pass Ezra's Tomb on the way forward. By the evening of the 4th the occupation of Amara was complete without a single casualty, thanks mainly to the uninterrupted and relentless pursuit by the naval flotilla. As a piece of impudent bluff the capture of Amara with its garrison of forty officers and at least 750 soldiers and countless Arabs of unknown tendencies can only be compared with some of the exploits of Lord Dundonald. Its audacity richly deserved its success.

Meanwhile the 43rd bravely bore its new quarters. Once the stimulus of action had been superseded by the monotony of inaction, the Regiment began to feel the heat more intensely, and cases of fever and heat-stroke began to increase considerably. Its quarters in the dilapidated cells of the two-storeyed *Khan* were infested with every known crawling and winged insect and parasite. Mosquito-nets were impracticable, as the heat beneath them became intolerable, and sleep consequently quite impossible. However, the protection from the blasting sun which any roof supplied was something not to be lightly refused.

For three days the 43rd sweltered and dripped with sweat in the precincts of the Tomb, until at 3 p.m. on the 5th the *Blosse Lynch* arrived and orders were received to embark. At 5 p.m. the 43rd, less "S" Company, went aboard to spend a hell-born night in a crowded ship amid a vertiginous swarm of mosquitoes. Starting again at 5 a.m. on the 6th, the 43rd steamed on into a new country without marshes and flanked with hills in the far distance. Here were grazing cattle and sheep and ponies—a sight which had not been seen during the seven months of liquid isolation at Qurna. The inhabitants thronged the banks to watch the ships pass, banks which actually sported green grass. Leaving the 119th Infantry to garrison Qala Salih, the rest of the brigade reached Amara at 8 p.m. and started to disembark the next morning. As the Regiment was billeted in two granaries at the back of the town

---

[36] *Ibid.*, Vol. I, pp. 259-263, and Birch Reynardson, pp. 152 and 156-157.

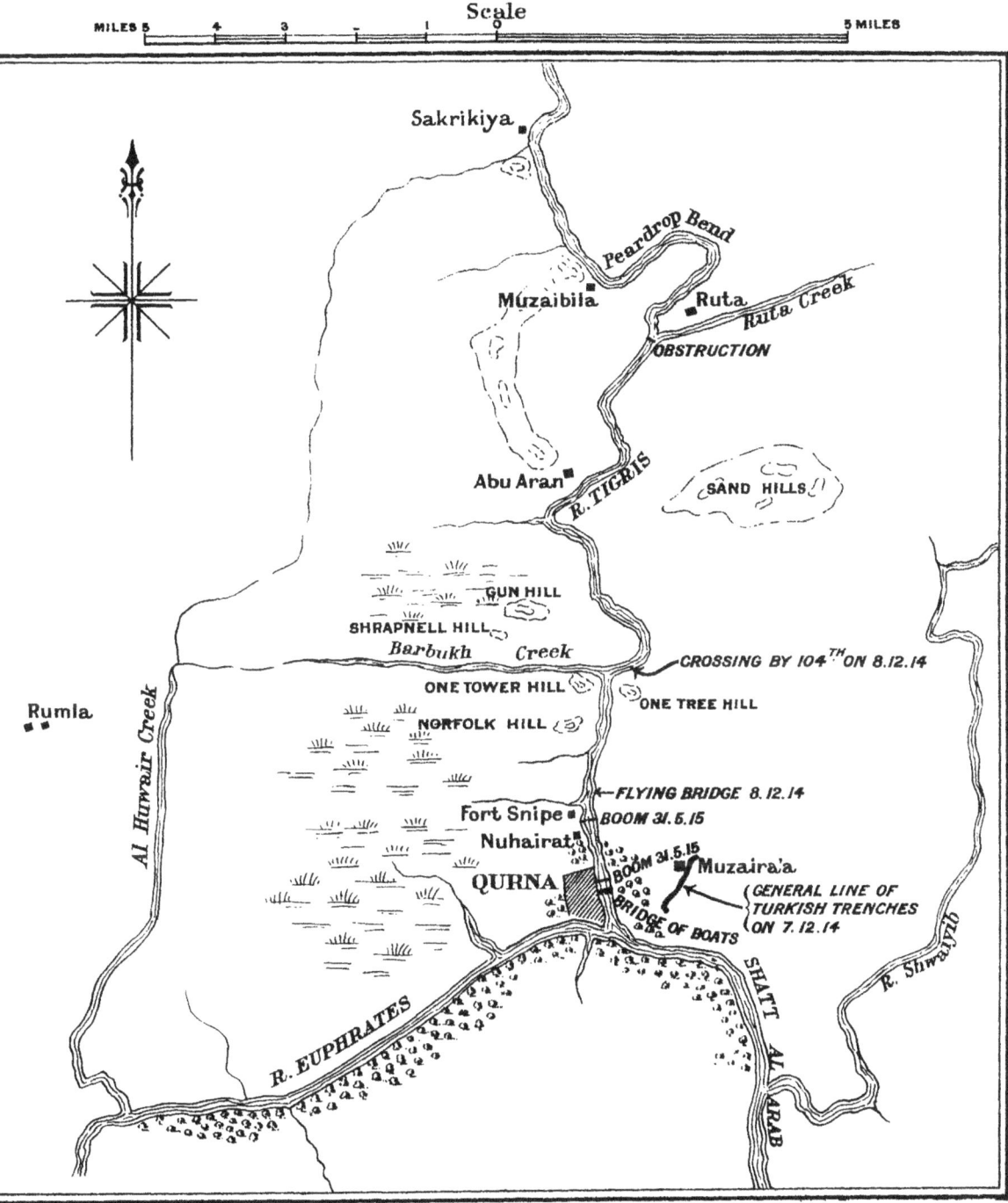

on the Jahalah canal, debouching from the Tigris, all the troops and equipment had to be transhipped into the *Sumana*, so that it was after 4 p.m. before the last platoon reached its quarters. On the 9th the 43rd was allotted No. 10 Blockhouse in the defences.

Thus ended the *regatta* operations, the success of which General Nixon attributed to " a careful study of detail in the initial stages of the organization, the skilful manner in which these details were worked out, and to the loyal co-operation of all concerned in putting the whole machine in motion."[37] In his despatch on these operations Colonel Climo, commanding the 17th Brigade, laid stress on the excellent example the 43rd had given to the rest of the brigade in its attack on Norfolk Hill and in its careful preparations for amphibious warfare. He also praised the officers for their care of their men whereby much sickness from fever and heat-stroke had been prevented.

For their services in these operations the following were mentioned in despatches: Captain R. R. M. Brooke, killed, the 31st May; Lieutenant J. H. Courtis, machine-gun officer; Captain C. F. Henley (wounded); Lieutenant-Colonel E. A. E. Lethbridge, D.S.O.; Captain W. E. T. Morland; Lieutenant J. J. Powell, signalling officer; 5766 Serjeant H. Arlett; 5787 C.S.M. T. J. Shilcock; 8041 Serjeant A. H. Cowley; 6907 Corporal A. E. Pursglove; 7478 Serjeant E. W. Stevens.

Captain F. H. Stapleton, D.A.Q.M.G., 6th Division.

Captain G. E. Whittall, military landing officer, Basra.[38]

---

[37] *Official History*, Vol. I, p. 265.
[38] *Chronicle*, 1914-15, p. 113.

CHAPTER XI.

I.—June and July in Amara.

Torrid heat—Casualties—Medical arrangements inadequate—Operations on Tigris and Euphrates—Arrival of Dunlop's force at Amara—Reconnaissance of Ali Gharbi by party of 43rd—Turkish threat from Nasiriya—Operations on the Euphrates—Capture of Nasiriya.

(See Map facing page 1.)

" THE story of June in Amara would be but one long chronicle of hot days and breathless nights, of sickness and boredom, and shortage of most things which make hot weather bearable," wrote Lieutenant Birch Reynardson.[1] However, the conditions required courage and patience and are therefore as important as hard fighting. The heat was recorded on the 11th at 119 degrees in the shade, and even the short nights provided little relief or respite. The sun was too hot by 5 a.m. to allow of sleep on the flat roof which was capacious enough to accommodate the whole Regiment. Parades consisted of an hour's work in the morning and evening, as all men were ordered to be under cover between 9 a.m. and 6 p.m. The enforced inactivity and monotony caused much sickness both of mind and body. An incubus of depression weighed upon the garrison, causing " restlessness, anxiety, and . . . shortness of temper." Trifles assumed an inordinate importance and grousing gave place to intolerance, while the mainspring of vitality was inexorably retarded by the sapping heat. Against this enemy not even the bodies of the garrison, however willing, could fight, for " vegetables were short, almost unobtainable; a much-boomed ice machine broke down after a fortnight's spasmodic activity, never to work again; there were no such luxuries as electric fans."[2] Here, then, in the garrison of Amara disease found ready victims. " Sickness of all kinds became rife, sunstroke and heat-stroke were common, fever and dysentery and paratyphoid "[2] took their toll.

On the 7th Colonel Gamble assumed command of the 17th Brigade in place of Colonel Climo, but he succumbed before the end of July. A week later General Townshend went down with fever and was sent down to Basra. By the end of the month Lieutenant-Colonel Lethbridge, Captain Stephens, Lieutenants Horan, Kearsley and Ivey, and one hundred and twenty men,

---
[1] Birch Reynardson, p. 163.   [2] *Ibid.*, p. 164.

had been recommended for sick leave in India. Scarcely a man in the 43rd escaped the visitations of sickness of some form or another. The Divisional Staff was undermanned, and by the 19th half the 103rd Mahratta Light Infantry was down with fever.

On the 28th a party paraded at 5.30 p.m. to bury Private Wells of "R" Company who had died of dysentery that morning. On the way to the cemetery " a man went down with heat-stroke, and was carried back, limp and twitching, to hospital. As the corpse was lowered into the grave, one of the men on the ropes stumbled forward and fell limply into the grave on top of the dead body, and as we fell in to march back, another man went down " who was carried back on the stretcher lately occupied by the corpse. " We had buried one man, and lost three others over the job."[3]

And what of the medical and transport arrangements to cope with this decimating sickness? There were only twenty-one river steamers and tugs in the country.[4] General Nixon had asked for more on the 27th May, but the Indian Government had been unable to procure any of suitable draught. Though Expeditionary Force " D " had by now swollen to two divisions, there were only field ambulances sufficient for one division. On the 18th June General Nixon applied urgently for more medical personnel on account of the great incidence of sickness which had incapacitated many of the medical corps. Added to this there was no place within the country where cases could convalesce from their sickness, and so many were invalided to India that General Nixon was compelled to refuse sick leave to India—except in urgent cases—in order to prevent the depletion of his force. Consequently, the country " was full of crocks."[5]

Such medical personnel as was dispatched originally was only equipped for frontier warfare " when India, with her railways and resources, lies close at hand."[6] The scale was not altered for the expedition to a climate known to be one of the most trying and difficult in the world. And this is not all, for the British General Hospital was not up to establishment, being " short of personnel and equipment for fifty beds."[6]

In this outbreak of devastating sickness, the staff and the Indian and British Governments had an earnest of the difficulties to be overcome in the event of heavy or unexpected battle casualties. A warning, not to be lightly disregarded, was kindly vouchsafed to the authorities by Providence, a lucky warning which gave them a chance to set their rearward services in order before embarking on further enterprises, such a warning as is not usually

[3] *Chronicle*, 1914-15, p. 110, and Birch Reynardson, p. 165.
[4] *Official History*, Vol. I, p. 268, cannot apportion the blame for the shortage, as the relevant facts were not brought to light by the Mesopotamia Commission.
[5] *Chronicle*, 1914-15, p. 111.
[6] Birch Reynardson, p. 164.

granted to politicians and commanders in the field, but we shall see, in due course, what attention was paid to it.

While the sickness raged in Amara, dying men were laid on rush mats in a scarcely sun-proof tent; the officers' hospital consisted of "two ill-ventilated rooms, without beds, and for a long time without punkas '"[7]; doctors prescribed " chicken or fish diet, when neither was available, and there was only one small stove and a native cook who could not even make soup."[7]

II.—JUNE AND JULY. MILITARY OPERATIONS ON TIGRIS AND EUPHRATES.

On the 14th June the 7th Hariana Lancers, the advance guard of Colonel Dunlop's force which had chased Daghistani's force from Khafajiya and Bisaitin, reached Amara in a sorry plight. They were only two hundred and fifty strong, with three of their own British officers. Later followed the 67th Punjabis, 2nd Royal West Kent Regiment and 82nd Battery, R.F.A. This column, by threatening the Turkish left flank communications, had materially assisted the *regatta* operations, but it requires a fertile imagination to gauge the distress of its march across the desert, combined with a shortage of fresh water.

The defences of Amara consisted of a chain of block-houses built by the Turks on both banks of the Tigris. These were occupied to protect the town from Arab raiders who were more likely to offend than the Turkish forces. In addition there was a movable column always prepared to move at short notice to deal with any more serious danger. The bridge over the Tigris was repaired, and a pontoon bridge soon spanned the Jahalah Canal. As in India so in Mesopotamia, rifle thieves became a menace. Jackals by nature, the Arabs were masters of the art of noiseless movement by night and often raided units in search of arms. Their method was to crawl up to a tent, tickle a soldier's back and quietly remove his rifle, on which he was sleeping, directly he rolled over. Rifles so stolen were rushed from Amara by relays of Arabs and by morning were miles away, bound for the North-West Frontier of India where they commanded a high price. Not always, however, were the thieves content with rifles: on one occasion they entered the 43rd transport lines by night and stole a mule, which they took across the Jahalah Canal.

On the 30th June a reconnaissance consisting of Captain Simpson, Lieutenant Price and fifty men of " P " Company, together with Lieutenant Courtis and the machine-gun section, advanced eighty miles upstream to Ali Gharbi and found it unoccupied except for half a dozen officials who were taken prisoners. Later on the 3rd July, General Delamain, who was temporarily in command of the 6th Division, established an advanced post

---

[7] *Ibid.*, p. 165.

at Kumait, but this had to be evacuated on the 20th, because troops were required on the Euphrates front. As Turkish troops from Kut al Amara were reported to be reinforcing their right at Nasiriya by way of the Shatt al Hai, the 17th Brigade was ordered to create a diversion against the enemy at Fulaifila. Accordingly the 43rd was ordered to be ready to embark at 4.30 p.m. on the 15th, but when the Regiment with all kits and stores was on board, the move was postponed till 4 a.m. the next day. At 3 a.m. however, the whole advance was cancelled because more troops were required on the Euphrates front where operations were not progressing too favourably. It was immediately after the capture of Amara that General Nixon determined to advance to Nasiriya which was included in the Basra *vilayet*. At the same time, he suggested to the Indian Government that the capture of Kut al Amara would more effectively secure the control of the *vilayet* as, by so doing, he would hold both ends of the Shatt al Hai, that channel which connects the Euphrates with the Tigris at Kut al Amara.[8] The rumour of this advance had already reached the 43rd towards the end of June,[9] though by then the advance was still under discussion and had not been officially sanctioned.

On the 26th June the 30th Brigade and naval flotilla concentrated at Kubaish on the Euphrates, preparatory to an advance across the Hammar lake.[10] The advance across the lake was unmolested, and the force entered the Akaika channel where a dam prevented further movement until a passage was blown through it by the sappers. The general advance continued on the 5th July, when the force defeated the Turks in a sharp engagement and captured Suq ash Shuyukh the following morning. In the further advance, however, General Gorringe soon met with a stiffer resistance than he ever expected, and was compelled to request reinforcements which arrived, in the shape of the 12th Brigade, on the 12th and 13th.

" It was soon found that the enemy was in force, and had taken up strong positions astride the Euphrates below Nasiriya. General Gorringe disembarked his troops on both banks, and halted to reconnoitre. Making frequent reconnaissances, and gradually advancing his trenches, he made an attempt on July 13th-14th, with a small force, to capture the position on the enemy's right flank."[11] At 12.30 a.m. on the 14th the 76th Punjabis and half the 48th Pioneers skilfully seized the enemy's advanced position, but the 24th Punjabis with two sections of the 30th Mountain Battery failed in a

---

[8] *Official History*, Vol. I, p. 270. The Intelligence Branch believed that Sulaiman Askari Bey transferred his troops from in front of Qurna to Shaiba in March by way of Kut and the Shatt al Hai.
[9] *Chronicle*, 1914-15, p. 109.
[10] See Map No. 1, facing p. 1.
[11] *Chronicle*, 1914-15, p. 57.

gallant *bellum* attack on the sandhills. Forced to retire, the 24th were harassed by Arab tribesmen on all sides, and were with great skill extricated from a very precarious position. During the next week the 18th Brigade, withdrawn from the Tigris front, arrived, and at 5 a.m. on the 24th July General Gorringe launched his attack on both banks of the river with the co-operation of the naval flotilla.

The attack, carried out in extreme heat by troops weary after long days in the trenches and hard work, was completely successful. " Resisting stubbornly, the Turks were driven from successive positions during the day, and by 6.30 p.m. were in full retreat across the marshes,"[12] having lost about " two thousand in killed and wounded, all their fifteen guns, five machine guns, a large quantity of arms, ammunition and stores and three motor boats,"[13] while the British casualties amounted to 104 killed and 429 wounded.[13] On the 25th July Nasiriya, a centre of considerable trade and the Turkish headquarters in the Muntafik country, was occupied and garrisoned. The bulk of General Gorringe's force was thereafter withdrawn to guard the lines of communication on the Tigris.

By the capture of Nasiriya General Nixon completed his instructions to compass the effective security and control of the Anglo-Persian oilfields and pipe-line. The original objective was therefore attained by the 25th July, but in the meantime further enterprises had been mooted.

Meanwhile in Amara the 43rd, plagued with flies, mosquitoes and sickness, was still suffering badly from the heat and inaction. On the 31st July the following officers were doing duty with the Regiment:—

Major A. C. Hyde, in temporary command.
Captain C. E. Forrest, D.S.O.
Captain R. V. Simpson.
Captain Hon. J. C. W. S. Foljambe, adjutant.
Captain F. M. Davenport.
Captain J. H. Courtis.
Captain S. C. B. Mundey.
Lieutenant F. C. W. Wynter.
Lieutenant H. T. Birch Reynardson.
Lieutenant J. S. Kearsley.
Second Lieutenant G. Naylor.
Second Lieutenant D. Murphy.
Second Lieutenant F. Brown.
Captain and Quartermaster T. E. Ivey.

[12] *Ibid.*, 1914-15, p. 58.
[13] *Official History*, Vol. I, p. 297. For Nasiriya operations see *Official History*, Vol. I, pp. 274-298.

Attached—

Captain J. Startin, R.A.M.C.
Captain W. W. Meldon, 3rd Durham Light Infantry.
Lieutenant H. B. L. Hind, 3rd Somerset Light Infantry.
Lieutenant S. L. Webber, 2nd Duke of Cornwall's Light Infantry.
Second Lieutenant A. Price, 2nd Royal Sussex Regiment.
Second Lieutenant A. J. Hazell, 2nd West Riding Regiment.

And there were the following on sick leave in India:—

Lieutenant-Colonel E. A. E. Lethbridge, D.S.O.
Major L. J. Carter.
Captain C. F. Henley, wounded.
Captain R. Stephens.
Lieutenant K. Horan.

Of the others who embarked with the 43rd in November 1914, Captain F. H. Stapleton had been appointed deputy assistant quartermaster-general on the 21st April 1915; Captain W. E. T. Morland was appointed general staff officer, 3rd Grade, on the 20th June; Captain G. E. Whittall military landing officer, Basra, on the 23rd February; Captain J. J. Powell was brigade signalling officer; and Second Lieutenant R. C. Loverock assistant military landing officer at Basra.[14]

---

[14] *Chronicle*, 1914-15, pp. 115-116. Services of Officers of 43rd, November 1914 to 31st July, 1915.

[JUNE/AUG.

CHAPTER XII.

I.—POLITICAL AND MILITARY ASPECTS OF AN ADVANCE TO KUT AL AMARA.

THREAT TO OILFIELDS AND PIPE-LINE—BRITISH GOVERNMENT AGREES TO CAPTURE OF KUT—THE ADVANCE TO KUT AL AMARA—TURKISH STRENGTH—ORDERS TO ADVANCE—HEAT AND DUST—SECOND-LINE TRANSPORT—CAPTURE OF SHAIKH SAAD—TURKS HOLD ES SINN—THE 6TH DIVISION HALTS AT SANNAIYAT—TOWNSHEND'S PLAN—FEINT MARCH ON THE RIGHT BANK—THE 18TH BRIGADE ADVANCES—THE 17TH BRIGADE CONCENTRATES—THE NIGHT MARCH—THE BATTLE OF KUT AL AMARA OR ES SINN—THE 43RD ATTACKS—SUCCESS—THE 43RD'S CASUALTIES—THE FINAL ATTACK—INCIDENTS OF THE BATTLE—THE NIGHT AFTER THE BATTLE—THE PLIGHT OF THE WOUNDED—GENERAL NIXON'S DESPATCH.

(*See Maps facing pages* 1 *and* 88, *and on page* 206.)

IN his appreciation of the situation on the 24th of June General Nixon considered that Kut al Amara was the key to the interior lines of Lower Mesopotamia, for, so long as the Turks held the head of the Shatt al Hai at Kut, strong garrisons would be required at Amara and Nasiriya with reserves at Qurna. Inversely, were Kut in his hands, General Nixon would be able to concentrate troops more easily at any threatened point either on the Tigris or Euphrates. Unfortunately, however, he did not then know that the Shatt al Hai was only navigable for five months in the year and then not along its whole length to Nasiriya. He also pointed out, at the same time, that the Basra *vilayet* could not be properly secured until the powerful Bani Lam tribe, which inhabited the northern portion of the *vilayet*, was placed under our authority; and he averred, in support of an advance to Kut, that the corn lands of the Shatt al Hai would thereafter be available to supply large quantities of valuable cereals.

The disadvantage of an advance to Kut lay in the extension of the lines of communication by 153 miles, but he was confident of being in a position to reduce the garrison at Nasiriya for the purpose of guarding them.[1]

Meanwhile the British and Indian Governments were advocating an advance to Baghdad, mainly owing to the great moral effect it would have on Musalmans in Mesopotamia, Afghanistan, India and Persia, with the last of which relations were becoming distinctly strained.[2] At the same time the General Staff in India gave as their reasons for an advance on Baghdad: the position of the Russians who were gradually approaching Baghdad; the demoralization of the Turks by their defeats at the hands of the British and

---

[1] *Official History*, Vol. I, pp. 301-302.   [2] *Ibid.*, Vol. I, p. 272.

Russians; and their inability to reinforce Mesopotamia so long as their attention was held by the Dardanelles campaign.² The General Staff further considered that Kut was advantageously placed as a base for a future advance and for control of Lower Mesopotamia. In fact the primary object of the expedition was being expanded into a new and more ambitious enterprise.

By the middle of August the feasibility of an advance to Kut had been thrashed out by the British and Indian Governments and the advantages of such an advance thoroughly appreciated. But during the correspondence the situation in Persia had become critical owing to the activities of German agents and Austrian escaped prisoners. As a result of this the British Government once again became fearful for the safety of the oilfields and pipe-line, and requested an assurance that they could be properly protected by the force in Mesopotamia. General Nixon answered on the 13th that he could not undertake the responsibility for operations so far inland and that " it was only on this understanding that he could undertake an advance on Kut."³ At the same time he suggested that an advance on Baghdad provided the best means of counteracting the unrest in Persia by cutting the German communications with that country. Finally, to effect the occupation of Baghdad, he requested another division.

On the 20th the British Government agreed to General Nixon's plans, except the advance to Baghdad; and also agreed to the payment of a subsidy to the Bawi tribe to protect the oilfields.⁴ Three days later General Townshend received his instructions to destroy and disperse the enemy who, according to the intelligence reports, were prepared to dispute his advance; and to occupy Kut al Amara, " thereby consolidating our control of the Basra *vilayet*."⁵

By the 28th General Townshend had planned his campaign in which he proposed to take advantage of the Turkish dispersal of force on both banks and attack them on their left flank. For his advance on Kut, General Nixon gave him the whole of the 6th Division and appointed General Gorringe to the defence of the lines of communication with the 30th Brigade of the 12th Division.⁶

II.—THE ADVANCE TO KUT AL AMARA.

As has been seen,⁷ the advanced positions on the Tigris above Amara had been withdrawn owing to Turkish pressure and lack of troops. " The Turks had then occupied Kumait, but only for a few days," for the news of

² *Ibid.*, Vol. I, p. 272.   ³ *Ibid.*, Vol. I, p. 307.
⁴ *Ibid.*, Vol. I, p. 308.   ⁵ *Ibid.*, Vol. I, p. 312.
⁶ *Ibid.*, Vol. I, p. 314.   ⁷ See p. 69 *ante*.

the Nasiriya victory put a completely different complexion upon operations at Amara. The Turks soon began to retire towards Kut, and General Nixon issued orders to General Fry, in command at Amara, to send detachments to support the river column and make touch with the enemy. Accordingly on the 30th July General Delamain, with the 16th Brigade and artillery, advanced in steamers and occupied Ali Gharbi without opposition.[8] A further reconnaissance by the Navy disclosed the nearest Turks to be in position at Shaikh Saad.

The Turkish strength and dispositions were estimated at this time to be as follows: " At and near Kut, the re-formed 38th Division with a strength of about 5,000 rifles and 19 guns; retiring on Kut from Nasiriya, the remnants of the 35th Division, consisting of about 2,000 rifles, and at or near Baghdad, the 37th Division totalling about 2,700 rifles with two guns."[9]

In the first week of August the 18th Brigade began to return from Nasiriya, thus reuniting the 6th Division; and Brigadier-General Hoghton took over command of the 17th Brigade on the 7th. The following week the 43rd was ordered to train two more machine-gun sections, increasing the establishment to six guns; at the same time the machine-gun sections of all three regiments of the brigade—the 22nd Punjabis were at Ali Gharbi—were brigaded together under the command of Captain Courtis of the 43rd.

On the 28th General Townshend reached Amara, much to the joy of all the troops, who already had great confidence in him. A few days later he paid a visit to the 43rd officers' mess and expatiated on his plans, to the interest of all. The Regiment had been carrying out company training and brigade exercises all through August, and had profited considerably from the slightly cooler and longer nights and shorter days. A large draft[10] arrived on the 28th, and the health of the Regiment had steadily improved since July. The stage was now set for the advance to Kut.

Orders to move on the 3rd of September were received on the 1st. The horses and mules were embarked by 6.45 a.m. on the 2nd on P1, and all baggage on barges and the P3. Leaving Amara at 8.30 a.m. the following day, the 43rd steamed upstream all day against " a tearing, scorching wind," and suffered great discomfort from exceedingly cramped conditions on board. Reaching Ali Sharqi at 7 p.m., the steamers tied up for the night to the left bank just above the village, and those who wished were allowed to sleep on shore while "S" Company found the piquet. The following day "the same burning north-west wind was blowing again, with a breath like the blast

[8] *Official History*, Vol. I, p. 300, and Birch Reynardson, p. 184.
[9] *Official History*, Vol. I, p. 301.
[10] The draft consisted of 65 reservists, 40 1st/4th Somerset Light Infantry, 37 1st/4th Border Regiment, 15 2nd/4th Border Regiment, 40 2nd/4th Wiltshire Regiment. Total, 197.

ADVANCE FROM AMARA

from a furnace door, and the air was so thick with dust that often the farther bank was invisible."[11] At 9 a.m. the starboard barge stuck on a sandbank—the level of the Tigris was noticeably lower—and here the Regiment remained for four hours obnoxious to the continuous and withering sandstorm which choked the eyes, throats and ears, and frayed the tempers of all. At length a tug pulled the barge off, and the long-suffering Regiment was able to continue its journey to Ali Gharbi which was reached at 4.30 p.m. Disembarking at once, the 43rd unloaded its baggage and bivouacked on the right bank below the town, with two piquets posted for protection. Unloading was a long and difficult task as there were no arrangements for the disembarkation of animals and stores, etc., except for some decrepit brows which provided a steep and insecure communication with the bank. In the bivouac camp " the overpowering stench of mud and garbage, combined with swarms of active sand-flies, made sleep out of the question,"[11] though the Regiment was spared the usual sniping.

The following morning the 43rd moved from the unsavoury bivouac ground to quarters within a big walled garden and spent the whole day in pitching camp. Eastern pattern tents were now available, which added to comfort though the thermometer still registered 121 degrees. The 43rd supplied three piquets.

Ali Gharbi was now the centre of concentration of the 6th Division, and a stream of troops kept arriving. On the 6th headquarters of the 17th Brigade and the 119th Infantry arrived, the latter taking over No. 3 piquet from the 43rd. The same day a small column went out to try to round up some hostile cavalry which had been reconnoitring in the neighbourhood, but met with no success and suffered severely from the heat for their pains.

Orders to march on the 12th were received on the 7th, and at the same time the Regiment was informed that it would be provided with camels for second-line transport. As land transport with Force "D" scarcely existed,[12] camels had to be collected from neighbouring villages. " A general round-up of every four-footed beast for miles round was instituted—camels for choice, but donkeys and cows accepted."[13] But no sooner did the rumour of this intention spread round the neighbourhood than the Arabs found urgent business outside of the area, which necessitated transport. Some, however, were persuaded and cajoled into hiring their beasts at high prices. These reached Ali Gharbi on the 10th. " They were not baggage camels at all, and most of them had never carried a load before, so that the Transport Sections spent a gay and giddy time trying to induce them to accept

---

[11] Birch Reynardson, p. 190.
[12] The original camel transport of the force had succumbed to a disease called *surra*.
[13] Birch Reynardson, p. 193.

loads."[13] Tents were struck at 4.30 p.m. the same day and loaded on to P2 the following day.

At 5 a.m. on the 12th the Cavalry Brigade, guns and 16th and 17th Brigades started the forward march towards Shaikh Saad, and halted for the day at 9 a.m. on account of the torrid heat. As the troops had done no marching for a year, this march was particularly trying, and the heat caused many casualties not only among the British but also the Indian regiments. Two men in the Dorsetshire Regiment died, and the 43rd had twenty-four sick at the end of the march. As P2 was very late arriving with the tents, it was past 10 a.m. before the 43rd encamped south of Fail village. That night " Q " Company found three piquets on the left bank of the river, and General Townshend paid the Regiment a visit.

Starting at 4.15 the following morning, the column had a long march over bad ground and through a suffocating dust-storm. Halting at 9 a.m., the Regiment encamped six miles below Shaikh Saad,[14] where "Q" Company rejoined in the steamer *Mosul*. The same day an aeroplane reconnoitred Shaikh Saad and reported it unoccupied. Accordingly General Townshend went forward in H.M.S. *Comet*, and ordered the two brigades to follow on the 14th. Shaikh Saad was occupied at 8 a.m. on the 14th after another grilling march, in the course of which twelve men of the 43rd collapsed with heat-stroke. Once again the unfortunate troops were tentless, for the P2 ran aground on the way up. Without food or cover the 43rd was fired under the blistering sun until 3 p.m. when the P2 arrived at last. No sooner had tents been pitched than a withering sandstorm with a scorching wind descended on the camp, penetrating eyes, noses, ears and mouths. The officers were even worse off than the men, for the boat with the mess stores[15] was blown on to a sandbank and did not arrive until the evening. The low state of the water and the shifting channels in the Tigris made navigation extremely difficult; added to which some of the steamers which had plied successfully in high water were now found to draw too much. Consequently the river transport, already short enough, was still further curtailed. All these deficiences of transport, shortcomings and omissions recoiled upon the troops who suffered and became casualties before being required to fight. The same story can be read in practically any British campaign, and it is only the indomitable spirit of the British soldier which has never failed those who have so often failed him.

[13] *Ibid.*, p. 193.
[14] See Map No. 12, p. 206, showing Tigris from Shaikh Saad to Kut.
[15] This *mahaila*, acquired by the foresight of Captain Foljambe, was the private property of the 43rd and contained, besides mess stores, such delicacies as champagne, a soda water factory, coffee shop stores for the troops, and at least one cow. Being unauthorized, it caused the staff and divisional commander much annoyance on more than one occasion; but it fulfilled its mission admirably.

Here at Shaikh Saad without a " vestige of shade or shelter . . . the sun and dust had to be endured all day, with a consequence that a lot of men went down."[16]

That evening an aeroplane reported that the Turks were evacuating Es Sinn, and so General Townshend determined to press on, and abandoned his project of concentrating at Shaikh Saad. Starting at 3.45 a.m. the next day, the Regiment halted at 8.30 a.m. and camped at 10.30 north of Ora ruins. Despite the aeroplane report the Cavalry Brigade gained touch with the enemy in the Es Sinn position. On the 16th a short march brought the Regiment to Sannaiyat, twelve miles short of Es Sinn. By this time patrols had discovered that the Turks were holding the Es Sinn position in strength, and therefore General Townshend halted the division. The halt was badly needed, for the men, still unfit from long inaction, had sore feet and many mules of the first-line transport had sore backs; besides which, the improvised camel transport had given endless trouble. The wake of the marching column had been characterized by strings of wandering camels, donkeys and cows, apparently unattended and without escort. As there was only one Arab ruffian to twenty beasts, this was not surprising; but more surprising was it that they all eventually reached Sannaiyat.[17]

As General Townshend did not propose to occupy Sannaiyat for any length of time a perimeter was not built. Shallow trenches, however, were dug to accommodate the outpost line and supports, and preparations made for the offensive in the near future. At first the general hoped that the Turks would advance from their position and attack, but aerial and naval reconnaissances on the 14th and 15th had reported that the Turks were digging trenches with all speed. General Townshend, thereupon, made his plan after a cavalry reconnaissance had reported that the route running from Nukhailat, on the left (north) bank, between the Suwada and Suwaikiya marshes was fit for three arms.[18] These reconnaissances had all disclosed the fact that the Turks had been reinforced and that their position was much stronger than any encountered hitherto.[18]

Owing to the enemy's strength General Nixon gave General Townshend two more battalions from the 30th Brigade, then on the lines of communication. By the night of the 25th General Townshend's force had concentrated at Sannaiyat, consisting of " one flight of four aeroplanes [and a flight of four seaplanes]; three and a half squadrons of cavalry (7th Lancers and 16th Cavalry); 10th Brigade, R.F.A. (eighteen guns); 1st/5th Hampshire Howitzer Battery; 86th and half 104th Heavy Batteries (six guns); Maxim battery; 17th and 22nd Companies, Sappers and Miners; 16th, 17th,

[16] Birch Reynardson, p. 194.
[17] *Ibid.*, p. 195.
[18] *Official History*, Vol. I, p. 316.

18th and half 30th Infantry Brigades; and 48th Pioneers," amounting to nearly 11,000 men with 28 guns and 40 machine guns.

The Turkish position ran roughly north and south astride the Tigris.[19] On the right bank the Turks had entrenched the high Sinn banks—formerly a high-level canal—for a distance of five miles. These trenches, flanked with redoubts, commanded a good field of fire and view over the open desert. The river on the left flank had been blocked by a boom made of barges and cables, and commanded by fire from both banks.

North of the river the enemy's trenches extended over seven miles but were intersected by two marshes, known as Horse Shoe and Suwada marshes. The left—that is, the extreme north—section " consisted of a chain of redoubts, connected by a maze of trenches, and reached to within two thousand yard of Ataba marsh."[20] The whole enemy position had been well and carefully constructed, and was covered by barbed wire entanglements and other obstacles. The rear was also well organized and provided with communication trenches, pumping stations for water supply, brick gun emplacements, and landing stages. Still further in rear and upstream, a bridge of boats connected the two banks.[21] In fact, the position was nothing if not formidable.

The enemy's total strength[20] was estimated at two divisions (twelve battalions) divided equally on both banks, with a reserve of four battalions, two cavalry regiments and four hundred camelry, and an unknown number of Arab horsemen near the bridge of boats. The two divisions amounted to about six thousand infantry, mostly Arabs. The enemy artillery actually consisted of " three heavy guns, two howitzers, eight field guns, sixteen 15-pounders, two mountain guns and seven old muzzle-loaders, that is a total of thirty-eight,"[22] though the preliminary reconnaissance underestimated the artillery by thirteen pieces at twenty-five.

To deal with this situation General Townshend determined to deceive Nur-ud-Din, the Turkish commander, into believing that he was going to attack on both banks; this was to be effected by a demonstration on the right bank, under cover of which the weight of the force was to be transferred to the left bank, where it was to fall upon the extreme left flank of the enemy, and thereafter cut his communications with Kut.[23]

Meanwhile the troops at Sannaiyat had several alarms of Turkish attacks from the 18th onwards, and adopted the routine of front line work by standing to arms every morning at 4 a.m. But the Turks showed no signs of

---

[19] See Map No. 4, facing p. 88.
[20] *Official History*, Vol. I, p. 317.
[21] The site of this bridge was a tactical error, as was proved later. It was too far in rear to influence a battle on either bank.
[22] *Official History*, Vol. I, p. 318.
[23] *Ibid.*, Vol. I, p. 319.

moving out of their defences though our cavalry patrols had several brushes with the enemy.[24] At least two of these alarms were due to illusions created by mirage. On Sunday morning, the 19th, when all ranks were breakfasting after the usual stand to arms a sudden order turned out the whole division to repel a large body of mounted Arabs and Turkish cavalry reported to be advancing towards the camp. The guns opened fire and appeared to register direct hits, yet the hostile cavalry continued to advance. Under cover of the gun fire a cavalry patrol went out to investigate, and soon afterwards the " dismiss " was sounded. The enemy cavalry was a harmless flock of sheep. On the other occasion, at midday there suddenly appeared to the north across the river a large Turkish encampment filled with moving figures, whereas in fact the nearest Turks were some miles to the west. This illusion must have been deflected through about ninety degrees.

All through this time the Royal Flying Corps were making reconnaissances and taking photographs[25] of the enemy positions, which greatly assisted General Townshend.

By the 25th all was ready for the feint march on the right bank and a demonstration on the left bank by General Fry's force of the 18th Brigade with guns. Starting at 5 a.m. on the 26th, the 43rd, with the rest of the 17th Brigade, reached Chahela Mounds, about 6,000 yards from the enemy, after two hours' marching. Here the two brigades, the 16th and 17th, made much show by pitching all the available tents along the perimeter of the camp—in order to delude the Turks into thinking that a permanent camp was being erected, while the 103rd Mahrattas advanced still further towards the enemy and went through the motions of digging trenches.[26]

Meanwhile the bridging train was towed up, and a bridge constructed soon after 4 p.m. at Nukhailat—6th Divisional Headquarters—on a sharp curve of the river but screened from the Turks and out of range of their shrapnel.

During the afternoon the camp at Chahela Mounds succeeded in attracting the attention of the enemy who proceeded to shell the tents without doing much damage; the ruse was evidently beginning to work according to plan.

That night orders were issued to the 43rd and the plan explained. Meanwhile, across the river a right flank guard advanced from Nukhailat and established itself at Clery's Post at the south-east corner of the Suwada marsh.

Next morning the 43rd, under Major Hyde, with the 119th Infantry and one section of guns and a squadron of cavalry, all under Colonel Darley of the 119th, moved out of Chahela camp at 4 a.m. to make a demonstration against the Turkish right. As soon as it was light the column deployed

[24] Birch Reynardson, p. 197.
[25] The maps used in the battle of Es Sinn were produced from these photographs.
[26] *Official History*, Vol. I, p. 319.

when four thousand yards from the Sinn banks, while the guns opened fire to cover the advance of the demonstrators. Meanwhile the 18th Brigade across the river advanced from Clery's Post towards the Turkish centre or " horse-shoe " position, supported by the weight of the naval and military artillery.[27] Driving in the enemy's advanced troops with very little opposition, the 18th Brigade advanced to within two thousand yards of the Turks and suffered no more than twenty-five casualties in spite of heavy shell-fire from the Turkish guns.[28] Early in the afternoon the 18th Brigade dug itself in, while the 63rd Field Battery commander reconnoitred positions for his guns some three thousand yards from the enemy's lines.

On the right bank the 43rd did its best to advertise its presence and delude the enemy. Owing to the mirage it was impossible to spot the enemy's gun positions, or, indeed, to see whether the Sinn banks were held in force or not: so the column returned to camp at 1.15 p.m. without having met with any opposition.[29]

At 5 p.m. part of the 16th Brigade—the Dorsetshire Regiment and 20th Punjabis—and half the 30th Brigade moved up the right bank again and began to dig trenches in full view of the enemy. " They failed to draw the enemy's fire, however, and after dusk the 16th Brigade withdrew to camp, leaving the 30th Brigade to hold these trenches and the bridge-head near Nukhailat."[30] This demonstration, though appearing to fail, did actually delude Nur-ud-Din into thinking that the right would be attacked.

" All day working parties had been employed in building roads and cutting a ramp down to the river,"[29] and at 3.45 p.m. the second-line transport was sent over the pontoon bridge to the left bank. At 6.30 p.m. the 43rd paraded to assemble with the rest of the 17th Brigade at the bridge-head, preparatory to its march by night across the enemy's front to the extreme right flank of the British force. " The large camp pitched the day before was left standing, the tents tenantless, to impose upon the Turks."[29] The safety of the right bank, the bridge and communications was entrusted to the 2nd/7th Gurkhas and half the 67th Punjabis when the 16th and 17th Brigades shuffled off through the darkness in the wake of the cavalry and artillery.

III.—The Night March.[31]

Absolute silence was ordered during the night march and no light of any sort was to be shown. There was a delay before crossing the bridge, owing to the steepness of the ramps, which necessitated great care being

---

[27] *Ibid.*, Vol. I, pp. 319-320.   [28] *Chronicle*, 1915-16, p. 55.
[29] Birch Reynardson, p. 206.   [30] *Official History*, Vol. I, p. 320.
[31] *Chronicle*, 1915-16, pp. 55-56, Captain Powell's account. *Ibid.*, p. 61, Lieutenant Birch Reynardson's account. Birch Reynardson, pp. 206-209. See Map No. 4.

taken by the transport carts to avoid noise. The bridge itself had been strewn with earth and straw to deaden the sound of wheels and tramping feet. Once safely across, the Brigade formed up at Nukhailat and marched out towards Clery's Post[32] under Captain Davenport's guidance. On reaching Clery's Post soon after 9 p.m., loads were removed from the mules, and all animals were sent off to water while the two brigades formed square with piquets out on all flanks. During the halt food was served out, but fresh water was unobtainable as the marsh water which had been reported drinkable proved to be brackish. Strict conservancy of water was therefore imperative as only the company *packals* and each man's waterbottle were available for all needs for an indefinite length of time.[33] The night was so intensely cold that, instead of being able to snatch a few hours' sleep, the Regiment paced up and down in grim silence trying to keep warm.[34]

One consolation, however, was provided by the Turks who vigorously shelled the vacant standing camp across the river during the night.

By midnight General Delamain's force, consisting of three and a half squadrons of cavalry (7th Lancers and 16th Cavalry), two batteries of 18-pounders and a section of howitzers, 22nd Company, Sappers and Miners, 16th and 17th Infantry Brigades, Maxim battery, signal and medical units, had assembled at Clery's Post. This force was to deliver the flank attack on the Turkish left at dawn, while General Fry, with a force consisting of the 63rd Battery and one section of howitzers, 17th Company, Sappers and Miners, 18th Infantry Brigade and 48th Pioneers, was to pin the enemy to his centre section, north and south of Horse Shoe marsh.[35]

At 1 a.m. on the 28th General Delamain's force formed up and started the last and most difficult lap. From now onward its left was completely open to the Turks, except for a flank guard. The force marched in two columns, "A" and "B," at about two hundred yards' interval, with a small advance guard out in front while the 43rd scouts provided a guard for Lieutenant Matthews, R.E., who was leading the columns with Captain Davenport, of the 43rd, checking distances covered.[36] " The night was very still, and nothing was to be heard, except an occasional rattle of the packs on the mules, or the distant sound of the artillery."[36] The Regiment " plugged on in suffocating dust through the darkness. The atmosphere was damp and heavy, like clammy cotton-wool, and at every halt the men would fall asleep at once, some of them as they stood, overcome by the closeness of the air."[37]

At 4.45 a.m. scouts picked up the south-western edge of Suwaikiya marsh. Marching along the edge of the marsh, the two columns halted at

[32] See Map No. 4.
[34] *Chronicle*, 1915-16, pp. 56 and 61.
[36] *Chronicle*, 1915-16, pp. 56 and 61.
[33] Birch Reynardson, p. 208.
[35] *Official History*, Vol. I, p. 318.
[37] Birch Reynardson, p. 208.

5 a.m. This was to be the point of deployment for the frontal attack on the Northern and Centre Redoubts by Column "B," consisting of the Dorsetshire Regiment, half the 117th Mahrattas, 22nd Company, Sappers and Miners, two guns of the Maxim battery with the 76th and 82nd Field and 1st/5th Hampshire Howitzer Batteries, under the personal direction of General Delamain himself.[38] Between 5.15 and 5.30 a.m. General Hoghton, in command of the enveloping attack, preceded by the cavalry who were to guard his flank, moved off with his force, Column "A," to take post opposite the gap between Northern Redoubt and Ataba marsh.[39] With him he had his own, the 17th, Brigade, consisting of the 43rd, 22nd Punjabis, 103rd Mahrattas and 119th Infantry, as well as two regiments of the 16th Brigade, the 20th Punjabis and 104th Rifles.[38] Having reached what he considered to be Point "A,"[40] General Hoghton deployed his force in two lines on a 1,200 yards' frontage, the front line from the right consisting of the 20th Punjabis, 43rd and 22nd Punjabis, and the second line of the 104th Rifles, 103rd Mahrattas and 119th Infantry.

IV.—THE BATTLE OF KUT AL AMARA OR ES SINN.[41]

Just after 6 a.m., when the sun rose, General Hoghton realized that he had led his column too far, and that instead of being south of Ataba marsh he was very nearly round the northern flank of it. At 7 a.m. the cavalry drove back some hostile mounted troops, and General Hoghton's force wheeled round the marsh and threatened the north-west flank of Northern Redoubt. During this long and trying march the force kept its formation very well, except that the 104th Rifles were now echeloned in rear of the right of the 20th Punjabis. However, just as the attacking lines advanced on the enemy's rear, the cavalry and 20th Punjabis on the right flank reported the presence of enemy in an entrenched position to the westward, hitherto unlocated.[42] General Hoghton immediately detached the 104th Rifles to deal with this thorn in his side. Advancing with great dash under supporting fire from the 76th Battery and Maxim battery, the 104th Rifles carried the position at 9.10 a.m., capturing one officer and 111 men.

Meanwhile General Delamain was in an awkward quandary owing to the delay caused by General Hoghton's wide enveloping march. He had intended to attack the Centre and Southern Redoubts with his own small force at dawn in co-operation with General Hoghton. "He therefore

[38] *Official History*, Vol. I, p. 322.   [39] *Ibid.*, Vol. I, p. 323.
[40] See Map No. 4.
[41] *Chronicle*, 1915-16, pp. 56-59, Captain Powell's account. *Ibid.*, pp. 61-65, Lieutenant Birch Reynardson's account. Birch Reynardson, pp. 210-214. *Official History*, Vol. I, pp. 316-336.
[42] *Official History*, Vol. I, p. 324.

advanced deliberately from the position of deployment,"[43] reconnoitring with the help of two armoured cars and an aeroplane sent up from divisional headquarters. By 8 a.m. he had reached a position 2,000 yards north-east of Northern Redoubt. At 8.20, when General Hoghton was halted pending the result of the attack by the 104th Rifles on the outlying redoubt, General Delamain ordered an attack by his small force before Turkish troops could reinforce the redoubts. In this attack the 117th Mahrattas and 22nd Company, Sappers and Miners, were to capture Northern Redoubt while half the Dorsetshire Regiment attacked Centre Redoubt. Advancing at 8.45 a.m., the attack on Northern Redoubt was stoutly resisted by the tough Ottoman Turks, but help was at hand, for General Hoghton's force was now nearing its objective. Pushing on southward, General Hoghton first detached the 103rd to help General Delamain's attack on Northern Redoubt and then the 119th Infantry to attack Centre Redoubt, with the 43rd in support.[44] The 43rd received its order at 9.45 a.m. by which time the 119th Infantry had already advanced some distance. However, like true light infantry, " Q " and " R " Companies, with " P " and " S " in support, dashed forward in time to cover the last advance of the 119th.

The battle was now raging furiously. Advancing with the utmost gallantry, General Delamain's force together with the 103rd, well supported by the 76th Field Battery, carried the north and north-west of Northern Redoubt at about 10 a.m. Meanwhile the 43rd was nearing the rear of Centre Redoubt in conjunction with the 119th. Steadily the two regiments[45] advanced and captured two lines of trenches west of Centre Redoubt, but they could go no farther for heavy artillery fire from the south was switched on to them. The Turks were fighting stubbornly to the south-west and south of Centre Redoubt, and Southern Redoubt was strongly held.

Meanwhile the Turks were massing to counter-attack from Southern Redoubt; the aeroplane reported that reinforcements were being hurried across the river in support of their left flank. General Hoghton, alive to this danger, formed a defensive flank with the 20th and 22nd Punjabis and 104th Rifles.[46]

Meanwhile, owing to lack of artillery support, the advance against Southern Redoubt had almost been brought to a standstill. The Turks started to counter-attack, and the British could make no headway against the accurate and heavy artillery fire.[46] Things were not going too well; the decisive moment had arrived. At about 12.30 p.m. a new firing line was formed from the 43rd, 119th and 103rd.[47] The attack on Southern Redoubt was launched under the covering fire of the 82nd and Hampshire Batteries

[43] *Ibid.*, Vol. I, p. 325. [44] *Ibid.*, Vol. I, p. 326.
[45] War Diary : " R " and " Q " Companies in front line, " P " and " S " in support.
[46] *Official History*, Vol. I, p. 327. [47] War Diary.

which redoubled their efforts. Gallantly the 43rd, steady as of old, advanced through the Turkish fire, with " P " and " S " Companies in the front line and " R " and " Q " in the second line. When within four hundred yards of Southern Redoubt, Captain Davenport with some men of " Q " Company worked up a communication trench, surprised and captured two Krupp guns and killed or captured the gunners.[46]

Meanwhile the order to fix bayonets was passed down the lines, and then with a roar the lines surged forward, stormed the entrenchments and captured the redoubt and two hundred prisoners.[47] The observer in the aeroplane described the attack: " A forest of rifles is pointing at us from the centre trenches, but the Turks will have no time to think of aeroplanes when the Oxfords get amongst them with cold steel. Our troops have deployed and are advancing steadily, wave after wave of gallant men marching through the Turkish fire as if they were on a King's parade. Wonderful. The first wave has reached the trenches. Never shall I see such things again. . . . The opposing forces look like ants, tapping each other with their feelers. Some of the ants lie still. Hurrah, the Turks are leaving their trenches and the Oxfords are bayoneting them as they run. . . . The Oxfords have won the main trenches."[49]

This attack by the Regiment was also described by General Nixon in his report " as particularly fine," and General Delamain, following the attack, congratulated the 43rd on the spot.[50]

In Southern Redoubt an hour was spent in reorganizing and collecting arms, wounded and prisoners, three hundred of whom had been taken. The casualties in the Regiment up till now amounted to one officer—Captain Meldon—and about thirty-five men wounded.[50]

During the process of mopping up the northern section of the Turkish position, General Delamain ordered General Hoghton to push on southward with his own force, less the 43rd, 103rd and 119th which were now under General Delamain's command. At 1.45 p.m. the advance was resumed by General Hoghton's force until 3.30 p.m. by which time the men were completely exhausted from long marching, hard fighting, lack of water, heat and dust. He therefore halted his troops north-west of the Horse Shoe marsh.[51] As the need of water was now vital, General Hoghton retired towards the Suwada marsh at about 4 p.m., where he met, near Point " B," General Delamain who was advancing to his support with the troops which had lately captured Southern Redoubt.[52]

[47] War Diary.
[48] *Chronicle*, 1915-16, p. 67.
[49] *Bengal Lancer*, by F. Yeats-Brown, pp. 180-182.
[50] War Diary.
[51] *Official History*, Vol. I, p. 328.
[52] See Map No. 4.

HARD FIGHTING

Farther south the holding attack by the 18th Brigade had been hampered by the initial delay of General Delamain's enveloping movement. Advancing methodically at 6 a.m. the 18th Brigade reached a point fifteen hundred yards from the enemy's trenches north of Horse Shoe marsh but was unable to progress farther. At noon General Fry, in command, was requested to press his attack again in order to assist General Delamain in his southerly advance from the northern section. This request, however, proved premature. Nevertheless by 4.30 p.m. the 18th Brigade had managed to advance to within nine hundred yards of the trenches between the Suwada and Horse Shoe marshes,[53] but its left was being severely enfiladed from the trenches immediately north of the river.

At about 4 p.m.[54] General Fry sent a message by aeroplane, asking General Delamain to co-operate by a flanking attack. General Delamain agreed to advance at 5.30 p.m. and take in reverse the position which General Fry intended to attack, between the Suwada and Horse Shoe marshes. His troops had had an hour's rest, and movement towards water was imperative by this time. At about 4.50 p.m. General Delamain set his troops in motion. " The three battalions[55] of the 17th Brigade led the advance. The 22nd Punjabis, on the left of the leading line, moved along the western edge of the Suwada marsh, with the Oxfords on their right, and the 103rd and Brigade machine guns following in support."[56] The 16th Brigade marched in echelon on the right rear of the 17th Brigade. The two brigades, advancing in artillery formation, soon spotted " a large force of the enemy moving up as if to reinforce the Turks opposite General Fry."[54] General Delamain, forced to change his intentions, immediately wheeled his force round to the right to meet this threat. The guns "promptly opened fire on the enemy, and soon silenced his four guns."[57] As soon as the wheel had been completed, the two brigades made straight for the Turks; " the 17th Brigade on the left with the 43rd and 22nd Punjabis in front line,[58] and 103rd in support; the 16th Brigade on the right, with the Dorsets and 104th leading."[59] The two brigades advanced methodically in artillery formation until a heavy burst of rifle fire was opened from a patch of parched grass about six hundred yards to their front. " It needed no orders to make the men extend; they did so automatically and within a few seconds all were lying flat, and the column,

---

[53] *Official History*, Vol. I, p. 332.
[54] *Chronicle*, 1915-16, p. 58.
[55] The 119th were left behind to hold the captured northern section.
[56] *Official History*, Vol. I, pp. 332-333.
[57] *Chronicle*, 1915-16, p. 59.
[58] War Diary. The 43rd, with "P" and "R" Companies in front line and "Q" and "S" in support, was on the left of the 22nd Punjabis. "S" Company was eventually sent to prolong the line to the left.
[59] *Chronicle*, 1915-16, p. 59. Captain Powell's account.

except for the ammunition mules, seemed to have disappeared into the earth."[60] There was now no alternative: the Turks had to be defeated in the short half-hour of daylight that still remained. The men, though utterly exhausted and parched with thirst, responded gallantly to this call to new endeavours, and swept forward at an amazing pace under the covering fire of the 76th, 82nd, 1st/5th Hampshire Howitzer and Maxim Batteries, until failing light made it impossible to distinguish friend from foe and the guns and Maxims were forced to cease fire. The Turks, meanwhile, took up a position along a dry canal running north-west from the Tigris. In the long advance over completely open ground a gap began to appear between the 43rd and 22nd Punjabis. This was filled by the 103rd from support. For a thousand yards the irresistible and indomitable regiments swept on—now without artillery support—straight into the Turkish fire and the blinding rays of the setting sun. "Some men suddenly collapsed never to rise again; others shouted in pain as they were hit; one or two, although wounded, completed the attack."[60] Nothing could stop them; they charged all the way in a manner conceived impossible on peace manœuvres; and then, at assaulting distance, with a roar of many voices they were at the Turks' throats. "Some got away, some were bayoneted, and the rest, together with a battery of guns and two machine guns, were captured."[61] And then night came down like a pall upon the battlefield.

V.—INCIDENTS OF THE BATTLE.

Before dealing with the night after the battle mention must be made of the part played by the regimental machine-gun section during the battle. In the initial deployment for the attack on the northern section of the enemy's position, the brigaded machine-gun sections under Captain Courtis, 43rd, had been placed on the right flank in echelon behind the 20th Punjabis. While Column "A," General Hoghton's force, was halted north-west of Ataba marsh the regimental machine-gun section, under Lieutenant Birch Reynardson, spotted three or four hundred enemy infantry moving into a trench on its right flank. Soon after, when the brigade major came up to order the machine guns to co-operate in the attack on Northern Redoubt, Captain Courtis pointed out that three hundred of the enemy were sitting on the flank. The brigade major thereupon ordered Captain Courtis to capture the position, and then co-operate in the attack on Northern Redoubt.

Without any infantry escort, but nothing daunted, the six machine guns were marched off "in artillery formation, over ground as flat as a billiard table, towards the objective."[62] When about 800 yards distant, the

---

[60] Lieutenant Naylor's diary.   [61] Birch Reynardson, p. 214.
[62] *Chronicle*, 1915-16, p. 62.

Turks opened fire. In a trice the 43rd machine guns were in action, Lance-Corporal Upstone's gun being the first in the brigade to open fire. Meanwhile the mules, which had never been under fire before, dug in their toes and refused to be led away to the rear. The enemy by this time had ranged and was hitting the sections. Corporal Barford and Mills were the first to be wounded.

After about five minutes of rapid fire from the guns the Turks hoisted a white flag. A second later Private Miles was hit, so the white flag was disregarded. A little later the 76th Battery opened on the enemy with shrapnel. The result was instantaneous; they immediately started to bolt, giving the men behind the machine guns that target which is generally only encountered in dreams. Running back to the trenches, the Turks hoisted more white flags. The machine guns ceased fire.

Captain Courtis was now faced with the problem of attacking and capturing the enemy position with the guns' teams alone.[63] Luckily it was then that the 104th Rifles appeared, having been detached by General Hoghton to capture the outlying redoubt as has already been described.[64] Thereafter the brigade machine guns came under General Hoghton's orders, and fought with the 20th and 22nd Punjabis and 104th Rifles for the rest of the day. All the morning the regimental section manhandled its guns and ammunition from position to position in support of the infantry and yet no sooner had the guns been mounted than the infantry advanced again, masking its fire. So exhausted did the team become that Lieutenant Birch Reynardson gave up his attempts to get into action.

When General Hoghton ordered the withdrawal to the Suwada marsh at about 4 p.m. the pack mules gave great trouble. Mad with thirst, they nearly stampeded as soon as they saw the water, and the drivers had great difficulty in preventing their being bogged in the marsh.

In the final attack the machine-gun section, in between the two brigades, supported the initial advance, but so impetuous was the attack that the section was soon left behind, unable to compete with the pace. While following as best it could, the section lost one man and four mules killed.

During the battle Captain Powell, 43rd, was brigade signalling officer to General Hoghton. Communications were of vital importance in a battle waged over such a vast area by moving columns. The seven miles of heavy cable was expended early in the operations and visual signalling, except within brigades, was impossible owing to mirage. Communication, however, with headquarters was maintained with great difficulty by light telephone cable, but eventually even this method had to be discarded as the Arabs, who hovered like vultures on the rear of the battle, continually cut

[63] *Ibid.*, 1915-16, pp. 62, 63.   [64] See p. 82 *ante*.

the line despite the efforts of patrolling linesmen. In the later stages of the battle all communication between Generals Delamain, Fry and Townshend was effected by aeroplane.[65]

VI.—THE NIGHT AFTER THE BATTLE.

We left the Regiment in the captured Turkish position at nightfall. At first the dry canal was thought to be the bank of the Tigris with sorely needed water close at hand. The disappointment of the troops on finding no signs of water anywhere can only be faintly imagined.

First of all the wadi had to be cleared of the Turkish dead and wounded, and then organized for defence against possible counter-attacks. For this the machine guns were sent back to their regiments by General Hoghton, and sentries were posted every six yards. Unfortunately it was impossible to send out patrols to find water and locate the position now held, for "re-action had set in. The men were so dead-beat that they literally could not understand an order: thirst and exhaustion had produced a stupefying effect."[66] After a few hours' rest General Delamain sent a staff officer with a cavalry escort to try to communicate with General Townshend and tell him what had happened, " but all the horses were killed on the way by enemy fire."[67] Consequently the party had to lie out all night, unable to communicate with either of the generals.

To add to the already unspeakable discomforts of the troops the temperature dropped 50 degrees that night. Without food, water, jackets or blankets the 43rd shivered in the bitter cold, the sweat of battle drying in black streaks on the faces and cracking the lips of the exhausted officers and men.

The casualties in the battle were not so severe as might have been expected from the hard fighting. Major R. V. Simpson, commanding "S" Company, was killed in the final stage of the battle, hit through the head. Four other ranks were killed and three died of wounds, namely:—

    8993 Private Brazier, Albert Henry—killed.
    8037 Corporal Dixon, D.C.M., Albert—died of wounds.
    6742 Bugler Harper, Frederick George—killed.
    7884 Lance-Corporal Keinch, Joseph—died of wounds.
    8460 Private Little, Herbert—killed.
    8335 Private Rout, John Alfred—died of wounds.
    8985 Lance-Serjeant Wright, John—killed.

Captains Powell and Meldon and eighty-two other ranks were wounded.

---

[65] For a graphic description of this intercommunication see *Bengal Lancer*, pp. 175-184.
[66] Birch Reynardson, p. 214.
[67] *Official History*, Vol. I, p. 334; *Chronicle*, 1915-16, p. 65; Birch Reynardson, pp. 214-215.

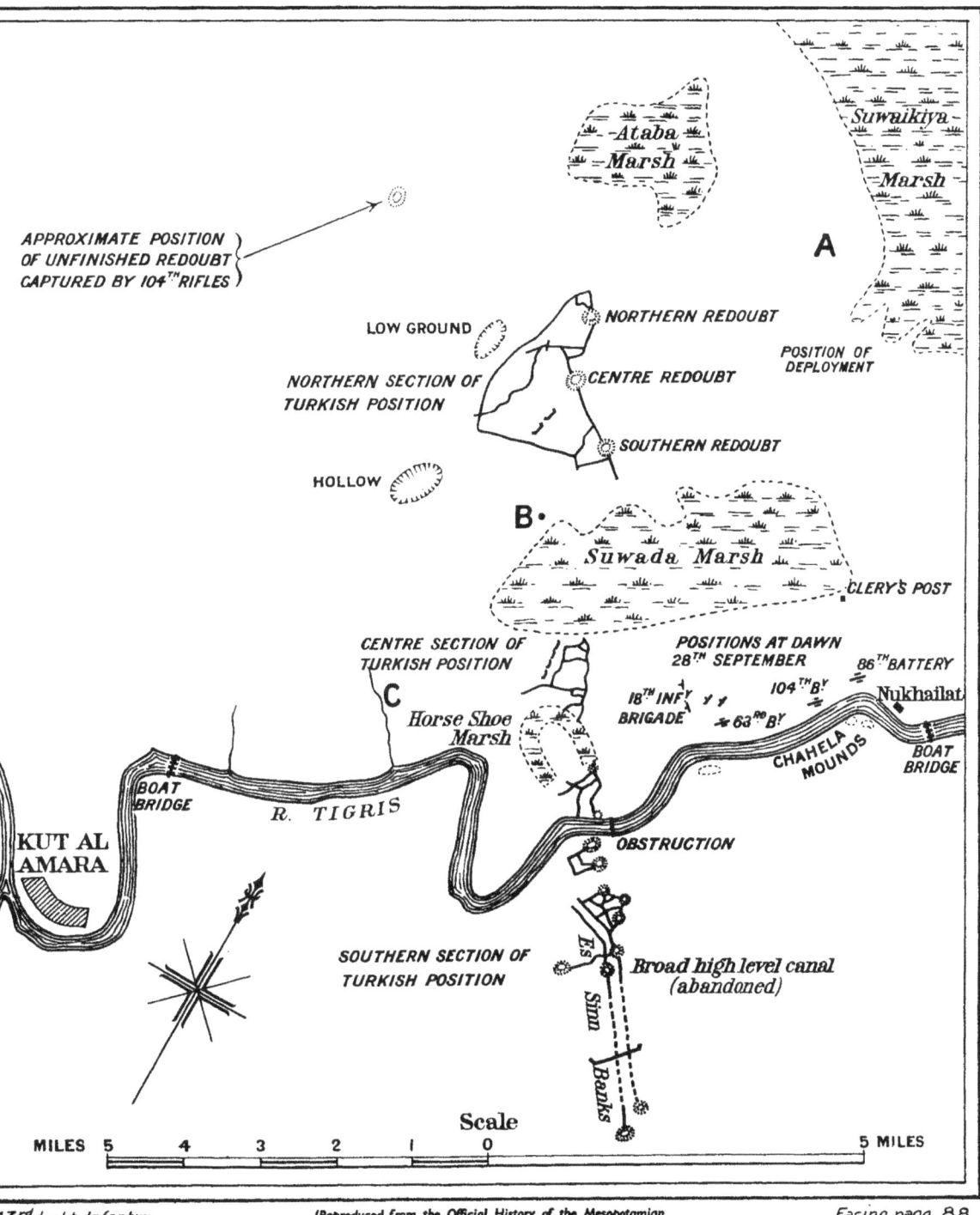

And what of the wounded? In front the groans of the Turks alone disturbed the stillness of the night; to the flank unknown numbers of our men were lying out in the bitter cold unattended. A few volunteers searched over a wide area. No one knew whither the ambulances had moved, but the wounded had to be found as Arabs were known to be on the prowl for loot. At about 11 p.m. Captains Foljambe and Startin, the medical officer, found Captain Powell lying in the long grass, grievously wounded. He had been carried more than a mile by Corporals Pursglove, Ballard, Olliff and Cave after being bandaged by Private Stevens. With him were more wounded men of the Regiment. Captain Foljambe sent out some mule rugs to protect them from the cold.[68] Previously to this a mounted Turkish officer retreating with one or two men had stumbled over the party of wounded in the dark. One of the guard promptly shot at them; whereupon the Turkish officer fell off his horse and was captured; his greatcoat was taken from him and laid over the wounded. But many of the wounded were robbed and murdered that night by the Arabs who were, as usual, impartial alike to British and Turks; while others succumbed to the cold and exhaustion.[69] Bodies were found the following day foully mutilated. Three Arabs were caught in the act of butchering the wounded and were publicly hanged, a punishment too humane for such bestiality.[70]

During the battle the collecting stations and field ambulances were soon lost, and all day wounded men and stretcher-bearers wandered over the battlefield searching for them. "The improvised arrangements for the reception and accommodation of the wounded proved inadequate,"[71] and this is hardly surprising considering that makeshift arrangements were made for "six per cent. casualties, whereas they actually amounted to double this number."[70] There was only one motor ambulance in the country for the transport of sick or wounded by land, and there was no hospital ship for river work.[72] The wounded were laid out on the iron decks of any steamer, launch or barge that was available, and there left to rot of gangrene, bred of foul bloated flies, under a thin awning if they were lucky. The hot decks,

---

[68] *Chronicle*, 1915-16, p. 59.
[69] Birch Reynardson, p. 215.
[70] *Official History*, Vol. I, p. 337.
[71] *Ibid.*, Vol. I, p. 336.
[72] Birch Reynardson, p. 214. *Official History*, Vol. I, p. 343. A hospital ship had been provided in India in March, but she sank on the ocean voyage. General Nixon was vitally aware of the need of river transport. In May he asked for six tugs and some motor launches. On the 8th July he urgently requested nine light-draught steamers. On the 17th he demanded six paddle steamers, three sternwheelers, eight tugs, forty-three barges and six launches. Hospital barges were available locally, but tugs of three feet six inches' draught were not procurable in India to tow them. Long ocean voyages, the peculiar types of ships required, the exigencies of the war elsewhere, all militated against General Nixon's efforts to provide adequately for the needs of his troops.

" slippery with blood and diarrhœa,"[73] were piled high with helpless men whose wounds were infected by their neighbours if not already septic and gangrenous. To cope with this spate of agonized humanity the overworked medical personnel was entirely inadequate.

The following officers and men of the 43rd were mentioned in General Nixon's despatch which covered the operations up to and including the battle of Es Sinn:—

    Lieutenant-Colonel E. A. E. Lethbridge, D.S.O.
    Major A. C. Hyde.
    Captain R. R. M. Brooke, killed in the Qurna *Regatta*.
    Captain C. F. Henley.
    Captain W. E. T. Morland.
    Captain J. H. Courtis.
    Captain Hon. J. C. W. S. Foljambe.
    Lieutenant J. J. Powell.
8037 Corporal A. Dixon, D.C.M.
7452 Lance-Corporal W. E. Donohoe.
8347 Private G. F. Draper, D.C.M.
8929 Lance-Corporal W. J. Farrant.
6830 Serjeant H. Grace, D.C.M.
9037 Lance-Corporal J. Horwood, D.C.M.
8777 Private F. J. Hussey.
 793 Serjeant J. Kidd, D.C.M., attached from 1st/4th Border Regiment.
8732 Private J. W. Neale.
8986 Lance-Corporal J. Upstone, D.C.M.
9166 Lance-Corporal R. Parkes, D.C.M.

The following were awarded the *Distinguished Conduct Medal* for their gallantry in the battle of Kut al Amara or Es Sinn:—

8986 *Lance-Corporal J. Upstone*: for conspicuous gallantry and initiative at Kut al Amara on the 28th September 1915. He brought his machine gun quickly into action under heavy fire, and worked it with great effect against the enemy.

8037 *Corporal A. Dixon*: for conspicuous gallantry at Kut al Amara on the 28th September 1915. Although wounded, he continued to lead and encourage his section with great determination until the evening, when the fight closed.

8347 *Private G. F. Draper*: for conspicuous gallantry and devotion to duty at Kut al Amara on the 28th September, 1915. He tended a badly

---

[73] *Bengal Lancer*, p. 183.

wounded man under heavy fire, helped him to a trench and then returned immediately to the firing line.

6830 *Serjeant H. Grace*: for conspicuous gallantry at Kut al Amara on the 28th September 1915. He sent messages to the artillery by heliograph under heavy fire, although he had to stand in full view of the enemy's redoubts in order to do so.

9037 *Lance-Corporal J. Horwood*: for conspicuous gallantry at Kut al Amara on the 28th September 1915. He both carried messages and sent them by heliograph and flag under heavy fire when in close proximity to the enemy's trenches.

793 *Serjeant J. Kidd*, attached from the 1st/4th Border Regiment: for conspicuous gallantry at Kut al Amara on the 28th September 1915. Although wounded, he took part in the final charge, and showed a fine example to those around him.

CHAPTER XIII.

I.—Results of the Battle : Capture of Kut al Amara : Concentration at Aziziya.

Turkish retreat—Pursuit—The 43rd clears the battlefield—Turks evade pursuit—
—The 43rd rejoins at Aziziya—General Nixon's memorandum—Sir Beauchamp
Duff warns the Viceroy—Memorandum by General Staff—Cabinet authorizes
advance on Baghdad—Concentration at Aziziya—Townshend's estimate of Turkish
strength—The advance to Ctesiphon—Capture of Zor—Townshend's preparations.

(*See Maps facing pages* 1 *and* 88, *and on page* 130.)

Anxiously the Regiment awaited the dawn and a sight of the river. For thirty-six hours all ranks had subsisted without water; for those who had sampled the marsh water to slake their thirst found that it contained properties as cathartic as Epsom salts.[1]

When at last dawn came there was still no sign of the river; only open desert strewn with the débris of the Turks' precipitate retreat of the previous evening.

Soon after dawn, however, an aeroplane dropped a message ordering General Delamain to press on to the river immediately, as the Turks were in full retreat to Kut. The river proved to be only about a mile from the outpost position, and that mile was covered without opposition. The Turks, slipping away from their positions north and south of Horse Shoe marsh during the night, had evaded the two brigades lying north of their line of retreat. Had General Delamain been able to locate his position before nightfall, the tale of the Turkish discomfiture might well have been complete.

On reaching the river, it was found that there was only one place where the men could wade in and drink their fill, but regiments patiently awaited their turns. This was a hard test of discipline, when lips were black with thirst and tongues felt like wads of hot cardboard[2]; but not a man in the 43rd moved until he received an order. *Packals* were filled at the same time and water taken back to the wounded, who received their first drink at about 10.30 a.m.

Meanwhile the cavalry and naval flotilla took up the pursuit, and the 18th Brigade was ordered to embark and follow up the Turks, who were reported by aeroplanes to be retreating on Baghdad. For the march on Kut

---
[1] *Chronicle*, 1915-16, p. 65.   [2] Birch Reynardson, p. 216.

the 16th Brigade was chosen by General Townshend, while the 17th Brigade went into camp about two miles above the Es Sinn position, as there was insufficient transport to take it forward. The Regiment received the news that it was to stay behind and clear up the battlefield with some disappointment. But after a good meal and a sound sleep the situation was viewed in a better light. At 6 p.m. the Regiment's parent ship—P2—arrived with tents, and General Nixon visited the mess and explained the reason for detaining the brigade at Es Sinn.

For five days the 43rd cleared the battlefield and buried the dead. There was little of value to be salved after the Arab vultures had had their pick. But it was possible to examine carefully the position which the 43rd had stormed with such signal success. It was indeed imposing: the trenches were well sited, deep, traversed and supplied with jars of water every fifty yards. The redoubts were provided with dug-outs and wells, and were protected with wire, in front and on the flanks, and land mines which luckily were not exploded in the heat of the battle. All the loop-holes were well protected with concrete overhead cover. From the front-line redoubts a very complete system of communication trenches, ten to twelve feet deep, led back to the rear. Those on the north-west flank of the north section had fire positions, thus producing a strong defensive flank. Considering that throughout the actual battle dust and mirage had often prevented artillery observation and consequently co-operation, the casualties sustained by the 43rd were amazingly light. "The infantry had often to advance without any artillery support whatever."[3]

By the 2nd October the left bank had been cleared up, and orders received to cross the river to the right bank and there salve military material. On the 3rd regimental headquarters, " Q " and " R " Companies and the machine-gun section, mule-cart transport and one section of guns set off to cross by the Turkish boat bridge which was found to be impassable by artillery. So rotten was it that the medical cart with its mules went through the planking. After a hot march of eight miles the Regiment halted at 3 p.m. on the river bank. Meanwhile " P " and " S " Companies started at 7 a.m. to march to Kut with the rest of the 17th Brigade.

"Q" and "R" Companies found very little material of military value on the right bank and, beyond salving two old 7-pounder brass muzzle-loading guns dated 1802 and suffering the tortures of the damned from a plague of sand-flies, accomplished little worthy of record. However, Lieutenant Birch Reynardson visited the defences and recorded his impressions of them.[4] These are interesting in the light of future events, for in the attack on these defences the 2nd/43rd was destined to take part in March 1916.[5] On

[3] *Ibid.*, p. 217. [4] *Ibid.*, 223.
[5] *Chronicle*, 1915-16, p. 69.

the 5th regimental headquarters and " Q " and " R " Companies hauled the two brass cannon over the bridge with some difficulty, and marched to Kut al Amara.

Meanwhile the pursuit of the beaten Turks by the naval flotilla and the 18th Brigade had been much impeded by the fall of water in the Tigris; difficult navigation had prevented the ships from harassing and demoralizing the Turkish retreat still further. Consequently the enemy had been able to keep ahead of the pursuit with an organized rear guard. By the 3rd October General Nixon realized that " there was no longer any chance of surprising and stampeding the retreating enemy, who would probably stand and fight at Ctesiphon."[6] He therefore determined to concentrate his striking force at Aziziya, in case a further advance on Baghdad should be authorized by the Indian Government.

On the 6th the 16th Brigade with the guns and a column of cavalry with half " S " Battery, R.H.A., left Kut for Aziziya, and two days later the 17th Brigade was ordered to follow. The 43rd started by land at 7 a.m. on the 8th with insufficient transport for its needs. The Regiment marched till noon through torrid heat and suffocating dust as the result of which twelve men collapsed, though the distance was only about ten miles. That night the 17th Brigade received orders to push on with all speed, as the Arabs had reported to General Townshend that the Turks intended to attack his weak force, the 18th Brigade, which numbered only 2,200 effectives. Starting at 5.30 a.m. on the 9th, the 43rd marched till 9.30 a.m., when a halt was called to rest and unload the transport animals. By this time the sun was exceedingly hot for the troops lying on the shadeless desert. The route chosen was direct, regardless of the serpentine course of the river, with the result that the supply of water was restricted during the march across the bends. The march was continued at 1 p.m., and according to supposition the camping-ground should have been reached at 5 p.m. However, this was not to be, for the column lost direction in crossing the desert and the 43rd, parched with thirst, was still marching at 6 p.m. The Regiment " plugged on, occasionally cheered for a moment by a glimmer in the distance which appeared to be the river, but always we found that it was only a white salt deposit shining in the moonlight," wrote Lieutenant Birch Reynardson.[7] This happened repeatedly, but still the men of the 43rd refused to be disappointed. They marched splendidly. " It had been a very hot day with a dust storm most of the time, and water bottles, full at dawn, had proved a short ration."[7] However, at about 7 p.m. men began to fall out, dead-beat and complaining of a " terrible stiffness and numbness in their legs." For these men guards had to be found as a protection from the prowling Arabs,

---

[6] *Official History*, Vol. II, p. 6.   [7] Birch Reynardson, p. 229.

for no one knew exactly how far off the camping-ground lay. When this was eventually reached at 7.45 p.m. the parent ship had not arrived, having gone aground downstream; and "there was no food to be had until late when most of the men were too tired to eat."[8] At 11 p.m. the ship arrived, by which time most of the sick had managed to make their way to camp; they were put on board, and their sickness was diagnosed as the first symptoms of beri-beri. At the same time the weary Regiment was warned that the march was to be resumed the next day to Aziziya, twenty-five miles upstream. Very fatiguing conditions were experienced on this march, similar to the previous day. Direction was again lost on leaving the river, so that night had fallen before the 43rd reached Aziziya. At 5.30 p.m. some water-carts from the camp met the column with the news that there were only two more miles to go; yet the Regiment stumbled on for another five miles to prove the messengers to be the usual liars. During the whole march the Regiment had been buoyed up by the rumour that its presence was urgently needed to participate in an attack on the 11th, but when it was discovered that the rumour was started to encourage the men to march and that there was not to be an attack the Regiment felt aggrieved that such a primitive method of encouragement should ever have been considered necessary.

Aziziya on the left bank proved to be the usual village of ruined mud huts. Planted on the wind-swept desert it had not a redeeming feature. " The prospect was depressingly featureless and bare, blue sky and brown earth with only the yellow river . . . to vary the monotony; a dust-laden wind seemed to blow almost continuously, until earth and sky and river became a monochrome in khaki."[9]

II.—Political and Military Considerations of an Advance to Baghdad.

As has been seen already, the possibility of an advance to Baghdad had been discussed and received with favour by the General Staff in India and the British and Indian Governments.[10] In August General Nixon had advised the capture of Baghdad in order to counteract the unrest in Persia, but he had emphasized the need for reinforcements, were he to be ordered to advance. In giving its permission to advance to Kut al Amara, however, the Indian Government had, on the 6th September, forbidden General Nixon to advance upstream therefrom without reference to it.[11] A week earlier General Nixon had forwarded a memorandum on an advance to Baghdad. In this he reported that he did not expect enemy reinforcements to arrive within two months, and he considered that there would be a good

---

[8] *Chronicle*, 1915-16, p. 70.   [9] Birch Reynardson, p. 230.
[10] See pp. 72-73.
[11] This instruction was misunderstood by General Nixon, who, as we have seen, ordered General Townshend to advance to Aziziya.

chance of chasing the demoralized and routed enemy into Baghdad after a crushing victory at Es Sinn. If, however, the enemy were allowed time to reorganize and recuperate, any advance from Kut would entail a series of expensive engagements. In conclusion he asked for sufficient troops to allow of the concentration of two divisions in Baghdad.[12]

His immediate pursuit of the enemy turned out to be a failure through no fault of his own. The ships were unable to harass the enemy, who retired in good order. As soon as this was apparent on the 3rd October, General Townshend advised General Nixon to content himself with the occupation of the entire Basra *vilayet* by consolidating his position at Kut; but if Government ordered a further advance, then two divisions with land transport would be needed, as the river was impassable by laden ships.[13] To the best of his ability General Townshend, as a subordinate, tried to dissuade General Nixon from committing himself without the necessary force. In answer to this advice, General Townshend was told to submit a plan for opening the road to Baghdad, as General Nixon had private information that another division was to be sent from France and he considered the enemy to be inferior both in numbers and morale.[14] In answer, General Townshend disagreed with General Nixon's estimate of the enemy's strength,[15] but made no further comment. He had warned the Army Commander and could do no more.

Meanwhile the report of General Nixon's forward move from Kut had galvanized the British Government into considering the situation in Mesopotamia. Though advocating a cautious policy, the British Government emphasized at the same time " the political advantages of a British capture of Baghdad,"[16] and the effect that such capture would have on Persia and German intrigues in the East. Though desiring the capture, yet the British Government would not promise the means of achieving it because of uncertainty in the Dardanelles and Bulgaria's ambiguous attitude at the moment.

On the 5th October the India Office wired that " Kitchener can hold out no hope of reinforcements from Europe or Egypt."[17] On the same day Sir Percy Lake, Chief of the General Staff in India, advocated the possession of Baghdad in an appreciation, in that it would deprive the enemy of a place of concentration and base, cut communication between Germany and Persia, increase our prestige and counterbalance the failure in the Dardanelles.

[12] *Official History*, Vol. II, pp. 4-5.
[13] *Ibid.*, Vol. II, p. 6. *My Campaign in Mesopotamia*, pp. 124-125.
[14] *Official History*, Vol. II, p. 7.
[15] *My Campaign in Mesopotamia*, p. 123.
[16] *Official History*, Vol. II, p. 9.
[17] *My Campaign in Mesopotamia*, p. 124-125.

But he, too, averred that reinforcements could only be sent from France, as India's strength had been reduced to the minimum compatible with security. In conclusion, he advised that General Nixon should be told not to go beyond Kut until another Indian division had been promised from France.[18] As a result of this appreciation General Nixon was warned on the 6th October not to go beyond Kut, until the reinforcements from France had been definitely assured.[19] On the same day Lord Hardinge informed the British Government that " Nixon with forces at his disposal could without much difficulty capture Baghdad," but could not maintain his advantage without the addition of one division. " It would be a grave political error to advance to Baghdad and to retire later under pressure from the Turks," he added. Incidentally, the Turkish strength at this time was estimated at 8,500 rifles, 600 sabres and 28 guns.[20] Finally, he reiterated the political importance of an advance to, and capture of, Baghdad.

In reply to the order to stand fast at Kut, General Nixon pointed out that a withdrawal from Aziziya would be interpreted as a sign of weakness by the Arabs who had come to consider the British irresistible; that the enemy was demoralized and shaken; and that there was nothing to " justify letting slip such an opportunity "; that Baghdad was the focus of Turkish lines of advance and a large supply centre which from a military point of view should be wrested from the enemy.[21]

Not, however, until the 7th October was transport mentioned in these discussions. On that day Sir Beauchamp Duff[22] warned the Viceroy that the adequate supply of any troops in Baghdad would be well-nigh impossible with " our present insufficient number of light-draught steamers," but for some unaccountable reason the Viceroy never mentioned the subject in his telegram to the British Government.[23]

The following day, the 8th October, the Secretary of State wired direct to General Nixon asking what reinforcements he required wherewith to capture and hold Baghdad. His reply was very important: he could capture Baghdad with the 6th Division, but required one additional division and one British cavalry regiment to hold it.[24]

By this time the British Government were definitely interested in the Mesopotamia campaign. Here there appeared to be a chance of a great

---

[18] *Official History*, Vol. II, pp. 9-10.   [19] *Ibid.*, Vol. II, p. 10.
[20] *Ibid.*, Vol. II, p. 11.   [21] *Ibid.*, Vol. II, p. 12.
[22] When on sick leave at Simla in August Lieutenant-Colonel Lethbridge lunched with Sir Beauchamp Duff, who informed him that " no advance beyond Kut al Amara was contemplated, that the line of communication was long enough and that India had no more troops or material with which to reinforce the force in Mesopotamia."
[23] *Official History*, Vol. II, p. 13.   [24] *Ibid.*, Vol. II, p. 15.

success at a critical period when Bulgaria was tending towards hostilities, and when the Austro-German drive against Serbia greatly imperilled the position of the Dardanelles force. Rather than lose this opportunity for a diversion in our favour they were prepared to send even two divisions so as to ensure success.[25] The whole question was thereupon delegated to an Inter-Departmental Committee which reported in favour of the capture of Baghdad provided it could be held. The Committee assumed that General Nixon's river transport was adequate for all exigencies.[26] The Cabinet considered this report on the 14th, together with a memorandum by the General Staff at home, who considered reinforcement by two divisions to be necessary to ensure absolute success. In the meantime General Nixon reported that enemy reinforcements had not reached Baghdad. At the Cabinet meeting it was decided that the whole question should be considered by the Admiralty and War Office Staffs, and a report rendered. In their report the Staffs were of the opinion that General Nixon might be strong enough to hold Baghdad by the addition of two divisions to his command, but they favoured a raid on Baghdad and a withdrawal at will if necessary; that an advance would be definitely advantageous at the moment, but if the power to withdraw were not left in the hands of the military authorities they opposed either raid or occupation; that none but Indian troops should be diverted from the main theatre of war for any purpose in Mesopotamia.[27]

In considering these two reports the War Committee came to the conclusion that the advantages of an advance outweighed the disadvantages of a possible withdrawal at a later date. But before giving the order the British Government asked India again for concurrence in their decision, stressing Persia's tendency to drift into war against us, and the necessity of inducing wavering Arabs to join us.[28] The Viceroy replied that he was "confident that the right policy at the present time is to take the risk and to occupy Baghdad with the least possible delay."[29]

On the 23rd the Cabinet authorized the fateful march on Baghdad and promised two divisions as soon as possible.[29] Against this force of a possible three divisions the General Staff at home had calculated that the Turks might concentrate 60,000 men by the end of January 1916.[30] The die was cast, and thereafter the Secretary of State authorized that "no expense should be spared in ensuring that everything necessary and possible should be done to make the medical arrangements adequate and complete in Mesopotamia."[31]

[25] *Ibid*, Vol. II, p. 15.
[26] For questions and answers, see *ibid*., Vol. II, pp. 16-18.
[27] *Ibid*., Vol. II, p. 26.
[28] *Ibid*., Vol. II, p. 27.   [29] *Ibid*., Vol. II, p. 28.
[30] *Ibid*., Vol. II, p. 25.   [31] *Ibid*., Vol. II, p. 32.

III.—At Aziziya: Advance Authorized.

Meanwhile at Aziziya the 43rd had been told by General Townshend that no forward movement was contemplated without reinforcements, and that he wanted the Regiment to make itself comfortable and get up tents and heavy kits. A rest was badly needed by now, as the climate was telling on the health of the Regiment. Beri-beri, which broke out in the 43rd on the march up from Kut, spread with alarming speed among the British regiments and gunners, causing a number of deaths. The weather, too, had changed and nights were now cold, with the result that the incidence of malaria increased considerably.[32]

On the 18th the 43rd moved to a less dusty camp near the 120th, but farther away from water, and here settled down to the routine of digging redoubts for the defence of the permanent camp. Lieutenant-Colonel Lethbridge returned on the 23rd from sick leave in India and assumed command of the Regiment.[33] He found the Regiment in a sick state, the epidemic of beri-beri causing the doctors much anxiety. " The fact was that the troops had outstripped supplies and had to exist on what rations they could get. Foljambe had acted with great energy in this matter. He had found a man who had contracted to bring up in a *mahaila* a quantity of coffee shop stores." Colonel Lethbridge obtained permission for this *mahaila* to be sent up in the first convoy. The fresh food proved a godsend to the men and reduced the incidence of sickness.[34]

On the 27th the 43rd, as part of the 17th Brigade, paraded at midnight to take part in a night march against Kutuniya which had been occupied by a small observing force of the enemy, consisting of 1,500 cavalry and 2,000 infantry. For this attack General Townshend employed the same tactics as had been so successful at Es Sinn. The Turks were completely surprised, but were just able to fly before the turning movement cut off their line of retreat to Zor.[35] By this time it was known in the Regiment that the standfast had been altered to advance. The glamour of the name Baghdad fascinated all ranks. At last the 43rd was going to the capture of a place which folks at home had heard about, after fighting their way across nameless deserts to places not marked on maps. Hitherto the Turks had not proved themselves in any way capable of withstanding a British attack, and perhaps the outstanding success of the British campaign had caused all, the British and Indian Governments, the higher command and the soldiers themselves, to under-estimate the enemy's powers of resistance. The 6th Division with

---

[32] Birch Reynardson, p. 232.
[33] War Diary.
[34] Colonel Lethbridge's Memoirs.
[35] *My Campaign in Mesopotamia*, p. 147, by Major-General Sir Charles Townshend, and *Official History*, Vol. II, p. 49.

first and second-line transport, and the 30th Brigade without transport, were to capture Baghdad.[36]

Though official sanction for the advance had been given on the 23rd October, three weeks elapsed before a forward movement could be made. During this time twenty-one days' supplies were brought up to Aziziya, and two months' supplies collected at Kut.[37] For these river transport was entirely inadequate, only eight steamers being able to work above Kut with any certainty.[38]

The difficulty of supply, so seldom mentioned by the Governments in their discussions, was also greatly increased by the hostility of the Arabs, who continually sniped at the convoys from coigns of vantage at sharp bends in the river. And though every day of delay meant that the Turks would be more strongly entrenched at Ctesiphon and the rainy season more imminent, yet the preparations could not be accelerated. Bullocks for the heavy guns, transport animals and reinforcements to supplement wastage in the 6th Division had to be catered for as well by the overworked steamers over a prodigious length of communications. It seems surprising that so great a concentration of supplies of all sorts was actually completed in three weeks.

Moreover, other difficulties than those of supply were encountered at this time. Certain Musalmans objected strongly to advancing on Ctesiphon, where a devoted servant of the Prophet lay buried. These had to be sent down to Basra and replaced by another regiment. Also the brigadiers of the three brigades had reported earlier that their men were not really fit and required a long rest before being capable of prolonged exertions. But in spite of weakness and staleness, the morale of the troops was good.

On the 30th General Townshend estimated that the enemy had a maximum strength of 12,300 with 30 guns, but reports of the arrival of reinforcements came in in the first week of November. From the Caucasus, Egypt and his own agents General Nixon received news. On the 4th an agent reported the arrival at Baghdad, towards the end of October, of 8,000 Turks with 12 guns. On the 15th the Caucasus reported the departure of 15,000 Turks from Mosul for Baghdad. But the " Intelligence Staff came to the conclusion that the reinforcements indicated had not yet reached Baghdad."[39] On the eve of the advance General Townshend's force amounted to

[36] *My Campaign in Mesopotamia*, p. 152.
[37] *Official History*, Vol. II, p. 35.
[38] Birch Reynardson, p. 232. *Official History*, Vol. II, pp. 41-44. Grave misunderstanding had arisen between General Nixon's Staff and the Indian authorities on the subject of river transport. On the 24th of October General Nixon wired asking for any craft that was available. Previously India had been unable to supply craft to his specifications.
[39] *Official History*, Vol. II, p. 52.

17,000 (with 35 guns and five aeroplanes), of whom about 14,000 were combatants; of these only 8,500 were infantry.[40]

IV.—THE ADVANCE TO CTESIPHON.[41]

On the 11th November the advance guard, consisting of the 18th Brigade, Cavalry Brigade and 63rd Field Battery, left Aziziya to capture Kutuniya, and reconnoitre Baghdadiya and Zor. By the 13th the concentration of the rest of the force was completed, together with a naval flotilla consisting of H.M. Ships *Firefly, Comet, Shaitan* and *Sumana,* and four barges armed with 4.7 naval guns and towed by the *Shushan* and *Mahsoudi.* There were also five river steamers, three tugs and seven supply barges. Two of these steamers, the *Blosse Lynch* and *Mosul,* were to be prepared as hospital ships capable of accommodating 800 and 700 cases respectively.[42]

The land transport consisted of numerous mules, camels and donkeys; and 666 carts to carry water, supplies and ammunition and thereafter to evacuate the wounded. Four heavy guns, however, were left behind, as there were only sufficient bullocks to draw two. In like manner the force was short of pontoons.[43] On the 13th General Townshend issued a special order, thanking the troops for their past efforts and calling on them again for further exertions on the march to Baghdad.[44]

On the 15th final preparations were made in a tearing gale and sandstorm, but, owing to the delay caused by the head-wind which forced the supply barges ashore downstream, it was not till 1 p.m. on the 17th that the 43rd marched out of Aziziya *en route* for Kutuniya, which had already been occupied by the 18th Brigade. The following day the 43rd crossed the river, as the 17th Brigade (less the 119th Infantry) was to be employed in an attack on Jumaisa fort and village on the 19th. But in the evening the aeroplanes reported that the Turkish reinforcements were moving down both banks of the river.[45] The 17th Brigade was therefore ordered to entrench opposite Kutuniya to cover the shipping. Two regiments were sent forward immediately, " while the 43rd formed up in reserve on the river bank. The men were allowed to lie down, and, later, to remove their equipment."[46] All night the Regiment waited, but nothing untoward occurred. At 5 a.m. the 43rd was sent forward about two miles to the neck of the loop in the river and there ordered to dig trenches against the threatened enemy attack. While the three regiments of the 17th Brigade were digging like badgers, the rest of the 6th Division continued its march along the left bank to attack Zor

---

[40] *My Campaign in Mesopotamia,* p. 153.
[41] Appendix III, Composition of Force. See Map No. 7, p. 130.
[42] *Official History,* Vol. II, p. 54.   [43] *Ibid.,* Vol. II, p. 54.
[44] *Chronicle,* 1915-16, pp. 73-74.   [45] *Official History,* Vol. II, p. 55.
[46] *Chronicle,* 1915-16, p. 75.

and so cut in behind the enemy on the right bank. By 2.30 p.m. the Regiment had dug a good system of trenches, and had stopped work for dinners and a rest when the brigade major galloped up with orders to fall in and march immediately. Though the 43rd had had nothing to eat hitherto, dinners had to be abandoned. After a sleepless night and a meatless day of hard labour the 43rd " plugged along the river bank with scarcely a halt,"[47] until sunset, as it was necessary to catch up the rest of the division which had occupied Zor with very little opposition. At sunset the 43rd halted in mass, and it was hoped that the brigade would bivouac for the night; but half an hour later the Regiment was ordered to continue in column of route. The weary Regiment stumbled through the pitch-dark night, unaware of what was happening or where it was going; losing its way and fouling high liquorice bushes. Now and then the moonlight glittered on the river and rockets soared into the sky far away to the north. On and on the 43rd trudged, utterly worn out, through the silent night, not a man having the energy left to talk. After what seemed to be an interminable age the Regiment reached the river bank and descended to the shore, along which it trudged through soft sand, about a foot deep, towards the twinkling lights of the camp at Zor, which was eventually reached at about midnight.[48]

General Townshend had decided to concentrate the whole of his force and employ it against the Turkish left; and so on the following day, after a deep sleep, the 43rd crossed the pontoon bridge to the left bank. Thereupon transport carts were redistributed; each camel carried forty blankets in two rolls; donkeys and cows were loaded with tools, reserve ammunition was piled into carts; and rations and coats were stacked in the second-line carts.[49] Meanwhile the *Blosse Lynch* and *Mosul* were hastily converted into hospital ships, that is to say " canvas windscreens were rigged along the sides and medical equipment put aboard."[50] At 12.30 p.m. the 43rd marched to Lajj, eight miles upstream, without interference from the enemy.

At Lajj General Townshend made his final preparations for the attack. Here it was that he received apparently trustworthy information that large Turkish reinforcements had already reached Baghdad or south of it.[51] He immediately sent this news to General Nixon, who, however, scouted it and still reckoned the enemy strength at about 13,000 with 38 guns.[52] In all his

---

[47] Birch Reynardson, pp. 249-250; *Chronicle*, 1915-16, p. 75.
[48] *Chronicle*, 1915-16, p. 76.
[49] *Ibid.*, 1915-16, p. 76.
[50] Birch Reynardson, p. 250.
[51] It was one of Captain Morland's Arab agents who first reported the arrival of two divisions at Baghdad.
[52] *Official History*, Vol. II, p. 58. Reports of the arrival of Turkish reinforcements had been proved incorrect on many occasions since the beginning of the campaign.

reports to India General Nixon had affirmed that he would receive a fortnight's notice of any concentration of the enemy at Baghdad.

On the 21st General Townshend ordered an air reconnaissance of the Ctesiphon position. This reported no change. But a long aerial reconnaissance of the neighbourhood of Baghdad disclosed to Major Reilly of the Royal Flying Corps that the enemy's position consisted of two main lines, one to the south of the Arch of Ctesiphon, and the other to the north on the line of the Diyala river where large reinforcements had arrived. By a stroke of ill-luck his engine was put out of action when he was in the act of examining the northern position, and he, together with his invaluable information, was captured. Had General Townshend received the news of these reinforcements on the eve of the battle, it is extremely doubtful whether he would have launched an attack against an entrenched position held by greatly superior numbers.[53] Actually, the Turkish forces consisted of the 35th, 38th, 45th and 51st Divisions, amounting to 18,000 rifles exclusive of Arabs and irregular cavalry and camelry. Of these infantry divisions the 45th and 51st were immeasurably superior to any that the British had hitherto encountered.[54]

---

[53] *Ibid.*, Vol. II, p. 59.   [54] *Ibid.*, Vol. II, p. 60.

[NOVEMBER

CHAPTER XIV.

I.—THE TURKISH POSITION AT CTESIPHON.[1]

THE PLAN—ORDER OF BATTLE OF THE 43RD—THE APPROACH MARCH—THE BATTLE OF CTESIPHON —ATTACK BY " R " AND " S " COMPANIES UNDER CAPTAIN WYNTER—LIEUTENANT-COLONEL LETHBRIDGE'S EXPERIENCES—THE 43RD'S CASUALTIES—THE AFTERMATH OF THE BATTLE— TURKISH COUNTER-ATTACK—PLIGHT OF THE WOUNDED.

(See Maps facing page 120, and on page 130.)

THE Turkish position, as at Es Sinn, lay astride the Tigris. The course of the river originally described a long, narrow loop between Ctesiphon and Bustan, but in 1912 the Turks changed and shortened the course by cutting through the neck of the peninsula. It was at this point that the main line of defence crossed the Tigris. Behind this line were two others: one north of Ctesiphon, and the other some miles in rear on the line of the Diyala river. On the right bank the front line extended along the western bank of the old course for a distance of about one and a half miles and then turned westward, refusing the right flank; " behind its northern end were emplacements for two field, and one heavy, batteries."[2] In front of this position was an outpost line with two battery emplacements and infantry fire trenches. The line of approach to this flank of the enemy was extremely difficult, the terrain being so intersected by dry water courses and gaping fissures that it was impassable by troops.

On the left bank the front line " extended for over six miles in a northeasterly direction following generally a line of a few low mounds,"[2] fortified with redoubts connected by fire trenches. These redoubts and trenches were so well sited that they were invisible except at very close range. The whole system, moreover, was protected with entanglements except for about a mile at the southern end near the river. The extreme north flank, that is to say the enemy's left flank, lay on low mounds and was protected by two redoubts considered by the Turks to be exceptionally strong. This point came to be known by the British attackers as " V.P.," that is " vital point." This north section commanded an extensive field of fire over the open flat plain on which there was no cover to be found by the attackers except in patches of low scrub. It was also supplied with a complete system of communication trenches leading towards reserve positions in rear, and was

---

[1] See Map No. 5.   [2] *Official History*, Vol. II, p. 63.

covered by six and a half field batteries concealed in emplacements. The whole system was, moreover, well supplied with water from a pump installed near the Ctesiphon Court House.[3]

The second line, north of Ctesiphon and running parallel to the front line, was not extensively fortified; "and the Diyala line was also very incomplete."[4] Behind the second line was a bridge of boats connecting the two wings.

The 35th Turkish Division,[5] with eight field and three heavy guns, occupied the defences on the right bank. The left bank was divided into four sections: the south, south-central, central, and north sections. The first three were held by the 38th Turkish Division (six battalions in the front line and one in divisional reserve at Ctesiphon), and the north section was occupied by the 45th Division with two battalions in front, one in local reserve behind V.P. and six in divisional reserve in front of the left of the second line. The Iraq Cavalry Brigade, reinforced with one camel regiment, guarded the extreme left flank. The general reserve consisted of the 51st Division with seven battalions, a machine-gun company and fourteen field and mountain guns. The third line, on the Diyala, was held by an Arab tribal brigade.[6] The Diyala river, with only two bridges, formed a dangerous obstacle in the Turkish rear in the event of the British attack being successful.

II.—THE PLAN OF ATTACK.[7]

General Townshend organized his command in four columns, consisting of :—

>Column "A," under General Delamain, with the 16th and 30th Brigades and two batteries, the 82nd and 1st/5th Hampshire Howitzer Batteries;
>Column "B," under General Hamilton, with the 18th Brigade and 63rd Battery;
>Column "C," under General Hoghton, with the 17th Brigade and 48th Pioneers, and 76th Field and 86th Heavy Batteries;
>Flying Column, under General Melliss, V.C., with the 6th Cavalry Brigade, Maxim Battery, motor machine-gun section, and 76th Punjabis in transport carts.

Column "C," the 17th Brigade, was to pin the enemy down in their central section and make such a show of force as to induce the enemy to

---
[3] *Ibid.*, Vol. II, p. 64.   [4] *Ibid.*, Vol. II, p. 63.
[5] Seven battalions: three in front line and four in reserve.
[6] *Official History*, Vol. II, p. 68.
[7] *Ibid.*, Vol. II, pp. 67-68, and Appendix IV of this Volume.

reinforce that sector from his reserves. After the 17th Brigade's holding attack had started, Column " B " was to make for the enemy's left and rear, while the Flying Column threatened the enemy's second line and reserves at Qusaiba by enfilade and reverse horse-artillery fire. As soon as the enemy felt the effect of Column " B's " turning attack, Column " A " was to march against the enemy redoubts at V.P.; and this advance was to be the signal for a united attack by all three columns. At this moment every available gun was to switch on to V.P. The holding attack by the 17th Brigade, Column " C," was to begin at dawn at 6.30 a.m., and the turning movement by Column " B " an hour later.[8]

It will be seen from this that General Townshend's plan was very similar to that which had been so successful at Es Sinn, but, reckoning that the Turks would expect him to repeat his tactics, he arranged that the principal mass under General Delamain, and not the turning attack under General Hamilton, should give the *coup de grâce*. By this subtle difference in his tactics he hoped to deceive and confound the enemy.[9]

Though he inspired the troops under his command with great optimism during the preparations for the battle, yet General Townshend was by this time aware of the " extreme gravity of the results of this advance . . . undertaken with insufficient forces."[10]

The order of battle of the 43rd Light Infantry at the Battle of Ctesiphon was as follows:—

Lieutenant-Colonel E. A. E. Lethbridge, D.S.O., commanding.
Major A. C. Hyde, senior major.
Captain Hon. J. C. W. S. Foljambe, adjutant.
Captain F. C. W. Wynter, transport officer.
Lieutenant H. T. Birch Reynardson, machine-gun officer.
Captain T. Ivey, quartermaster.
Captain J. Startin, R.A.M.C., medical officer.
Captain J. H. Courtis, " Q " Company, Maxim Battery.

" P " Company.

Lieutenant S. L. Webber, attached from 46th Light Infantry.
Lieutenant A. E. Mason.[11]
Lieutenant D. Murphy.
Lieutenant G. L. Heawood, attached from 4th Wiltshire Regiment.[12]

---

[8] *Ibid.*, Vol. II, pp. 69-70.
[9] *My Campaign in Mesopotamia*, pp. 165-166.
[10] *Ibid.*, p. 161.
[11] Employed with brigade reserve ammunition column.
[12] Employed with the boats at Lajj.

"Q" COMPANY.

Captain F. M. Davenport.
Lieutenant H. B. L. Hind, attached from 3rd Somerset Light Infantry.
Second Lieutenant A. J. Hazell, attached from 76th Regiment.

"R" COMPANY.

Lieutenant J. S. Kearsley.
Lieutenant J. S. P. Mellor, attached from 2nd/5th Somerset Light Infantry.

"S" COMPANY.

Major C. E. Forrest, D.S.O.
Lieutenant G. Naylor.[13]
Second Lieutenant F. Brown.[13*]
Second Lieutenant A. P. Wilson, attached from 4th Border Regiment.

THE APPROACH MARCH.

On the 21st November the 43rd, well rested and cheerful, paraded at 10.30 a.m. and marched one and a half miles out of Lajj along the Baghdad road, and then halted. From here it was just possible to see the ruin of the palace and arch of Chosroes standing nearly a hundred feet above the plain, a fine example of the ancient Sassanid civilization. Once again was this plain to witness battle and sudden death, this plain which had been plundered and conquered by Asshur, Cyrus and Alexander the Great many ages ago. For five hundred years it had been the battlefield of the Middle East. Originally a Parthian suburb of the more ancient Greek settlement of Seleucia across the river, which was destroyed by the Romans in A.D. 164, Ctesiphon became the centre of the Sassanid empire in 226. Thereafter it became the prize for plundering Roman and Persian armies until finally reduced to dust and ashes by Omar and his destroying Arabs.

Starting again at about 2.30 p.m. the 17th Brigade, accompanied by General Townshend and his divisional headquarters and General Nixon and his staff, moved off on a widely extended front towards Bustan. On reaching the river two miles south-east of Bustan, the 43rd halted to water the transport animals. Hitherto there had been no opposition from the enemy, but a British gunboat, mistaking the column for the enemy, fired two shells—

[13] Employed with the brigade salvage section. Of this party, Lieutenant Naylor says in his diary: "After previous battles in Mesopotamia great trouble had been caused immediately after our troops had driven the Turks from the main battlefield by large numbers of Arabs who followed behind, sometimes murdering our wounded, and always looting and getting away with a large number of rifles. I was therefore given a number of carts and ordered to follow just behind my brigade with a small party of men . . . and collect such rifles and equipment as I could, and stack them in a central position where they could be properly looked after."

[13*] Employed as galloper to Brigadier-General Hoghton during the battle.

which luckily did no damage—before realizing its error. At 9 p.m. the march was resumed in a northerly direction towards the appointed rendezvous—about two miles north-east of Bustan—which was reached at about 11.30 p.m. after a rather trying march. At the rendezvous Lieutenant-Colonel Lethbridge received his orders for the attack. Thereupon he explained the plan to the officers and detailed companies to their places. The baggage came up, including mails from England, and the Regiment rested for the remainder of the night.[14]

Meanwhile Columns " A " and " B " were being led to their assembly positions by Captain Morland of the 43rd, who was now on General Townshend's staff, and Lieutenant Matthews, R.E.[15] By 3 a.m. all four columns had reported themselves in position, and the stage was set for the battle.[16]

III.—THE BATTLE OF CTESIPHON.

Though the 43rd had nearly six hours' rest before the battle, the freezing wind made sleep difficult even for tired men. The enemy appeared to be unaware of our approach, but it is now known that news of the advance of the Flying Column was reported to Nur-ud-Din at about 5 a.m. Early in the morning, at about 5 a.m., the 43rd loaded its baggage, fell in at 6 a.m. and moved off at 6.20 a.m. A thick mist which overhung the Tigris and the enemy's position immediately north of the river did not disperse when the sun rose over the battlefield at 6.30 a.m. The 17th Brigade started its advance cautiously towards the Ctesiphon Arch on a front of 1,500 yards. The 43rd was on the right on a frontage of 400 yards with " P " and " Q " Companies in the front line, in that order from the left, under Major Hyde; and " S " and " R " Companies in support, in that order from the left, 400 yards in rear. On the left were the 119th Infantry, and in rear of the advanced line were the 22nd Punjabis and 48th Pioneers in support.[17] Farther in rear came the 76th Battery, R.F.A., and farther back still near General Townshend's headquarters were the two 5-inch guns of the 86th Battery.

At 7 a.m. the battle began with a bombardment of the south central section of the enemy's position by the naval flotilla which was seriously handicapped by the high banks of the river and could only fire indirectly. But no reply came from the enemy in front. At 7.15 a.m. the 76th Battery opened fire, and the advance continued through the mist without opposition. At 8 a.m., however, the mist lifted, disclosing the immense Arch which

---

[14] *Chronicle*, 1915-16, p. 76, and Colonel Lethbridge's Memoirs.
[15] *My Campaign in Mesopotamia*, p. 171.
[16] *Official History*, Vol. II, p. 72.
[17] *Ibid.*, Vol. II, p. 74 : Colonel Lethbridge's Memoirs have the order of battle as follows: 43rd on the right, 48th Pioneers on the left, 22nd Punjabis and 119th Infantry in brigade reserve. I have accepted the *Official History* dispositions.—J. N.

reared its huge bulk above the desert and showed its façade and recesses clearly against the blue sky. By this time the 43rd had closed to within 2,000 yards of the enemy and there were still no signs of him. In fact Captain Foljambe turned to Lieutenant-Colonel Lethbridge and said that he thought the Turks had evacuated their position, for a line of barbed-wire entanglements alone indicated where their trenches lay. Hitherto the advance had not succeeded in drawing the enemy's fire, but at about 8.30 a.m. Major Hyde went forward with two or three men to reconnoitre. Immediately in front was a belt of broken ground where the scrub had been burnt by the Turks to give a field of fire. No sooner had Major Hyde crossed into the open than the enemy's guns and machine guns opened fire from the left, and he was killed instantaneously.

As the 17th Brigade was not to make a frontal attack until General Delamain's Column advanced, General Hoghton issued orders to the front line to dig in. At 8.30 a.m. the 43rd halted in a nullah, and the range-takers of the machine-gun section reported the distance to the Arch to be 2,500 yards.

Meanwhile General Townshend had determined to delay the turning attack no longer, and at 7.45 a.m. had permitted Column "B" and the Flying Column to advance.[18] General Hamilton's advance began at 8.30 a.m., and soon a roar of musketry proclaimed that the turning attack on the Turkish rear was hotly engaged. So successful did this attack appear to Generals Delamain and Townshend from the numbers of Turks seen flying from the front to the second line that General Townshend ordered General Delamain to deliver his decisive attack on V.P. at 9 a.m.[19] and at the same time ordered General Hoghton to push home the frontal attack.[20]

At about 9 a.m. the Colonel received the message " The Turks are leaving their trenches. Pursue," and accordingly the 43rd advanced from the nullah in two lines of half-companies in fours with " P " and " Q " Companies in the first, and " S " and " R " in the second, line at 100 yards' interval and 450 yards' distance.[21] The machine-gun section followed in rear of Major Forrest's " S " Company.

For about a thousand yards the Regiment continued over ground intersected by small nullahs, two to three feet deep. Then suddenly it met with heavy and accurate gun, machine-gun and rifle fire. It was at about this time that Captain F. M. Davenport, commanding "Q" Company, was mortally wounded. Deploying immediately, the Regiment occupied mounds and ditches running parallel to the enemy's trenches. These gave excellent cover from fire and view, but the transport animals in rear were palpably conspicuous and were heavily shelled. By 10.30 a.m. the Regiment had managed to

[18] *Official History*, Vol. II, p. 75.
[19] *Ibid.*, Vol. II, p. 76.
[20] *Ibid.*, Vol. II, p. 77.
[21] *Chronicle*, 1915-16, p. 76.

get to within seven hundred yards of the enemy trenches, but the guns had to cease fire at this point, as the gunners could not see owing to the mirage. Here the Regiment remained for about half an hour replying to the enemy's fire and awaiting the moment to assault in conjunction with Column " A." In spite of heavy and accurate shrapnel fire the 43rd suffered few casualties at this time.[22]

Meanwhile the turning attack had been launched on the left of the enemy second-line position, and the troops had managed to fight their way forward until held up by strong opposition at 10 a.m. At about the same time, the Flying Column, which had found the enemy's left, was held up and forced to dig in.[23]

In the meantime General Delamain had advanced at 9 a.m. against V.P. over completely open and flat country under cover of the artillery and brigaded machine guns, posted wide on the right flank. So rapid was this advance over a distance of 5,000 yards that the enemy's wire, forty yards in front of the trenches, was soon reached and the Indian infantry proceeded to force its way through, not without casualties. At 10 a.m. the vital point was captured, and the Turks, who had suffered severely, fled in disorder towards their second line.[24]

By this time the whole of the British force was engaged and General Townshend had no reserve. As against this, Nur-ud-Din had two battalions on the left bank and three on the right, which were on their way to reinforce his left.[25]

As soon as V.P. had been captured General Townshend moved his headquarters thereto; and realizing that " the battle was by no means finished " and that the order to pursue was premature, he ordered General Hoghton to concentrate at V.P.[26]

" The order meant moving to a flank in front of an entrenched enemy "[27] at a distance of not more than a thousand yards. By the time Lieutenant-Colonel Lethbridge received the order to advance with left shoulders up, the 119th Infantry had passed to the right between the front and second lines of the Regiment. The Colonel sent off Captain Foljambe and R.S.M. Love to the companies with orders to push on as quickly as possible in the direction of Water Redoubt, on their right front. While carrying this order Captain Foljambe was wounded and the Colonel was consequently left without an adjutant. A few detachments and machine-gun

[22] Birch Reynardson, p. 257. *Chronicle*, 1915-16, pp. 76-77.
[23] *Official History*, Vol. II, pp. 77-78.
[24] *Ibid.*, Vol. II, pp. 78-79. The trenches were so piled with Turkish dead that it was impossible to avoid treading on them.
[25] *Ibid.*, Vol. II, p. 81.
[26] *My Campaign in Mesopotamia*, p. 174.
[27] *Official History*, Vol. II, p. 82.

sections were left behind to keep up covering fire while the 17th Brigade moved off across the open plain. The Turks were not slow to seize their opportunity; every form of fire swept the ground as the troops side-slipped across the enemy's front. Luckily the ground became less exposed as the Regiment advanced, patches of scrub from four to five feet high providing a certain amount of cover. The steadiness of the Regiment was wonderful despite intense and accurate bursts of shrapnel, rifle and machine-gun fire. With an exposed flank the 43rd advanced for all the world as if nothing was happening. It was not as if it had been called upon to charge a strongly held position: that was to come later. Now it was to accomplish a manœuvre both difficult and dangerous. However, it was executed with comparatively small losses by the 43rd. When opposite Water Redoubt the 22nd Punjabis were sent up to prolong the right of the Regiment and then, turning to the left, the whole line advanced towards the redoubt. Expecting the redoubt to be either unoccupied or only lightly held, the 43rd advanced quickly towards its objective over ground as flat as a billiard table, but was met with a hail of bullets which inflicted very severe casualties. The Regiment pressed on until the front line reached a small water cut running parallel to the enemy's wire and not more than one hundred and fifty yards from the redoubt. Here Lieutenant-Colonel Lethbridge found Major Forrest with his company, and told him to wait until the attack on the right was launched, the fire from the redoubt being at this time extremely intense. While discussing the situation with the Colonel Major Forrest and another man were both shot through the head.[28]

By this time the second-line companies, " S " and " R " had closed up on the front-line companies in the water ditch. Lieutenant Mellor, attached from the 2nd/5th Somerset Light Infantry, worked his way down the ditch which was only sufficiently deep when in a stooping position to provide cover from the bullets cracking like stock-whips overhead. On his way he found Lieutenant Kearsley mortally wounded in the neck, and he therefore assumed command of " R " Company. Still without orders he continued towards the left. On the way he met Lieutenant Hind, commanding " Q " Company, who was peering over the top of the ditch now and again to see what was happening. But any advance at this time would have been sheer madness, so hot and accurate was the fire; yet Lieutenant Hind heeded not Lieutenant Mellor's advice to take cover, and a second later a bullet went through his head. Crawling back to his company area, Lieutenant Mellor waited for the order to assault.

From V.P. the situation in front of Water Redoubt appeared at this time to Generals Townshend and Delamain to be very serious, for large bodies of the enemy had been seen advancing towards the line south of

[28] Colonel Lethbridge's Memoirs.

V.P. Accordingly General Delamain ordered heavy artillery fire to be directed against the advancing Turkish lines, and sent his last troops, half the 22nd Company, Sappers and Miners, and two companies of the Dorsetshire Regiment to help the 17th Brigade's attack on Water Redoubt.[29]

The advancing Turkish reinforcements were soon stopped by the artillery fire; and after a short bombardment of the redoubt with 5-inch howitzers, which reduced the enemy's rifle fire, the 43rd rose from its shallow ditch and, charging over the last hundred yards, clambered through the wire and captured the position. But at very grievous cost.[30] The important northern section of the enemy's position was now in British hands, and the Turkish 45th Division had been practically destroyed.[31]

Meanwhile General Hamilton's 18th Brigade had managed to clear the advanced positions of the enemy's second line at severe cost; but the Flying Column, still farther out to the right, in trying to get round the enemy's left flank had been heavily counter-attacked and itself outflanked by infantry of the 51st Turkish Division and the Iraq Cavalry Brigade, and had been forced back to its original position of assembly.[32]

But as soon as V.P. was in British hands, Colonel Climo, commanding the 30th Brigade, pushed his troops on towards the Turkish second line[33] under heavy shell fire and captured eight guns and a number of prisoners by 11.30 a.m. The Turks, however, fought so stubbornly that the attack was held up when eight hundred yards from the enemy's second line. Here the troops remained under a gruelling fire until a strong counter-attack at 2 p.m. by enemy reinforcements[34] compelled them to abandon the captured guns and withdraw towards V.P.

Meanwhile the attack by the 17th Brigade on the redoubts south of V.P. had so shaken the Turks of the 38th Division that they had retreated in disorder to Ctesiphon village, leaving behind two field batteries in their flight.[34] By 1.30 p.m. the whole of the Turkish front line had been abandoned, but there were no British troops available to occupy it and to capture the field batteries. Directly after the successful attacks on the redoubts, General Hoghton met Lieutenant-Colonel Lethbridge in Water Redoubt and told him to reorganize preparatory to sweeping down the Turkish front line in a southerly direction in order to mop up any enemy garrisons still holding out.[35] In the redoubt was Captain Wynter—who had succeeded to the command of " S " Company—Lieutenant Mellor and the remnants of

[29] *Official History*, Vol. II, p. 83.
[30] Colonel Lethbridge's Memoirs.
[31] *Official History*, Vol. II, p. 84.
[32] *Ibid.*, Vol. II, p. 84.
[33] *Ibid.*, Vol. II, p. 83.
[34] *Ibid.*, Vol. II, p. 85. Reinforcements consisted of 1st/44th, 3rd/9th and one battalion of the 105th Regiments with two field batteries. Two battalions and a field battery ordered from the right bank did not reach the left bank until the evening.
[35] *Ibid.*, Vol. II, p. 87.

"R" and "S" Companies. Ordering Captain Wynter to remain in the redoubt, the colonel set off to reorganize the 43rd on "S" Company.[36] In the meantime, however, General Townshend ordered General Delamain to collect all available troops and capture the Turkish second line. Having no reserve of his own upon which to call, General Delamain sent a message to General Hoghton asking him to co-operate in the attack. Then General Delamain collected his signallers, orderlies and any parties of troops in the neighbourhood of V.P. and, putting them under the command of his staff officers, launched the attack.

On receipt of the message General Hoghton, who was preparing to attack the redoubts south of Water Redoubt, ordered his nearest troops to concentrate at V.P.; and so it was that Captain Wynter and Lieutenant Mellor, with about forty to fifty men of "R" and "S" Companies, were ordered to V.P.,[37] while the colonel was absent trying to collect the rest of the 43rd. The colonel, returning with about twenty men, found that "R" and "S" Companies had disappeared.

Meanwhile General Delamain's thin line, suffering severe casualties, finally managed to come up on the left of the 7th Rajputs, of Column "B," who gallantly accepted the call to try again. But the enemy's resistance was far too strong to be broken by the attack of so few and weary men; and therefore, when a heavy Turkish counter-attack was seen to be advancing on his left flank towards his guns and V.P., General Delamain ordered the line to withdraw.

It was at this moment that General Hoghton's troops came to the rescue. General Hoghton had managed to collect about two hundred and fifty men from six different regiments.[38] These he ordered to advance on the left of General Delamain's line and so relieve pressure. The attacking line consisted of about fifty men of the 2nd Dorsetshire Regiment on the right, "R" and "S" Companies in the centre, and about as many of the 22nd Punjabis and other Indian regiments on the left.[39] Led by the British this little band advanced across the open expanse of desert with the greatest gallantry towards the enemy ensconced on some sandhills twelve hundred yards from V.P. The advance was unmolested for nearly a thousand yards, but when the troops were within three hundred yards the enemy opened a hot fire. Halting, the line returned the enemy's fire for some time. But there could be no weight in the attack; for General Delamain's party on the right had been definitely checked, and there were no reinforcements of any sort to be had. Heavy casualties also had been incurred and further forward movement was impossible. However, Captain Wynter, regardless of personal safety, rose to his feet and walked across towards the right in order to

[36] Colonel Lethbridge's Memoirs.
[37] Sir John Mellor's Memoirs.
[38] *Official History*, Vol. II, p. 87.
[39] Sir John Mellor's Memoirs.

discuss the situation with the officer commanding the line of the Dorsetshire Regiment. But when about forty yards from Lieutenant Mellor he staggered and fell and never moved again. Lieutenant Mellor, having seen Captain Wynter killed, now assumed command with R.S.M. Love as his second-in-command. By this time the sun was beginning to sink in the sky; no reinforcements arrived to make an assault practicable; and therefore when the troops on the flank began to fall back Lieutenant Mellor got into touch with the officer commanding the Dorsetshire Regiment's line, and later withdrew the remnants of the 43rd, together with about six wounded men, to V.P., leaving Captain Wynter and about three men dead on the battlefield.[40] The casualties in this forlorn hope had been very heavy. General Hoghton lost his brigade major, and two out of the four British officers and about sixty men, mostly from the Regiment and the Dorsetshire Regiment, had been killed or wounded. When the brigade major was killed, Company Serjeant-Major Arlett, of the 43rd, acted as brigade major, " performing excellent work, and also distinguished himself by taking command of a large body of Indian infantry which had lost all its officers and leading them with the greatest courage and dash." He was subsequently awarded the *Distinguished Conduct Medal* for his conspicuous services.

Soon after 5 p.m. General Townshend decided to break off the battle, occupy the ground won, and resume his offensive on the 23rd. Accordingly all troops were warned to concentrate on V.P.

On arrival at V.P. with the remnants of " R " and " S " Companies Lieutenant Mellor met General Hoghton, who ordered him to take up a position in V.P. the defence of which had been allotted to the 17th Brigade. Thereupon he took up a position in the original Turkish support trenches, supported by the machine-gun section and protected by outposts.[41] On the left of the 17th Brigade General Delamain's troops held the line with General Hamilton's still farther south towards the river.

To return to the actions of the rest of the 43rd after the capture of Water Redoubt; "R" and "S" Companies having disappeared, Lieutenant-Colonel Lethbridge joined up with Colonel Harward, commanding the 48th Pioneers, and led his small party of the 43rd in a southerly direction from Water Redoubt. In another redoubt he found Captain Wallace with some of the 22nd Punjabis. Colonel Harward, being the senior officer, thereupon told off the garrison to their places. Soon after, General Delamain arrived alone and told the two colonels the situation as far as he knew it, adding that the redoubt must be held at all costs. Taking command himself, he redistributed the little garrison to its posts. All day this mixed force waited for what appeared to be the inevitable attack from a large body of Turks

---

[40] Sir John Mellor's account, 5/6/34.   [41] R.S.M. Love's account.

clearly visible beyond an abandoned battery of guns which could not be brought into our lines for lack of troops to capture it. At first it seemed probable that the counter-attack would be launched in daylight; but it did not materialize. The early evening and night, therefore, became all the more anxious, as it was obvious to the Colonel that a determined attack would overwhelm the garrison. All night the troops stood to arms expecting the attack which never occurred. This was extremely lucky for the whole of the 6th Division, for the Turks could hardly have failed to interpose themselves between the main body and High Wall whither the rations had been brought. The night, however, was strangely quiet, and when morning came there were neither signs of the battery nor of Turkish troops.[42]

The concentration at V.P. was unmolested by the Turks, whose losses during the day had been twice as heavy as ours; in fact such was the condition of their troops that Turkish headquarters were seriously alarmed, and Nur-ud-Din was only too willing to break off the action and withdraw to the second line. By 11.30 p.m. all the troops of Column " B " and the Flying Column had reached V.P., and then it was that General Townshend was acquainted with the serious casualties incurred, and realized that he was far too weak to resume the attack on the Turkish second line the following day.

The work of reorganization was extremely difficult, for regiments were dispersed over the whole length of the battlefield and casualties in officers had been particularly heavy. Furthermore, the trenches when captured at 10 a.m. had been full of Turkish dead and wounded, to which the British had added their quota during the hard fighting at midday and in the afternoon. These had to be cleared and evacuated before the position could be occupied and organized for the defence by the survivors. The confusion was indescribable. The casualties were over double the number catered for, in all 4,511. The 43rd had only six officers left; seven—Majors Hyde and Forrest, D.S.O., Captains Courtis, Davenport and Wynter, and Lieutenants Kearsley and Hind—had been killed; Captain Foljambe and Lieutenants Birch Reynardson, Murphy, Webber, Hazell and Wilson had been wounded; 72 other ranks had been killed, 190 wounded, and 29 were missing—a total of 304 out of 638 who had gone into action, or 47.6 per cent.[43] Some of the Indian regiments had fared still worse: the 110th had

[42] Colonel Lethbridge's Memoirs.
[43] These are the official casualties taken from the *Official History*, Vol. II, p. 486. The casualties suffered are variously given in *Chronicle*, 1915-16, pp. 9, 81, 84, wherein it is stated that only about 137 to 140 survived the battle out of the whole of the 43rd's strength. Moreover, on the 25th November General Townshend reported to General Nixon that the 43rd had lost 450 killed and wounded and only had 140 fit for duty. All these figures were necessarily inaccurate, being assessed immediately after the battle; and it seems that the parties with the baggage at Lajj and with the brigade ammunition reserve were omitted altogether from the computation. For the names of those killed and died of wounds, see Appendix V.

one British officer and the 104th only two. The 66th, 117th and 2nd/7th each lost all their officers but four. The ambulance transport of riding mules and *dhoolies* soon broke down during the battle. " There was little or no water or food " for the wounded, " and the cold was intense."[44] Many of the Regiment's casualties inevitably occurred when it was ordered to march across the enemy's front. The badly wounded lay out in the open all day, while those who could crawled to the cover of the shallow irrigation ditch from which the Regiment assaulted the Water Redoubt. The Turks immediately began to flood the ditch, and the wounded were faced with the problem of keeping their heads under cover and their mouths above water. Only by the efforts of the less severely wounded were many badly wounded men prevented from drowning; and to show a head spelt certain death for any man who was still capable of using his rifle. The icy water was crimson with blood long before the wounded were rescued some three hours later after the Turkish front line had been cleared. Then, and not till then, first field-dressings were applied to their wounds,[45] and they were laid out on the edge of the ditch, until carried on stretchers to a collecting station a thousand yards south of V.P. Here the short-handed medical personnel, regardless of personal danger, worked like beavers with an inadequate supply of material all through the day and night. Elsewhere on the battlefield the wounded experienced the same conditions as had obtained at Es Sinn. " Walking wounded wandered about looking in vain for collecting stations which could not be found."[46] All night long search parties scoured the battlefield for groups of wounded, and brought them in on springless carts whose jolting caused excruciating agony.

Lieutenant Naylor in his diary describes his experiences with the salvage section : " When the attack commenced I followed close behind my brigade, but the fire was so heavy and my carts such good aiming marks that for a considerable time I could not get on with my work : and plenty of work there was too. The whole area was strewn with dead and wounded, discarded equipment, rifles, and wounded ammunition mules, so that I did not know where to begin first. I detailed half my party to carry on with their own work and collect what material they could in Water Redoubt, while the other half I used to help the wounded who were so numerous that it was quite beyond the power of the ambulance staff to look after them all."

That night he spent in Water Redoubt with his party, fully expecting a counter-attack; but the night fortunately was quiet. The Turks' casualties[47] had been heavier even than the British, and they too spent the hours of darkness collecting their wounded.

[44] *Official History*, Vol. II, p. 90.   [45] *Chronicle*, 1915-16, p. 78.
[46] Birch Reynardson, p. 260.
[47] They had also lost 1,200 men taken prisoners in the battle, in addition to 9,500 casualties.

OFFICERS' MESS, EZRA'S TOMB, 3rd JUNE 1915.
Captain Morland, Lieutenant Mundey, Lieutenant Courtis, Lieutenant Birch Reynardson, Lieutenant Davenport, Major Hyde, Captain Foljambe.

THE GREAT ARCH OF CHOSROES AT CTESIPHON.

IV.—The Aftermath of the Battle.

On the morrow General Townshend was able to appreciate the situation. He realized at once the futility of trying to advance with a force of men and animals utterly exhausted and still disorganized. Also all the carts were required for the evacuation of the wounded.

When, therefore, his air force reported that the Turks had retired to the line of the Diyala, leaving only a rear guard in their second line to collect wounded, he determined to concentrate his troops between Water Redoubt and High Wall, leaving the remnant of the 17th Brigade to garrison V.P. until all the wounded had been evacuated from the vicinity.

At dawn on the morning of the 23rd, all being quiet and no enemy in sight, Lieutenant-Colonel Lethbridge with Captains Ivey and Startin—the medical officer—and about one hundred men of the 43rd whom he had managed to collect, started in search of the rest of the Regiment. On his way to V.P. he passed over the stricken field. In front of Water Redoubt the Regiment's dead lay thick, and just beyond were rows of our wounded who had been left out all night in the bitter cold. At V.P. he learnt of the terrible losses in officers and men, and found Lieutenant Mellor, the sole surviving officer of the battle besides himself, with the remnants of " R " and " S " Companies.

The remaining officers[47*] were called up to command companies: Lieutenant Mason from the brigade reserve ammunition column; and Lieutenant Heawood from the boats at Lajj. The Colonel appointed Lieutenant Mason acting adjutant in place of Captain Foljambe, who had been wounded; Lieutenant Heawood took over " Q " Company and Lieutenant Mellor remained in command of " R " Company. The Regiment, now only about two hundred strong, took up a position on the right face of V.P. looking north and with its back towards the river.

There was still a very large number of wounded at V.P. awaiting evacuation when, for no apparent reason, the 76th Field Battery opened fire on the Turkish position.[48] This produced instant and accurate retaliation on V.P. from the enemy guns, and caused havoc among the unfortunate and helpless wounded. During this bombardment Lieutenant Naylor and his party of the 43rd rendered conspicuous service to the wounded. Regardless of their own personal safety, this party helped to carry many of those who were still lying out exposed in the open to cover within the trench system, and in so doing incurred a number of casualties themselves.[49]

While the reorganization of the defence was taking place, a detachment of the 2nd/7th Gurkhas and 24th Punjabis advanced westward towards the Arch and occupied a mound (subsequently known as " Gurkha Mound ")

[47*] Second Lieutenant Brown on rejoining from the brigade staff was given the command of " P " Company.
[48] R.S.M. Love's account.
[49] Sir John Mellor's account.

a few hundred yards south of the Arch, covered by the Maxim Battery and a section of the 82nd Field Battery. The 16th Brigade now occupied Water Redoubt, and by 2 p.m. the 18th Brigade and 76th Punjabis had marched off for High Wall.[50]

Meanwhile Nur-ud-Din, realizing that the British must have suffered heavy casualties, ordered a counter-attack to be made at 2.30 p.m. to capture his old front line. The 35th and 38th Divisions were to attack the centre while the 45th and 51st enveloped the northern sector. At about 3 p.m. the counter-attack started. As soon as this movement was descried, an order was passed down the British line commanding all those wounded who could walk or ride to make for Lajj, ten miles distant, as best they could. Thereafter a crowd of limping and bandaged figures made its way to the rear, while the seriously wounded were left at the bottom of the deep trenches at V.P.[51]

The Turkish attack on the centre,[52] however, was extremely half-hearted and was checked in front of Gurkha Mound by the fire of " S " Battery, R.H.A., and the two guns of the 82nd Field Battery until 5 p.m. At 4 p.m. the enveloping counter-attack was launched on Water Redoubt and V.P. At V.P. the 43rd was covered by the 76th Field Battery and two guns of the 86th Heavy Battery, and this being also the vital point for the enemy it was subjected to considerable shell fire during the Turkish advance, shell fire which killed many of the grievously wounded men still lying in the trenches. An hour later the 35th and 38th Turkish Divisions were persuaded to advance again on seeing the withdrawal of the guns from Gurkha Mound, but they were successfully repulsed by rifle fire from the Mound.[53] By dusk the 45th Turkish Division had got to within six hundred yards of V.P. on the left of the Regiment's position; but not till 7 p.m. did the attack develop. This was heralded by heavy rifle fire from all along the Turkish line. But the British held their fire until the Turks were within five hundred yards and then let fly, while the guns sprayed them with shrapnel. The attack petered out, to be followed by intermittent and spasmodic attacks all through the night until 2 a.m., when the enemy withdrew in confusion; only a few had managed to advance to within two hundred yards.

In the repulse of these several attacks the Regiment was not seriously involved,[54] though an outstanding example of tenacity and leadership was

[50] *Official History*, Vol. II, pp. 93-94.
[51] By sunset only about half the wounded had been evacuated.
[52] By five battalions of the 35th Division with two batteries and nine battalions of the 38th Division.
[53] Although surrounded during the night the detachment at Gurkha Mound repulsed all attacks.
[54] Accounts of the night 23rd-24th differ considerably. Colonel Lethbridge and Sir John Mellor affirm that the 43rd hardly fired a shot; but R.S.M. Love is emphatic that the Turks were repulsed by the Regiment's fire when within 500 yards of V.P. This may be so, but I have taken the evidence of the majority.

provided by Lance-Corporal Upstone, D.C.M., who assumed command of the machine-gun section after Lieutenant Birch Reynardson was wounded. All through the night, with coolness and courage, he maintained the guns in action and covered the Regiment's left front. This was no mean feat, for ammunition was at one time during the night extremely scarce, as was water also wherewith to keep the barrel casings of the guns filled. But he contrived to maintain the supply of ammunition; and to keep the guns cool he adopted an insanitary but extremely efficacious method. The enemy's failure to assault the 43rd on the night of the 23rd can be attributed in great measure to this gallant lance-corporal's action and initiative; and also to the fact that the Turkish 51st Division, which was to have made a turning attack on V.P., lost its way in the dark, luckily for the 17th Brigade. Had the handful of men been assailed simultaneously from front, flank and rear, it is doubtful whether even their stout hearts could have prevailed against such overwhelming odds.

Meanwhile Lieutenant Naylor, aware of the need of carts for the collection of wounded and the Regiment's shortage of men, handed over his carts to No. 1 Field Ambulance and led his little party to V.P. and rejoined the 43rd at dusk. The colonel was naturally pleased to find another survivor and put him in command of the remnants of his old "S" Company. Without food and with only water polluted by divers animals to drink, he and his party had spent the whole day collecting the human and material litter of the battlefield.

During the first attack the padre, the Rev. H. Spooner, stood on the parapet under heavy fire, giving tidings to the wounded men of the Regiment in the trenches " just as if he were on the stand of a race-meeting, and we down in the crowd below."[55]

At the same time, farther to the southward, six furious attacks were made by the enemy on Water Redoubt. Six times were the assailants repulsed with heavy loss, and driven back in hand-to-hand fighting. By the early hours of the morning the British were running out of ammunition both for guns and rifles, and volunteers took cart-loads of ammunition from High Wall to V.P. and brought back wounded.

By the time these several attacks had ceased the British were almost completely exhausted. But the Turks were exhausted too; their casualties in their massed attacks had been prodigious[56]; and we now know that despondency reigned supreme at Turkish headquarters. Nur-ud-Din had lost another division in trying to break the British defence, but it had been touch and go with the gallant 6th Division.

[55] *Chronicle*, 1915-16, p. 79.
[56] Estimated at 6,188. *Official History*, Vol. II, p. 108.

" When dawn broke on the 24th quiet reigned along the British front." The Cavalry Brigade moved out early to a position north-east of V.P. to cover the flank while the wounded were being evacuated. " Of water there was none," wrote Lieutenant Naylor, " and the condition of the wounded was pitiable. Owing to the Turkish counter-attack the previous evening the ration carts which were on their way had to go back; but at 8 a.m. they came along and we got something to eat, some sixty-three hours after our last settled meal."

The 43rd was detailed to hold the trenches of V.P. which faced north, and to watch the flank. Meanwhile the evacuation of the wounded to Lajj was successfully completed during the afternoon despite some shelling and sniping, as well as a sandstorm.

The discomfort, not to say agony, which these seriously wounded men suffered beggars description. Loaded with three lying and three sitting cases in each, the iron-tyred A.T. carts started on their ten-mile journey to the river " over rough desert, in places sun-baked plough, and everywhere intersected by dry ditches, with here and there deep nullahs."[57] Though the cases were all serious, " fractured limbs, abdominal wounds, head wounds," there were no mattresses available, except as provided by dead bodies. "The carts bumped and clattered over the rough soil "; every few hundred yards a ditch had to be crossed, when the iron bottom of the cart seemed to rise up and hit the wounded a stunning blow on the head; and, in addition, the ponies or mules were nervous and often broke into a bucketing trot.[57] The deep nullahs had to be rushed to get the carts up the other side. Some of the wounded, unable to bear the protracted torture, threw themselves off and had to be collected again. All along the track, too, wounded men who had been missed by the search parties crawled towards the convoy and were added to the congestion. Truly a *via dolorosa*.

At Lajj the ships were waiting. As has been recorded, only two ships had previously been prepared for the accommodation of the wounded, namely, the *Blosse Lynch* and *Mosul*. As these were, of course, hopelessly inadequate for the evacuation of the casualties, " the local medical officers had to crowd . . . the wounded into six other steamers and into barges, which had not been prepared for their reception and which, in some cases, were even hardly fit for ordinary passenger traffic."[58]

Relieved from the excruciating jolting in the springless carts, the wounded were again piled upon the decks. There were some straw mat-

---

[57] Birch Reynardson, p. 264. Methods had not improved since the days of the Peninsular War, in which wounded were similarly treated. *Cf.* George Simmons's experiences after being wounded at Almeida in 1810 (*A British Rifle Man*, pp. 93-94).

[58] *Official History*, Vol. II, p. 109. The barges had been used for stores and the transport of animals.

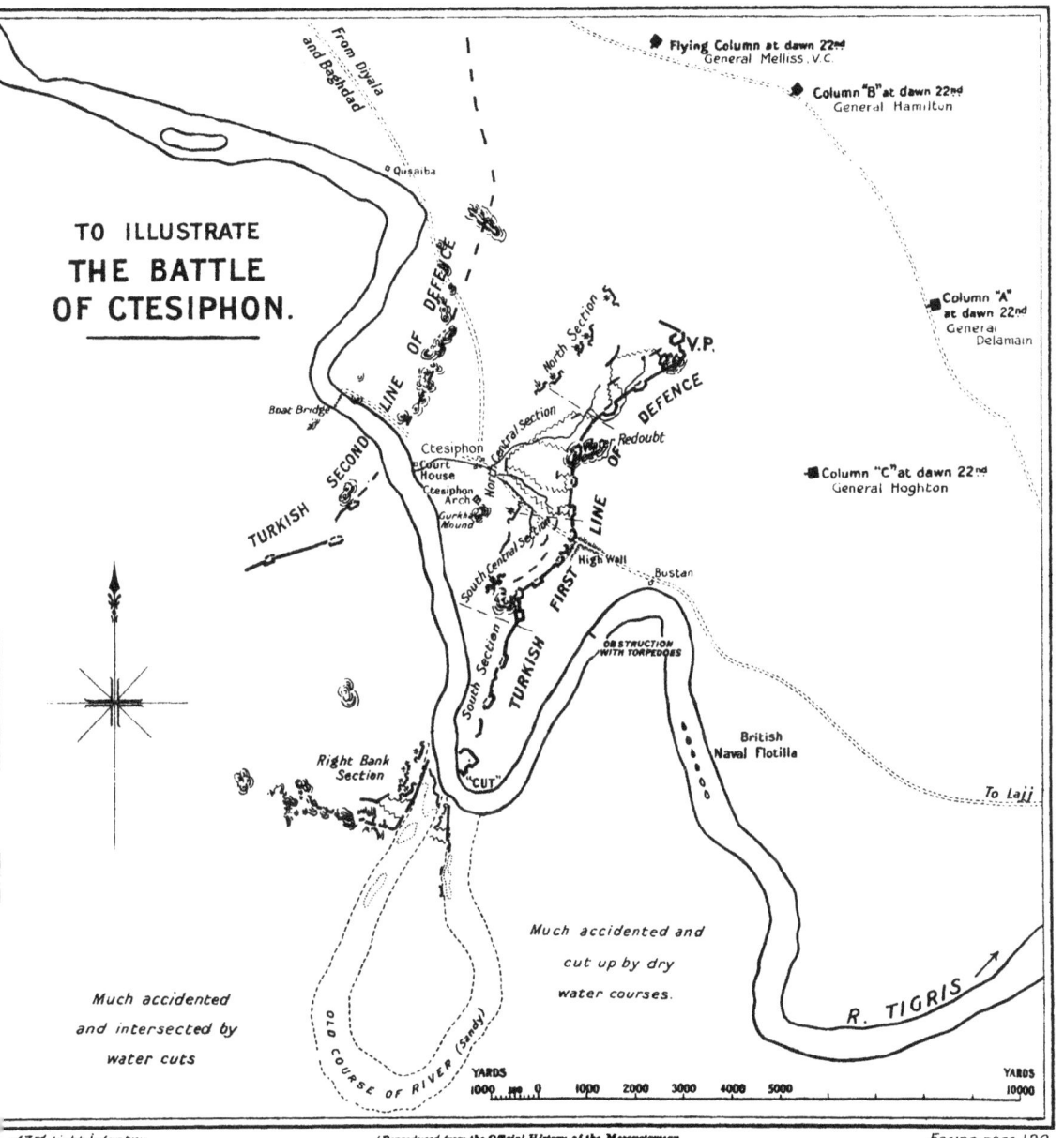

tresses, but not enough to supply all. The medical personnel, short-handed and overworked, were powerless to alleviate suffering owing to shortage of materials. Despite their untiring efforts many men suffered the refinements of torture. As after the Battle of Es Sinn gangrene spread from dirty to clean wounds, and many succumbed who should have lived.

The military situation demanded the evacuation of the wounded without delay so as to leave General Townshend free to manœuvre. In his report to the Mesopotamia Commission General Nixon stated: " The alternative before us . . . was to bring the wounded down . . . at any cost of suffering to them, or of leaving them exposed [to death or mutilation by Arabs] before the regular Turkish troops had the chance to protect them."[59] That the occasion for such a decision should ever have occurred can be attributed in the main to the resolve *to take the risk* of an advance on Baghdad.[60]

Packed like pulled figs, the wounded left Lajj on the morning of the 25th. When the convoy reached Aziziya, the heavens opened and rain poured through the thin awning in an icy stream, drenching the blankets which could neither be replaced nor yet dried. At Kut al Amara all the casualties were transhipped on to the P5 and *Julnar,* in which stretchers were provided for the serious cases. After two false starts[61] the convoy left for Basra on the 2nd December. " There were only two doctors, an assistant surgeon, a British orderly and four native sweepers to deal with all the cases on the ship " and the two barges lashed to her side. The wounds of the worst cases could only be dressed every other day, such was the congestion and shortage of medical stores. Day and night the doctors worked on deck, labouring against almost superhuman difficulties.

The wounded reached Basra on the 7th December, sixteen days after the Battle of Ctesiphon. While the ships were lying in midstream waiting to disembark their mangled freight, a nauseating stench emanated from the iron decks whereon the wretched cankerfret men lay crowded and huddled in indescribable filth. When admitted to the hospital ship *Varela* and the hospital at Basra, several men with slight wounds were found to be dying from huge bed-sores. And yet a report was sent to India: " General condition of wounded very satisfactory. Medical arrangements under circumstances of considerable difficulty worked splendidly."[62] That telegram pronounces its own condemnation.

---

[59] *Ibid.,* Vol. II, p. 109 *note.*
[60] See p. 98 and *Official History,* Vol. II, p. 28: Viceroy of India to the British Government.
[61] *Chronicle,* 1915-16, pp. 81-82. On the 29th November the ships were attacked when aground by Arabs ; one man was killed and five wounded again in the P5.
[62] Birch Reynardson, pp. 270-271.

CHAPTER XV.

I.—The Retreat from Ctesiphon.[1]

Townshend's communiqué—The 43rd reaches Lajj—Advance of enemy forces—Retreat continued—Affair at Umm at Tubul—The 17th Brigade acts as rear guard and 43rd as rear party—Lieutenant Heawood's description—The 43rd reaches Kut.

(*See Maps facing page* 1, *and on pages* 126 *and* 130.)

Now that the battlefield was cleared of its human litter, General Townshend could decide on his future action. About 4 p.m. General Delamain advanced from High Wall with a mixed force to cover the withdrawal of the 17th Brigade from V.P. to High Wall. During the day seven air reconnaissances reported that the Turks were retiring to the Diyala line.[2] The advance of the Cavalry Brigade in the morning and of the covering force in the afternoon so deceived the Turks that Nur-ud-Din, suspecting that the British intended to attack again, ordered a general retirement to the Diyala in the early hours of the 25th. As the result of the air reports General Townshend decided to bring up his ships to Bustan and hold the battlefield. But it so happened that the Turkish cavalry never received Nur-ud-Din's order to retire, and at 5 a.m. on the 25th it sent a message to say that V.P. had been evacuated and that the British showed no signs of advancing. Nur-ud-Din promptly issued orders to his army to turn about and reoccupy the second line without delay. This advance started between 3 and 4 p.m.[3]

In the meantime General Townshend had decided to retire on Lajj, the need for so doing being emphasized by the air reports of the advance of superior enemy forces. In the evening the air force reported that the Turks had reoccupied their second line with an advance guard pushed out towards Ctesiphon.[4] Before ordering the retirement General Townshend issued a *communiqué*[5] to the troops explaining the situation. In it he said, " I cannot express my admiration and gratitude for the heroism displayed by all ranks. To show with what stern valour you fought, you drove four divisions out of a very strong position and forced them to retire beyond the Diyala river. But our numbers were too few to put them to rout; we have had 4,000

---

[1] See Map No. 7, p. 130.
[2] This was incorrect news. The Turks did not retire till early on the 25th.
[3] *Official History*, Vol. II, p. 102.
[4] *Ibid.*, Vol. II, p. 106.   [5] *Ibid.*, Vol. II, p. 105.

killed and wounded, the Turks losing many more than this figure.⁶ You have added a brilliant page to the glorious battle roll of the Army in India and you will be proud to tell them at home that you fought at the Battle of Ctesiphon.

" The troops must know that I have ordered a move back to Lajj for the following reasons :—

"(1) Food and supply question. The ships are exposed to fire on the river at Bustan, and the enemy can with cavalry accompanied by guns stop their progress upriver to opposite their camp.

"(2) At Lajj I can await in security the arrival of reinforcements at Basra from France and Egypt due in a week's time.

" The ships at Lajj are in security. Three more monitors are promised to me in a few days."

The 43rd spent the day digging additional trenches in the neighbourhood of High Wall whence a good view of the country to the north could be obtained. Not till 6 p.m. did the Colonel issue orders for the night march to Lajj. Thereupon carts were redistributed, and everything of military value, such as ammunition, biscuits, bully beef, rum and entrenching tools, which could not be taken away was either buried or destroyed. At about 7 p.m. the 43rd moved off with strict orders to be silent and show no lights. Behind followed the 16th and 18th Brigades as rear guard. Reaching Lajj at 1 a.m. on the 26th the 43rd was told off to its bivouac, where the company cooks, already installed, had hot tea ready for the men and where the blankets were also found. As so often happens in war, a heavy downpour of rain conspired to make the wearisome task of disposing the troops even more difficult, but the blankets luckily were still rolled so that only those on the outside were wetted. The 43rd was detailed to hold the north-east corner of the perimeter, but it was not until well on into the early hours that sentries were posted. For the rest, the hot drink and warm blankets were indeed a luxury.

As General Townshend intended to hold Lajj while the necessary reinforcements for the resumption of the offensive were being concentrated at Aziziya, a scheme of defence was issued and adopted under cover of the Cavalry Brigade which reported no enemy movements, except by Arab horsemen. Late in the afternoon the Regiment took up an outpost position with three piquets, found by " Q " Company. These were relieved in the morning when the cavalry and observation troops watched the front.⁷

Shortly after 9 a.m., however, an air reconnaissance reported the advance of about 12,000 Turkish infantry in two columns and 400 cavalry.

⁶ Turkish accounts estimate them at 9,500.
⁷ *Chronicle*, 1915-16, p. 93.

This confirmed General Townshend's opinion that it would be impossible to stand anywhere north of Kut, as he reckoned that reinforcements could not reach him before late in December.[8] Orders were therefore issued at once to continue the march. For this the 16th and 18th Brigades with the Cavalry Brigade and divisional artillery were to form the rear guard, and the 17th and 30th Brigades the main body in two columns abreast. The advanced parties with the prisoners moved off at about 2 p.m., but it was nearly dusk before the 43rd cleared the camp. The march was particularly dreary, as it was an intensely dark night and no one in the 43rd knew how far the column had to march. The pace was slow with frequent halts. From 2 a.m. till 5 a.m. the column halted, and then, under pleasanter conditions, resumed the march to Aziziya, which was reached at 8 a.m. on the 28th.

The fatiguing march of twenty-five miles was thus accomplished without any interference, except from a few Arab snipers on the flank and rear. The prospect of plunder in the abandoned camp at Lajj had lured the Arab cavalry from its task of pursuit.

General Townshend and his staff stood at the entrance to the camp at Aziziya and watched each regiment march in. By 9 a.m. the 43rd had settled down in its bivouac, and was ready for breakfasts.

At Aziziya were sundry reinforcements consisting of the 14th Hussars and half the 2nd Royal West Kent Regiment, as well as those who had been sick when the 6th Division marched up to Ctesiphon.

Meanwhile the Turks, now consisting of two army corps, moved to Lajj and then continued southward, camping in the neighbourhood of Zor.

At Aziziya all the troops were detailed to evacuate the supplies which had been concentrated there a month previously. But once again, owing to the shortage of suitable craft, much useful material had to be destroyed, those boats which could still ply in the shallow waters being already crammed with wounded.

At midday the 43rd received orders to retreat the following day as part of the main body to Umm at Tubul, about ten miles downstream. The shortness of the march considering that the Turkish advance guard had reached the neighbourhood of Kutuniya was due to a misunderstanding between General Townshend and Captain Nunn, senior naval officer, whose ships had to be protected by the Army. Above all things, General Townshend was afraid of being pinned down and subsequently surrounded by the enemy; and this misunderstanding nearly resulted in the fulfilment of his fear.[9]

The 43rd, however, was quite content to retreat only a short distance after its extremely fatiguing march of twenty-five miles from Lajj on the

[8] *My Campaign in Mesopotamia*, p. 188.
[9] *Official History*, Vol. II, p. 115.

night of the 27th/28th November and two days spent in loading stores, destroying equipment and dismantling the perimeter camp. Starting at 9 a.m. on the 30th the Regiment reached Umm at Tubul without incident at midday and went into bivouac on the river bank. The afternoon and evening were spent in digging trenches round the camp, and within the camp for shelter. The camp[10] was roughly rectangular with its southern face on the river where H.M. Ships *Firefly* and *Comet* were anchored to protect the left rear of the perimeter. The western face was held by the 18th Brigade, the northern by the 16th Brigade and the eastern by the 17th Brigade. The 43rd made itself comfortable with straw and hay found in a deserted Arab village; and as there was plenty of food a welcome rest on full stomachs appeared likely. But this was reckoning without the Turks. At nightfall they were known to be in Aziziya. At sunset Nur-ud-Din ordered an advance on Umm at Tubul.[11]

II.—THE AFFAIR AT UMM AT TUBUL[10]; AND RETREAT TO KUT.[12]

At about 7 p.m. the leading regiments of the 45th and 51st Turkish Divisions bumped into the British outposts, who fired upon them. This was the end of the 43rd's comfortable night, for an order was immediately issued to man the trenches; but, except for spasmodic shelling, the night was quiet. At 9.15 p.m. General Townshend issued orders for the transport and ships to be ready to retire at dawn on the 1st under cover of an attack by the rest of the 6th Division, if the enemy were found to be present in force. At 3 a.m. a party of the 7th Lancers volunteered to take a message to General Melliss ordering him to march back to the rescue with the 30th Brigade,[13] and, by keeping well to the north, to fall upon the left flank of the enemy in an enveloping manœuvre.

In the grey light of early morning the Cavalry Brigade moved out of camp towards the north to envelop the enemy's left, followed by the 17th and 18th Brigades, while the 16th Brigade remained in the camp holding the western face.

The Regiment was barely clear of the camp when bullets began to fall, but it succeeded in occupying a deep, dry water channel on the extreme right of the divisional front without much trouble. Meanwhile the transport was filing out of the perimeter *en route* for Kut. At 6.45 a.m. the sudden daylight disclosed the situation to both sides. Each was ready to advance

---

[10] See Map No. 6, p. 126.
[11] *Official History*, Vol. II, pp. 116-117.
[12] See Map No. 7.
[13] This brigade had been sent on to Kut independently on the 30th November in response to an urgent appeal from General Nixon for troops to open the threatened communications between Kut and Basra.

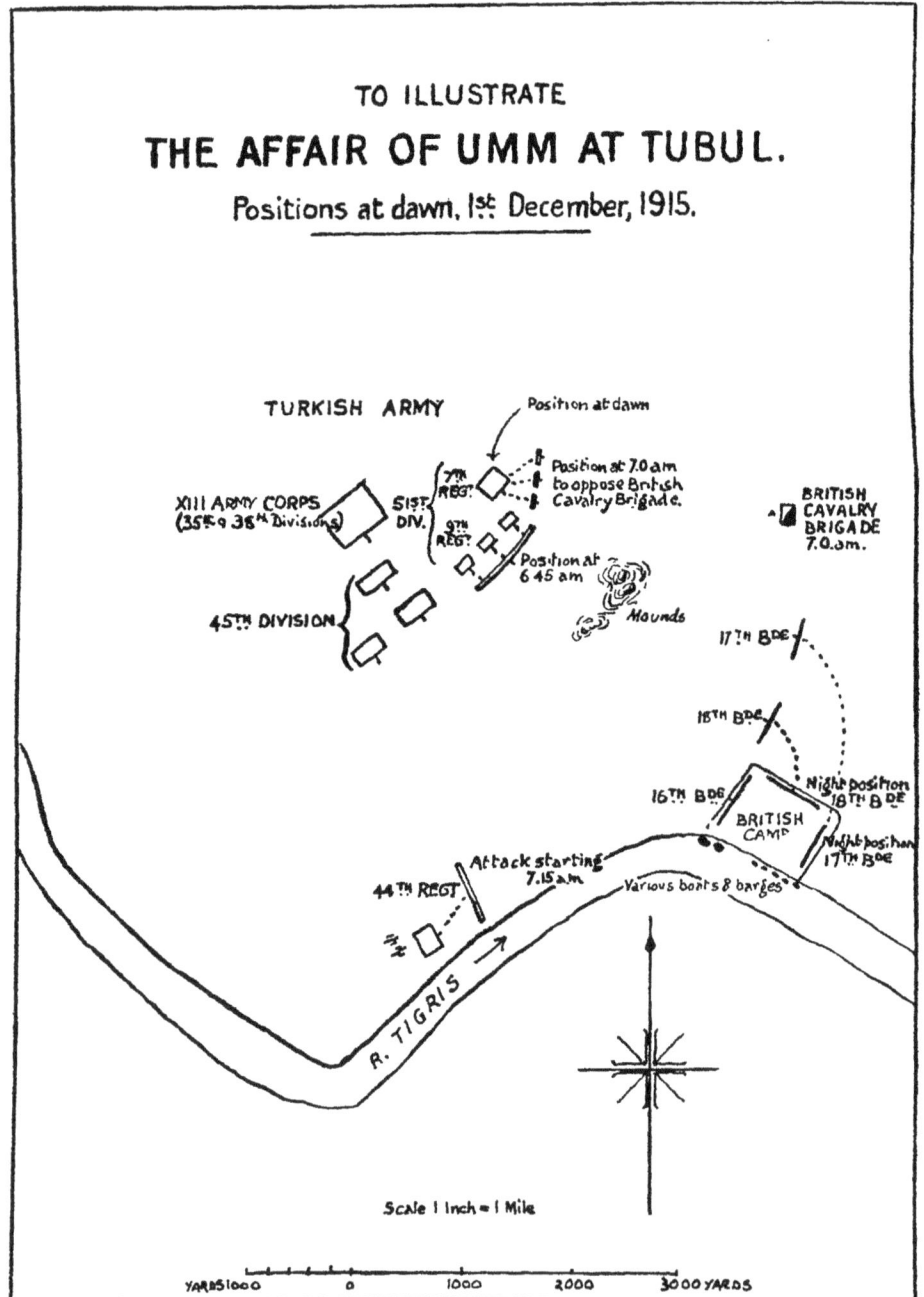

against the other. But when General Townshend noticed that the Turkish XIII Army Corps[14] and transport were massed in rear of their front-line divisions, he ordered rapid fire to be opened at 3,500 yards by every available gun. The field batteries, one in close support of each brigade, opened fire with such great and immediate effect that the Turkish advance was stopped and the whole of the Turkish XIII Army Corps fled panic-stricken. This allowed General Townshend time to break off the engagement and retire in echelons of brigades. The first brigade to move was the 16th at 7.30 a.m., followed by the 18th at 8 a.m.

At this time the 43rd was holding a nullah with " S " and " P " Companies in the front line and " R " and " Q " in support. Just before 8.30 the 22nd Punjabis took up a position about 120 yards behind the nullah to cover the withdrawal of the 43rd. But when the retirement began at about 10 a.m. the 43rd became the rear party to the division, the 103rd Mahrattas alone rendering assistance on occasions. Directly the 43rd moved, presenting " excellent targets for the enemy infantry, the rifle fire greatly increased, and the Turks began to follow . . . up. Their shrapnel was particularly accurate, bursting exactly over the retiring lines, and we suffered a good few casualties," wrote Lieutenant Naylor. " Unfortunately a number of men who had been hit were left behind; but one of my men went back and brought in a wounded comrade who had dropped some two hundred yards behind our last line, and this in the face of advancing Turks and a heavy fire." For a considerable distance across open, flat desert the 43rd covered the withdrawal of the 17th Brigade, the rear guard.

During the whole of the retirement the 17th Brigade acted as rear guard to the division. During each halt to allow the supporting battery time to retreat to another position the Turkish advanced troops pressed more closely, but in spite of the accurate shrapnel fire the casualties in the 43rd were very light; and with great steadiness and precision the distance from the enemy was gradually increased.[15] Meanwhile General Melliss's column, the 30th Brigade, came up and reinforced the rear guard, having moved well inland. By 11 a.m. the Turks had ceased to press the pursuit closely, and it was now possible for the 43rd to march in artillery formation. The 6th Division had thus extricated itself from a perilous position. Not so the naval flotilla; two gunboats and two barges[16] ran aground and had to be abandoned. On one of the barges were all the Regimental orderly room papers and documents, as well as all the company pay sheets and nominal rolls. This loss entailed endless work when the Regiment reached Kut. Among the crews of the two gunboats, *Firefly* and *Comet,* who were rescued

[14] The 35th and 38th Divisions.
[15] *Official History*, Vol. II, p. 122.
[16] One contained the stores of the Royal Flying Corps detachment.

by the *Sumana* under point-blank rifle and artillery fire was Colour-Serjeant H. Gibbs, of the 43rd, who had been lent to the Navy as machine-gun serjeant of H.M.S. *Firefly*.

It must have been nearly midday when the Regiment halted for half an hour on the river bank where the wounded were put on board a boat and sent off downstream.

General Townshend had decided to shake off the enemy completely by marching to Qala Shadi, twenty-six miles distant. This meant a real test of endurance for the regiments of the 17th Brigade which had already fought a rear-guard action for nearly five hours. The 17th Brigade still marched in rear, " though now more or less closed up, as our cavalry were protecting our flanks and rear," wrote Lieutenant Heawood.[17] " The track now lay inland across the desert, which, except for scattered low scrub bushes, was bare and dry. All the regimental horses (even the Colonel's) had been sent on with the transport, so everyone had to foot it. Occasionally, a transport cart or one of the three motor cars which were in the country, turned back to pick up stragglers; for, as the day advanced, it became more and more difficult to keep the men going, in spite of their knowledge that if they dropped out they would have a short shrift from the merciless Arabs.

" Later we were encouraged by the announcement that, after seven more miles, we should halt on the river bank, get water, and rest for three hours. Our spirits revived, and, after a rather weary drag, we found ourselves close in to the river again, near a clump of trees. Mules were off-loaded, water drawers detailed, and equipment loosened. But fate was against us once more. Before the water parties had reached the stream, there was a rattle of musketry, and, though the offenders were only Arabs, our machine guns were unable to suppress the firing. Our prospect of water and a rest had vanished, and within half an hour we were off again on another slow night march.

" The night was black, and it was impossible to see men at any distance in front . . . ; consequently the pace averaged barely two miles an hour. Obstacles, such as dry nullahs or clumps of low scrub, constantly caused checks to the column, and it was no easy matter to keep the company closed up, especially as the men were . . . only half awake. In this way we plodded slowly on until, at about 2 a.m., we saw bivouac fires ahead, and were told that we might lie down, as we were, in column of route. Food was not forthcoming, as the transport was a long way ahead; water, we were promised we should get soon after we started again. It was a bitter night with a strong north wind, and our cotton uniform did not help us to keep out the cold. Three of us tried to make a fire, but it would not burn, so we

---

[17] *Chronicle*, 1915-16, pp. 96-97.

gave up the idea, and sat round and dozed—but not for long, for soon the order came to be ready to move in five minutes' time. The mules were loaded up, and we were off again."[18]

The division had marched twenty-six miles, and there were still more than twenty between it and Kut. General Townshend, for safety's sake, determined to cover this distance in one forced march. The 17th Brigade again found the rear guard. The 43rd " moved across the desert," wrote Lieutenant Heawood, " in parallel columns of companies, with the cavalry covering our left flank. For breakfast the men were allowed to eat their emergency rations, but the promise of water remained only a promise. It grew harder and harder to keep the men going, as they were quite ready to fall out, and prepared to risk everything for a rest and a drink of water; but the non-commissioned officers were magnificent, and it was due to them that we managed to get along. Twice we approached the river and had to go on,"[19] as General Townshend was afraid the men " would lie by the water, drink and fall asleep like logs."[20] Of this Serjeant A. C. Munn, of the 43rd, wrote that it was the most cruel instance " in the whole of the cruel march. . . . I believe if we had turned and fought the Turk then we'd have torn him to bits."[21]

Towards midday many of the exhausted troops began to fall out, but transport carts had been provided for this contingency, and no man was left behind the rear guard. Eventually the 43rd halted at a watering-place, and water parties were detailed to go down to the river bank. At this moment Arabs began to snipe from the right bank, but they were quickly dispersed by machine-gun and artillery fire; and the exhausted troops were allowed a rest of nearly three hours, spent in drumming-up cocoa in mess-tins. There were still nine miles to go before reaching the outskirts of Kut. The head of the division halted at Shumran towards dusk after a march of about eighteen miles,[22] but the 17th Brigade did not arrive till much later.

At dusk the 43rd was still marching, finding rear parties and flank guards, for the cavalry were withdrawn as soon as night came on. Just short of Shumran more carts met the column to pick up the most footsore of the tired and famished troops—they had had no food since the early morning of the 1st—and the stragglers from other brigades. Major Henley brought out food from Kut for the Regiment.

Early the next morning the 43rd covered the last two miles to Kut and, marching straight to the camping-ground,[23] had a good hot breakfast; then the weary men rolled themselves up in their blankets and slept soundly until midday.

---

[18] *Ibid.*, 1915-16, p. 97.
[19] Lieutenant Heawood's account.
[20] *My Campaign in Mesopotamia*, p. 196.
[21] *Chronicle*, 1915-16, p. 127.
[22] *Official History*, Vol. II, p. 124.
[23] On the river bank south of the Fort.

MAP No. 7

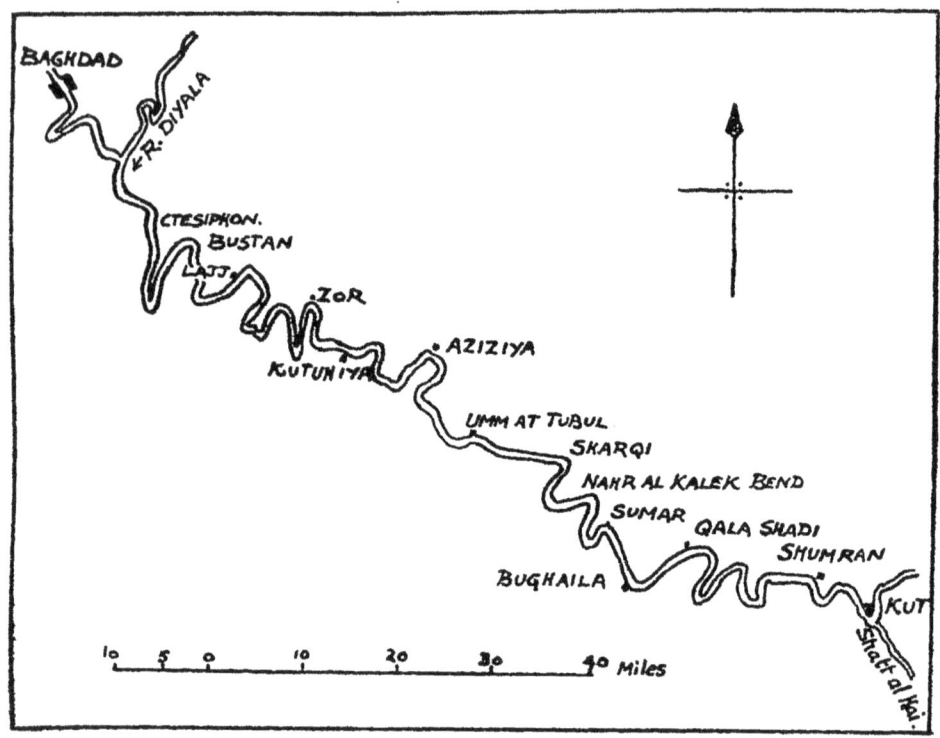

THE TIGRIS FROM KUT TO BAGHDAD.

The 43rd now consisted of Lieutenant-Colonel Lethbridge, D.S.O., Major Henley,[24] Captain Ivey (quartermaster), Lieutenants Mason (acting adjutant), Naylor ("S" Company), Mellor ("R" Company), Heawood ("Q" Company), Second Lieutenant Brown ("P" Company), Captain Startin (R.A.M.C.), and 332 rank and file. Major Henley became second-in-command.

So ended a memorable retreat under conditions as arduous as any in the 43rd's long war history. For twelve consecutive days the Regiment had fought, marched and worked under extremes of heat and cold with insufficient food and water. The stale and war-worn troops had been called upon to execute one of the most difficult manœuvres in war when, at Umm at Tubul, they were ordered to withdraw in echelons of brigades in the face of the enemy. Of this movement General Townshend said : " I have never

[24] Rejoined at Kut from wounds and sick leave.

seen, even in peace manœuvres, a retirement carried out better, both as regards steadiness and suppleness in manœuvre, than was executed by the Sixth Division at this critical moment. The sight of the brigades falling back steadily in echelon, with the precision of clockwork, and the gradual development into one steady flow of retreat in perfect order—guns, everything, in their proper places—filled me with pride."[25]

None of the wounded in this action was left behind, nor did any but a few Indian followers fall into the hands of the treacherous Arabs to have their throats cut and be otherwise mutilated according to Musalman customs. The forty-four-mile retreat under continual pressure from a merciless enemy was accomplished in thirty-six hours, which not only was a severe test of discipline, but also of the traditional marching powers of the 43rd. The 43rd, as usual, marched magnificently; and the pluck, endurance and fortitude of all ranks cannot but be admired by those who come after. Retreats are always a sterner test of discipline and endurance than victorious advances; "courage and firmness in adversity is more honourable than enthusiasm in success," and with courage and firmness the gallant remnants of that gallant 43rd upheld the traditions that are inseparable from its name.

There are no records of the number of men of the 43rd who were wounded in the retreat and at Umm at Tubul.[26]

---

[25] *My Campaign in Mesopotamia*, p. 194.
[26] *Official History*, Vol. II, p. 125. The casualties in the division on the retreat were 37 killed, 281 wounded and 281 missing; of the missing 81 were followers and many others were on the abandoned barges. See Appendix V.

CHAPTER XVI.

I.—POLITICAL AND MILITARY ASPECTS: DECEMBER 1915.

TOWNSHEND'S REASONS FOR STANDING AT KUT—THE TURKS INVEST KUT—TURKISH ATTACK ON THE 10TH—THE 43RD IN THE FORT—THE TURKS ATTACK THE FORT—THE 43RD'S DEFENCE—CASUALTIES—RELIEF PREPARATIONS—NIXON'S PROBLEMS—TRANSPORT DIFFICULTIES—AYLMER COMMANDS RELIEF EXPEDITION—DETAILS OF THE 43RD OUTSIDE KUT—DRAFT FROM ENGLAND.

(*See Maps facing pages 1 and 216, and on page 218.*)

MEANWHILE General Nixon had returned to Basra to expedite the dispatch of reinforcements, having established an advanced post with some cavalry, infantry and guns at Ali Gharbi. Wires buzzed between Basra, India and London, but little or no concern for the safety of the 6th Division in Kut seems to have been entertained as yet. The advanced troops of the 3rd (Lahore) and 7th (Meerut) Divisions were expected by the 15th December; and at long last the Viceroy had, on the 30th November, wired that the " ruling factor in rapidity of our concentration is the supply of additional river transport."[1] At the same time the Viceroy again urged the need of capturing Baghdad as being the only means whereby to keep Persia, Afghanistan and India quiet. As an immediate reinforcement the 1st Home Counties Field Artillery Brigade (T.F.), the 13th Company, Sappers and Miners, and the 34th and 35th Infantry Brigades were ordered to embark.

For many reasons General Townshend had determined to stand at Kut which was the key to the interior lines of Lower Mesopotamia. There were many senior officers who considered that the strategical importance of Kut was greatly exaggerated and that the occupation of Kut, surrounded on three sides by the river, was a tactical mistake denying power of manœuvre except on the north side, which was quickly closed by the enemy. In their view the force should have taken up a position on the right bank, with the river between it and the enemy, and a clear line of retreat downstream. The factors militating against such a plan were undoubtedly the lack of time to prepare and dig such a position; the exhaustion of the troops, especially the Indians; the large stores of food and ammunition concentrated in Kut, which could not be evacuated in time; and the optimistic opinion of the Staff that relief would be brought within six weeks.

[1] *Official History*, Vol. II, p. 131.

General Townshend considered that the state of extreme exhaustion of the men demanded instant rest,[2] and as he had " one month's full rations for British troops and two months' for Indian, as well as ample ammunition " he wired his intention to General Nixon. When, however, General Nixon replied on the same day that relief might be expected within two months, General Townshend began to waver in his decision, and proposed retiring on Ali Gharbi after destroying heavy guns and small arms ammunition.[3] Moreover, river transport was available and the details for the complete evacuation of the force had been worked out by Major Julius and Lieutenant Parsley of the staff of the Inspector-General of Communications. These plans entailed the destruction of the bridge of boats and a march down the right bank to Amara. But the proposal did not meet with the approval of General Nixon, who warned General Townshend that by holding Kut he would be fulfilling the duties of a detachment by containing superior numbers.

On the same day the Viceroy wired to the British Government asking for the dispatch of yet another division—making five in all—and the all-important river transport on which the relief of Kut so much depended. Though the danger of General Townshend's position was now causing grave anxiety in London, it must be remembered that there were many calls upon the man-power and resources of the Empire at this time. The tide of war was flowing against the Allies in the Balkans; Egypt required reinforcements; the British force at Salonika was in a precarious position; and the British regiments already in Mesopotamia, which had been sadly neglected, also required reinforcements. The 43rd had only received one draft of any size during a year's campaigning.

So it was that another division could not be found immediately; and when it was too late the War Committee in London advised the retirement of the 6th Division from Kut to a position downstream whence it could cover the concentration of reinforcements for another march on Baghdad. When, on the 14th, General Nixon reported the probable concentration of eight Turkish divisions on the Baghdad front owing to the release of troops from the Dardanelles, which the British were about to evacuate, the British Government was not a little concerned, but was fain to refuse his request for two more divisions, making seven in all. Instead the British Government guaranteed to send twelve garrison battalions to India to allow of the retention of the 34th and 35th Brigades in Mesopotamia and the dispatch of the 36th Brigade, thus creating the fifth division.

By the end of the month the War Committee had come to the conclusion that, after relieving General Townshend, General Nixon should act on the defensive; and that defensive positions should be forthwith prepared on

[2] *Ibid.*, Vol. II, p. 134. [3] *Ibid.*, Vol. II, pp. 136-137.

the line Qurna—Shaiba and possibly the Karun valley so as to protect effectively the oilfields and pipe-line, in case a withdrawal from Kut should be necessary.

II.—IN KUT, DECEMBER 1915.[4]

In Kut the situation was very difficult for General Townshend to compete with. The town lay on the left bank of the peninsula of land formed by the river which here describes a bend like the letter U. He found no defences prepared, except a mud-walled fort at the northern end of the peninsula connected by a barbed wire fence with four blockhouses built to accommodate ten to twelve men each. Such was the exhaustion of the troops that only the British regiments were fit to do any digging on the 4th December while most of the Indian troops could not move at all.[5] This complete immobility paralysed General Townshend, who was consequently compelled to abandon all hope of conducting an active defence by throwing a bridge across the river, and of breaking out to co-operate with the relief force. He was fain, in fact, to adopt a passive defence. The position was ideal as a base and easily defensible against Arabs without artillery, but it was another matter to organize it against the Turkish main army. The existing blockhouse barrier was too far forward, and needlessly lengthened the divisional front, but it could not be abandoned because the Fort at the northern end contained large quantities of supplies and stores. Men could not be spared from the vital task of entrenching in order to move these elsewhere. Another disadvantage was a line of low sandhills which, though too distant to be occupied by our troops, would offer cover to the enemy and limit the power of the garrison to sally out by the only land exit on the left bank.[6]

On the right bank above the Shatt al Hai lay the village of Yakasub, commonly known as Woolpress village. This General Townshend decided to hold and to connect with a bridge of boats. The left bank was to be further fortified by a Middle and Second Line behind the existing barrier.

For this purpose the whole area was divided up into three sectors[7]:—

(a) *The North-East Sector.* This included the river line from the Fort to the Second Line, and from the Fort inclusive to Redoubt " B " exclusive. This was held by the 17th Brigade throughout the siege.

(b) *The North-West Sector.* The rest of the first line and the western river front, held by the 16th Brigade.

(c) *The Southern Sector.* The Second Line and Woolpress village,[8] held by the 18th Brigade.

[4] Order of battle of the 6th Division. See Appendix VI. See Map No. 13, facing p. 216.
[5] *My Campaign in Mesopotamia*, p. 212.
[6] *Official History*, Vol II, p. 161.   [7] See Map No. 13.
[8] Woolpress village was held throughout the siege by the 110th and 120th, who were supplied by night by the *Sumana*. It is sometimes called Liquorice Factory on maps.

The general reserve consisting of the 30th Brigade was posted by night at the north end of Kut and in the town itself by day, and the artillery occupied some brick kilns to the north-east of the town.[9]

The town of Kut lies in the south-west corner of the U peninsula. At each end of the town there are palm groves, fruit orchards and vegetable gardens. The best houses, built of mud bricks, lay on the river frontage, but there were other respectable buildings including a bazaar, caravanserai, the shaikh's house, two mosques and a few wool presses. Most of the inhabitants, however, lived in small mud huts.

There was absolutely no sanitary system in the town; the whole place was indescribably filthy with heaps of refuse and garbage in the roads and on the river banks. It was, in fact, the vilest place that British troops had yet occupied.

The town and suburbs contained just under 7,000 inhabitants when the 6th Division arrived. Of these, only the genuine householders and their families were allowed to remain, with the result that about seven hundred strangers were expelled after a survey of the food resources had been made. From this survey, it was reckoned that " there were two months' full rations for the whole force, excepting firewood, medical comforts "[10] and vegetables; and in view of the prospect of relief within two months, General Townshend decided to maintain the full ration so as to preserve the vitality of his command."[11] There were also about 800 rounds per rifle, and about 600 per gun.

On the 4th all the sick and wounded and the flotilla of ships, except the *Sumana* and twelve other craft, were sent downstream to Amara, and the Cavalry Brigade was ordered to be prepared to retire to Ali Gharbi on the 6th. On the 4th General Townshend issued a special order, as follows:—
" I intend to defend Kut al Amara, and not to retire any further; reinforcements are beginning to be sent up from Basra to relieve us. The honour of our Mother Country and the Empire demands that we all work heart and soul in the defence of this place. We must dig in deep, and dig in quickly, and then the enemy's shells will do little damage. We have ample food and ammunition, but Commanding Officers must husband the ammunition, and not throw it away uselessly.

" The way you have managed to retire some eighty or ninety miles under the very noses of the Turks is nothing short of splendid, and speaks eloquently for the courage and discipline of this force."[12]

[9] *Official History*, Vol. II, p. 162.   [10] *Ibid.*, Vol. II, p. 163.
[11] At this period the British troops received: 1 lb. meat; 1 lb. bread; 3 oz. bacon; butter or cheese; 6 oz. potatoes; 4 oz. onions; 2¼ oz. sugar; 3 oz. jam; 1 oz. tea; ½ oz. salt.
[12] *Chronicle*, 1915-16, p. 100.

On that afternoon the Regiment dug trenches for four hours along the river bank between the Fort and the brick kilns, thus encircling the bivouac ground. The Turkish main force was reported to be fifteen miles upstream, with an advanced force some five miles from Kut.

On the 5th the 43rd improved its position and completed its trenches, but was relieved in the evening and ordered back to the Second Line where it occupied two dry water channels facing north. This line, on the right, joined the southern end of the Regiment's previous line, and on the left was in touch with the 63rd Field Battery in the neighbourhood of the brick kilns. These two nullahs were occupied by three companies: " P " on the right, " Q " in the centre and " R " on the left, with " S "[13] in support behind " P " and " Q." This position became the 43rd's headquarters throughout the siege, and the rest position after spells of digging and holding the front-line trenches. " The trenches were eventually roofed over, as were also the various dug-outs between the two lines, such as the mess, dressing station, orderly room, quartermaster's stores, officers' quarters, etc."[14]

Meanwhile other regiments were entrenching the existing barrier and constructing redoubts in place of the blockhouses which were not proof against artillery fire.

On the 5th a bridge was thrown across the river opposite the Fort, and on this day the Turks shelled the cavalry outposts and the infantry working parties in the First Line. In fact, the enemy was so close that the Cavalry Brigade only just got away in time on the 6th.

From the 5th onwards the whole force worked like beavers, for time for work above ground was becoming limited. From the Second Line the Regiment started digging a communication trench to the Fort, and henceforth life for the 43rd became one of digging. Under the glare of the sun the Regiment dug; it dug in the bitterly cold nights of darkness, and under the pale light of the moon it was still digging.

On the 6th more shells landed in Kut from the north and north-east, and General Townshend therefore ordered the bridge to be dismantled and re-erected in a less exposed position upstream. This was done on the night of the 6th/7th; and, to cover the work in the new position, Major Henley with " R " Company was ferried across by the *Sumana* on the 7th to hold the right bank. This company was withdrawn at nightfall, having seen no signs of the enemy on that bank.[15]

[13] Lieutenant Naylor records that "S" Company was 82 strong. His order of battle was as follows: Serjeant (acting C.S.M.) Adby; C.Q.M.S. Voller; No. 13 Platoon, Serjeant Barfoot; No. 14 Platoon, Serjeant Woollard, a reservist; No. 15 Platoon, Serjeant Ballard; No. 16 Platoon, Serjeant Dawson, a reservist.
[14] *Chronicle*, 1915-16, p. 100.
[15] *Official History*, Vol. II, p. 166.

On the left bank, however, it was not safe to move about above ground even at the double. Trenches, three feet deep, were scratched in the ground by night and improved by day. From the very outset of the siege, the Turks paid particular attention to the Fort which required much improvement and hard work, as it lay in an exposed position, liable to be cut off. On the other hand, its position was valuable in that it commanded two long reaches of the river and enfiladed the sandhills in front of the First Line. The garrison formed a separate command under Lieutenant-Colonel Brown, 103rd Mahrattas, and consisted of two 15-pounder guns of the Volunteer Artillery Battery, the Maxim Battery, fifty bombers of the 43rd, the Sirmur Sappers and Miners, 103rd Mahrattas and 119th Infantry. The trenches and Redoubt "A" on the left of the Fort were occupied by the 43rd in conjunction with the 22nd Punjabis in spells of forty-eight hours on duty and forty-eight hours in brigade reserve. By this time the First Line redoubts had been constructed but had not been connected by trenches nor had support and reserve trenches been started.[16] Many casualties were incurred from machine-gun fire which swept the flat ground before the system was perfected.[17]

Meanwhile, the Turks were digging themselves in and sapping forward to closer quarters on the left bank; and at the same time a force, estimated at a division, crossed the Shatt al Hai and approached the eastern flank, threatening the bridge of boats and cutting off the line of retreat to Ali Gharbi. However, they showed no inclination to come to closer quarters as yet.

On the evening of the 8th the boat bridge was finished, and a detachment of two hundred rifles from the 67th Punjabis was sent across to establish a bridge-head and hold a line of sandhills beyond.

It had been General Townshend's intention to construct three redoubts at the bridge-head, but neither the troops nor the time were available owing to the amount of work urgently required on the left bank.[18] Early on the morning of the 9th the Turks advanced against the 67th who had only had the night in which to entrench themselves. As soon as General Townshend saw the lines of Turks advancing, he ordered the 67th to withdraw, and at the same time the 43rd from the general reserve of the 17th Brigade was warned to line the river bank and prevent the Turks from effecting a lodgment on the bridge-head.[19] "S" Company (Lieutenant Naylor) was detailed for this task. Moving out from the bivouac under cover of some mud walls, the company extended along the bank of the river under a heavy fire. "Then ensued an interesting sniping duel, my best shots availing themselves of every case of careless exposure by the Turks on the other bank, while the remainder of my men dug themselves in as they were, lying flat on their

[16] *Ibid.*, Vol. II, p. 167.
[18] *My Campaign in Mesopotamia*, pp. 214, 220.
[17] *Chronicle*, 1915-16, p. 101.
[19] *Chronicle*, 1915-16, p. 140.

stomachs. . . . It was very unpleasant while it lasted " wrote Lieutenant Naylor. Eventually the 67th regained the left bank, having suffered severe casualties, including the company commander and two other officers killed. That night the bridge was successfully destroyed by a party of volunteers, and the investment of Kut was complete.

During the whole of the 9th the position, especially the Fort, was subjected to heavy shell fire from all directions. At 3 p.m. the Turks attacked the north-west sector in extended lines, but were quickly repulsed by rifle fire. During the night they entrenched themselves about six hundred yards from the First Line. In the evening headquarters and " P," " Q " and " S " Companies took over Redoubt " A " and the flank trench on the left of it until the 12th. Soon after dawn on the 10th the whole of the front was subjected to heavy shell fire under cover of which long lines of the enemy, widely extended, advanced towards the British trenches. It was, however, soon realized that the enemy was not attempting a determined attack but was merely bent on investing the position more closely. The men of the 43rd took full advantage of the opportunity; " the least movement by one of the enemy was answered by a hail of bullets, our men thoroughly enjoying themselves in this glorious chance to pay back the Turk in his own coin. . . . The Turks by persevering eventually established . . . a thin line of skirmishers within an average distance of 300 yards from our barbed wire."[20] In front of Redoubt " A," however, the Turks approached nearer, for at this point the redoubt formed a slight salient. The apex of the triangular redoubt being on high ground provided an excellent observation post; and here it was that Lieutenant Naylor and Second Lieutenant Brown were spotting for their snipers through field glasses. While so doing a bullet penetrated Second Lieutenant Brown's cap. This, however, did not deter him, and half an hour later when looking over the parapet again he was shot through the head by a sniper who had managed to crawl up to within 150 yards. And so died a gallant officer. " He was all that a good officer should be, was liked and trusted by his men, and was a sad loss to our already badly depleted ranks."[20] The same day Major Henley and Q.M.S. Burbidge were wounded in the bivouac line.[21] These bombardments caused 199 casualties in the force on the 9th, and 331 on the 10th and 11th; while the expenditure of rifle ammunition on the 10th alone amounted to 61,000 rounds. On the evening of the 12th and morning of the 13th the Turks made yet other attempts to storm the First Line of the north-west sector, but were again repulsed by steady rifle fire.

The next days were unusually quiet, and the troops were able to obtain the rest so sorely needed. On the 16th Lieutenant Mellor with " R " Com-

---

[20] Lieutenant Naylor's diary.   [21] *Chronicle*, 1915-16, pp. 102, 140.

pany reinforced the Fort.[22] By this time the necessary trenches and communication trenches had been dug, and work was concentrated on the completion of the Second and Middle Lines.

In the north-east sector the Fort[23] gave cause for anxiety. As early as the 7th the Turks had occupied a position four hundred yards from the wire. Within ten days they had sapped forward so close that a raid was made by some 43rd and Indian soldiers with great success at dawn on the 18th. The raiders reached the Turkish trench a hundred yards away before being discovered by the sentries, and thereupon set to work with bombs. Having cleared the trench and inflicted several casualties on the enemy, they returned with their prisoners at the expense of only one man hurt. But this did not deter the Turks, for they soon started to cut our wire with bombs, thus presaging an attack. As the walls of the Fort would not stand heavy shelling, " trenches and low-level loopholes had been constructed along the walls and inside the fort, and a stockade with head cover of bales of forage had been built across the gorge of the north-east bastion."[24] Saps had also been dug under the walls across the ditch towards the wire and opposite the enemy's saps. This entailed hard work for the garrison who by night had to repair the damage done by the daily shell fire as well as construct new defences. The enemy's snipers and machine guns, which swept our trenches with the greatest accuracy, also contributed to the difficulties of making the Fort really strong.

On the 22nd the Turks began a heavy artillery bombardment on the Fort and First Line trenches, as a result of which the 43rd lost two men killed and wounded in Redoubt " A." On the following day the 43rd was relieved by the 22nd Punjabis and went into brigade reserve. The heavy shelling continued and predicted an attack in the near future. On Christmas eve, before it was light, a heavy artillery bombardment was opened on the town, the First Line and Fort. This bombardment disabled the two 15-pounders in the Fort very early and cut telephonic communication with the rest of the artillery and brigade headquarters. By 11 a.m. the mud walls of the Fort had been completely destroyed and the north-east bastion was evacuated, and its garrison withdrawn to the trenches on either side of the stockade. " This bastion and the northern wall were held by the 103rd Mahrattas, and the north-eastern wall was held by the 119th Infantry, whose Rajput company held the trenches outside the eastern corner of the fort."[25] The stockade was held by thirty men of the 43rd.

Between 11 a.m. and 12 noon the bombardment ceased, and the Turks immediately launched a heavy attack on the north-east bastion and wall. There was furious hand-to-hand fighting at the bastion. The advancing

[22] *Ibid.*, 1915-16, pp. 102, 140.
[24] *Official History*, Vol. II, p. 175.
[23] See Map No. 14, p. 218.
[25] *Ibid.*, Vol. II, p. 177.

Turks were met by a hail of bullets and improvised bombs. At the stockade the party of the 43rd, seizing its opportunity, poured " mad minutes "[26] of rapid fire into the compact masses of the enemy, while the bombers of the 43rd, 103rd and volunteer gunners hurled bomb after bomb where none could fail to find a billet. Four machine guns on the flanks ploughed through the enemy ranks while all the available guns plastered the Turkish trenches. But despite this withering rain of fire, some brave Turks managed to reach the bastion and north-east wall; while wave after wave of reinforcements surged forward in support. For half an hour this deadly combat continued until the Turks, no longer supported, began to waver, and finally ran back.

Meanwhile a dangerous situation on the right along the north-east wall had been restored by the gallantry of Major Anderson, of the Volunteer Artillery Battery, and the Rajput company of the 119th. " At 1 p.m. the 43rd moved out of bivouac, and was stationed at the junction of the main communication trench and Gurkha communication trench, in order to be handy for reinforcing the Fort if need be."[27] Shortly afterwards the 43rd was sent forward. On arrival it was detailed to hold from the north-east bastion to the eastern corner in relief of the 119th, who had suffered heavily. The whole Regiment filed into the front line, and by 4 p.m. the relief was completed with companies in the following order from the right: " P," under Captain Gilchrist, 52nd Sikhs, lent by divisional headquarters; " Q," under Lieutenant Heawood; " S " under Lieutenant Naylor; and " R " under Lieutenant Mellor, whose company, reinforced by ten men of " P " Company, held the stockade in the north-east bastion. The afternoon was spent in collecting the wounded and in repairing the defences against another attack which was obviously intended. Lieutenant-Colonel Lethbridge was now in command of the north-east corner of the Fort. In front of the stockade was a party of the 103rd holding the battered walls of the bastion. In case of an attack the Colonel arranged that the 103rd " should retire right and left to the side galleries thus uncovering the stockade and allowing of a cross fire from three directions to bear on the assailants."[28]

Meanwhile the enemy shelled intermittently during the afternoon, and Lieutenant Naylor was wounded in the face by shrapnel. At about 8 p.m., just as the moon was rising, the second enemy attack was launched, led by bombers who advanced on the bastion. As arranged, the 103rd withdrew to the flanks of the stockade. Here the fight raged for the greater part of the night. The 103rd in the side galleries were practically wiped out, and for some time it seemed doubtful whether the handful of " R " Company and volunteer gunners would be able to hold the stockade when it was out-

---

[26] The " mad minute " before the war was 15 rounds per minute.
[27] *Chronicle*, 1915-16, p. 141.   [28] *Official History*, Vol. II, p. 179.

flanked. But a barricade of bales, tins, and flour bags was hastily erected, and the unconquerable troops held on.

For an hour the gallant defenders held their ground amid the infernal din of gun, machine gun, bomb and rifle fire. Then the machine gun in the centre of the stockade was disabled, and the enemy rushed forward to within more effective bombing range. One of their bombs fell in the middle of the defenders and " killed or wounded most of those on the right half of the stockade, including Major Anderson and Lieutenant Mellor,"[29] commanding " R " Company. Still the 43rd held on although reduced by over half, and with steady rifle fire kept the Turks at bay. At the critical moment the 48th Pioneers arrived to reinforce the stockade, and were immediately involved in heavy fighting as the result of which the first thirty of them were either killed or wounded. But others took their places, and still the stockade was unconquered. At about midnight the Turks[30] withdrew, only to resume their attacks at 2.30 a.m.; but the line held.

The Turkish attack on the north-eastern wall, delivered in driblets at different times, was never dangerous, thanks to the disposition of the men of " P," " Q " and " S " Companies who were able to sweep all the exits from the Turkish trenches with machine-gun and rifle fire. At 3 a.m. a company of the Norfolk Regiment took over the stockade, and the remainder of the night was quiet.

The casualties in the Regiment in this defence amounted to about thirty men. Of these most belonged to " R " Company which lost twenty-three killed or wounded from the gallant party of thirty who had defended the stockade with invincible tenacity. That fine fighting regiment, the 103rd Mahratta Light Infantry, suffered even more severely, ninety-three casualties being reported. The total loss in the garrison amounted to 315, including seventeen British officers.

This magnificent defence of the 43rd was eulogized throughout the garrison. " The repulse of the Turkish assault proved afresh the valour of the troops composing the Sixth Division, and especially did the men of the Oxford Light Infantry add more glory to the history of that famous regiment, so renowned in the Peninsular War," wrote General Townshend.[31] The official history states bluntly : " the Oxfords maintained fully their reputation as one of the old Light Brigade; as an officer of another corps who had been alongside them since their landing in Mesopotamia describes their conduct, ' They need no mention—they were the Oxfords.' "[32]

[29] *Ibid.*, Vol. II, p. 130. Lieutenant Mellor was wounded in the wrist.
[30] One, at least, of the Turkish attacks on the night of the 24th-25th December was launched by the Turkish 43rd Regiment of the 52nd Division. The Turkish casualties were 907 all ranks. *La Campagne de l'Irak*, p. 137, by Commandant M. Moukbil Bey.
[31] *My Campaign in Mesopotamia*, p. 233.
[32] *Official History*, Vol. II, p. 181.

When dawn broke on Christmas Day the Turkish dead and wounded lay thick in front of the Regiment's trenches. Attempts were made to bring them in, but the Regiment's chivalry was rewarded with a hail of bullets. However, more humane than their countrymen, who omitted to help even those wounded who could crawl back to the parapet of their line, the men of the Regiment managed to pass water and food to the Turks hanging on our wire.

The afternoon was uncannily quiet; silence to the mind inured to the din of continual battle can be ominous and even oppressive, presaging something worse than previous experiences; but by evening the familiar rattle started again with rifle and machine-gun fire, and artillery bombardments at regular intervals.[33] The artillery employed by the Turks at the outset of the siege consisted for the most part of 40-pounder and 18-pounder Krupp guns, neither of which fired high-explosive shells. The 40-pounder shells, filled with black powder, burst on percussion with a terrific explosion, but had a moral rather than a material effect. The 18-pounders fired mostly shrapnel of fair quality and percussion shells. Later the Turks employed some howitzers and more modern field guns of high velocity, firing high-explosive shells of small calibre. They also used some trench mortars as well as a large bronze mortar which threw a round shell of large diameter but did little damage.[34]

After dark further efforts to bring in the wretched Turkish wounded were more successful. All those who could be moved without a stretcher were brought in, but the seriously wounded perforce had to be left to a lingering death and exposure to the extremes of heat and cold.

The rest of the night was spent by the 43rd in repairing the damage to the defences. " The mud walls had either great holes or huge breaches, and piles of debris lay about " everywhere. Roofing timbers, corrugated iron, equipment and stores lay buried under heaps of bricks and rubbish, blocking the trenches which had been practically obliterated by the bombardment. Reorganization entailed considerable work, and the garrison of the Fort was fully employed for several days. Parties crawled out at night with muffled mallets on the unenviable task of replacing the wire which had been demolished during the attack. Days were spent in deepening old trenches, shovelling out mud after rainstorms or digging new trenches; and nights found the Regiment completing tasks which could not be safely done by day, while an officer of the Regiment, armed with a Very pistol, kept watch all night along the regimental front. The 43rd was now reduced to six combatant officers, of whom only Lieutenant-Colonel Lethbridge, Lieutenant Mason, his adjutant, and Lieutenant Heawood were fit for duty. Captain

---

[33] *Chronicle*, 1915-16, p. 103.   [34] *Ibid.*, 1915-16, p. 137.

Gilchrist, 52nd Sikhs, made the grand total up to four. The night was apportioned into four-hour watches up to 5.30 a.m., when the whole Regiment stood to arms.

Although the week following Christmas was tense, nothing of moment happened. Sniping, however, increased and worried the Regiment considerably, but the 43rd soon organized a team of sharpshooters[35] who quickly gained the upper hand.

Meanwhile the Sappers had commandeered all mirrors in Kut, and had improvised effective periscopes. They also manufactured jam-tin bombs, and devised ingenious trench mortars, first of wood and later from cylinders of an aeroplane engine.

By the end of this eventful year the 43rd was still on full rations and confident of relief by the force under General Aylmer, which was known to be concentrating at Ali Gharbi.

III.—DECEMBER 1915.

GENERAL NIXON'S PROBLEMS: SHORTAGE OF TRANSPORT: BAD COMMUNICATIONS: PLANS FOR THE ADVANCE OF THE RELIEF FORCE.

As has already been told, General Nixon started downstream to organize the reinforcements as soon as he realized that the advance on Baghdad had failed. On the 2nd December the advanced troops of the 7th Division arrived at Basra. These consisted of the headquarters of the 28th Brigade, under Major-General Sir George Younghusband, and the 51st Sikhs. They were immediately transhipped and dispatched upstream the same day to Ali Gharbi, where General Nixon ordered General Younghusband to establish the 28th Brigade[36] as a covering force to the main concentration.

On the 11th General Townshend reported that he had fifty-nine days' full rations for British and Indian troops, though this estimate later proved to be very erroneous and contributed largely to the disasters experienced by the relief force.

General Nixon was now faced with a very awkward problem. He had calculated on capturing in Baghdad enough river craft[37] to enable him to send up the two reinforcing divisions. He had not made any special arrangements for a rapid concentration of the reinforcements. Indeed, he was powerless to do so without suitable craft.

[35] These used captured Turkish rifles with their flat trajectory up to 400 yards in preference to their own S.M.L.E. rifles.
[36] 2nd Leicestershire Regiment, 51st and 53rd Sikhs, 56th Rifles.
[37] What justification he had for this calculation is not at all clear; the Turks had only two steamers and a launch or two.

At this stage it will be convenient to consider the whole transport problem. Sir Beauchamp Duff, Commander-in-Chief in India, had rightly appreciated that success in Mesopotamia depended on the adequacy of river transport,[38] and had reported his opinion that an advance on Baghdad was fraught with danger on account of the shortage.

It has been seen from this history that the advance on Baghdad was undertaken with first-line land transport of mules and carts. The second line consisted of *mahailas* towed by the few light-draught steamers. General Nixon's request in August for the construction of a railway from Basra to Nasiriya was refused on the 14th November on account of expense,[39] and therefore a railway from Basra to Amara was not mooted, although engineers had reported favourably on the proposal. As the problems of supply and maintenance by river had proved so difficult, and by land almost insuperable,[40] it is strange that the higher command should not have realized that a railway provided the solution of them all, long before disaster overtook the Army. The wastage of men by sickness and wastage of time through difficult navigation with unsuitable craft on hundreds of miles of communication were appalling, and General Nixon was fain to improvise methods of concentrating the relief force. In December the importance of time, that unconquerable factor in war, was paramount if he was to be able to march to the relief of Kut before the Turks could establish themselves athwart the communications south of the town. At Basra there were as yet no facilities for the disembarkation of reinforcements. Valuable time was again wasted in this task.

By the 14th December a track up the right bank from Basra to Amara, a track which included eleven bridges over otherwise impassable creeks, was fit for use, thanks to the tireless energy and efforts of the 12th Company, Sappers and Miners, and 107th Pioneers of the 7th Division.[41]

As the result of the retreat from Ctesiphon and the investment of Kut, the British and Indian Governments increased their efforts to provide river transport. By the middle of December the Admiralty had arranged to send six Thames steamers, forty flat-bottomed boats, six motor lighters and twenty small barges; Egypt was to provide ten river steamers; and India had discovered forty river steamers, twenty-four of which were stern-wheelers.[42] But there were still vast difficulties to surmount. The delivery of boats promised in March was postponed till May owing to labour shortage in England; and the construction of those boats sent out in parts for completion in

---

[38] See p. 97. [39] *Official History*, Vol. II, pp. 45-46.
[40] Some of the difficulties of land transport were: superabundance of water in the flood season; shortage of water in the dry; shortage of carts, drivers and animals; shortage of local fodder and grazing whereby much of an animal's burden consisted of its own rations; lack of roads; impassable creeks, etc.
[41] *Official History*, Vol. II, p. 187. [42] *Ibid.*, Vol. II, p. 188.

Mesopotamia was delayed because the plans and details for assembling them were not forwarded.[43] The six Thames steamers did not arrive until the end of May, which is hardly surprising considering that they sailed under their own steam and were not seaworthy; and of the fifty earmarked in Egypt and India five arrived in January, three in February, fourteen in March and seven in April; and seventeen foundered and three were burnt en route.

By December the strength of the river flotilla was: thirteen paddle steamers, three stern-wheelers, nine tugs, three screw boats and fifty-seven barges, exclusive of *mahailas*. During December only two barges were added.

This flotilla was patently and lamentably inadequate for supplying the needs of five divisions, should Kut be relieved, or four if the 6th Division were forced to capitulate. Moreover, the vessels of the flotilla had been ceaselessly employed for many months without the chance of overhaul or repairs, and were consequently in very bad condition.[43]

So much for the question of river transport, from which it will be seen that General Nixon did all in his power to procure an adequate supply. Misunderstandings, however, occurred between the authorities in India and Mesopotamia on the subject of specifications. India accused General Nixon's Staff of being too rigid in these, and the Staff retaliated by complaining that India was not helpful.[44] Whether personal contact between the two was ever effected is not stated, but it might conceivably have eased the difficulties which, early in 1915, were not insuperable. By the time the large reinforcements arrived it was impossible to make good the shortage, and the troops consequently suffered greatly, as we shall see in due course.

General Nixon reached Basra on the 6th December, the same day as many of those wounded at Ctesiphon. Some of the extra wharves, which he had ordered General Gorringe to construct, were already in use, and five others were erected at Maqil within twelve days. Ocean steamers could now berth alongside the shore, instead of having to anchor in midstream. From now onwards reinforcements arrived almost daily, and were pushed on upstream as transport became available.[45]

General Nixon's health by this time was very poor. The strain of the operations had been severe, and soon after his arrival at Basra his health further deteriorated. But, thinking that a change at such a crisis would be undesirable, he gallantly, but perhaps injudiciously, retained command.[46]

Meanwhile Lieutenant-General Sir Fenton J. Aylmer, V.C., K.C.B., had arrived from India, and had been appointed to command all the British troops upstream of Ezra's Tomb. His instructions were to relieve Kut, for which purpose he would have the 3rd Division—7th, 8th and 9th Brigades—

[43] *Ibid.*, Vol. II, p. 189.
[45] *Ibid.*, Vol. II, p. 190.
[44] *Ibid.*, Vol. II, p. 44.
[46] *Ibid.*, Vol. II, p. 187.

and 7th Division—28th, 35th and 19th or 21st Brigades—and the cavalry and details at Ali Gharbi.[47]

On his arrival at Amara on the 12th December, he was told that the Turks opposing him amounted to the same force as General Townshend had fought at Ctesiphon, namely, the 38th, 35th, 45th and 51st Divisions, with possibly another, the 52nd Division. Even before his arrival he received telegrams from General Townshend on the 9th and 11th urging him to come to his relief within fifteen days. General Aylmer rightly answered that it would be foolhardy to attempt relief before a sufficient force had been concentrated to ensure success, on the principle of economy of force. How far urgent appeals from Kut for a speedy relief militated against this principle will be seen hereafter.

In his appreciation General Aylmer reckoned that the whole of the 7th Division and Cavalry Brigade should be concentrated at Ali Gharbi by the 3rd January and the whole corps by the end of January. He was averse to making any attempt to relieve Kut until he could advance with the whole corps; but in view of General Townshend's straits, which at this time were more imagined than actual, he was prepared to advance with one division and the Cavalry Brigade.[48] To this plan General Nixon agreed.

For the rest of the month telegrams were exchanged between Generals Townshend and Aylmer on the best method of advance; and General Townshend reported all enemy troop movements by both banks, for towards the end of the month large bodies had been seen marching downstream towards the old Es Sinn position. He also urged an early relief on account of the impaired morale of some of the Indian troops in his garrison. This last news greatly added to General Aylmer's desire to effect the speedy relief of Kut. However, by the 1st January 1916, all three generals, Generals Nixon, Aylmer and Townshend had agreed that the relief should be effected by the whole corps, and not piecemeal by divisions, unless General Townshend found himself in dire necessity.

IV.—DETAILS OF THE 43RD OUTSIDE KUT: THE DRAFT FROM ENGLAND.

Meanwhile a draft of about twenty-five men of the 43rd, who had recovered from wounds or sickness, had been on its way upstream to rejoin the Regiment when it was invested at Kut. These men, together with similar drafts for the other British regiments in Kut, were formed into a provisional battalion at Ali Gharbi and were officered by territorials sent from India. These last were:—

[47] *Ibid.*, Vol. II, p. 191.
[48] *Ibid.*, Vol. II, p. 194. In his wire to General Townshend on the 30th General Aylmer said: "It is essential to postpone adoption of actual method of advance as long as possible, as hurry means inevitable want of organization and consequently decrease of efficiency" (*My Campaign in Mesopotamia*, p. 237).

Lieutenant L. de Selincourt, 2nd/7th Hampshire Regiment;
Lieutenant H. C. Butcher, 2nd/5th Hampshire Regiment;
Lieutenant D. G. Firth, 1st/5th Hampshire Regiment;
Lieutenant E. C. Kinghorn, 2nd/4th Border Regiment;
Lieutenant S. Wilson, 1st/4th Somerset Light Infantry;
Lieutenant F. C. Staley, 1st/5th Somerset Light Infantry;
Lieutenant K. R. Murray, 2nd/4th Wiltshire Regiment[49];
Lieutenant W. Gilchrist, 1st/4th Duke of Cornwall's Light Infantry;
Lieutenant C. E. Elliott, 1st/7th Hampshire Regiment;
Lieutenant A. H. Seymour, 2nd/4th Duke of Cornwall's Light Infantry.

In the meantime, too, a large draft had at last left England on the 11th December, bound for the 43rd, consisting of:—

Major Hon. W. R. S. Barrington;
Captain S. F. Hammick;
Second Lieutenant G. R. Grosvenor;
Second Lieutenant S. J. Griffin;
Second Lieutenant W. Rance;
Second Lieutenant D. A. T. Wilmot;
Second Lieutenant A. E. Gardner;
Second Lieutenant H. T. C. Field;
Second Lieutenant G. F. Garrard;
Second Lieutenant G. C. Huggard;
Second Lieutenant W. W. Wooding;

and 298 non-commissioned officers and men. At the same time eight other officers from the 3rd Battalion of the Regiment at Portsmouth left for Mesopotamia in command of a large draft of men for the 2nd Royal West Kent Regiment. The officers were:—

Captain R. H. G. Tatton;
Lieutenant J. W. Meade;
Second Lieutenant C. I. Widcombe;
Second Lieutenant A. H. Truman;
Second Lieutenant C. H. Riley;
Second Lieutenant C. T. Davenport;
Second Lieutenant E. B. Parkinson;
Second Lieutenant E. F. Coulthard.

These drafts reached Basra on the 6th January 1916, and disembarked on the 8th.

[49] *Chronicle*, 1915-16, p. 187.

CHAPTER XVII.

I.—January with the Relief Force: First Attempt to Relieve Kut.

Aylmer's difficulties—Townshend urges relief—The action at Shaikh Saad—Turks retreat—The action of Wadi and first attack on Hanna—General Nixon hands over command—Political and military aspect—The draft for the 43rd—Its experiences—January in Kut—Floods—Townshend finds supplies of food—His communiqué to the garrison.

(*See Maps facing pages 1 and 216, and on pages 152, 154 and 158.*)

On the evening of the 3rd General Townshend reported that a large body of the enemy, estimated at two divisions, had been seen moving down the left bank. As it did not attack him, he assumed that it had advanced to the Es Sinn position.

Meanwhile General Nixon had ordered General Aylmer to advance on the 3rd to the relief of Kut. In his instructions General Nixon estimated the enemy maximum force between Shumran and Shaikh Saad at about 30,000 with 53 guns. General Townshend's estimate was between 16,000 and 17,000 with 32 guns, and the Turkish account gave it as 20,000 with 50 guns.[1]

Now it is as well to take a peep at the forces concentrating at Ali Gharbi, and to consider some of General Aylmer's difficulties which contributed to the failure of the relief measures.

First, General Aylmer had no trained corps staff; secondly, General Younghusband, now in command of the 7th Division, had no staff, and a staff had to be improvised; thirdly, the division sent from India, consisting of the 34th, 35th and 36th Brigades, was not provided with a staff at all. Therefore General Aylmer had to retain some of these formations under his personal command. Besides this, units were sent forward as and when they reached Basra, and, owing to the shortage of river transport, often arrived before their brigade staffs, and often without their full equipment.[2] The weather was very cold, and as " medical and supply arrangements were generally inadequate " there were many cases of sickness among the new arrivals. Of the three brigades composing the 7th Division the regiments of the 28th had served together, but the 35th, allotted temporarily, was ill-trained, and the 19th " was an improvised formation, with a temporary

[1] *Official History*, Vol. II, p. 202.   [2] *Ibid.*, Vol. II, p. 203.

brigadier and staff" and only the 72nd Highlanders properly belonged to it. There was also a certain amount of discontent among some units which, having served in France, considered that they had been relegated to a sideshow, and, unmindful of their fate, to operations of an inferior type.

Moreover, the brigades had not worked together as a division; nor had they even had similar and consistent training. The methods applicable to France, Egypt and the North-West Frontier were widely diverse. Yet haphazardly these troops were thrown together and bidden to call themselves a division.[3] With a force lacking experience, cohesion and the necessary equipment, it was no enviable task that faced the conscientious general. He had only first-line land transport, and, though sufficient carts and animals were available at Basra for the second line, yet there was not enough river transport to maintain the animals in forage. They were vicious circles with which he had to contend, circles concentring on the permanent and vital question of river transport. It is not too much to say that he was houghed, and yet he was bidden to advance as if he were not halt. Short of land transport personnel, gun ammunition, telephone equipment, engineers, pontoons, medical personnel and equipment, short, in fact, of all but the least of the vital needs of a force which had to deal with a stiff-kneed enemy, General Aylmer gallantly accepted the risks imposed upon him in the firm belief that it was imperative to advance to Kut's relief. But, like most other improvised British expeditions, it was foredoomed to failure at great cost in life and money. Had it been known on the 3rd January that General Townshend had the means of holding out for four months how differently would Generals Nixon and Aylmer have acted!

II.—The Action at Shaikh Saad.[4]

On the 3rd January General Aylmer issued his instructions for the advance the following day. General Younghusband with the 6th Cavalry Brigade and 7th Division[5] was to advance to Shaikh Saad, accompanied by H.M. Ships *Butterfly, Cranefly* and *Dragonfly*. The enemy's total strength was estimated at 22,000 and 67 guns,[6] together with sundry local Arab irregulars and a mixed brigade of cavalry and camelry. The force at Shaikh Saad was reckoned to be 900 cavalry, 1,100 camelry with two light guns, and a battalion of infantry. There was, however, the possibility that the enemy had pushed forward a division to the neighbourhood of Shaikh Saad. On his arrival at Shaikh Saad General Younghusband was to make land and air reconnaissances of the old Es Sinn position and report on the state and position of the Suwaikiya and Ataba marshes.

[2] *Ibid.*, Vol. II, p. 204.
[3] See Appendix VII.
[4] See Map No. 8, p. 152.
[6] This was an over-estimation.

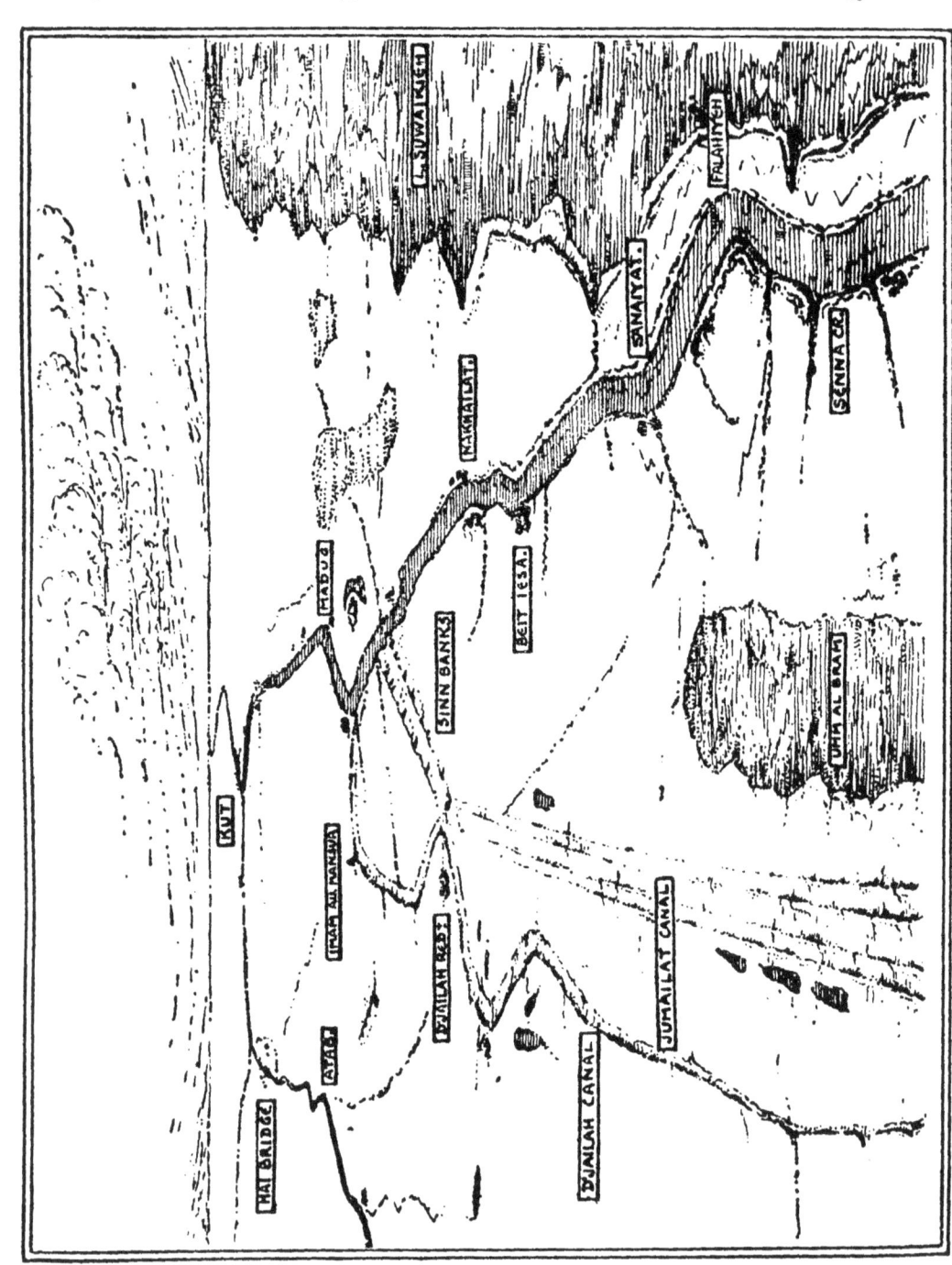

BIRDSEYE VIEW LOOKING TOWARDS KUT.

General Aylmer hoped to advance in support on the 6th with the rest of the Tigris Corps, amounting approximately to two infantry brigades, one cavalry regiment, a howitzer battery, four mountain guns and details.[7]

In his orders issued on the same day, the 3rd, General Younghusband estimated the enemy force at Shaikh Saad to be 2,500, entrenched and supported by two guns. The advance was to begin on the 4th up both banks of the river. Major-General Kemball, with the 28th Brigade and Cavalry Brigade, was detailed to march up the right bank, while the 35th Brigade, under Brigadier-General Rice, advanced up the left, with the 19th Brigade in general reserve.

A gale of wind on the morning of the 4th delayed the start until 10.45 a.m., but the columns reached their destinations on both banks without serious opposition. On the 5th the division reached the east end of the Musandaq reach and encamped at 2.30 p.m. Meanwhile General Townshend reported that large bodies of troops had been detached from the siege of Kut to oppose General Younghusband's advance. On the 5th airmen reported great enemy activity at Shaikh Saad, and estimated their numbers to be 10,000. Thereupon General Younghusband made his plan: General Rice was to threaten the enemy's left on the left bank, while the 28th Brigade was to drive the enemy into Shaikh Saad loop, and there annihilate it. The advance was to begin at 8.30 a.m. on the 6th.[8]

Owing to a thick mist the advance did not start until 9 a.m., and for an hour continued without opposition. By 11 a.m. General Kemball had reached the western end of the Musandaq reach, and issued his orders for the attack. By these, the 56th Rifles and one company 128th Pioneers were to hold the enemy in front, while the main attack by three regiments and the Cavalry Brigade was to be launched against the Turkish right. The advance began at about noon, and soon came under heavy fire. Moreover, the cavalry in trying to outflank the enemy found themselves outflanked by large bodies of Arabs. On the left bank the attack had also been held up by 3.30 p.m. and heavy casualties incurred owing to the flatness of the country, devoid of any kind of cover. A situation of stalemate had been reached when at 3.45 p.m. General Younghusband broke off the action, and ordered the force to establish battle outposts.[9]

Meanwhile, early on the 6th, General Aylmer advanced with those troops which had arrived during the previous two days, and reached the eastern end of the Musandaq reach. His force consisted of the 7th Lancers, two sections of the 23rd Mountain Battery, 21st Brigade[10] and an improvised

---

[7] *Official History*, Vol. II, p. 213.   [8] *Ibid.*, Vol. II, p. 215.
[9] *Ibid.*, Vol. II, pp. 217-220.
[10] 2nd Black Watch, 6th Jats, 9th Bhopal Infantry, 41st Dogras.

MAP No. 8

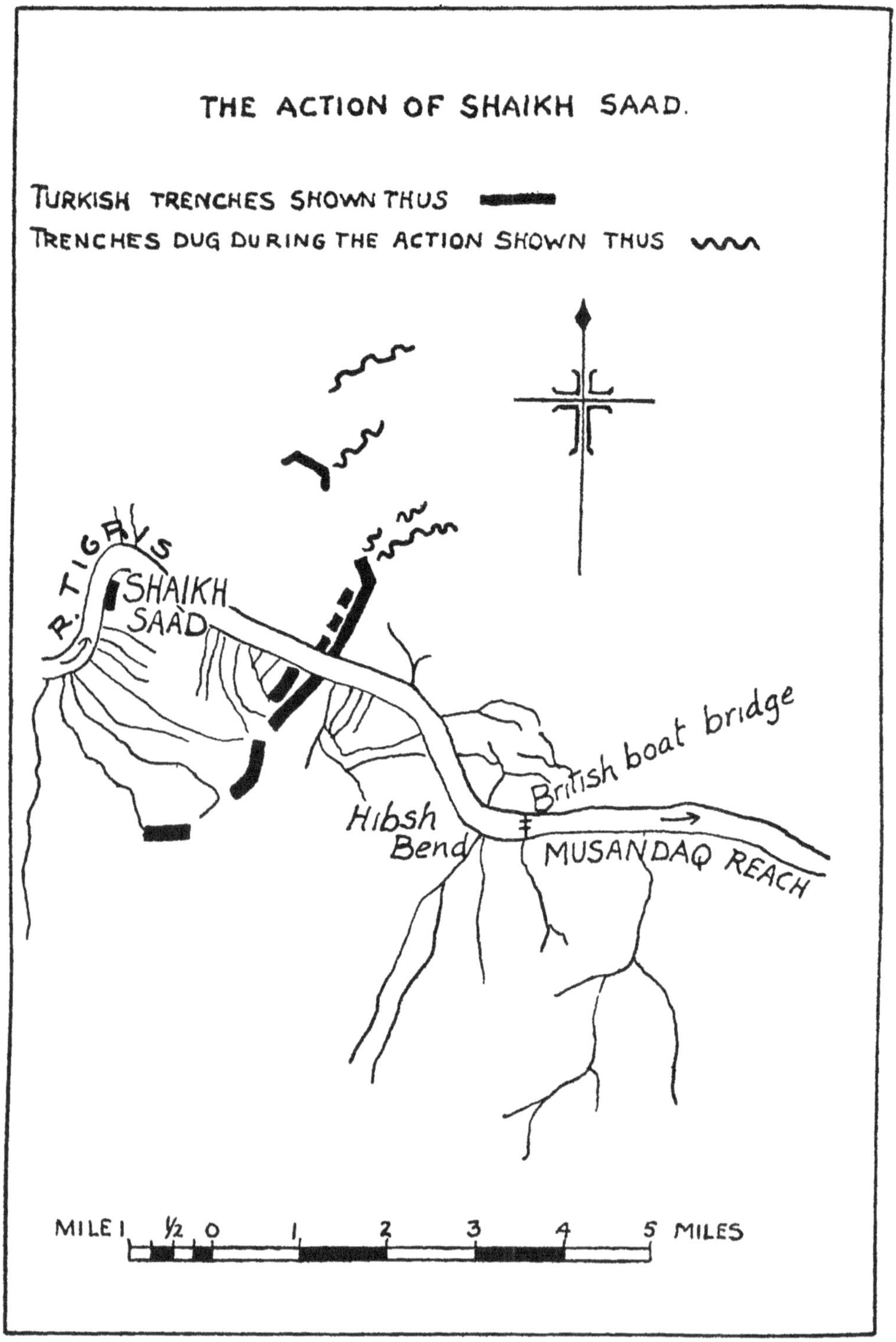
THE ACTION OF SHAIKH SAAD.
TURKISH TRENCHES SHOWN THUS
TRENCHES DUG DURING THE ACTION SHOWN THUS
R. TIGRIS
SHAIKH SAAD
British boat bridge
Hibsh Bend
MUSANDAQ REACH
MILE 1 ½ 0 1 2 3 4 5 MILES

Based upon The Official History of the Mesopotamia Campaign by permission of The Controller of H.M. Stationery Office.

9th Brigade,[11] while the *mahaila* convoy was escorted by the Provisional Battalion in which about one hundred men of the 43rd were serving. At 8 a.m. on the 7th this force advanced again to join up with the 7th Division, the details of the 43rd marching on the right bank with the 9th Brigade. Meeting General Younghusband at 7.30 a.m., General Aylmer decided to attack on the left bank; the 35th Brigade was to pin the enemy down while the 19th and 21st Brigades executed a turning movement against the enemy's left; on the right bank the 28th Brigade and 92nd Punjabis[12] were to attack vigorously in co-operation.[13] In reserve, in his own hands, General Aylmer kept the 9th Brigade, to which had been added the 62nd Punjabis and the Provisional Battalion.

The columns moved off at 11.45 a.m. in a north-westerly direction until at about 1.30 p.m. the 19th Brigade was ordered to wheel to the left and turn the enemy's flank. This movement was met by a heavy cross-fire from the north-west and west, and between 2 and 2.30 p.m. a strong counter-attack so threatened the right flank of the gallant attackers that the 21st Brigade was brought into line facing north. On the right bank the attack of the 28th Brigade was more successful. In a gallant assault the Turkish trenches were captured, together with 600 prisoners, three machine guns, two mountain guns and much equipment. Unable to advance farther the brigade consolidated the ground won. The casualties on both banks were prodigious; nearly 50 per cent. of the 28th Brigade were either killed or wounded, and on the left bank many regiments were decimated.

The Provisional Battalion was held in reserve all day, and at night provided protection for the camp and bridge on the right bank. The wet, cold night was spent in collecting wounded and in consolidation.

The troops were so exhausted that further movement on the 8th was impossible; rest, and replenishment of ammunition, food and water were urgently needed. However, reports from the front line indicated that the Turks were about to retire. These were confirmed on the 9th; and the 28th Brigade occupied Shaikh Saad before 2 p.m. without interference. But such was the viscosity of the ground owing to the recent rains, and the exhaustion and unfitness of the troops, that General Aylmer decided to halt on the 10th, reconnoitre the next position of the enemy, and evacuate the wounded.

On the 11th he reported to General Nixon by wire that he intended to continue the advance, though he realized that it was " a most precarious undertaking "[14] for which he accepted full responsibility, as he considered that a supreme effort was required to relieve Kut. He was prepared to accept the known risks because he had been informed on the 10th by General

---

[11] 1st/4th Hampshire Regiment (less one company in Kut), 107th Pioneers.
[12] Lent to the 28th Brigade from the 19th Brigade on the 6th.
[13] *Official History*, Vol. II, pp. 226-227.   [14] *Ibid.*, Vol. II, p. 240.

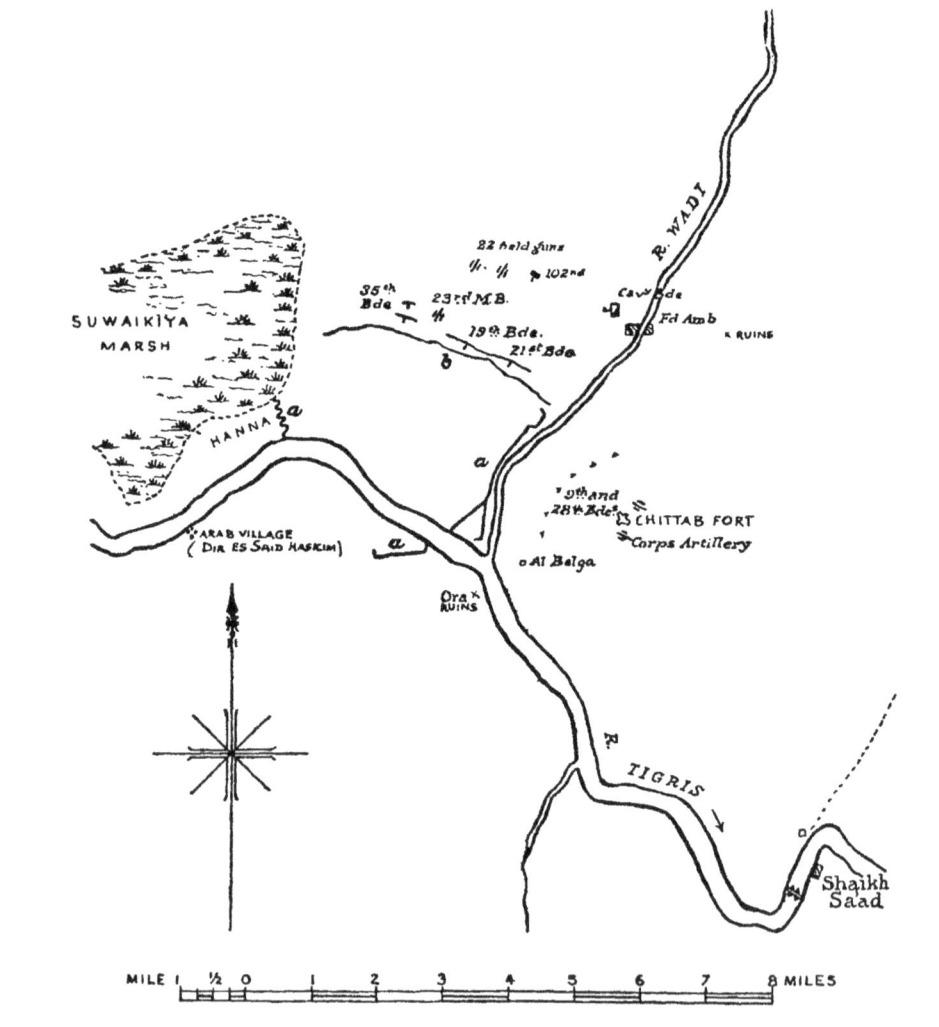

Townshend that another corps was due at Kut on the 20th, and because he was still under the impression, erroneous as it proved, that General Townshend had only sufficient food to last till the end of the first week in February.[15] On the same day an air reconnaissance reported that the enemy was entrenching behind the Wadi, a stream on the left bank, three and a half miles east of " the long and narrow Hanna defile formed by the Suwaikiya marsh and the Tigris."[16]

III.—THE ACTION OF THE WADI.[17]

The Turkish main trenches extended along the western edge of the Wadi for a distance of over two miles, with the left of the line in a redoubt. On the right bank there was a small force estimated at about 500 men. On the 12th January the Cavalry Brigade advanced about ten miles and made a reconnaissance without opposition. General Aylmer therefore determined to attack the exposed left flank of the enemy, and by a wide turning manœuvre obtrude his force across the Hanna defile, thereby surrounding the enemy completely. The Turks, by boldly offering a flank when a large and impassable marsh lay in their rear, seemed to present that chance of a decisive victory which General Aylmer had failed to achieve at Shaikh Saad.

In his orders, issued on the evening of the 12th, General Aylmer detailed the Cavalry Brigade and 7th Division—19th, 21st and 35th Brigades—to execute a turning movement while the 28th Brigade made a frontal attack. In reserve he held the 9th Brigade at Shaikh Saad where the Provisional Battalion and 13th Company, Sappers and Miners, protected the bridge and camp.

That night the 7th Division made a night march to a position of assembly three miles east of some ruins which lay another three miles northeast of the Turkish left redoubt. At 6.30 a.m. the division was to march due west, cross the Wadi and fall upon the Turkish left.

At 7.30 a.m.[18] the 7th Division infantry started its march due westward and crossed the Wadi without opposition or difficulty by 10 a.m. Not so the artillery and transport which, owing to the steepness of the banks, were unable to cross until nearly 1 p.m.

At 11 a.m. the leading brigade, the 21st, met with considerable opposition, but managed to contain the enemy's left so as to allow the 19th, 35th and Cavalry Brigades to manœuvre against the enemy's rear.[19] By 1.30 p.m. the 19th Brigade had come up on the right facing south, and an hour later

---
[15] *Ibid.*, Vol. II, p. 241.   [16] *Ibid.*, Vol. II, p. 243.
[17] See Map No. 9, opposite.
[18] *Official History*, Vol. II, p. 246. A thick mist prevented the start from being made at the scheduled time of 6.30 a.m.
[19] *Ibid.*, Vol. II, p. 247.

both brigades were pressing the enemy who was rushing reinforcements towards his left flank.[20] At 4 p.m., when the two leading brigades were closely engaged and suffering severe casualties, General Younghusband ordered the Cavalry Brigade and 35th Brigade to close the gap between the 19th and the Tigris, thus encircling the enemy position. But this enveloping manœuvre was soon checked.[21] Meanwhile General Kemball ordered the 28th Brigade, supported by the 9th Brigade from reserve, to make a frontal attack at 4 p.m. in co-operation with the enveloping manœuvre. In a most vigorous and gallant attack over the bullet-swept plain, the 28th Brigade managed to reach a shallow nullah within three hundred yards of the enemy. The Turks, entrenched behind the formidable stream as obstacle, were perfectly safe from assault. They had marked the different ranges with white posts, and spent the late afternoon in target practice with rifles and machine guns as the 28th Brigade attacked across their model field-firing range. It was not war; it was butchery and massacre; and it requires little imagination to estimate the casualties suffered in this attack. The 28th Brigade, decimated at Shaikh Saad, was decimated again to no purpose.[22]

At dusk all the attacks had been checked, and the troops took up night outpost positions.

It is now known that this action was very nearly decisive, and that the failure of the turning manœuvre can be attributed in great part to the inaccuracy of the maps. Had the 7th Division made a wider march and turned south along the eastern edge of the Suwaikiya marsh, it would have achieved a real decision, for the Hanna defile was held by only two hundred engineers. But the gods fought against us on the 13th, and the Turkish resistance in hastily dug trenches on their exposed flank was stout and admirable. During the night the Turks evacuated their position and retired to the Hanna defile.

After a bitterly cold night with some rain, the 7th Division started early in pursuit and got into touch with the enemy at the eastern end of the Hanna defile soon after 9 a.m., and prepared to attack the position. But General Aylmer sent a cautionary message to General Younghusband to concentrate ample artillery before attacking. Tied as he was to the river owing to the inadequacy of his land transport, General Aylmer was now faced with a formidable obstacle. Added to this, on the evening of the 14th it began to rain hard, converting the desert into a clinging mud through which the transport could scarcely move, wagons, carts and artillery sinking axle-deep in the glue. Once again the gods turned their hands against the gallant but ill-found relief force, and by torrential downpours of rain allied themselves to its enemies. The blustering gale of wind which accompanied the rain not only wrecked the boat bridge and frustrated the tireless efforts

[20] *Ibid.*, Vol. II, p. 248.   [21] *Ibid.*, Vol. II, p. 249.
[22] *Ibid.*, Vol. II, pp. 251-252.

of the sappers to re-erect it, but also, with a preternatural and malicious fury, drove the waters of the marshes before it, further flooding the sodden plain.

Hardly surprising was it that the troops were in no fit state to attack a strongly entrenched position, and the forced inaction was spent in re-organizing the Tigris Corps.[23] For five days the advance was delayed, five days during which the Turks vastly improved their defences. Meanwhile, too, General Aylmer received another importunate message from General Townshend requesting relief by the 7th February according to his promise. Owing to the weather General Aylmer could not transfer the weight of his artillery to the right bank so as to enfilade the Hanna position, nor could he make the fifty-mile march round the Suwaikiya marsh on the enemy's left flank owing to shortage of transport. Fully realizing that a frontal attack would mean the destruction of half his force, he wired his appreciation to General Nixon on the 16th/17th.[24] By this time General Nixon was a very sick man and unable to make a personal reconnaissance of the enemy's position, but, taking the line that such positions had been captured in the past by the 6th Division, bade General Aylmer employ part of his force on the right bank and turn the enemy out with his main force on the left. On the 19th January General Nixon handed over his command to Lieutenant-General Sir Percy Lake and sailed from Basra.

On the 19th the weather cleared, and the 7th Brigade advanced on the right bank and took up a position enfilading the enemy at Hanna[25] on the left bank.

At 6.30 a.m. on the 20th General Aylmer issued his orders: the guns were to bombard the enemy's trenches from 9 a.m. to dusk; and on the 21st the cessation of the fire on the enemy's first and second lines was to be the signal for the 7th Division to assault the Hanna position.[26]

At 7.45 a.m. the forty-odd guns of the force opened on the enemy and bombarded for twenty minutes; and then the 7th Division launched its attack. Across a flat and muddy expanse of three hundred yards the condemned troops marched into a hail of lead. Only on the left were they able to penetrate the enemy's trenches, but, unsupported, were bombed out by the stout Anatolian Turks who had lately fought in Gallipoli. Had the supports arrived in time, it was said, the enemy front line might easily have been won. But what of the supports? They had been ordered to advance across a thousand yards swept by cross-fire from machine guns. All the enemy had to do was to keep the thumb-piece pressed and change the belts when empty. The supports were mown down like corn before a scythe or ever they had a sight of the concealed trenches. That familiar of a frontal attack was, of course, present—uncut wire; and that the troops ever reached

[23] See Appendix VII.
[25] See Map No. 10, p. 158.
[24] *Official History*, Vol. II, p. 261.
[26] *Official History*, Vol. II, pp. 266-277.

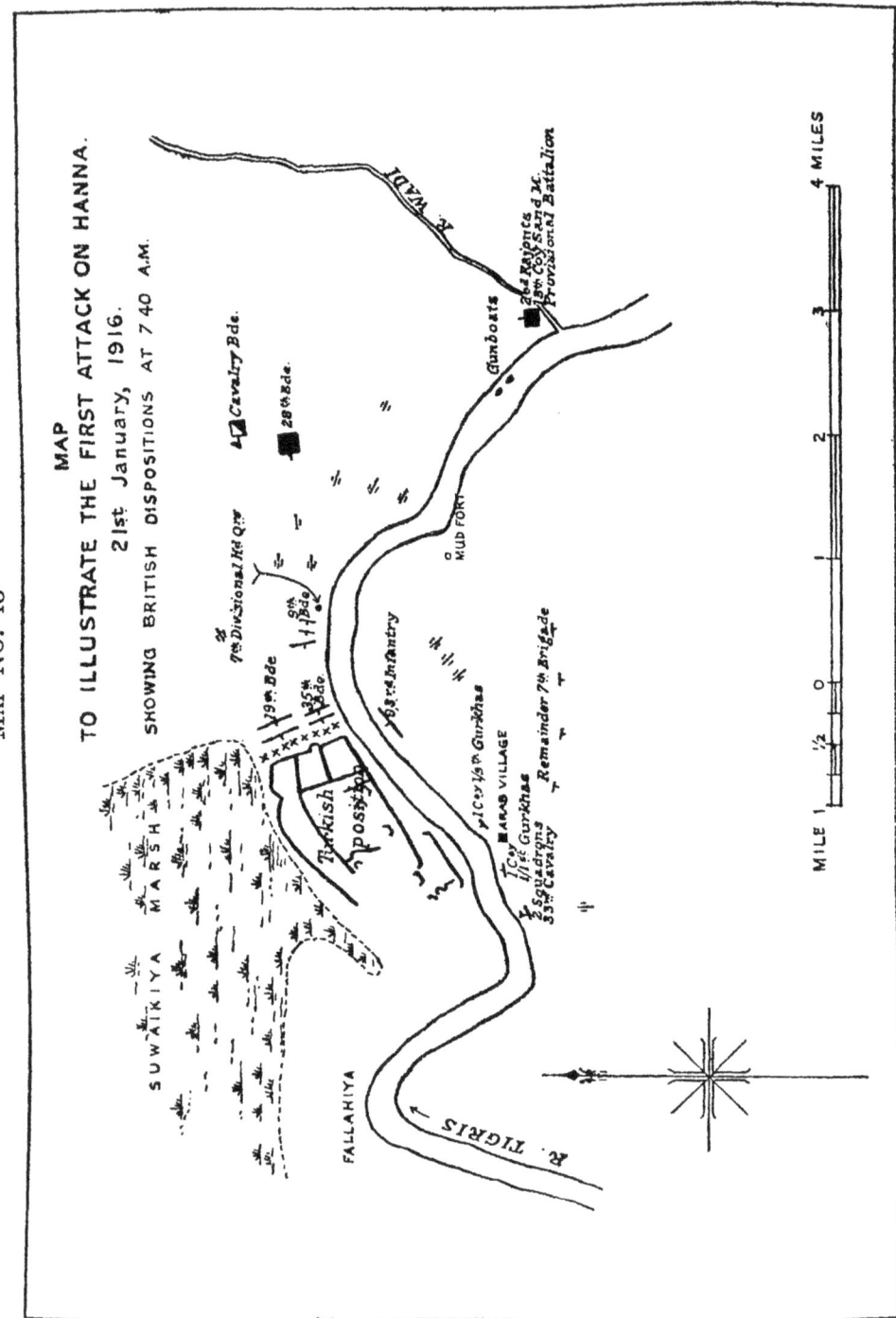

it on the right is more surprising than the fact that some of them lived to tell the tale. To make everything worse, " before noon the rain had settled into a steady downpour, the plain had become a lake of mud, and the wounded lay in pools ankle-deep."[27]

At 12.50 p.m. another bombardment of a half-hearted nature was opened on the enemy, and a second attack was ordered at 1 p.m. The troops responded to the call, rose to the assault and tried to plough their way through the sucking morass of glutinous mud which reduced their numbed and drenched bodies to impotence and immobility. The attack petered out. The troops were withdrawn whence they had started, and the attack was postponed indefinitely. Luckily for the details of the 43rd the Provisional Battalion was not involved in this grim and disastrous action. It was held in reserve near the Wadi junction, together with the 13th Company, Sappers and Miners, and the 2nd Rajputs. On the following day a six-hour truce was arranged with the Turks when both sides collected their dead and wounded.

IV.—POLITICAL AND MILITARY ASPECT, JANUARY 1916.

General Lake, on his arrival in Mesopotamia, immediately sanctioned the construction of additional wharfage and landing-stages, roads and camps to facilitate the disembarkation and accommodation of the reinforcements. Basra was badly in need of reorganization into an efficient base of operations.[28] He also considered the possibility of a railway up the Tigris, but decided against it because time was pressing if he was to succeed in relieving Kut. He did, however, demand a light railway for the work of Basra and also a railway to Zubair,[29] south-west of Basra.

He soon realized his impotence owing to the shortage of transport. On the 21st—the day of the disastrous attempt to break the Hanna line—there were 10,000 troops in Basra immobile for lack of transport.[30] But on the 24th the urgency of the situation was greatly eased by the receipt of a wire from General Townshend stating that he had found quantities of food which, with his horses and mules, gave him provisions for another eighty-four days.[31] That vital urgency, which had appeared to demand the sacrifice of thousands of men in frontal attacks foredoomed to failure, was now reduced after the damage had been done, as so often happens in war. This was intelligence of first importance, as was the news, received on the 10th February, that the War Office had decided to take over the control of the Mesopotamia campaign.[32]

[27] *The Long Road to Baghdad*, by Edmund Candler, p. 96.
[28] *Official History*, Vol. II, p. 279.   [29] *Ibid.*, Vol. II, p. 281. See Map No. 1, facing p. 1.
[30] *Ibid.*, Vol. II, p. 280.   [31] *Ibid.*, Vol. II, p. 283.
[32] *Ibid.*, Vol. II, p. 288.

Meanwhile, as the result of anxiety in England, the War Office ordered the transfer of the 13th British Division from Egypt to Mesopotamia[33]; and the British Government guaranteed twelve battalions for service in India so as to allow of the dispatch of the 37th, 41st and 42nd Brigades to Mesopotamia.[34]

On the 28th January General Lake visited General Aylmer's headquarters and realized that the organization of the rearward services was imperative if he was to overcome the phenomenal difficulties. He realized, too, that pressure had been put upon the unfortunate General Aylmer " to advance promptly without waiting to organize his force properly."[35]

On the same day General Gorringe arrived to assume the temporary appointment of Chief of Staff, so as to help in the reorganization of the Tigris Corps, which had been so haphazardly formed to prosecute the advance.

It was during this reorganization that Major L. J. Carter rejoined from India, and was ordered to form a provisional battalion of the Regiment from the details—already part of the Provisional Battalion of drafts for regiments in Kut—and the large draft which had reached Basra on the 6th January and was on its way up by march route. To obviate confusion this provisional battalion of the Regiment will be called the 2nd/43rd.

V.—THE DRAFT OF THE 2ND/43RD ARRIVES.

The draft for the 2nd/43rd, having disembarked on the 8th January, was accommodated at Askar Barracks, and remained at Basra a week, during which route marches were made to harden the men's muscles after their long sea voyage. On the 12th Major Barrington was warned that the draft would march to the front on the 15th. Two days later rations, tents and heavy kits were stowed on *mahailas,* and at 1.30 p.m. on the 15th the draft marched out of Basra for Kurmat Ali,[36] seven miles distant. The day was fine and the mud had fortunately dried up. The column consisted of 500 men each for the Royal West Kent Regiment and Hampshire Regiment and 350 for the 2nd/43rd, all under the command of Major Barrington, with Captain Hammick as his adjutant.

On the 16th misfortunes were heaped upon the drafts. Owing to lack of wood fuel many men started the march at 9 a.m. with only a couple of biscuits and a little tea inside them. After crossing the new Euphrates channel it began to rain, and the ground soon became a bog. For ten miles the unfit men, soaked to the skin and hungry, ploughed their way through the mud, stumbling and floundering under the weight of their full packs and

---

[33] *Ibid.*, Vol. II, p. 289.
[35] *Ibid.*, Vol. II, p. 292.
[34] *Ibid.*, Vol. II, p. 284.
[36] *Chronicle*, 1915-16, pp. 164-167.

equipment. Instead of reaching camp at 2 p.m. the column arrived at 5.30 p.m., only to find that the *mahailas* with the tents were missing. There was no shelter, and no food because the transport carts were bogged miles behind. For over an hour the troops waited in the rain for the *mahailas* which eventually arrived at 6.30 p.m. The transport, however, never put in an appearance.

The men were so exhausted that a halt of a day was found to be imperative on the 17th. All day it rained, turning the camp into a quagmire; and at night a still heavier downpour flooded the drafts' tents and drenched any kit hitherto dry. These conditions soon produced sickness amongst the men in such alarming numbers that the medical officer was fain to hail a passing hospital boat to evacuate the worst cases.

The 18th was fortunately fine with a high wind which soon dried the ocean of mud within the camp, but the forward march was still impossible because the transport carts were still bogged axle-deep. Owing to this enforced delay rations were running short, Qurna, the next supply depot, being two days' march distant. Major Barrington therefore wired to Basra for more, and was told in reply to get them at Qurna. The weather, however, remained fine, and on the 19th the column started again under better conditions, though the transport carts were frequently bogged. During the march on the 20th the column lost its way and floundered in a bog for over an hour. The hot sun after the recent cold and drenching rain had the attendant effects upon many men, who collapsed from exhaustion as they tried to forge through the mud underfoot. After a fourteen-mile march the column straggled into Qurna five hours ahead of the tents. The carts never arrived at all.

Here at Qurna the drafts remained until the 25th, experiencing all the discomforts so well known to the 1st/43rd. Rain cascaded from above, water flooded the tents and the wind blew bitterly, bringing with it sleet and snow. Starting on the 25th the column reached Ezra's Tomb on the 27th after two days' marching in better weather, though numberless streams had to be crossed hip-deep.

Crossing to the left bank of the Tigris at Qala Salih, the column eventually reached Amara on the 31st after four days of varying vicissitudes produced by mud, flood, tardy boats and land transport. Here the drafts stayed until the 2nd February, when the march was resumed in lovely weather. A divergence from the track, however, in order to cut a corner, resulted in the column marching into a bog in which several mules were nearly lost.

On the 7th Ali Gharbi was reached, and there orders were received to push on to Shaikh Saad, twenty-eight miles distant. The march was a story of rain, mud, bogged transport, beached *mahailas*, and the usual short rations. But even when Shaikh Saad had been reached the journey was not completed, for the base camp had been moved forward to Ora.[37] On the 12th, after a trek lasting twenty-nine days, the draft marched into camp on the left bank and was absorbed into the 2nd/43rd Light Infantry. The draft for the 2nd Royal West Kent Regiment under Captain Tatton and seven subalterns of the Regiment reached Ora on the 14th and was attached to the 1st Connaught Rangers.

VI.—JANUARY 1916 IN KUT.

Meanwhile during January the garrison in Kut was on the tip-toe of expectation of relief by General Aylmer. It soon became evident to the observers that the Turks were sending many of the besieging troops downstream to oppose the relief force. But up till the 19th the siege was definitely active; the town and trenches were shelled intermittently, and the Turks showed no signs of desisting from their entrenching operations. Three lines of trenches with the necessary communications now encompassed the garrison.

By the end of the first week in January the outer defences of the Fort had been adequately strengthened and the nightly fatigue parties instead of being employed in the front line were put to work in rear of the Fort where work could not be done by day. All night carrying parties hodded baulks of timber from the river face of the Fort, where the *mahaila* convoy had stacked it just before the siege began. " These parties had to work very quietly so as not to draw attention, and they almost gave one the impression of ghosts as they flitted silently about in the still moonlight with the softly flowing river in the background."[38] The river communication trench also required plenty of work which was invariably carried out at night under heavy sniping fire.

Meanwhile the news, picked up by wireless, of the advance from Ali Gharbi and of the actions at Shaikh Saad and the Wadi enheartened the garrison; but General Townshend was not so sanguine of the success of the relief force. If it was not possible now to force a passage to Kut, how much more difficult would it be when the enemy reinforcements released from Gallipoli arrived on the Mesopotamia front ![39] And when the news of the unsuccessful attack at Hanna came through, the garrison realized that no help could be expected until the weather improved and reinforcements reached General Aylmer.

For the remnants of the 43rd in Kut the wet weather was very discouraging. The torrential deluge of rain soon produced standing water in the trenches which were on such a low level as to preclude drainage. The

[37] See Map No. 9, p. 154.
[38] Lieutenant Naylor's diary.
[39] *My Campaign in Mesopotamia*, p. 245.

Turks, on a higher level, merely diverted the surface water into the First Line, and the sides of the trenches began to cave in and create a glutinous porridge of mud at the bottom. At the same time the river began to rise alarmingly, and the 43rd found itself at its old mud-larking operations again. By the 21st the river had overflowed its banks and flooded the First Line, which had to be evacuated. It was impossible to build a *bund* along the river bank owing to the attention paid by the Turks to any party exposing itself by day. However, the sauce for the goose was applicable to the gander; the Turks were likewise flooded and had to withdraw. Moreover numbers of them were cut off and drowned. Captain Morland counted forty corpses on the left of the line on the morning after the floods rose. But despite of continual labours against the malicious and relentless elements, the 43rd kept its cheerfulness. There were now two more officers available for duty, Major Henley and Lieutenant Naylor, who had been discharged from hospital.

Life in the Fort, though monotonous, was not allowed to pall; a plague of frogs even provided amusement; infinite patience was expended on the adornment of dug-outs; and amongst the officers Lieutenant Mason, a highly talented man, gave lessons in shorthand.

On the 18th the Turks withdrew from contact with our troops on the northern lines of defences to some redoubts about two thousand yards in rear.

As the result of General Aylmer's failure to force a passage at Hanna, General Townshend had to consider his position and what steps he was to take with his command. It appeared that three courses were open to him: first, make a sortie, as General Aylmer had suggested on the 17th January, with all the able-bodied men in the garrison and leave the sick and wounded behind; secondly, hold Kut to the last man and the last round; thirdly, negotiate with the enemy for surrender with the honours of war.[40] On the 24th he informed General Aylmer that he was prepared to try the first alternative and sortie by the right bank, though he emphasized that luck alone could bring success.[41] However, owing to the local conditions, namely, the great rise in the river and lack of bridging material and therefore the impossibility of ensuring the transfer to the right bank of a sufficient force during the hours of darkness to cut a way through to Shaikh Saad, he gave up the idea.[42] In the meantime, too, a house-to-house search for food had produced good results, and he was informed that he could hold out for eighty-four days. He therefore wired on the 25th that he intended to hold Kut to the bitter end.[43]

When the floods inundated the First Line a new system of defence had to be improvised. From near Redoubt "B" a line was dug towards the

[40] *Ibid.*, p. 257.
[41] *Ibid.*, p. 259.
[42] *Ibid.*, p. 261.
[43] *Ibid.*, pp. 262-263.

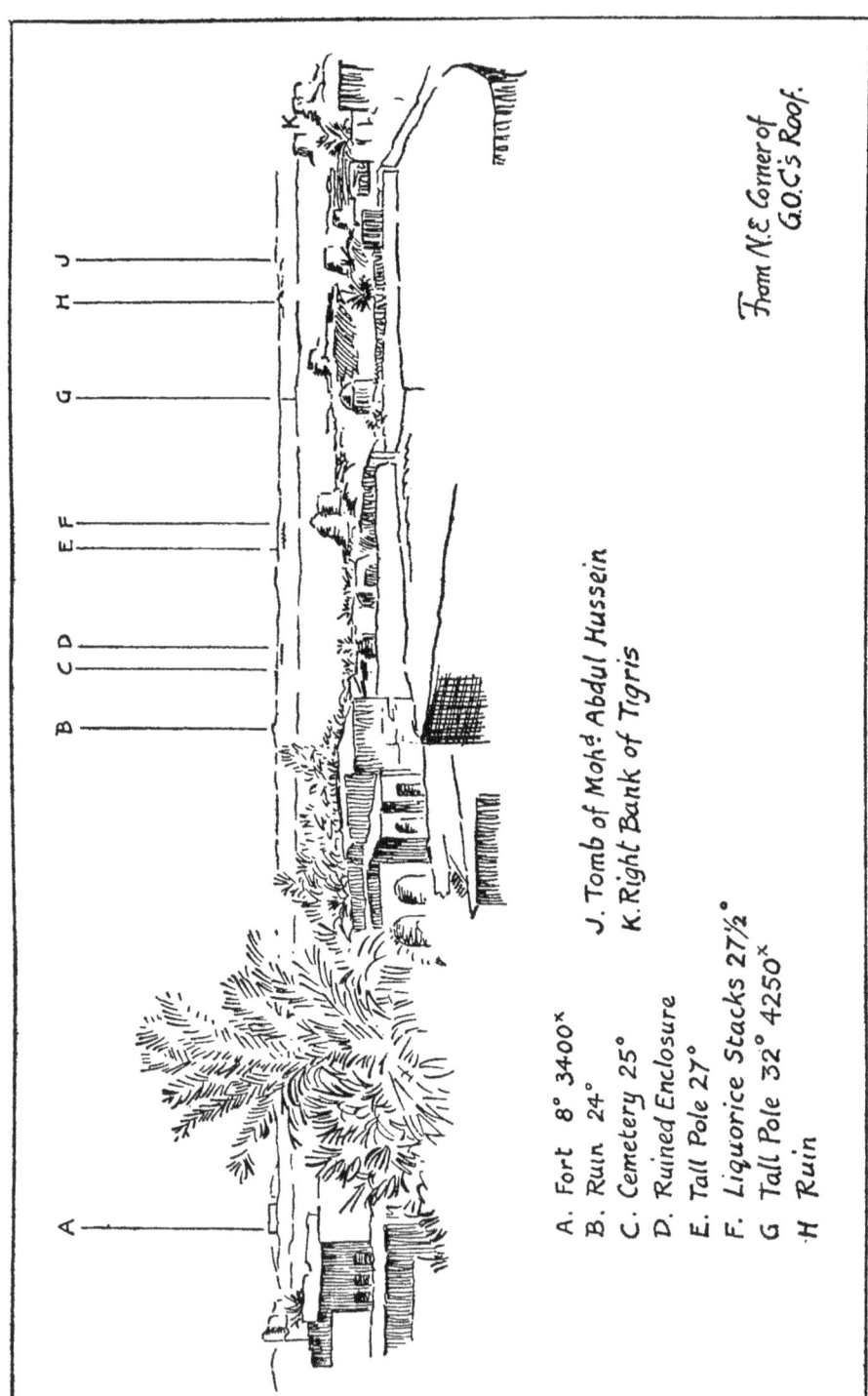

PANORAMA FROM KUT LOOKING TOWARDS THE FORT.

A. Fort 8° 3400×
B. Ruin 24°
C. Cemetery 25°
D. Ruined Enclosure
E. Tall Pole 27°
F. Liquorice Stacks 27½°
G. Tall Pole 32° 4250×
H. Ruin
J. Tomb of Mohᵈ Abdul Hussein
K. Right Bank of Tigris

From N.E. Corner of G.O.C's Roof.

[After a panorama by Major N. V. L. Rybot, D.S.O.]

Middle Line. The new trench then continued parallel to the flooded Reserve Communication Trench till it joined the Middle Line trench by a straight length of 300 yards giving flanking fire along the Middle Line.[44]

The troops still had fairly substantial rations, but fuel had become a problem. " Firewood for cooking was almost unobtainable, and doors and even windows were being impressed for the work."[45] Fortunately, however, a barge full of crude oil from the Anglo-Persian Oilfields had been left at Kut, and this was utilized by the cooks. It was exceedingly dirty to use, and the regimental cooks looked like sweeps; but it served its purpose. By the 26th the garrison was still eating the oxen from the heavy-gun teams, but two days later the less valuable horses were slaughtered, and the 43rd was issued with one pound of horseflesh and twelve ounces of bread, made of *atta*, per man.[46] Tobacco had become increasingly difficult to obtain.

On the same day, the 26th, General Townshend issued a *communiqué* to his troops, as follows :—[47]

" The relieving force under General Aylmer has been unsuccessful in its efforts to dislodge the Turks entrenched on the left bank of the river some fourteen miles below the position at Es Sinn, where we defeated them in September last, when the Turkish strength was greater than it is now. Our relieving force suffered severe loss, and had very bad weather to contend against—they are entrenched close to the Turkish position. More reinforcements are on the way up river, and I confidently expect to be relieved some day during the first half of the month of February.

" I desire all ranks to know why I decided to make a stand at Kut during our retirement from Ctesiphon. It was because as long as we hold Kut the Turks cannot get their ships, barges, stores, and munitions past this place to attack Amara, and thus we are holding up the whole of the Turkish advance. It also gives time for our reinforcements to come up river from Basra, and so restore success to our arms; it gives time to our Allies the Russians, who are now over-running Persia, to move towards Baghdad, which a large force is now doing. I had a personal message from General Baratoff, in command of the Russian Expeditionary Force in Persia, telling me of his admiration of what you men of the 6th Division and troops attached have done in the past few months, and telling me of his own progress on the road from Kermanshah towards Baghdad.

" By standing at Kut I maintain the territory we have won in the past year at the expense of much blood, commencing with your glorious victory at Shaiba, and thus we maintain the campaign as a glorious one, instead of letting disaster pursue its course down to Amara, and perhaps beyond.

" I have ample food for eighty-four days, and that is not counting the

[44] *In Kut and Captivity*, p. 177.
[46] *Chronicle*, 1915-16, p. 143.
[45] *Ibid.*, pp. 174-175.
[47] *Ibid.*, 1915-16, p. 106.

three thousand animals which can be eaten. When I defended Chitral twenty years ago, we lived well on *atta* and horseflesh, but, as I repeat above, I expect confidently to be relieved in the first half of the month of February.

" Our duty stands out clear and simple. It is our duty to our Empire, to our beloved King and Country, to stand here and hold up the Turkish advance as we are now doing; and with the help of all, heart and soul, together we will make this defence to be remembered in history as a glorious one. All in England and India are watching us now, and are proud of the splendid courage you have shown; and I tell you, let all remember the glorious defence of Plevna, for that is what is in my mind.

" I am absolutely calm and confident as to the result; the Turk, though good behind a trench, is of little value in the attack. They have tried it once, and their loss in one night in their attempt on the Fort was two thousand alone; they have had very heavy losses from General Aylmer's musketry and guns, and I have no doubt they have had enough.

" I want to tell you all that, when I was ordered to advance on Ctesiphon, I officially demanded an Army Corps, or at least two divisions to do the task successfully. Having pointed out the grave danger of attempting to do this with one division only, I had done my duty. You know the result and whether I was right or not, and your name will go down to history as the heroes of Ctesiphon, for heroes you proved yourselves in the battle. I perhaps by right should not have told you of the above, but I feel I owe it to you all to speak straight and openly, and take you into my confidence, for God knows I felt our heavy losses and the sufferings of my poor, brave wounded, and shall remember it as long as I live; and I may truly say that no general I know of has been more loyally obeyed and served than I have been in command of the 6th Division.

" These words are long, I am afraid, but I speak straight from the heart, and you will see that I have thrown all officialdom overboard. We will succeed—mark my words—*but save your ammunition as if it were gold.*

" CHARLES TOWNSHEND, *Major-General,*
" Commanding 6th Division."[48]

The atrocious weather which had started on the 16th had not improved much by the end of the month, for, though there was less rain, the cold at night was intensely bitter. In the early morning there were eleven degrees of frost and a film of ice over the water-logged area. When such an extreme of cold followed the suffocating heat of summer, it speaks much for the hardihood of the Regiment that its health was not seriously impaired. The health of the 43rd, on the contrary, was definitely good.

[48] *Ibid.*, 1915-16, p. 106.

CHAPTER XVIII.

I.—FEBRUARY WITH THE RELIEF FORCE.[1]

FEBRUARY IN KUT—THE SIEGE BECOMES PASSIVE—TOWNSHEND DECIDES TO ISSUE HORSEFLESH.

(See Maps facing pages 182 and 216, and on page 218.)

ON the 4th General Aylmer received General Lake's approval of his plan for the resumption of the offensive. In this he proposed to leave a containing force on the left bank, while the principal mass with all available transport was to march across the desert and fall upon the Turkish right at Es Sinn; and then, crossing the Shatt al Hai, attack the enemy at Shumran and effect the relief of Kut. He expected to take the offensive about the middle of February, and arrangements were discussed with General Townshend who was asked to co-operate by a movement against the enemy on the right bank opposite Kut. The limiting factor in the plan was the shortage of land transport which could only carry one day's rations besides those on the soldier. Therefore the forcing of the Hai bridge-head might prove impracticable, in which case General Aylmer determined to try to rescue the Kut garrison by bridging the Tigris south-east of the town.[2]

Eventually the date of the offensive was postponed until the maximum force commensurate with the transport available could be concentrated. This force amounted to two additional infantry brigades and an artillery brigade. As the flood season was expected to begin on the 15th March, it was arranged that the relief operations should be concluded by that date.[3] The month was spent in reorganizing and training the Tigris Corps.

With the arrival of the large draft from England, the 2nd/43rd numbered just over three hundred rank and file. Major Carter formed the Regiment into two companies, " A " and " B," under Captains Hammick and Tatton.[4] Equipment, *packals* and machine guns were drawn. The Regiment was constituted as follows :—

---

[1] See Appendix VIII.
[2] *Official History*, Vol. II, pp. 294-295.
[3] *Ibid.*, Vol. II, p. 299.
[4] Captain Tatton on his arrival with the draft for the 2nd Royal West Kent Regiment was temporarily attached to the 1st Connaught Rangers until the 29th February, when with the other subalterns who accompanied the draft he joined the 2nd/43rd at Ora Camp.

Headquarters.

Major L. J. Carter, commanding;
Major Hon. W. R. S. Barrington, senior major;
Captain S. F. Hammick, acting adjutant;
Lieutenant F. C. Staley, 1st/5th Somerset Light Infantry, machine-gun officer;
Second Lieutenant W. W. Wooding,[5] acting quartermaster;

Captain R. H. G. Tatton;
Second Lieutenant G. R. Grosvenor;
Second Lieutenant A. E. Gardner;
Second Lieutenant S. J. Griffin;
Second Lieutenant H. T. C. Field;
Second Lieutenant G. F. Garrard;
Second Lieutenant D. A. T. Wilmot;
Second Lieutenant G. C. Huggard;
Second Lieutenant W. Rance;
Lieutenant W. Gilchrist, 1st/4th Duke of Cornwall's Light Infantry;
Lieutenant C. E. Elliott, 1st/7th Hampshire Regiment;
Lieutenant A. H. Seymour, 2nd/4th Duke of Cornwall's Light Infantry;
Lieutenant K. R. Murray, 2nd/4th Wiltshire Regiment;
Lieutenant D. G. Firth, 1st/5th Hampshire Regiment;
Lieutenant E. C. Kinghorn, 2nd/4th Border Regiment;
Lieutenant S. Wilson, 1st/4th Somerset Light Infantry;
Lieutenant H. C. Butcher, 2nd/5th Hampshire Regiment;
Second Lieutenant L. de Selincourt, 2nd/7th Hampshire Regiment;

making a total of 23 officers and 288 other ranks. Serjeant-Major Dancey was appointed to the acting rank of regimental serjeant-major, and Captain Foljambe, the adjutant of the 1st/43rd, who had been wounded at Ctesiphon, was then on his way to rejoin from India. In the meanwhile Captain Hammick filled the post.

On the 18th the 2nd/43rd, as part of the 28th Brigade of the 7th Division, was ordered into the trenches on the left bank opposite Hanna. From the reserve trenches the Regiment supplied working parties to dig trenches in the front line.[6]

On the 21st there was considerable shelling in the afternoon, which increased in intensity after dark; as the result of it the Regiment lost Private

---

[5] Promoted rom the ranks of the 52nd for service in France.
[6] *Chronicle,* 915-16, pp. 156-157.

The Shatt al Hai.

YAKASUB, commonly known as Woolpress village or the Liquorice Factory.

Kut town.

The Fort.

By permission of Imperial War Museum.

KUT AL AMARA FROM THE AIR, FEBRUARY 1916.

MAJOR L. J. CARTER, D.S.O.

Ford killed, and C.S.M. Smith and Private Lambourne wounded. Lieutenant Elliott was wounded when out with the digging party.

The following day a very successful demonstration was carried out. While the 28th Brigade contained the enemy at Hanna, the 21st Brigade made a feint at crossing the Suwaikiya marsh. Meanwhile during the night of the 21st/22nd a force under General Gorringe, consisting of the Cavalry Brigade, 36th Infantry Brigade and two batteries of artillery, had marched up the right bank. At dawn on the 22nd, while the guns bombarded the enemy camps in rear of the Hanna position, part of the column pushed upstream to a point opposite Sannaiyat. " As the first shells began to fall among their tents there was a stampede of transport animals. Horses, mules, camels, donkeys . . . began to streak across the plain."[7] Completely taken by surprise, the Turks found that they had no means of moving their guns to deal with the British intruders. " The country on the opposite bank was clear; . . . there was no opposition,"[8] and had General Gorringe had three pontoons he could have made a flying bridge and transferred a brigade to the left bank in a day. But such pontoons as he had were only dummies wherewith to delude the Turks into thinking that he was going to effect a crossing. Meanwhile on the front of the 28th Brigade the guns, by plastering the enemy's trenches from 6.30 a.m. onwards, attracted a good deal of shell fire in retaliation up to 11 a.m. The Regiment spent the rest of the day and the ensuing two days in digging trenches.

On the 25th the Regiment moved into the front line for four days, which likewise were spent in intensive digging by day and night. On the 29th Major Carter handed over to the composite battalion of the Norfolk and Dorsetshire Regiments, familiarly known as the " Norsets." Heavy rain fell during the relief, and the trenches became so water-logged that movement was exceedingly difficult. It took two hours to reach the reserve trench, where the Regiment waited till 8.30 p.m. for the transport carts. As these failed to appear, Major Carter marched back to camp, the four miles taking nearly four hours to cover, so heavy was the going. Waiting for the Regiment's arrival in camp were the officers who had been attached to the Royal West Kent Regiment, namely, Captain Tatton, Lieutenant Meade and Second Lieutenants Widcombe, Riley, Parkinson, Coulthard, Truman and Davenport.

The end of the month found the relief force disposed with the 7th Division on the left bank in front of Hanna, the 3rd Division on the right

[7] *The Long Road to Baghdad,* pp. 123-124.

[8] *Ibid.,* p. 125. General Aylmer hoped that this threat to their communications might induce the Turks to evacuate the Hanna position and allow of his advancing to Kut, where the garrison was ready to sortie on the left bank. It was also intended to distract the Turks' attention from the right bank whereon General Aylmer intended to attack in force.

bank and an infantry brigade and battery of guns forward in the Fallahiya loop.[9] The Turks showed no signs of abandoning their Hanna position, but General Aylmer had succeeded in establishing himself nearer the starting-point which he required for his attack on the Turkish right at Es Sinn.

II.—FEBRUARY IN KUT.

During the first week the sound of the distant gun fire downstream enheartened the garrison, but when heavy rain fell on the 8th and 9th hopes of relief were again dashed to the ground. " The perpetual alternation of hope and disappointment was one of the most trying features of the five months' siege of Kut," wrote Major Sandes.[10]

The 1st/43rd was still holding the Fort, but when the floods inundated the First Line " Q " Company, under Lieutenant Heawood, was detailed to hold the newly constructed Redoubt " B." Here this company remained for the rest of the siege. As the trenches on each flank were only lightly held at night the men of " Q " Company were set to make an all-round defence and such improvements as would enable the occupants of the redoubt to hold out indefinitely. This entailed considerable labour and the garrison was never idle.

Lieutenant Naylor was now the only company officer left with " P," " R " and " S " Companies in the Fort, as Major Gilchrist, 52nd Sikhs, had been recalled to Kut to resume his staff duties. In his place Major Booth, Army Signal Corps, was sent up. This officer took over command of the bastion with one company and a half, and Lieutenant Naylor with the other company and a half occupied the wall from the bastion to the north-east corner exclusive. The western face from the bastion to the north-west corner was held by the Norfolk Regiment from the end of January to the end of February, when it was relieved by two companies of the 67th Punjabis. These two companies remained in the Fort until the end of the siege.[11]

The trenches opposite the Fort had been evacuated by the enemy on account of the floods, the nearest Turkish piquet being about 900 yards away. The opportunity was therefore seized to fill in the enemy's saps. At night a large party of the 43rd and Sirmur Sappers and Miners under Lieutenant Naylor went out and succeeded in obliterating the saps, but the main trenches, eight feet wide and six feet deep, presented too formidable a task to be undertaken in two hours. It " was an eerie time; dead bodies were lying about all over the place, reminders of the 24th December, and as it was now nearly six weeks since that day the still night was heavy with the sickly smell of decomposing bodies."[12]

---

[9] See Appendix VIII.
[11] Lieutenant Naylor's diary.
[10] *In Kut and Captivity*, p. 188.
[12] *Ibid.*

One afternoon news reached the Fort that an officer had penetrated 1,000 yards into the evacuated Turkish trenches on the left of the front line and had brought back useful information. Lieutenant Naylor was detailed to take out a similar patrol in front of the Fort. At about 4 p.m. with two stout-hearted volunteers, Serjeant Ballard and one other, he crawled out over no man's land to the Turkish first trench. This proved to be full of mud and water; the patrol therefore kept to the ground level, and by making use of the "cover provided by the parapets of the numerous fire and communication trenches eventually reached a point some five hundred yards from the Fort."[12] Hitherto no sign of the enemy had been seen, but now the Turkish piquet spotted the patrol and opened fire. Unable to penetrate farther the patrol made for the Fort, now sprinting over open ground, now wallowing knee-deep in the mud and ooze of the trenches, and all the while under a hail of bullets. Eventually the patrol reached safety unscathed, but not before the leader was nearly cut off by a party of Turks from the west. After this the Turks established a piquet and snipers' post within 300 yards of the Fort.

Food was still fairly plentiful. Horse provided good soup and edible steaks and joints. "Potatoes had disappeared, but a fair quantity of potato meal was available instead. . . . Puddings were made of *atta* with a flavouring of ground ginger. These were very solid, but they helped to fill up corners. . . . English tobacco had long since given out, but there was plenty of Arab tobacco in the town, and this though very poor stuff helped to make up the deficiency."[13]

By the 13th the Tigris began to rise and it was clear that the real floods were on their way. "The *bund* along the river bank had been practically completed . . . and a strong *bund* was now built along the whole length of the Middle Line. Thus Kut was amply protected; but the whole of the original front line in the North-West Sector had been evacuated except for piquets and echelon trenches which ran back from Redoubt 'B' towards the left end of the Middle Line. The remainder of the front line from Redoubt 'B' to the Fort remained intact."[13]

In anticipation of the floods an inner keep had been started in the Fort in January. "This consisted of a high loopholed parapet which performed the dual function of a defence against water and fire. This keep entailed endless work, for it was scientifically constructed of mud bricks, properly moulded and mixed with *boosa* retrieved from the ruins of the bastion, and was *bunded* in order to localize any sudden inrush of water. Thus the three companies in the Fort spent weary days fighting the floods which had become more irritating than the Turkish snipers. By the middle of

[12] *Idem.*, p. 170.   [13] *Ibid.*

February, however, the floods had subsided considerably, thanks to a spell of fine weather, and the days began to get warm.

On the 17th General Townshend received a message from His Majesty The King-Emperor which ran: " I, together with your fellow-countrymen, continue to follow with admiration the gallant fighting of the troops under your command against great odds, and every effort is being made to support your splendid resistance.—GEORGE R.I." In his reply General Townshend said : " It is hard for me to express by words how profoundly touched and inspirited all ranks of my command have been by His Majesty's message. The knowledge that we have gained the praise of our beloved Sovereign and fellow-countrymen will be our sheet anchor in this defence."

About this time the besieging Turks were informed of the so-called German success at Verdun; whereupon they raised three half-hearted cheers which were plainly heard by the garrison. It was rumoured that General Townshend sent a message in clear to the relief force reporting that " the Turks have to-day given three stage cheers. This may be due to one of the following reasons :—

" 1. That it is a Turkish pay-day.
" 2. That they are being inspected by von Pilsener.
" 3. That Enver Pasha is dead."

By this time the siege had become entirely passive; and when even the spasmodic shelling ceased on the afternoon of the 19th leaving an ominous and deathly stillness General Townshend issued an order for all the troops to stand to arms, as he considered that the silence boded ill. So the Regiment slept in the trenches fully accoutred in case of attack, but the night passed without incident.

On the morning of the 20th news was received from General Aylmer that he intended to try to find a way across the Suwaikiya marsh so as to reach Kut by the left bank. Confidential instructions were issued to the company commanders, and on the 22nd the whole garrison was agog with excitement when the order was received to stand to arms. At 6 a.m. the bombardment of the Turks' rear by General Gorringe's column was plainly audible. " Q " Company was relieved by a company of machine guns in Redoubt " B," and the whole Regiment concentrated ready to sally out and join hands with the relief force. All day the Regiment waited, but when at dusk companies were ordered back to their positions the disappointment was abysmal.

The flood water had by now risen so high that the piquets in front of the North-West Sector were withdrawn, leaving the Middle Line as the front line of defence.

One afternoon the Turkish trenches were so inundated that the garrisons were forced to leave hurriedly over the open ground to the line of redoubts, 1,500 yards distant, providing excellent targets for the British artillery and machine guns as they went. The sniping post about 300 yards north of the Fort was, however, still held.

It was quite conceivable at this time that the Fort might be so flooded as to necessitate withdrawal to the inner keep, which naturally could not contain the normal garrison. Therefore such timber as could be spared from the defences was carried back to the 43rd's old bivouac line where a reserve system of trenches with dug-outs was constructed in case of need.

During the month the food question became more acute. On the 6th tinned milk became scarce, and fresh milk was reserved for the sick and wounded in hospital; sugar and eggs were unobtainable, and the jam ration was reduced to a minute portion.[14] Potatoes and vegetables had long since been exhausted, and horseflesh had become the main ration; but most of the Indian troops, for religious reasons, refused to touch it in spite of dispensations from their pundits in India.[15] Tobacco, of course, was the first item to fail, and all manner of substitutes were being tried at this time, including green leaves dried over a fire, tea leaves mixed with sawdust, and ginger cut up into small lumps. By the end of the month the ration of each man of the 1st/43rd consisted of one pound of horseflesh, three-quarters of a pound of inferior bread, one ounce of jam, and a small issue of dates and tea. The shortage of sugar and tobacco was particularly hard to bear.[16] Those who had shotguns managed to eke out the meagre rations by shooting the murmuration of starlings which used to collect in the palm groves at dusk. By careful alignment as many as thirty-seven starlings were killed with two shots on one occasion.[17]

As there were no vegetables whatsoever, scurvy broke out in the garrison as a natural corollary. By the middle of the month there were 140 cases, and about five new cases per day thereafter.[18] Other diseases which became epidemic by the end of the month were gastro-enteritis, dysentery, diarrhœa, malaria and pneumonia; and the men of the Regiment suffered terribly from lice—" millions of 'em," wrote Serjeant Munn, which " caused us more trouble than all the Turks on earth."[19] Turgid water from the filemot Tigris, vermin and inadequate rations were beginning to sap the Regiment's vitality; but for all that the men's morale was excellent, as one would expect of the 43rd.

The casualties in the siege up to the 29th February amounted to 2,927, of whom 846 had been killed or had died of wounds, 1,608 had been

[14] *In Kut and Captivity*, p. 188.
[16] *Ibid.*, Vol. II, pp. 307-308.
[18] *Official History*, Vol. II, pp. 307-308.
[15] *Official History*, Vol. II, p. 307.
[17] *In Kut and Captivity*, p. 192.
[19] *Chronicle*, 1915-16, p. 131.

wounded, 30 missing or deserted, and 443 had died of disease.[20] Colonel Lethbridge's diary gives the following data:—

"10th. Rations to-day, ½ lb. bread; 1 oz. jam.

"14th. Rations for British infantry hold out well; 8 oz. meat, 12 oz. bread, 2 oz. jam, 2 oz. cheese or dates."

On the 28th, the anniversary of the relief of Ladysmith, a dinner was held in Kut. The menu and entertainment were as follows:—

SIXTEENTH ANNIVERSARY DINNER
RELIEF OF LADYSMITH

To be Held at Hotel Optimus, Kut.
February 28th 1916 at 8 p.m.

MENU.

HER'S D'ŒUVRES

| Olives | ... | ... | ... | ... | ... | ... | All Nations |

SOUP

Cheval ... ... D'Artillerie

FISH

Sole ... ... Trench Sabot

ENTREE

Cutlets ... ... Jaipur Pony Superb

JOINT

Horse Loin ... ... Shell trimmings
Mule Saddle ... ... Bhoosa Sauce
Vegetable au Cotton

SWEETS

Windy Lizzie Pudding   Flatulent Fanny Sauce

SAVOURY

Whizz Bangs with Starlings on Toast

DESSERT

Liquorice Root   Mahailah Squares
Coracle-chunks   Bomb shells

COFFEE

S. & T. Special and Arabian

WINES

Liquorice, Tigris Water, Date Juice, etc.

Cigars ... ... Relief Special
Cigarettes ... ... Kut Favourites

Bellums, Mahailahs, A.T. Carts, G.S. Wagons at 3 a.m. sharp.

GOD SAVE THE KING EMPEROR

[20] *Official History*, Vol. II, p. 308.

By kind permission of FRITZ and FRANZ (*the two German aeroplane pilots*) the KUT ORCHESTRA *will render the following programme during Dinner.*

PART I

1. OVERTURE ... ... " Here we are again " ... ... *Aylmer*
2. WALTZ ... ... " Tantalising Aeroplanes " ... ... *Turco*
3. SELECTION ... ... " Shelling Recollections " ... ... *Windy Lizzy*
4. SONG ... ... " I'm a long way from Kut al Amara " ... ... " *J. N.*"
5. FANTASIE ... ... " The Whizz Bang Glide " ... ... *Woolpress Bill*
6. WALTZ ... ... " Those Tinkling Geggs " ... ... *Observer*
7. SELECTION ... ... " Bombing Memories " ... ... *Miles Running*
8. TWO STEP ... ... " Be quick and get under " ... ... *A. Dugout*

INTERVAL

During the Interval the Anti-Aircraft Squadron, ably supported by 13 pounder, will give a short Sketch entitled " *Aeroplanes and how to scare 'em.*"

PART II

1. MARCH ... ... " Over the hills not far away " ... ... *Percy Lake*
2. CORNET SOLO ... " I hear you calling me " ... ... *Aylmer*
3. SELECTION ... ... " Odoriferous Kut " ... ... *A. Smell*
4. SONG ... " We don't want to lose you, but we think you ought to go " *Von der Goltz*
5. WALTZ ... ... " Mail Time Dreams " ... ... *I. E. F.*
6. ROMANCE ... ... " When shall we three meet again " ... *Weston-Kee-Craw*
7. GALLOP ... ... " The GEE HEE'S Lament " ... ... *Stewpot*
8. REGIMENTAL MARCHES ... R.F.C. Mechanical Transport
" Maxim Gun Battery "

CHAPTER XIX.

I.—MARCH WITH THE RELIEF FORCE: SECOND ATTEMPT TO RELIEVE KUT: ATTACK ON THE DUJAILA REDOUBT.[1]

THE TURKISH POSITION ON THE RIGHT BANK—AYLMER DECIDES TO ATTACK DUJAILA—THE APPROACH MARCH—DUJAILA REPORTED UNOCCUPIED—ATTACK POSTPONED—TURKS REINFORCE—ATTACK FAILS—AYLMER WITHDRAWS—CAUSES OF FAILURE—GORRINGE SUPERSEDES AYLMER—REST AND TRAINING—MARCH IN KUT—TOWNSHEND'S COMMUNIQUÉ—RATIONS REDUCED—FLOODS.

(See Maps facing pages 182 and 216, and on pages 206 and 218.)

AT the beginning of March the enemy was estimated to have five divisions at least on the Mesopotamia front, with an effective strength of about 1,500 sabres, 25,000 rifles and 80 guns. The troops were thought to be divided into three approximately equal columns: investing Kut, holding Hanna and holding Es Sinn. It was calculated that the Es Sinn position was occupied by about 1,500 sabres, 8,500 rifles and 32 guns; and it was upon this force that General Aylmer determined to descend with every available man.

By this time the enemy trenches on the left bank had been greatly improved and provided with covered communication from Nukhailat, Sannaiyat and Fallahiya up to the front line at Hanna. These trenches were also an effective protection against flanking and enfilade fire and a surprise crossing by the British.

On the right bank the Es Sinn position had also been lengthened and more strongly fortified since the 1st/43rd cleared the area after the battle in September 1915. The line, formidable then, was more so now that it was flanked by the Sinn Abtar and Dujaila Redoubts. Till the beginning of March the Dujaila Redoubt formed the right of the position, but in the first week a defensive flank, running south-west towards the Shatt al Hai, was started. In front of the main Es Sinn position were two advanced positions at Bait Isa and opposite Nukhailat. The terrain in front, which had proved too difficult to traverse in September, was the usual open plain intersected by old irrigation channels and dotted with sandhills, mounds and banks. Behind the Sinn banks lay the Dujaila depression, a feature, said to be an old bed of the Tigris, which followed a tortuous course from Maqasis in a south-westerly direction and disappeared south of the Umm al Baram marsh.

[1] See Map 11, facing p. 182.

THE PLAN OF ATTACK

On the left bank the British had sapped forward towards the Turks so that, by the beginning of March, the opposing trenches lay three hundred yards apart. On the right bank General Keary, with the 3rd Division, held positions just east of Sannaiyat.

As the flood season was expected to develop about the 15th March, General Aylmer determined to make his attempt on the 5th before the enemy had time to reinforce Es Sinn or build a bridge at Maqasis. From his total force of 1,400 sabres, 24,000 rifles and 92 guns, he decided to attack the Turkish positions—now estimated to contain about 11,000 rifles—with the cavalry, seven brigades[2] and sixty-eight guns.

To conceal his intention and delude the enemy, many ruses, feints and stratagems were employed on the left bank in the hope that deceptive information would reach Turkish headquarters. On the 6th General Aylmer issued his orders: General Younghusband with a skeleton force was to contain the enemy at Hanna and guard the camp and bridge; the rest of the Tigris Corps was to cross the river and carry the Dujaila position.

On the 1st March the 2nd/43rd was at Wadi Camp on the left bank. Captain Hon. J. C. W. S. Foljambe had rejoined and resumed the appointment of adjutant. This day Second Lieutenant H. E. F. Smyth arrived with a welcome draft of one hundred men, having left three officers[3] and a number of men at Basra where they were required to escort certain Indian details who were disaffected. The Regiment's strength was now nearly four hundred, of which over thirty were officers, so that many of the subalterns were supernumerary.

The Regiment received orders to move on the 2nd at 4 p.m., but these were cancelled owing to threatening weather, which delayed the move until the 6th. At 7 p.m. on that day the 2nd/43rd with 29 officers and 406 other ranks[4] paraded in pitch darkness, crossed the river and promptly lost its

[2] Total of over 20,000 fighting men.
[3] Lieutenant Radford and Second Lieutenants Davis and Roberts.
[4] *Official History*, Vol. II, p. 514; *Chronicle*, 1915-16, p. 169. The officers who went into action were:—
  Major L. J. Carter, commanding;
  Major Hon. W. R. S. Barrington, senior major;
  Captain Hon. J. C. W. S. Foljambe, adjutant;
  Lieutenant Anderson, R.A.M.C., medical officer;
  Second Lieutenant D. A. T. Wilmot, transport officer;
  Captain S. F. Hammick, commanding "A" Company;
  Captain R. H. G. Tatton, commanding "B" Company;
  Lieutenant J. W. Meade;
  Lieutenant H. C. Butcher, 2nd/5th Hampshire Regiment;
  Lieutenant D. G. Firth, 1st/5th Hampshire Regiment;
  Second Lieutenant L. de Selincourt, 2nd/7th Hampshire Regiment;
  Lieutenant E. C. Kinghorn, 2nd/4th Border Regiment;
  Lieutenant A. H. Seymour, 2nd/4th Duke of Cornwall's Light Infantry;

[*Continued on next page*

way in the maze of trenches on the right bank. However, after a march of about six miles, the Regiment reached camp near the Senna canal at about 3 a.m. After dark on the 7th the whole striking force was concentrated on the right bank, screened by the 35th Brigade which had taken up a line running south from the Tigris towards the Pools of Siloam.[5]

The striking force was organized in three groups. The first group, under Major-General Kemball, which was to make the turning attack south of the Dujaila Redoubt, consisted of two columns: Column "A," under General Christian, comprised the 36th Brigade, half the 34th Pioneers, 8th Battery, R.F.A., a section 12th Company, Sappers and Miners, and a field ambulance; Column "B," under General Kemball's own orders, which was to make a flank attack on the Dujaila Redoubt, consisted of the 9th and 28th Brigades, 9th Brigade, R.F.A., a section 61st Howitzer Battery, 12th Company, Sappers and Miners (less two sections), and three and a half field ambulances.

The Cavalry Brigade composed the second group; and the third group, known as Column "C," consisted of the 3rd Division[6] under Major-General Keary. This last group was to make the frontal attack on the Dujaila Redoubt simultaneously with General Kemball's turning attack.

The 2nd/43rd spent the day in camp, and experienced difficulty in getting enough water to fill its bottles. Parading at 5.30 p.m., the Regiment started the night march, with "A" Company escorting the 28th Brigade first-line transport and "B" Company the guns. The whole force marched in one column until a point about four and a half miles east-north-east of the Dujaila Redoubt, known as the point of divergence, was reached at 2.30 a.m.[7] Here Column "C" halted, and hence General Kemball was to

Continued from previous page]
   Lieutenant S. Wilson, 1st/4th Somerset Light Infantry;
   Lieutenant K. R. Murray, 2nd/4th Wiltshire Regiment;
   Second Lieutenant E. F. Coulthard;
   Second Lieutenant C. T. Davenport;
   Second Lieutenant H. T. C. Field;
   Second Lieutenant A. E. Gardner;
   Second Lieutenant G. F. Garrard;
   Second Lieutenant S. J. Griffin;
   Second Lieutenant G. R. Grosvenor;
   Second Lieutenant G. C. Huggard;
   Second Lieutenant E. B. Parkinson;
   Second Lieutenant W. Rance;
   Second Lieutenant C. H. Riley;
   Second Lieutenant H. E. F. Smyth;
   Second Lieutenant A. H. Truman;
   Second Lieutenant C. I. Widcombe.
 Lieutenant F. C. Staley, 1st/5th Somerset Light Infantry, was employed with the brigade machine guns.

 [5] *Official History*, Vol. II, p. 315. [6] 7th, 8th and 37th Brigades.
 [7] *Official History*, Vol. II, p. 321; and see Map No. 11.

move on independently with his own two columns and the Cavalry Brigade, which was to operate on the left and reconnoitre the Hai. Every precaution had been taken by General Aylmer to ensure secrecy, silence, surprise and complete co-ordination of all three columns[8]; but though the wheels of all the carts had been carefully greased, yet some of them made raucous noises. Occasionally, too, mules broke loose and careered away into the darkness, flinging their loads far and wide, in perverse contempt of the plans of man.[9] However, up to the point of divergence the march was successfully carried out; and here, before advancing further, General Kemball gave orders for most of the transport to remain, so as not to encumber his attack. But so somnolent were the drivers that it was no easy matter to withdraw the unwanted transport from its position in the line of march; and it was not until 3.55 a.m. that General Kemball was able to resume his march. Hardly had "A" Company of the 2nd/43rd accomplished its thankless task when General Kemball was notified by the Corps Staff that the transport was not to halt at the point of divergence after all. Thus was valuable time wasted. Next in the sequence of hitches, Column "A" struck a deep line of trenches which so delayed it that the Dujaila depression was not reached until 5.10 a.m., whence it had to march another three miles before reaching its position of deployment.[10]

At 6 a.m. the Dujaila Redoubt was plainly visible to the 26th Punjabis, who reported that it was unoccupied. When General Christian reported this, General Kemball was sceptical and ordered the 26th Punjabis to be withdrawn. "By 7 a.m. the whole column was under cover in the Dujaila depression and the brigade and battalion commanders were taking their bearings,"[11] while the Turks, alive to the danger and thankful for an undeserved respite, hastily rushed troops into the Dujaila and Sinn Abtar Redoubts and prepared for the set-piece attack.

Meanwhile Column "C" was in its position ready to co-operate as soon as Columns "A" and "B" launched their attacks. Since 6.30 a.m. the enemy redoubts had been clearly visible and obviously unoccupied, but no forward movement was made to capture the position, offered as a gift to anyone advancing, because such movement was not scheduled on the programme. The success of the night march was beyond all hopes, the road to Kut lay bare, and yet the opportunity was not gladly seized. Reconnaissances, bearings, registrations by artillery—all the advertisement possible—were carefully carried out with the inevitable result. The surprise so carefully prepared, the initiative so ably won were jettisoned for the sake of a programme.

When General Kemball's columns eventually attacked at 9.35 a.m., the

[8] *Ibid.*, Vol. II, p. 320.
[9] *Chronicle*, 1915-16, p. 170.
[10] *Official History*, Vol. II, p. 322.
[11] *Ibid.*, Vol. II, p. 324.

Turks were ready for them, and the advancing troops soon met with heavy rifle fire. For an hour and a half the 9th, 28th and 36th Brigades struggled against increasing opposition, while, away on the right, the 37th Brigade reported at 9.50 a.m. that the Dujaila Redoubt was still only lightly held. But still the troops were leashed because Column "B" was not yet near enough to assault the redoubt. So it was that for another four valuable hours the troops of the 3rd Division were held in check and had the mortification of watching the Dujaila Redoubt being reinforced from all points.

Between 2 and 2.15 p.m. General Kemball's force made a gallant attempt to storm the line of trenches south-west of the Dujaila Redoubt, but without success; for during the initial bombardment the guns concentrated on the redoubt instead of on the trenches which were holding up the advance.[12] By this time the troops were nearly exhausted after the long night march and heavy fighting, and had suffered severe casualties. The 3rd Division, meanwhile, was still waiting for the order to attack.[13] Eventually the 8th Brigade, when it was too late, launched a frontal attack at 4.30 p.m. Soon after passing the Dujaila depression the attackers encountered severe cross-fire from north and south, but, advancing steadily, managed to get within assaulting distance; then, in a gallant charge, the 1st Manchester Regiment entered the enemy's trenches. But, deficient of bombs owing to heavy casualties among the carriers, the troops were unable to stem heavy counter-attacks on both flanks, and were driven out of the hard-won redoubt just as dusk was coming on.[14] In co-operation with this attack General Kemball's force made yet another attempt to reach the enemy's trenches but, under accurate artillery, rifle and machine-gun fire and without artillery support, the troops never reached within 1,500 yards of the Turkish line.

As the result of this failure General Aylmer decided to concentrate the whole force and retire to Wadi the next morning. Heavy casualties, shortage of transport for the wounded, danger of being cut off and shortage of water were factors contributing to his decision. The retirement was to start at 5 a.m.

The order to concentrate did not reach General Kemball until 7.50 p.m., at which time his troops were occupying night outposts and collecting the wounded. The 2nd/43rd, which in brigade reserve had watched the whole day's operations from some high ground whence the minaret in Kut could be seen in the distance, had been ordered up to dig an outpost line round Brigade Headquarters at 5 p.m. But on receipt of the order to concentrate the Regiment was withdrawn to Column Headquarters where it found three piquets. The night was mercifully quiet and the search parties were able to bring in all the wounded without further casualties.

[12] *Ibid.*, Vol. II, pp. 335-336. [13] *Ibid.*, Vol. II, p. 338.
[14] *Ibid.*, Vol. II, pp. 340-341.

At 7 a.m. the Regiment moved out to cover the retirement of the 36th Brigade. The Turks showed no signs of attacking, but hordes of Arab horsemen hovered on the rear and left flank like vultures. At 9 a.m. the main body started the retirement, followed at 11.50 by Column "B," while the 3rd Division guarded the northern flank. Meanwhile the Regiment, digging in across a deep nullah to cover the retirement, was subjected to intermittent shell fire which did little damage. But when the Regiment as rear guard began to retire, at about 1 p.m., the shelling increased considerably. By this time all ranks were suffering terribly from lack of water. None had been procurable since leaving Senna for the night march on the 7th, and all efforts to strike water in the nullah bed had been fruitless. However, on the way back the Regiment fell in with the water *packals,* and each man was given a little water inspissated with mud but none the less welcome. Scattered hereabouts was the charred debris of much second-line transport material which had been burnt so as to provide more carts for the carriage of the wounded.

From this point the whole force retired in three columns, and the Regiment was detailed to form the personal escort to General Aylmer. Suffering terribly from thirst, heat and dust, the 2nd/43rd marched continuously throughout the afternoon, and did not reach Wadi Camp until after midnight. Utterly exhausted, all ranks lay down and slept anywhere. The Regiment's casualties in this action were fortunately very light, three men wounded and five missing.[15] But Lieutenant Staley was killed by a chance bullet when with the brigade machine guns.

Thus ended the second attempt to relieve Kut. At one time it promised complete and overwhelming success. There is no doubt but that the Turks were taken unawares, and there is little doubt but that the 3rd Division could have captured the Dujaila Redoubt at 7 a.m. with insignificant loss. But the orders deprived subordinate commanders of the initiative. General Aylmer had his own very good reasons for limiting the powers of his commanders, for he considered that the lack of co-ordination and co-operation between different columns had contributed to the failures in the past. Had General Kemball's columns reached their position of deployment at the scheduled time, the attack could have been launched according to the programme. But these two columns were hampered by the transport which should have been in the rear of the striking force,[16] and the orders allowed no time for any unforeseen hitch in the last stage of the night march. The time lost in sorting the transport at the point of divergence was never made good; and valuable time was wasted by the needless bombardment of the

[15] *Ibid.,* Vol. II, p. 523.
[16] The order for the alteration of the position of the first-line transport in the line of march was actually issued on the 7th, but was not received in time to accomplish it.

unoccupied redoubt early in the morning. Moreover, the bombardment was ineffectual.

Much strong—nay venomous—criticism has been heaped upon the plan and conduct of this attack, and the theory has been propounded that a bold leader could have evaded the Turks and marched straight to Kut instead of " whittling away our reinforced strength in more frontal attacks."[17] War is not an exact science, and in this battle ample proof is provided of the disorganization which can be caused by an apparently small hitch at an early stage in a timed advance and attack. The troops fought with valiant courage and suffered heavily in their gallant attempts. But when it was reported that they had retired " ' through want of water,' there was much irony, blasphemy and derision in the camp."[18] Fourteen thousand casualties had already been incurred in the attempts to relieve nine thousand, but further sacrifices were fain to be made in the hope of relieving the starving garrison in Kut.

This last failure well-nigh caused consternation in India and London, and a scapegoat was hunted. Unsympathetic with his difficulties, the authorities fixed upon General Aylmer and visited upon him the punishment richly deserved by themselves. It is unnecessary to labour the point, and it is best left to individuals to judge for themselves the justice meted out to him. Without trained staffs for his formations, and without adequate transport he was pressed by those behind to go forward and beckoned by those beleaguered to come on. The urgency compelled him to take risks which he would never have taken under normal circumstances, and " our sympathies must go with the soldier whose past service had been so fine and gallant, deprived of his command at such a critical juncture."[19]

On the 11th of March General Aylmer handed over his command to General Gorringe, who had succeeded in the early operations in Arabistan and near Nasiriya. When he took over, the 7th Division was holding the trenches opposite the Hanna position, and the 3rd Division on the right bank occupied an advanced line, Thorny Nala to Twin Canals, with supports on the line of the Senna Canal. Meanwhile, there had reached Basra 12,000 infantry, 26 guns, 2,000 mules and a large number of carts which could not be sent to the front in time for the attack on Dujaila owing to shortage of transport. As usual they had been immobilized when their presence in the crisis of the battle might well have turned the scale in General Aylmer's favour. The critics at home did not realize the magnitude of the impasse. Troops unfed are troops useless. General Lake at Basra was experiencing all the difficulties of his predecessors. The promised craft did not arrive in time; vessels had to be repaired though spare parts were

---

[17] *The Long Road to Baghdad*, p. 146.   [18] *Ibid.*, pp. 156-157.
[19] *Official History*, Vol. II, p. 352.

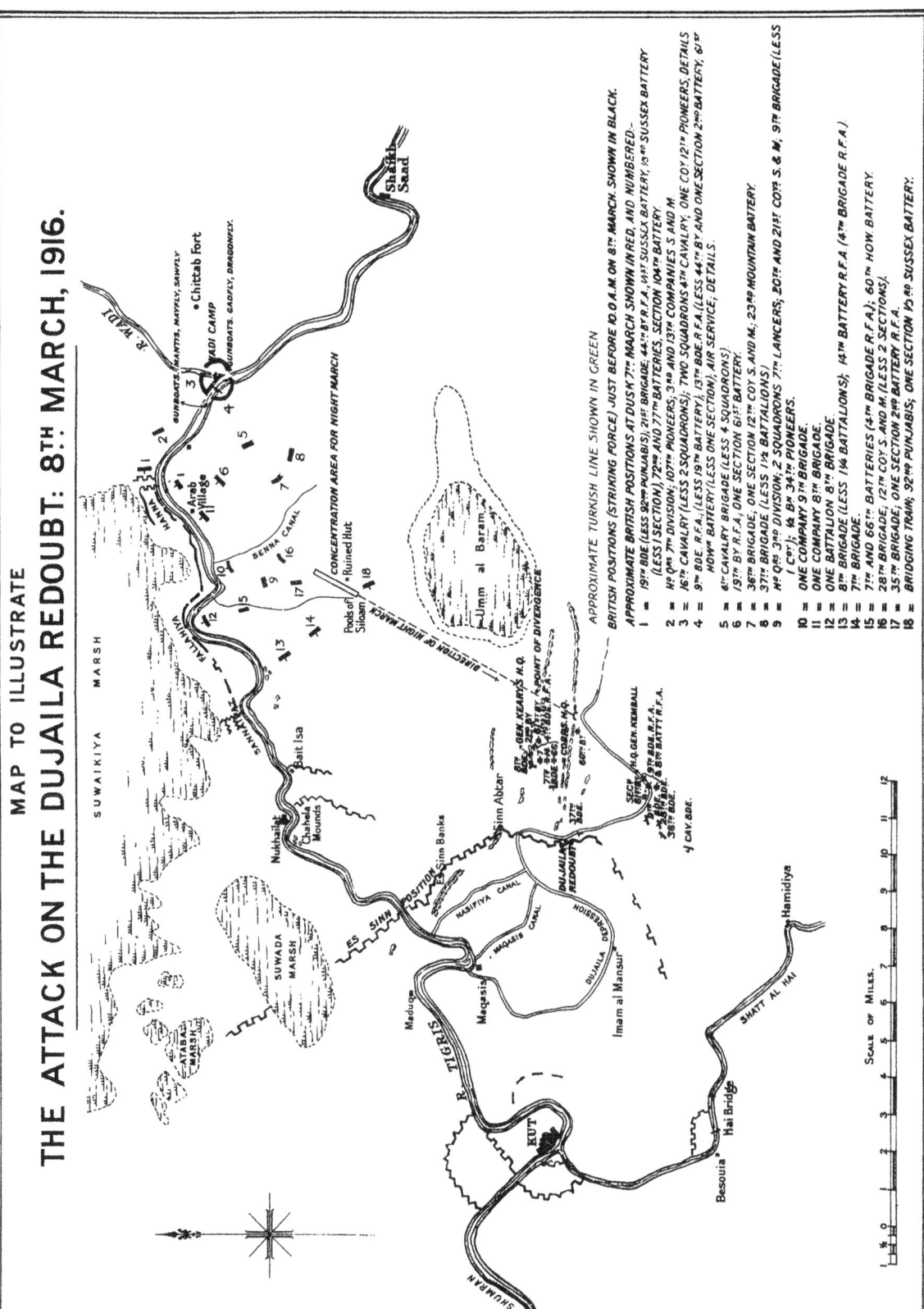

not procurable. On the 11th of March the total available ships were 37 steamers and tugs and 68 barges which were capable of a maximum daily delivery of " 300 tons against a requirement of 468 tons "[20] without allowing for the transport of troops. And though by the 25th of March the number of steamers and tugs had increased to 45 with 79 barges, the increase in craft was still disproportionate to the increase in troops. It was in fact impossible to send reinforcements upstream by river and supply them as well. Therefore the troops had to march as we have seen. But the rain had precluded movement by road for a month past, and General Lake could not hope to concentrate his available force before the floods came.[21] In addition to these transport difficulties, " neither the base nor its facilities were adequate to support the traffic."[22]

General Gorringe's policy on taking over command was to creep forward on both banks, utilizing by means of two bridges a superior force against each enemy position on both banks; and he calculated to be able to start his offensive on the 1st April, by which time the 13th Division would have arrived. By sapping forward on the left bank he proposed to assault the Hanna position and then Sannaiyat before attacking the Es Sinn position.[23]

On the left bank the 7th Division was waging trench warfare. The area covered by the trenches " was deeper than anything on the same line of front in Flanders."[24] Days and nights were spent in sapping forward to within seventy yards of the Turkish wire on a front of 1,200 yards. The result was a system of trenches measuring sixteen miles. The front was held by two brigades with one in reserve in Wadi Camp.

From the 10th to the 13th the 2nd/43rd rested in Wadi Camp. On the 14th the Regiment paraded at 8.30 a.m. and marched up to the front line by platoons to take over from the Norfolk Regiment of the 21st Brigade on the left of the divisional front. The relief was completed by 1 p.m. "A" Company, under Captain Hammick, went into the front line, King's Trench; and "B" Company, under Captain Tatton, into the second line known as Queen's Trench. On the left was the 2nd Leicestershire Regiment, and on the right were the 51st Sikhs. Sniping was heavy and continuous but there was little shell fire. As usual water was a problem in the front line. Water parties had to make a long journey through the line of the Leicestershire Regiment on the left, then down Tigris Street to the fourth line whence water could be drawn direct from the river.

In dealing with the monotonous period of trench warfare which lasted

[20] *Ibid.*, Vol. II, p. 358. This estimate was made by Captain Whittall, then D.A.Q.M.G. (Embarkation).
[21] *Ibid.*, Vol. II, p. 357.
[22] *Ibid.*, Vol. II, p. 359.
[23] *The Long Road to Baghdad*, p. 164.
[24] *Official History*, Vol. II, p. 350.

on the left bank from the 21st January to the 5th April, it must be remembered that when the Regiment went into rest in divisional reserve there were no billets, amusements, canteens and other relaxations as in France for officers and men, who had no relief from stringent war conditions, no periods of short leave, and " often increased discomfort if they fell ill or were wounded."[25]

On the 11th the 3rd Division had been ordered to advance from Thorny Nala and occupy Mason's Mounds and Abu Rumman, but rain on the 12th compelled a postponement. Then on the night of the 14th/15th the floods descended in heavy spate, and, partially inundating the trenches held by the Regiment, successfully prevented any forward sapping. At the same time the terrific weight of water damaged the boat bridge, and floods closed the road from the advanced base at Shaikh Saad and isolated the Turks holding Mason's Mounds. The sudden rise in the river brought the water-level above that of the surrounding country and constant supervision and labour were required to prevent the *bunds* from bursting.[26]

On the 16th the general inspected the trenches, and remarked unfavourably on the effluvium which emanated from sundry Turkish and British corpses lying out in no man's land. To remove the causes of offence, a party was detailed that night under Second Lieutenant de Selincourt to bury the dead within the Regiment's barbed wire. In brilliant moonlight the party set to work, but the officer's tall figure must have been spotted by the enemy who opened fire with a machine gun and severely wounded 21452 Pte. Ruck.[27] Second Lieutenant de Selincourt went back to call for stretcher-bearers, and on returning was himself hit.

On the 17th an inter-company relief took place, " B " relieving " A " in the front line. The day and night were quiet, and the floods subsided sufficiently to allow sapping to be resumed. The following day General Gorringe inspected the trenches and saps; and a heavy thunderstorm that night caused extra discomfort and labour, for the walls of the trenches began to cave in. On the 22nd the Regiment was relieved by the 21st Brigade at 10 a.m., and marched back to Wadi Camp having lost two men, died of wounds, and one officer and one private wounded.

The remainder of the month, spent in rest, was devoted to regimental and brigade training in preparation for the ensuing operations against Hanna. By the 24th the all-British 13th Division (except one battalion) and the 66th Brigade, R.F.A., had reached Shaikh Saad. But the floods were threatening to close the road from Amara to the front; indeed, on the 25th the Tigris rose to such an alarming level that all troops were detailed to

---

[25] *Ibid.*, Vol. II, p. 350.   [26] *Ibid.*, Vol. II, p. 366.
[27] *Chronicle*, 1915-16, p. 172 : War Diary. Private Ruck died of his wounds on the 17th.

strengthen and raise the *bunds* on the river bank to prevent the camp from being completely flooded. However, the Turks were in worse plight, for on the 24th the guns successfully breached the *bunds* built to keep the floods out of the Hanna trenches.

On the 28th Lieutenant Radford and Second Lieutenants Davis and Roberts joined the 2nd/43rd from escorting a disaffected Indian regiment to Bombay.

II.—March in Kut.

The month of March was ushered in with a heavy bombardment of the town of Kut by the Turkish artillery on all sides, but the damage done was surprisingly small. The garrison was now living in hopes of early relief and, as far as it was able, was co-operating with General Aylmer by sending information, etc. The sappers concocted an ingenious mine and floated it down the Hai in the hope of it striking and destroying the bridge of boats which the Turks had built.

By the 8th arrangements had been made for co-operation with the relief force after the attack on the Es Sinn position. A force from the garrison was to cross the river and attack the right flank of the Turks as they retired towards the Hai bridge.

The 1st/43rd, 22nd Punjabis and Sirmur Sappers and Miners were withdrawn from the Fort and Redoubt "A" before daylight, and a small party from an Indian regiment took over Redoubt "B" from "Q" Company. Then the whole Regiment concentrated in Kut and awaited developments. All day the Regiment remained mewed up in an " old stable-yard, in a somewhat restless state, occasionally climbing up to the one safe coign of vantage on a wall from which little could be seen owing to a very thick mirage."[28] All day the guns of the relief force, nearer and more audible than hitherto, rumbled and drummed to the southward. Towards evening the mirage cleared; the artillery fire intensified and the Regiment could see the smoke of the battle. Tidings, reassuring but ambiguous, came through; and the Regiment hoped on, and the night found all ranks still hoping and still ready to play their part. The next morning the bombardment started again to southward but it died away, and left the Regiment, " if not actually gloomy, at any rate more anxious and pensive as the day dragged on."[29] At dusk the Regiment realized its fate when orders were received to return to its old position. Its disappointment was abysmal.

The following day, 10th March, General Townshend again took the garrison into his confidence and issued a *communiqué* :—

" As on a former occasion, I take the troops of all ranks into my confidence again and repeat the two following telegrams received from General

[28] *Ibid.*, 1915-16, p. 111.   [29] *Ibid.*, 1915-16, pp. 111-112.

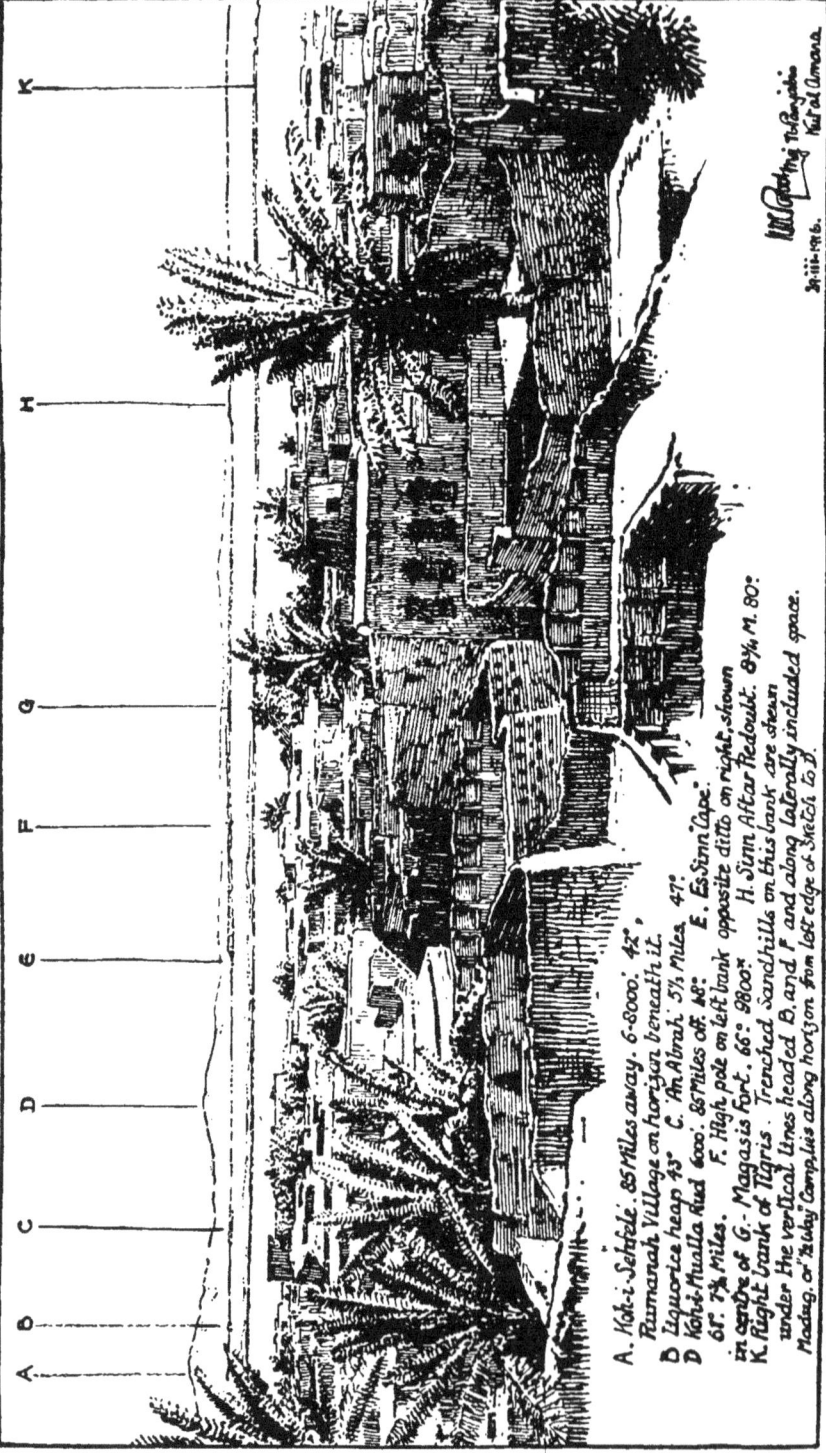

PANORAMA FROM KUT LOOKING TOWARDS ES SINN.

Aylmer from which they will see that our relieving force has again failed to relieve us:—

"*First Telegram, 8th March.*

"'To-day's operations terminated in a gallant but unsuccessful attempt to storm Dujailah Redoubt. Troops pushed home attack and carried out the operation with great gallantry, but the enemy was able to mass reinforcements which arrived from the left bank at Maqasis and Shumran, and we were unable to break through. Unless the enemy retires from his present position on the right bank, which does not seem probable, we shall be unable to maintain ourselves in present position, owing to lack of water; and unless the enemy evacuates the Es Sinn position, we shall be obliged to withdraw to our previous position at Wadi.'

"*Second Telegram, 8th March.*

"'We have been unable to break through to relieve you to-day, and may have to withdraw to Wadi to-morrow, but hope to make another attack before long and relieve you at an early date. Please wire movements of enemy, who, in any case, suffered most severely, as their repeated counter-attacks have been repulsed with heavy loss.'

"I know you will all be deeply disappointed to hear this news. We have now stood a three-months' siege in a manner which has called upon you the praise of our beloved King and our fellow-countrymen in England, Scotland, Ireland and India, and all this after your brilliant battles of Kut al Amara and Ctesiphon, and your retirement to Kut, all of which feats of arms are now famous. Since the 5th December 1915 you have spent three months of cruel uncertainty and to all men and all people uncertainty is intolerable; as I say, on top of all this comes the second failure to relieve us. And I ask you also to give a little sympathy to me who have commanded you in these battles referred to, and who, having come to you as a stranger, now love my command with a depth of feeling I have never known in my life before. When I mention myself, I would couple the names of the Generals under me, whose names are distinguished in the Army as leaders of men.

"I am speaking to you, as I did before, straight from my heart, and, as I say, ask your sympathy for *my* feelings, having promised you relief on certain dates on the promise of those ordered to relieve us—not their fault no doubt—do not think that I blame them—they are giving their lives freely and deserve our gratitude and admiration.

"But I want you to help me again as before. I have asked General Aylmer for the next attempt, which must be made before the end of this month, to bring such numbers as will break down all resistance and leave no doubt of the issue. Large reinforcements are reaching him, including an

English division of 17,000 men, the leading brigade of which must have reached Wadi by now—that is to say, General Aylmer's headquarters. In order, then, to hold out, I am killing a large number of horses so as to reduce the quantity of grain eaten each day, and I have had to reduce your ration. It is necessary to do this in order to keep our flag flying—I am determined to hold out, and I know you are with me in this, heart and soul.

"CHARLES TOWNSHEND,
"*Major-General Commanding, 6th Division.*
"KUT AL AMARA,
"*10th March*, 1916."

As the result of the failure at Dujaila, " each British officer and soldier now received a small loaf of about ten ounces weight per diem, the bread being composed of a mixture of wheat and barley—very coarse and very heavy. The Indian troops were given an equivalent of flour and made their own *chupatties* as usual."[30] The issue of dates and the ration of jam and butter ceased altogether, but one pound of horseflesh was still issued to those who would eat it. Those Indians who refused it were " now mere bags of skin and bone " and were a gruesome sight.

On the 18th the allowance of bread was reduced to eight ounces and further reduced to five on the 20th so as to allow of the garrison holding out till the 17th April. Tea had given out early in the month, and by the 29th, when the rations were reduced to four ounces of bread and one and a quarter pounds of horseflesh, dried ginger was being boiled and used as a substitute for tea. Tobacco of any sort was, of course, unobtainable, and dried leaves of apricot trees became the favourite substitute."[31]

Meanwhile, on the 12th, the Turks for the second time sent over a flag of truce proposing that the garrison should surrender now that honour was satisfied. This was refused by General Townshend in firm phrases.

The 22nd brought another heavy bombardment of Kut and its defences, and when an Arab rumour was bruited abroad that the Turks intended to assault, the whole garrison was ordered to stand to arms; but nothing unusual occurred.

From the 23rd onwards the flood problem commanded all attention. For three days heavy rainstorms combined with the river spate threatened to flood Redoubt " B." Constant back-breaking labour was necessary to bale out the water, which reached the fire-step in the redoubt; and even then, owing to the lie of the land, much of the water dribbled back into the trenches. " Q " Company, in Redoubt " B," worked ceaselessly trying to keep the position dry and habitable, but the echelon trenches on each flank had to be evacuated. Eventually Lieutenant Heawood managed to

[30] *In Kut and Captivity*, pp. 209-210.   [31] *Chronicle*, 1915-16, p. 145.

borrow a pump from the sappers; he then drained the trenches by sections, filled them up and then redug them. On the 26th the flood crept across the peninsula from the west, and a party had to be ready at any moment " to block up a trench wherever an inrush of water seemed imminent." As the water had the habit of percolating through the porous soil and also through rat-holes, an inundation had to be expected anywhere. The flood advanced steadily at the rate of about one yard per hour on so vast a front that any attempt to check it was impossible. Suddenly from the least expected quarter the flood burst in and swamped the redoubt completely. Lieutenant Heawood forthwith withdrew "Q" Company to the Middle Line, and subsequently occupied a piece of the line between Redoubts "B" and "A," as well as part of the Retrenchment.

The floods showed no signs of abatement, and by the end of the month all hope of saving the advanced trenches was abandoned. "Q" Company was therefore detailed to hold the sandhills between the Fort and Middle Line. Here this company entrenched in the friable soil with great difficulty, making mud bricks by day wherewith to revet the trenches by night.

The Middle Line now became the main line of resistance, with the two forward positions in the Fort and sandhills in advanced isolation. Eventually "Q" Company managed to make a passable fortification with barbed wire protection, and from its position above the floods was able, to its unbounded satisfaction, to watch the discomfiture of the enemy from the rising waters.

Meanwhile "P," "R" and "S" Companies in the Fort were faced with the same problem of how to stem the rising floods. The inner keep was by now proof against the floods but required much work on the parados and loop-holes. This kept the three companies busy in the morning and afternoon. The trench was also revetted with mud bricks, each man's task being 250 bricks per day. But as the rations were reduced so the task became impossible of completion, and the number of bricks was reduced until no man had the strength to make more than ten.[32]

It was an uncomfortable period to say the least of it. Soaked from above by torrential downpours, paddling about in slush, mud and water up to and over their ankles, without dry quarters to sleep in, the men of the Regiment worked by day and night under ceaseless sniping fire until bodily exhaustion and empty stomachs reduced them almost to impotence. Not only was there endless work in the Fort itself, but also men were required to patrol and repair the *bunds* on the river bank when high winds and rough water threatened to erode the banks. " Water began to percolate through into the river communication trench; and as this had to be filled in gradually to give

[32] *Ibid*, p. 131.

a comparatively dry footing it soon ceased to be a trench."[33] The lack of food was by now so definitely reducing the vitality of all, that eventually " three or four hours' work by day and two to three at night was fixed as the maximum " for the Regiment in the Fort, " but in the last fortnight of the siege the night work was reduced to one hour."[34] Lieutenant Naylor describes in his diary a day's food in the officers' mess at this time. It only differed from the men's in the method of cooking and in the addition of a cup of tea or coffee and sometimes a very little rice. " The ration of bread was eight ounces. Each officer had his own small loaf which was divided in the morning into four equal parts. Breakfast consisted of a quarter of the bread, a small piece of horse meat usually fried as a steak, and a cup of tea. Lunch: the same as breakfast except for the tea. About once every ten days the quartermaster gave us a tin of bully beef from a small store he had, and this was a welcome addition to the midday meal. Tea: another quarter of the bread ration and a cup of tea. Dinner: horse soup, meat, perhaps a minute quantity of potato meal, some green stuff,[35] a small savoury, a cup of tea, and the last of the bread. The whole day's food would not have made one decent meal. The doctor, Captain Startin, ran the messing and always included a savoury in the dinner. Very often it was less than one inch square, and more often than not consisted of a small piece of horse cooked differently from the main dish; but still he continued to include it in the menu even up to the very last just for the sake of appearances. . . In the summer the mess had bought some cows so that we could always have fresh milk. These were with us in Kut [jealously guarded and cared for by Captain Morland], and we were lucky enough to have a bottle of milk in the mess every day. This was usually more than we required and often we were able to exchange a little for some rice or *atta*. Sometimes therefore we could have a little so-called pudding for dinner though the quantity was very minute."

By the end of the month the stench of the decomposing Turkish dead in front of the Fort was so overwhelming, so revolting and noisome that efforts were made to remove the cause. Every night for a week a fatigue party went out and dragged the mangled remains of the enemy into the ditch which skirted the walls. Having lain exposed for three months the bodies disintegrated as soon as they were touched, and it was therefore not an easy task. Altogether the parties buried ninety-seven Turks on a front of about one hundred yards. The result was a comparative purification of the air and was well worth the unpleasant labour.

[33] Lieutenant Naylor's diary.   [34] *In Kut and Captivity*, p. 218.
[35] This was a weed picked at night. Later it was forbidden on account of the difficulty of distinguishing at night between esculent weeds and others of strongly cathartic properties.

CHAPTER XX.

I.—SECOND ATTACK ON HANNA.[1]

STRENGTH OF 43RD—FIRST ATTACK ON SANNAIYAT, 6TH APRIL—2ND/43RD WIPED OUT—ITS CASUALTIES—SECOND ATTACK ON SANNAIYAT—CAPTURE OF BAIT ISA—TURKISH COUNTER-ATTACK—FLOODS—THIRD ATTACK ON SANNAIYAT FAILS—*Julnar* ATTEMPTS TO RUN THE BLOCKADE—LAST DAYS IN KUT—NEGOTIATIONS FOR SURRENDER—THE 43RD MARCHES TO SHUMRAN—CASUALTIES DURING THE SIEGE—HONOURS AND AWARDS.

(*See Maps facing page 216, and on pages 206 and 218.*)

IT will be remembered that General Gorringe, on taking over command of the Tigris Corps, had calculated that he would be able to resume the offensive on the 1st April[2]; but he was compelled to postpone operations until the 4th by which time three aeroplanes, of which he was badly in need, would have arrived.[3] The Tigris Corps now had an available strength of 30,000 rifles and 127 guns, but it might have been considerably stronger had not the shortage of transport prevented the concentration of 32 guns, 350 sabres, 2,600 rifles, 1,400 carts and 900 pack mules, which were immobilized downstream owing to heavy rain and floods. Once again bad weather and inadequate transport prevented the concentration of the maximum strength at the decisive point.[4] Opposing him, General Gorringe estimated that the enemy forces amounted to 30,500 infantry and 88 guns, which proved to be an over-estimation.[5]

In his operation orders General Gorringe detailed the newly arrived 13th Division, supported by the 7th Division, to attack the Hanna position without a previous bombardment, while the 3rd Division on the right bank was to contain the enemy.[5] From the night of the 31st March/1st April onwards the 13th Division took over the trenches in front of Hanna, having marched up through mud and floods from Shaikh Saad.[6]

The 2nd/43rd, meanwhile, practised attacks as part of the 28th Brigade, and furnished fatigue parties to clean up the reserve trenches. The floods at this time were very serious, delaying not only the arrival of ships with stores of every kind but also their unloading owing to the fact that they could not berth near dry land.

---

[1] See Map No. 12, p. 206.
[2] p. 183.
[3] *Official History*, Vol. II, p. 369.
[4] *Ibid.*, Vol. II, p. 371.
[5] *Ibid.*, Vol. II, p. 373.
[6] *Ibid.*, Vol. II, p. 370.

On the 4th April the orders for the assault on the Hanna position were received.[7] The day was spent in loading up the *mahailas* with heavy kits; and Captain Foljambe assigned a goodly supply for the officers and men of the 1st/43rd in case the operations were successful.

As Major Carter had orders to take only one officer per forty men—exclusive of regimental staff—into action, there was much heart-burning among the subalterns who were detailed as first reinforcements. The ten officers, however, to be left out of action were easily selected from among those who were sick. Captain Foljambe should have been included, for he was suffering from an acute attack of dysentery; but he refused to be left out of action, being determined to see the 2nd/43rd through its ordeal.

At 8.30 p.m. the 2nd/43rd marched out of camp to take up its position in brigade reserve in H.L.I. Trench. The strength going into action was 266 non-commissioned officers and men, with the following officers:—

Major L. J. Carter, commanding.
Captain Hon. J. C. W. S. Foljambe, adjutant.
Lieutenant A. H. Seymour (2nd/4th Duke of Cornwall's Light Infantry), machine-gun officer.
Second Lieutenant A. H. Truman, bombing officer.
Lieutenant Anderson (R.A.M.C.), medical officer.
Captain S. F. Hammick, commanding " A " Company.
Captain R. H. G. Tatton, commanding " B " Company.
Lieutenant D. G. Firth (1st/5th Hampshire Regiment).
Lieutenant E. C. Kinghorn (2nd/4th Border Regiment).
Lieutenant H. D. H. Radford.
Second Lieutenant C. I. Widcombe.
Second Lieutenant E. F. Coulthard.
Second Lieutenant A. H. Davis.
Second Lieutenant A. E. Gardner.

Four officers—Second Lieutenants Parkinson, Davenport, Grosvenor and Griffin—were detailed to the second-line transport; Lieutenant Meade was with the first line; and Major Barrington and Second Lieutenants Smyth, Roberts and Wilson (4th Somerset Light Infantry) were with the third-line *mahailas*.

Second Lieutenants C. H. Riley and H. T. C. Field were attached to the 2nd Leicestershire Regiment and 28th Brigade respectively as bombing officers; and Second Lieutenant W. Rance was detailed as orderly officer to Major-General Kemball, commanding the 28th Brigade.[8]

At 4.55 a.m. the 13th Division attacked the Hanna position and quickly captured the first and second lines with trifling loss. Further progress, how-

---

[7,8] *Chronicle*, 1915-16, pp. 173-174.

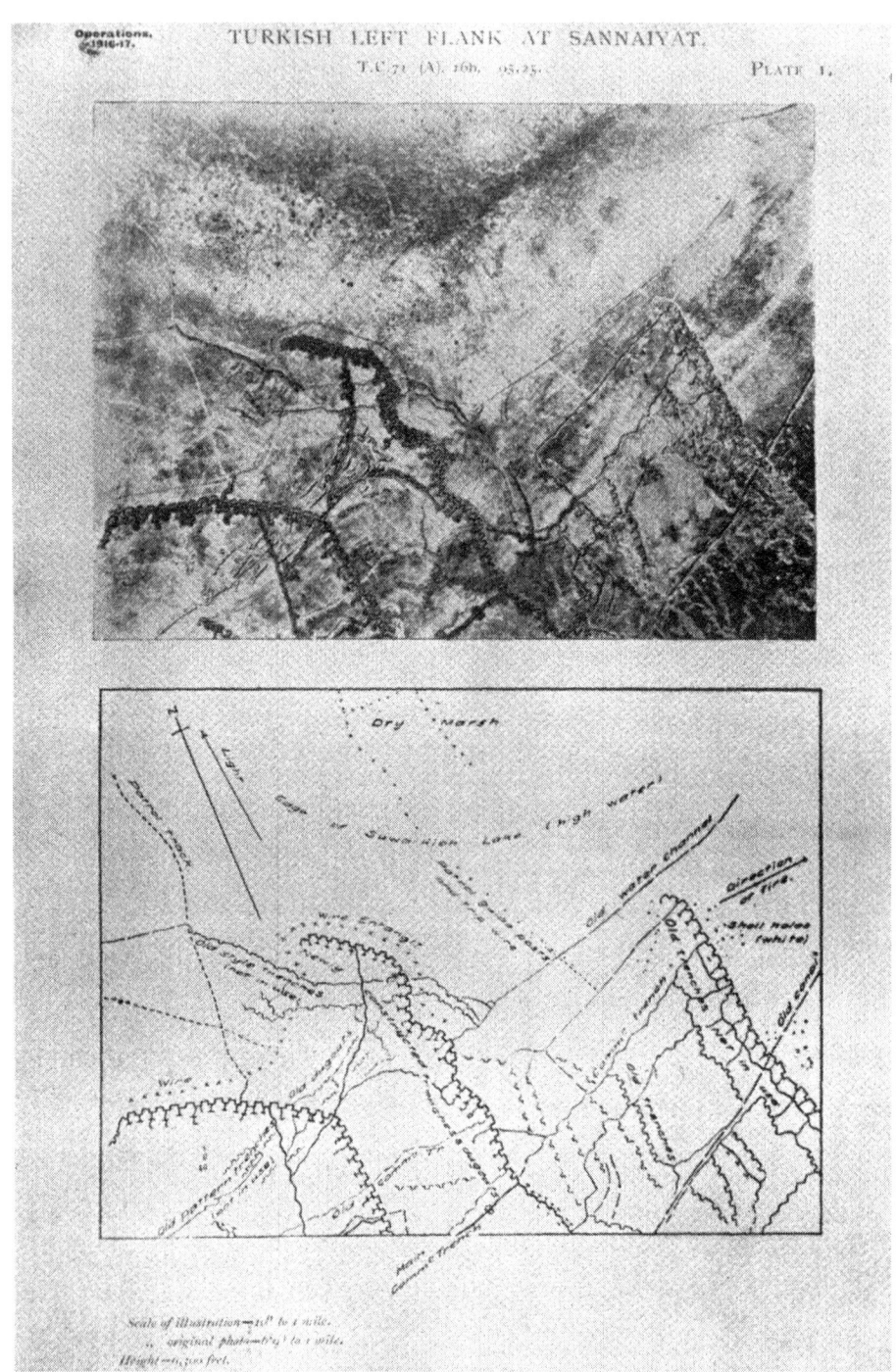

AEROPLANE PHOTOGRAPH AND KEY MAP OF THE TURKISH POSITION AT SANNAIYAT,
showing the enemy's left flank which the 43rd was ordered to attack.

ever, was delayed by the bombardment of the third line by our guns, which did not lift their fire until 5.35 a.m. A few minutes later the third line was found empty, the Turks having effected a masterly withdrawal during the night in the nick of time. At 7.30 a.m. Major-General Stanley Maude, commanding the 13th Division, sent forward his 40th Brigade to occupy a line between the Tigris and Suwaikiya marsh, about two thousand yards from the enemy's position at Fallahiya. This advance, meeting with stubborn resistance, was held up. Three hours later the 38th and 39th Brigades were ordered forward on each flank of the 40th Brigade, but they were held up about three hundred yards short of the 40th Brigade and forced to dig in.[9] On hearing of this check, General Gorringe ordered General Maude to attack at nightfall.

Meanwhile the 3rd Division on the right bank made progress and occupied the whole of the Abu Rumman position, whence it was possible to bring enfilade fire on the Sannaiyat, and reverse fire on the Fallahiya, positions.[10] At 7.35 p.m. the 13th Division began its attack on the left bank, supported by all the artillery in the Corps. In a fine advance against stubborn opposition the 38th and 39th Brigades captured the Fallahiya position soon after 8.15 p.m., but at severe cost.[11] Soon after capture the 21st Brigade of the 7th Division took over the line from the 13th Division, which withdrew to bivouacs in rear. The relief, however, was not completed until after midnight.

II.—First and Second Attacks on Sannaiyat.[12]

During the day air reconnaissances reported that, owing to the recession of the Suwaikiya marsh, the Turkish left at Sannaiyat was not entrenched. These tidings suggested that the line might be successfully turned. The distance from Fallahiya to Sannaiyat according to the sketch maps was about two and three-quarter miles, but, " as the main communication trench from Fallahiya alongside a flood embankment led directly into the Sannaiyat position," the likelihood of losing direction was considered negligible, and General Gorringe ordered the 7th Division to make a night march and turn the Turkish left flank.

At 7.30 p.m. General Younghusband issued his orders for an attack at 4.55 a.m. on the 6th. Having been prevented from making a reconnaissance by the night attack on Fallahiya, he ordered his troops to advance with their left on the main communication trench. The 19th and 28th Brigades were to assemble two miles east of Fallahiya and advance in line at 1.15 a.m., the 19th being on the directing flank—that is to say, the left.

[9] *Official History*, Vol. II, pp. 375-376.   [10] *Ibid.*, Vol. II, p. 377.
[11] The casualties in the 13th Division amounted to 1,868.
[12] See Map No. 12.

The Regiment paraded in ample time, and the two brigades arrived punctually at the position of assembly. But from the very outset hitches occurred and misfortune dogged the project's footsteps. Such delay and confusion first occurred at the assembly point, owing to the withdrawal of the 13th Division and the wounded down the line of advance, that the 19th and 28th Brigades did not move off until 2 a.m. The night was pitch-dark.

General Kemball ordered both brigades to advance in fours, as he considered it impossible to move as ordered. At last the troops moved forward; but still further delay was caused by parties of the 13th Division marching back or bivouacked in nullahs across the line of advance. On reaching the Fallahiya line there was yet another disastrous delay when the two brigades lost their way in the maze of captured trenches and had to counter-march. By the time the brigades were clear of the Fallahiya line so much time had been lost that General Kemball told the 7th Division staff officer accompanying the column that in his opinion it would be impossible to attack before dawn; and he suggested that General Younghusband should come forward and give a decision. General Kemball was in favour of advancing under cover of darkness and entrenching before dawn.

About 4 a.m. a platoon of the Highland Battalion, composed of the remnants of the 73rd and 72nd Highlanders, of the 19th Brigade, encountered an enemy piquet which promptly withdrew. At 4.45 a.m.—that is to say, ten minutes before zero hour as ordered—the guides of the 19th Brigade on the left calculated that two miles[13] had been covered since leaving Fallahiya; and consequently both brigades were ordered to deploy into lines of platoon columns. The 28th Brigade formed in three lines: the 51st Sikhs on the left and the 2nd/43rd on the right in the front line; the 2nd Leicestershire Regiment in the second line; and the 53rd Sikhs and 56th Rifles in the third.[14]

At this point the 19th Brigade halted to make a wider deployment. The 28th Brigade, however, continued its advance. When trying to close the lost distance orders were received to deploy into attack formation.

As the first streak of dawn tinged the sky of the anniversary of the storming of Badajoz, the regimental descendants of those valiant stormers deployed into attack formation to storm a line of trenches well concealed and commanding a vast expanse of open, flat country without a vestige of natural cover. Unlike their ancestors, the officers and men were not veterans of three years' experience. Many of them were young soldiers, as young in

---

[13] It has been seen that the original estimate of the distance between Fallahiya and Sannaiyat was $2\frac{3}{4}$ miles. Actually an air reconnaissance on the 5th proved this distance to be a mile longer, namely $3\frac{3}{4}$ miles. Therefore, at this point, there was still over 3,000 yards to cover instead of about 1,300 as calculated.

[14] *Official History*, Vol. II, p. 381.

the matter of arms as they were in years; but there was a leaven of those fine men, the pre-war non-commissioned officers. Yet the spirit of all ranks was the same as of old. Probably few had been soldiers long enough to know intimately the history of the Regiment they were serving. We know that Lieutenant-Colonel Charles Macleod, before leading the 43rd to the breach at Badajoz, " long and earnestly addressed his men, expressing entire confidence in the result of the attack, and concluded by impressing that he trusted to the honour of all listening to preserve discipline."[15] Whether Major Carter on the eve of Sannaiyat also earnestly impressed on the 2nd/43rd the need of discipline we do not know; but we do know that he impressed on all ranks the vital importance of silence, quickness and dash, those qualities which go to the making of true light infantry. As the 43rd at Badajoz obeyed the gallant Charles Macleod to the death, so did the 2nd/43rd obey the gallant Lindsay James Carter one hundred and four years later.

It was well past 5 a.m., and the 2nd/43rd was still in column, when General Younghusband reached the front to see for himself. General Kemball hazarded the opinion that the Turkish trenches were over a mile distant, when the actual distance was over three thousand yards. General Younghusband, on the contrary, believed them to be less than a mile away. In spite of the hour—thirty-five minutes after the scheduled zero hour for the attack —in spite of the imminence of dawn, of the uncertainty of the distance yet to be covered and of the exact position of the enemy's trenches, General Younghusband ordered General Kemball to assault. The die was cast and two brigades marched to their foregone destruction.

In the dawning light the 13 officers and 266 men[16] of the Regiment advanced quickly on the extreme right of the attacking line. The Regiment was still over a mile from the Turkish trenches and still pressing forward, giving the lead the Regiment has always given in a forlorn hope: for forlorn hope it was to expect even British troops, and light infantry at that, to cross over a mile of open country in broad daylight and assault frontally a line of strong trenches defended by a stout enemy armed with modern weapons.

In this impetuous advance the leading lines of the 2nd/43rd and 51st Sikhs—on the Regiment's left—so outstripped the 19th Brigade that General Kemball was fain to call a halt to allow the 19th Brigade to close the four hundred yards' distance. Thus again were valuable minutes lost—minutes which might have been spent in covering a few of the intervening hundreds of yards before dawn disclosed the vanity of the enterprise.

[15] Levinge's *Historical Records of the 43rd Regiment*, p. 161.
[16] See Appendix IX.

By 5.30 a.m. the 19th Brigade had come up on the left, and both brigades advanced together. Still the enemy trenches could not be seen. But on the right the Regiment could see that the open passage between the Turkish left and the marsh did not exist; for the marsh, driven southward by the strong north wind, had closed the vital gap on the enemy's left flank. The gods again had come to the aid of our enemies and in the nick of time had conjured a defence more formidable than any of which the Turks were capable. The incursion by the Suwaikiya marsh had also contracted the front of the attackers, who were now cramped on a front of about 350 or 400 yards.

All night the Turkish listening posts and observers with telephones had lain out in front, passing back information of the advance of the luckless troops. From before dawn the enemy had stood to arms awaiting our brave folly. They held their fire until the 28th Brigade was within 700 yards, and then at about 5.35 a.m. " poured in one solid sheet of lead,"[17] closely followed by concentrated gun fire from both banks. Though bewildered and staggering under this withering hail of fire, the Regiment, true to its tradition, did not falter; with only their rifles and bayonets and their own strength of heart and will to rely on, without that covering fire from artillery and machine guns which previous experience had proved vitally necessary in the storming of entrenched positions, the officers and men of the 2nd/43rd pressed on towards the unseen enemy amid the din of cracking bullets and the crash of bursting shells, the while gallant men continually crumpled up with sickening grunts under the impact of solid lead.

The official historian has paid a generous tribute to the gallantry of the Regiment in this forlorn hope: " The enemy trenches could still not be discerned, but the gallant 28th Brigade dashed forward in a desperate attempt to carry out their orders. . . . On this same date, one hundred and four years previously, at Badajoz, the Oxfords—then the 43rd and 52nd Regiments of Light Infantry—had covered themselves with glory by their stern endurance of extraordinarily heavy casualties; and their successors now displayed no less unyielding fortitude."[18] Brave and chivalrous words.

For two hundred pitiless yards the indomitable officers and men of the 2nd/43rd and 51st Sikhs struggled against what the official eye-witness called a " torrent of death."[19] When within five hundred yards of the enemy's position, now faintly discernible, the Regiment halted in lines, the impetus of its attack crushed by sheer weight of lead and steel. There was no retaliatory fire from these lines: they showed no signs of scratching holes in the featureless plain; their strength was now spent and they could

[17] *The Long Road to Baghdad*, pp. 179-180.
[18] *Official History*, Vol. II, p. 381.
[19] *The Long Road to Baghdad*, pp. 179-180.

do no more; there were but one officer—Lieutenant Kinghorn—and a mere handful of men still able to use their weapons. It was as if the angel of death had blasted the Regiment to annihilation with one thrash of his pinioned wings.

The leading lines of the 28th Brigade being ahead of the 19th Brigade on the left attracted the concentrated fury of the enemy fire. Captain Foljambe was shot through the head; Captain Hammick was hit through the chest and arm; and Captain Tatton through both hands and one leg in the first burst of fire. Of the subalterns, Second Lieutenants Widcombe, Davis, Coulthard and Truman[20] were killed. Soon afterwards Major Carter, Lieutenant Firth and Second Lieutenant Gardner were wounded. The heavy casualties were not confined to the leading lines: Major-General Kemball and all his staff were wounded, including Second Lieutenant Field of the Regiment.[21] But although unsupported by artillery fire the remnant of the Regiment hung on between five and six hundred yards from the enemy's trenches. Indeed, the hail of death prevented any movement either forward or back.[22] The same eye-witness, Edmund Candler, who was watching this amazing example of courage, has recorded that:

" A staff officer handed me his glasses.

" ' Do you see that line of khaki,' he asked, ' about five hundred yards from the enemy ? '

" ' Yes. Why haven't they dug themselves in ? '

" He explained that they were our dead."[23]

On the left the 19th Brigade had also been held up by the Turkish fire, but having been outstripped in the advance by the 28th Brigade the leading lines were echeloned in rear of the 28th Brigade at a distance of about eleven hundred yards from the enemy. General Kemball, though wounded, was still at duty; and, realizing the futility of trying to advance farther in the face of such devastating fire, ordered his third line, the 53rd Sikhs and 56th Rifles, to halt and dig in. The 19th Brigade followed suit. Not until it was light was the 9th Brigade, R.F.A., able to move forward into action; but when the artillery on both banks was able to open fire the enemy's attention was slightly diverted from the exposed lines of troops.

---

[20] These four officers were buried the night after the battle by Second Lieutenant Rance, who records that each of them was hit several times.

[21] *Chronicle*, 1915-16, p. 175, and Appendix IX. Second Lieutenant Field was hit in the mouth by a bullet which passed out through his neck and shoulder without shattering anything vital.

[22] Sir Arnold Wilson writes in *Loyalties*: " Napier has recounted in deathless prose the heroism that marked the conduct of those regiments on that occasion [the 43rd and 52nd at Badajoz]; a pen no less brilliant is needed to do justice to those who maintained on the banks of the Tigris the reputation of their forbears."

[23] *The Long Road to Baghdad*, p. 180.

Meanwhile General Gorringe ordered General Younghusband to arrange for a night attack by the 28th Brigade supported by the 40th Brigade of the 13th Division.

As if it were not enough that the wounded and dying could not be succoured in the tornado of lead, the gods again intervened against them; for the waters of the Suwaikiya marsh, driven by the fury of the north-west wind, began to flood the advanced trenches scratched by the survivors, inundating the plain and threatening with yet another type of doom those, the hale and the helpless, who hitherto by sheer luck had escaped annihilation. The Regiment was forced to evacuate the ground won at such shattering cost, leaving many seriously wounded men to die by drowning or suffocation in the mud, while the troops in the rear had to protect themselves from fire and water simultaneously. The guns were soon surrounded by water and were only kept dry by *bunds* hastily built round them.

This sudden incursion on the north flank, together with a threatened flood from the Tigris to southward, called for the efforts of all survivors; and therefore General Gorringe was compelled to cancel his orders for the night attack.[24]

Lieutenant E. C. Kinghorn brought back the remnants of the Regiment, numbering seventeen, into divisional reserve. The surviving officer had been saved from almost certain death by his belt buckle; for a bullet which hit it was so deflected that it travelled round his body and passed out through the back of his jacket. Of the sixteen officers of the 2nd/43rd who went into this First Battle of Sannaiyat, five were killed, Captain Hammick died of his wounds, and six were wounded. Lieutenants Kinghorn, Seymour[25] and Radford,[26] and Second Lieutenant Rance[27] escaped. Of the 266 non-commissioned officers and men who went into action, 51 were killed, 170 wounded and 14 missing—a total of 235, or 88 per cent. Of the fourteen missing, eleven were officially reported killed in the War Office list of casualties issued after the war; of the wounded, ten at least died of their wounds and probably more.[28] At Badajoz on the 6th April 1812 the 43rd lost 20 officers and 335 serjeants and men, but we do not know what the strength of the Regiment was on going into action. The percentage of casualties was probably slightly less.

After being wounded Major Carter received from the brigade commander the following message, written on a sheet of a field service message book:—

[24] *Official History*, Vol. II, pp. 382-383.   [25] Machine-gun officer.
[26] Was at headquarters delivering a message.
[27] Orderly officer to brigade commander.
[28] *Official History*, Vol. II, p. 382, gives the casualties as " all the officers and 220 other ranks . . . either killed or wounded." The statistics, as far as I am able, are fully presented in Appendix IX.

" *To* O.C. Provisional Battalion, Oxford and Bucks L.I.
" On the Field, Sannaiyat.
" *6th April,* 1916.

" I regret that, owing to a wound in the ankle, I am unable to visit the firing line, and thank you all for the gallantry and tenacity you displayed this morning. I am afraid it has been at very heavy cost, but I should like to place on record that you have done credit to the fine Regiment which many of you have not yet joined. I saw the attack of the 1st Oxford and Bucks Light Infantry at Ctesiphon, and I should like that Battalion to know that you are worthy to join them. With best wishes to you all for the speedy relief of Kut, I must bid you farewell.

" G. V. Kemball, *Major-General.*"

At 7.40 p.m. the British artillery on both banks bombarded the Sannaiyat position to cover an advance by the 3rd Division on the right bank. When the bombardment ceased there was little firing, and the night was spent in collecting the wounded under cover of patrols.

The *communiqué* which appeared in *The Times* of the 8th April was as follows: " During the 6th April and the night of April 6/7 operations on the north (left) bank of the river were confined to close reconnaissance of the Sanna-i-Yat defences, and the execution of the necessary measures, movements of artillery preparatory to the assault of this latter position." Three days later on the 11th April another *communiqué* gave this information: " No attack on the Sanna-i-Yat position was made on April 6th, as reported in the Turkish *communiqué* of the 10th."

So ended the First Battle of Sannaiyat. For conspicuous services the commanding officer of the 2nd/43rd, Major Lindsay James Carter, was awarded the *Distinguished Service Order,* Captains Hammick and Foljambe were mentioned in despatches, and the only man of the Regiment recommended for gallantry, Private Golding, a stretcher-bearer, received the *Distinguished Conduct Medal.* Of other distinctions there are no records. The reward of those who survived and those who died must therefore come from succeeding generations of their Regiment, who by remembering their deeds of tenacity and sacrifice in a forlorn hope for all time can give them a memorial more lasting than any decoration or distinction. With the storming of Badajoz the storming of Sannaiyat should be linked, despite the fact that the one contributed towards a success and the other a failure. There is no official battle honour[29] for Sannaiyat: platoons of recruits at the Depot are not named " Sannaiyat " in due succession; yet it is hard to find such

[29] A claim for the battle honour " Tigris 1916 " to include " Sannaiyat " was preferred in 1935 to the Battle Honours Committee.

another example of indomitable courage in the face of almost certain death throughout the history of the 43rd. May the remembrance of it never fade.

The following morning at 9.15 a.m. the three brigades of the 7th Division were ordered to advance again across the bullet-swept plain, and entrench a starting-line for a night attack by the 13th Division. There was no decrease in the valiant courage of the advancing troops, though bidden to do what had been proved impossible the day before. It was the same story—a story of sickening waste of life. Gallant men were fed to Moloch in broad daylight as if they were fuel for a blast furnace. They managed only to move forward some three hundred yards before the enemy's guns, machine guns and rifles by sheer weight of lead forced the survivors to lie down where no reinforcements could reach them.

It was now arranged that a second assault on the Sannaiyat position should be made at dawn on the 9th. On the night of the 7th/8th the three brigades advanced more successfully, and dug a new line between five and six hundred yards from the enemy. After dark on the 8th the 13th Division took over the new line, and at 4 a.m. advanced to the assault. On reaching a line some three hundred yards from the enemy, the Turks, evidently fully alert, sent up Very lights and opened a heavy fire. Yet the first line pushed on and managed to assault and capture a portion of the position, but, unsupported, was unable to hold its ground. The supports, disorganized by the first bursts of fire, hesitated and fell back, and something very near to a panic seems to have ensued. Before the officers could rally their men, those of the front line who had effected a footing in the Turkish trenches were overpowered and very few of them emerged alive. Eventually a line was dug about four hundred yards short of the enemy trenches.[30]

On the morning of the 7th Major Barrington went up from the third-line transport to take over command of the Regiment. On his way he collected all the officers and as many men as could be spared from the second-line transport. This party found the Regiment in hastily dug trenches in the fourth line. It consisted of Lieutenant Kinghorn, in command, and Lieutenants Seymour and Radford with about thirty men, including machine gunners. Here the Regiment remained during the night, and sent out all available men in search of wounded. The medical officer, Lieutenant Anderson, spent hours out in front doing all he could to ease the wounded, many of whom had been caught by the flood waters of the marsh. Incidentally, many helpless wounded must have been drowned.

From the Regiment's position the front line was plainly visible, and beyond it a long row of green canvas bomb buckets marking the lines of dead. The following day, the 8th, Major Barrington sent back the super-

---

[30] *Official History*, Vol. II, pp. 384-391.

numerary officers, Second Lieutenants Parkinson, Davenport, Grosvenor and Griffin, to the second-line transport; and retained Lieutenants Meade, Seymour and Radford only, as the strength of the Regiment, now about sixty all told, required no more officers. On the 9th Lieutenant Meade was hit in the shoulder by a shrapnel bullet and Private Sturge was also wounded. The Regiment spent the day digging and improving trenches. That night the 7th Division took over the front line from the 13th Division, and the Regiment occupied trenches in the third line in brigade reserve.

As the result of the failure of this third attempt to relieve Kut, the situation was very serious, and General Lake asked General Townshend to try to extend the time limit. General Townshend consented to cut down the rations still further so as to hold out until the 29th, provided food were dropped by aeroplanes. This allowed General Lake another three weeks' grace, and he ordered General Gorringe to plan an attack on the right bank, as it was obvious that a forward move on the left bank would involve lengthy sapping operations.

The weather at this time was becoming very hot in the day-time. The glare of the sunlight in, and the dust outside, the flooded areas were very trying to the Regiment, few of which had been salted in India. Besides which the plague of flies had to be seen to be believed. Of this and other plagues Edmund Candler wrote vividly in his book, *The Long Road to Baghdad*:—[31]

" The flies in the tents, dug-outs and trenches, unless seen, were unbelievable. To describe them is to hazard one's reputation for truth. You could not eat without swallowing flies. You waved your spoon of porridge in the air to shake them off; you put your biscuits and bully beef in your pocket, and surreptitiously conveyed them in closed fist to your mouth, but you swallowed flies all the same. They settled in clouds on everything. When you wrote you could not see the end of your pen. . . . The Mesopotamian variety is indistinguishable from the English horse-fly except that many of them, one in twenty perhaps, will bite. . . . At night the flies will disappear, and the mosquitoes and sand-flies relieve them, completing the vicious circle. Mosquitoes are local. . . . The sand-fly is another and more insidious plague. A net with a mesh fine enough to exclude him is suffocating, and he will keep one awake at night with a hose of thin acid playing on one's face. He is also the transmitter of a microbe which will lay you out by the heels for three days with a virulent fever. . . .

" The morning's work done, you lay in your tent with the flaps open and the side-flies lifted up, and gasped through the long day waiting for the sun to go down. . . . You were clothed in dust and sweat. . . . You eat

[31] Vol. I, p. 235 *et seq.*

sand, breathe sand, lie in sand, have sand in your ears and eyes and clothes. Sand-flies by night; flies by day, until they shrivel up; sand and suffocation by day and night."

III.—Final Attempts to Relieve Kut.

In the attempt to force a passage on the right bank the extensive floods " continued to impede all movement across country; but General Keary, with the 3rd Division, succeeded in capturing the Bait Isa position on the morning of the 17th April, after killing some three hundred Turks and taking one hundred and eighty prisoners."[32]

General Gorringe had already transferred the 13th Division to the right bank to exploit any advantage. But at about 7 p.m. the Turks launched a furious counter-attack and succeeded in breaking the centre of the 3rd Division line. All through the night the battle raged, and at one time the confusion was complete. At the critical moment, however, the 13th Division came to the rescue, and, though the original line, west of Bait Isa, was not regained, the situation was restored by daylight. By this time the troops were utterly exhausted and incapable of further offensive action. Valuable time was flying; every day brought capitulation nearer to the gallant defenders of Kut; and therefore General Gorringe decided to make a third and final attempt to break the Turkish resistance on the left bank at Sannaiyat. But here the conditions were not conducive to success. On the 12th a north wind sprang up and drove the marsh southwards, flooding the Regiment's trenches. All ranks were compelled to leave their cover and work above ground in the rain in the vain hope of stemming the flood. But it was to no purpose, and the Regiment had to evacuate the position and retire behind an old Turkish communication trench where another *bund* was built, " which successfully checked the flood, but not before two batteries had been completely isolated and abandoned."[33] During the enforced evacuation of the line and the ensuing mud-larking operations the Turks shelled the Regiment caught in the open, but luckily without causing casualties. In this the Regiment was fortunate, for some other regiments suffered considerable losses. All that night a constant watch was kept on the *bund* to guard against another inundation.

Sapping operations perforce had to be abandoned by the front-line troops, and once again the gods conspired against us. On the 17th the Tigris overlapped its banks and, rushing northwards, joined the Suwaikiya marsh water which had been driven southwards, so that there was now a continuous sheet of water one hundred yards wide between the opposing forces.

[32] *Chronicle*, 1915-16, pp. 153-154.
[33] *Ibid.*, 1915-16, p. 176. These batteries were later retrieved.

The following night, the 18th/19th, patrols managed to find a strip of ground about six hundred yards wide whereon the water was only a few inches deep. Astride this General Younghusband proposed to attack with two brigades on the 20th. But this had to be postponed, for on the 18th " at 3 p.m. the wind veered round suddenly to the northward, driving the water of the Suwaikiya marsh . . . into the 7th Division trenches and right across the shell-pitted area to their front to join the Tigris flood."[34]

On the 21st orders were issued for the attack on the 22nd by the 19th and 21st Brigades, supported by the Corps artillery, on a front of three hundred yards each, with the 28th Brigade in support. Behind, in reserve, the 35th and 36th Brigades were to be concentrated. The enemy's numbers were estimated to be approximately equal to the British.

For this attack the 2nd/43rd was detailed as reserve to the 28th Brigade. Its strength was now 16 officers and 219 other ranks,[35] for three officers—Lieutenants Titherington, Adams and Milford—with 90 men had joined on the 20th, and 41 men had rejoined from hospital.

Early on the 22nd a report from the 21st Brigade on the right stated that an advance over the front allotted was impracticable owing to the floods. Consequently General Younghusband ordered the 19th Brigade to assault, supported by the 28th.

At 7 a.m., under the concentrated fire of the artillery on both banks, the assaulting infantry covered the four hundred yards to the enemy front line with comparatively light casualties; and quickly captured the first and second lines of trenches, which were found to be completely water-logged. Here the attackers floundered in a quagmire up to their armpits, but, slowly and tenaciously struggling on under an increasing hostile fire, managed to reach the third line. But such was the severity of the enfilade and cross-fire that the 19th Brigade reserve was unable to reach the Turkish third line, held by the Highland Battalion and 92nd Punjabis. The Turks counter-attacked, but were severely punished by the machine-gun battery firing from Crofton's Post on the right bank and by artillery fire. By now the struggling troops, except with bombs and bayonets, were practically unable to defend themselves, for the breeches of their rifles, clogged and jammed with mud, would not work.[36]

At 8 a.m. the Turks again counter-attacked heavily. Fighting valiantly with such weapons as were serviceable, the 19th Brigade managed to hold its own, and beat back the attack at close quarters. Meanwhile the 21st Brigade on the right had begun to retire, and the front-line troops of the 19th Brigade found themselves isolated, just when it seemed likely that a counter-attack

[34] *Official History*, Vol. II, p. 423.
[36] *The Long Road to Baghdad*, Vol. I, p. 202.
[35] *Ibid.*, Vol. II, p. 533.

by the 28th Brigade—which was moving forward—would restore the situation on the left. It is not known whence the order to retire emanated, but suffice it to say that the assaulting troops were back in the front line by 8.20 a.m., and the attack by the 28th Brigade was cancelled.[37]

At 7.15 a.m. the Regiment had moved forward behind the 19th Brigade and had occupied the British third-line trenches,[38] remaining there until the attackers retired, when, as part of the 28th Brigade, it took up a position on the left of the line, with the 19th Brigade on the right.[39]

At about 11.20 a.m. the Turks suddenly raised two Red Crescent flags, and medical parties advanced to attend to their wounded. The British ceased firing, and collected the wounded under Red Cross flags as far as the Turkish second line only.[39]

This final attack, as so often in the past, only just failed to be a success. To those on the right bank the enemy resistance appeared to be crushed, their enfilade fire causing untold havoc among the Turkish counter-attackers. Also it appeared to them that " it was entering hell fire for the Turk to expose himself in the third line trench, or in the long communication trench which ran obliquely from their position."[40] On the left of the 19th Brigade the ground was dry, and it is conceivable that supporting brigades advancing on the left could have captured the entire position under the covering fire of the machine guns on the right bank. To those floundering in the mud and unaware of the dry ground to their left front any advance appeared hopeless. In any case the complete change of plan at the last moment from an assault on a two-brigade to a one-brigade front probably contributed to the failure, for " in an attack through floods on a two-brigade front, the odds were all against us; on a one-brigade front they might well appear insuperable."[41]

In the evening the Regiment moved up to the second line and took over from part of the 19th Brigade.

The following day General Gorringe reported that it was useless to call upon the troops for further efforts " within the time limit imposed by the food supply of Kut." General Lake transmitted this opinion to India and London.

[37] *Official History*, Vol. II, p. 430. [38] *Chronicle*, 1915-16, p. 177.
[39] *Official History*, Vol. II, p. 431.
[40] *The Long Road to Baghdad*, Vol. I, p. 206. This is corroborated by Commandant Moukbil Bey in *La Campagne de l'Irak* : " Nos mitrailleuses de l'aile droite prennent alors cette brigade [that is, the 19th] sous leur feu d'enfilade et elles l'auraient sans doute anéantie, *si elles n'avaient pas été immédiatement contrebattues et criblées de projectiles par les batteries anglaises postées sur la rive droite du Tigre.*"
[41] *The Long Road to Baghdad*, Vol. I, pp. 207-208. Edmund Candler gives a review of the two opinions gathered from officers who took part, and affirms that the Turkish truce was intelligible owing to the terrific casualties incurred by them from the enfilade fire from the right bank. The machine guns fired 165,000 rounds at good targets.

On the 23rd General Townshend asked whether he should open negotiations with the Turks to prevent the starvation of the garrison. On the 24th General Lake replied that another attempt would be made, this time by the Navy, who would try to run the blockade and revictual the garrison with one month's supplies and so allow time for the concentration of reinforcements for further operations. At 7 p.m. that night the *Julnar*, under Lieutenant H. O. B. Firman, R.N., with two other officers and twelve unmarried ratings and a cargo of 270 tons of supplies, started upstream on her forlorn hope. Though riddled by rifle and machine-gun fire from Sannaiyat, she approached Maqasis whence a shell hit her bridge and killed her gallant commander. Undaunted, she still steamed on until she fouled a cable at Maqasis and, swinging round with the current, ran firmly aground near the fort. The failure of this heroic attempt rang down the curtain on the relief operations, for on the night of the 25th/26th the British Government authorized General Lake to open negotiations with the Turks for the surrender of the garrison of Kut.

On the 29th April General Townshend capitulated. The relief operations incurred 23,000 casualties in officers and men; just double the number of men whom they were endeavouring to succour. Before recording the tale of the last month spent by the 1st/43rd in Kut it will be convenient to note the military causes of the failures to relieve the garrison.

Mesopotamia became at one time the grave of military reputations, but such another campaign may well have to be faced by us in the future. Two principles of war were violated by each commander in turn—the principles of concentration and mobility. It was through no fault of theirs that they were violated. Owing to lack of river and land transport neither General Nixon nor General Lake was able to concentrate his maximum force at the decisive point at any time during the relief operations. For the same reason the principle of mobility was automatically broken. Never were they able to make wide turning movements for lack of adequate land transport to carry the necessary water. Towards the end food and ammunition were running short, and the fighting troops' rations had to be reduced, and the expenditure of 60-pounder ammunition seriously decreased. Early—too early, in fact,—urgency of relief was impressed on them by General Townshend. Tidings of the imminent arrival of strong Turkish reinforcements from Gallipoli also spurred them on to attack while yet there was time. Yet each attack minimized the chances of success; each attack reduced the force whereas an increase was required. Risks had to be taken which would have been unjustifiable under any other circumstances.

The difficulties were inconceivable and, when the floods came to supplement them, the problems became inextricable. Time became the governing factor; time, the unconquerable factor in war. The floods threw in their

MAP No. 12

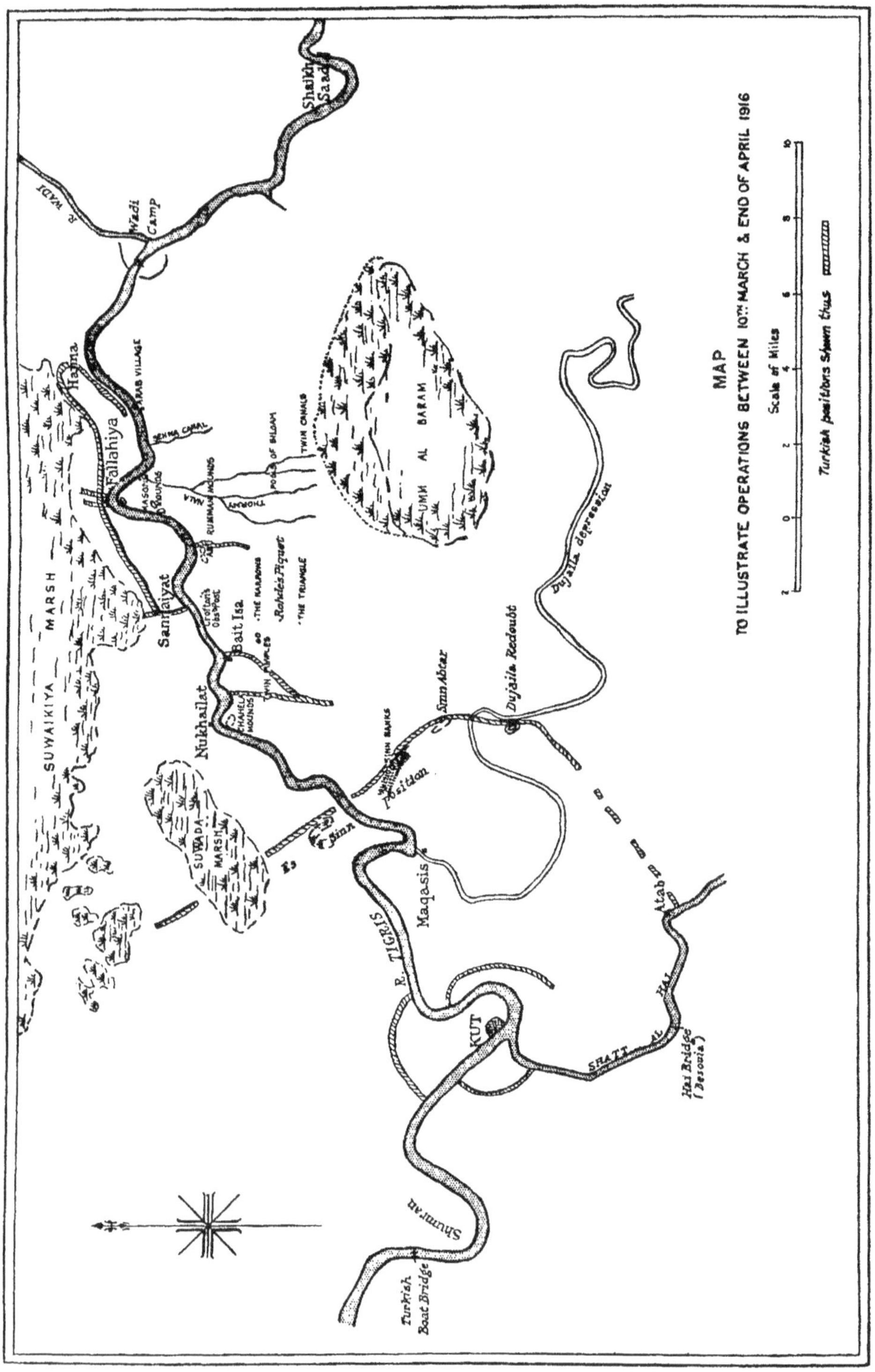

MAP TO ILLUSTRATE OPERATIONS BETWEEN 10TH MARCH & END OF APRIL 1916

weight in defence of our enemies; simple movements became matters of difficulty; the strong current delayed the supply ships; the mud immobilized wheeled traffic; away from the mud and floods, driven dust and burning sand parched and stifled moving troops, demanding for them ample supplies of water which could not be carried.

It is idle to speculate on the result of the relief operations had it been known in December that the food supply would suffice in Kut until the end of April, but it is likely that many lives would have been saved with that knowledge. Those who argue this should remember that General Townshend's force was liable at any moment to be overwhelmed by sheer weight of numbers.

It is easy to be wise after the event and to sit in judgment on those responsible for these operations. The causes of failure were intimately correlated and are worth analysing from both points of view: those of the relief force—which have been roughly sketched—and those of the beleaguered. Let us turn to the gallant defender of Kut, and analyse his errors in the light of after-events.

First, there is little doubt but that General Townshend was obsessed by his successful defence of Chitral when he decided to stand at Kut. As a captain he had withstood a siege and been awarded the C.B. for his services: Kut might well be another Chitral.

Secondly, the civilian inhabitants should have been turned out. General Townshend originally intended to clear the town, but was dissuaded by Sir Percy Cox, his political officer, who pointed out that the inhabitants would starve during the winter months. Thus over 6,000 useless mouths had to be fed for humanitarian reasons. It does not pay to be sentimental in war; and, moreover, the loyalty of the population was more than doubtful.

Thirdly, it should have been realized at once that the Arab custom is to bury grain in holes in the ground; and strong pressure should have been put upon the population to disclose the caches before being expelled. Had this last step been taken at once, operations for the relief of Kut would not have been undertaken until a sufficiency of men, equipment, armaments and transport had been concentrated; and the disastrous piecemeal attacks by the ill-found relief force would have been avoided.

Fourthly, had a less optimistic view of the prospect of relief been adopted by General Townshend he would have earlier started the slaughter of those animals which consumed the staple food of his Indian troops.

But in fairness to General Townshend it should be noted that he had justification for his optimism: had not his division proved irresistible until opposed by four times its strength? Was he not therefore entitled to expect the relief force to be equally successful against the Turks who were compelled to disseminate their forces owing to his holding Kut?

In conclusion, the one bright page in this chapter of failures was the indomitable courage and tenacity of the troops. Never for one moment did they relax their efforts to break through. Underfed, ill-supplied, they fought magnificently and valiantly, not only against the enemy but also against the elements, the rain, wind, floods, dust, flies, mosquitoes, and sickness, always willing—nay, enthusiastic—to answer every call no matter how forlorn the hope, and fain to die in their attempts. Primarily the stolid defence of Kut, and secondly the indefatigable efforts of these troops maintained the prestige of British arms in the East.

* * *

The end of the month found the 2nd/43rd in the trenches with two companies, each about sixty strong, " A," under Lieutenant Titherington and Second Lieutenant Griffin, being in the front and " B," under Lieutenant Radford and Second Lieutenant Davenport, in the second line. On the night of the 29th/30th the Regiment stood to arms expecting an attack which never materialized. Then a ten-day truce was proclaimed on the 30th, and the Regiment was relieved by the 19th Brigade and went back into the fourth line. From the 6th April up to the 30th the Regiment lost one man killed and Lieutenant Meade and five men wounded. With the capitulation of Kut the old 43rd ceased to exist, and its mantle fell upon the 2nd/43rd, which officially became the 43rd.[42]

IV.—THE LAST DAYS IN KUT, APRIL 1916.

" They that did feed delicately are desolate in our streets ; they that were brought up in scarlet embrace dunghills . . . their skin cleaveth to their bones ; it is withered, it is become like a stick. . . . The kings of the earth, and all the inhabitants of the world, would not have believed that the adversary and the enemy should have entered into the gates. . . . In our watching we have watched for a nation that could not save us . . . our end is near, our days are fulfilled ; for our end is come."
—*Lamentations of Jeremiah*, Chapter iv.

April came in with wet and windy weather which added greatly to the discomfort of the anxious and half-starved garrison. Those Indians who refused to eat horseflesh were daily losing strength, for their ration of ten ounces of *atta* and half an ounce of *ghi* was insufficient to maintain vitality.[43] Furthermore, scurvy had attacked the whole garrison.[44]

Before dawn on the 5th the garrison heard the bombardment downstream and were greatly encouraged when tidings were received at 8.35 a.m. that the 13th Division had captured the first lines of the Hanna position. All day the garrison observed the bombardment, ready to co-operate if the

---

[42] The official notification was not received until the 6th July (G.H.Q. Telegram 1172/20/75A).
[43] *In Kut and Captivity*, p. 226. [44] *My Campaign in Mesopotamia*, p. 310.

relief force should break through the Turkish defence; and the 5-inch guns bombarded the Maqasis ferry at long range. No further tidings of the battle, however, came through until early on the 7th, which was a day spent in anxious excitement.

Meanwhile, as has been recorded, the Tigris began to throw its weight into the scales against the British. On the 7th it exceeded the level of the March flood, and burst its bank below the Fort, flooding the peninsula again.[45] " The Fort ditch on the north-east and western faces was flooded, and the river water rose right up to the river face of the fortification."[45] The inner keep, occupied by three companies of the 1st/43rd, was to some extent protected by the old walls of the Fort; but one evening the water burst through into the Regiment's dug-outs. The draining of this entailed much arduous labour for which the Regiment was not, by now, fit. For weeks all ranks had been overworked, underfed, and harassed by snipers who prevented work in daylight by their accurate fire. " All dug-outs within fifty yards of the Tigris were gradually flooded."[45]

On the 9th the garrison stood to arms again as usual, while guns rumbled to southward; but no message came through for many hours, and then only the bad news that the 13th Division had failed to break through. There was now no longer any doubt in Kut. It was certain that the garrison would not be relieved by the 15th.[46] In a *communiqué* to the troops, issued the following day, General Townshend appealed to all ranks to husband their scanty rations and so enable Kut to hold out until the 21st. Thus the daily ration of grain was reduced to five ounces for British and Indians alike; and Indians were no longer favoured on account of their religious prejudice against horseflesh. He reminded them that their religious leaders had authorized them to eat it, and that their refusal to do so had weakened his power of resistance.[47] This abstention from meat was a real problem to General Townshend, as, by the 10th, the situation among the Indian regiments had become serious: men were fainting at work and literally dying of starvation.[48] General Townshend, therefore, had to rely almost entirely on the English units of the garrison. He said " without the (now—alas!—skeleton) battalions of Norfolks, Dorsets, Oxfords (who showed magnificent courage and bravery at Ctesiphon, where they bore the brunt of the battle), the wing of the West Kents . . . the Hampshire Territorial Infantry, and the detachment of bluejackets of the Royal Navy, Kut would have fallen, in my opinion, at the end of March."[49] However, this appeal bore good results, for on the following day 5,135 Indians applied for an issue of horseflesh; but by now they were too weak to derive benefit from the better ration. Two days

[45] *In Kut and Captivity*, p. 230.
[47] *Ibid.*, p. 321.
[49] *My Campaign in Mesopotamia*, p. 320.
[46] *My Campaign in Mesopotamia*, p. 318.
[48] *Official History*, Vol. II, p. 444.

These statistics, printed in Secunderabad soon after the war, were taken from the diary of Captain Peel of the 119th who was on the staff in Kut. A copy came into the possession of Private Thatcher who gave it to Brigadier Stapleton. Many inaccuracies of spelling and arithmetic will be noticed but these have not been edited.

TROOPS OF THE KUT GARRISON

Duration of Seige, Dec. 6th 1915 to April 29th 1916 —146 days. Ladysmith was 120 days.

Royal Navy S.N.O. Lt. Tudway, R.N.
H.M.S. "Samana," 1 12pr. (8 cwt.)   1 8pr.
4 4.7 Guns on Horseboats.
1 12pr. (12 cwt.) mounted on shore.

Artillery (GUNS)

		Guns.
R.F.A.	63rd Battery ⎫ 76th ⎬ 10th Bde. R.F.A. 82nd ⎭ Lt.-Col. Maule Hants Howitzer Battery, Major H. G. Thompson	18 (18pr.) 4 (5")
R.G.A.	86th Heavy Battery, Lt.-Col. Courtenay 104th " , (1 Sec.) Major Martin Calcutta Vol. Art., Major Farnar Spare 18pr. (from store)	4 (5") 2 (4") 2 (15pr.) 1 (18pr.)
Also	Sect. 'S' By. R.H.A. (left us no horses) (see above)	
Add	Naval Guns	2 (18pr.) 7 — 43 —

AMMUNITION STATISTICS
1 Gun
(Authority, Lt.-Col. Maule, R.A.)

Battery	No. of guns	Rds. on Dec. 4th	Rds. per gun	Rds. destroyed on April 29th	Rds. per gun	Expended during Siege	Rds. per gun
10th Bde. R.F.A.	19	11,400	600	5,200	275	6,200	326
"S" Battery	2	1,600	800	900	450	700	350
Hants Howitzer	4	960	240	240	60	720	180
4" (104th)	2	970	485	210	105	760	380
5" (86th)	4	1,624	406	560	140	1,064	266
Vol. Art'y	4	900	225	84	21	816	204
Naval 12pr.	2	700	350	500	250	200	100

N.B.—Figures for the 4 Naval 4.7's not available.
11 S.A.A.

At the beginning of the Seige we had about 6,000,000 rounds S.A.A. or 800 rounds per man.
At the end of the Seige we had about 740 rounds per *effective* rifle.

SEIGE STATISTICS.

A. SUMMARY OF CASUALTIES from 4th December 1915 to 28th April 1916.
(OFFICIAL)

	Killed A	Wounded	Died of Wounds B	Missing C	Died of Disease D	Total	Remarks
British Officers	9	44	10	1	4	68	These totals do not include the Casualties of Oxfords and 119th Infy. after 21st April. Probably 6 Oxfords and 15 of the 119th.
Indian Officers	8	21	7	1	5	42	
British Ranks	84	351	105	2	68	610	
Indian Ranks	369	1,253	278	64	531	2,495	
Followers	67	229	88	4	123	571	
Totals	537	1,958	488	72	731	3,786	Say 3,800

A	B	C	D
Lieut. Haddon, 119th	Col. Courtenay, R.G.A.	Capt. Gribbon, 67th Pun.	
Capt. Baillie, Dorsets	Capt. Garnet, "		
Lt. Nuran, I.A.R.O., 120th	" Anderson, I.M.S., 2/7th G.	Lt.-Col. Codrington, 120th Infy.	
Lt. Brown, Oxfords	Lt. Arbuthnot, 67th P.	Lt. Wood, I.A.R.O., 119th	
Lt. Russell, Norfolks	" Head, 117th Infy.	Br.-Gen. Hoghton	
Capt. Beg, D.A.D.O.S.	" Badelow, R.F.A.	Capt. Lambert, I.M.S.	
Lt. Dwyer, I.A.R.O., 108rd	" East, R.E.		

FOOD SUPPLIES DURING THE SEIGE OF KUT (BRITISH TROOPS)

FROM JANUARY 21st, 1916

DATE	Jan. 21	Jan. 22	Jan. 23	Jan. 26	Jan. 31	Feb. 3	Feb. 8	Feb. 15	Feb. 23	Mar. 5	Mar. 8	Mar. 10	Mar. 12	Mar. 27	Apl. 12	Apl. 16	Apl. 22	Apl. 23 to 25	Apl. 26 to 29
Bread	Full Ratn. 1 lb.	12 oz.	12 oz.	12 oz.	12 oz.	12 oz.	12 oz.	12 oz.	12 oz.	12 oz.	12 oz.	10 oz.	10 oz.	8 oz.	8 oz.	5 oz.	4 oz.	Emergency and Reserve Rations, 6 oz. Biscuit, 1 lb. meat, nothing elce.	Aeroplane rations—4 oz. bread, 1 oz. cocoa, ¼ oz. sugar, 1 lb. meat.
Meat	1 lb.	1 lb.	1 lb.	1 lb.	1¼ lb.	1¼ lb.	1¼ lb.	1¼ lb.	1¼ lb.	1¼ lb.	1¼ lb.	1¼ lb.	1¼ lb.	1¼ lb.	1¼ lb.	1 lb.	1 lb.		
Bacon or	3 oz.	3 oz.	3 oz.	2 oz.	2 oz.	2 oz.	1 oz.	1 oz.	1 oz.	nil	nil	nil	nil	nil	nil	nil	nil		
Cheese or	4 oz.	4 oz.	4 oz.	2 oz.	2 oz.	2 oz.	1 oz.	1 oz.	1 oz.	nil	nil	nil	nil	nil	nil	nil	nil		
Jam or	4 oz.	4 oz.	4 oz.	4 oz.	2 oz.	2 oz.	2 oz.	1½ oz.	1 oz.	1 oz.	1 oz.	1 oz.	nil	nil	nil	nil	nil		
Butter	3 oz.	3 oz.	3 oz.	2 oz.	2 oz.	2 oz.	1 oz.	1 oz.	1 oz.	nil	nil	nil	nil	nil	nil	nil	nil		
Vegetables	nil	nil	nil	nil	nil	nil	nil	nil	nil	nil	nil	nil	nil	nil	nil	nil	nil		
Sugar	2½ oz.	2½ oz.	½ oz.	½ oz.	½ oz.	nil	nil	nil	nil	nil	nil	nil	nil	nil	nil	nil	nil		
Dates	4 oz.	4 oz.	4 oz.	4 oz.	4 oz.	4 oz.	4 oz.	4 oz.	4 oz.	4 oz.	nil	nil	nil	nil	nil	nil	nil		
Tea	1 oz.	½ oz.	½ oz.	½ oz.	½ oz	½ oz.	½ oz.	½ oz.	½ oz.	½ oz.	nil	nil	nil	nil	nil	nil	nil		
Saccharine via Aeroplane	.	.	.	.	.	.	.	.	.	.	.	.	.	.	a few	grain	s		

P. 295

TOTAL STRENGTH OF KUT GARRISON AT SURRENDER

April 29th, 1916. (Official figures)

British Officers	227	N.B. The Turks always pretended that they did not know what "Followers" (*i.e.* Transport Drivers, Stretcher bearers and Hospital employee, private servants, etc.) meant, and included them in the total of "Fighting men" captured.
" Ranks	2592	
Indian Officers	204	
" Ranks	6988	
Followers	3248	
Total	13,309*	Arab inhabitants numbered about 6,000.

C. *Some Auction prices.* (in Rupees—1/4)

Revolver	150	1 lb. Coarse sugar	20
Camp Bed	50	2½ lbs. Arab tobacco (usual 1½) price	54
6d. Packet Chocolate	8½		

Above prices about February 1st.

Very small sponge	12		

February 8th.

Packet Brome† ...	9	100 Arab Cigs. (usual ½) price	1½
100 Cigarettes ...	100		

April 1st.

½ lb. A. & N. Tobacco	47	100 Cigarettes	109

April 15th.

½ lb. Butter ...	12	Arab Cigs. ½ rupee *each.*	

April 26th.

1 bottle Whiskey (offered but accepted)‡ ...	50	100 "Planter" cheroots	200
		50 "3 Castle" Cigarettes	60
		3 Packets "Scissors" Cigarettes	£1 Gold

* Adds up to 13,259.
† Bromo.
‡ Should probably read "offered but *not* accepted."

later General Townshend issued an appeal to the Indians, and a threat to promote others in the place of those who still refused to eat horseflesh. This had a good effect; 7,054 and later 9,329 Indians coming on the meat ration list. This state of semi-starvation naturally reduced the troops' powers of resistance against disease. Colic and dysentery, complicated by jaundice, became epidemic; add to these a plague of fleas, swarms of sand-flies and parasitical lice, and the picture of the *Mesopotamian picnic*[50] is almost complete.

Tobacco was, of course, unprocurable; ginger, tea leaves, apricot and lime leaves were tried as substitutes. As an instance of the value of tobacco, one box of a hundred cigarettes belonging to a deceased officer fetched Rs100 (£6 13s. 4d.) at an auction.[51]

The craving for sugar, as the result of lack of starch in the rations, and for green food became very strong towards the end. Dandelion leaves were concocted into a spinach, and, indeed, any green vegetation was utilized. But when Brigadier-General F. A. Hoghton suddenly and mysteriously died on the night of the 11th/12th from having eaten some poisonous vegetation, it was said, Colonel Lethbridge stopped the Regiment gathering " green stuff."[52] General Hoghton, who had commanded the 17th Brigade at Es Sinn and Ctesiphon, was very popular among all ranks of the Regiment. He never missed visiting the Regiment in the Fort, or "Q" Company when in Redoubt " B " and its later position in the sandhills. He was buried in the cemetery at the north end of Kut in the presence of all officers of the garrison who were not on duty.[53]

On the 14th when the grain belonging to the town population was finished, General Townshend wired that he could hold out until the 24th by making the emergency rations last two days but that beyond that date he would have to rely on supplies dropped by air.[54] The first sacks of flour were successfully dropped on the 15th, but, instead of the 5,000 lb. required, only 3,350 lb. arrived. The following day the supply amounted to only 1,333 lb.[55] General Townshend was therefore forced to reduce the ration again to five ounces of bread and one pound of meat for British troops and four ounces of barley meal, four ounces of barley for parching and nine ounces of meat for the Indians.

The officers and men of the Regiment were now so thin and weak that to walk a few hundred yards required a great effort. " Not only was the

[50] The campaign was so described by a journalist.
[51] *In Kut and Captivity*, pp. 233-234.
[52] *Chronicle*, 1915-16, p. 119.
[53] *In Kut and Captivity*, p. 236.
[54] *My Campaign in Mesopotamia*, pp. 327-328.
[55] *Ibid.*, p. 330.

bread ration so small," wrote Lieutenant Naylor, " but also the meat ration was only about half of what it had previously been. Officially we received 1 lb. of meat and bone; but as the horses were in such a poor state . . . the greater part of the ration was composed of bone . . . we were receiving just about enough to keep us alive and no more."

There was a certain amount of trouble over a deficiency of hand grenades in a certain native regiment, but it was discovered that the disappearance of the bombs coincided with fish for breakfast in the officers' mess, proving that " there are more ways of catching fish than by hooking them." Two

[By permission of Major N. V. L. Rybot, D.S.O.

young dogs brought out from Kut by some men of the 43rd earlier in the siege also disappeared though they never left the Fort. Timber from bridges also mysteriously walked away at night to the native cooking-places to such an extent that sentries had to be posted over the bridges to preserve the communications and an order issued threatening any wood thief with death. Nevertheless, wood continued to disappear.

On the morning of the 17th the garrison stood to arms as soon as the bombardment of Bait Isa was heard. Such tidings as were received were very reassuring and raised the spirits of the garrison, for the weather was now fine and considerable casualties had been inflicted on the enemy. But the food question was now critical, and a proposal was mooted that H.M.S.

Sumana should run the gantlope downstream with a complement of the most useful troops of the garrison. This suggestion was vetoed, however, and another discussed, namely, that H.M.S. *Sumana* should try to destroy the Maqasis bridge and, by depriving the Turks of communication between their two wings, render a great service to General Gorringe. This plan was also considered impracticable.

When on the 22nd tidings of the failure at Sannaiyat reached Kut, all food except meat had been finished. On the evening of the 24th tidings were received of the *Julnar's* projected attempt to run the gantlope of the Turkish lines. Lieutenant Naylor was detailed to take twenty-five men of " S " Company and report to Major Gilchrist at a point just upstream of the retrenchment. This party was to guard the stores when they had been unloaded. Greatly to his surprise he was given a whole pound of *atta* and two ounces of chocolate for each man as the following day's ration.

At the rendezvous other troops assembled and positions were allotted. The river bank from the Fort to the Middle Line was lined by native troops and machine guns to cover the opposite bank, while the 30th Brigade which was to unload the ship was concentrated at the *Julnar's* berthing-place. Roadways, brows, a darkened signal lamp and all necessary arrangements for her arrival had been prepared. Here let Lieutenant Naylor speak : " The hours passed away slowly; midnight came with no sign of anything un- usual, and it was with difficulty that we could conceal our impatience. In the direction of Bait Isa large flare lights would now and then soar into the air. . . . These lights were so powerful that they seemed no more than half a mile away from us. . . . Around Kut was absolute stillness . . . one might have imagined that all was peace in the world.

" About 2 a.m. we heard a faint crackle of rifle fire in the far distance . . . as the minutes passed it gradually became louder. . . . Louder and louder it grew until it seemed as if a large number of machine guns were at work, and the shrapnel began to burst. The noise of the shrapnel and rifle fire continued to increase until it seemed as if it was no further away than the Fort . . . then there came a sudden and complete silence. What had happened we hardly liked to guess; there was no sign of the *Julnar* and the night was as quiet as it had been before. We strained our eyes into the night, but there was nothing to disturb the silvery sheen of the moon on the river. At dawn . . . we received orders to disperse." And with the failure of this last magnificent attempt the last sparks of hope flickered and went out.

Lieutenant Naylor records that on return to the Fort he made *chupattis* with his extra pound of *atta*, cooking them in the lid of a tobacco tin over a tin of dubbin with a wick in it. Between the 22nd and 25th the garrison subsisted on two days' emergency rations; and from the 26th to the 29th it relied entirely upon the food dropped from the air, which allowed each man about five ounces per day.[56]

On the 23rd General Townshend suggested that negotiations should be opened with the Turks for an honourable capitulation. After the failure of the *Julnar* to reach Kut he wired that an armistice should be arranged, and ten days' supplies sent up at once; that the garrison was emaciated, " the Indians unfit to fight and the British, though retaining their pluck, dejected and very weak."[57] Men were dying from dysentery at the rate of fifteen a day; scurvy was raging, and the foul, fetid stenches in the town were likely to cause a pestilence.

At 10 a.m. on the 26th negotiations were opened, and on the morning of the 27th there was a cessation of hostilities. " The stillness after so many months of noise was quite extraordinary. The day was calm, the weather fine, and the river-flood had fallen considerably; the atrocious weather and flood conditions had lasted just sufficiently long to prevent our relief."[58]

In his letter to Khalil Pasha[59] on the 26th General Townshend asked for a six-day armistice, and permission for ten days' food for the garrison and inhabitants to be sent up from the British lines; he hoped, too, that the Turks would be generous and allow the garrison to retire to Amara with their arms, as they were too weak from want of food to march into captivity.

On the 27th General Townshend, with his staff,[60] proceeded upstream and met Khalil alone on board a Turkish launch about one and a half miles above Kut. Khalil at first demanded unconditional surrender, but, when General Townshend suggested a ransom in gold, he said that better terms might be made. He insisted, however, that the garrison should quit Kut at once, and he promised to supply tents and the food from the captured *Julnar*. General Townshend thereupon consulted General Lake, and suggested that he, General Lake, should carry out the negotiations because he was in a position to argue whereas he, General Townshend, without a biscuit up his sleeve, was not.[61] General Lake answered the same day, and suggested that General Townshend should offer Khalil his guns, money and exchange of prisoners as the price of a free pass to India on parole.

" The bread ration had entirely failed, and for the last four days we had what were called emergency rations for two days and reserve rations for two days. These rations differed very slightly and consisted of such odds and ends of stores as had not been large enough for an ordinary issue. Such things as Huntley & Palmer's biscuits, a few ration biscuits and a little

---

[56] *Official History*, Vol. II, p. 449. [57] *Ibid.*, Vol. II, p. 451.
[58] *In Kut and Captivity*, p. 247.
[59] Khalil Pasha succeeded Nur-ud-Din in command of the Turkish VIth Army in January.
[60] Captain Morland was present. [61] *My Campaign in Mesopotamia*, p. 335.

chocolate were among these scraps. Actually from the point of view of food, Kut could not have held out a day longer than it did."[62]

Very early on the morning of the 28th General Townshend sent a letter by Captains Morland (43rd) and Shakeshaft (Norfolk Regiment) to Khalil, offering him £1,000,000, his fifty guns, and the parole of his force not to fight against Turkey for the rest of the war, in exchange for the freedom of the troops.

Khalil, according to German accounts, recommended in his report to Enver Pasha that the garrison of Kut should be allowed to go on parole to India; but Enver's reply was not encouraging. He demanded unconditional surrender, but offered General Townshend his personal liberty in exchange for the guns and material. This suggestion was, of course, refused by General Townshend.

Meanwhile, on the 26th and 27th much gun ammunition had been dumped into the Tigris, but, when hopes of good terms of surrender were frustrated, orders were issued for the systematic destruction of all war material. On the last night in Kut, the 28th/29th, fatigue parties emptied vast quantities of ammunition into the river. The 1st/43rd spent the night dumping ammunition, destroying documents, revolvers, machine guns, rifles and bayonets. Carts were broken up and harness cut to unserviceable ribbons. The scene was one of desolation and destruction. On the morning of the 29th the muzzles of the forty-two guns were blown away one by one; the launches were blown up in deep water, and all bridging material and engineers' stores were destroyed.[63]

General Townshend issued a last *communiqué* to his hard-fighting division, and thanked the troops for their devotion, discipline and bravery. A message was also received from the Army commander, General Lake, as follows: " The Commander-in-Chief [Sir Beauchamp Duff] has desired me to convey to you and your brave and devoted troops his appreciation of the manner in which you together have undergone the suffering and hardships of the siege, which he knows has been due to the high spirit of devotion to duty in which you have met the call of your Sovereign and Empire. The Commander-in-Chief's sentiments are shared by myself, General Gorringe, and all the troops of the Tigris column. We can only express extreme disappointment, and regret that our efforts to relieve you should not have been crowned with success."[64]

General Townshend also received a message from Captain Nunn, C.M.G., D.S.O., R.N., as follows: " We, the Officers and Men of the

[62] Lieutenant Naylor's diary.
[63] *In Kut and Captivity*, pp. 251-258. The officers were forced to surrender their swords to the Turks.
[64] *Chronicle*, 1915-16, p. 122.

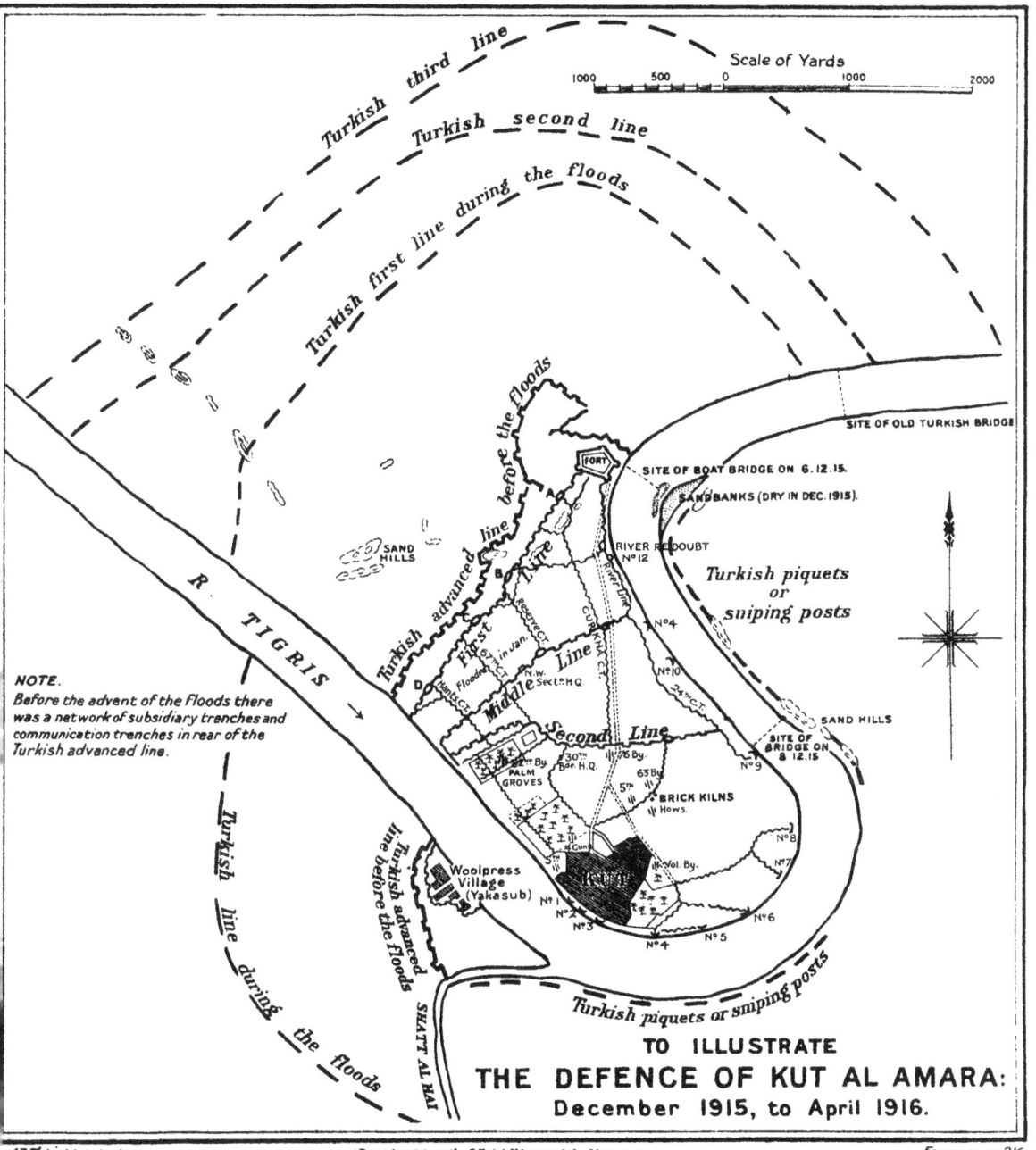

Royal Navy, who have been associated with the Tigris Corps, and many of us so often worked with you and your gallant troops desire to express our heartfelt regret at our inability to join hands with you and your comrades in Kut."[64]

Before noon the launch containing Major Gilchrist and Captains Morland and Shakeshaft landed Colonel Nazim Bey (commanding the regiment which was to march into Kut) below the Fort, and then proceeded upstream to the Fort to warn Colonel Brown, commanding the Fort, to admit the Turks in one hour's time.[65] No more destruction was thereafter possible.

At 12.42 p.m. a Turkish regiment approached the Fort. " White flags were hoisted on the walls . . . and the Turks piled arms and sat down round the outside."[66] The Regiment then collected its kits and marched by companies into the inner keep of the Fort, and there piled those few arms[67] which had been kept in case of trouble with the Arab population or any unforeseen occurrence, and deposited the remaining ammunition—between 150 and 200 rounds per man—which was to be taken over by the Turks. At 1 p.m. the wireless winged its last message to the relief force: " Good-bye," and was then destroyed.[68]

Skeletons of their former selves, weak and sick, conquered by hunger and disease, but still unconquered by the enemy, the 1st/43rd Light Infantry awaited courageously the last act in the tragic drama. How bitter was the sight of the Turks squatting like vultures round the Fort so long and so gallantly defended by the Regiment, no one who was not present can possibly imagine. All noonday and afternoon the Regiment waited, and not till 5 p.m. did the Colonel receive orders to move. At 5.30 p.m. the Regiment, with belts, water-bottles and haversacks, marched out of the Fort, staggering under its kits. There was no transport.[69] Then the regiment of " thick-set, dusty, dirty, and tired looking Turkish infantry, laden with their full field-service kits "[70]—the type which the Regiment had helped to defeat on three occasions—marched in and took over the defences.

Unfortunately the Regiment was not allowed to collect any of its belongings from the Middle Line, which had been used as a depot for surplus clothing, the Colonel having orders to march direct to the palm groves on the north of Kut town. Thus many useful personal articles were perforce left to the enemy. On reaching the palm groves at about 8 p.m. the Regiment bivouacked with the rest of the 17th Brigade, and the quartermaster

[64] *Ibid*, 1915-16 p. 122.
[65] *In Kut and Captivity*, p. 256.
[66] *Chronicle*, 1927, p. 183.
[67] The sights of these had been methodically deranged.
[68] *Official History*, Vol. II, p. 457.
[69] *Chronicle*, 1927, p. 184.
[70] *In Kut and Captivity*, p. 255.

MAP NO. 14

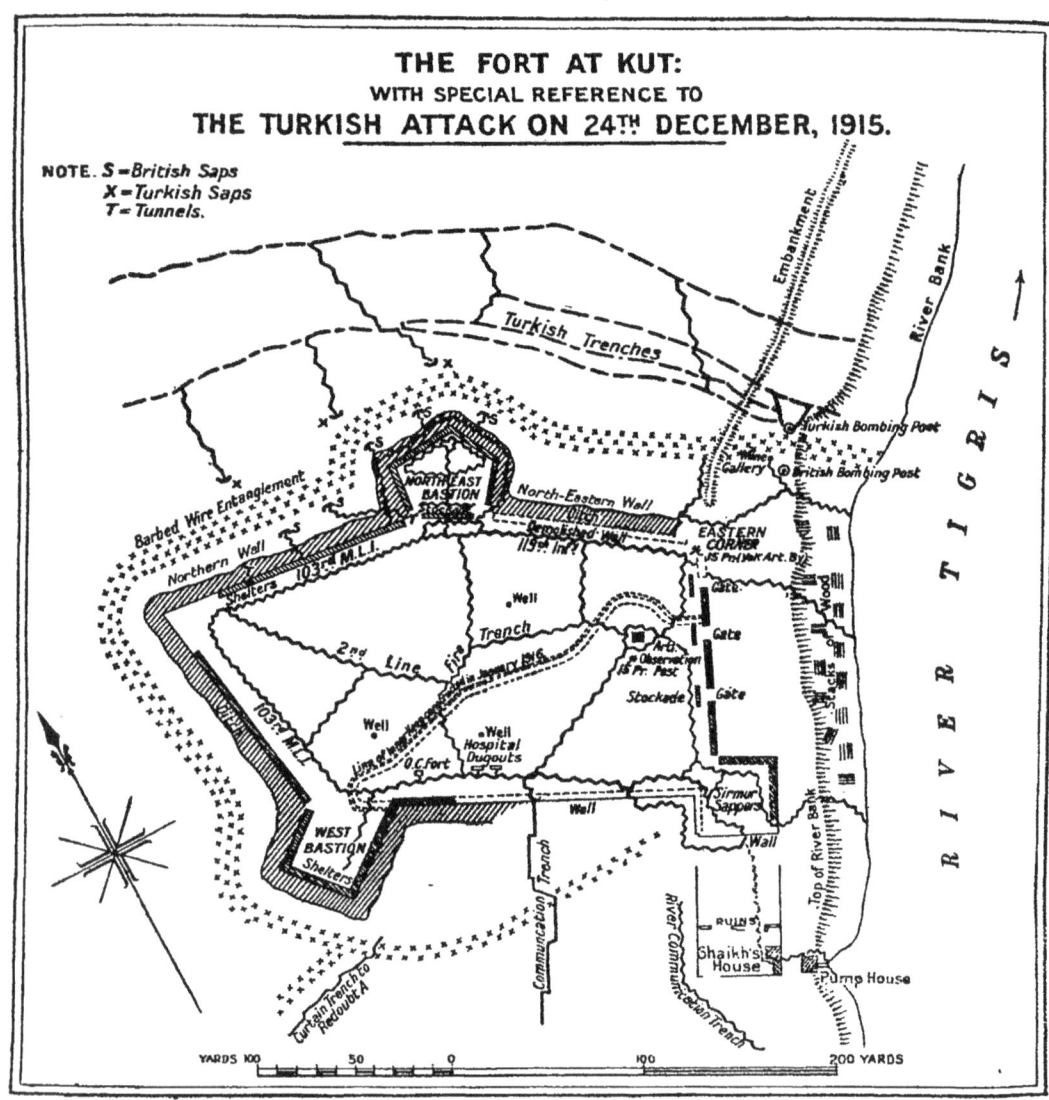

distributed the contents of parcels belonging to those who had died during the siege. These had been stored pending the issue of the siege and were only shared out on capitulation. The Regiment's portion was a little tobacco and a few cigarettes which were a welcome change from dried apricot leaves. " That night the men slept heavily and peacefully, but one or two men who visited the latrine . . . were waylaid by Turks and robbed of their [money] belts." Here Captain S. C. B. Mundey, who had been attached to the Flying Corps, rejoined the Regiment.

On the 30th the 18th and 30th Brigades and divisional troops embarked on a river steamer *en route* for Shumran, nine miles upstream. The 16th and 17th Brigades were ordered to march, as there was no transport available. Captain Mundey and Lieutenant Heawood, however, went on ahead with the baggage in the steamer. At 3.30 p.m. the Regiment marched out of Kut, the strength being 385, including those sick and left in hospital in Kut and 77 attached from other regiments.[71] It must be remembered that the Regiment had had no food supplied by its captors, and was still subsisting on its emergency siege rations and a few luxuries saved from parcels. The march was therefore another great test of endurance and pluck. Unused to marching and starved, the Regiment wound its slow and infinitely weary way in single file along the river bank, and eventually reached the camp at Shumran at 7 p.m.[72]

Soon after arrival the Regiment received its first ration of Turkish food: six brown biscuits per man, made from barley flour, chaff, mud and lard according to Serjeant A. C. Munn.[73] In his own words, " the British Army biscuit is no doughnut, but it is a sponge cake compared with the Turkish variety." This was hardly the fare for starving men; but the biscuits were soaked and eaten with the inevitable result. Stomachs were too weak to digest the food, and eight men of one company alone died during the night.[73]

Meanwhile negotiations had been carried on between General Lake and Khalil Pasha. Arrangements were made to exchange the sick and wounded in Kut for as many unwounded and healthy Turkish prisoners of war of specified regiments; but General Lake, himself short of transport, was unable to accede to Khalil's request for ships to carry the garrison of Kut to Baghdad. The following day General Lake reminded Khalil that he had given General Townshend assurances that the Turks would feed, transport and pay the Kut garrison.[74]

And so ended the siege of Kut, and for the third time in its history the 43rd was taken prisoner through stress of circumstances over which it had

[71] *Chronicle*, 1916-17, p. 103.
[73] *Ibid.*, 1915-16, p. 132.
[72] *Ibid.*, 1927, p. 185.
[74] *Official History*, Vol. II, p. 458.

no control after an historic siege lasting 143 days.[75] It is doubtful whether the 43rd in its long and glorious history has ever had to endure such vicissitudes as in the eighteen months' campaign in Mesopotamia; and this is postulated with due regard to its services in the unhealthy West Indies in the eighteenth century and in the Peninsular War. The conditions were, in fact, inconceivable by any who was not present.

The strength of the Kut garrison on the 29th April was:—

British officers	277
Indian officers	204
British rank and file ...	2,592
Indian rank and file ...	6,988
Total	10,061

with 3,248 non-combatant followers.

The casualties sustained during the siege amounted to 3,776, "of whom 1,025 had been killed or died of wounds, 721 had died of disease, 2,446 had been wounded (including 488 who died of wounds) and 72 were missing." At the time of the surrender there were 1,450 sick and wounded in hospital, of whom 1,336 were exchanged and sent down river from Kut.[76]

The 43rd's casualties during the siege were:—[77]

Officers killed	1
Officers wounded	3
Rank and file killed	17
Rank and file died of wounds	14
Rank and file wounded	52
Rank and file missing	1
Rank and file died of disease	7
Followers wounded	3
Followers died of disease	2
Total	100

[75] Under similar circumstances the remnants of the 43rd were taken prisoners at Yorktown in 1781, and in Guadeloupe in 1794. The description by Sir John Fortescue—*History of the British Army*, Vol. IV, Part II, p. 381—of the capitulation of the garrison of Berville, Guadeloupe, on the 6th October 1794 is extraordinarily applicable to the surrender of the 43rd's descendants at Kut on the 29th April 1916. The officers and men of that old 43rd surrendered on condition that they "should march out with the honours of war and be shipped by first opportunity to Great Britain. Thereupon one hundred and twenty-five ghastly figures staggered out of the lines, 'fitter for hospital than to be under arms' . . . For a whole year . . . they were detained as prisoners; but they died so rapidly in the weeks that followed the surrender that probably few of them ever saw England again. . . . The records of the British Army contain no grander example of heroism than this of the dying garrison of the Camp of Berville."

[76] *Official History*, Vol. II, p. 459.

[77] *My Campaign in Mesopotamia*, p. 356.

V.—HONOURS AND AWARDS.

The following honours were awarded to officers and other ranks for their services up to the capitulation of Kut al Amara:—

Companion of the Order of St. Michael and St. George, and promoted brevet colonel.

Lieutenant-Colonel E. A. E. Lethbridge, D.S.O.

Companion of the Distinguished Service Order.

Captain W. E. T. Morland, M.C., who had received his *Military Cross* for " conspicuous gallantry and resource in action when rallying and leading men up to the firing line. Later he assisted his brigadier with great ability. His horse was shot under him. On another occasion he distinguished himself by marked courage."

Major L. J. Carter, who commanded the 2nd/43rd from February up to the First Battle of Sannaiyat on the 6th April, in which he distinguished himself.

Brevet of lieutenant-colonel.

Major F. H. Stapleton.

Brevet of major.

Captain Hon. J. C. W. S. Foljambe.

Awarded the Military Cross.

Captain G. E. Whittall.
Lieutenant G. Naylor.
Captain J. Startin, R.A.M.C.

Awarded the Distinguished Conduct Medal.

5574 Acting Regimental Serjeant-Major T. A. Love.
6414 Serjeant A. Barlow (acting pioneer serjeant).
5407 Regimental Quartermaster-Serjeant J. W. Burbidge.
9143 Private P. R. Miller.
6334 Serjeant W. Ward.

The following were brought to notice for gallant and distinguished service in the field from the 5th October 1915 to the 17th January 1916:—

Lieutenant-Colonel E. A. E. Lethbridge, D.S.O.
Captain Hon. J. C. W. S. Foljambe.
Second Lieutenant F. Brown (killed in action 10/12/15).
Hon. Captain and Quartermaster T. Ivey.
8034 Serjeant R. J. Adby, D.C.M.
8361 Private A. Apps, D.C.M., " Q " Company.
5766 Acting Company Quartermaster-Serjeant H. Arlett, D.C.M., "P" Company.

8397 Serjeant T. W. Armitt, D.C.M., " R " Company.
9099 Private H. T. Day, " S " Company.
7452 Lance-Corporal W. E. Donohoe, D.C.M., " Q " Company.
9015 Private A. S. Evans, " Q " Company (killed).
8540 Private L. P. Grey, D.C.M., " R " Company.
8687 Private J. H. Harvey (Sherwood Foresters), " P " Company.
7315 Private E. G. H. Leach, " Q " Company.
5574 Acting Regimental Serjeant-Major T. A. Love, D.C.M.
6907 Lance-Serjeant A. Pursglove, D.C.M., " R " Company.
8148 Acting Company Quartermaster-Serjeant W. E. Robins, D.C.M., " R " Company.
8057 Lance-Serjeant F. Smith, D.C.M., " R " Company.
Captain W. E. T. Morland (Staff).
Captain S. C. B. Mundey (Royal Flying Corps).

Relief Force Despatch.
Major L. J. Carter.
Captain S. F. Hammick.
Captain and Adjutant Hon. J. C. W. S. Foljambe.

* * *

The following were recommended by Major-General Townshend for distinguished service during the defence of Kut al Amara, covering the period from the 19th January to the 30th April 1916 :—

Lieutenant-Colonel E. A. E. Lethbridge, D.S.O.
Lieutenant A. E. Mason.
Captain W. E. T. Morland.
Captain S. C. B. Mundey.
Lieutenant G. Naylor.
Captain J. Startin, R.A.M.C.
9046 Lance-Corporal (temporary corporal) S. N. Ballard.
16140 Lance-Corporal R. W. Compton.
845 Private P. Devanney.
8654 Lance-Corporal (temporary corporal) A. Evenett.
8987 Private W. Hicks.
9673 Private E. G. Merritt.
6907 Corporal (temporary serjeant) A. E. Pursglove.
9020 Lance-Corporal W. G. Rakestrow.
8848 Private R. W. Rankin (killed).
8592 Private W. H. Saxby.
8484 Private C. Stokes.
8395 Lance-Corporal T. Swift.
10497 Corporal (temporary serjeant) G. Trine, Highland Light Infantry.

GROUP OF PRISONERS AT KASTAMUNI.
1. Private Knox. 2. Lance-Corporal Young. 3. Lance-Corporal Miller.
4. Serjeant F. Ponting. 5. Serjeant W. Finch.

CHAPTER XXI.

The 43rd in Captivity.

" They that be slain with the sword are better than they that be slain with hunger: for these pine away, stricken through for want of the fruits of the field."
—*Lamentations of Jeremiah.*

OFFICERS SEPARATED FROM MEN—MORTALITY IN THE 43RD—THE MARCHING-OUT STATE—THE MARCH INTO CAPTIVITY—BRUTALITY OF ARAB ESCORT—THE PRISONERS REACH BAGHDAD—THE TRAIN JOURNEY TO SAMARRA—THE MARCH TO TIKRIT—SHARQAT—MOSUL—TERRIBLE SUFFERINGS—THE MARCH TO RAS AL 'AIN—THE TRAIN JOURNEY TO ISLAHIYA—THE JOURNEY TO MAMOURA AND MARCH TO BAGHCHE—THE 43RD PRISONERS DETAILED FOR WORK ON RAILWAY AT AIRAN—RAVAGES OF DISEASE—TREATMENT AT AFIUN QARAHISAR AND ANGORA—NEWS REACHES ENGLAND—THE PARLIAMENTARY REPORT—THE REGIMENTAL CARE COMMITTEE—STATISTICS OF PARCELS—THE JOURNEY OF THE OFFICERS INTO CAPTIVITY——ECHELON " A " AND " B "—YOZGAD—SECRET COMMUNICATION WITH ENGLAND—COLONEL LETHBRIDGE'S SUMMARY OF THE TURKS' CHARACTERISTICS.

(*See Maps on page* 130, *and facing pages* 274 *and* 302.)

It is the intention of this chapter to include the whole period of the captivity. Though it is a subject on which any prisoner could write a book, statistics and diaries never wholly escaped the knavery and thievery of the Turkish jailers.

Early in the morning the Regiment started sorting out its kits which had been transported by river under Captain Mundey the previous day. Luckily most of the kits arrived safely, but the officers lost the mess *yakdan* in which were all the cups, plates, knives, forks, etc.[1] The Turks provided no tents, shelters or blankets, and many weak men suffered considerably from exposure to the sun.[2] Both General Townshend and General Melliss were sick at this time, and all the responsibility devolved on General Delamain, who did his utmost to rouse the Turks to an appreciation of the needs of the starving troops. " In fairness to the Turks it should be remembered that they were hard put to it to maintain their own field army in food and ammunition with their very inadequate shipping and land transport "[3]; also they did not realize that the British and Indian soldier could not subsist on the meagre fare on which they themselves throve; nor did they realize the effect of the summer heat on the British soldier. General Melliss left hospital and joined the men in camp, where he used all his influence to alleviate

---

[1] *Chronicle,* 1927, p. 185.   [2] *Official History,* Vol. II, p 461.
[3] *In Kut and Captivity,* pp. 262-263.

conditions. " But he soon fell ill again and the apathy of the Turks was too great to overcome."[4]

There is little doubt but that the rations ordered by Khalil Pasha were sold by the Turks, who wandered round the camp hawking dates, onions, *chupattis* and bread, the free and rightful ration of the troops. Such was the hunger of many of the soldiers that they bartered their clothes for a handful of food.[5] Fuel, however, was issued free, and the camp was organized and administered by our staff. At this time the Turks had no possible excuse for underfeeding our troops, as the *Julnar* with ample stores on board was in their possession. She, however, was detained until the 3rd, when some British and Indian troops were issued with a good, if small, ration.[6] The same day General Townshend with Colonel Parr and Captain Morland, of the 43rd, passed Shumran on his way upstream. The officers and men of the 6th Division lined the bank and cheered loud and long as the launch went by, but it was a sad-hearted General Townshend who stood to attention at the salute and acknowledged the cheers. As he rightly said in his book, " never had any man a finer command."[7] But, though with the Turks he had great prestige as a fine tactician and fighter, he was powerless to ameliorate the lot of his gallant command and henceforward fades out of the picture.

Despite of many protests, the Turks issued orders separating the officers from the rank and file,[8] and on the 4th the first batch of British and Indian officers—to be known as Echelon " A "—embarked on the *Burhanieh* with General Delamain in command. Each regiment was, however, allowed to leave one officer to take charge of the men until they marched to Baghdad. Major Henley was detailed to look after the men of the 43rd, and remained with Echelon " B " at Shumran until the 10th.

The officers of the 1st/43rd who embarked on the 4th were: Colonel Lethbridge, Captains Mundey and Ivey, Lieutenants Mason and Naylor; and of the attached officers Captain Startin, R.A.M.C., and Lieutenants Mellor and Heawood.

On the 6th tidings were received that a large barge containing private regimental stores[9] was expected. But when the barge arrived at about 10 a.m. and was unloaded by the Turks, it was found that there was nothing for the 43rd. However, the Norfolk Regiment, which had more stores than it could carry, handed over a large quantity and the Regiment received ample sup-

[4] *Official History*, Vol. II, p. 461.   [5] *In Kut and Captivity*, p. 270.
[6] There is no record of the 43rd having received an issue.
[7] pp. 240-241.
[8] A similar separation occurred after the surrender at Saratoga in 1777 with the same results. The rank and file prisoners were brutally maltreated by the American colonists.
[9] From the captured *Julnar*.

plies of "butter, milk, biscuits, cake, plum pudding, and several odd luxuries, but no tobacco." This consignment[10] was probably the means of enabling many a starved soldier to survive a little longer; it also had a psychological effect so that the men seemed cheerful when the column paraded to march out at 2 p.m.

Several men were too ill to march and were left at Shumran. The mortality was particularly severe while the Regiment was in camp, fifty-three men, according to Serjeant Munn's account,[11] dying of enteritis due to bad or inappropriate food taken on starved stomachs.

At 2 p.m. the Regiment paraded in column of companies under Major Henley, who, standing on the top of a bottomless bucket, spoke a few words to the men wishing them farewell and above all a quick release from captivity by the victory of the Allies. Little did he know what tragic irony he was uttering. The marching-out state of the Regiment was as follows:—

Acting Regimental Serjeant-Major T. A. Love, D.C.M. ("P" Company), commanding	1
"P" Company, under command of 8093 Serjeant Richardson	61
"Q" Company, under command of 6334 Serjeant Ward, D.C.M.	58
"R" Company, under command of 8397 Serjeant Armitt, D.C.M.	67
"S" Company, under command of 5235 Company Serjeant-Major Voller	66
	253[12]
(Orderly Room Quartermaster-Serjeant White and Regimental Quartermaster-Serjeant Burbidge, D.C.M., were included in the above total.)	
In hospital[13]	42
Detained as unfit to march[13]	16
	311
Native followers, including Regimental Jemadar Bhisti Rustum	25

[10] Major Henley discharged the debt to the Norfolk Regiment when the 43rd was stationed at Limerick after the war.

[11] *Chronicle*, 1915-16, p. 132. This figure, large though it is, is probably not exaggerated; the names of thirty-three other ranks—namely, twenty-seven of the 43rd, three reservists and three attached—have been traced. See Appendix XI for fuller statistics.

[12] The strength of companies, taken from Major Henley's diary, *Chronicle*, 1927, p. 187, agrees with R.S.M. Love's parade state in 1916-17, p. 103.

[13] These men went to Baghdad by boat.

For an hour and a half the troops stood under the full force of the sun awaiting the order to move. When at last it came, at about 3.30 p.m., the men of the 43rd shouldered their few small possessions and marched off in column of fours, saluting Major Henley as they passed through the gap in the perimeter bank. Outside the Arab guards took charge, and they started their journey into captivity, a journey which was to test the very foundations of their English lineage, their pluck and powers of endurance. For a parallel to this march it is necessary to go back to the earliest days of history, when prisoners were treated like cattle without souls of their own; to the triumphs of the Cæsars, to the conquests of Alexander the Great, Genghis Khan and Tammerlane, when captives were scourged from place to place regardless of humanity. That such methods should have been employed in the twentieth century may seem strange without reckoning with the Turk, who for unknown centuries had become inured to the barbarity of his rulers and thought nothing of meting out to prisoners what he would expect to receive in their place.[14]

I.—The March of the Rank and File into Captivity.[15, 16]

When the column started this terrible march, 300 of the garrison had already died of disease and starvation at Shumran. The Turks refused to listen to the earnest entreaties of General Delamain that a proportion of officers should be allowed to march with the men. The only concessions allowed were that those unfit to march should be sent by river, and that the distances to be covered daily should not exceed eight miles.[17] The first march from Shumran was about nine miles. On arrival Regimental Serjeant-Major Love was told by the adjutant of the escort that the Regiment was to march to Baghdad by easy stages, but this proved to be a cruel lie. During the night several men approached Regimental Serjeant-Major Love with complaints that the escort had stolen their property, and in the morning two men found that their boots had disappeared. Thereafter the men seldom took off their boots; or, if they did, they tied them to their persons during the night.[18]

Starting at 6 a.m. on the 7th, the column was kept moving until 4 p.m.

---

[14] There is a misleading note in the *Chronicle*, 1927, p. 195, wherein it is suggested that the Turks did not *wilfully* illtreat the men of the Regiment in the first phase of the march. All the evidence of survivors and history goes to prove conclusively the reverse. The only explanation open to the Turks and Arabs for their treatment is that, being Turks and Arabs, they knew no better. But that they did wilfully maltreat our men every line of the records of this march will prove beyond doubt. The degree of ill-treatment alone differed in the subsequent stages of the march. Unfortunately, this misleading note has never been corrected in later numbers of the *Chronicle*.

[15] The march of the rank and file has been recorded first, though it took place last in point of time, because in importance it holds first place.

[16] See Maps 7, p. 130; 16, facing p. 274; 19, facing p. 302.

[17] *Official History*, Vol. II, p. 462.   [18] *Chronicle*, 1916-17, p. 103.

through intense and suffocating heat. The distance to Bughaila was fifteen miles—fifteen miles without water or shade—fifteen miles of which every step was a struggle for the weak, diseased and emaciated men. They stumbled and staggered, parched with thirst, blinded with the sun, choked with dust. Those—and they were many—who had already contracted dysentery were scourged with whips and sticks or clubbed with rifle butts[19] by the Arab escort until, infinitely exhausted, they managed to rejoin the column. Several men of the Regiment who fell out for this reason were never seen again. Those who fell off the camels provided for the worst cases were left to die unless rescued by their comrades. The track of the column was sprinkled for miles with human litter, with men in the last stages of exhaustion. Private Carter, " R " Company cook, died within three miles of camp and was buried where he fell. It was only owing to the indomitable spirit of the men that any managed to struggle into camp. As it was, some men did not arrive until well after dark. The following day it was obvious even to the Turkish commandant that the prisoners could not march for two days. " They had been issued with three days' rations (six Turkish biscuits and a handful of dates per man) on leaving Shumran, and were thirty-six hours in camp near Bughaila before they received any more; each man was then given a few mouldy *chupattis* and could only purchase extra *chupattis* from the Arab guards at three for a rupee (ten times the actual cost)."[20] Until the rations were issued, the men of the 43rd subsisted on the remains of the Norfolk Regiment's gift, but these were soon exhausted. A few black *chupattis* were issued to the dying men, but not to those who were sick. During the halt ten men were admitted to hospital, and of these Serjeant Barfoot and 9302 Lance-Corporal Williams, " P " Company, died.[21]

Two ghastly marches brought the column to Aziziya which was reached on the 12th. By this time many men had neither boots nor water-bottles, and wrapped their bleeding feet in the shreds of their puttees. The Arab escort made several false reports against the men, alleging that they had been threatened with knives by the prisoners of the Regiment. Consequently the Turkish commandant confiscated all knives and sharp instruments, allowing only one blunt table-knife per twenty-five men. When Regimental Serjeant-Major Love saw the serjeant of the escort, Shiaba by name, beating Armourer Quartermaster-Serjeant Packer, who had fallen out owing to dysentery, he reported the Turk to the commandant. For satisfaction Regimental Serjeant-Major Love was told that there was no cause for complaint; the Arab had done his duty; this was Turkish discipline, and, while

---

[19] *Official History*, Vol. II, p. 463. *In Kut and Captivity*, p. 281. *Chronicle*, 1915-16, p. 132.
[20] *In Kut and Captivity*, p. 281.
[21] *Chronicle*, 1916-17, p. 104.

prisoners, the Regiment would be subject to Turkish discipline.[22] At Aziziya 350 men unfit to march were left behind, " crowded together in miserable insanitary buildings," to await river transport. The rest staggered on past Zor and through Ctesiphon, where they had so soundly thrashed their present captors. It was a bitter sight as they neared the great Arch and crossed the battlefield—a ragged and exhausted column of starved men.

Further evidence of this stage of the march has been supplied by Captain E. O. Mousley,[23] who has given a vivid description of the captors' behaviour and the suffering of our men:

" We tingled with anger and shame at seeing on the other bank a sad little column of British troops who had marched up from Kut driven by a wild crowd of Kurdish horsemen who brandished sticks and what looked like whips. The eyes of our men stared from white faces, drawn long with the suffering of a too tardy death, and they held out their hands towards our boat. As they dragged one foot after another some fell, and those with the rear guard came in for blows from cudgels and sticks. I saw one Kurd strike a British soldier who was limping along, he reeled under the blows. . . . Some had been thrashed to death, some killed, and some robbed of their kit and left to be tortured by the Arabs. Men were dying of cholera and dysentery and often fell out from sheer weakness. . . . Enteritis, a form of cholera, attacked the whole garrison after Kut fell, and the change of food no doubt helped this. . . . A man turned green and foamed at the mouth. His eyes became sightless and the most terrible moans conceivable came from his inner being. . . . They died, one and all, with terrible suddenness. One saw British soldiers dying of enteritis with a green ooze issuing from their lips, their mouths fixed open, in and out of which flies walked."

Turkish and German flags were flying in Baghdad on the 17th when the column was driven through the streets—a " dreadful spectacle to see British troops in rags, many barefooted, starved and sick wending their way under brutal Arab guards through an Eastern bazaar."[24] Like cattle the men were marched through the streets amid the mocking jeers of the Baghdadi scum to an exposed enclosure on the right bank of the Tigris while cinematograph operators recorded the first success of Turkish arms for many decades. Here the men were visited by General Delamain and Colonel Hehir, the A.D.M.S. in Kut, who managed to arrange for eleven of the British medical officers to remain in Baghdad and look after the sick. General Melliss, V.C., was also tireless in his efforts on behalf of the men, but to no purpose. Here too the

---

[22] *Ibid.*, 1916-17, p. 104. [23] *Secrets of a Kuttite.*
[24] *Official History*, Vol. II, p. 534. From the diary of Captain Shakeshaft, 2nd Norfolk Regiment.

American Consul, Mr. Brissell,[25] visited the men of the 43rd, encamped near the railway station with negligible protection from the sun and absolutely no sanitary arrangements. Amid the stench and flies the men remained for nearly three days, and for the first time received a ration of bread—two small loaves daily per man. Leaving 500 sick at Baghdad, the remainder were packed into trucks and dispatched in batches to Samarra, *en route* for Mosul and Anatolia.

Meanwhile the sick in Baghdad, bad as their treatment was, were immeasurably more comfortable than their supposedly hale comrades. Serjeant Munn, who was admitted to hospital with dysentery, was dieted on five loaves of brown bread and five cigarettes daily.[26] But when the British medical officers took charge of the sick prisoners, conditions improved at once, thanks to the freemasonry of medicine. They spent their money on the men, and Captain Clifford even sold his kit to buy extra milk for one of his patients. Eventually Serjeant Munn and a few others of the 43rd were among the 345 sick or convalescent prisoners who were exchanged.[27]

On reaching Samarra the men of the 43rd were allowed to rest for two days before beginning the march to Mosul. Here the prisoners were organized in two columns, the Regiment being with the first column. On account of the intense heat by day the column marched by night; and on the 22nd May the men of the Regiment set out for Tikrit, about thirty miles distant. The track lay over very rough and stony ground, and cut the feet of those who had no boots to veritable ribbons, for strips of blanket are no protection against sharp stones. For rations the men were given a double handful of *atta*, a handful of wheat, a spoonful of *ghi* and some salt, but no firewood.[28] The men were therefore forced to sell the clothes they wore to avoid starvation.

At Tikrit the men of the 43rd were joined by Company Serjeant-Major Butcher and about seventy non-commissioned officers and men of various units. From Tikrit they marched through Sharqat to Mosul, a distance of about 130 miles as the crow flies, averaging over twenty miles a day on the six stages.[29] General Melliss and his aide-de-camp, Captain Shakeshaft, followed in the wake of this tragic march; and Captain Shakeshaft recorded some of the sights they saw. At Tikrit they met " a number of unfortunate British and Indian soldiers who were standing at the door of a miserable yard, where they were herded together. . . . They were in a miserable plight, many suffering from dysentery. Others . . . had no boots for

[25] He managed to prevail on the Turks to admit the worst cases to hospital.
[26] *Chronicle*, 1915-16, p. 133.   [27] See Appendix XI.
[28] *In Kut and Captivity*, p. 311.
[29] *Chronicle*, 1927, p. 199. The distance by road from Samarra to Mosul was 180 miles.

marching. . . . They received only a ration of wheat. The Arabs used to bring milk and eggs to sell and ask exorbitant prices; consequently they would soon have no money and would die of starvation and neglect. . . . Sometimes, when a sick man would crawl out of the hovel they lived in, Arabs would throw stones and chase him into the yard. I will spare . . . any description of the dark, filthy hovel where they slept."[30]

General Melliss protested strongly in a letter to Khalil Pasha, who eventually sent a British medical officer with a hospital establishment to Samarra. Many of the men who fell out on the first stages of the march to Mosul were collected by this party, " but many more had passed on out of reach."[31] Owing to General Melliss's exposures of the sufferings of the rank and file, subsequent parties of officers were sent from Baghdad to Anatolia by another route so as " to prevent any further discovery of what had happened."[30] The men of the Regiment halted for two days at Mosul. " Every one was now suffering from diarrhœa, and about twenty men were admitted to hospital, including C.S.M. Butcher and Serjeant Gibbs."[32]

At Mosul Regimental Serjeant-Major Love was told that the men were to march across the desert tableland to Ras al 'Ain, where they would work on the Baghdad railway. The prisoners were here divided into three groups: English, Musalman and Hindu. This was a matter of religious policy, for the Musalmans were potential allies and had from the outset received better treatment from the Turks than English or Hindus. Before leaving Mosul twenty-five men of the Volunteer Artillery Battery were attached to the men of the 43rd, increasing the strength to about 300. The march across the desert through Dolabia,[33] Rumailan Kabir,[34] Nisibin, Kochhisar[35] to Ras al 'Ain was a *via dolorosa* over a distance of about two hundred miles. On one march the men had to cover forty-five kilometres—nearly thirty miles—between 4 p.m. and 11 a.m. " At the end of this march seven men were reported as having fallen out sick, and they never rejoined "[36] the 43rd; two of them were 8210 Private Wilson and 7740 Private Taylor. On or about the 19th June the survivors of the 43rd reached Ras al 'Ain. Private Harding—8668, " Q " Company—died on the last march, but the escort refused to allow his body to be brought into camp for burial.

It is probable that the column started the march from Mosul on the

---

[30] *Official History*, Vol. II, p. 534. General Melliss in a letter says that the men " were afraid to go any little distance alone to relieve themselves for fear of being murdered for their clothes."

[31] *Ibid.*, Vol. II, p. 464.   [32] *Chronicle*, 1916-17, p. 106.

[33] I have been unable to trace this place on modern maps of Turkey.

[34] This place has been spelt Rumala and Rumelat.

[35] Sometimes spelt Kotschissar.   [36] *Chronicle*, 1916-17, p. 106.

31st May or the 1st June.[37] The distance was therefore covered in about twenty days, an average of twenty miles a day. Fortunately for posterity and future generations of the 43rd accounts of this terrible march, written by Captains Shakeshaft and Mousley of General Melliss's party, are available. Though they mention no regiments in their accounts, what is true of one is true of all. Many men of the 43rd never survived the march from Mosul to Ras al 'Ain. General Melliss started across the desert about three weeks after the 43rd column. On the 20th June Captain Shakeshaft records that " we found six British soldiers in a fearfully emaciated condition lying in a filthy stable. Of course, the Turks had done nothing for them. One of them said, ' We are like rats in a trap and they are slowly killing us.' "[38] All the way across the desert the Arabs singled out the English for cruel and barbarous treatment. On one occasion the escort was seen burying a British soldier " who was foaming at the mouth and moving." When his comrades went to his help, they were driven off with loaded rifles.[39] At Nisibin a party of sick men " too weak to stand were knocked about " by a Turkish serjeant while awaiting admittance to hospital. Even when admitted they " received no medical treatment whatsoever . . . helpless dysentery cases were neither washed nor tended in any way."[39] The only sympathy and help the prisoners received came from Germans serving in Turkey.

Captain Mousley also visited the hospital at Nisibin and recorded what he saw:

" A bare strip of filthy ground ran down to the river some two hundred yards off. Along the wall, protected by only a few scanty leaves and loose grass flung over some *tatti* work of branches through which the fierce sun streamed with unabated violence, I saw some human forms which no eye but one acquainted with the phenomenon of the trek could possibly recognize as British soldiery. They were wasted to wreaths of skin hanging upon a bone frame. For the most part they were stark naked except for a rag around their loins, their garments having been sold to buy food, bread, milk, and medicine. Their eyes were white with the death hue. Their sunken cheeks were covered with the unshaven growth of weeks. One had just died and two or three corpses just been removed. . . . But the corpses had lain there for days. Some of the men were too weak to move. The result of the collection of filth and the insanitary state in the centre of which these men lay in a climate like this can be imagined. Water was not regularly supplied to them and those unable to walk had to crawl to the river for water. One could see their tracks through the dirt and grime . . . other forms near by I thought dead, but they moved unconsciously again. One saw the beehive pheno-

---

[37] *Ibid.*, pp. 103-108. R.S.M. Love gives few dates in his description of the march as his diaries were invariably stolen by the Turks.
[38] *Official History*, Vol. II, p. 535.   [39] *In Kut and Captivity*, p. 343.

menon of flies which swarmed by the million going in and out of living men's open mouths."

As the party travelled on they overtook more human derelicts lying in the track of the plodding columns. Captain Mousley has said:

"I shall never forget one soldier who could go no further. He fell resignedly on to the ground, the stump of a cigarette in his mouth, and with a tiredness born of long suffering, buried his head in his arms to shut out the disappearing column and smoked on. We were half a mile behind the column. . . . One sick soldier was hanging on to a strap of my donkey, my orderly on another. His feet were all blood, as his boots had been taken from him. A soldier went to the sick man behind, but I did not see him again. Shortly after . . . I saw another man crawling on all fours over the desert in the dark quite alone. He said he hoped to reach the next halt, and get his promised ride for half an hour. . . . We picked him up, and I gave him my strap. Another sick orderly held him up. He was all bone, and could scarcely lurch along. At another place we came across a British soldier. . . . He had been left in a cave, and had evidently eaten nothing for days, but had crawled down to the river. He was delirious and jabbering, and thought he was a dog."

General Melliss, in a letter, said: "At Nisibin was a hospital [sic], so Padre Spooner told me afterwards, where a number of our men were lying in a terrible state of dysentery, with flies crawling in and out of their mouths and eyes; and in an inner room into which he managed to enter before the Turks could stop him he found a number of our men; corpses stripped; and one poor fellow opened his eyes and said, 'O pray God, sir, that I may die quickly.'"

On arrival at Ras al 'Ain the men of the 43rd were given "a 2-lb. loaf of coarse bread and received no more for forty-eight hours." At about 3 p.m. they were herded like cattle into a train, each truck containing an average of forty men. Some wagons were closed and some open. The doors of the closed wagons were locked and only opened at stations, although among the occupants were many men in advanced stages of dysentery. One wagon, containing fifty-two men, was not unlocked until Islahiya was reached, twenty-four hours later, "in spite of the shouts and appeals of the occupants."[40] There was no room for the men to lie down. They sat on top of each other throughout twenty-four hours of summer heat amid an indescribable stench. At Islahiya twenty sick men of the 43rd were left behind, including Orderly Room Quartermaster-Serjeant White and Company Serjeant-Major Voller.[41] The sick were left in "Arab tents on the ground without bedding, and in some cases absolutely naked." Men died at the

[40] *Ibid.*, p. 344.   [41] They died at Mamoura.

rate of three or four a day, and were " often laid outside the tent naked, and had to be buried in the evening by the patients."[42]

On the 23rd June when General Melliss arrived, a German warrant officer reported that the prisoners were being starved to death, and " promised to do what he could for our men."[43] The general protested again to the commandant, but to no purpose. On the road from Islahiya this gallant general befriended many exhausted prisoners. At Hassan Begli he found twenty-seven sick men of the 43rd, Royal Artillery and Royal Navy who were unable to march. He procured rations for them through the agency of a German under-officer and refused to move until he had seen the invalids safely off to Mamoura[44] in carts.

Leaving Islahiya at 8 p.m. the men of the 43rd started to march across the Amanus mountains and, after halting for three hours during the night, arrived in camp at 1 p.m. The following day the column marched to Mamoura where it rested for two days. Here it was that General Melliss came up with the main body of the prisoners. The men of the 43rd " made a rush to see him. His kindness to us will never be forgotten. He was greatly touched by our wretched condition, and he offered the men a few words of advice, giving them at the same time all the money he possessed—I believe five Turkish pounds in gold," wrote Regimental Serjeant-Major Love. " The commandant of the escort, observing what was taking place, ordered the men away, and the general was not allowed to see us again."[45]

On or about the 24th the men of the 43rd entrained for Adana, where orders were received to return at once to Mamoura. The following day at 2 p.m. Regimental Serjeant-Major Love was told to move to a camp about one hour's march distant. This was a cruel lie, for the survivors were forced to march to Baghche,[46] about thirteen miles distant, which took about nine hours to cover. On this march Regimental Serjeant-Major Love witnessed " a most brutal attack by the same Arab—Shiaba—on a young Australian of the Royal Flying Corps. He was sick at the time, and Shiaba struck him across the head with a large stick and knocked him down. Several of our men rushed to the lad's assistance, but they were driven back by the escort, and were forced to leave him where he fell." Regimental Serjeant-Major Love was suffering from dysentery himself during this march, and " was obliged to fall out for ten or fifteen minutes, but was able to keep up with the party for a time." Eventually, however, he lost sight of the party going round a bend in the road, when Shiaba struck him over the head with a big stick and knocked him senseless. He says: " When I came to myself I

---

[42] *In Kut and Captivity*, p. 357.
[43] *Official History*, Vol. II, p. 535.
[44] Spelt Mamourie in the *Chronicle*. At this time it was railhead from the Amanus mountains to the Cilician plain.
[45] *Chronicle*, 1916-17, p. 107.
[46] Spelt Bagtchi in the roll books.

found my arms, back and head bleeding, and the khaki coat which I was wearing had been stolen off my back."[47]

The following day, the 26th, the party was paraded and handed over to the German engineer, Herr Klaus, for work on the railway line. This day the Australian lad died of his injuries, and Regimental Serjeant-Major Love reported the case to Herr Klaus.

The rank and file of the Regiment, with the non-commissioned officers and men attached to them, were sent to Airan[48] to work on the railway. The strength of the party was now only 104. At Airan the men were allowed to rest for seven days; tents were issued and a bread ration of one kilo per man was given out. They were then detailed for tasks according to their trades before enlistment, and work was started on the 3rd July. The day's work began at 6 a.m. and ended at 6 p.m. " with half an hour off for breakfast and an hour for dinner, Sundays included." Although anxious to work in order to earn a few piastres wherewith to buy extra food, the men of the Regiment were in no way fit for any manual labour. It must be remembered that it was now the height of the Anatolian summer. Fever and beri-beri broke out among the survivors.[49] Those who went to hospital received no treatment. They were given rice water and a quarter of a loaf.[50] One or two men died daily either from cholera, dysentery, enteritis or beri-beri. Between July and October twenty-three non-commissioned officers and men of the Regiment died from one or other of these diseases.[51]

Despite of the ravages of diseases the men were driven to work for two months, and the mortality in the camp became terrible. Gradually, however, the engineer became less exacting when he realized that it was impossible to work moribund men.

The hospital arrangements at Airan were conspicuous by their absence. At first the sick were sent by train over the eight miles to Baghche; and when the hospital there became overcrowded a large German tent was pitched in Airan as a hospital. A Swiss, Vogt by name, was appointed medical officer to this hospital by virtue of the fact that he had been a masseur before the war. Of medical qualifications he had none. A cruel sadist, he used to strike the weak and sick without provocation, but Regimental Serjeant-Major Love reported him to the German chief engineer who successfully prevented repetitions of his brutality.

By September most of the men were sick and incapable of work. They were therefore handed back to Turkish custody. The Turks then decided to

[47] *Chronicle*, 1916-17, p. 107.
[48] I have not been able to find this place on modern maps of Turkey, and I have therefore used R.S.M. Love's spelling.
[49] *Chronicle*, 1916-17, p. 108.   [50] *In Kut and Captivity*, p. 357.
[51] From R.S.M. Love's roll book in the Regimental Museum. *Chronicle*, 1916-17, gives the number as 24. See Appendix XI.

disperse the prisoners to various camps in the interior. On the 7th September the seventy-six men of the 43rd were sent away from Airan to such places as Konia, Mamoura, Afiun Qarahisar and Angora, while a few of the sick and stragglers were lucky enough to be sent to Adana and Tarsus, where, thanks to the exertions of the American Consul at Mersina and American doctors and ladies, some of them were saved from inevitable death.

The journey of the rest into the interior differed not one whit from the journeys in the past. Without doctors, without medicines, our men " were packed in railway wagons without food and then driven across the Taurus mountains, where there was a break in the line, by gendarmes with the butts of their rifles. . . . An Austrian officer who saw part of this journey likened it to a scene from Dante's *Inferno*."[52]

At Afiun Qarahisar and Angora our men received brutal and cowardly treatment from the Turks. But eventually the flogging and maltreatment of the prisoners by the commandant at Afiun Qarahisar became so notorious that even the Turkish Government was constrained to dismiss him. This satanic sadist sold the men's clothes, and had them bastinadoed if they did not hand in their blankets. In the bitterly cold winter months they were allowed one blanket and a quilt, but no mattress; and were crowded in small rooms with an inadequate supply of fuel. One prisoner was flogged and imprisoned on a bread-and-water diet for a fortnight for burning verminous clothing. The hospital resembled a shambles rather than a house of healing. The weak were beaten because they were helpless. They were injected with some brandy-coloured fluid from the effects of which they never recovered. Those who could not feed or wash themselves were left to die of starvation in their own ordure. The story is one of nauseating barbarity,[53] but some lion-hearted men survived.

Colonel Lethbridge was commandant of the prisoners in 1917, and in his memoirs he says:

" The Turkish commandant treated our private soldiers grossly, and was a drunkard. When in this state he was not accountable for his actions. The story was current that he was one of Enver Pasha's men, hired by that worthy to do his dirty work in the capacity of assassin, and that, being in his power, Enver had given him the appointment." It was said that he had served many years in the Yemen where he had had sunstroke which was assumed to have affected his brain. " There was no crime that this individual was incapable of, including grossly immoral and unnatural conduct." Colonel Lethbridge collected the evidence of this brute's barbarity and

---

[52] *Official History*, Vol. II, p. 465.
[53] *In Kut and Captivity*, pp. 370-373, and Appendix XI. At least thirty-four non-commissioned officers and men of the 43rd died at Afiun Qarahisar, and at least thirteen at Angora.

handed it over to the Dutch office. " The Turk," he says, " was tried afterwards . . . for appropriating the money sent from England for our private soldiers."

For months the Turks would not allow neutral consuls to visit the prison camps; complaints and appeals by the prisoners were treated with studied indifference and supine apathy. But gradually tidings of the conditions leaked through to England, and the Turks " were forced to open up their country to Red Cross delegates."[54] Conditions gradually improved; parcels of food and clothing for the men of the 43rd began to arrive in February 1917, thanks to those ladies of the Regiment who worked on the Regimental Care Committee. The joy, when life held but few joys, which these parcels brought to the men was unbounded, and that they were grateful Regimental Serjeant-Major Love testifies in his account. " But for them [the Committee] very few would ever have reached home," he wrote.[55]

As the war dragged on British doctors were allowed to take medical charge of the British prisons, and the Turkish guards gradually began to fraternize with our men. By 1918 the men in most of the camps " were warmly clothed, cheerful and had sufficient food and money."[56]

At the cost of the charge of redundancy, the Parliamentary report on the march into captivity may here conveniently be quoted :—

" Their state of preparation for a march of five hundred miles, the health and strength and equipment which they possessed for withstanding one of the fiercest summers of the globe, can be pictured from what has been described already; and the efficiency of the Oriental care to which they were entrusted is as easily imagined. The officers who were left in Baghdad, and who watched them depart, could only feel the deepest anxiety and dread.

" The truth of what happened has only very gradually become known, and in all its details it will never be known, for those who could tell the worst are long ago dead. But it is certain that this desert journey rests upon those responsible for it as a crime of the kind which we call historic, so long and terrible was the torture it meant for thousands of helpless men. If it is urged that the Turkish powers of organization and forethought were utterly incapable of handling such a problem as the transport of these prisoners, the plea is sound enough as an explanation; as an excuse it is nothing. There was no one in the higher Turkish command who could be ignorant that to send the men out on such a journey and in such conditions was to condemn half of them to certain death, unless every proper precaution were taken. And there were precautions which were easy and obvious, the chief one being that the prisoners should not be deprived of the care of their

---

[54] *In Kut and Captivity*, p. 433. [55] *Chronicle*, 1916-17, p. 108.
[56] *In Kut and Captivity*, p. 434.

health which their own officers could give them. Yet even this plain opportunity was sacrificed, as we have seen, with perfect indifference to the fate of the mere rank and file. Here, as always, we find that Turkish apathy is not as simple as it seems; it betrays considerable respect of persons, and it contrives to evade the most dangerous witnesses of its guilt."[57]

All the way from Shumran, through Aziziya, Baghdad, Tikrit, Sharqat, Mosul, Nisibin, Ras al 'Ain, Islahiya, Mamoura, Baghche and Airan to the prison camps of the interior, men of the 43rd left their bones. Lucky were they who died early on that blood-stained journey.

We have rightly been taught to regard the retreat of the two battalions of the 43rd to Vigo and Corunna in 1809 as a feat of supreme endurance under terrible conditions. That retreat alone can bear any comparison with the march into captivity. Then the officers—the soldiers' best friends—were present to lead and inspire; but one hundred and seven years later the men were deprived of their officers, as were Burgoyne's men after Saratoga in 1777 with similar results. Upon Regimental Serjeant-Major Love, D.C.M., descended the mantle of leadership, and, as ever in the history of the 43rd, this gallant warrant officer assumed it and all its responsibilities. Sick though he was, he never spared himself in his efforts to protect those in his charge. Quick to realize that the lives of his men depended on him, he enforced discipline and self-control with all the strength of his character and training at the cost of his popularity, ably supported in his endeavours by Quartermaster-Serjeant Burbidge, D.C.M., Serjeant Ward, D.C.M., and the non-commissioned officers. Vilified, insulted and reviled by the Turks, he never for one moment surrendered to the enemy, though their prisoner, nor gave up the unequal contest. His wholly admirable conduct under treatment which few Englishmen have ever been called upon to endure should be remembered by those who have the honour to serve in the 43rd as an example of leadership, courage and determination comparable to that of Serjeant Newman.

Before reverting to the officers of " A " and " B " Echelons, it will be convenient at this point to record the activities of the Regimental Care Committee[58] which rendered such conspicuous help and service to the prisoners of the Regiment. The committee consisted of :—

Lieutenant-Colonel Sir Charles Cuyler, Bart. (chairman).
Mrs. C. M. Wilson, O.B.E. (General business).
Mrs. H. R. Davies (Parcels).
Mrs. A. J. F. Eden (Clothing).
Miss Audrey Ashhurst (Propaganda).

Also many others who in a lesser capacity assisted the committee.

[57] *Official History*, Vol. II, pp. 463-464.
[58] For full report see *Chronicle*, 1919-20, pp. 42 *et seq.*

Started in March 1915, this Care Committee was recognized in February 1916 by the War Office, which required, and was prepared to supply, information concerning prisoners of war. The committee had two main tasks: the location of the prisoners and provision of comforts when discovered. " The location of prisoners required an immense amount of heavy correspondence and considerable tact."[59] It will readily be realized that the committee had the greatest difficulty in tracing the whereabouts of the wretched prisoners in Turkey. Sufficient evidence has already been produced in these records to prove the barbarity of the Turks, high and low, in their treatment of our men. Not only did the Turkish officials shut their eyes to the needs of our men, but also with studied apathy " frustrated many of the attempts made by the British Government, the Red Cross, the Regimental Care Committee and others to feed and clothe the prisoners and to supply them regularly with money."[60] But eventually, thanks to the help of the American Embassy and later the Dutch Legation, parcels found their way through, and conditions for the rank-and-file prisoners improved considerably from the spring of 1917 onwards. Regular food parcels were sent once a fortnight and were " supplemented by regular remittances of money through the Red Cross, Geneva." But owing to delays in transport through Austria and Turkey the parcels were received anything but regularly by the prisoners. When, however, the Austrian railways were blocked, the money remittances were doubled. Between the 8th January 1917 and the 19th September 1918 2,536 food parcels were sent to Turkey for which 418 acknowledgments were received. Evidence from released prisoners proved that " less than a third of the food sent reached them "; as an example: of 247 parcels sent to eleven prisoners at Angora, only seventy-two were acknowledged. As many as 434 clothes parcels were sent in 1916 and 1917, forty-three being addressed to prisoners who died before receipt of them; but 118 were definitely acknowledged, " some men saying that the warm English clothing had helped to save their lives."

The stupendous work of the Care Committee can hardly be realized nor sufficiently appreciated. For four long years the ladies of the Regiment and counties worked with tireless energy so that, if possible, no one prisoner should think that he had been forgotten. And not only to the prisoners themselves did the Care Committee render signal service but also to their anxious families. The work naturally increased year by year, food prices soared, yet the provisions were regularly dispatched in hopes that they would ultimately be received and acknowledged. This voluntary work should be remembered with deep gratitude by all ranks of the Regiment.

[59] *Chronicle*, 1919-20, p. 43.
[60] *Ibid.*, p. 44.

II.—THE JOURNEY OF THE OFFICERS INTO CAPTIVITY.

On the 4th May Echelon " A " under General Delamain, consisting of 100 British and 60 Indian officers with their servants and orderlies, embarked on board the paddle steamer *Burhanieh*. The accommodation was entirely inadequate, the British officers being packed like sardines on the upper deck and the Indian officers on the lower deck.

Passing Bughaila on the 5th, Umm at Tubul on the 6th, Lajj and the battlefield of Ctesiphon on the 8th amid the abusive jeers of Arabs thronging the banks, the party reached Baghdad on the 9th and moored alongside the British Residency.

Having disembarked, the junior officers were marched through the main bazaar roads of the city to the Cavalry Barracks. Though the whole route was thronged with spectators, " the general behaviour of the crowd was excellent," and there was no organized demonstration of hostility. For a Turkish building the barracks were clean and well ventilated, but as usual without any proper sanitary arrangements. During the stay in Baghdad the Turks, either by ignorance or intent, tried to treat British and Indian officers alike, insisting that all should feed together from the same crockery. Thanks to the courtesy and good manners of the Indian officers the difficulties were obviated.

Meanwhile the senior officers, with whom were Colonel Lethbridge and his servant, Lance-Corporal Swift, were accommodated in the Grand Babylon Hotel, whose illustrious title belied its bare and filthy interior. The stay in Baghdad, however, was short, for on the 12th all the officers were packed into the train for Samarra which was reached that night at 9 p.m.

Three officers of the 43rd—Captain Ivey and Lieutenants Naylor and Heawood—were left behind sick in hospital. Eventually Lieutenant Heawood had the good fortune to be exchanged, but Captain Ivey and Lieutenant Naylor were sent on later to Kastamuni.

Echelon " B," with which were Major Henley, Lance-Corporal Ponting and Private Finch, embarked on the same ship at Shumran on the 10th. Though crowded, there was slightly more space for this echelon, as it numbered about ninety British and fifty Indian officers with their servants. Echelon " B " reached Baghdad on the 13th and marched to the Cavalry Barracks lately occupied by Echelon " A."

At Samarra Echelon " A " spent the night of the 12th on the platform or in the offices of the station. The following morning General Townshend with his staff, consisting of Lieutenant-Colonel Parr (7th Rajputs) and Captain Morland of the 43rd, left in carriages for Mosul. He was not allowed to say good-bye to the assembled officers. He and his staff spent the years of captivity on the island of Prinkipo in the Bosporus in comparative comfort.

On the 15th the prisoners were warned to start at 4.30 p.m. for the march to Mosul. Previously the junior officers had been ordered to reduce their kits to 66 lb., which necessitated the disposal of many useful articles. The discarded clothes and belongings were either sold or given to the rapacious Turkish guards.

For the journey the junior officers were allotted one donkey each, on which to load their kits, cooking utensils and the kits of their orderlies. The officers paired off and shared two donkeys, one being used for baggage and the other for riding. At 6 p.m. the column moved out from the dusty station precincts on to the plain to northward and halted to adjust loads. As the sun was sinking in the summer sky the prisoners started the march, none knowing the length of the journey ahead of him. Hour after hour the march continued across the desert of coarse, brown grass. Halts for ten minutes every hour seemed to pass quicker and occur less often as the weary prisoners trudged on and on through the night, parched with thirst and suffocated with the dust of the column. At 2 a.m. the column halted and was allowed to rest for two hours. Soon after 4.30 a.m. the half-starved and unfit officers were plodding along the stony track. At 10 a.m. the column halted alongside the Tigris and water-bottles were filled and welcome drink allowed. For another two hours the march continued under a torrid sun and brazen sky. With blistered feet, staggering and stumbling, the officers limped into Tikrit amid the ribald jeers and laughter of the Arab women thronging the street. After a march of fifty-six kilometres (thirty-five miles) the prisoners were packed into a filthy courtyard wherein there was practically no shade from the burning sun except that provided by unventilated cattle sheds, fetid with stale air. The officers of the Regiment now consisted of Colonel Lethbridge, Captain Mundey and Lieutenant Mason. Lieutenant Mellor, unfit to march, had been left behind in the *serai* at Samarra.

The prisoners remained at Tikrit for just over twenty-four hours during which little sleep or rest was possible owing to the cramped and exposed quarters allotted to them. Starting before dusk on the 17th, they reached Kharnina[61] near the river the next day, where they remained exposed to the full force of the heat without a vestige of shelter other than what they could concoct themselves. Early on the 19th the column marched again, this time only about five miles to Sunaidij[62] on the Tigris. Leaving Sunaidij in the evening, the column marched " for hour after hour in heat, dust, and dark-

---

[61] About twenty miles north-north-west of Tikrit; spelt Kharinina by Major Sandes in *In Kut and Captivity*.

[62] About twenty-five miles south-south-east of Mosul; spelt Sanaich by Major Sandes.

ness "[63] until 2 a.m. on the 20th, when it halted on a stony spur, about twenty miles from Sunaidij, called by the Arabs Wadi Khanana. From here the prisoners covered the twenty-six miles to Sharqat during the night of the 20th/21st, and halted until the evening of the 22nd.

As the column approached Mosul, the country began to change and the climate became more bearable. The monotonous expanse of flat desert gave place to undulating country with a slightly keener atmosphere; green fields and even orchards bordered the rapid stream of the Tigris. Mosul was entered on the 25th, and the prisoners were taken to the barracks. Thus was the march of " 170 miles completed in seventy-seven and a quarter hours of actual marching time, including hourly halts,"[64] an average of seventeen and a half miles per day of twenty-four hours. Colonel Lethbridge, in his memoirs, remarks that after fatiguing marches " we had no sleep, or very little. This kind of thing can go on for a day or two, but, longer than that, the weariness becomes well-nigh intolerable. One's eyes smart, one has a feeling of intolerable lassitude and to do anything requires a monstrous effort. In addition to this, our food was very poor. From Tikrit to Mosul there is no village of any importance and supplies, therefore, were non-existent. Some of these disadvantages the Turks perhaps could not remove, but they could have palliated them by letting us have a halt for an extra night at certain specified places, and so get some sleep."

Fortunately the prisoners were allowed to visit the bazaars in Mosul, and were consequently able to eke out their meagre rations with purchases of sugar, dates, raisins, etc., at reasonable rates. They were also allowed to feed at a restaurant near the barracks where the food appeared so palatable that many suffered from severe indigestion as a result. The barracks, according to Turkish standards, were exceptionally clean, but infested with bugs for all that. These and other vermin were ubiquitous and the natural inhabitants of all the buildings occupied by the prisoners during the march. Indeed, they came to be treated with indifference before the captivity ended. But despite of the prolificacy of lice, the carriers of the dreaded typhus fever, there were few cases among the officers during the whole of the captivity.

On the 27th, after the column had been warned to march that evening, Enver Pasha, the Turkish Minister of War, who was on his way back to Constantinople from Baghdad, addressed the prisoners. While the officers were packing their kits he appeared on the veranda with a numerous staff and spoke in fluent French. He said that he had the highest admiration for the British officers; that while they were in Turkish hands they should be treated as the precious and honoured guests of the Ottoman Government; that he had heard with displeasure that the officers had been deprived of

[63] *In Kut and Captivity*, p. 302.   [64] *Ibid.*, p. 309.

their swords, and that he would take steps to have them returned. Needless to say, he never kept his word, and the officers' swords have not been seen from that day to this.

For the journey across the desert to Ras al 'Ain one light four-wheeled wagon was allotted to three officers,[65] and one *arabiya*—a light victoria—to each general officer. The carts were so small that when the valises of three officers had been loaded aboard there was scarcely room for two riders. The third had to march and take turn and turn about to ride.

From the 27th to the 31st the prisoners trekked across the desert on long and infinitely fatiguing night marches, often without fresh water, and bivouacked by day without shelter from the sun so that sleep was an impossibility.

Passing Rumailan Kabir at 8 a.m. on the 31st, where fresh water was available, the weary column pushed on for another three hours before reaching the post of Damir Qapu[66] which lay at the bottom of a green valley watered by a pure stream. This was a particularly long march of about thirty-six miles which had been covered in fourteen marching hours. Hence the column continued across the deserted Armenian plateau, the inhabitants of which had lately been massacred by the Turks or their gallant henchmen, the Kurds and Arabs. On the 3rd June Nisibin—120 miles from Mosul—was reached. Here was an " oasis in the desert. A purling stream of clear water runs past the village. There are trees of various kinds clustered round the houses, and the place has a welcome change of air about it, compared with the flat monotonous and uncultivated plain through which we had passed," writes Colonel Lethbridge. " Cherries were in full bearing when we passed through, a welcome change of diet for all of us."

Starting again on the evening of the 5th the prisoners reached Kochhisar[67] on the 6th, and railhead at Ras al 'Ain early in the morning of the 8th, where they camped near the railway station.

Two days later the prisoners entrained for Aleppo in horse-boxes, the generals and senior officers being given the luxury of a passenger carriage. On arrival the senior officers were taken to hotels, and the captains and subalterns to a great barrack on a hill outside the town, which proved to be alive with every known species of human parasite. However, the British officers were soon moved to hotels in the town, and the short stay was spent in making purchases in the European shops to make good the wastage of the march.

Without previous warning the prisoners were ordered, early in the morning of the 13th, to entrain at 6 a.m. for Islahiya, at the foot of the

---

[65] Colonel Lethbridge's memoirs. *In Kut and Captivity*, p. 321, gives the distribution as one per six officers.

[66] Sometimes spelt Demir Kapu or Demikapu.   [67] South-west of Mardin.

Amanus mountains, which was reached soon after noon. Here there was a break in the line, which at that time had not been linked up to the railhead at Mamoura across the mountains. On the 14th the column started on its journey across the mountains with one wagon allotted to four junior officers. As usual the march was carried out by night to avoid the heat of day; but, when the prisoners found themselves at the top of a pass after a steep ascent of 2,000 feet, the cold was intense while waiting for the wagons which had to wind their way up the mountain road. A halt was called at 3.30 a.m. near Hassan Begli and the weary prisoners were allowed to encamp near a pure stream in the shade of mulberry trees. The following day the column reached Mamoura where a train was already waiting to take the prisoners across the well-watered, fertile, but intensely hot, plain of Cilicia to Kulek, a few miles from the small town of Tarsus. At Kulek the prisoners experienced the influence of Germans and Austrians, for arrangements for their accommodation had been made and a line of bell-tents pitched close to the station. Colonel Lethbridge and other senior officers were allowed to spend the night in Tarsus.

From Kulek the prisoners were taken in motor lorries, driven by Germans or Austrians, over the Taurus mountains to Bozanti.[68] The mountains had not been tunnelled at this time, and there was thus a second break in the railway communications between Ras al 'Ain and Constantinople. Along the rough, narrow, mountain road bordered on one side by sheer precipices, the lorries negotiated countless hairpin bends at a foot's pace until, at about 3 p.m., the summit of the barren Cilician Gates, 6,000 feet above sea-level, was reached and passed. Then the road fell sharply away at steep gradients to Bozanti. Here the prisoners were once again crammed into the train for the journey across Asia Minor. Passing through Konia and Afiun Qarahisar, they detrained and spent the night of the 19th in a verminous hotel at Eskichehir. From here the general officers, Delamain, Hamilton, Evans and Grier, household names in the 6th Division, were separated from the party and sent to Brusa, near the Sea of Marmora. The rest entrained again on the 20th and reached Angora the following day. Here the prisoners, bereft of their servants and orderlies, who had been marched off elsewhere, were herded into a barrack some distance outside the town. Two small oil lamps were provided for the room, 66 feet long by 40 feet wide, wherein sixty-eight officers were crowded. " The sanitary arrangements will not bear description, and there were no facilities for washing."[69] Nor were the officers allowed to go down to wash in a stream which ran past the barrack some 500 yards distant. Even the supply of drinking water was inadequate, and no food was issued until the evening of the 22nd. From an arrogant Turkish

[68] Variously spelt Posante and Pozanti.   [69] *In Kut and Captivity*, p. 377.

serjeant the prisoners had to bear many humiliations and petty tyrannies, for the Turks, either by neglect or intent, omitted to appoint an officer commandant. The same day Echelon " B " arrived, including Major Henley and Lieutenant Mellor. At this point it will be convenient to trace the fortunes of this party on its march from Baghdad.

Echelon " B " left Baghdad on the 16th May for Samarra, where Major Henley found Lieutenant Mellor and Lance-Corporal Young sick in the *serai*. Here the prisoners made themselves as comfortable as possible in spite of intense heat and innumerable flies. The *serai* consisted of four walls with a very light brushwood roof. Parties of officers were allowed the luxury of a bathe in the Tigris, half a mile distant, in the evening. On the evening of the 19th 8472 Private Burke of the rank-and-file column managed to evade the guard when drawing rations in the town, and reached the *serai* with news of the men of the Regiment. He told of the march from Shumran and the deaths of Serjeant Barfoot, " S " Company, and Private Carter.

By the 20th, when the prisoners were ordered to lighten their kits preparatory to marching to Mosul, Lieutenant Mellor had recovered sufficiently to join the column. Lance-Corporal Young, however, was admitted to hospital. Tikrit was reached on the 21st at about noon, and a halt was allowed for two days. By this time the prisoners had supplemented the allotment of donkeys by hiring animals at two lira for the journey to Mosul. Thus there were three animals per two officers. Marching all through the night of the 23rd/24th without water, the column halted at 9 a.m. near some brackish water. The following evening the prisoners reached Sharqat and drank fresh water for the first time for two days. On the 27th they started again and marched by day for two days, only halting during the extreme heat of the days. Mosul was reached on the 30th, and the prisoners were allowed to buy their food in " horrid little places more like a fried fish shop than anything else . . . they gave us country wine, compared to which vinegar is nectar," wrote Major Henley.[70] While resting at Mosul awaiting transport, Lieutenant Spackman (I.M.S.), who had been left in charge of the sick of Echelon " A," visited the new arrivals of Echelon " B," and brought the news that Corporal Read, of the 43rd, was dangerously ill and raving from sunstroke.[71]

Leaving Mosul on the 3rd June the column followed the same route as Echelon "A," and reached Nisibin on the 6th where good and cheap victuals were procurable. Moving on again on the 8th through Tel Ermin,[72] the column reached Ras al 'Ain on the 9th late in the evening, and bivouacked

---

[70] *Chronicle,* 1927, p. 200.   [71] He died on the 6th June. See Appendix XI.
[72] I have not been able to trace this place on maps of Turkey. Major Henley spells it Talameh in his diary.

near the railway station. On reaching Aleppo on the 12th the party came up with Echelon " A," which, however, left the following morning for Islahiya. Echelon " B " moved on on the 14th, following in the tracks of Echelon " A," and experienced similar discomforts. On the journey from Islahiya across the Amanus mountains Major Henley records that near the top of the pass the prisoners came upon " some dead bodies in the gutter, apparently Armenians." Traces of the recent massacres of Armenians were found all the way along the route from Mosul. Early in the journey across the Armenian plateau the prisoners discovered bodies in the wells of the deserted villages, on one occasion *after* water had been drawn and imbibed.

On the 15th Echelon " B " reached Hassan Begli and encamped at 3.30 a.m. Daylight disclosed another camp near by, composed of Armenian men, women and children. These wretched people were being driven from their homes by the Turks. Those who could not march because of sickness, old age or weakness were left to die by the roadside or were murdered by their Turkish guards. At this time our own men were experiencing similar treatment in their march into captivity.

On reaching Angora on the 22nd Echelon " B " joined up with Echelon " A," as has been recorded. Here in the uncomfortable barrack the officers remained until the 25th. Only at midday did the Turks provide a meal, when the prisoners assembled in the central hall, floored with pebbles, and sat round " like a lot of school children, while Turkish soldiers in the dirtiest apparel dished out food, which consisted of a plate of coarse meat cooked in oil, followed by a plate of cherries and a loaf of bread," but without vegetables. Before continuing the journey the prisoners were deprived of their servants, who were sent to Kastamuni[73] with Echelon " B." On the 25th the officers were warned to prepare for the last lap to Yozgad; and that day the commandant of the town, safe in his knowledge that the prisoners were leaving his area, paid his first and last visit to the barrack.

For the journey the officers were allotted one small cart between four in which to ride, and others for their kits. For two days they travelled before reaching Maaden[74] on the 27th. Here they were dispersed for the night among different *serais*, each of which was as verminous as its neighbour and quite uninhabitable. Hence they went over barren, rocky hills and through fertile valleys, rich in fruit trees of all kinds, cherries, apricots and plums, until they reached their prison at Yozgad[75] at about noon on the 30th. Here the

---

[73] About 110 miles north-east of Angora and seventy miles south-west of Sinope. See Map 19, facing p. 302.

[74] This is probably Denek Maaden, thirty-five miles south-east of Angora as the crow flies, which is marked on the map dated 1932.

[75] About one hundred miles east of Angora and roughly half-way to Sivas. See Map 19.

officers were separated, Colonel Lethbridge and Major Henley being accommodated in one house, and the captains and subalterns in another. The rooms allotted, though surprisingly clean, were bare of furniture; but the officers were given a mattress, quilt, sheet and pillow. Here in Yozgad, situated in one of the deep valleys of the desolate country of Anatolia, the remnants of the officers of the 43rd languished for over two years, cut off from all intercourse with the outside world and unaware of the course of the war. Deprived of everything that makes life worth living, hope alone remained to all ranks of the 43rd—hope that the Turkish resistance would crumble; hope that eventual exchange would materialize. To the younger officers, unable perhaps to view their conditions philosophically, the enforced inactivity became extremely irksome. The senior officers were more able to exercise the cardinal virtue of patience. Yet none, from the commanding officer downwards through each rank of the Regiment, ever surrendered in spirit though his body was imprisoned. None gave his parole not to attempt to escape. Books have been written giving minute details of the daily life of the officers while in prison, books which bring out the ingenuity and boundless resource of the human mind when put to the test.[76] Even cameras were manufactured and used with success. They made their own chessmen, played hockey and football, lectured each other on technical subjects, instituted a debating society and theatricals; in fact, by all means in their power sought to break the monotony of inaction and idleness by preserving the functions of the mind and by maintaining interest in subjects beyond the prison doors. Furthermore, as the war dragged on, communication with folks at home by means of cryptograms, cunningly devised and as cunningly noticed and decoded in England, was successfully established, and news of the war was transmitted to the prisoners by code.

Another party of officers left for Samarra by train on the 30th May. This included Captain Ivey, Lieutenant Naylor and those officers who had been admitted to hospital on arrival at Baghdad. At Samarra the party was kept waiting until the evening of the 4th June. As usual the Turks failed to provide sufficient donkeys for the exiguous belongings of the officers, who were therefore compelled to leave behind much of what they still possessed. Not unnaturally this dereliction was loudly resented and an altercation with the Turkish commander ensued and was only settled by the guards driving the prisoners out at the point of the bayonet.

At the filthy little village of Tikrit, which was reached on the evening of the 5th, Lieutenant Naylor, hearing that there were some British soldiers on the river bank, went down to see them and found fifteen men. " Two of them were dead. Arabs refused to bury them unless they could have the clothing.

---

[76] Two good accounts can be found in *In Kut and Captivity* and the *Road to En-dor*.

Others were at their last gasp including Lance-Corporal Gunter and Private Merritt. When they moved into the shade of the river bank they were stoned by Arab children who were encouraged by their elders." The dead and dying were almost hidden beneath a buzzing swarm of loathsome flies which crawled with impunity all over their pathetic bodies.

The party left Tikrit the next day, and after three particularly severe marches reached Sharqat on the evening of the 9th and were allowed to rest for forty-eight hours. From Sharqat to Hamam Ali, a distance of forty-seven miles, the party marched in two days without water in an intense heat and with only two hours' halt at noonday. On the 14th they entered Mosul, where the conditions were appalling. There were about fifty British soldiers in barrack rooms (lately occupied by Arab convicts) without any sanitary arrangements whatsoever. " The floors . . . were inches deep in filth " and on these the prisoners had to lie. For food they were given a bowl of rice soup and a small loaf of bread per day provided they had the strength to fetch it. Those who were too weak to move went empty. It was here that Lieutenant Naylor saw two men, of whom one was in the Regiment, raving mad as the result of the barbarous treatment meted out to them. " Most of them could show wounds where they had been beaten, whipped or struck with a bayonet." After this one visit the officers were forbidden all further intercourse with the wretched men.

Six days later, the 20th, the party started on the desert march across Anatolia. It was on the third march out from Mosul that they also found the man of the Norfolk Regiment living in a cave, as recorded on page 232. " He had been left for dead and had had no food or water for days. He was just like a wild animal." At the end of the fourth march they found eleven sick and dying men at a police post. It was the same story : little food and no hope. At Damir Qapu, reached on the 25th, the few sick men were in better way. They were getting a little food and were able to bathe in a stream ; moreover, some Germans passing through had befriended them. But at Nisibin, four days later, they found conditions similar to those at Mosul. " They were just waiting their turn to die and be buried." Mortally sick, helpless and hopeless though they were, a column of about four thousand Turkish troops had robbed them of everything they yet possessed the day before Lieutenant Naylor and his party arrived. At Tel Ermin on the 2nd July they found two men with nothing but a shred of blanket to cover them. They were just able to support life in the blistering heat.

At Ras al 'Ain the party entrained for Islahiya where there were about twenty-five men in a wire enclosure with a little thatch propped on sticks as their only shelter. These men crawled on their hands and knees to a stream about fifty yards away, and among them Lieutenant Naylor found his company quartermaster-serjeant, Voller, who had a large festering wound on the left side of his head where he had been hit with a rifle butt; and his back was a mass of red weals where he had been whipped.

Henceforward this party of officers travelled by train and road in the tracks of Echelons " A " and " B " and saw no more of the rank-and-file prisoners. Eventually they reached Kastamuni on the 28th after a stay of ten days at Angora between the 14th and 23rd. Major Naylor in notes lately made on the terrible march into captivity emphasizes that " few stages were under twenty miles, and the one into Sharqat was forty-two. On practically all of the marches water was not procurable until the end of the stage was reached. . . . Except at Tikrit, Mosul and Nisibin there were no trees or shade of any sort. . . . One small loaf—about half a pound—and a few dates was the daily ration when it was issued. Often it was not issued." He corroborates all the terrible details of the march into captivity as already recorded; and further recounts that the soldier servant of Askari Bey (the Turkish commander at Shaiba), who deserted to the Regiment and was employed as a handyman in the officers' mess at Amara, donned the uniform of the Regiment at the end of the siege of Kut and marched as a prisoner into Asia Minor. By the end of 1917 he was still successfully masquerading as a British soldier.

In September 1917 Colonel Lethbridge, Major Henley and other officers were transferred to Afiun Qarahisar whither a party of twenty prisoners was dispatched. Here Colonel Lethbridge remained until early in 1918, when he applied to join a party of senior officers due to go to Brusa; from Brusa he was released in November 1918, and by way of Salonika and Taranto journeyed to England.

In appreciating the ill-treatment meted out to the prisoners of all ranks in greater and smaller degree it is necessary to consider the Turkish characteristics which are clearly described by Colonel Lethbridge in his memoirs. One of the chief of these is that apathy which resisted complacently the entreaties not only of the prisoners themselves but also those of the neutral Powers. Semi-barbarous, the descendants of the Tatars who brought fire and desolation to the civilizations of Asia Minor, the Turks were not civilized according to Western standards. They had little regard for human life or the palliation of human ills, sicknesses or wounds. Indeed, had they possessed the best will in the world, the materials for the alleviation of suffering were not available and never had been available in adequate quantities. Being innately respecters of persons, they treated all prisoners according to rank and not civilized standards of humanity. When one considers that the word for prisoner in Turkish is synonymous with slave, it is hardly surprising that our rank-and-file prisoners were treated like cattle. But the policy adopted by the Turks of putting Arabs, whom they hated and despised, in charge of our men was completely unpardonable; for if they did not know the habits of the Arabs when in authority, then there was no one in the world competent to do so.

Then, again, our officers and men were continually overcrowded. This overcrowding is natural to the Turks as to all Eastern races. They required little space themselves and allotted to our men what would be sufficient for themselves in like circumstances. Vermin to them was of no more consequence than smuts to Londoners. They knew no sanitation, and they had neither beds nor tables in their own homes; therefore they provided none for our men.

The same applies to food. The Turkish soldier can subsist on the coarse ration biscuit, march untold miles in his thick uniform without transport, and be fit to fight where a European would be incapacitated from further action for some time. The Turks considered that our officers and men should be capable of similar accomplishments.

Theft, peculation, embezzlement, graft, bribery and all forms of corruption as well as procrastination, natural to all Orientals, were as common as flies in Turkey. Their code of honour, if any, was entirely different from ours. It was proved that the Turkish contractor who supplied the food to the officers at Yozgad at exorbitant price shared the profits with the commandant. " Graft is rampant in Turkey, and bribery will take you very far in most projects," says Colonel Lethbridge. Suspicious of anything they did not understand, yet sometimes credulous and simple-minded, those in authority were tyrannical to a degree almost inconceivable during the first year of the captivity. Exercise for health's sake was not understood by them. " The Turk is an extraordinary mixture of sloth and energy. If put to it, no people can put up with more hardship and physical toil."

Until pressure was put upon the Turkish Government by neutral and belligerent Powers, the treatment as recorded herein was brutal, cowardly, tyrannical and wholly inexcusable judged by any, but inconceivable by European, standards. The Turks never took the slightest trouble to examine the needs or to appreciate the culture of their prisoners, and they never can be acquitted of the indictment of murder, of which all civilized countries will accuse them for the treatment of the defenceless rank-and-file prisoners. That as many as seventy-six of the 43rd survived the captivity is surprising when it is realized what privations the prisoners suffered during the first winter alone. The cold was intense, fuel unobtainable, and clothing, threadbare from hard service, totally inadequate to protect their emaciated bodies from the rigours of the climate.

These characteristics applied more to the official than to the peasant class, which the prisoners found more friendly and trustworthy. The official was underpaid and was allowed to eke out his income by illicit means.

CHAPTER XXII.

I.—Reorganization and Preparation.

THE 43RD AT SANDY RIDGE—SHORTAGE OF RATIONS—SICKNESS AND DISEASE—THE 43RD DETACHED—THE TOLL OF DISEASE—TRAINING—DRAFTS—LIEUTENANT-COLONEL POPE-HENNESSY ASSUMES COMMAND—SPECIALISTS—MAUDE SUCCEEDS GORRINGE—MAUDE BECOMES COMMANDER-IN-CHIEF—POLICY—ORGANIZATION OF THE TIGRIS DEFENCES—THE 43RD MOVES INTO FORWARD SECTION—MAUDE'S OFFENSIVE IN DECEMBER 1916—THE 43RD TAKES OVER A SECTION OF THE BLOCKHOUSE LINE—MAUDE ORDERED TO DEFEAT THE TURKS—THE REGIMENTAL SCHOOL AT DUJAILA.

(*See Maps facing pages* 1, 270, 274 *and* 302, *and on page* 206.)

AT the time of the capitulation of Kut the 2nd/43rd was in the reserve trenches opposite Sannaiyat, and, as recorded, became the official 43rd. During the armistice the hospital ship *Sikkim* plied to and fro bringing sick and wounded from Kut.

On the 1st May thirty men from each regiment of the 28th Brigade were ordered to attend an inspection at Wadi by General Lake. The few men of the 43rd who survived the operations of March and April attended. In his address General Lake expressed his admiration for all ranks in their efforts to relieve Kut. Private Golding, a stretcher-bearer, who acted with conspicuous gallantry at Sannaiyat on the 6th April, was decorated with the *Distinguished Conduct Medal*.

The following day Second Lieutenant H. E. F. Smyth took over command of " A " Company from Lieutenant G. W. Titherington, who became adjutant.

When resting in the fourth line, about a thousand yards from the enemy, the Regiment was allowed to bring up 40-lb. tents and make itself comfortable. The weather was intensely hot and the usual routine was a parade in the early morning, followed by a prolonged period of inaction under cover until 5 p.m. when the Regiment was usually employed in making up barbed-wire bales or digging trenches.[1]

Lieutenant T. P. Williams, who joined from England on the 26th April, records in his diary of this time: " Flies simply awful and swarming everywhere. We live on rations and some extra tinned stuff of which we have to make very sparing use." Later he remarks: " Our mess is very frugal;

---
[1] *Chronicle*, 1915-16, p. 178.

there is no proper process at present of filtering water, and we drink pure (!) Tigris which has stood for a time and so lost the sediment to a certain extent. Twice a day we each draw lime juice sufficient for a glass of water. Tea is the chief drink." Is it surprising that dysentery, boils and paratyphoid were rife among the officers and men ? There were rumours of ice and soda-water factories, but these were merely as abstract as the rumours.

On the 10th the armistice ended, by which time the 28th Brigade was holding the front line once more; but the Regiment did not have to move, one company occupying the third line by night.

The Tigris Corps was now on the defensive. This policy had been dictated by the British Government when authorizing General Lake to open negotiations for the surrender of Kut on the 25th April. At the same time General Lake was ordered to hold as forward a line as possible so as to minimize the effect of the surrender, prevent extensive rebellions of the Arab tribes on the line of communications which any withdrawal would be certain to produce, and, by containing a large body of Turks, assist the Russians in their intended offensive. On the 30th April Lord Kitchener sent further detailed instructions. In these he emphasized the fact that the British Government attached no importance to the capture of Kut or Baghdad, that signs of weakness in the Turks should only be exploited if practicable without incurring heavy losses, and that it was " undesirable and impossible to reinforce "[2] General Lake.

But in the meantime the advance of the Russians under General Baratoff towards Khaniqin had attracted Turkish troops from the Kut area. On the 19th May British aeroplanes reported that the Bait Isa and Chahela positions had been evacuated, but that the Sinn Abtar redoubt was still occupied. Owing, however, to the great heat, lack of drinking water, and the danger of further " infection with cholera[3] from the evacuated Turkish trenches," General Gorringe decided to postpone an advance until nightfall when he intended to send the Cavalry Brigade from Shaikh Saad, the 3rd Division and 36th Brigade round the infected areas to seize the bridge in the rear of them at Abdul Hassan. Accordingly the following day the force advanced and seized the line Maqasis—Dujaila. During the advance the troops suffered terribly from the heat and lack of water due once again to shortage of transport. But the line which had defied assault for so long was now in our hands. The heat was increasing considerably, the day temperature being officially recorded between 105 and 107 degrees. The heat inside tents was becoming so unbearable that many officers had their heads shaved to the skin. Those officers of the 43rd in the second line at Wadi used to bathe in the

[2] *Official History*, Vol. III, p. 3.
[3] Cholera was rife at this time in the Tigris Corps. The supply of serum was, however, insufficient to inoculate all the troops against it.

evening in the Tigris whence came drinking water; and it was when they encountered inflated, bloated corpses floating downstream that they realized the origin of the flavour peculiar to Tigris water. Yet all ranks drank of the Tigris by the gallon day in day out as though it were not a main sewer.

On the 19th Lieutenant Williams took over command of " A " Company from Second Lieutenant Smyth, who was admitted to hospital. On the same day the Regiment prepared for action, and all tents and spare kit were sent down to the quartermaster's stores. The next day orders were received to attack Sannaiyat at 3.30 a.m. on the 21st supported by the 19th Brigade; but this attack was postponed for twenty-four hours and cancelled on the 21st, as the Turks were still holding the left bank and the orders from home precluded any attack which might incur heavy casualties. General Gorringe, therefore, decided to continue pressure upon the right bank, and on the 22nd the 28th Brigade was relieved by the 19th. Moving off at 7.45 p.m., the 43rd crossed the river and took over Sandy Ridge—in the loop of the river opposite Fallahiya—from the Highland Battalion and provided piquets with the 2nd Leicestershire Regiment.

At Sandy Ridge the Regiment was able to settle down and make itself comfortable. Tents were brought up and thatched roofs were made to keep out the heat. There were two large Eastern pattern tents available for the officers' mess and canteen stores. Luckily for all ranks, ample stores, consigned from India, began to arrive from Basra where they had been lying for months. The officers' mess indulged in luxuries previously unknown in Mesopotamia, and the men found the barrels of beer a perfect godsend after the ration lime juice and Tigris water. The health of the Regiment was far from good, but in that respect differed not from the rest of the Tigris Corps. Owing to shortage of land and river transport and congestion of shipping at Basra, the troops at the front were not supplied on an adequate scale. The drafts of fine material which, it was hoped, would allow of the much-needed rest and reorganization merely added to the difficulties by falling victims to the intense heat and disease. " The cursed country continued to receive, consume, invalidate and reject draft after draft of our best blood."[4] The Government now spared no expense to alleviate the conditions, but no improvement was possible because an increase in river craft before the cold weather could not be effected. The boats were packed with humanity going upstream, and nearly as crowded with sick on the return journey. A draft of ninety doctors landed at Basra on the 15th May. " In three months ten had died and forty had been invalided out of the country."[5] The number of old soldiers, either officers, non-commissioned officers or men, who still survived was by this time hardly sufficient to leaven the lump of unsalted per-

[4] *The Long Road to Baghdad*, p. 288.   [5] *Ibid.*, p. 290.

sonnel. Besides which the failures to relieve Kut after many attempts, grievous losses and severe hardships reacted adversely upon the mentally and physically fatigued troops. In the 43rd the sick list began to swell rapidly. Lieutenant Seymour contracted enteric fever. Boils and septic sores became prevalent, causing the admittance to hospital of officers and men.

On the 1st June the 28th Brigade relieved the 19th in the trenches on the left bank, but the 43rd was detached for duty and reorganization on the line of communications. Handing over the camp at Sandy Ridge to the Highland Battalion, the Regiment crossed to the left bank and there encamped to await transport. The following day a body of hale Turkish prisoners to be exchanged for British sick and wounded disembarked opposite the Regiment's camp. "They were marched off by a company of Black Watch. . . . They were all blindfolded; there were two officers . . . a curious sight it was to see these two walking closely arm-in-arm with our officers. The men looked healthy enough, and all had blankets, waterproof sheets and mosquito nets."[6] Embarking at 2 p.m. on the 5th the Regiment, with 15 officers and 330 other ranks, reached Shaikh Saad at 6 p.m. the same day, and Amara two days later. Having disembarked on the 8th on the right bank, the 43rd pitched camp.

The 8th was a heavy day spent in unloading stores and kit and pitching camp in a temperature of 108 degrees. The camp was on the outskirts of the town of Amara and therefore exposed to the predatory Arabs; consequently precautions had to be taken to safeguard arms and equipment. That night when the weary troops eventually got under cover they dug trenches in their tents and slept on their accoutrements. On the night of the 9th/10th the Gurkhas alongside the Regiment snaffled three Arab thieves and "took a corpse up to their officers' mess tent for their edification." Working hours were now modified to meet the torrid conditions; the Regiment had gunfire at 6.30 a.m., breakfast at 10 a.m., and its next meal at 4 p.m. The temperature was now 110 degrees by 10.30 a.m.

By the 13th some of the deficiencies of kit and equipment such as shaving-brushes, water-bottles, saddlery, etc., had been made good; but the supply of the all-important helmets was not equal to the demand, thanks partly to the large number issued to the sotnia of Cossack cavalry which arrived unexpectedly on the 20th May. As a makeshift helmet flaps were issued and these together with spine-pads provided welcome protection from the sun. Ice was still precious as gold; yea, as much fine gold; but it was known in Amara at infrequent intervals.

On the 19th the Regiment started building a breastwork round the new camp site one thousand yards south of the bridge, hitherto occupied by the

[6] Lieutenant Williams's Diary.

9th Gurkhas; and marched in on the 21st to find the tents pitched so gloriously askew by the Territorials that many had to be repitched by the blaspheming troops. Here the Regiment settled down to a routine of training, fatigues and a soul-destroying monotony.

As early as the 11th June the spectre of cholera stalked abroad in the Regiment's camp, and sickness of all sorts took heavy toll of both officers and men. More cases of cholera were recorded on the 26th. Four men of " A " Company died within a week. The heat in the tents was terrific and the health of the Regiment suffered accordingly. " How one longs for the evenings now," wrote Lieutenant Williams in his diary; " everything gets so hot: chairs, camp bed, shirts, cups and plates. The hair on my head is very hot. . . . The only bearable time now is before 7 in the morning and after 6 at night."

But improvements to the camp and work on barbed-wire entanglements continued while every day the sick list became longer. Not only was cholera common but also enteric, dysentery, paratyphoid, malaria, sand-fly fever, and such minor ailments as septic sores and intumescent boils, abscesses and ulcers. Out of a draft of four hundred men for another regiment one hundred were admitted to hospital within the first fortnight. In the 43rd Lieutenants Kinghorn and Radford and Second Lieutenant Davenport were admitted to hospital during the month. The drafts of employed officers and men hardly replaced the deplorable wastage among all ranks. Second Lieutenants Watts, Rock and Hardie joined from England and Field rejoined from hospital, but by the end of the month the strength of the 43rd was only 16 officers and 315 other ranks; 4 officers and 91 other ranks had been admitted to hospital, of whom 21835 Lance-Corporal Burton, 18551 Lance-Corporal Lacy, 21163 Private Brown, 21883 Private Smith, 21997 Private Webb and 17402 Private Boswell died of unrecorded diseases between the 14th and the 28th June.

The regimental war diary for July makes sorry reading. The entries consist of such items as:

" 2nd.—Captain G. W. Titherington and Lieutenant Williams to hospital.
" 6th.—Second Lieutenant Riddle to hospital; 2857 Private Lockhead, A., died of enteric; 20107 Private Allen, A., died of enteric.
" 17th.—8765 Private Rice, C., died of cholera.
" 19th.—8903 Private Wilks, H., died of enteric.
" 27th.—29038 Private Scrivens, W., died of dysentery and Major Barrington to hospital."

To quote Lieutenant Williams's diary again : " A stifling day [the 1st July]. . . . Titherington has just gone into hospital with [jaundice]. . . .

We don't live here now : we just endure life. The official shade temperature about midday the other day was 115 degrees, but it is a good deal more than that in tents . . . a glass of water taken cool from a *charghal* . . . will be hot in a quarter of an hour. . . . The 43rd long ago . . . ordered all sorts of drinks. . . . We are now reaping the benefit. We can get mineral waters here too. . . . We haven't had any potatoes for a long time. . . . It's a pity the bread is so nasty, made as it is of potato meal ; it leaves a beastly taste in one's mouth."

Medical arrangements were still inadequate to cope with the pathetic spate of human suffering. In Amara there were but twelve nurses to five hundred patients; and these gallant women worked ceaselessly through the heat of day till noon and again from 5 p.m. onwards. There were as many as ten funerals per week through no fault of the enemy. Shades of the Crimea !

Even at the end of the month the 43rd was still badly in need of helmets, but there was none to be had; and men just died because this essential part of their equipment was not vouchsafed.

The strength by the end of July was still further reduced to 13 officers and 287 other ranks, and Captain Titherington, but lately returned from hospital, was in command of the Regiment. On the 14th August, however, Major R. H. Crake (King's Own Scottish Borderers) arrived from Basra and took over command of the 43rd. The whole of August was spent in training and was not wasted. The 43rd was really only a cadre when it reached Amara, and much time and work was required to re-form it into a fighting unit with its necessary specialists, such as machine gunners, signallers and transport drivers. While these were being trained, the two companies were employed on tactical exercises and musketry. On the 22nd a big draft of 220 other ranks from Maqil and England reached Amara, thus allowing of the formation of two more companies, " C " and " D," which were commanded by Second Lieutenant Field and Lieutenant Kinghorn respectively. By this time old soldiers, who had recovered from wounds received in the earlier Tigris battles, began to return to duty, and added a stiffening to the ranks. The health of the Regiment, moreover, seems to have improved during August, for the wastage from sickness, hitherto barely replaced by drafts, was checked and the Regiment began to swell in numbers until, by the end of the month, there were 15 officers and 530 other ranks on the strength.

September from the point of view of military operations was also uneventful. Training continued and the strength increased, while sickness was negligible, 23425 Private Keeling, who died of cholera at Amara, being the only casualty.

On the 5th October Lieutenant-Colonel L. H. R. Pope-Hennessy, D.S.O., joined from England and took over command of the Regiment from Major Crake. Captain W. E. C. Terry, also from England, took over " C " Company. Early in the month a large draft of 300 men from various regiments reached Amara from England under Second Lieutenants J. R. Brown, F. E. Anderson and H. W. Bleeze, of the 9th Battalion of the Regiment. These men had an average of three months' service only.

On the 23rd the Amara Column, consisting of the 43rd, 2nd/7th Gurkhas and 2nd/119th Infantry, with one troop of the 10th Lancers, mobilized to raid an Arab village, fourteen miles east of Amara, where rifles were reported to be hidden. The Gurkhas, who had started the previous evening, failed to surprise the village, but succeeded in capturing three hundred sheep.

The Regiment, with the 2nd/119th Infantry and half a troop of 10th Lancers, left camp at 5 a.m. to support the Gurkhas, who were encountered at 9.30 a.m. returning to camp. The day was hot and still, and the Regiment's marching powers were tested and found wanting, for about fifty men fell out, three of whom were admitted to hospital. The untrained men were, as yet, not equal to the conditions of heat and dust. The process of hardening and acclimatizing the Regiment continued with company training; and the specialist classes began to show good results. By the 18th November there were sixteen qualified instructors in the Lewis gun, thirty-two first-class bombers and sixteen first-class snipers, but the Regiment, as yet, had no Lewis or Vickers guns. At the end of October the strength was 22 officers and 914 other ranks.

During the period from May to November the conduct of the war in Mesopotamia was vitally changed with benefit to all the fighting troops; and the foundations of success were well and surely laid when the reorganization of the rearward services was taken in hand.

At the beginning of the hot weather the mental and physical condition of the whole of Force " D " was far from good. The troops at the front were not on full rations owing to shortage of river steamers, and the vegetables sent up from Amara in sacks were rotten on arrival.[7] " There was no place of decent rest . . . increasing heat and few decent tents, with a dull ration, absolutely no canteen arrangements, nowhere to go to for rest billets. The men were wonderful considering, . . . but . . . there was no other word for it—stale. . . . India had begun to send canteen stores, but *more suo* without any distributing organization."

[7] *Behind the Scenes in Many Wars,* by Lieutenant-General Sir George MacMunn, K.C.B., K.C.S.I., D.S.O., gives a vivid description of the state of transport, line of communication, etc., and the methods adopted to reorganize the whole system of supply and maintenance, but it must be remembered that he arrived when the responsible Governments were determined to retrieve the situation in Mesopotamia.

MAJOR-GENERAL L. H. R. POPE-HENNESSY, C.B., D.S.O.

In May two new divisions were formed: the 14th, under Major-General Egerton, consisting of the 35th, 36th and 37th Brigades and other units from the Tigris Corps; and the 15th on the Euphrates, consisting of the 12th, 34th and 42nd Brigades, under Major-General Brooking.

Behind the fighting troops General Lake's strong representations concerning the transport shortage began to bear fruit; for towards the end of the months of April and May permission was given for the construction of a metre-gauge railway to Nasiriya to obviate the navigation of the shallows of the Hammar Lake and Lower Euphrates, and a 2 ft. 6 in. gauge line from Qurna to Amara. The light railway from the advanced base at Shaikh Saad to Sinn, which was started in June, reached Twin Canals on the 20th July and thus eased the problem of land and river transport.

On the 11th July the first of many changes in the higher commands took place when General Maude superseded General Gorringe in command of the Tigris Corps, and Major-General A. S. Cobbe succeeded General Younghusband in command of the 7th Division. Modern 18-pounder guns and 4.5-inch howitzers, Stokes mortars, Vickers and Lewis guns began to arrive; moreover, the vexed and difficult question of control of the campaign was definitely settled when, in mid-July, the commander-in-chief in India became responsible to the Army Council in all matters of personnel, administration and supply of Force " D." India was to remain the main base and was to continue to administer the force in Mesopotamia as far as her resources would allow.[8]

By July the Royal Flying Corps had been reinforced with pilots and modern machines, and it was not long before the airmen definitely established their superiority in the air.

The general policy of the campaign was still one of active defence while the means for active offence were being reconstructed behind the line. Then in August General Sir Charles Monro was appointed commander-in-chief in India, succeeding Sir Beauchamp Duff, who was recalled to England to give evidence before the Commission set up by Parliament to inquire into the conduct of the operations which had caused our men so many hardships, sufferings and privations. Not long afterwards General Lake was relieved in command by General Maude, a junior major-general who had had no experience of India or Indian troops. These changes produced changes elsewhere, and General Cobbe assumed command of the Tigris Corps.

Between April and August General Lake " had laid the foundations of the organization which finally brought us success." In spite of his urgent

---

[8] *Official History*, Vol. III, p. 24. The War Office had taken over the general direction of the operations in February, 1916, though India administered the force. This division of responsibility had proved impracticable.

requests, the river fleet had only increased from forty-five to fifty-six vessels by the time that the monsoon prevented ocean voyages. By the end of August this total had risen only to sixty-four. During the same period only eleven barges had been added, bringing the total up to ninety. " Twenty-seven steamers and tugs and twenty-six barges had sunk at sea; and of the seventeen steamers and tugs and forty-three barges ordered from the India Office in August 1915 and expected to arrive in Mesopotamia by May 1916, none was in commission when General Lake left Mesopotamia."[9] Between May and July, when the troops required between 500 and 560 tons of supplies daily, the maximum tonnage which could be delivered daily averaged 300.[10] Before he left General Lake had reduced this discrepancy between requirements and receipts, and he had arranged for " large tents, material for hot weather shelters, railway material, pumps, water pipes and motor lorries."[11] A considerable addition to the fleet of steamers and barges was expected by the end of the monsoon, and General Lake also arranged for the construction of a shipyard at Maqil. At Basra, too, he had caused many improvements to be effected whereby large bodies of troops could be accommodated, and ocean-going ships could berth alongside suitable wharves; and he had materially improved the hospital arrangements. Major-General G. F. MacMunn was now Inspector-General of Communications, and the formation of the Inland Water Transport was about to be effected. Basra, in fact, bade fair to become " an adequate and efficient base " in the near future. General Lake's desire to improve the land transport at the front was limited by his inability to feed more animals, but he had managed to organize local transport, and had received two mechanical transport companies and had requested three more, as well as motor ambulances, cars, bicycles and armoured cars.

Though the medical arrangements still left much to be desired, great improvements in them had been made already, and a thorough reorganization was in hand at this time. Amara and Basra were still the main hospital centres, and arrangements were made to accommodate 20,000 cases. But during the hot weather, when, as has been recorded, the incidence of sickness was appallingly great, the medical personnel was not adequate to cope with the casualties.[12]

II.—POLICY.

Meanwhile long discussions on the future conduct of the war in Mesopotamia were passing between the Chief of the Imperial General Staff—Sir William Robertson—and General Maude. Soon after assuming supreme

[9] *Ibid.*, Vol. III, p. 31.
[10] Captain Whittall as D.A.Q.M.G. Embarkation made up the figures daily.
[11] *Official History*, Vol. III, p. 31.
[12] Nearly 11,000 officers and men were invalided in June, over 12,000 in July, and 11,000 in August.

command, General Maude had deprecated any offensive action until the communications had been developed and the morale and training of the troops improved. To this end he proposed to form the four divisions on the Tigris —the 3rd, 7th, 13th and 14th—into two corps; and the two cavalry brigades into a cavalry division.

At the same time the War Committee was urging an advance to Baghdad against the wish of Sir William Robertson, who deplored the drain on resources with poor return and the dissemination of forces. He was in favour of a withdrawal to Amara and the concentration of a strong central reserve capable of acting either north, west or east. By these dispositions General Maude would protect the oilfields and command both rivers, and so obviate " the present difficult, costly and objective-less plan."[13]

General Maude, who had quickly proved himself equal to all difficulties, expressed his views early in September, and considered that the advantages of the forward policy outweighed the disadvantages. The forward policy " menaced Baghdad and prevented the Turks detaching troops to Persia," whose attitude was still giving considerable anxiety. Owing to the retreat of the Russians the way through Persia to Afghanistan now lay open, and the Indian Government expected Afghanistan to be drawn into the war against us. In his opinion any withdrawal would enable the Turks to overwhelm the Russians under General Baratoff and make an anxious situation critical. Alternatively he proposed to establish a footing on the Hai and to occupy Samawa on the Euphrates, thus threatening Baghdad still further. Nevertheless, Sir William Robertson was still opposed to any offensive when General Monro sailed for India via Mesopotamia. Sir William Robertson " had been unable to find any clear instructions defining exactly the mission of Force ' D ' which appeared to have been sent originally for protection of the oilfields and pipe-line,"[14] and to be certain that he thoroughly understood the policy of the British Government it was essential that it should be defined. His proposal of a withdrawal was strongly opposed by the War Committee, who demanded General Monro's opinion. In a telegram sent on the 30th September to General Monro, who was on his way to Mesopotamia, the policy of the British Government was stated clearly at long last: the mission of Force " D " was to protect the oilfields and pipe-line; to hold and control the Basra *vilayet*; no fresh advance to Baghdad was to be undertaken, but, if and when possible, British influence was to be established in the Baghdad *vilayet*; heavy casualties were to be avoided, as no reinforcements were available. Sir William Robertson, with his eyes fixed on the main theatres of war in Europe, concluded his message by saying that he had informed the War Committee that he considered that we neither had,

[13] *Official History*, Vol. III, p. 43.   [14] *Ibid.*, Vol. III, p. 45.

nor ever would have, adequate forces in Mesopotamia to seize and hold Baghdad.

General Monro reached Basra on the 10th October, and on the 19th communicated with Sir William Robertson, stating as his considered opinion that the forward positions could be maintained and properly supplied, and that a withdrawal would neither effect economy of force[15] nor permit the necessary command of the rivers and approaches to the oilfields. Sir William Robertson concurred in this opinion, and gave General Maude a free hand to assert British influence in Mesopotamia provided he realized that no reinforcements would be forthcoming and that heavy casualties must be avoided. His reluctance to increase our commitments at this time is easily comprehensible when it is realized that the situation in Europe was far from good. The German drive against Verdun had been countered by the Somme offensive at great cost; Rumania had been virtually annihilated; the internal situation in Russia was causing anxiety; the Serbian Army had practically ceased to exist; and the Germans and Austrians were preparing strong offensives against the Russians and Italians. Besides which, troops had been diverted to Salonika, and the tribes on the North-West Frontier of India were giving considerable trouble.

III.—THE 43RD ON THE TIGRIS DEFENCES.

The period of reorganization, preparation and concentration in Mesopotamia was completed early in December, and on the 12th General Maude telegraphed to Sir William Robertson that he was ready to operate on the Hai. To counter this threat no steps were taken by Khalil Pasha, who considered that the " British force on the Tigris was inferior, demoralized and totally incapable of taking Kut."[16] But in fact the cause of failure in the past—shortage of transport—had been practically eliminated when the railways from Qurna to Amara and from Shaikh Saad to Imam al Mansur were completed on the 28th November and the 20th December respectively. River and mechanical transport had also arrived in sufficient numbers to supply the forward troops with adequate rations and render them mobile at last. Also the Tigris Line of Communication Defences had been organized in three sections spread over the line from Qurna to Twin Canals. No. 1 Section comprised Qurna, Ezra's Tomb and Qala Salih; No. 2 Section had posts at Fulaifila,[17] Mudelil[17] and Amara, where Tigris Defence Headquarters were situated. The Amara post consisted of:—

---

[15] For the reason that a withdrawal would cause the tribes of Mesopotamia and South Persia to join the Turks and so necessitate increased forces for protective duties.
[16] *Official History*, Vol. III, p. 61.
[17] See Map No. 19, facing p. 302.

Headquarters, No. 2 Section, Tigris Defences.
One squadron, 10th Lancers (less two troops). ⎫
One pack station, " A " Troop, 2nd Wireless Signal ⎪ Mobile
 Squadron. ⎬ Column.
43rd Light Infantry. ⎪
One section, No. 22 Indian Field Ambulance. ⎭
Anglo-Indian Battery (less detachments)—two post guns.
1st/6th Devonshire Regiment.
4th Rajputs.
Half battalion, 96th Infantry.

No. 3 Section was responsible for the forward posts at Ali Gharbi, Omaiya and Shaikh Saad. Into this forward section the 43rd was ordered to move on the 28th November, but it did not embark until 8 p.m. on the 29th on board P52, one of the new class of steamers which had lately arrived. The Regiment left Amara at 6 a.m. on the 30th, and stopped for the night at Ali Gharbi; and on the following day reached Shaikh Saad where it disembarked. Meanwhile Captain Kinghorn and Second Lieutenants Roberts and Parkinson, with 60 men of the machine-gun section, 16 followers, 10 grooms and 74 men of " D " Company, followed the Regiment by march route. On arrival at Shaikh Saad[18] the 43rd proceeded to pitch camp eight hundred yards from the river, but its efforts were frustrated because the Ordnance at Amara had omitted to issue poles for the tents. Having borrowed tents from its old friends the 2nd Dorsetshire Regiment, the Regiment settled in, and took over the internal defence guards, amounting to about one hundred men nightly.

From Shaikh Saad the 43rd, now having a strength of 24 officers and 918 other ranks, was called upon to find various detachments. On the 11th December Second Lieutenant Grosvenor and one platoon, " C " Company, left by road for Advanced General Headquarters at Sinn, and the rest of " C " Company, together with two platoons of " A " Company, under Captain Terry, left the following day to provide guards for the army commander and prisoners. Two platoons of " B " Company under Second Lieutenant Wilmot left by river the same day to take over General Headquarters' guard at Arab Village.

On the 14th General Maude opened his offensive by throwing a bridge across the Hai at Atab and by advancing astride that river to make touch with the Turks in the salient which guarded both its effluence from the Tigris and Woolpress Village. At the same time troops of the 14th Division—now forming with the 13th Division, III Corps—advanced towards the Khudhaira

[18] See Map No. 15, facing p. 270.

bend, which was found to be strongly held.[19] The same day half of the 43rd, with a section of the 2nd/105th Battery—as a mobile column—marched out of Shaikh Saad at 7 a.m. in support of the 10th Lancers, who were patrolling towards Lot's Mounds, south-west of Shaikh Saad. This was part of General Maude's plan for the protection of the left flank and rear of the troops operating on the Hai. The Regiment halted from 9 a.m. till 3 p.m., when the cavalry returned, having seen no signs of the enemy; and the column marched back to camp, arriving at dusk.

As a result of the successful operations on the Hai, the General Officer Commanding Tigris Defences, Brigadier-General H. H. Austin, took over the defence of the light railway from Shaikh Saad as far as Imam al Mansur on the 17th December. The previous day the Regiment was warned to move on the 17th and take over the blockhouse line from No. 66 near Imam al Mansur to No. 30 near Twin Canals. Accordingly, on the 17th, the detachment of " C " Company and two platoons of " A " Company already at Sinn moved westward and took over blockhouses numbered 66 to 55 inclusive. " A " Company took over Nos. 54 to 45 inclusive, with company headquarters at Sinn in No. 51 Blockhouse, and " D " Company Nos. 44 to 30 inclusive, with company headquarters at Twin Canals. At the same time the two platoons of " B " Company on detachment at Arab Village took over Strong Point No. 4. Regimental headquarters remained at Shaikh Saad.

The garrison per blockhouse was two non-commissioned officers and ten men with one officer in command of three blockhouses. Each company headquarters moved complete with first-line transport, stretcher-bearers and two signallers; and the move was completed by 3.30 p.m. without incident.

The following day, the 18th, the signallers, machine-gun section, and thirty men of " B " Company left Shaikh Saad for Strong Point No. 4, which was reached on the 19th. That day regimental headquarters also moved to the same strong point, having left the surplus stores at Shaikh Saad to await transport; and " C " Company with one machine gun took over Strong Point No. 12. At 7 p.m., however, one hundred men of the 2nd Norfolk Regiment arrived at Strong Point No. 4 with orders to relieve the garrison and the garrisons of Blockhouses 31 to 42, which were to concentrate at the Dujaila Redoubt. After this redistribution regimental headquarters moved to a central point on the 21st at Blockhouse 55; and Major Crake was sent to take command of the Dujaila Redoubt, the garrison of which was responsible for providing piquets along the old Turkish line of trenches from Dujaila towards Atab. These piquets, however, were withdrawn on the 22nd.

[19] See Map No. 15.

The distribution of the 43rd was now as follows:—

"A" Company holding Blockhouses 43 to 54 with three platoons; one platoon at General Headquarters.

"C" Company holding Blockhouses 55 to 66 at Imam al Mansur where it connected with the left of the 2nd/119th Infantry.

"B" and "D" Companies and machine-gun section at Dujaila under Major Crake.

Meanwhile, on the 20th, the guns of the Cavalry Division had broken the Turkish bridge on the east of the Shumran peninsula, and heavy bombardments on the Hai salient, the Khudhaira bend and Sannaiyat had begun to shake the nerves of the stout Turks whose forces, inferior both in numbers and artillery, were holding an attenuated front from Sannaiyat on the left bank to west of the Shumran peninsula on the right bank.

On the 22nd Sir William Robertson telegraphed saying that the time had come for General Maude to make up his mind to fight for a decision, as it appeared that the Turks were not to be frightened into the abandonment of their present positions by threats to their communications; and that substantial advantages, worth the cost, would be gained if General Maude could drive the enemy from Sannaiyat and Kut. This was just the encouragement which General Maude needed. He thereupon ordered the consolidation of the new positions and the improvement of communications preparatory to launching a determined offensive. On the 26th the rain came, and continued intermittently until the 6th January 1917, converting the whole area into a glutinous amalgam. "Camels and motor lorries were immobilized, carts carried less and stuck frequently, pack mules had to make fewer or slower journeys, and even the railway trains, carrying half loads, took double the usual time over their journeys, the engines being frequently held up by the mud on the rails, left in some cases by infantry crossing the line."[20] But the supply service did not break down.

On the 23rd the 43rd came under the command of Lieutenant-Colonel Darley, 2nd/119th Infantry, commanding the west sector of No. 3 Section, Tigris Defences. The following day regimental headquarters evacuated Blockhouse 55 and took over the III Corps camp, which was found to be in a most insanitary condition; and on Christmas Day the whole of the Regiment was concentrated by the relief of the platoon of "A" Company from G.H.Q. guard. The 43rd had recently been issued with four Lewis guns with thirty-six magazines apiece, and four Vickers machine guns to replace four Maxims of which two were unserviceable. The parties in charge of these held the Dujaila Redoubt whence field firing practice could be carried out.

[20] *Official History*, Vol. III, p. 89.

On the 26th " B " Company took over the prisoners-of-war camp at Sinn from the 10th Lancers, and the following day the 43rd began to wire the front of the blockhouse line eastward from Imam al Mansur. The wet weather necessitated much work on the blockhouses; and, in addition, the Regiment was allotted the task of constructing a new blockhouse line south of the Dujaila depression between Sinn and Imam al Mansur.

The strength of the Regiment at the end of the year was 22 officers and 860 other ranks. The officers serving with the 43rd were:—

Lieutenant-Colonel L. H. R. Pope-Hennessy, D.S.O., commanding.
Major R. H. Crake, King's Own Scottish Borderers, senior major.
Captain G. W. Titherington, adjutant.
Lieutenant F. E. Anderson, sniping officer.
Second Lieutenant B. F. Roberts, machine-gun officer.
Second Lieutenant E. B. Parkinson, transport officer.
Second Lieutenant H. W. Bleeze, bombing officer.
Second Lieutenant T. R. Milford, signalling officer.
Lieutenant G. Dancey, D.C.M., quartermaster.

" A " Company.

Captain (Hon. Major) Hon. W. R. S. Barrington.
Lieutenant P. G. Wells, 2nd King's (Liverpool Regiment).
Second Lieutenant F. M. Hardie.

" B " Company.

Captain T. H. Wheelwright.
Lieutenant H. E. F. Smyth.
Second Lieutenant D. A. T. Wilmot.
Second Lieutenant J. R. Brown.

" C " Company.

Captain W. E. C. Terry.
Lieutenant W. W. Wooding.
Second Lieutenant L. J. Rock.

" D " Company.

Captain G. E. Whittall, M.C.
Lieutenant E. C. Kinghorn, 2nd/4th Border Regiment.
Second Lieutenant G. C. Huggard.

On the 4th January 1917 the whole Regiment was employed on the new Blockhouses 50 and 60. The following day the 2nd Norfolk Regiment took over the blockhouse line from 43 to 50 inclusive, and the Regiment started work on a new strong point on Stable Ridge, which was occupied on the 9th. The work on the new line employed the Regiment throughout January, for, though the new blockhouses were ringed with barbed wire and occupied by the 11th, the wire fence along the whole front took much time to complete. In this fence bombs were fixed to trap inquisitive Arabs, and other ruses devised to warn the garrisons of the approach of raiders. Wood for fuel, being very scarce, was highly prized; " and it was almost impossible to keep roads and camps properly signposted, as the boards were removed nightly. . . . " One night the 43rd serjeant in charge of the commander-in-chief's camp was dumbfounded at seeing General Maude's own private convenience moving apparently of its own volition. Rather shaken, he watched until there was no doubt: the tent was moving by slow bounds towards the barbed-wire fence. Once satisfied, he called out a file of the guard, and fixing bayonets the three charged the tent. The result was immediate: the tent collapsed and out rushed two yelling Arabs, who escaped in the confusion. But raids were not always so comic as this; for on Christmas night an orderly of the 43rd, on his way between the blockhouses, ran into a party of marauding Arabs who shot him in the thigh and took his rifle.

By the 17th a searchlight had been installed in the position on Stable Ridge. This was very useful, for the Arabs were active at night during the second week in January. On the 16th they cut the wire and entered the line near Blockhouse 66, and succeeded again on the 18th. But a third attempt on the 20th to enter the line near Stable Ridge was spotted and a Lewis gun opened fire, hitting at least one of the marauders.

Meanwhile a regimental school was established at Dujaila to train such specialists as snipers and bombers under Second Lieutenants Anderson and Bleeze respectively. The machine-gun section, now armed with Vickers guns and numbering forty-five other ranks under Second Lieutenant Roberts, was also at Dujaila whence guns could be registered. The companies were also training reserve Lewis gunners under their own arrangements, and carried out field firing from their own areas in the blockhouse line. In the meantime also the old blockhouse line and strong points were dismantled by the Regiment.

The front for which the Regiment was now responsible was organized in three sectors with " B " Company holding the left, " D " the centre and " C " the right. " A " Company was held in reserve at regimental headquarters. The school of instruction flourished exceedingly, material and necessary equipment and appliances for specialists were generously supplied, and the Regiment was fast becoming fit to take its place in a formation. The companies holding the blockhouse spent mornings on intensive training, and afternoons on fatigues improving the blockhouse line and the blockhouses. Training included trench storming in co-operation with bombers; encounter and deliberate attack schemes combined with field firing; route marching and the training of Lewis-gun teams and reserve Lewis gunners. It was found that the system of splitting up companies to occupy blockhouses three to six hundred yards apart put difficulty in the way of training, nor was the scheme particularly efficacious in frustrating the attempts of Arabs to cut the wire and enter the line. It was thought, however, that when once a continuous fence of apron wire should have been constructed there would be little fear of serious attack on the line from this class of enemy. But marauding Arabs very soon learned to recognize bomb traps which were, moreover, useless unless placed in every bay, involving great waste of bombs which deteriorated when exposed to rain or sun.

The solution[21] to the difficulty of holding an extensive line suggested by the commanding officer was as follows: when a unit is allotted a line for protection against Arabs, an efficient fence should first be erected. Small posts to hold three men each should be constructed along this line at intervals of not more than one hundred yards; and at every thousand yards a post to hold twelve men or more with a machine or Lewis gun. Special attention to be paid to nullahs, etc., leading through the line, not to be blocked but used as traps. These posts should be occupied by night and should make it impossible for Arabs to remove horses and large gear, although they might still be able to crawl through singly. Should, however, a few be shot by the occupants of the posts, the survivors would find that the raids were not worth the risk. By day companies on blockhouse duty should return to a central camp, near the line and equipped with a crow's-nest, whereby training, supervision, rationing, watering, etc., should be greatly simplified; and the tendency which the prolonged occupation of detached posts has towards lowering discipline should be obviated. In flat country a crow's-nest lookout thirty feet high should give ample warning of the approach of enemy, mounted or otherwise.

On the 28th February Major Crake left the 43rd to take command of the 8th Cheshire Regiment; and Captain Whittall took over the duties of senior major and retained command of " D " Company.

On the 1st March the following officers were serving with the Regiment:

Lieutenant-Colonel L. H. R. Pope-Hennessy, D.S.O., commanding.
Captain G. W. Titherington, adjutant.
Lieutenant F. E. Anderson, sniping officer.
Second Lieutenant B. F. Roberts, machine-gun officer.
Second Lieutenant E. B. Parkinson, transport officer.
Second Lieutenant H. W. Bleeze, bombing officer.
Second Lieutenant T. R. Milford, signalling officer.
Lieutenant G. Dancey, D.C.M., quartermaster.

[21] War Diary.

"A" Company.

Captain C. Fitzgerald.
Lieutenant D. Murphy.
Lieutenant P. G. Wells, 2nd King's (Liverpool Regiment).
Second Lieutenant F. M. Hardie.

"B" Company.

Lieutenant H. T. C. Field.
Lieutenant H. E. F. Smyth.
Second Lieutenant D. A. T. Wilmot.
Second Lieutenant J. R. Brown.

"C" Company.

Captain W. E. C. Terry.
Lieutenant W. W. Wooding.
Lieutenant S. J. Griffin.
Second Lieutenant L. J. Rock.

"D" Company.

Captain G. E. Whittall, M.C.
Captain H. K. Bicknell.
Lieutenant E. C. Kinghorn, 2nd/4th Border Regiment.
Second Lieutenant G. C. Huggard.

CHAPTER XXIII.

The Offensive:

Second Battle of Kut al Amara.[1]

Fourth attack on Sannaiyat—Fifth—The passage of the Tigris—Capture of Kut—Turks escape annihilation—Pursuit—Attenuation of communications—Halt—Pursuit restarted—Capture of Baghdad, March 11th.

(See Map on page 130, and facing page 270.)

AFTER the preliminary advance in December General Maude decided to clear the right bank by an attack on the Khudhaira bend, a position which threatened his communications with the Hai.

On the morning of the 9th January the 3rd Division assaulted the Khudhaira position while feints were made on the two flanks of the enemy line, by the Cavalry Division on the left towards Shumran and Bughaila, and by the 7th Division on the right at Sannaiyat.

After ten days of severe fighting the 3rd Division drove the enemy from the Khudhaira bend by the 19th. Anxious to give the enemy no time to recuperate, General Maude next turned to the Hai salient. A week was spent in consolidating the ground won and in preparing for the next advance, which was to be deliberate and systematic and supported by great preponderance of artillery.

The battle of the Hai salient opened on the 25th with an attack by the 3rd Division on the enemy positions on each bank of the Hai, while feints were made on the flank positions at Shumran and Sannaiyat. Once again the Turks fought stubbornly, and not until the 4th February did they evacuate the east bank of the Hai. They then took up a line from Woolpress Village to the southern end of the Shumran bend, and showed no signs of withdrawing farther on either bank of the Tigris.

The next step was to clear the Dahra bend. On the 9th the two divisions of the III Corps, with an overwhelming superiority of artillery, attacked the numerically inferior Turks. By the 16th the Dahra bend had been cleared of the enemy, and the III Corps encircled the Shumran peninsula on the right bank. But the Turks still held the Sannaiyat position in spite of the threat to their communications. General Maude therefore determined to attack both

---

[1] See Map No. 15, facing p. 270.

flanks, at Sannaiyat and Shumran, simultaneously. Accordingly, on the 17th, the 7th Division made the fourth attempt on Sannaiyat. The Turks were taken by surprise, and the 21st Brigade occupied the second line near the Tigris with only slight casualties. The first counter-attacks were successfully repulsed, and all seemed well until the Turks, following up a heavy bombardment in the early afternoon, drove the 20th Punjabis and 1st/8th Gurkhas out of the captured trenches. Once again Sannaiyat refused capture. But this failure served General Maude's purpose by attracting the Turks' attention to their left flank. He therefore decided to make a crossing of the river at Shumran on the 23rd, and to attack Sannaiyat again on the 22nd.

This fifth and last attack by the Seaforth Highlanders and 92nd Punjabis achieved immediate success. This time the 72nd was not to be denied. By 5 p.m. the 19th and 21st Brigades were firmly established in the first and second lines of trenches. At long last Sannaiyat, the Thermopylæ which had defied four assaults, was in the hands of the troops which had failed so often to capture it.

Meanwhile, miles farther west, the troops of the 14th Division were assembling for their attempt to cross the Tigris. Just before dawn on the 23rd the covering parties were ferried across, but not without severe casualties among the gallant rowers of the pontoons. On the left the 2nd Norfolk Regiment succeeded in establishing a bridgehead. At 4.30 p.m. the bridge was completed and ready for traffic; and by midnight all the infantry battalions and divisional headquarters had crossed to the Shumran peninsula.[2] The position of the Turks was now critical, but once again the Turks showed their fine fighting qualities: dogged tenacity and refusal to panic. On the night of the 23rd/24th they evacuated their positions on the left bank and retired north of Kut towards Qala Shadi, while a stout-hearted rear guard held the neck of the Shumran peninsula during the 24th. The stubborn action of this rear guard prevented the annihilation of the enemy.

At 7 p.m. on the 24th the naval flotilla reached Kut, and a party from H.M.S. *Mantis* hoisted the Union Jack. In his daily report of the 24th General Maude said: " As a result of these operations we now have the whole of the enemy's positions from Sannaiyat to Kut; and Kut itself to which no interest but a sentimental one attaches, passes automatically into our hands. . . . We have also secured navigation of the river up to Shumran."[3]

On the night of the 24th/25th the Turks withdrew from Shumran, and the 13th Division took up the pursuit at 10.30 a.m. on the 25th. On the 26th

[2] *Official History*, Vol. III, pp. 162-170. The account of the crossing is well worth reading.
[3] *Ibid.*, p. 184.

the III Corps took Imam Mahdi and Qala Shadi[4] with little opposition. But the Turkish rear guard, by withdrawing during the night, had evaded the infantry and cavalry pursuit.

Meanwhile General Maude had called upon Captain Nunn, R.N., to push on with the naval flotilla, and harass the retreating enemy. At full speed H.M. Ships *Tarantula, Mantis, Moth, Gadfly* and *Butterfly* steamed upstream. As he approached the Nahr al Kalek bend Captain Nunn ordered all his guns to fire on the Turkish position, and led the fleet on without a moment's hesitation. The enemy's fire at ranges averaging from one to five hundred yards caused many casualties, but each ship, finely handled, managed to swing round the bend and run the gauntlet of the concentrated fire without being incapacitated. Thereafter the fleet soon overtook the Turkish main body and opened rapid fire with every available gun with terrific effect. Completely demoralized by this fire, the Turks broke their formations and abandoned their guns; and their retreat soon became a rout. But for the fleet there was still other game ahead—the enemy's flotilla. One after the other his ships were captured: first the *Sumana* which the Turks had captured on the surrender of Kut; then the *Basra* with many wounded on board, including a few British lately taken prisoners; the *Firefly*, a few miles from where she was lost in 1915; the *Pioneer*; and several barges.

By this action Captain Nunn's fleet exterminated the enemy's flotilla in one day and rendered services beyond the scope of cavalry in a waterless country.

The Turks were now in a sorry plight, panic-stricken at last. Harried by the British cavalry and infantry, plundered, murdered and mutilated by their erstwhile allies, the Arabs, " no sign remained that this was the fine army which had held us in check for over a year."[5] On the night of the 26th/27th this rabble retreated to Aziziya.

But what of the communications? In a single day the line, so carefully prepared and organized for the maintenance of supplies of all descriptions, was rendered almost completely otiose. The railway from Shaikh Saad to Atab[6] automatically ceased to serve its purpose directly the III Corps crossed to the left bank and started the pursuit. Henceforth the Tigris became the artery of supply. On the 26th General Maude issued orders that the general officer commanding Tigris Defences was to take over the defence of the line of communications as far as Shumran on the 27th. By this time the advanced troops of the Cavalry Division had reached Aziziya, which was found to be held by the enemy rear guard.

Keen as he was to advance and give the enemy no respite, General Maude was fain to call a halt on account of the difficulty of supply.

[4] See Map No. 7, p. 130.   [5] *Official History*, Vol. III, p. 195.
[6] The railway from Imam to Atab was in use by the 3rd February. See Map 15.

TO ILLUSTRATE OPERATIONS ON THE TIGRIS.—13TH DECEMBER 1916, TO 25TH FEBRUARY 1917.

NOTES.—(a) For detail of trenches, etc., in the Hai Salient, Dahra Bend, and Shumran Peninsula, see Map 23.
(b) British advanced general line on 13th December 1916, shown by thick Red line ———
   Extension of British advanced general line by 9th January 1917, shown by thin Red line ———
   " " " " " 22nd February 1917. ·········
   British advanced line at northern end of Shumran Peninsula at nightfall 24th February 1917 shown by red line ———
   (c) Turkish advanced general line on 9th January 1917 shown by Green line
   General line of Turkish rearguard on evening 24th February 1917 shown in green (It is not known exactly how far north it extended)

Scale ½ Inch = 1 Mile.

(Reproduced from the Official History of the Mesopotamia Campaign, by permission of H.M. Stationery Office.)

BAGHDAD CAPTURED

By the 4th March the naval flotilla, Cavalry Division and III Corps had concentrated at Aziziya, whither four days' reserve supplies had been forwarded. On the 5th March the British force moved forward, and occupied Zor that night after a trying march such as the 43rd experienced eighteen months earlier. The following day the Cavalry Division passed through Lajj and rode over the field of Ctesiphon, through the village and up the Baghdad road to Bawi, within eight miles of the Diyala river whither the Turks had retired. The Diyala provided a formidable obstacle to negotiate, but on the night of the 8th/9th a party of the 6th Loyal Regiment managed to cross and hold a lunette against repeated and heavy counter-attacks, in which it inflicted severe casualties on the enemy.

However, the Turks evacuated their position on the left bank at 6.30 a.m. on the 10th. That night, the 10th March, Khalil Pasha was persuaded of the futility of trying to protect Baghdad with the troops at his disposal. At 8 p.m. the commander of the XVIII Turkish Corps issued orders to retreat, but not until 2 a.m. were the rear parties clear of the suburbs of Baghdad.

Meanwhile between 1.30 a.m. and 2 a.m. on the 11th British patrols occupied the vacated Turkish lines on both banks. At 6 a.m. a patrol of the 73rd Royal Highlanders entered Baghdad railway station and asked for a cup of tea. Three hours later the 35th Brigade, led by the 1st/5th The Buffs, marched into the city, and the Union Jack was hoisted on the Citadel. For the thirtieth time Baghdad had fallen to the hand of a conqueror, but never to such a merciful hand. Except for marauding Arabs and Kurds, who had seized their opportunity to plunder and loot as soon as the Turkish police had been withdrawn, there was little disorder and much enthusiasm from the Christian and Jewish populations.

CHAPTER XXIV.

OPERATIONS FOR THE PROTECTION OF BAGHDAD.

CO-OPERATION WITH THE RUSSIANS—OPERATIONS ON THREE FRONTS—HEAVY FIGHTING.

(See Map facing page 274.)

THE immediate benefits reaped by the capture of Baghdad were twofold: the Turks were robbed of their base for operations; and the tension on the North-West Frontier was relaxed, for the possession of the city threatened the rear of the Turkish XIII Corps which was invading Persia and causing anxiety in India. But the ultimate benefits were manifold: many Arab shaikhs in Lower Mesopotamia, who had been sitting on the fence, offered their doubtful allegiance; the Amir of Afghanistan received encouragement in his attitude of neutrality; and the agitators and malcontents in India were conversely disheartened.

After the capture of Baghdad General Maude's immediate objects were to consolidate his position and co-operate with the Russians in their offensive towards Mosul. Baghdad was not easy to hold, for many possible lines of advance converged on the city which had neither natural nor artificial defences. There was, however, no waste of time. The military and civil administrations were soon planned; police were formed for the control of the city; and communications and hospital arrangements were quickly and effectively improved. In spite of the greatly increased length of communications the troops now lacked for nothing, for in the Baghdad *vilayet* meat, vegetables, forage and fuel were abundant, and these naturally reduced the strain on the supply system.

Basra was now a great port; metal roads linked the depots and hospitals; and steamers unloaded their cargoes at wharves served by railways. And what was true of Basra was true of the various posts on the long line of communications. The river was by this time divided into sections which had their own pilots; the channels were buoyed and lighted; and shipyards in Basra and upcountry were capable of repairing steamers and erecting new craft sent out from England in sections. The railways by supplementing the river craft further facilitated supply.

Medical arrangements had almost been perfected. Hospitals at Basra and Amara now had water and electric light laid on; and ice factories had

BRIGADIER F. H. STAPLETON, C.M.G.

been erected. There were now hospital launches for the medical service, and hospital steamers for the evacuation of casualties. The old bad days had passed, and now the soldiers' comforts, and with them their health, were studied with a consequent increase in morale. The fighting men no longer had to fear the results of wounds, which had in the past been almost worse than the wounds themselves; and the Army knew that proper requisites were available for the treatment of the many diseases and disorders to which it was liable in that climate. Everything that was humanly possible was now done to ease the lot of the troops, but it had taken two and a half years to effect and at ghastly cost to our man-power.

To complete the picture it is necessary to give here a brief outline of the operations[1] undertaken immediately after the capture of Baghdad, though the 43rd took no active part in them.

On the 13th troops of the I Corps marched up the Tigris right bank to attack the enemy rear guard at Hassaiwa. Storming this line with the greatest gallantry, the troops drove the enemy from the field; and the following day occupied Mushahida station. Having achieved his purpose, General Maude instructed General Cobbe to leave a brigade to ensure the security of the river embankment and to withdraw the rest of his force to Baghdad.

A column under Brigadier-General Davidson was dispatched on the 18th towards Nukhta, due west of Baghdad, to prevent the enemy from further inundating the country by cutting the Sakhlawiya canal. Little opposition was encountered, and on the 19th the force entered Falluja on the Euphrates. Next morning the mouth of the Sakhlawiya canal was secured, but the damage done to the embankment by the Turks was too extensive to be repaired.

On the third front, the Diyala, more extensive operations were undertaken for political and strategical purposes. On the 18th troops of the III Corps occupied Baquba. From here a force was ordered to advance towards Khaniqin. Advancing on the 20th, it occupied Abu Jisra that night and Shahraban in the early morning of the 23rd. When, on the 24th, a brigade group occupied the area between Diltawa and Sindiya, the British forces formed a protective fan north-east of Baghdad.

At this point General Maude determined to try to defeat the Turks in detail before their two corps—the XVIII on the Tigris and the XIII in the Jabal Hamrin area—could effect a junction. While the Cavalry Division contained the Turkish XIII Corps, the 13th Division fell upon the enemy on the left bank of the Tigris at Mara and drove him back to the line of the Shatt al Adhaim. Having disposed of the enemy's right wing, it now remained to crush his left. On the 31st some Russians reached Qasr-i-Shirin,

[1] See Map No. 16, facing p. 274.

east of the Jabal Hamrin, but the Turkish XIII Corps managed to escape the nutcrackers, which at one time seemed likely to close on it with deadly effect, by marching north towards Kifri. As a result General Maude suggested that General Raddatz should pursue the Turks to Kifri, while he with his main force undertook operations towards Samarra. But owing to the revolution which broke out in March, the morale and discipline of the Russian troops were far from satisfactory. This secession from the Allied cause put a completely different complexion upon the conduct of the war in Mesopotamia and placed the onus entirely upon the British. At the same time the Russian defection—for defection it eventually became—prevented what easily might have been an overwhelming victory.

Nevertheless, General Maude operated towards Samarra in April to assist the Russians in establishing themselves on the Tigris. On the 8th the 7th Division drove the Turks from Balad station on the right bank and occupied Harba next day. Meanwhile General Marshall drove the enemy back towards the Jabal Hamrin on the 11th, and on the 15th forced a passage across the Adhaim. On the right bank General Cobbe's[2] column defeated the Turkish XVIII Corps on the 22nd April and occupied Samarra two days later.

---

[2] *Official History*, Vol. III, p. 325. General Cobbe took over command of operations from General Fane on the 16th April.

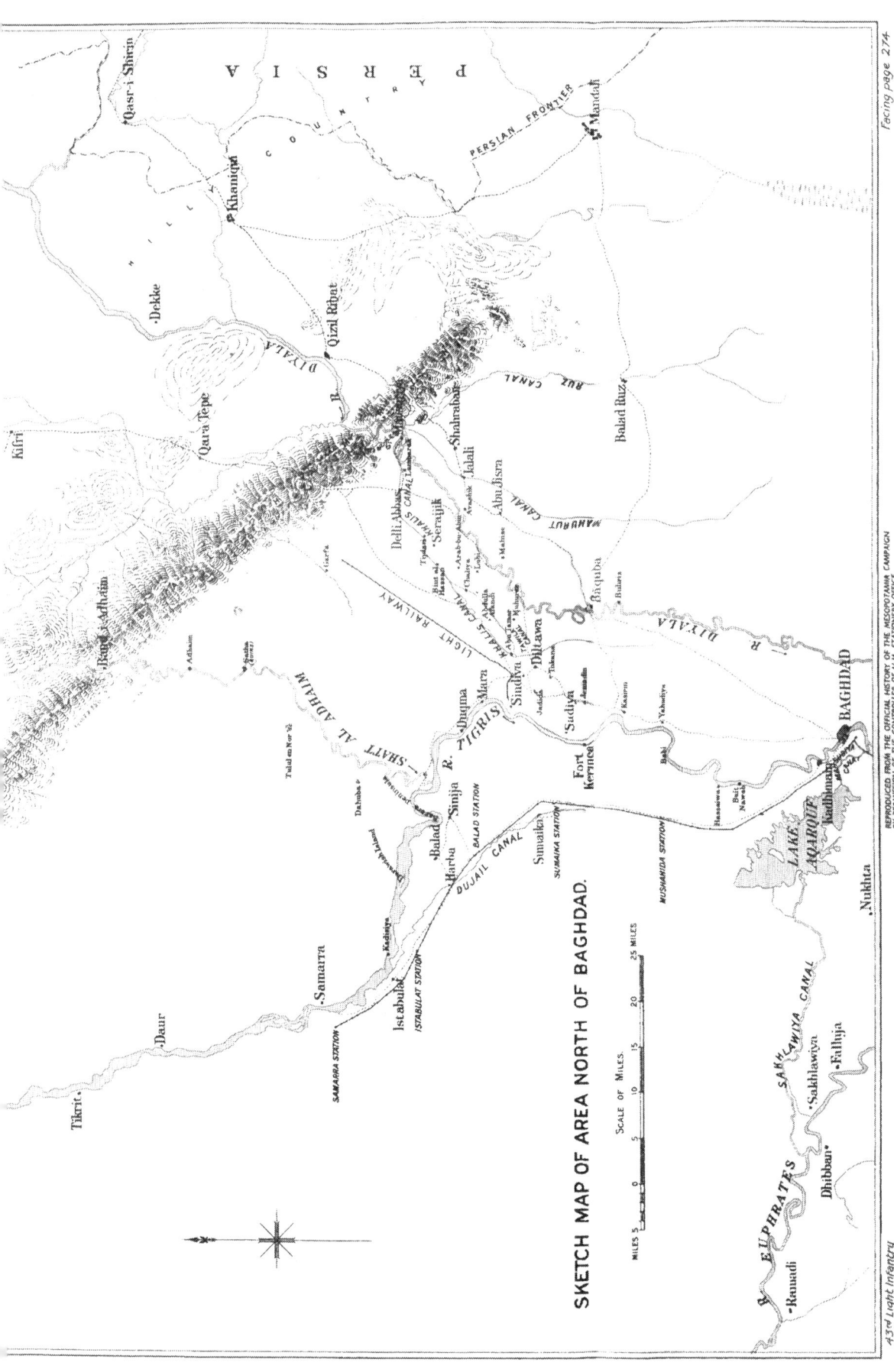

1917]

CHAPTER XXV.

I.—March to July with the 43rd.

Redistribution of the Tigris Defences—The 43rd dismantles the light railway—The line of Communications—The 43rd moves to Aziziya—Weather conditions—Yilderim—The Russians retreat—Mesopotamia reinforced—Improvements in communications—The Mesopotamia Commission—Defection of the Russians—The 43rd attempts to capture Turkish agent—Sickness in the 43rd—The 43rd moves to Hinaidi—Turks defeated at Ramadi—Death of Sir Stanley Maude—Appreciation—General Marshall assumes command—Birth of Bolshevism—Russian armies disintegrate—Dunsterforce—Withdrawal of 7th Division to Egypt.

(*See Maps facing pages* 1, 270 *and* 274, *and on pages* 130 *and* 300.)

MARCH found the Regiment still holding the blockhouse line with regimental headquarters at Sinn. As has been recorded,[1] the general officer commanding Tigris Defences was ordered to take over, on the 27th February, the line of communications as far as Shumran, which necessitated a reshuffle. Accordingly regimental headquarters moved on the 6th March to Imam al Mansur.

Arabs at this time were causing trouble by grazing their herds nearer to the blockhouse line, but they were kept at a respectful distance by machine-gun fire; and a few surrendered in obedience to the proclamations which were dropped by aeroplanes. But others continued to raid the line. On the 13th a party of about fifty attempted to penetrate near Blockhouse 75, and one was found dead on our wire the next morning. A week later another party succeeded in penetrating the wire, but, on being fired on as they departed, they dropped much valueless material collected from old trenches in Abdul Hassan bend. Their ingenuity was certainly praiseworthy; for instance, on the 21st a party removed donkeys from the Labour Corps without cutting the wire by tying the beasts' feet together and dragging them *under* the wire. On the 27th Private A. V. Spencer was shot by an Arab when a sentry on guard at regimental headquarters and died of his wounds.

Meanwhile the railway from Shaikh Saad to Atab, now useless, was being taken up to be transported for use upstream between Baghdad and Baquba and other outlying posts. By the end of March it had been dismantled as far as Imam, and Blockhouses 81 to 69 had been abandoned. Consequently " D " Company moved from Atab to Sinn on the 30th. As

[1] See p. 270.

the work of dismantling progressed, so the companies of the Regiment concentrated at Sinn. On the 3rd April Dujaila Redoubt was abandoned, and the Regiment, less " C " Company, marched to Twin Canals, arriving at 10.30 a.m. Marching to Shaikh Saad the following day, the 43rd encamped near the old site of the previous December, but not until the 12th were all the companies concentrated at headquarters.

The 43rd was now under the command of Brevet Lieutenant-Colonel F. H. Stapleton, who had arrived on the 22nd March in relief of Lieutenant-Colonel L. H. R. Pope-Hennessy, D.S.O., who on the 14th March had received orders to join the 3rd Division as G.S.O.1.

At Shaikh Saad the 43rd carried out company and individual training, hoping to be sent to a fighting formation like its old friends the 2nd Norfolk Regiment and 2nd Dorsetshire Regiment of the original 6th Division. But the Regiment was not yet destined to achieve its wish.

By this time the line of communications, greatly lengthened, had been reorganized in four sections[2] :—

 I. Basra (exclusive) to Amara (inclusive).
 II. Amara (exclusive) to Shaikh Saad and Dujaila (inclusive).
 III. Wadi to Bughaila (both inclusive).
 IV. Bughaila (exclusive) to Diyala (inclusive).

Into this last section the 43rd was ordered to move. On the 28th April " A " and " D " Companies embarked for Aziziya, to be followed on the 30th by headquarters and " B " and " C " Companies. By the evening of the 3rd May the whole Regiment had reached Aziziya, headquarters of No. 4 Section, Tigris Defences.

This post consisted of a half-squadron, 10th Lancers; one 4-inch post gun; 43rd Light Infantry; 1st/6th Gurkhas; one pack station, 1st Wireless Signal Squadron; " L " Company, Supply and Transport; and No. 7 Combined Field Ambulance.[3]

From the point of view of military operations the ensuing months were devoid of interest for the 43rd, which was occupied in routine duties. These consisted of perimeter guards, weekly practice parades of the mobile column, and sundry escorts to parties and transport bound for the next post upstream at Zor. Training, however, in open warfare and musketry continued all through the hot weather. In June the Regiment set to walling its tents as a protection from the great heat, which, as usual, incapacitated many men of the drafts received at this time. One such draft arrived on the 26th June with 2 officers and 213 other ranks, having left Basra 254 strong. In the Regiment there were seventy other ranks sick and off duty on the 30th, when the strength was 27 officers and 1,026 men.

[2] *Official History*, Vol. III, p. 295.   [3] *Ibid.*, Vol. III, Appendix XXXIX, p. 413.

The summer of 1917 was considerably severer than in either of the two previous years, and the intensely hot weather started earlier than usual. Between the 12th March and the 3rd April there were as many as 37,400 officers and men admitted to hospital.[4] " According to the Baghdadis it was the hottest season in the memory of man. Most things were too hot to touch. The rim of a tumbler burnt one's hand in a tent. The dust and sand burnt the soles of one's feet through one's boots. . . . In July the temperature rose to 122.8 degrees in Baghdad. . . . In tents and dug-outs it was often ten degrees higher than the standardised official reading."[5] On the 10th July the regimental war diary records that the temperature was 126 degrees in the shade. Captain Whittall recorded that it rose on one occasion to 131 degrees and that nights averaged 80 degrees.

II.—YILDERIM; COMMUNICATIONS; REPORT OF THE MESOPOTAMIA COMMISSION.

General Maude's intentions at the end of April were to consolidate his positions and rest the troops during the great heat of the summer. Meanwhile, however, the German supreme command agreed in April to shoulder the responsibility for operations to recapture Baghdad.[6] For this purpose General von Falkenhayn was appointed to the command of the Turco-German force which came to be known as *Yilderim*—that is, thunderbolt. The recapture of Baghdad would not only be a great triumph for Enver Pasha, but also it would allow of an invasion of Persia; and the Germans had not yet resigned their hopes of eventually dominating the East.

On the 3rd June General von Falkenhayn reported that an offensive against Baghdad was practicable; and preparations were at once made for the improvement of the Turkish communications, which alone could bring success to the project. These were as long as, and even more awkward than, the British communications, for the railway tunnels through the Taurus and Amanus mountains were not yet completed. With thoroughness and energy the Germans set to work on their herculean task, but they and the Turks made incompatible bedfellows. Early in June Enver Pasha explained to the commanders concerned that *Yilderim* would march down the Euphrates, concentrate at Hit and proceed to cut the communications of the British.

Meanwhile considerable improvements in the British communications were being effected. By the end of July the metre-gauge railway from Kut to Baghdad and the 2 ft. 6 in. lines from Baghdad to Baquba, and from Sumaika to Sadiya had been completed. A metre-gauge line from Qurna

[4] *Ibid.*, Vol. III, p. 296. [5] *The Long Road to Baghdad*, Vol. II, p. 179.
[6] *Official History*, Vol. IV, p. 8.

was under construction, and further lines from Baghdad to Falluja and Musaiyib as well as an extension beyond Samarra of standard gauge were projected. Roads were likewise improved, and steps were taken to control the floods which appeared likely to be extensive in the winter of 1917-18. The river transport had increased so enormously that in July 1917 it could deliver 2,000 tons daily in Baghdad whereas in July 1916 it could land only 300 tons daily at Shaikh Saad, less than half the distance from Basra. Basra was still further extended by the construction of wharves and unloading facilities for six ships at Nahr Umar, twelve miles above the town. In fact, within a year Basra and its immediate neighbourhood had been completely transmogrified. Anyone of the old 6th Division, languishing in prison in Anatolia, would have been justifiably astounded at the improvements.

In June the Report of the Mesopotamia Commission,[7] dealing with the operations up to the fall of Kut, was published. The rumours of the sufferings of the wounded and the conduct of the operations which, after victory, culminated in the capitulation of Kut, had caused considerable indignation at home; and the Commission was set up in August 1916 to examine " the origin, inception and conduct of the operations in Mesopotamia,"[8] and to apportion responsibility and blame. The Commission was in the nature of an autopsy to inquire into conditions which were at the time—that is August 1916—in process of being rectified, and no longer obtained when the report was issued. Lord George Hamilton, chairman of the Commission, only undertook the duty in order to avert a political crisis. Of the other seven members of the Commission, Lord Donoughmore was chairman of Committees of the House of Lords, four were Members of Parliament, one was an admiral, and General Sir Neville Lyttelton had served in India as a young officer; " but none of the others had any practical experience in that country of military or civil administration."[9] Witnesses were sworn, but the Commission did not observe the rules of evidence; and those whose conduct was questioned were given little opportunity to clear themselves. Owing to the exigencies of the war it was naturally impossible to examine all those witnesses whose evidence could contribute to a just finding. For instance, General Townshend, one of the most important witnesses, was a prisoner. The finding, based neither on civil nor military law, was valueless and unjust, for the Commission, sitting on soft seats in London, judged conditions in Mesopotamia and India which they did not visit before recording their finding. The Quartermaster-General in India, who was responsible for transport, was not called; yet gallant fighting soldiers lost their military reputations as a result of the report. " That the Commission did not always

---

[7] See *Chronicle*, 1916-17, pp. 70 *et seq.*
[8] *Official History*, Vol. IV, p. 28.   [9] *Ibid.*, Vol. IV, p. 29.

appreciate the true significance of what it learnt, lends force to the criticism, often made, that, generally speaking, the members of the Commission were lacking in the technical and up-to-date knowledge of military operations and military war organization required in an enquiry of this nature. It is undoubtedly true that, in a military sense, its report was incomplete and in a few cases inaccurate."[10] The issue of the report, however, raised a storm of indignation in England, which was visited upon the servants of the Crown, just as in 1756 the loss of Minorca resulted in the execution of Admiral Byng on the quarterdeck of the *Monarque* and the dismissal of Lieutenant-General Thomas Fowke, first colonel of the 43rd, *pour encourager les autres*. The popular rage, as voiced by the Press, was focused on the sufferings of the wounded. A separate Commission[11] had made an exhaustive inquiry both in India and Mesopotamia into the causes which led to the breakdown of the medical arrangements, and had rendered a true account which was incorporated in the finding of the Mesopotamia Commission. And when blame was apportioned, the scalp hunters with facile pens called for the punishment of those deemed responsible by the Commission; but they forgot, if indeed they ever knew, that India had rendered invaluable assistance in the hour of need, for which she was, like England, wholly unprepared; that the Army in India was organized only for the protection of the Frontier and the maintenance of internal security; and that India willingly and ungrudgingly, at the call of the Viceroy, had shouldered many external responsibilities and had sent troops to Europe, Egypt, East Africa, Aden and Mesopotamia.

III.[12]—ON THE DEFENSIVE: THE 43RD MOVES TO HINAIDI: OPERATIONS AT RAMADI AND ON THE RIGHT FLANK: POLICY REGARDING PERSIA: GENERAL MILITARY SITUATION.

In August when it was clear that a Russian offensive against Mosul was extremely unlikely General Maude determined to form another division and omit the Russians from all his calculations. Consequently he ordered the occupation of Shahraban in order to secure his right flank where the Russians should have been.

During August the first brigade, the 50th, of the new 17th Division was formed and sent to relieve the 7th Brigade in the Falluja area; and in September it was decided to send a new 18th Division from India to Mesopotamia early in 1918.

During this period the rôle of the Army in Mesopotamia was defensive owing to the defection of the Russians, the uncertainty of the direction of

[10] *Ibid.*, Vol. IV, p. 30. [11] The Vincent-Bingley Commission.
[12] See Map No. 18, p. 300.

the Turkish offensive, and the diversion of British offensive action from Mesopotamia to Palestine whence the British Government deemed an offensive towards Aleppo more likely to strike at the heart of Turkey. But General Maude was instructed to take advantage of any Turkish mistakes and prevent the incursion of parties of Germans or Turks into Persia for the purpose of stirring up trouble in Afghanistan and Turkestan. In fact, the Army in Mesopotamia was to become the guarantor of India's security.

In the second week of September General Maude decided to occupy Ramadi on the Euphrates, and detailed the 15th Division, under General Brooking, for this operation.

Meanwhile the 43rd spent July and August in tents at Aziziya, and many of its days working on the railway to Baghdad. On the 12th July a small operation was undertaken to arrest a Turkish agent, nephew of Shukri Bey, the Turkish commander of the Euphrates force. At 8.45 p.m. on the 11th " B " and " D " Companies, each of 125 rifles, embarked on P32, and Lieutenant J. R. Brown with twenty men on H.M.S. *Sedgefly*. This detachment, together with one troop and machine-gun section of the 10th Lancers, an armoured car and a section of a field ambulance, sailed at midnight under the command of Major Whittall. At 5 a.m. the next day the party disembarked on the right bank twelve miles downstream from Aziziya and four miles above Tubal post; but owing to the high river bank the armoured car took five hours to land. The cavalry, however, supported by the 43rd in three columns, moved off to surround the suspected village four miles inland. No resistance was offered, but the bird had flown; and the column marched back, reaching Aziziya at 3.15 p.m. Three days later the Turkish agent was handed over by the Arabs.

On the 21st July Lieutenant-Colonel Stapleton was called to Baghdad to take up the appointment of G.S.O.1 at G.H.Q., Baghdad, and Major Whittall assumed command of the Regiment. In August one company was quartered at Railway Camp to find escorts to trains and working parties, while the rest of the Regiment concentrated on company training in open warfare.

The sickness in the Regiment, though not so great as in 1916, was considerable. The average weekly sick in July was: officers, 2; other ranks, 88; and 23 were detained in hospital. Privates Phillips and Nicholls, Corporal Gibson and Captain H. K. Bicknell, acting military forwarding officer in Baghdad, died of heat-stroke during the month. In August the average of sick per week increased to over one hundred, and the admittances to hospital increased in proportion. But the strength of the Regiment did not vary materially. In August the chief cause of sickness was sand-fly fever which incapacitated many men for about a week; but there were no deaths from heat-stroke.

THE 43RD AT KARADA

On the 14th September the Regiment received orders to hand over to the 2nd/7th Hampshire Regiment, lately arrived from India, and to move to Hinaidi.[13] Kits were immediately sorted, and the heavy baggage was loaded at 5 p.m. on board P35. At 6 p.m. the next day the first train left for Hinaidi carrying " C " Company, one platoon of " A " Company and baggage. The same night the first party of the 2nd/7th Hampshire Regiment reached Aziziya and took over the standing camp. At 1 a.m. " B " and " D " Companies with 20-lb. kits left by the same train, to be followed at 7 a.m. by the rest of the Regiment. On arrival the 43rd took over the camp at Karada, half a mile from Hinaidi station, in relief of the 1st/4th Dorsetshire Regiment which, as part of the 42nd Brigade, had left for Falluja the previous day.

The next day, the 17th, the Regiment was put under orders to go to Falluja to join the 50th Brigade, then in the newly formed 17th Division. It therefore appeared likely that the 43rd would take part in the forthcoming operations at Ramadi. But at Hinaidi the Regiment remained for another month, a month spent in bringing the companies and headquarters up to establishment in specialists, in route marching and training of all descriptions. At Hinaidi the incidence of sickness decreased considerably, and at the end of the month, when the strength was 26 officers and 1,195 other ranks, there were seventy-four off duty.

On the 28th/29th September General Brooking inflicted such a decisive defeat on the Turks at Ramadi[14] that Ahmed Bey, the Turkish commander, and his entire force surrendered. This victory secured the left flank and forced the enemy to divert troops for the security of the upper reaches of the Euphrates.

After the Ramadi operations had begun, General Maude ordered the occupation of Mandali, east of Balad Ruz. This place was successfully seized on the 28th. These two strategical and tactical successes on the extreme flanks of the Army greatly aggravated the difficulties of the Turks, and by the end of September they had abandoned the idea of an offensive in Mesopotamia. As the result of Falkenhayn's inspection of the Euphrates front, the *Yilderim* Army which was to recapture Baghdad was transferred to Palestine, and henceforth the preparations in Mesopotamia were only continued half-heartedly. At this point that friction which eventually culminated in open hostility between the Turks and Germans was probably worth a division of troops to the British in Palestine and Mesopotamia.

Though General Maude was relieved of anxiety about a Turkish offensive in Mesopotamia, nevertheless there were indications that parties were about to enter Persia. Consequently he ordered the III Corps to occupy the

[13] Two and a half miles south-east of Baghdad on the line to Diyala.
[14] See Map No. 18.

Jabal Hamrin. This was done between the 16th and the 20th October. A fortnight later he seized Tikrit on the 5th November and destroyed much material before withdrawing to Samarra. This was General Maude's last success, for on the 18th November he died of cholera in Baghdad after an unbroken series of victories. His death caused consternation among the troops under his command. His attitude towards the fighting troops can be compared with that of that great soldier of the Regiment, Sir John Moore. " His care for all that concerned their well-being, his constant sympathy with their hardships, difficulties and dangers, and his ready and generous acknowledgment of their work had endeared him to all ranks in Mesopotamia."[15] There was not a man who did not realize the part he had played in converting defeat into victory, and his name had become "synonymous with success." His reputation could scarcely have been greater than when he died, and he died with the knowledge of victory won after great and terrible privations and hardships. To his place Lieutenant-General Sir W. R. Marshall, K.C.B., succeeded.

From now on the situation in Mesopotamia became exceedingly intricate and complex. Policy rather than military necessity dictated the measures adopted. It seemed unlikely that the Turks would be able to take the offensive again for many months, but the Army in Mesopotamia was still the guarantor of India's security, and at this point disturbing things were happening elsewhere. Amongst the most important was the counter-revolution in Russia, which took place in October, when a coterie of international Jews overthrew the Provisional Government and instituted what we now call Bolshevism. Towards the end of December the Bolsheviks opened peace negotiations at Brest-Litovsk, and as a natural corollary the Russian armies began to disintegrate. This defection completely uncovered the British right flank, and the outlook as regards Persia, Afghanistan and the North-West Frontier became serious. The mischievous Bolshevik propaganda which was immediately disseminated in Persia was likely to find its way into India if measures were not adopted to counteract it at once.[16] Hence the formation under the command of Major-General L. C. Dunsterville—the *Stalky* of Mr. Rudyard Kipling's stories—of that force which came to be known as " Dunsterforce."

But not only in Mesopotamia and India were the Bolshevik peace negotiations causing anxiety. Now that Russia had seceded from the Allied cause

[15] *Official History*, Vol. IV, p. 85.
[16] *Ibid.*, Vol. IV, p. 98. " There were also several thousand Austrian and German prisoners of war at this time in Trans-Caspia and Russian Turkestan, who, if Russia made peace, might cross into Persia and enter into anti-British activities." There was also the fear of a Pan-Turanian movement, and there had been signs of unrest among Musalmans since the Russian counter-revolution.

LIEUTENANT-COLONEL G. E. WHITTALL, M.C.

as a formed entity, it was obvious that Germany would be able to withdraw many divisions from the Eastern Front and concentrate them on the west for a decisive attack on the British and French. The general situation in Europe was far from good. France was war-weary; Italy had to be stiffened with British and French divisions after the debacle at Caporetto; Rumania had to be saved if possible; and we had to prevent supplies reaching Germany. To meet this altered state of affairs and the threatened German onslaught, English troops had to be recalled from all fronts. Thus the 7th Division was withdrawn to Egypt at the end of December and a new division, the 18th, was formed at Baghdad.[17]

---

[17] The 3rd Division was withdrawn for transfer to the Palestine front in March, 1918, and its place in the I Corps was taken by the 18th Division.

CHAPTER XXVI.

I.—THE 43RD JOINS THE 50TH BRIGADE ON THE EUPHRATES: OCCUPATION OF HIT.[1]

CAPTURE OF KHAN ABU RAYAN—THE 43RD PATROLS TOWARDS HIT—CAPTURE OF HIT—THE COUNTRY—THE TURKS HOLD KHAN BAGHDADI—CONCENTRATION OF SUPPLIES—THE ENEMY'S STRENGTH—THE 11TH CAVALRY BRIGADE ARRIVES—ENEMY'S DISPOSITIONS—GENERAL BROOKING'S PLAN—THE BATTLE OF KHAN BAGHDADI—ROUT OF THE TURKS—PURSUIT—CAPTURE OF HADITHA AND ANA—TURKISH LOSSES—THE 43RD WITHDRAWS TO SAHILIYA—SUMMER OPERATIONS—RECONNAISSANCES—THE 43RD RAIDS ENEMY CAVALRY—THE BEGINNING OF THE END—THE BATTLE OF SHARQAT—THE TURKISH ARMISTICE—THE GERMAN ARMISTICE—DEMOBILIZATION—THE CADRE LEAVES FOR ENGLAND—ARRIVES AT ALDERSHOT.

(See Maps on page 300, and facing pages 296 and 302.)

AFTER a month at Hinaidi the 43rd was ordered, on the 14th October, to reduce kits of men and officers to 20 lb. and 80 lb. respectively, and the following day the Regiment was rearmed with high-velocity rifles and Mark VII ammunition. Movement was afoot at last. Seventy-six mules were also drawn from the 15th Divisional Transport Depot.

Having loaded the first-line carts on the 16th, the 43rd was roused at 3.30 a.m. on the 17th and marched out of camp at 5 a.m., crossed the river and proceeded via Baghdad railway station and Ironbridge to Temple Post, eighteen miles distant. The following day the Regiment marched through Nukhta to Mahratta Post, a distance of twelve miles; and moving off again at 5 a.m. on the 19th joined the 50th Brigade at Falluja on the right bank of the Euphrates, and pitched camp. At long last the 43rd was in a formation after eighteen months on line of communication duties.

The 50th Brigade, commanded by Brigadier-General A. W. Andrew, now consisted of the

    43rd Light Infantry;
    6th Jat Light Infantry;
    24th Punjabis;
    1st/97th Infantry;
    256th Machine Gun Company;
    50th Brigade Supply and Transport Company.

By the end of the month the 43rd was further armed with one Lewis gun per platoon.

[1] See Map 18, p. 300.

November and December were uneventful, but another of Mesopotamia's plagues—smallpox—carried off two men, Privates Bishop and Boddington; and during this time Armourer Staff-Serjeant Sherlock died of cholera. The Regiment spent the months in training Lewis gunners, route marching, company training and fatigues on the new railway from Baghdad, which reached Falluja on the 22nd December.

On the 11th January 1918, Lieutenant L. J. Rock and Second Lieutenant C. H. Murray, with four selected non-commissioned officers, returned to Baghdad to join "Dunsterforce," which was to organize the Armenians and Georgians—in fact, all those in Trans-Caucasia who were hostile to the Bolsheviks and desirous of forming republics friendly to their late Allies.

On the 2nd February the Regiment, with first and second-line transport, marched via Dhibban to Madhij in relief of the 42nd Brigade. The road was good, the weather cool, and the men, lightly equipped, marched well and arrived without a casualty. Platoons were now organized in two sections of riflemen, one section of bombers and rifle grenadiers and one section of Lewis gunners.

After a fortnight of training and routine, the Regiment was ordered, on the 20th, to be prepared to move the following day as part of the 50th Brigade to Ramadi. At 8 a.m. on the 21st the 43rd moved out of Madhij at field service strength—24 officers and 855 other ranks—leaving Lieutenant Riddle and 217 other ranks in charge of kit, baggage and tents.

For the past two months the Turks had been reinforcing their troops in the Hit area; and at the beginning of February their strength was estimated to be between 4,000 and 5,000 men of the 50th Division. Hit was a town of strategic value, being connected by desert tracks with Tikrit on the Tigris and Karbala in the Middle Euphrates area; and therefore, early in February, General Marshall ordered General Brooking, commanding the 15th Division, to capture the town and its garrison. On the 18th General Lucas's 42nd Brigade advanced from Ramadi, seized Khan Abu Rayan and took up a position ten miles south of Hit. As soon as he ascertained that the enemy was holding a depression known as Broad Wadi as well as the village of Sahiliya, General Brooking set about improving his communications[2] before attacking.

On the 22nd the 50th Brigade, now known as Andrew's Column, advanced from Ramadi to Khan Abu Rayan, which was reached without incident. Two days later the brigade, with two batteries of the 215th Brigade, R.F.A., advanced to Uqbah and pitched camp east of the 42nd Brigade, now known as Lucas's Column. The next day the 42nd Brigade withdrew to Khan Abu Rayan, leaving the 50th Brigade in observation. In the afternoon

[2] The railway reached Dhibban on the 18th February.

" D " Company and the regimental scouts advanced four miles towards Hit as escort to a reconnaissance party of the 215th Brigade, R.F.A. That evening the camp was raided by Turkish aeroplanes and three casualties were incurred in the 43rd: 9528 Corporal Dredge died of wounds, and 28315 Private Hunter and 28150 Private Purvey were killed.

On the 26th a reconnaissance in force, composed of the 43rd, 97th Infantry, two batteries of field artillery and two light armoured motor battery cars, was made towards Hit. Leaving camp at 8 a.m., patrols from the Regiment entered the enemy's front line without opposition, and succeeded in penetrating his second line, which was found to be partially wired and only very lightly held. Particularly good work in this reconnaissance was done by 9136 Serjeant W. Bull, who, with the regimental scouts, carried out a daring patrol. For his fine leadership he was given an immediate award of the *Military Medal* on the 10th March. As soon as the patrols entered the second line the Turkish guns opened fire from near Broad Wadi, but without inflicting casualties. The Regiment took four prisoners.

The ensuing week was uneventful, but on the 8th March an air reconnaissance reported that the enemy had evacuated his Broad Wadi position and was retiring on Sahiliya and Khan Baghdadi. A cavalry patrol, however, from south of Hit saw about 150 Turks along the Broad Wadi position.

At 10 p.m. the 50th Brigade, 215th Brigade, R.F.A., and six light armoured motor battery cars advanced towards Hit and halted at 2 a.m. on the river bank four miles south of the town. Meanwhile the 90th Punjabis from the 12th Brigade had advanced up the left bank.

At 7.30 a.m. that morning the column advanced again, preceded by " D " Squadron, 1st/1st Hertfordshire Yeomanry, and a squadron of the 10th Lancers, and supported by the details of the 42nd Brigade, then at Khan Abu Rayan. Feeling its way carefully, the column halted at 10 a.m. outside the town, having encountered no opposition. Two hours later Hit had been captured, and the troops were bivouacking on the river bank one mile north of the town.

At noon an air patrol reported that the enemy was retiring on Khan Baghdadi, twenty-two miles upstream. In their retreat the Turks were constantly attacked by our aeroplanes, and they suffered considerable casualties and inconvenience.

" At Hit we entered a new country, a land of limestone and gypseous clay, where the river winds in a valley between low hills. It is built of grey limestone as compact as a castle within its walls; the small minaret stands out like a campanile. . . . Hit marks a dividing line on the Euphrates. Here the river leaves its rocky bed and emerges into the alluvial plain of Mesopotamia." But as usual the beauty of the town, as viewed from a distance, was soon dispelled on closer acquaintance. The smell of refuse in the narrow streets of tightly packed houses was overpowering. " The houses are built on refuse. The Hit of to-day is built on strata of Hits dating back to Ava of the Bible. The debris without grows until it threatens to dominate the walls of the town; yet the debris never decreases, and being more recent is more offensive."[3] Other causes of offence are the bitumen wells in the neighbourhood, known to the Arabs as the " mouths of hell." A foul miasma pervades the atmosphere, " gas spouts up in intermittent gushes, raising the scum in bubbles like gigantic black boils, which distend and burst with a hissing sound. . . . Bitumen, waterwheels and dirt are likely to be the abiding impressions that the Euphrates Force will carry away from Hit."[3]

On the 11th the Regiment advanced again and occupied Sahiliya. The same day a conference was begun between Generals Marshall and Brooking at Baghdad. As the result General Brooking was instructed to drive the enemy as far as possible from Hit and defeat him if possible before withdrawing to a position covering Hit.[4]

During the preparations for this offensive every precaution was taken to keep our intentions secret and to delude the enemy into thinking that we were preparing summer quarters. To this end the Regiment was employed in digging a dummy defensive position and improving roads.

Meanwhile reports of the enemy's movements were somewhat conflicting; on the 12th aircraft reported that the Turks were retiring northwards of Khan Baghdadi, but two days later, when the Regiment made a route march towards Khan Baghdadi, a Turkish deserter found *en route* reported that two battalions with four guns were still holding the town. On the 15th two companies of the 43rd made another reconnaissance towards Khan Baghdadi, but returned with nothing to report. Thereafter forward movements were forbidden so as to lull the enemy into a false security, while the energies of the troops were concentrated on improving the roads and making dumps of supplies. By the night of the 25th/26th a reserve of five days' supplies for the whole striking force had been collected.

The latest information was to the effect that the whole of the enemy force was in the Khan Baghdadi area; that Nazim Bey had recently assumed command of the Turkish 50th Division in place of Shukri Bey, who had been superseded on account of his hasty retreat from Hit; and that reinforcements of two heavy guns and 1,000 infantry had left the Tigris for Haditha and Khan Baghdadi. To divert the attention of the enemy still further from the attack which was due to start on the 26th, General Brooking arranged with General Marshall for demonstrations on the Tigris and in the Jabal Hamrin

[3] *The Long Road to Baghdad*, Vol. II.
[4] *Official History*, Vol. IV, p. 121.

by the I and III Corps respectively on the 23rd. These were entirely successful and caused the enemy to discount the possibility of a concentration on the Euphrates to such an extent that he withdrew nearly all his aeroplanes from that front.

Not until the last moment was the concentration effected. The 11th Cavalry Brigade left Falluja on the 22nd, and, digressing to westward to avoid observation, reached the palm groves of Sahiliya on the 25th after a twenty-mile night march. The rest of the force, consisting of two brigades of artillery and a siege battery, engineers and pioneers, the 12th, 42nd and 50th Infantry Brigades, 275th Machine Gun Company and the Light Armoured Motor Brigade, concentrated on the nights of the 23rd/24th and the 24th/25th.

General Brooking estimated that the enemy then had the Turkish 50th Division and between 17 and 21 guns on the Euphrates. Of this total, 100 sabres, 2,800 rifles and 12 to 16 guns were believed to be holding the Khan Baghdadi position. This had been photographed by the Royal Flying Corps. It consisted of an advanced line south-east of the town, known as " P " trenches, and another line west of Baghdadi known as " Q " and " R " trenches.[5]

General Brooking's plan was to annihilate all the enemy forces downstream of Ana. The advance was to be led by the 50th Brigade at 9 p.m. on the 25th, followed by the 42nd Brigade at midnight and the rest of the division in the early hours of the 26th. The 13th and 14th Light Armoured Motor Batteries and the 11th Cavalry Brigade were to attack the enemy's right flank and rear; and lastly a mobile column in Ford vans, consisting of half the 1st/5th Queen's Regiment and 2nd/39th Garwhalis, two machine-gun sections and a detachment of sappers, together with the 8th Light Armoured Motor Battery and a battery of field guns, was formed for a special rôle.[6]

The 43rd was now at complete war establishment, its first reinforcement, amounting to about 20 per cent. of its strength, having been left behind at Madhij in February. Those officers who went into action were :—

Lieutenant-Colonel G. E. Whittall, M.C., commanding.
Major C. Fitzgerald, second-in-command.
Captain G. W. Titherington, adjutant.
Lieutenant T. R. Milford, signalling officer.
Lieutenant E. B. Parkinson, transport officer.
Lieutenant B. F. Roberts, Lewis-gun officer.
Lieutenant G. Dancey, M.C., D.C.M., quartermaster.

[5] See Map No. 17, facing p. 296. [6] *Official History*, Vol. IV, pp. 122-124.

ON THE MARCH TO FALLUJA.

HIT FROM THE EUPHRATES.

THE APPROACH MARCH

"A" Company.
Captain A. Price, commanding.
Lieutenant L. R. Watts, No. 1 Platoon.
Lieutenant D. S. Northcote, No. 2 Platoon.
Lieutenant H. C. Joyce, No. 3 Platoon.
Lieutenant S. J. Griffin, No. 4 Platoon.

"B" Company.
Captain H. T. C. Field, commanding.
Lieutenant A. E. S. Riddle, No. 5 Platoon.
Lieutenant H. E. F. Smyth, No. 6 Platoon.
Lieutenant J. G. Shepherd, No. 7 Platoon.
Lieutenant D. A. T. Wilmot, No. 8 Platoon.

"C" Company.
Captain H. W. Bleeze, commanding.
Lieutenant C. M. Banks, No. 9 Platoon.
Lieutenant A. L. Thompson, No. 10 Platoon.
Lieutenant H. N. Burrell, No. 12 Platoon.

"D" Company.
Captain J. W. Meade, commanding.
Lieutenant J. S. Fenwick, No. 13 Platoon.
Lieutenant L. V. Steele, No. 14 Platoon.
Lieutenant E. G. Vine, No. 15 Platoon.
Lieutenant T. P. Williams, No. 16 Platoon.

II.—THE BATTLE OF KHAN BAGHDADI.[7,8]

At 9 p.m. on the 25th the 6th Jat Light Infantry, followed by the Regiment, 24th Punjabis and 97th Infantry, moved off up the Aleppo road under a bright full moon. The 50th Brigade marched in column of route without an advance guard, strange as it may seem. At 1 a.m., when about ten miles from Sahiliya, General Andrew halted the column to reconnoitre the enemy's "P" trenches which had been reported to be only lightly held, probably by a cavalry piquet. He accordingly ordered one company from each of the 43rd, 6th Jats and 24th Punjabis to rush the position and so clear a way for further progress.

Lieutenant-Colonel Whittall thereupon detailed Captain Price's "A" Company and, in giving the officers their orders, warned them all emphati-

---
[7] See Map No. 17.
[8] For the order of battle of the 15th Division, see Appendix XII.

cally to avoid the Aleppo road during their advance inasmuch as this would certainly be watched and covered by the Turkish outposts.

With only vague information and still vaguer orders, the three companies advanced blindly on their errand, " A " Company of the 43rd being in the centre between the Jats and Punjabis. Not knowing the direction Captain Price had no other alternative than to disregard the commanding officer's warning and advance astride the Aleppo road. For about one and a half miles the three companies progressed without opposition, but at about 2 a.m. they were checked by heavy gun, machine-gun and rifle fire at close range. Without faltering "A" Company continued to advance and managed to enter the enemy's first two lines and take some prisoners at the expense of two killed and four wounded. Further penetration, however, was impossible, owing to heavy enfilade fire from the third line of the enemy's trenches. Captain Price thereupon sat down on a boulder to write a message to the commanding officer, but was unceremoniously dislodged by a belt of machine-gun fire which shattered the boulder beneath him. In the meantime the colonel, on hearing the heavy firing, had sent up the regimental scouts to order Captain Price to withdraw. This withdrawal was completed without incident by about 4.30 a.m.

Soon after the reconnoitring companies had disappeared the rest of the 50th Brigade came under artillery fire and consequently wheeled off to the left of the Aleppo road and took up a position amongst some hillocks at Point " A,"[9] behind which the troops were covered from view and partially from fire. The brigade staff, however, failed to warn the 42nd Brigade following behind of this halt; and consequently the 48th Pioneers in the van all but blundered into " P " trenches.

At 6 a.m. when the 50th Brigade artillery began to register on " P " trenches the situation was as follows: Lucas's Column, the 42nd Brigade, was south-east of General Andrew's headquarters; the 11th Cavalry Brigade, with the armoured cars, was moving westward to turn the enemy's right flank; the rest of the force was either at or leaving Sahiliya.

At daylight a British aeroplane reported that " P " trenches were strongly, but that " Q " and " R " trenches were but lightly, held. Consequently at 7.45 a.m. General Brooking ordered Andrew's Column to attack the right of " P " trenches while Lucas's Column pinned the enemy astride the Aleppo road. Meanwhile the Cavalry Brigade and armoured cars were moving north and west of the right flank of " Q " and " R " trenches.

Here a digression must be made to record the excellent work done for the 43rd on these exacting operations by Lieutenant Dancey, who, as quartermaster, was with the first-line transport of the 50th Brigade, Lieutenant

---

[9] See Map No. 17.

Parkinson, the transport officer, being with the second line a long way behind. Despite of strict orders against moving out of the line and a threat of arrest if he disobeyed them, he brought up the cookers and served out breakfast to the Regiment at 7.30 a.m., thus enabling all ranks to fight on full stomachs.

At 10 a.m. the 50th Brigade advanced against " P " trenches, with the 24th Punjabis, 97th Infantry and 6th Jat Light Infantry, in that order from the right, in the front line and the 43rd in support. This threat caused the Turks to retire towards their main position. Thereupon General Andrew ordered a general advance, and " P " trenches and about one hundred prisoners were captured with only slight opposition. Advancing rapidly about one and a half miles ahead of Lucas's Column, the 50th Brigade reached by about 12.30 p.m. a plateau extending south-westward from Khan Baghdadi, where it was held up by gun, machine-gun and rifle fire.

" The Turkish position was a strong one and from their trenches, sited on and near the crests of the cliff-like slopes rising from a deep ravine, they were able to sweep with fire the plateau on the southern side of the ravine."[10] The distance from the front line on the plateau to the ravine called Wadi Brooking was about one thousand yards, and the Turkish " Q " and " R " trenches lay another thousand and thirteen hundred yards respectively beyond it.

From a scrutiny of map No. 17 it should appear that the obvious tactics to employ to capture the Turkish position were to contain the front and turn the enemy's right flank, especially as the cavalry brigade was known to be encircling the enemy by that flank without hindrance. But to have adopted such a plan with infantry would have entailed a long march over difficult ground without the means of providing a sufficiency of water for the troops. General Andrew was therefore compelled to remain within easy reach of the river; and decided to wait until the 42nd Brigade arrived and until effective artillery and machine-gun fire could be arranged before launching the frontal attack in which heavy casualties were expected.

From 12.30 p.m. till about 4 p.m. the 43rd in reserve remained in mass behind the hill at the point marked " B,"[10] covered both from fire and view. It was while the Regiment was waiting on events that a woebegone Turk crawled out of a hiding-place and surrendered to " A " Company; whereupon Captain Price tried to interrogate him in Arabic, which he did not understand. Lieutenant Griffin came over from his platoon area to join in the discussion. Later the prisoner was marched off to the rear and the officers returned to their posts. No sooner had Lieutenant Griffin reached his platoon than a shell hit the top of the hill and splinters were deflected almost perpen-

[10] See Map No. 17.

dicularly downwards. Lieutenant Griffin, before he had time to take cover, was so grievously wounded in the back of his head that he died soon afterwards and another man of " A " Company received a flesh wound in the shoulder.

At about 4 p.m. the leading regiment of Lucas's Column, the 1st/4th Dorsetshire Regiment, reached the line and took up a position on the right of the 50th Brigade; and at the same time the reserve reached " P " trenches. At 4.20 p.m. General Brooking instructed General Andrew to use the Lewis and Maxim guns of the Mobile Column to enfilade " R " trenches from the neighbourhood of the Aleppo road. Nearly an hour later he received a report from the 11th Cavalry Brigade and armoured cars saying that they were engaging the right flank and rear of the enemy from a position about six and a half miles north-west of Khan Baghdadi. From this report it was clear that the cavalry had succeeded in cutting off the enemy's line of retreat.

Soon after 4.30 p.m. the Regiment was ordered forward from reserve to take up its position in the front line. In succession the companies moved across the open in artillery formation and again formed up in mass at the point marked " C." The front line now consisted of the 1st/4th Dorsetshire Regiment, 24th Punjabis, 43rd Light Infantry and 6th Jats in that order from the right. The line thus held faced " R " trenches (" Q " trenches being to the left front) and in support were the 97th Infantry of the 50th Brigade and the 2nd/5th and 2nd/6th Gurkhas of the 42nd Brigade.

At 5.30 p.m. the whole line advanced from the plateau. The 43rd with " A " and " C " Companies under Major Fitzgerald in front, and " B " and " D " in second line in that order from the right deployed under cover and, moving round the spur, passed through the batteries and down the open descent towards Wadi Brooking.

Simultaneously the artillery, and machine guns from a position about six hundred yards west-north-west of point " C," opened rapid and intense fire on the enemy position on the opposite side of Wadi Brooking. " C " Company on the left, passing to the right of one of the covering batteries, topped the crest and for the first time was confronted with its objective and the formidable obstacle intervening. To Captain Bleeze the most disquieting feature of this preliminary advance was the absence of hostile fire. The reason for this lack of retaliation was, however, soon apparent, for the barrage fire was so accurate and effective that the Turkish position, dug out of chalk and plainly visible, was completely obliterated within a few minutes as the storm of high-explosive shells burst in fountains of tawny sand and dust, blinding those of the enemy who yet remained. Efficiently screened the Regiment covered the thousand yards of bare slope without casualties and then for the first time realized the magnitude of the obstacle presented by the ravine. It was about forty yards wide and thirty feet deep, the north

TURKISH OFFICERS, PRISONERS AND TRANSPORT CAPTURED AT KHAN BAGHDADI.

slopes being precipitous with only three or four exits. Into this chasm—for such it proved to be—" A " and " C " Companies tumbled helter-skelter, formations being momentarily lost in the headlong descent. But before the leading companies had time to re-form at the bottom the second-line companies likewise dropped into the ravine to increase the difficulty of reorganization. It is a miracle to this day that the Turkish howitzers and machine guns did not make of that ravine a living hell; but mercifully the shelling was slight and ineffective and machine-gun fire was altogether absent.

After a necessary delay to re-form, the Regiment, clambering with difficulty up the friable face of the wadi, advanced again up the steep, open and featureless ascent towards " Q " trenches while the barrage of shells and machine-gun bullets screamed and cracked overhead. For one thousand yards the advance progressed with slight losses; and when the lines were within about fifteen yards of their objective the barrage lifted, the breathless attackers topped the crest and, unhampered by wire entanglements, were on the Turks as quick as the light on their bayonets.

Meanwhile " C " Company on the left, having lost touch with the companies on its right, found itself on the left of the whole line. Just as the barrage lifted as the troops were scaling the face of the ravine, Captain Bleeze received a message from Serjeant Green, his Lewis-gun serjeant, saying that he had spotted an isolated machine-gun nest wide on the Turkish right flank and ideally sited to enfilade the whole advance once the attackers debouched from the wadi. At the same time the serjeant asked leave to work round the rear of this strong point with four Lewis-gun sections. Captain Bleeze halted Nos. 9 and 10 Platoons with orders to contain the front while Nos. 11 and 12 Platoons wheeled to the left to form a defensive flank and cover the advance of the Lewis-gun sections. Serjeant Green's manœuvre was so entirely successful that he captured the Turkish machine-gun section intact without suffering any casualties. For this exploit he received an immediate award of the *Military Medal*.

The delay caused by this digression to the flank separated " C " Company from the rest of the Regiment, and darkness had fallen by the time it stumbled upon the 43rd's battle outposts.

Altogether about eight hundred prisoners were taken as well as several machine guns and three field guns. The prisoners were in a pitiable state of demoralization, clothed in rags and underfed. These were not the Turks of Ctesiphon and Sannaiyat, and so little stomach had they for the fight that the 6th Jats on the 43rd's left captured the entire 169th Regiment and four machine guns. The casualties in the 43rd amounted to one officer, Lieutenant S. J. Griffin, and two men killed, and five men wounded; of these two men were killed and four wounded in the night attack on " P " trenches.

Having overrun the enemy's " Q " trenches, the Regiment continued its rapid advance until checked by precipitous ground and darkness at about point " D." Here, among the enemy's artillery animals, Major Fitzgerald halted the leading companies and placed piquets facing north. Under cover of these the Regiment re-formed, a tedious task in the dark after action.

However, by 8 p.m. the companies, weary but elated, were ready for further action, if need be. At 8.20 p.m. General Andrew issued orders for the troops to bivouac on the ground, and to be prepared to continue the advance at 5 a.m. on the 27th.

At 10.15 p.m. General Brooking issued his orders: the 11th Cavalry Brigade was to block all lines of escape to the northward by road and river; Andrew's, Lucas's and the Mobile Columns were to maintain constant pressure upon the enemy all night despite fatigue. General Andrew thereupon ordered the Mobile Column to move forward and get clear of the road, and his own brigade to assemble on the Aleppo road. The 43rd received this order at about 1 a.m.; the 24th Punjabis never received it; and the 6th Jats[11] did not move until 3.30 a.m. At 2 a.m. the 43rd moved down to the river bank whither the Lewis-gun mules were brought up; and once again the quartermaster, Lieutenant Dancey, supplied the weary troops with hot tea from the cookers. Two hours later, at 4 a.m., the 43rd advanced at the head of the 50th Brigade.

Meanwhile the Cavalry Brigade was covering all possible lines of escape. On the right, south of Wadi Hauran, were the Guides Cavalry and a squadron of the 23rd Cavalry; the 7th Hussars straddled the Aleppo road; the right and the road were each covered by a section of "W" Battery, R.H.A., and the 15th Machine Gun Squadron. One squadron, 23rd Cavalry, was in reserve behind the left centre. But the net was laid right across the only exits from the Turkish positions when General Cassels later extended his line towards the river.

Just before midnight the Turks tried to force their way through the cavalry right centre where it was strongest, and, on failing in their attempts, over 1,000 with several machine guns surrendered.

At 5.45 a.m. General Cassels, commanding the 11th Cavalry Brigade, let go eleven armoured cars which captured a mass of demoralized Turks, numbering over 2,000, at the crossing of the Wadi Hauran. Then, turning about, the cars made off up the road towards Haditha to cut off any enemy who might have succeeded in evading the cavalry. Meanwhile General Cassels ordered the Cavalry Brigade to rendezvous at the Alus bend preparatory to pursuing to Ana, and General Brooking ordered a battalion of the 42nd Brigade forward to take charge of the prisoners. At 6.30 a.m. General Brooking released the Mobile Column with orders to seize and hold Haditha

---

[11] The orderly sent to warn them was afraid to wake his commanding officer.

while the cavalry and armoured cars pursued to Ana; and he also ordered the reserve group with a battery of guns to march to the Wadi Haqlan, about four miles south of Haditha.

By 7 a.m. the Light Armoured Motor Brigade was careering up the Aleppo road, causing alarm and despondency amongst the enemy; and the Cavalry Brigade was re-forming at Alus. By this time the captures amounted to between 3,000 and 4,000 Turks, ten guns, many machine guns and much material. At 8 a.m., by which time the 50th Brigade had reached the Wadi Hauran, the Regiment rested and watered from pools in the wadi, and the first and second-line transport arrived. There was now no manœuvre that the slow-moving infantry could perform to add to the Turkish discomfiture, and therefore Andrew's and Lucas's Columns were ordered to clear the battlefield. But in the meantime the pursuit by the 11th Cavalry and Light Armoured Motor Brigades was pressed relentlessly throughout the day, and the rout of the enemy was complete.

"The same undulating country extends beyond Khan Baghdadi in a succession of wide plateaux, intersected by ravines with steep cliffs. We scaled one of these and saw in front of us black masses of the enemy's transport and infantry, dotted like ants on the face of the ridge beyond . . . it was the most complete rout imaginable. There were ambulances, field kitchens, water carts and convoys of lagging bullock wagons with their bullocks yoked and the drivers standing by their side; wounded men, dead men and sick men, who had fallen out; also bombs and live shells, boxes of ammunition, portmanteaux and office paraphernalia, and books and papers."[12]

By noon the pursuing troops were beyond Haditha; at nightfall they bivouacked in the neighbourhood of Fuhaima. At 8.30 a.m. on the 28th the armoured cars seized Ana. Thereupon General Cassels dispatched some armoured cars to pursue and capture a party of Germans, which had retreated the previous evening in charge of the dismantled wireless installation and two British airmen, captured on making a forced landing behind the enemy's lines on the 25th. The rescue and capture of the wireless were effectively carried out after a pursuit of thirty-two miles to the west of Ana. As it was not intended to hold either Ana or Haditha, all the war material which could not be evacuated was destroyed. The stores at Ana were blown up on the 30th, and thereafter the force gradually withdrew until, on the 6th April, the 15th Division was disposed with brigades at Haditha and Khan Baghdadi.

At the Battle of Khan Baghdadi General Brooking achieved his purpose, the annihilation of the enemy opposed to him. The enemy's communications were raided to a depth of 130 miles behind his battle front. "The endurance

---

[12] *The Long Road to Baghdad*, Vol. II, p. 268.

and rapidity of movement of the troops were extraordinary. The infantry were marching two days and two nights with little or no sleep, and fighting all day and part of two nights."[13] General Brooking issued an order of the day on the 27th March in which he said: " I asked you to march hard and hit hard. You have done so. . . . My thanks to you for your fine response to the call made on you." During the battle practically the whole of the Turkish 50th Division was captured, including its commander, Nazim Bey, at the expense of 159 casualties. Prisoners totalled 5,254, including 18 Germans; and in addition 12 guns, 47 machine guns, much war material, and upwards of £3,000 in gold and notes were captured.

On the 1st April the 43rd was withdrawn from its position on the river bank two miles upstream of Khan Baghdadi to a standing camp at Sahiliya where it remained throughout April working on the defensive position. During April Khan Baghdadi was evacuated and Sahiliya established as the advanced post of the 15th Division.

Lieutenant-Colonel Whittall has written that the salient features of the Battle of Khan Baghdadi were: the disinclination of the Turks to fight; the amazing endurance of the 43rd[14]; and the fact that, had the Turks placed machine guns in Wadi Brooking and sited their trenches differently, the attack would certainly have been wiped out. During the operations he spoke to some German and Turkish prisoners, who said, " Why fight? The war is over and we have won." They then showed him the wireless reports of the 25th/26th dealing with the German offensive in France.

III.—SUMMER OPERATIONS: THE TURKISH ARMISTICE.

When, early in May, information was received that there were thirty enemy cavalry at Khan Baghdadi and two infantry regiments at Haditha, it was decided to establish contact.[15] At 7 p.m. on the 10th a force, consisting of the 43rd—844 strong—one company 48th Pioneers, 1088th Battery, R.F.A., one section 256th Machine Gun Company, one squadron 10th Lancers, and a combined field ambulance, moved out of Sahiliya and marched up the Aleppo road. At 2 a.m. the Regiment encountered on the Wadi Brooking bridge an enemy patrol which opened fire and then promptly retired. At 3.20 a.m. " B " and " D " Companies advanced astride the Aleppo road and came under fire from a Turkish cavalry patrol which also retired. Two men were slightly wounded in the forward companies. Soon after, the armoured cars which had left Sahiliya at daybreak passed through the 43rd and captured a Turk at Wadi Hauran. This man gave the information that there were thirty mounted men at Khan Baghdadi, two hundred at

---

[13] *The Long Road to Baghdad.*
[14] Not a single man fell out during the operations.
[15] War Diary, and *Chronicle*, 1917-18, p. 76.

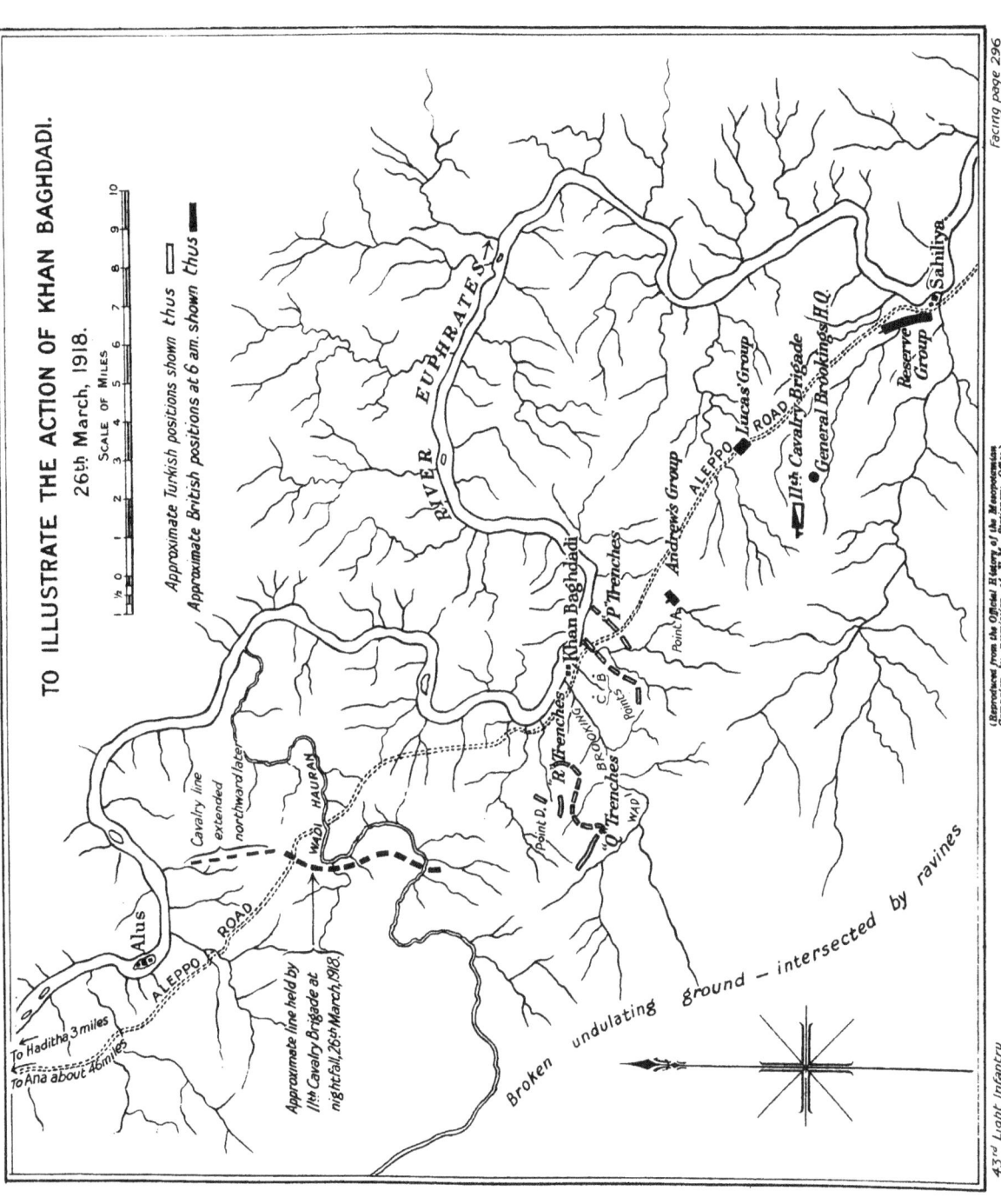

Haditha and a division of infantry at Ana. Bivouacking on the night of the 11th the column continued its reconnaissance inland from the river, but encountered no greater force of the enemy than a cavalry patrol two miles above Khan Baghdadi. The next morning, at 4.45 a.m., it withdrew, reaching Sahiliya at 10 a.m. without incident.

The next six weeks—that is, until the end of June—were spent in work on the defensive position and training of specialists. Parties of officers and men were sent on leave to India.

In the *London Gazette* of the 8th March, six officers, one warrant officer and one non-commissioned officer were mentioned in despatches.

On the 24th June another raid was made upon the enemy cavalry at Khan Baghdadi. The force parading at 8 p.m. for the night march comprised the 43rd, less one company and three platoons, with cavalry and machine guns. Advancing up the road in bright moonlight the force halted from 11.30 p.m. to 2 a.m., and men and horses were watered from *chagals* slung on poles across A.T. carts. Moving off again soon after 2 a.m., the 43rd crossed Wadi Brooking without opposition. As soon as it got light the cavalry moved on ahead, while " A " Company and one platoon of " C " Company, with a sub-section of machine guns, made for the old enemy position west of Khan Baghdadi whence they fired at long range on enemy cavalry patrols. Soon after, touch was gained with our cavalry which had captured one officer and sixteen men, and the whole force retired to bivouac at Khan Baghdadi. Leaving the bivouac ground at 6 p.m. the cavalry marched straight back to Sahiliya, but the Regiment halted from 9 p.m. until 4.30 a.m. in the desert, and marched back to Sahiliya in the morning, having covered about thirty miles in high summer. Casualties from sore feet amounted to nine men, but there were no cases of heat-stroke. The days of parching thirst on marches were now happily past, and the need of water when covering long distances through suffocating dust was at this time fully realized and was, moreover, fully supplied : so much the better for the troops and their fighting capacity.

July was completely uneventful from the point of view of military operations. On the 12th Captain Titherington was appointed acting brigade major, and Captain Smyth took over the duties of acting adjutant. Work on the defensive position and training continued throughout August. On the 31st the strength was 17 officers and 807 other ranks, the following officers being present :—

Lieutenant-Colonel G. E. Whittall, M.C., commanding.
Major C. Fitzgerald, senior major.
Captain J. W. Meade.
Captain A. Price (attached from 2nd Royal Sussex Regiment).

Captain H. E. F. Smyth, acting adjutant.
Captain W. Rance.
Lieutenant A. L. Thompson.
Lieutenant B. F. Roberts.
Lieutenant E. G. Vine (attached from 10th Duke of Cornwall's Light Infantry).
Lieutenant H. V. Smith.
Lieutenant T. R. Milford.
Lieutenant J. G. Shepherd.
Lieutenant E. B. Parkinson.
Lieutenant A. L. Tompkins.
Lieutenant H. N. Burrell (attached from 60th Rifles).
Second Lieutenant P. J. Andrews.
Lieutenant and Quartermaster G. Dancey, M.C., D.C.M.

Elsewhere in Mesopotamia there was little fighting during the summer months, as the right flank commanded General Marshall's attention. " Dunsterforce," from small beginnings, had developed into the North Persia Force charged with the frustration of a Turco-German-Bolshevik invasion of Persia and Trans-Caspia. This force, operating on long communications, dealt successfully with the whole gamut of political intrigue, revolution and counter-revolution, and thereby shielded the North-West Frontier of India from disturbing influences.

But September saw the beginning of the end, the disintegration of our enemies. The Allied advance from Salonika forced Bulgaria to her knees; the crushing victory of Lord Allenby in Palestine annihilated the right wing of the Turkish armies; and in France and Flanders the Allies were advancing to victory. To complete the discomfiture of the Turks, the War Office, at the end of September, ordered General Marshall to take the offensive up the Tigris.

On the 23rd October the British started to advance, and by the evening of the 28th the Turkish Tigris Group was caught between the 17th Division (I Corps) and the cavalry to northward, leaving it but one line of escape and that through the difficult and waterless country to westward. After heavy fighting throughout the 29th, the whole of the Turkish force surrendered early on the 30th, and the cavalry and armoured cars scoured the country northward towards Mosul. This overwhelming victory which, like Khan Baghdadi, was completely decisive set the seal to Turkish resistance. The Turks concluded an armistice on the 31st, exactly four years after the opening of hostilities.

In October the 43rd moved from Sahiliya to Hit, and it was on the 1st November that the tidings of the signing of the Turkish armistice were

GROUP OF OFFICERS, SOUTHAMPTON.

From left to right. Captain Meade; Lieutenant Booth; Lieutenant Giles; Lieutenant Colvill; Captain Mason; Mrs. Dodington; Captain Baines; Colonel Dodington; Lieutenant Holt; Miss Dodington; Lieutenant Lethbridge; Lieutenant Warren; Lieutenant Eagle; Lieutenant and Quartermaster Dancey.

received. All military operations were now over for the 43rd, and little remained except monotony and the longing of all ranks for a sight of their homes.

At 11.30 p.m. on the 11th news was received of the signing of the armistice by the Germans, and a holiday on the 12th was granted. At 5 p.m. that day all the troops in the Hit area paraded, a salute of thirty-one guns was fired, and for the first time the land of the old River Euphrates heard the British National Anthem. It is not difficult to imagine the 43rd standing to attention in the dust of Hit while the curtain was being rung down on the Mesopotamia campaign. But, however much peace may have meant to the officers and men of the Regiment at that moment, it meant infinitely more to the prisoners of the old 43rd locked away in Anatolia where their safety in nowise compensated for the tortures of mind and body, the monotonous inaction and the gnawing pangs of hunger which they had been enduring for two and a half years.

Little now remains to tell. On the 3rd November Lieutenant Adams and a platoon of " A " Company carried out a notable march to Ana, ninety-one miles distant, in order to be present at the Durbar held by General Brooking. This march was rendered particularly difficult owing to heavy rains and flooded wadis, but the platoon returned to Hit on the 18th without having incurred a single casualty.

At the end of the year news was received that Lieutenant-General Sir William Marshall, K.C.B., K.C.S.I., had mentioned the following officers and non-commissioned officers of the Regiment for their services at Khan Baghdadi:—

Acting Lieutenant-Colonel G. E. Whittall, M.C.
Brevet Major G. W. Titherington.
Captain H. T. C. Field.
Lieutenant J. R. Brown.
Captain H. W. Bleeze.
8041 Regimental Serjeant-Major Cowley.
9075 Serjeant J. Green.
9479 Lance-Corporal A. Dean.
21565 Serjeant E. Davies.

In December demobilization began with students and pivotal men, and by the end of January so many men had already gone that companies were amalgamated, " A " and " C " becoming " A " Company under Captain Bleeze, and " B " and " D " becoming " B " Company under Lieutenant Banks. Local leave was opened in December, and many officers and men of the 43rd availed themselves of the opportunity of visiting Babylon and Hilla.

MAP No. 18

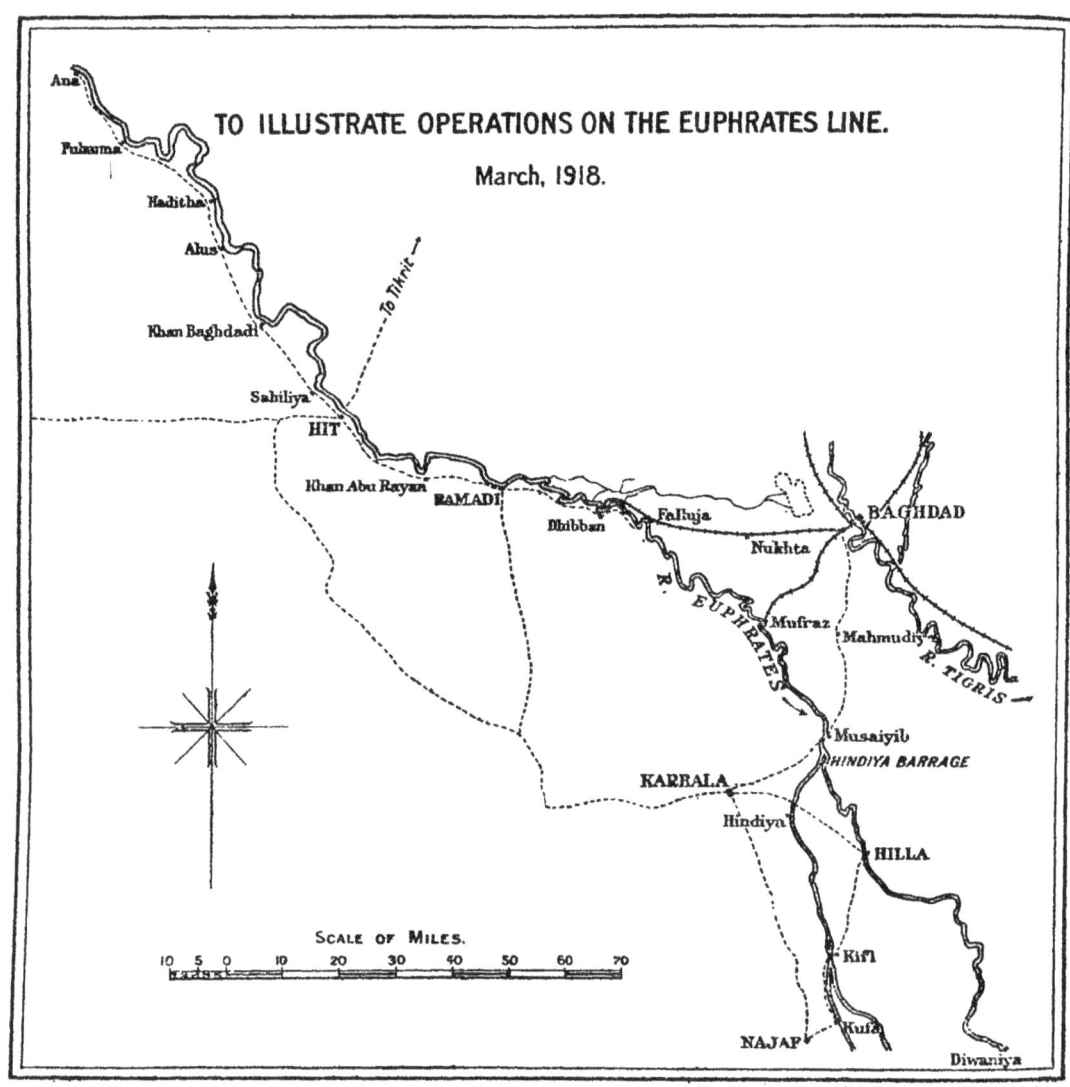

The period of demobilization was not an easy one, and every effort was made to organize classes of instruction in various trades so as to help the men on their return to civil life. Ordinary military training to men about to be demobilized and impatient for home naturally seemed pointless. But the 43rd was lucky in having a definite task, the construction of permanent huts for the Hit garrison. And many competitions were instituted for running, shooting, drill, marching and football, as well as pontoon races on the Euphrates. As might be expected, that mighty hunter, Captain J. W. Meade, soon collected a pack of long dogs, Arab and Persian greyhounds, with which he hunted jackal two days a week throughout the winter.

On the 20th February orders were received intimating that the 43rd was to go on foreign service again, and that the cadre of five officers and forty-six other ranks was to return home, leaving the rest of the Regiment behind at Dhibban.[16] Two days later the cadre, composed of Captains Meade, Murphy and Smyth; Lieutenant Lethbridge and Second Lieutenant Murray; Company Serjeant-Majors Bovington, Hodgson and Headdon; Serjeants Bull, Young, Keen, Prior and Sylvester; and thirty-six other ranks, started its homeward journey, and reached Ramadi that evening. Arriving at Baghdad on the evening of the 23rd, the cadre entrained the following day for Kut al Amara whence it travelled by steamer to Amara, and reached Basra on the 28th. Here Lieutenant-Colonel Whittall, who had just returned from leave, took over command.

On the 4th March the cadres of the 43rd, 2nd Norfolk Regiment and 7th Hussars embarked on board H.T. *Ellenga,* and at 6 p.m. that evening started downstream. Long before the transport gained the bar at Fao the black Mesopotamian night had enveloped that small nucleus of the 43rd. There was none on board who had shared all the Regiment's triumphs and disasters, but there were those with experience enough of Mesopotamia's vagaries to raise pious hopes that the land of the two great rivers would see the Regiment no more.

At Bombay the cadre transhipped into s.s. *Tahiti,* already packed to saturation-point, and, reaching Suez on the 25th, unloaded the six tons of baggage into a train bound for Port Said. Thence it crossed the Mediterranean, landed at Taranto and went by special train to Havre. It was the earnest hope of all ranks that their destination would be the Depot on arrival in England, but on landing at Southampton on the 12th April orders were received to go to Aldershot. At 6 p.m. that evening the train steamed into

---

[16] During the ensuing months those who remained were gradually dispersed, the demobilizable men being sent to the 1st/5th The Buffs. Many officers and men were eventually sent to India to man the frontier posts while operations against the Afghans were being undertaken. As a unit the 43rd ceased to exist from about the middle of March.

the station, where General Sir Archibald Murray was waiting to welcome the cadre. Having unloaded the baggage for the last time, the cadre, looking strange in their topis, fell in and, headed by a band, marched to Badajos Barracks, where yet another 43rd was already being formed for service in North Russia.

The journey from Hit to Aldershot had taken fifty-one days, during which the cadre had travelled in three river steamers, four ocean-going ships and eight trains; and had loaded and unloaded the baggage more than thirty times.

And here the story of the Mesopotamia campaign closes. The prisoners —those who survived—filtered back to England and were dispersed from prisoner-of-war camps in different parts of England. The bones of those who did not return lie scattered on the plains of Mesopotamia and on the uplands and in the valleys of Anatolia.

This campaign of the 43rd, however badly and inexpertly it may have been told, has this merit: it covers the whole range of military experience. In it we have seen the 43rd in attack and defence, in advance and retreat, fighting afloat, in static and open warfare, besieged and attempting to relieve, marching by day and by night, in captivity and on rearward service, in triumph and disaster; and we have seen the 43rd encountering other enemies —disease, thirst, starvation, plagues of flies and parasitical insects, the canker of monotony which the French call *cafard*, floods, drought, dust, blistering heat and bitter cold. All these and more the Regiment and those who served in Mesopotamia experienced during the campaign. It can truthfully be said that the 43rd endured all things, attempted all things and never faltered.

And now let us turn to the short campaign in North Russia wherein the Regiment learned something of forest fighting.

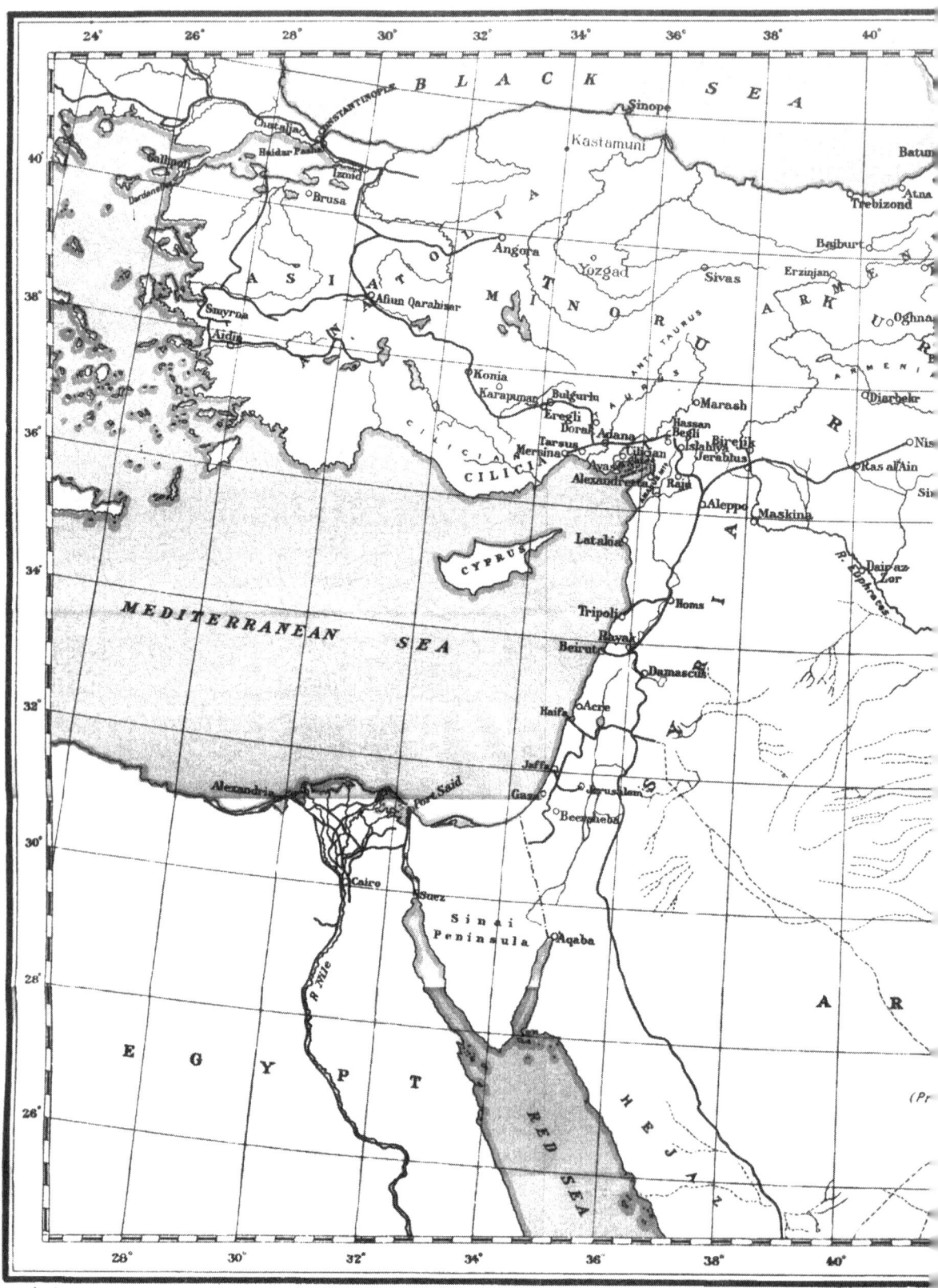

43rd Light Infantry.

MAP No 19

CHAPTER XXVII.

ORIGIN OF THE EXPEDITION TO NORTH RUSSIA.

THE RUSSIAN REVOLUTION—ITS EFFECT—THE BOLSHEVIK PARTY—GERMANY OVERRUNS THE UKRAINE—THE TREATY OF BREST-LITOVSK—BRITISH AND ALLIED FORCES OCCUPY MURMANSK AND ARCHANGEL—SUMMARY OF BRITISH AND GERMAN AIMS IN RUSSIA—GARRISON TROOPS' EXHAUSTION—PLIGHT OF EUROPE AFTER THE ARMISTICE—THE SITUATION IN RUSSIA IN APRIL 1919—THE 43RD DETAILED FOR ACTIVE SERVICE—LACK OF MEN OF THE REGIMENT—THE 43RD IS BROUGHT UP TO ESTABLISHMENT—MOVES TO CROWBOROUGH—INSPECTED BY GENERAL RAWLINSON—SAILS FOR ARCHANGEL—LIST OF OFFICERS—THE OUTWARD JOURNEY—MURMANSK—THE WHITE SEA—ARCHANGEL—THE 43RD DISEMBARKS—RUSSIAN WELCOME—GENERAL IRONSIDE—THE " HONOURABLE TEA "—PARADE OF THE 1ST BATTALION SLAVO-BRITISH LEGION—THE 43RD IS ORDERED TO LEAVE ARCHANGEL.

I.

WHY did the 43rd go to North Russia in 1919? The reason originated two years earlier when the Tsar abdicated in favour of the Tsarevitch, and revolution swept over Russia like a flood. The first news of the gigantic upheaval was received by the Allies with complacence for reasons that cannot easily be adduced. The instigators of it, it was said, were liberal patriots bent on abolishing the antiquated form of government which had been responsible to the Tsar alone; autocracy—an anachronism in the twentieth century—was to be superseded by a popular democratic government; the war was to be prosecuted with energy and better administration; the old corrupt practices were to be eradicated, and an era of enlightened progress was to be ushered in. So it was said. Such have been the aspirations of most revolutions. The simple were hypnotized by the word " democracy," and gave no thought to the history of revolutions.

In actual fact the Russian revolution of March 1917 prolonged the war considerably. The Germans regarded it as a merciful dispensation of Providence. It had the immediate effect of relieving pressure on their eastern front, and permitted the transfer of troops to the western battlefields. However, the Germans could not altogether neglect the Russian front so long as Kerensky led the country: far from it. Kerensky was determined to honour Russia's obligations and stand by the Allies. But with the revolution concerted action became impossible, and therefore, when the Russians attacked in July with all their old valiant courage and self-sacrifice the Allies were not ready to co-operate. Their attacks began to falter and finally ceased altogether. And then, as usually happens in revolutions when the pace of reform is not fast enough for the hotheads, a counter-revolution broke out in October. For this Germany was partly responsible. Determined that the tottering mass should crash, she had sent an international revolutionary, called Lenin, to compass its destruction. She did not foresee that the viper would bite her and accomplish her fall too. For the nonce she was content to be jesuitical.

By Lenin's agency the Bolshevik party was formed. Round him he collected his coterie of foreign anarchists, who accomplished the disintegration of the country. During the winter of 1917 blood flowed almost as freely as the waters of the Neva in summer-time. To show how much they cared for popular democratic government the Bolsheviks overthrew the Constituent Assembly in January 1918 and gathered the reins of power into their own gory hands. By inconceivable atrocities perpetrated by Chinese mercenaries the wretched inhabitants were terrorized into submission to a form of government such as the Tsar would never have tolerated.

Meanwhile, by fraternization and propaganda, the Germans were inculcating into the Russian soldiers the desire for peace at any price. By this time the Germans were feeling the pinch of the British blockade, and it was essential that they should have access to the granary of Europe, if possible, without fighting. In December peace negotiations were started, but before the terms were settled the Ukraine petitioned Germany's help against the Bolsheviks. This was in February when the negotiators were still haggling over the terms. Naturally it was a request with which Germany was only too willing to comply, for Austria-Hungary was as sorely in need of corn as she. By the end of April their troops had overrun the whole of the Ukraine and had even reached Odessa and the Crimea. On the 3rd March 1918 Trotsky at last signed the treaty of peace at Brest-Litovsk, but not before the Germans had resumed hostilities to end his methods of paltering procrastination.

Following the example of the Ukraine, Finland next asked Germany to deliver her from the scourge of Bolshevism. Thus by May, in spite of the peace treaty, Germany had become the enemy of the Soviet Government and the champion of the oppressed nationalities under Bolshevik hegemony. In Ludendorff's own words the Germans " held positions at Viborg [in Finland] and Narva which would at any time enable us to advance on Petrograd, in order to overthrow the Bolshevik Government or prevent the English from reaching there from Murmansk."[1] By this time Germany was determined to prevent the Bolsheviks from spreading their insidious propaganda

[1] *My War Memoirs*, Vol. II, p. 628.

among her own people, and for that purpose aided the different nationalities on the Baltic littoral to form their own buffer states on the principle of self-determination.

At this point, June 1918, the British appeared on the scene at Murmansk and later at Archangel. The original expedition to North Russia was amply justified by results. From September 1917 onwards the Germans had withdrawn divisions from the Russian front at the rate of six per month, but directly British troops landed in North Russia, in June and September 1918, the flow of reinforcements to the Western Front ceased, and that at a time when the German effort in France and Belgium demanded the concentration of its maximum strength. When Marshal Hindenburg requested the dispatch of ten divisions from the Russian front he was told that none could be spared, for the German Government could not afford to risk a popular rising in Russia backed by British troops.

The Allied force, which consisted of contingents of Italians, French, Americans and Serbians, besides the British contingent of officers and men marked fit only for garrison duty abroad, was placed, in September 1918, under the command of Major-General Edmund Ironside, who was himself able to speak all the languages of his force including Russian. This heterogeneous little army helped to contain a considerably superior force of Germans on a front where they could not possibly contribute towards a decision of the war.

Besides the military reasons for the expedition, there was also the urgent necessity of preventing the establishment of a submarine base on the ice-free Murman coast. It must be remembered that by May 1918 when the first British contingent sailed for North Russia the submarine campaign against British shipping had been going on for over a year. From significant beginnings, it had developed into a threat to our very existence. It was difficult enough for the Navy to watch all the submarine bases along the German and Belgian coasts, and another base far to the north, necessitating yet more patrols over a vast expanse of ocean, was not lightly to be allowed. Hence the race to occupy Murmansk, that wonderful natural harbour at the mouth of the Kola river.

Therefore, so long as the war lasted, the Allied force fulfilled a strategic purpose, and its right to occupy Russian territory was undeniable; but directly the Armistice was signed its presence ceased to have any military justification. How was it, then, that this force was allowed to remain in Russian territory?

By the time the Armistice was signed the Arctic winter had descended on it, freezing its communications with the outer world. Also, the continued existence, or rather the unexpected survival of Bolshevism, vastly complicated the policy of the British Government. From the political point of view the cult of Bolshevism was naturally received with diffidence by all the Allied countries. By ineffable cruelties, murder, torture and regicide; by disregarding the ethics of civilization; by the complete destruction or reversal of all modern institutions; by the proscription of religion and the priesthood; by the adoption of a system of free love; by spreading sedition and subversive propaganda broadcast; and by fostering discontent, the Bolsheviks shocked and alienated the whole of the civilized world. Their policy which branded as *intelligentsia* and condemned to death without trial all those who pretended to any education, however slender, was not calculated to inspire confidence in their future.

But the nations of the world, underfed and weary with many months of war, provided ideal breeding-grounds for their foul, insidious propaganda. Moreover, their avowed policy aimed at the overthrow of empires by bloody revolution and the infliction of the Bolshevik cult upon the resultant chaos, and was such a formidable foe that the British Government determined to oppose the authors of it by force of arms before its virus ran riot through the world.

But the Bolsheviks spared the British Government the pains of its decision by attacking all those who resisted their creed. Russians of all classes, imperialists as well as those who had supported the original revolution, banded themselves together to stamp out the rabies. Civil war raged all over Russia. In the north, on the Murmansk and Archangel front, the little Allied force provided a buttress for many Russians harried and harassed by the relentless Bolshevik hunters after blood. Thus a moral obligation to protect those who had fought so long and valiantly for the Allied cause was also forced upon the British Government. Added to which, the ports of Archangel and Murmansk contained great quantities of stores and munitions which the British Government had dispatched to the Russian Government for the prosecution of the war. To have left these unguarded would have added to our already great financial losses, for the Bolshevik regime, on usurping power, immediately repudiated all foreign liabilities.

Such were the considerations, political, moral and financial, which caused the British Government to intervene by force of arms in the internal affairs of another nation on which it had not declared war.

To summarize the situation : after the revolution and before the Armistice of November 1918 the Germans fought in Russia for four good reasons : to exploit the corn resources of the country and break the blockade; to forestall the formation of a new hostile Russian front; to prevent Bolshevik propaganda from poisoning their own people; and to create a chain of buffer states along their frontier between them and Bolshevism.

The British went to North Russia for three reasons : to support those Russian leaders who refused to accept the Bolshevik peace treaty; to prevent the Germans establishing a submarine base at Murmansk; and to contain German troops on the Russian front.

After the Armistice Germany changed her policy completely. She was quick to realize that in Russia she might find stepping-stones to the high fortune she had forfeited in the west.[2] Her policy was simple: "Great Russia for the Bolsheviks, and the Bolsheviks for us." The ruin of Great Russia provided Germany's opportunity, and the longer the Bolsheviks were free to destroy the less became the possible danger of Russia in the future. And when with ruthless barbarism the whole of Russia had been swept as bare as a prison cell, then would Germany come into her own, gather the reins of power into her hands, and by a subtle penetration rebuild on the ruins a dominion of her own conception. A German general became the chief of staff of the Bolshevik Army; its staffs were filled by German officers, and whole regiments of German prisoners marched in its ranks with Hungarians, Chinese and Turks as their companions-in-arms.[3]

The old enemy was wreaking his vengeance on our old ally, supporting the Bolshevik terror, and helping the disintegration of a great nation.

In the spring of 1919 there was scarcely a nationality in Central Europe and Asia Minor that was not seething with war fury owing either to injustices received or preconceived; and behind them all stalked Russia, urging the disaffected to revolution. In Asia Minor British troops were still operating on the line Baku—Batum; the inhabitants of Georgia and Azerbaijan were fighting for their own republics; Turkey had great internal troubles to contend with; there were serious riots in Egypt; there was fighting in the Ukraine and Rumania; Hungary and Austria were in the throes of civil war; Czechoslovakia, Poland, Lithuania, Latvia and Estonia were contending for their autonomy; there was fighting in Danzig and Courland; and the British force in Archangel was carrying on an Arctic campaign, bluffing and buccaneering for its very existence.

But the sorry plight of the world hardly affected England in the process of demobilizing her vast Army. Such troubles as there were were mostly petty and due to the belief of certain troops that they, above all others, had a prior claim to demobilization and repatriation. The petty troubles were, however, sufficient to divert the attention of politicians and people from the maelstrom of European affairs. Yet, in the Arctic circle, Englishmen of the garrison battalions[4] were suffering all the rigours of intense cold and the monotony of almost perpetual darkness with the knowledge that a wound in that temperature might well result in death by freezing. These invalids—men unfit for active service of any sort—had fought with the energy of the

[2] *The Times.* [3] *Ibid.*
[4] The Royal Scots, King's Liverpool Regiment, Yorkshire Regiment, Durham Light Infantry.

hale and active; they had in fact set an example of tenacity and determination to all the foreign troops under General Ironside's command, and had proved themselves to be the only truly reliable troops. But their powers of endurance were limited; and it was imperative to relieve them as soon as possible after the break-up of the ice.

During the war the Russians had captured from the Austrians a great number of Czechs—the equivalent of about two army corps—whose sympathies were with the Allies. These troops—fine fighters—tried to find their way out of Russia by way of Siberia and Vladivostok. Having no love for the Bolsheviks, they were a power in the land, and became the nucleus of Admiral Koltchak's army. This last took the offensive from Siberia, while in the south General Denikin from the Don Cossack country and General Yudenitch from the south-west co-operated. An end to the Bolshevik rabies seemed to be in sight.

II.—BEGINNINGS.

Towards the end of March all the Regulars of the 43rd, including some of those who had survived captivity in Turkey, were ordered to Aldershot. There Brevet Major G. W. Titherington, who had been home on leave from Mesopotamia, was told to organize the field service details of the Regiment preparatory to going on service on the 1st May. These details consisted of Captains Mason and Naylor, Lieutenants Tyrwhitt-Drake, Neville and Warren, Second Lieutenants Trengrouse and Sawyer, and about seventy other ranks, only a proportion of whom were fit for active service.

Meanwhile Brevet Colonel W. Marriott-Dodington, C.M.G., had been ordered to report at the War Office for a personal interview. At this he was told to assume command of the 43rd and prepare it for immediate service abroad, but the destination was not divulged. On arriving at Aldershot on the 1st April he took over command of the details from Brevet Major Titherington.

For a few days the future of the Regiment was wrapped in mystery. It was not even known for certain whether the Regiment was to go on active service or garrison duty, though it formed part of a brigade with the 67th (2nd Hampshire) Regiment and a battalion of the Machine Gun Corps, to which was attached a brigade of artillery.

But when each infantry battalion was ordered to raise and train its own light trench-mortar battery everything pointed to active service; but where? On the 3rd April the details were put under forty-eight hours' notice to go abroad. Without men enough to form a platoon the order was farcical. Rumours flew round Badajos Barracks like wildfire; first the special brigade was going to Caucasia; then to quell the riots in Egypt where there was already a vast number of troops; or to Rumania, Ukrainia, Siberia, Danzig,

Archangel; all of them in turn took pride of place with remarkable rapidity after the manner of barrack rumours. Nothing was certain except that the 43rd was unfit to go on active service anywhere. To speculate was vain. Europe was in a melting-pot; and any place or country was as likely a destination as any other.

But in the evening papers of the 3rd April there were large headlines:

" GRAVE PERIL OF OUR TROOPS IN NORTH RUSSIA.
" REINFORCEMENTS URGENTLY NEEDED."

The Times had a leading article on the subject the following morning with a headline in sufficiently big type to distract the eye from the six columns of other war news. There could no longer be any doubt about the Regiment's destination.

The harrowing accounts of the plight of our exhausted troops who had fought and held the line through the Arctic winter implied that they were in danger of being completely cut off. Recruiting offices were to be opened for the enrolment of volunteers to go to the rescue of these men. Relief was to be effected entirely by volunteers—that was emphatically stated—so as not to offend the susceptibilities of those patriots at home who, having escaped the war, declaimed loudly against militarism and military commitments. Little was said about the special brigade of Regulars at Aldershot. It escaped Socialist criticism by being dubbed a volunteer force. Actually, of course, it was nothing of the kind.[*]

But despite of the Press campaign, the special brigade had practically no men. The whole Regiment could not produce one battalion of regulars, and the 43rd cadre had not yet returned from Mesopotamia. The 52nd, being in the Army of Occupation on the Rhine, was unable to draft to the 43rd such regulars as it had. On the other hand, there was no scarcity of regular officers of the Regiment.

On the 8th April, however, the problem of personnel was solved when the Regiment received orders that it was to be known as No. 2 Composite Battalion, consisting of:—

Headquarters and " A " Company, 43rd Light Infantry;
" B " Company, Royal Warwickshire Regiment;
" C " Company, Devonshire Regiment;
" D " Company, Royal Berkshire Regiment.

Thereafter officers reported in great numbers, but other ranks arrived but slowly from their depots. The fact was that there was no Regular Army on

[*] One so-called volunteer, with War Office orders in his pocket to report to the Depot for duty, stupidly applied for leave to fetch his car before joining. The adjutant peremptorily ordered him to North Russia. Being more afraid of the adjutant than the War Office, he went; and bears the scar of his cowardice to this day.

which the Government could depend as soon as demobilization started in earnest. An expedient had to be found to tempt men to serve, and the inducement to stay on for four years took the usual form of a cash bounty and a period of furlough.

Before leaving Aldershot for Crowborough, the Regiment was inspected by Lieutenant-General Sir Archibald Murray, commander-in-chief at Aldershot; and on the 12th the cadre of the 43rd arrived from Mesopotamia and was sent on leave.

Training at Crowborough was almost impossible. The camp had been partially demolished by disgruntled Canadians earlier in the year; the weather was exceptionally bad with much rain and snow; and men reported one day and went on furlough the next. Organization of companies was all that could be accomplished.

Lectures on the state of Russia and gruesome details of the treatment meted out to the *intelligentsia* by the Bolsheviks were given in the afternoons by certain fortunate Englishmen who had escaped from the Terror. Thus was the fighting spirit inculcated, and any illusions about Bolshevism dispelled. But the Battalion was given to understand by these lecturers that the expedition was to be a picnic; that the Bolsheviks were cowards and would not fight; that at sight of an English force they invariably fled; and that forest fighting against them was not difficult. The officers were told that North Russia abounded in game, and were advised to take fishing-rods and guns, the better to enjoy a summer holiday; and that mosquitoes were likely to prove more formidable foes than the Bolsheviks. The Bolsheviks were good for nothing—as fighters negligible. And so on. The tone was always the same—flippant; to put the officers and men in good conceit of themselves. But the wisdom of such policy was doubtful.

On the 24th orders were received from the War Office that the Battalion was to be called the 1st Oxfordshire and Buckinghamshire Light Infantry after all. But still it was five hundred men below establishment. Early in May, however, drafts from many different regiments were received, bringing the strength up to about eight hundred, and all leave was stopped. Most of the men were young soldiers who had seen no active service; and altogether twenty regiments were represented. West Countrymen, East Anglians, Welshmen, Irishmen and Scotsmen complete with Balmoral bonnets and red hackles were drafted into the 43rd's ranks. When it is considered that each man of the drafts cherished his own regimental distinctions, customs, drill and dress peculiarities, it is not surprising that some gave trouble to officers whom they did not know. Moreover, the conditions of re-enlistment had not been fulfilled in some cases; the bounty had been paid, but the two months' furlough had been curtailed or stopped. A broken pledge is generally a cause of grievance.

On the 9th May the Regiment paraded for the first time at full strength when General Sir Henry Rawlinson came to inspect No. 238 Special Brigade. In front of the serried lines on a very restive horse sat the gallant brigadier, Brigadier-General G. W. St. G. Grogan, V.C., C.B., C.M.G., D.S.O., and while General Rawlinson declaimed that he had never seen a finer body of men, attention was riveted on the brigadier. Would he survive? He did. Perhaps the only sentence which made an impression was Rawlinson's last: "You are going out in the morning and will be home in the evening. Good-bye, and good luck to you." How many times had that been said in similar circumstances?

Two days later, in the middle watches of the night of Sunday, the 11th May, the collection of eight hundred men, called for euphony the 43rd Light Infantry, started on its journey to Southampton for embarkation on board the hired transport *Czar*, while thirteen officers and some other ranks proceeded in the opposite direction to embark at Newcastle. At both ports the troops received hearty farewells. Foghorns, sirens and whistles from every conceivable type of craft blared their good wishes to the cheering troops who occupied every vantage-point to be found in the ships, while the officers leant over the rails in stolid and strictly British silence.

The officers who embarked were:—

Brevet Colonel W. Marriott-Dodington, C.M.G., commanding.[5]
Major L. J. Carter, D.S.O., second-in-command.[5]
Lieutenant H. E. F. Smyth, adjutant.[5]
Lieutenant R. C. Warren, M.C., assistant adjutant.[5]
Lieutenant T. Tyrwhitt-Drake, M.C., intelligence and scout officer.[5]
Lieutenant H. S. Eagle, transport officer.[5]
Lieutenant A. B. Hamilton, Lewis-gun officer.[5]
Lieutenant D. J. L. Lethbridge, signalling officer.[5]
Captain A. E. Mason, messing officer.[5]
Captain J. W. Meade, supernumerary.[5]
Lieutenant F. C. L. A. Lowndes, M.C., supernumerary.[5]
Lieutenant and Quartermaster G. Dancey, M.C., D.C.M.[5]
Captain F. C. Chandler, R.A.M.C., medical officer.

"A" Company, 43rd Light Infantry.[5]

Captain C. S. Baines, D.S.O.	Lieutenant L. W. Giles, M.C.
Captain G. Naylor, M.C.	Lieutenant P. Booth.
Lieutenant E. Holt, M.C.	Lieutenant J. E. H. Neville, M.C.
Lieutenant O. H. M. Sturges.	Second Lieutenant C. A. Sawyer.

[5] Regular officers of the Regiment.

"B" Company, Royal Warwickshire Regiment.

Captain A. J. Peck.
Captain L. R. Swinhoe.
Lieutenant W. L. Dibben.
Lieutenant H. J. King.
Lieutenant J. E. W. Rance.
Second Lieutenant J. Clews, D.C.M.
Second Lieutenant H. G. Harbourne.
Second Lieutenant R. M. Harman.[*]

"C" Company, Devonshire Regiment.

Major A. F. Northcote.
Captain O. M. Parker.
Lieutenant M. H. C. Perry.
Lieutenant H. Gibbons.
Second Lieutenant J. Moulding.
Second Lieutenant N. L. Hughes.
Second Lieutenant J. W. Wadham.

"D" Company, Royal Berkshire Regiment.

Major A. G. MacDonald, D.S.O.
Lieutenant P. H. Hight.
Lieutenant W. S. McKay.
Lieutenant E. C. Denis de Vitré.
Lieutenant A. S. Denham, M.M.
Lieutenant H. E. Baldwin.
Lieutenant D. C. Colvill, M.C.[*]
Second Lieutenant F. W. Paines.

239th Light Trench Mortar Battery.

Captain J. L. Carr, Royal Berkshire Regiment.
Lieutenant J. C. Holberton, Devonshire Regiment.
Lieutenant M. G. Beck, Devonshire Regiment.
Second Lieutenant W. T. Trengrouse, 43rd Light Infantry.[*]
Second Lieutenant E. B. Dickenson, Royal Warwickshire Regiment.

Attached.

Rev. Ishmael Jones, C.F., chaplain.
Second Lieutenant N. Trewheler, interpreter.

Reinforcements.

Lieutenant L. H. M. Westropp, Devonshire Regiment.
Second Lieutenant F. C. Holland, 43rd Light Infantry.[*]
Second Lieutenant W. Maunder, M.C., Devonshire Regiment.
Second Lieutenant M. A. Wilcox, Devonshire Regiment.

III.—THE JOURNEY OUT AND ARRIVAL AT ARCHANGEL.

The course lay up the coast of Scotland, through double minefields, past Fair Island—a famous lair of German submarines—and the Orkney and Shetland Islands, roseate in a wine-dark sea; thence across the North Sea

---

[*] Regular officers of the Regiment.

to the coast of Lapland. On the 18th the weather changed from spring sunshine to bitter cold; and through rifts in the scudding clouds the great black rollers could be seen breaking furiously against the snow-capped cliffs of the coast. The following day the transports rounded the North Cape with ice glazing the windows of saloons and smoking-rooms.

The morning of the 20th found the expedition anchored in the spacious roadstead of Murmansk among supply ships and naval craft of all kinds. Murmansk, lying fifty miles up the Kola river, was a magnificent natural harbour. Enclosed entirely by low hills, still deep in snow, it seemed as if the convoy lay in a calm lagoon. The atmosphere was keen and frosty; and seals lolled for all the world like bored choirboys on the ice-floes which glided slowly downstream towards the sea.

Here the expedition waited for four days for ice-breakers to lead it through the White Sea. The time was not wasted. There was much to be learnt and more to be imagined of this land of extremes, midnight sun and perpetual darkness. Murmansk itself had little to commend it. It consisted of a landing-stage, a few log shacks, the important railway terminus of the Petrograd line, and much foul and odoriferous matter. But its inhabitants were interesting. Besides Russians, gorgeous or fearsome to behold, there were Americans, French, Chinese, Italians and Serbians, the last looking the brigands that they probably were in more peaceful times. Cosmopolitanism was personified in that small fishing village.

During the winter months all refuse, garbage and ordure is deposited indiscriminately in the snow, where it remains, preserved by the frost from putrefaction, until the thaw comes. By May the thaw had come; the deep snow, on melting, disclosed the filth that it had concealed for months. The tracks of grey sand which led up from the landing-stage were nothing better than drains of liquid sewage. And yet above the appalling stench there was another indefinable smell—less pungent but just as noticeable—the smell of Russia.

On the 24th the convoy weighed anchor and left the roadstead for the most interesting part of the journey through the White Sea. Ahead, the ice-breakers forged their way through the pack-ice wedged in the narrow entrance to the White Sea. Rearing their hulls out of the water, they seemed to crawl up the ice until their weight sundered it beneath them. Griding and groaning, the transports followed in their tortuous wake, now and then shuddering from stem to stern on impact with large packs of ice. It was an interesting but slow procedure. For over an hour one transport got wedged in the ice, unable to move, and had to be extricated by another ice-breaker following in rear of the convoy.

All day long the troops watched the progress in the brilliant sunshine, which, reflected from the ice, dazzled and blinded the eyes so that the clean, white paint of the superstructure appeared yellow or even orange. Colours lost their hues in that light, and men seemed to be as black-faced as negroes.

In the evening a most wonderful effect was produced by the fading rays of the setting sun when the north-west sky, still glowing, threw a golden light on the ice. The rugged lumps became a tender shade of blue, and the pools of water in the melting pack-ice appeared as liquid gold in goblets of turquoise. Beyond the ice and in sharp contrast lay the sinister and desolate shore, black and forbidding. Such a sight was it that even the soul of that prosaic officer, Lieutenant Tyrwhitt-Drake, was moved to poetry.

And so through the narrow neck the convoy passed, close to a shore that in its whole entirety seemed to boast but one building, a monastery standing alone in a howling waste; then through another belt of pack-ice, insignificant compared with the first, and so into the delta of the Dvina. Slowly the ships steamed up the river past low-lying marshes where, doubtless, duck abounded; past gigantic yards of stacked timber occupying many acres of reclaimed marsh-land, until, afar off, the towers and spires of Archangel could be spied gleaming in the brilliant sunshine. Gradually the broad river opened out into a vast lagoon crowded with shipping and busy launches, gaily dressed in honour of the Relief Force. On the far bank lay Archangel, liberally supplied with churches whose star-spangled domes, painted in different colours, stood out against a cloudless sky. Clustered round the churches were rows of low wooden houses whose white paint contrasted sharply with their green and vermilion roofs and shutters. From a distance it was a fairy city, medieval and clean in appearance.

At the quayside were many strange sights to be noticed: Russian sentries with bayoneted rifles slung and hands deep in pockets; officials in short, white jackets and caps, tilted at a stylish angle over one ear, who shouted to the pilot in their purring, spitting tongue; drosky drivers, furred up to their eyes lest they should lose one degree of heat so hardly preserved through the winter months; and lastly the smell of Russia which was wafted ever upwards from the crowd below.

On the 27th the brigade disembarked at the Sabornaya and Smolny Quays, and was officially welcomed under a triumphal arch by the Provisional Government, the Governor—General Miller—and Major-General Ironside, commanding the Allied forces. According to the ancient Slav tradition, General Grogan accepted the offering of bread and salt, after which patriotic speeches were delivered and duly interpreted. The ceremony ended with a march past of the brigade amid much enthusiastic cheering, and so through gaily flagged streets to billets at the far—north-eastern—end of the town.

The Regiment was billeted in Olga Barracks, a spacious brick building facing the lagoon, which had originally been the infirmary. Here a week

GOING THROUGH THE WHITE SEA.

ARCHANGEL, FROM THE SABORNAYA QUAY.

was spent unloading stores and attending ceremonial parades and functions. As there was no land transport, all stores and equipment had to be unloaded from the ships into barges, which were then tugged round and moored opposite the barracks. Here more fatigue parties man-handled the kit ashore—a slow and tedious business without cranes.

Concurrently with the arrival of the Relief Force pamphlets of welcome from the North Russian Provisional Government and from the Governor-General, printed in English, were issued to the troops. These, especially General Miller's, showed the implicit trust which the Provisional Government placed in the British soldiers. They ran as follows:—

"A FRIEND IN NEED IS A FRIEND INDEED.

"WELCOME TO OUR TRUE ALLIES!

"You, who have vanquished the German armies, have answered our call.

"You have not forgotten our sacrifices when we fought for the common cause and have realised our present need.

"Our struggles are not yet over. The German armies are gone, not so the German Agents.

"They still continue their dirty, traitorous German work.

"Our country is devastated, our strength is sapped by the awful war forced on the world by Germany.

"Thanks to your brothers in arms we have again risen.

"Our new armies are getting back their former strength.

"Our aim is to free Russia from the degradation of bolshevism.

"To free the heart of Russia—Moscow—from traitors and resurrect our native land.

"And now in the time of our need we greet our true friends.

"Thousands of miles away you heard us call.

"Your innate feeling of justice could not permit the violence of tyrants. And you voluntarily came to our aid.

"Your arrival will encourage us to new efforts and revives our faith in the good-will of our Allies.

"We remembered them during our darkest hours and were true to them.

"We always trusted our Allies and we receive you with joy.

"Russia knew how to fight during the first years of war. A Resurrected Russia will be able to appreciate the deeds of her true friends.

"ALL HONOUR TO YOU NOBLE SOLDIERS OF THE GREAT BRITISH ARMY.

"PROVISIONAL GOVERNMENT OF NORTHERN RUSSIA."

"NORTHERN RUSSIA'S WELCOME.

"Governor General Miller's Tribute to Britons.

"In the reign of Queen Elizabeth daring sailors and traders from England arrived in Archangel, which was then part of the dominions of the Muscovite Tsar, Ivan the Terrible. Here, on the banks of the Dvina, Englishmen and Russians met for the first time.

"Archangel received the strangers with courtesy, and they were regarded by the Terrible Tsar with favour. He invited them to visit him in Ancient Moscow, where he received them cordially and granted them, before they left his presence, a Trading Charter which assisted the relations between the two countries.

"Much time has passed since. England and Russia, guided by their statesmen, have pursued their own courses in history, more than once passing through historical crises which shook Europe—sometimes fighting shoulder to shoulder against a common enemy and sometimes meeting as opponents. And, as the political lives of our countries followed their own courses, so did the lives of our peoples.

"In Ancient Moscow, the heart of Russia, in St. Petersburg, the young and splendid Russian Capital, and in other parts of the immense Russian State, British Colonies appeared and flourished. The British brought us their knowledge, and sent to Russia the merchants she needed.

"On the field of battle and in peaceful work among our people, Englishmen, from time immemorial, have been known to us as people of undaunted courage, of practical working ability, always unswerving in their aims, and unwaveringly honest in their dealings. Russians came to value the word of an Englishman higher than any written bond. The English word 'Gentleman' was adopted into the Russian language, and in every Englishman, before all else, we always expect to see a gentleman.

"Three and a half centuries passed, and again the British landed on the banks of the Dvina, where their help was needed. Russia was under the heel of the Bolshevik—the Bolshevik who, in the middle of the great war, treacherously signed the Brest-Litovsk Treaty, committed the most unheard-of crimes in Russia (one of the victims was Captain Cromie of the British Navy), threw hundreds of innocent sons of Britain into prison, and finally aroused the indignation of the British Government which, a year ago, sent troops to the distant North of Russia—to Murmansk and Archangel.

"These troops formed the outpost, under the protection of which began the creation of the Russian Army for the struggle for the deliverance of Russia from the despotic power of the one-time German agents—the traitorous Bolsheviks.

"These tyrants and outcasts—mostly aliens—stained with the guilt of every kind of crime, helped by Germans and supported by Lettish and Chinese mercenaries, have, by deception, force and terror, enslaved a portion of the simple and ignorant Russian people.

"Now we have witnessed the arrival of further British troops. These soldiers volunteered to strengthen the 'outpost' in order to help Russia to free herself from the yoke of the Bolshevik.

"Welcome! Gallant British Soldiers, hastening in disinterested and self-sacrificing aid in the struggle for the deliverance of Russia from the miscreants under whose yoke the majority of the Russian people groan.

"Long live Great Britain, who helps us to re-build our Mother Country on a basis of Right and Justice.

"WELCOME! BRITAIN'S OUTPOST.

"(Signed) E. MILLER,
"Governor General North Russia."

On the 29th General Ironside addressed the whole Regiment, and later, in a talk to the officers, laid great stress on the importance of maintaining British prestige in so mixed a force. He described some of the many difficulties with which he had to contend: drunkenness, indiscipline of all kinds, and bartering of Government stores for furs with the Russian peasants. None of the Allies, he said, had been in a position in 1918 to send any but poor troops to North Russia; all but the British had given considerable trouble; and now, with the arrival of the Relief Force, he hoped to be able to pack the rest of the Allies off home; he relied on the British to set the Russians an example of soldierly qualities. Standing with his legs wide apart, wearing long, soft-leather, Russian boots half-way up his thighs, his hands thrust deep into his jacket pockets, this giant of a general, a commander every inch of him and commanding in appearance, could not fail to inspire and enthrall his listeners. This man, who with his two great hands could have wrung the neck of the tallest officer, placed his trust—implicit trust—in the Regiment. The Regiment would prove worthy of it.

At lunch that day each officer was issued with an invitation to an *honourable tea* at the Duma to meet the mayor and members of the Provisional Government. The invitation ran:—

"The Mayor of Archangel begs you to come to tea the 29.5.19 which is going to be held in honour of our friends the British Allies, who have come out to help us to fight with Bolsheviks. The beginning will be at 5 p.m."

The officers—forty-two from each of the three regiments of the brigade —assembled at 5 p.m. and marched up the stairs where the mayor shook each warmly by the hand. Having assembled, the mayor mounted his rostrum and read a speech of welcome to the " brave volunteers " which was interpreted at the end of each sentence. Next, a band, cramped in the corner of the crowded room, struck up and played three verses of *God Save the King,* followed by the old solemn Russian anthem.

Despite of the report that Archangel was short of food, the tables were loaded with dainties, and all the guests were bidden to sit and eat while Russian ladies and officers bustled round with samovars and glasses of the bitter-sweet tea that they delight in. In fluent and polished English many of the refugees made conversation with the British. Here were some of the last remnants of that old regime, that paradox of civilization and barbarism. General Savitch—at one time chief of staff to General Brusiloff—a fine old man with a long, neatly parted beard and a chest amply adorned with ribbons, medals and stars—had managed to escape the Terror a year before. He and many others made it quite clear that they regarded the Relief Force as their only hope of salvation from the Bolsheviks; that they knew the British would never desert them though others might. What these people had to say less than six months later has never been recorded.

The following day, the 30th, a party of the Regiment was detailed to attend an Allied parade, held to commemorate those who died in the American Civil War. Four miles the party marched down the dusty road of the Troitsky Prospekt, formed up at the Sabornaya Quay, and then waited for the ceremony. The parade, led by American soldiers and sailors, and followed by Russian soldiers and sailors, Royal Navy and Relief Force, French soldiers and sailors, Italians and Poles—in strict alphabetical order of countries—marched to the cemetery where a few Americans lay buried. More speechification and then back to barracks in the dust.

And that was not the last of the ceremonies. On the 1st June another parade was held, in honour of His Majesty's birthday. Once again the Regiment marched over the pot-holes and through the parching dust of the Troitsky Prospekt to the gardens of the cathedral where it formed up with the rest of the brigade. The parade was made the occasion for the presentation of colours to the 1st Battalion of the Slavo-British Legion. This had been raised by an Australian officer, Colonel Dyer, from those Russians and prisoners of war who professed to be anti-Bolshevik, and it was organized on the system of the Indian Army, having both Russian and British captains and subalterns. Its turn-out and drill were excellent, and its method of marching past in slow time slapping the butts of rifles as left feet went forward was most impressive. Much was expected of these troops. They were to be the nucleus of the new Russian Army which was to preserve North Russia from Bolshevism at least, if not conquer it.

No one was sorry when orders came for the Regiment to go up the line and relieve the garrison troops. The novelty of Archangel soon wore off. The dust, the tropical heat, the stench of rotting fish guts, the stinking trams, the complete absence of sanitation were not pleasant novelties. Yet there was a quaintness about the place which made impressions; strange sights to be seen, strange and incomprehensible lettering and relics of barbarism. It was immediately evident that Russians and soap were strangers to one another, but soap cost 4s. 6d. a cake. They were said to be in extreme want—yet all seemed well clad, nourished and cheerful; the priests—parasites, the Bolsheviks called them—with long locks of hair dangling on their shoulders and with beards, among the more ancient, reaching to their cummerbunds strolled about in shiny bowlers or inverted top-hats—a comical sight to strangers.

Superficially there did not seem to be much of which the peasants could complain; yet an example of old methods was vouchsafed even before the Regiment left for the front.

One evening, about three days after landing, the mess serjeant told the orderly officer that a Russian officer wanted to speak to him. Outside in the passage the officer found an extremely drunken Russian who, by his uniform, appeared to belong to the Russian Navy, which consisted of one obsolete battleship lately stripped of its breech-blocks on General Ironside's orders. In broken English he informed the orderly officer that he had just passed one of the sentries who had failed to salute him, and he wanted to know what the orderly officer was going to do about it. As there were many different types of badges of rank among the Allied forces, he was requested to be lenient in his censure and give the English time to recognize them. However, he would not be mollified and demanded that the man be placed in irons at once. At this, Lieutenant Trewheler, the interpreter, was called in to assist, and eventually the Russian officer was pacified. Having watched him stagger safely out of sight, the orderly officer visited the offending sentry and asked him for his story. He, at least, was sober. It so happened that he was a 43rd man who had served in India. He had seen the Russian approach his post and realized too late that he was an officer. Coming up to him, the Russian first purred in his own tongue and then in broken English asked why he—the dog—had not saluted him. " Then," added the sentry, " he spat in my face and walked away." The sentry was fulminating with fury and an international complication appeared likely if that Russian were to pass again. Luckily he reeled and lurched out of the Regiment's history, never to appear again. Such intolerable behaviour was common in the old Imperial Services.

[1919

CHAPTER XXVIII.

I.—Appreciation of the Situation.[1]

BOLSHEVIK STRENGTH—THE COUNTRY—COMMUNICATIONS—SUPPLY AND TRANSPORT—FRONT TO BE HANDED OVER TO ADMIRAL KOLTCHAK—THE PLAN OF CAMPAIGN—THE 43RD LEAVES ARCHANGEL—THE JOURNEY UPSTREAM—THE 43RD REACHES OSINOVA—LEAVES FOR THE VAGA FRONT—"A" COMPANY'S MARCH FROM UST VAGA TO MALA BEREZNIK—THE POSITION AT MALA BEREZNIK—PATROL WORK—MOSQUITOES—REGIMENTAL HEADQUARTERS COME UP TO SELTSO—THE BLOOD-SUCKING CLEGS—"A" COMPANY AT SELTSO.

(*See Maps on pages* 321 *and* 322, *and facing pages* 366 *and* 384.)

The object of the impending operations was to relieve the tired troops in the line, as has been explained, and then cover the evacuation of the whole Allied force. The factors which governed this object were many. Excluding the Murman front, which was a separate command, there were two fronts, known as the Railway and Dvina fronts respectively. Though the Allies were inferior in numbers they were infinitely superior in armaments, efficiency and morale. The naval flotilla, consisting of heavily armed monitors, motor-launches armed with machine guns, and coastal motor-boats as used against submarines in the German War, was a force with which the Bolsheviks had nothing to compare. Good news of Admiral Koltchak's advance had lately been received; and his mounted patrols from the direction of Viatka had joined hands with the Dvina force.

The Bolsheviks were underfed, ill-armed and disaffected, and as fighters of negligible value. On the other hand, they had unlimited resources in men, whereas the British were dependent on long sea communications.

Politically Bolshevism was expected to die a natural death and a revulsion of feeling was always a possible factor. No one believed that it had taken deep root in the heart of Russia. Great things were expected of Koltchak and Denikin. On the other hand, there were in England parties and sections of the Press which had already started to inveigh against the capitalist expedition to fight their brother-workers. These might, at any moment, prove extremely troublesome and add to the unpopularity of the operations.

The country can be described by two words: forest and swamp. The forest, consisting of pines and silver birches, was extremely thick and gave a

---

[1] See Map No. 20, opposite.

visibility of about fifteen to twenty yards in broad daylight. Added to which, impenetrable bramble undergrowth, ten feet high and more, was often encountered on any deviation from the tracks. Once in the forest it was very difficult to keep direction without a vestige of a landmark to march on and with forest tracks radiating in all directions. A compass was soon found to be essential. The forest tracks were only passable by men in single file, and it was therefore difficult to protect a column on the march. No matter how brilliant the sunshine, the forest was always dank, sombre and sinister; and teemed with all manner of insect life. To stray from a forest track often

MAP No. 20.

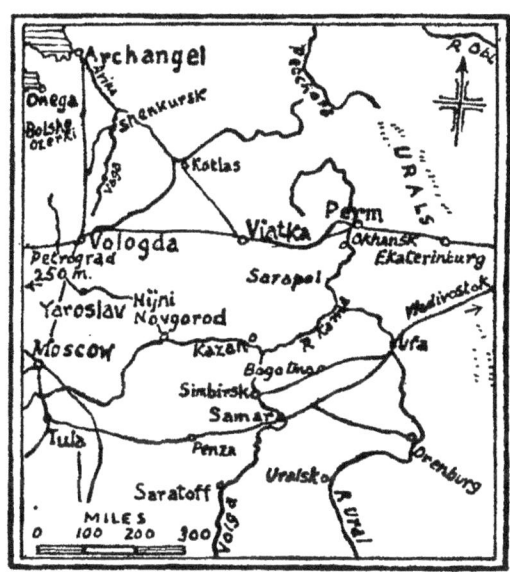

entailed floundering up to the knees in swamps, cunningly disguised by Nature with soft, spongy moss. The inhabitants lived only on the banks of rivers in clearings cut from the fecund forest, and there worked their rye fields and lumbered timber. Between villages there was generally a track, fit to take a cart, which was inches deep in sand in fine weather and conversely muddy in wet. Bridges over tributary streams were only fit to take light traffic.

The peasants in the villages were poor and badly supplied with domestic animals; consequently, horses, or rather ponies, for military transport were hard to replace. The peasants' loyalty to the Allied cause was always a doubtful quantity.

Owing to the nature of the country wide enveloping movements could not be undertaken, the difficulties of transport and direction being well-nigh insuperable far inland from the rivers. The fronts were therefore narrow and deep, and confined to the rivers.

The forest, however, was squared in certain places by broad fire-traces running for great distances in north-south and east-west directions, to localize forest fires, it was said; but these were not discovered until just before the evacuation.

The Russians, it should be remembered, were accustomed to the forest: they had lived in it and on it for countless generations, and they knew all the multitudinous tracks as well as if each had had a signpost. They had a sense of the forest just as some have an unerring sense of direction. Their

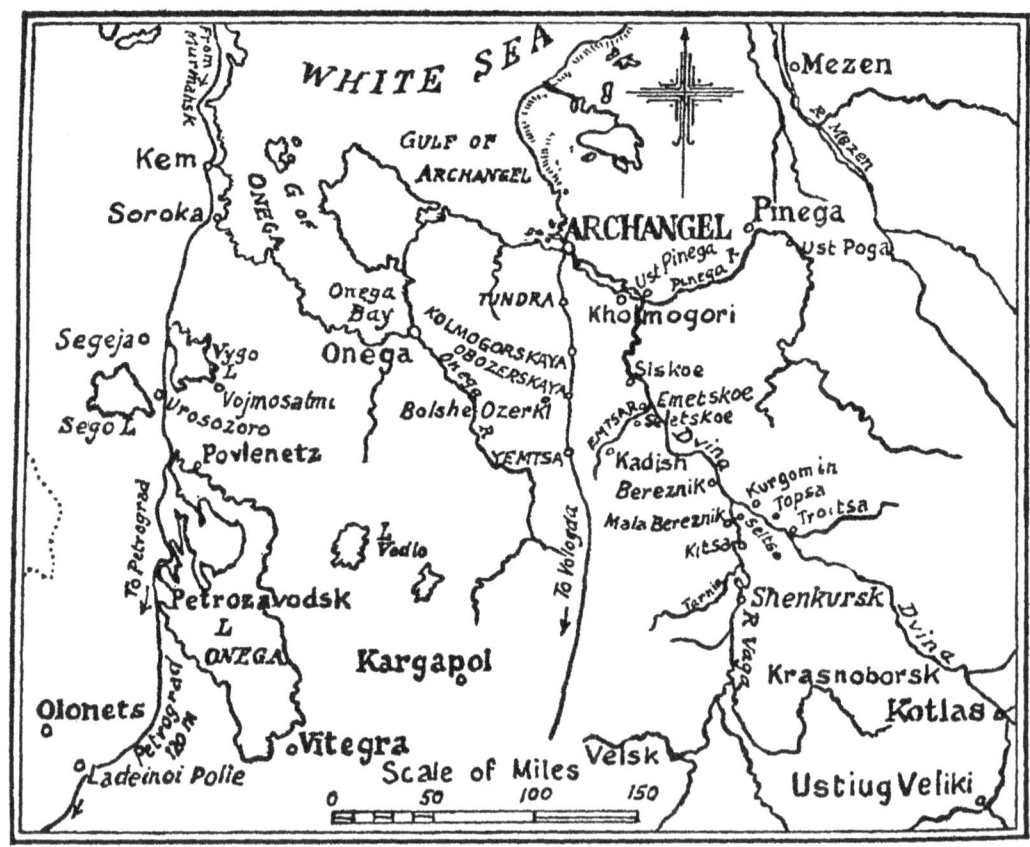

THE ARCHANGEL FRONT. Map No. 21.

familiarity with everything concerned with the forest was a factor in their favour whether as enemies or allies.

The enemy had the advantage of interior lines, though, for communication he only held the head waters of the rivers, of which the most important were the Dvina, Vaga, Emtsa and Pinega.[2] These last were the arteries of the country in the same way as the Tigris and Euphrates in Mesopotamia. In the summer the rivers were liable to fall to very low levels. All operations depended on them and the water they contained. The biggest, the Dvina, though navigable as far as Kotlas, was known to fall considerably in the summer months. A big fall might cause supply failures. Like the Tigris, its channels were liable to change very suddenly. The climate was one of extremes, confining operations to the late spring and summer months. In September heavy rains and flood waters in the rivers were to be expected and frosts at night. In October the rivers froze and finally communication with the outside world by way of the White Sea ceased in November.

The long lines of communication were always vulnerable throughout their length and caused considerable anxiety. It is obvious that an enemy, composed of trackers, lumbermen, hunters and foresters to whom the forest was an open field, was able, given the leaders and initiative, to harry if not cut British communications.

Added to which, signs of sabotage on the communications were not altogether absent. Bolshevik propaganda was insidious, the rear teemed with spies and agents—potential enemies who were not easy to capture on over two hundred miles of river communication. Mutiny had occurred among the Russian allies in the past, and, though Bolshevism was at this time at its greatest discount, a recrudescence was not an impossibility and had to be guarded against.

Supply and transport, as in Mesopotamia, was a difficult problem. There was a certain amount of native craft, tugs, launches and paddle-steamers which were capable of transporting up to fifty men each. Any greater numbers were moved in vast barges—in shape and appearance very like the biblical ark—capable of accommodating a complete regiment. This method of transport was naturally slow, and on the upstream journey the barges required two tugs.

Later stern-wheelers were brought over from England and were used on the Dvina.[3]

After relieving the front-line troops, there were two courses open to the British: either to act on the defensive as covering troops to the evacuation of all stores in rear while training the loyal Russians to fight their own

[2] See Map No. 21, opposite.
[3] I remember being told that they had been used in Mesopotamia.—J. E. H. N.

battles; or to attack as Sir John Moore attacked before retreating to Corunna, and so give the Russians a flying start.

The enemy had it in his power to mobilize immense, if raw, levies of men, and by sheer weight of numbers overrun the forward positions, always provided he could feed his troops. He had no chance of living on the country.

The plan adopted depended for success to a great extent on good luck. In co-operation with the naval flotilla it was decided to make a lightning advance up the Dvina as far as Kotlas and to Shenkursk on the Vaga—flanking the Dvina on the right—join hands with Admiral Koltchak, hand over the northern line to the Russians, start them on a concerted movement on Petrograd, and then evacuate via Archangel before the port froze up. To this end vast stores of ammunition, arms and war material of all descriptions had been accumulated at Archangel for Admiral Koltchak's eventual use, and the British Government was prepared to supply him via Murmansk with all his needs.

But even before the embarkation of the 238th Brigade at Archangel for the front, Admiral Koltchak, distracted from his true objective (the junction with General Ironside and the establishment of a sure chain of supply) by the lure of Moscow, had already been checked in his advance and had evacuated Viatka and was retreating towards the Ural Mountains. The news was not good, but, as yet, not hopeless.

II.—THE JOURNEY UPSTREAM AND OCCUPATION OF THE FRONT LINE.

On the 30th the advanced party, under Captain Mason, embarked at the Sabornaya Quay for Bereznik. The heavy baggage was loaded three days later on to a barge at Vodka Quay, leaving valises and blankets for officers and men on the journey upstream. On the same day, the 2nd June, the Regiment suffered a great loss. Lieutenant George Dancey, M.C., D.C.M., quartermaster of the Regiment, died as the result of a gunshot wound in the head. There is no doubt but that he overworked himself preparing for the move up the Dvina. He had been ill before leaving England, and the strain was too much for him. As in Mesopotamia in the early days, transport was conspicuous by its absence; and from the moment he rejoined the Regiment he had had no respite from arranging moves. His energy and experience were sadly missed at a crucial time. Lieutenant Warren was appointed acting quartermaster for the move; and later Captain Mason was confirmed in the appointment.

At about 8.30 a.m. on the 3rd the Regiment paraded and marched in sweltering heat to the unsavoury Sabornaya Quay where headquarters and

"A," "B" and "C" Companies[*] embarked in fifteen boats, already laden heavily with wood fuel. There were craft of all kinds: tugs, launches and paddle-wheelers, the last accommodating the company field kitchens and fourteen days' rations per man. After picking up stores and ammunition at Bakharitsa, on the other side of the lagoon, the assorted convoy started upstream. The launches quickly took the lead, followed by the tugs, while the paddlers groaned and grunted miles behind. Luckily the tropical heat abated in the early afternoon or those under the corrugated-iron awnings of the launches would have been roasted alive. It was strange to meet with such intense heat just outside the Arctic Circle.

The country on each side was flat or slightly undulating, and dotted with many villages along the river banks in the first reaches above Archangel. Each little village of gaily painted shacks nestled amid its sprouting rye fields, reclaimed from the forest. Here were bluffs and crags, shot with purple and silver in the sunset light; there, low-lying swamps and marshes surrounded by the inexorable forest, the larches crimson-tufted and dressed in living, vivid green. It was, indeed, a country released from a rigorous bondage, gasping, as it were, with relief from the iron grip of winter.

Late that night, when the beautiful weather had given place to a fine drizzle borne on an icy wind from the north, the fleet moored for the night, and the Regiment bivouacked in lush grass on a bluff.

Roused at 6 a.m., the Regiment, with boots full of water and soaked by a fine drizzle, embarked once again. After two hours' steaming the fleet put in to shore at Ust Pinega for necessary functions, as there were no latrines in the boats. Re-embarking at 11 a.m., the Regiment steamed ahead round sandbanks, over sandbanks, and on to sandbanks. Between 3 p.m. and 5 p.m. another halt was called, this time to reload with wood fuel from one of the many piles which each big village seemed to keep stacked ready for passing traffic. At this halt a chance was given of seeing the Russian peasants in their own surroundings. It was very difficult to buy eggs—even at 1s. 3d. each—and butter, because one and all were suspicious of rouble notes, and, without a word of the language, it was impossible to explain that the British roubles were guaranteed. Cigarettes and whisky proved far more negotiable than paper money.

In the heat of the early afternoon some officers visited the village. In every shack the double windows were tightly shut, and the heat in the low rooms, where a man of six feet could not stand up straight, was really appalling. Added to this was the stench of live-stock in a confined space.

At this point it is convenient to describe the construction of the Russian shack, as, on one occasion in September, it played an important part. It was

---

[*] "D" Company was left behind in Archangel in charge of Olga Barracks owing to shortage of river transport.

generally one-storeyed and divided into two halves—one for human and the other for animal habitation. The front half was raised about six feet from the ground to prevent the snow from blocking the windows. This half consisted of a living-room and bedroom with an attic above.

The stove, simple and effective though of considerable size, occupied much of the floor space in the living-room. The more pretentious shacks boasted stoves on the first floor too. The walls were unlined, the cracks and crevices between the stripped logs being stuffed with moss, chips and birch bark.

The ground floor of the back half sheltered the live-stock in the summer, and a ramp from the ground led up to the first floor where the cattle were accommodated in the winter months when the snow was thick on the ground. From the cattle floor the peasants relieved the needs of nature into the byres beneath all through the winter, but the result was not necessarily removed in the summer.

That night the Regiment bivouacked on the bank near Emetskoe. The following day the fleet moved off at 7 a.m. and reached Osinova,[5] on the right bank opposite Bereznik, Advanced General Headquarters, late in the evening, and the Regiment occupied a standing camp.[6] The colonel held a conference and warned the officers that the Regiment and No. 239 Light Trench Mortar Battery were to take over the line on the Vaga river on the 6th. Officers were then issued with maps, weird, inaccurate concoctions marked off in rectangles and without scales. It was immediately evident that little if any reliance could be placed upon them.

Meanwhile the baggage barge, which had arrived on the 4th, was being unloaded. This was an arduous task, as everything had to be carried ashore down a ramp. Even more difficult was the disembarkation of " A " Company's field kitchen from the paddle-steamer *Souhanets*; but a very efficient sailor superintended, and took the responsibility on his own shoulders. Under his expert directions the brows were made fast, and the cooker and Private Green—they always went everywhere together—were adjusted to the two ramps. " Now, boys," shouted the sailor, " let her go "; and go she did, remembering her sex. Quickly gathering impetus, she trundled down the gangway, bounced light-heartedly on to the landing-stage, ploughed her inexorable way through the joists, and, like a great battleship, settled herself in the water with a list of forty-five degrees to port. So much for the sailor. The land lubbers—" A " Company—were left to extricate her. But

---

[5] See Map No. 27, facing p. 384.
[6] Two days previously, at the moment when the advanced party was disembarking at Osinova, an aeroplane from overhead made a perfect nose dive into the middle of the Dvina. The pilot was Lieutenant S. C. P. Slattery.

it was midnight before the company's labours were finished and the cooker safely bedded down in the lines.

Twelve hours later the Regiment was once more employed in loading baggage and stores on to a vast biblical ark, moored alongside the shingle beach. Owing to her size, the brows leaned at steep angles, and up these four recalcitrant cookers had to be man-handled once again. In this herculean task Lieutenant Holt took a prominent part, exhorting the sweating men to further feats of strength. So long as there was heavy work to be done Lieutenant Holt was perfectly happy and in his element. Tall and wiry, he stood in the bowels of a barge with his head and shoulders above decklevel, and with untiring energy slung boxes of ammunition and trench-mortar bombs about as if they had been empty biscuit-tins. Such was his example that many men tried to emulate it without success. No officers competed.

At 2 p.m. the ark was taken in tow, but, against a strong wind and current, progress was very slow; and it was not until 6 p.m. that the Regiment reached Ust Vaga, about fifteen miles from Bereznik. Having arrived at the headquarters of the Vaga Column, no one seemed to know what was to happen next. For two hours the troops remained on board, expecting to bivouac for the night before taking over the line the next day. But that was not to be. An order came to say that " A " and " B " Companies were to move forward at 10 p.m. in a smaller barge. Forthwith the job of unloading began again: ammunition, kit-bags, cookers, all had to go ashore. To make the work less pleasant, mosquitoes—billions of them—appeared from nowhere to take their evening meal. Captain Mason promptly issued head-nets to all ranks, and the work proceeded amid a torrent of superlative oaths, for once justified. But before the unloading had been completed, Captain Baines received a message from regimental headquarters cancelling the move forward by barge, as there was none available. Instead " A " Company was to stack rations, Lewis guns, kits, and officers' valises on to drosky carts, and march up to the front at 10 p.m. This meant a complete sorting of essential from unessential kit, and it was past 11.30 p.m. before the company was ready to start on the seven-mile march,[7] as calculated by the staff.

Meanwhile regimental headquarters, " C " Company and half the trench-mortar battery moved into billets in Ust Vaga, and " C " Company took over the defences of the village.

" A " Company—the regimental company—started off in the midnight twilight up the broad, sandy road with No. 1 Platoon (Lieutenant Holt) as advance guard. Hemmed in by the everlasting forest, there seemed no air

[7] The distance was actually nine miles.

to breathe, and the men, already forespent with much manual labour, found the going most exhausting. It was impossible to see anything ahead when head-nets were pulled down, and so the advance guard was forced to tie them up, while the main body soon found that to use them as protection meant asphyxiation from dust and heat. At the halts they were immediately pulled down; yet swarms found their way through the meshes where the net itself touched the skin round the collar. Through the seams of trousers and breeches, through lacing holes, they found room for the insertion of their proboscides. They settled like hairs upon the troops' hands, and crawled up their sleeves and inside their shirts. " Added to this torture, there was the maddening wheezing hum of the little devils and the sudden intensified scream as one or more settled in your ears and buzzed out again," wrote an officer. " The air was charged with them, dancing in their myriads, and see-sawing up and down in front of your eyes." No description of them would be an exaggeration: they had to be seen and felt to be believed.

The troops were tired and nearly mad with irritation; mouths were parched with thirst from heat, sand and the smoking of numberless cigarettes and pipes to ward off some of the winged fiends. The track ahead never altered—a rise, a fall, another rise, and so on interminably. Two hourly halts came and went; a third and then a fourth. At last, after four hours of unmitigated purgatory, the column reached Mala Bereznik; and at 5 a.m. the gallant second-line Territorials—the 2nd/10th Royal Scots—marched out for home.

Though the Regiment's welcome at Archangel had been cordial, it was nothing compared with that of these Lowlanders who had been counting the hours to its arrival. Therefore it was not surprising that the relief was effected with the minimum delay.

The trenches and posts at Mala Bereznik[8] formed a semi-circle facing the forest with the Vaga as diameter flowing from south to north. The southern posts, nearest the Bolshevik position, commanded the road, euphemistically known as the Moscow Road. These were allotted to No. 2 Platoon (Lieutenant Sturges), and consisted of Scots Hill and Coswick posts. The western face, on rising ground, commanded the exits from the forest, and consisted of the Summer House, Banya, the Pimple, Horseshoe and Fort Garry posts. These were allotted to Nos. 3 and 4 Platoons (Lieutenants Giles and Booth respectively). No. 1 Platoon (Lieutenant Holt) held the northern face, and was responsible for the Road post, looking towards Ust Vaga, and the forest between the road and the river which was covered by a blockhouse—Wood post—with a good field of fire down rides of felled timber radiating in three

[8] See Map No. 25, facing p. 366.

1. Refuelling on way upstream.
2. Canadian Village, Mala Bereznik.
3. Road Post, Mala Bereznik.
4. Trenches in the Bolshevik forward position.
5. Taken during the raid on Ignatovskaya. No. 3 Platoon advancing from the captured Bolshevik forward position.
6. Lieut. Tamplin and Capt. Watson, intelligence officers of the Vaga Column, interrogating Bolshevik prisoners.

directions. Another blockhouse—Burchill's post—watched the north-eastern approaches, and Hale's post, on the river bank, watched no man's land across the river as well as the rear approaches. On the river bank, between Burchill's and Scots Hill posts, there was a machine-gun position which protected the left flank of Scots Hill and also commanded a wide arc across the river.

The field of fire from the trenches and posts was never more than five hundred yards and in places considerably less, but the whole perimeter was well and stoutly wired. In front of the Pimple there was a pocket of dead ground which played an important part in September.

The trench-mortar emplacement was roughly in the centre of the village between the road and river, and so sited that fire could be brought to bear along the edge of the forest in all directions. Close to this emplacement were the dug-outs belonging to the sappers and the regimental aid post. The distance from the most southerly to the most northerly posts was just over one thousand yards.

In the forest between Wood and Burchill's posts lay a collection of shacks known as Canadian Village. Here Forward Area Headquarters, commanding the forward positions on both banks, were established on the 7th under Major Carter, who had Lieutenant Tyrwhitt-Drake with him as adjutant. On the same day " B " Company left Ust Vaga at 4.30 a.m. by barge, and took over the right-bank positions with two platoons at Nijni Kitsa and two platoons in Koslovo and Seltso, villages lying in the bend of the river. By noon the relief of the forward area was completed.

In Mala Bereznik there was very little accommodation for officers, for, where the Royal Scots had three, " A " Company had eight officers, and there were no company headquarters as soon as Major Carter arrived. Captain Baines therefore decided to make his headquarters in the only shack which was not entirely demolished by shell fire. This stood on rising ground in the centre of the village, and came to be known as Château Rickety.

There was much work to be done in the tropical heat of that first day when all ranks were exhausted after their labours of the previous twenty-four hours. Captain Baines, with his reputation for the cleanliness of trenches, made a tour of the line between 5 a.m. and 7 a.m., detailed work, and reorganized the perimeter.

It was strange to be back among the old familiar sour smells and to be living on tinned rations without fresh meat or vegetables. Such a life below the surface of the ground had ceased with the Armistice six months before; yet here was the Regiment back at trench routine in a land of perpetual daylight, as if there had been no Armistice.

On the 9th " A " Company had its first casualty. A machine gun opened fire from the direction of the Brown Patch on to the Pimple and Banya posts, and wounded a man in the groin. The Brown Patch was a big expanse of burnt forest which extended the whole length of " A " Company's eastern flank on the opposite bank of the river. " B " Company in Nijni Kitsa was echeloned to the rear and unable to cover this flank. Though the Bolsheviks had no position on the right bank nearer than Kitsa, some miles upstream, they had the initiative to bring up light machine guns to the southern edge of the Brown Patch whence they could enfilade the position at Mala Bereznik with impunity. The forest undergrowth provided that cover which light machine gunners dream of but seldom find. From Mala Bereznik it was impossible to locate the enemy; only their general direction could be ascertained, and, though the river machine-gun post and the gunners searched likely places with fire and patrols went out from Nijni Kitsa, the Regiment never succeeded in catching any of the enemy in the act. The Bolsheviks employed similar tactics on the left bank. In the evenings and early mornings they had the habit of bringing up light machine guns to fire on Scots Hill and Summer House posts, and, though they never inflicted any casualties on " A " Company, they were a distinct nuisance.

Patrols went out during the twilight hours, between 11.30 p.m. and 1.30 a.m., and approached the Bolshevik position from all angles, hoping to take the enemy listening posts in rear. Patrolling was exciting but painful work. Head-nets could not be worn, but something had to be done to ward off the mosquitoes. Serjeant Bristow discovered that the bad margarine in the rations was effective, but the smell was so revolting that it was diluted with rifle oil. With this concoction the faces, necks and hands of the patrol were smeared.

The first long patrol went out in the twilight at 10.45 p.m. on the 10th from Scots Hill post, and took the line of the river bank. Descending into the little valley, it first encountered soft, swampy ground covered with spongy moss from which clouds of mosquitoes arose to the attack. Wading on, the patrol crossed the stream and ascended the higher ground in front of the enemy position. From here it crawled forward, waiting and watching in a magnificent position to scupper any enemy venturing to fire on the company's forward posts from the forest. Patience was one thing; the mosquitoes were another. Their continual whining, buzzing and humming made it impossible to listen. They danced into the men's eyes, ears and nostrils. The irritation was excruciating and more than human beings could be expected to endure for any length of time.

The men in the posts nearest the forest, such as Scots Hill, Coswick, Summer House and Wood posts, were tormented by mosquitoes. During the hours when the sun was least fierce—between 6 p.m. and 8 a.m.—they endured the tortures of the damned. At the end of forty-eight hours in the line many men could not see out of their eyes, and their hands were as swollen as if they had been inflated with bicycle pumps. But they suffered their trials with their usual good humour, and cursed the " ——— gnats " unceasingly.

Such was the heat that Captain Baines instituted unusual routine hours. The normal day when the heat drove the mosquitoes into the shade of the forest was spent under cover. The officers had breakfast at 11 a.m., lunch at 3.30 p.m., and dinner at 10 p.m., and after dinner the day's work began.

Occasionally between 4 p.m. and 7 p.m. the Bolsheviks shelled very erratically, but never did any damage. It was seldom that more than one out of six of their shells exploded in those days. One dud actually landed between Captain Baines's legs. Retaliation was invariably swift and effective, for the Russian gunners who covered Mala Bereznik were never so happy as when firing their English 18-pounders. These Russians were definitely loyal in those days, and were stout-hearted and very keen.

The artillery consisted of four 18-pounders, one 4.5 howitzer, and a 60-pounder, which outranged the Bolsheviks' guns and kept them at a respectful distance. The Bolsheviks were poorly supplied with artillery at this time, and appeared to have nothing bigger than Russian field guns.

On the 15th Lieutenant Giles took out a fighting patrol from Banya post to reconnoitre the enemy's forest flank. Discovering a sentry post, he took forward five men to surprise it; but the enemy opened fire with a machine gun and rifles, and he withdrew the patrol without incurring a casualty. This patrol proved that it was comparatively easy to approach within a few yards of the enemy without being detected.

Meanwhile, on the 11th, headquarters and two platoons of " D " Company had reached Ust Vaga, and on the same day the colonel and Captain Mason inspected Seltso with a view to moving Vaga Column headquarters forward from Ust Vaga.

On the 13th Captain Meade with two platoons of " C " Company left Ust Vaga by the routine steamer, and took over the defences of Seltso from one platoon of " B " Company.

Two days later Vaga Column headquarters moved to Seltso, leaving Ust Vaga to be held by two platoons from each of " C " and " D " Companies. The next day Forward Area Headquarters were abolished, and Major Carter left for Seltso. This relieved the congestion in Mala Bereznik, and left the shacks in Canadian Village free for company headquarters.

A Bolshevik of the 6th Soviet Regiment came over to Scots Hill post on the 17th and gave himself up to Serjeant Hunt. Lieutenant Trewheler managed to extract a certain amount of useful information from him, but he had been in the line only three days before deserting. That he was half-starved was quickly proved by his getting outside two canteens of tea, six Army biscuits and three rashers of bacon. And so ended " A " Company's first tour in the line.

There had been compensations for the heat of the day and the burden of the mosquitoes for those who could see and enjoy. The walks to and from the bathing-place near Burchill's post in that June spring were always delightful. It seemed that in a flash the forest had burst into life: fresh, young, green leaves on the silver birches, flowering shrubs, maidenhair ferns and sheets of golden anemones carpeting the mossy banks; the undergrowth, a mist of purple heartsease and violets; the smell of damp moss, as soft and spongy as a pile carpet, the woodland smells, and the coolth of the forest after a burning day, made the evening something to look forward to. " A " Company was a happy company with a very high morale.

Despite of great keenness on the part of all ranks, an encounter with the enemy was never effected; neither patrols, standing patrols, nor listening posts managed to ambush the elusive Bolsheviks.

On the 18th headquarters and two platoons of " C " Company from Seltso and two platoons from Ust Vaga relieved " A " Company, which crossed over to rest billets in Seltso. Here " A " Company had ten days of ideal weather with no responsibility. Bathing for all ranks in the rapidly falling river by day, and expeditions downstream in search of game by night, made the days pass quickly and happily. All the officers of the Regiment proper were gathered in one place, and there was little of war.

But where were the fish—the salmon and trout which had been reported to be so prolific before the expedition left England? And where were the flighting duck? Not on the Vaga. Certain enthusiasts, including the colonel, flogged the river every evening, but never caught anything more palatable than rudd, roach and perch. Fish and game were alike myths of fireside fabrication.

As the troops had not had fresh meat or vegetables since landing, the absence of fish and game was a serious loss. Rations consisted of bully beef, Maconochie, margarine—not always esculent—and a few biscuits. There was no bread because there was no yeast. As the river fell so canteen stores, always strictly rationed, became more difficult to procure, and so there was no means of varying the diet either of officers or men. It was left to the cooks to camouflage bully beef and concoct porridge from biscuits.

At Seltso the troops were introduced to a fearsome type of cleg, the size of a hornet, with black and orange stripes. They feasted and bit during the hours of sunlight and then handed over to the mosquitoes. As bathing was the chief recreation, they had splendid opportunities; and their bites were most painful, invariably drawing blood.*

The officers used to undress in their billet and, clad only in greatcoats, run down to the river, pursued by a host of " bloody bees," as the troops called them; then leap into the water, and rush back to safety without drying.

Those were halcyon days at Seltso. Nothing was allowed to spoil the enjoyment of the rest; even the news that the Regiment was to raid the Bolsheviks was taken light-heartedly and confidently. It would be a walk-over; why worry?

---

* A letter to *The Times* on blood-sucking flies, November 1934, states that " perhaps nowhere are these bloodthirsty insects a greater pest than in the forests of North Russia. So excessively numerous and aggressive are these flies in the Gdov district of the Leningrad Government during July that agricultural operations have perforce to be carried out at night; and in parts of Siberia, for the same reason, settlers have been compelled to abandon the infested zone."

CHAPTER XXIX.

I.—GENERAL SITUATION.

TRANSPORT DIFFICULTIES—COMMUNICATIONS—SITUATION ELSEWHERE—PLAN OF THE 43RD'S RAID—" A " COMPANY'S ROLE—THE RAID OF 26TH/27TH JUNE—ADVANCE TO IGNATOVSKAYA—BOLSHEVIK RESISTANCE—THE COMMANDING OFFICER'S GALLANTRY—CASUALTIES—PLIGHT OF THE WOUNDED—AFTERTHOUGHTS—" A " COMPANY DETAILED FOR SECOND RAID—THE ADVANCE THROUGH THE FOREST—THE ATTACK—CASUALTIES.

(*See Maps facing pages* 348, 366 *and* 384, *and on pages* 338 *and* 340.)

THE Vaga Column was subsidiary to the Dvina Column, which with the co-operation of the naval flotilla was in a better position to carry out major operations. The Regiment really provided flank protection to the main force. But no advance by the Vaga Column could influence the war to any appreciable extent. On the contrary, with the river falling, a lengthening of its communications with its base at Ust Vaga would have increased the difficulty of supply and put a severe strain on the transport, which consisted of only twenty-five drosky carts capable of carrying three hundred pounds apiece.

Lateral communication with the Dvina force had been proved impracticable on the 23rd June, when a mounted patrol of five other ranks under Lieutenant Eagle reconnoitred the Chamovo[1] trail and encountered deep swamps impassable by wheeled or foot traffic, when only six versts[2] from Nijni Kitsa.

The course of the Vaga was such that any advance would have increased the distance of these lateral communications without any compensating advantage except by decreasing the morale of the enemy, if that were possible.

Before being in a position to strike at the flank and rear of the Bolsheviks on the Dvina, the Vaga Column would have been compelled to fight its way to Shegovari and Evsyakovskaya whence the map showed trails leading to Yakovlevskoe and Puchega.[3] Whether these were any better than the Chamovo trail was extremely doubtful.

Apart from these facts, the situation elsewhere in Russia had not improved since the arrival of the Relief Force. Admiral Koltchak had shown

---

[1] A village on the left bank of the Dvina.
[2] A verst is 3,500 feet or roughly 1,200 yards—two-thirds of a mile.
[3] See Map No. 27, facing p. 384.

no signs of stemming the Bolshevik advance. His retreat from Viatka had balked an advance upstream to Kotlas, for there was now no hope of effecting a junction; besides which the Dvina was also falling rapidly, and the old problem of supply and transport would have been magnified by an advance. The Railway front, lying astride the Archangel—Vologda railway, appeared to provide the best line of attack, as supply was not dependent on the vagaries of a river; but this front was neglected, probably for very good reasons. The head-waters of the Vaga inclined towards this front many miles above Shenkursk.

Therefore General Ironside decided that raids should be made on the enemy's communications, and that Russians supported by British troops should carry them out. As yet the Vaga Column had no Russian troops attached to it.

II.—The Plan and the Raid.[4]

The plan was: on the left bank, to capture the Bolsheviks' front line at Mala Bereznik and proceed down the Moscow road to Ignatovskaya, spike their guns mounted on barges at Maksimovskaya still farther upstream, and then return to the original positions.

On the right bank, a small column was to enter Kitsa after the capture of Ignatovskaya, and then unite with the main column on the left bank and return to quarters.

The colonel decided that the raid should be carried out on the 25th by three companies, " B " on the right bank, and " A " and " C " on the left. On the 23rd he received an order to send back sixty-five non-commissioned officers and men under an officer to act as guard to General Headquarters which had lately arrived at Bereznik. " A " Company was warned to detail twenty other ranks two days before going into action. However, Providence intervened. General Ironside visited the Regiment on the 24th, cancelled the order then and there, and postponed the raid for twenty-four hours.

On the 24th the period of advertisement began, and lasted for two days. All day the guns barked and aeroplanes circled over the enemy positions dropping bombs. After a fortnight of tranquillity, such activity could only substantiate the information already received from their own agents in Ust Vaga which was a hotbed of espionage. All elements of surprise were eliminated by this system inherited from the German War.

The same day the colonel issued his orders: on the left bank two platoons of " A " Company were to capture the enemy's first position and under a protective barrage clear the road for the advance. The remaining two platoons of " A " Company were then to go forward as advance guard

[4] See Maps Nos. 25, facing p. 366, and 22, p. 338.

and engage the enemy at Ignatovskaya while " C " Company deployed to attack and capture the village. Meanwhile the first two platoons of " A " Company were to act as escort to the limbers for captured guns, aid post, sappers, and signal cart, and also as rear guard to the force advancing.

On the right bank, two platoons of " B " Company were to demonstrate in front of Kitsa to coincide with the main attacks and to act as escort to a section of 3.7 howitzers, 55th Mountain Battery, R.F.A., which was to be prepared to bombard Ignatovskaya on a timed programme unless otherwise ordered.

Artillery programme: six 18-pounders and three 4.5 howitzers[5] were to concentrate on the enemy's front line at Mala Bereznik from 11 p.m. to 11.5 p.m. while the two platoons of " A " Company were forming up. Barrage fire from 11.10 p.m. to 11.15 p.m., under which the platoons were to advance and capture the position.

At 11.15 p.m. to lift on to Moscow road and put down a protective barrage while the front line was being mopped up.

The 60-pounder to carry out long-range shoots on Ignatovskaya and Maksimovskaya.

Machine guns in Mala Bereznik were to co-operate with overhead fire on to the enemy front line and later to thicken the protective barrage. The trench mortars in Mala Bereznik and Nijni Kitsa were given the special task of bombarding a suspected blockhouse—known as Tin Hut—on the right of the enemy's front line. For this purpose the mortar in Nijni Kitsa was to take up a position on the Brown Patch.

The whole force was to start withdrawing at 3.30 a.m. Communication was to depend on a line run out from Mala Bereznik whence the C.R.A. was to transmit to Nijni Kitsa and so to the section of 3.7 howitzers, if need be.

Having received his orders, Captain Baines detailed the right half-company under Captain Naylor, consisting of Nos. 1 and 2 Platoons (Lieutenants Neville and Sturges), to the task of carrying the first objective. He gave Captain Naylor a free hand in the preparation of his plan.

After close study of the aeroplane photographs[6] Captain Naylor decided to attack the enemy's left flank by making a detour through the forest. Both platoons were to assemble in the forest at 10.30 p.m. and advance with No. 1 Platoon on the right as far as the hurdle fence, seven feet high, which protected the enemy's front and left flank. At this point No. 1 Platoon was to go farther forward with left shoulders up until reaching a point well on the enemy's flank and rear. At zero—11.15 p.m.—No. 1 Platoon with a

---

[5] One section of the 4th Russian Field Howitzer Battery, lent by Dvina Force.
[6] See Map No. 24, facing p. 348.

AEROPLANE PHOTOGRAPH OF THE BOLSHEVIK FORWARD POSITION.

Lewis gun on the right raking the enemy's trenches was to assault the two flanking positions, while No. 2 Platoon scaled the fence, also under Lewis-gun covering fire, and attacked the main line in enfilade. The plan was simple so long as direction in the forest was kept.

Meanwhile the left half-company under Captain Baines, consisting of Nos. 3 and 4 Platoons (Lieutenants Giles and Booth), was to assemble in the defences of Mala Bereznik and advance at 11.15 p.m.

The morning of the 26th was spent in discussing every detail of the plans while aeroplanes droned overhead on their way to bomb the enemy. At the end of the conference Captain Baines asked if there were any questions. Serjeant Bristow, with a broad grin on his jovial face, wanted to know whether " Chinks " were to be taken prisoners or otherwise disposed of. As the Bolsheviks were known to employ Chinese mercenaries[7] on account of their proficiency in the more refined forms of torture; and as they had been known to hand over prisoners to the Chinese when their own ingenuity failed them, it was unanimously agreed by all present that no trouble should be taken to preserve any Chinese prisoners from harm. On the other hand, the poor benighted Bolshevik was to be treated kindly, for he might be enlisted into the Slavo-British Legion as an ally. At the end of the conference Lieutenant Giles, with an air of detached boredom, voiced a bitter complaint that he had got " to walk the hell of a long way before he came into the scrap."

After a meal at 7 p.m. an anti-mosquito ointment, concocted by the doctor out of tar and lard, was issued to all ranks to smear on their hands, necks and faces. As a result, " A " Company looked very comical—more like a collection of seaside minstrels than fighting men—when it fell in at 8.30 p.m. in fighting order. Crossing the river in the routine steamer, the company fell out by platoons and waited for that last quarter of an hour before action.

At 9.15 p.m. Nos. 1 and 2 Platoons marched off past the artillery, whose Russian teams lolled among piles of shrapnel and high-explosive shells; then along the track through the rye fields and into the mosquito-infested forest; past Burchill's post and so to Canadian Village, where " C " Company dispensed hospitality.

After a quarter of an hour's halt the two platoons marched out of the forest into the open in single file down a camouflaged track into the trench leading to the Horseshoe post. Overhead hummed the aeroplanes on their last visit to the enemy. Suddenly there was a terrific crash behind the enemy's lines; then another—and another—until the Bolshevik position was blotted out completely in clouds of smoke and dust.

---

[7] These mercenaries were also responsible for the wholesale massacres of civilians.

THE VAGA FROM SELTSO TO MAKSIMOVSKAYA MAP No. 22.

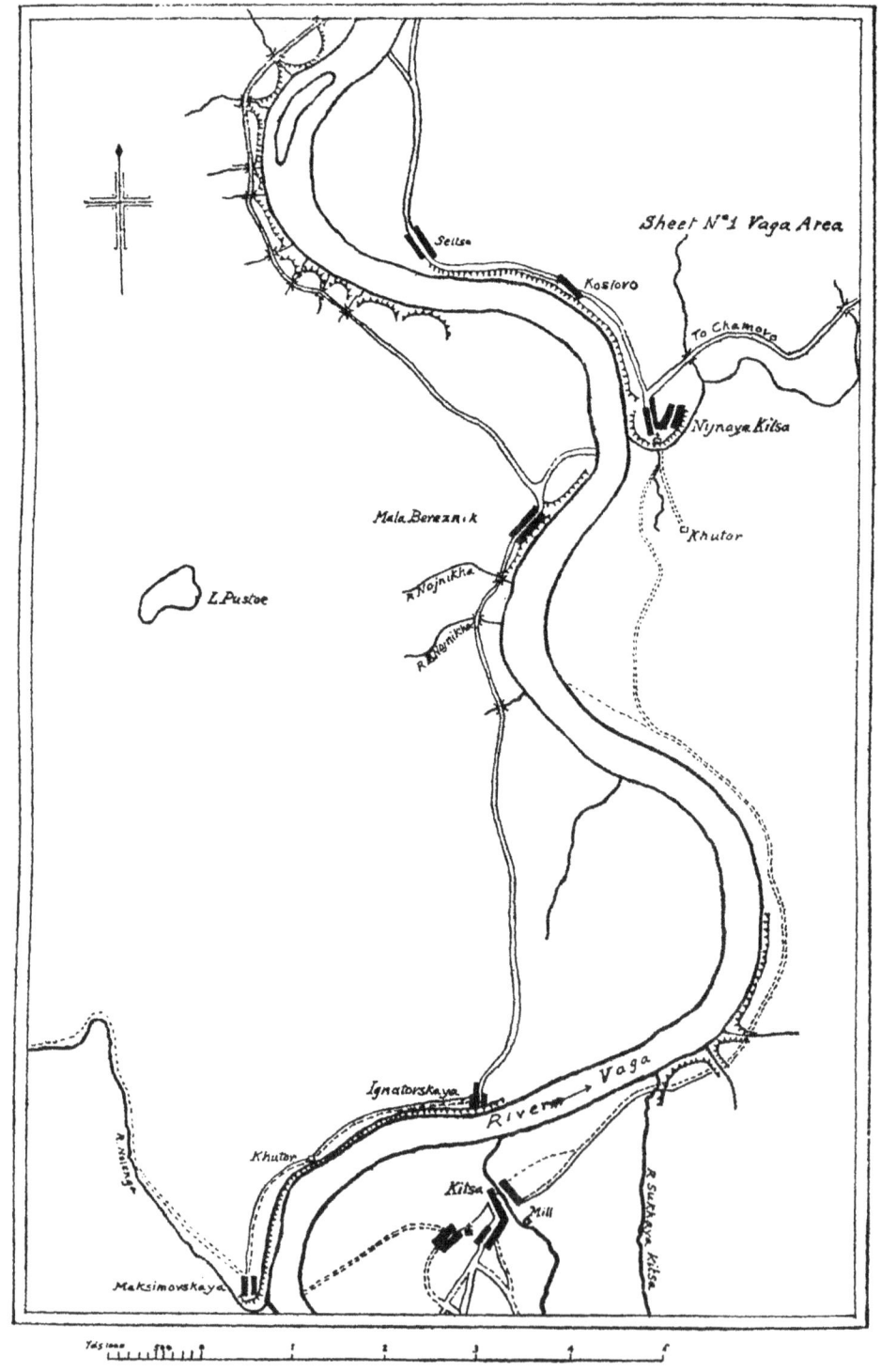

Punctually at 10.15 p.m. Lieutenant Neville led No. 1 Platoon out of Banya post through the wire into the pocket of dead ground in front of the Pimple, and so into the forest. By 10.30 p.m. the two platoons had assembled in the forest and the advance was begun in single file.

" I realized at that moment that we should be late on our jumping-off point.[8] My theoretical position was six hundred yards on Sturges's right, and he had to advance fifteen hundred yards before he reached his position. To my dismay, I realized that I had to lead my command over a mile through thick forest, taking necessary precautions in advancing; that I had to reconnoitre my jumping-off point; and that to do this I had only half an hour.

" Taking the bull by the horns, we floundered through the forest, chancing the presence of any Bolsheviks lying in ambush, and managed to get within two hundred yards of their position at 11 p.m.; from which point I was to advance still further to the right, and get well on the enemy's left flank. But before I could get my bearings the bombardment started.

" The noise was simply terrific when the guns and machine guns opened fire. The echo and reverberations of bursting shells and flying bullets were deafening, and, though there were only nine guns firing, it seemed as if there might have been nine hundred as the noise of each shot resounded through the forest."

By great ill-chance three shells in rapid succession crashed into the forest all round No. 2 Platoon, severely wounding Lieutenant Sturges in both legs and scattering the men of his platoon and three sections of No. 1 Platoon. At this moment the barrage ceased. " Then it was I found that there were only six men of the Lewis gun section behind me," wrote an officer. " I shouted to them to lie down, and went back to try to collect the rest of my platoon." There was " no sign of Naylor. . . . I collected a few men and advanced. . . . I found the Lewis gun team just as the bombardment stopped at 11.5 p.m., and we all lay down at the edge of the forest facing the front of the Bolo line. As soon as our guns stopped, the Bolos let fly into the forest with two machine guns. Bullets were cutting young fir trees in half and cracking and crashing through the forest like a young tornado." At 11.10 p.m. the guns opened fire again for the last five minutes, and the enemy fire ceased immediately. Lieutenant Neville's party then crawled forward to the high fence in front of the Bolshevik position. Meanwhile Captain Naylor had collected No. 2 Platoon and the rest of No. 1 Platoon; and, at the very moment when it was time to assault, suddenly appeared from behind. Scaling the high fence, the platoons attacked without opposition. The whole of the enemy line seemed to be deserted—but two machine guns were captured and seventeen very frightened Bolsheviks were

---

[8] *War Letters of a Light Infantryman*, p. 156.

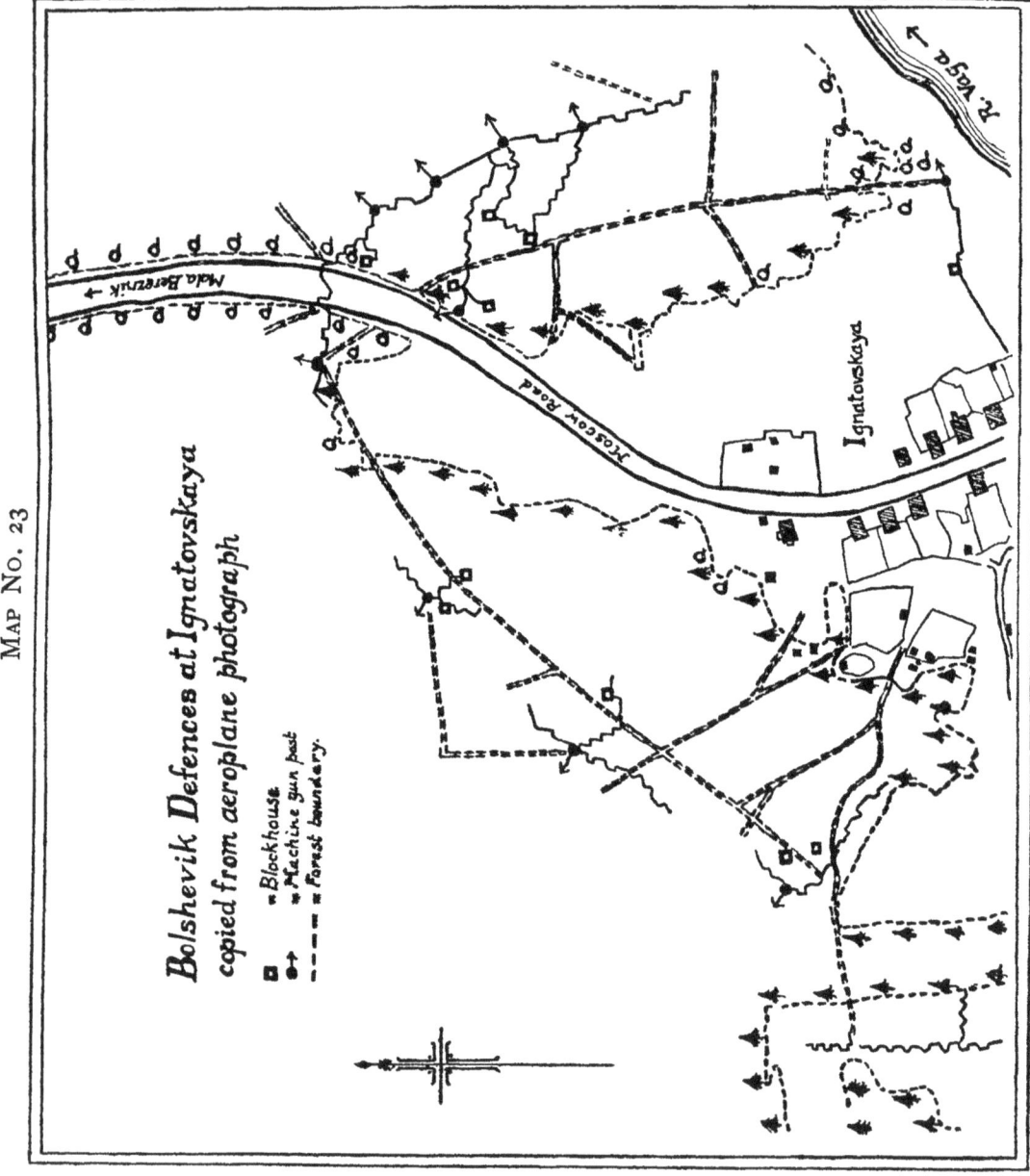

Map No. 23. Bolshevik Defences at Ignatovskaya copied from aeroplane photograph.

found cringing in funk-holes and were taken prisoners. While the leading platoons were mopping-up the first objective, Captain Baines, with Nos. 3 and 4 Platoons, passed through, but was held up until the protective barrage lifted. During the first attack the enemy concentrated all their guns on Nos. 1 and 2 Bridges in the little valley between the opposing positions. Though the shell fire was heavy, the left half-company managed to advance with the loss of one man slightly wounded.

As soon as the protective barrage lifted, Nos. 3 and 4 Platoons went forward as advance guard, followed by " C " Company, regimental headquarters, transport horses, gun teams for captured guns, and No. 1 Platoon as rear guard, while No. 2 Platoon remained in the first objective filling in the trenches, evacuating the wounded, and systematically destroying dugouts and equipment.

For a distance of about three miles the advance guard, with No. 3 Platoon (Lieutenant Giles) as van guard, and Serjeant Hunt's section as point, advanced without opposition, but on reaching the clearing in front of Ignatovskaya[9] the enemy opened heavy but inaccurate rifle and machine-gun fire. Thereupon the two platoons of " A " Company extended on each side of the road and worked forward by rushes to the Bolsheviks' wire which was strung out in a thin belt of forest in front of their position. On the left Serjeant White, platoon serjeant of No. 3 Platoon, tried to find the enemy's flank, and in doing so was shot in the head and killed instantly.

At this point they were held up, and the colonel sent forward " C " Company to capture the village. It was while he was explaining the situation to Major Northcote that Captain Baines, who had managed to survive the German War with a record of long and valiant service, was so severely wounded in the groin that later it was found necessary to amputate his right leg at Archangel.

Soon after 1 a.m. Major Northcote launched his company to the attack. With great gallantry the men tried to force their way through the enemy's line against heavy small-arm fire. In this attempt Second Lieutenant Hughes and a party of his men were shot down. Those who tried to extricate them were also shot down; and the colonel realized that the position could not be stormed without artillery support. But unfortunately all communication with the rear had broken down at the very inception of the operations when the enemy barrage so terrified the pony of the signal cart that it turned and bolted, to be no more seen.

The colonel was therefore compelled to rely on the prearranged time programme, whereby the section of 3.7 mountain howitzers from the right bank and all the artillery from Mala Bereznik were to open fire on Ignatovskaya between 1.45 a.m. and 2 a.m.

[9] See Map No. 23, opposite.

It was now past 1.30 a.m. and the firing line had to be withdrawn to safety while the artillery tried to cut the wire. Another effort to extricate the gallant Second Lieutenant Hughes—who was known to be severely wounded in the stomach—and his men before the bombardment was again frustrated by intense fire which killed or wounded every would-be rescuer.

Directly the bombardment began all enemy fire ceased abruptly; but the fire of the artillery was so weak and ineffective that, when " C " Company and Nos. 3 and 4 Platoons went forward to the assault the wire was still uncut; moreover, the cessation of the bombardment was the signal for the enemy to reopen intense and sustained machine-gun and rifle fire. It was now that the colonel ordered forward No. 1 Platoon—from reserve—to the edge of the clearing. Even at this distance from the firing line the enemy's bullets were kicking up the dust in the road all round regimental headquarters. The colonel, with his helmet tilted over his nose and a brightly coloured bandana handkerchief, soaked in tar and lard, hanging down over the nape of his neck, stood up in the open completely unperturbed and apparently oblivious of the fire. An officer wrote: " The Colonel was splendid, very cool and calm. It was not his fault that the show was not a howling success."

At about 2.30 a.m. No. 1 Platoon took up a position to cover the withdrawal; and at 2.50 a.m. the order was sent out to the front line to break off the engagement and retire through the rear guard.

All this time the enemy artillery had been strangely silent. But no sooner did the front line start filtering back than it opened fire on the road, luckily without inflicting casualties. The withdrawal was effected without incident, the pace being kept brisk by the enemy's chasing shell fire, and at 5 a.m. the column reached Mala Bereznik.

The casualties were:—

Killed—
    Second Lieutenant N. L. Hughes, Devonshire Regiment.
    9615 Serjeant John Henry White, M.M., 43rd Light Infantry.
    4 Other ranks, 43rd Light Infantry.
    1 Other rank, Machine Gun Corps.

Wounded—
    Captain C. S. Baines, D.S.O., commanding " A " Company, 43rd.
    Lieutenant O. H. M. Sturges, No. 2 Platoon, 43rd.
    Lieutenant W. Maunder, M.C., Devonshire Regiment.
    21 Other ranks.
    Lieutenant E. S. Browne (R.F.A.).
    3 Other ranks, Machine Gun Corps.
    1 Other rank, Royal Engineers.

Missing—
   7 Other ranks, of whom four were known to be wounded.

Though the casualties were light compared with those in the German War, they were considerably heavier than the column expected to suffer. The enemy's casualties, as ascertained later from a Bolshevik deserter, were 11 killed, including a regimental commander, and 50 wounded.[10] The result of the raid was a shock to all who had taken part; and there was little elation among the weary troops as they trudged through the dust down to the ferry and so to Seltso.

The journey of the stretcher cases from Ignatovskaya was an exact repetition of the journey of the wounded from Ctesiphon to Lajj. For three miles they were jolted in springless drosky carts over a road which was a road only in name. Captain Baines, severely wounded as he was, suffered indescribable agonies with every jerk of the cart. But on reaching Canadian Village he and Lieutenant Sturges were carried down to the hospital boat by Bolshevik prisoners. These were nothing more than impressed peasants without uniform; an unwashed, unshaved, underfed, malodorous, loathsome, and yet pitiful, mob.

There is nothing easier than being wise after the event, but the lack of success was due to the warning given to the enemy by bombing and bombardment; to the inadequate time allotted to the advance of the first two platoons whereby the Bolsheviks were not taken in flank and surprised before many had time to escape; to the delay to the advance on Ignatovskaya caused by the protective barrage; to the absence of a mounted party and howitzers on the left bank; and, above all, to the breakdown in communication.

Most of the mistakes were legacies of the German War, wherein bombardments and bombing became the natural preliminaries to an attack; wide turning movements were never possible; initiative, bluff and dash were at a discount. But in Russia there was no room for the old stereotyped forms of attack in which alone the troops had ever had any training. Held up by wire and without artillery to cut it, the best troops in the world can be expected to fail; and the Regiment was not strong enough to force its way through regardless of casualties. Such a procedure would have served no purpose. Doubtless the story would have been very different had a naval force been able to co-operate.

But with a vast forest at its disposal, providing the most wonderful covered approaches, it may well be asked why the Regiment did not fall upon the flanks and communications of the Bolsheviks without artillery support. On the face of it, it sounds a feasible suggestion. But those who

[10] See Appendix XVIII.

have never experienced forest fighting can have no conception of its difficulty nor of the length of time required to traverse trifling distances. It may be comparatively easy to surprise an enemy, but, by the same token, it is every bit as easy to be surprised when visibility is about fifteen yards; and the difficulty of keeping direction is almost insurmountable.

Nevertheless, on the way back to Seltso the colonel discussed with Captain Naylor plans for another raid on the Bolshevik first position—this time without any artillery support whatsoever—to be carried out the following week. It was obviously necessary to readjust the estimate of the enemy's power of resistance as advertised in England before the Regiment sailed. Their guns and machine guns had been surprisingly well served; and the enemy had repulsed a determined attack against all expectations. Before sailing, the Regiment had been told by those who professed to know, that the Bolsheviks invariably decamped on being attacked. Either the Relief Force troops had not the valour of the old, as alleged by *The Times,* or the Bolsheviks were better soldiers than had been reported. There is absolutely no doubt but that the Bolsheviks' morale had been underestimated.

III.—THE SECOND RAID.[11]

The casualties necessitated minor changes in " A " Company. Captain Naylor succeeded to the command, and Second Lieutenant Sawyer took over No. 2 Platoon. Lieutenant Giles became second-in-command, handing over No. 3 Platoon to Lieutenant Lowndes.

The weather remained torrid without so much as one hour of twilight; and the river continued to fall so rapidly that the routine boat which brought up rations, stores, and an occasional mail from Ust Vaga, ceased to run on the 28th. The following day Serjeant Warnock,[12] of No. 1 Platoon, embarked with twenty-nine men on a barge and floated down to Ust Vaga on the way to Bereznik for police and guard duties. The same day " D " Company headquarters and three platoons took over the defences of Mala Bereznik in relief of " C " Company.

On the 1st July a patrol of " D " Company reported that the enemy had reoccupied his front line; and then it was that the colonel decided to make another raid. The following day, when " A " Company was preparing to move up to Nijni Kitsa in relief of " B " Company, Captain Naylor warned Nos. 1 and 2 Platoons for action, as they knew the ground, or rather the forest.

The plan was essentially the same with the addition of one platoon from " D " Company, commanded by Lieutenant Colvill, 43rd. Now on the

---

[11] See Map No. 24, facing p. 348.
[12] He received the Meritorious Service Medal for his services at General Headquarters.

night of the 26th/27th June when the barrage broke up the formation of Nos. 1 and 2 Platoons, Serjeant Bristow, platoon serjeant of No. 2 Platoon, and four men from the rear files of the platoon got separated from the column and strayed through the forest in search of the Moscow road. In the course of their wanderings they happened upon a partially prepared position and a section of guns standing in a slight clearing with only two Bolsheviks in charge. Having ascertained the direction in which the enemy had retreated, Serjeant Bristow eventually managed to strike the Moscow road, and with his little party rejoined the column as it was returning to Mala Bereznik. But—a thousand pities—he never reported his adventure until reaching Seltso, and the opportunity of scouring the forest for the guns on the way back from Ignatovskaya was irretrievably lost. This information was of first importance, and Captain Naylor was ordered to find the new position and destroy it. Unfortunately Serjeant Bristow had very little idea of its whereabouts, but estimated it as being about four hundred yards behind the enemy's front line.

Captain Naylor—who was free to arrange the tactics of the raid—decided to start at midnight and work through the forest without a time limit. The attack was to be launched from the same flank by Nos. 1 and 2 Platoons—in that order from the right—which were to capture the two enemy flank posts and the trenches on the near side of the road; then Lieutenant Colvill's platoon was to go through as a second wave and capture the trenches and blockhouse on the far side of the road. The whole party was then to re-form at once and advance along each side of the road until reaching the partly constructed blockhouse in the middle of the road, at which point it was to reconnoitre for the new position. Having destroyed this, the raiders were to return along the river bank so as to avoid the barrage of the enemy guns which usually came down on Nos. 1 and 2 Bridges, and Scots Hill and Summer House posts.

The morning was spent in poring over aeroplane photographs, trying to recognize positions in the dark mass of forest.[13] The platoons were made up to thirty men each, and issued with bombs and wire-cutters, and all the impedimenta of modern war. After a late meal the platoons were ferried across the river in rowing-boats by Serjeant Swift and his henchmen. By 9.30 p.m. they reached Canadian Village and fell out for three hours, spent in explaining every detail of the plan to Lieutenant Colvill.

At 12.15 a.m., after a final application of the doctor's concoction of tar and lard, the platoons fell in in the dim twilight and made their way to Banya post whence they filed through the wire into the forest. Forming up in the forest with No. 1 Platoon on the right, No. 2 on the left, and the

[13] See Map No. 24.

platoon of " D " Company, detachment of Royal Engineers (Lieutenant Wakeford) and Intelligence party (Lieutenants Tamplin, R.F.A., and Tyrwhitt-Drake, 43rd) in rear of the centre, the raiders moved forward. Surprise being of paramount importance, the troops had been warned to pick their way carefully so as to avoid noise. Yet it seemed as if a herd of elephants were crashing through the undergrowth directly the column started to move. Before the raiders had advanced two hundred yards, three shots suddenly resounded through the forest. The column halted automatically, and Captain Naylor went forward to reconnoitre while the platoons followed within sight of him. Just when it seemed likely that the shots were mere coincidences, another three rang out in rapid succession. Again the column halted and lay down. Despite of all their care, the raiders knew that they had been spotted, probably when emerging from Banya post before entering the forest.

At this point Captain Naylor ordered Lieutenant Neville to lead off to the right, as he had farthest to go. Moving up a convenient ravine with flankers on his left, Lieutenant Neville led the column into the depth of the forest before wheeling to the left. With infinite care and caution the column toiled through the undergrowth, keeping to the ravines where possible; but the progress was tediously slow. By now it was impossible to recognize any landmark, as the column had deviated from the line of advance of the previous week, which hitherto had been faintly recognizable. There was now no alternative to advancing on a bearing. With his compass set to march south-south-east, and shorn of all steel trappings, the officer stood with his eye glued to the prism while the gnats swarmed all over his face. But when the view in the compass window consists of the trunks of trees, hundreds of trees of identical size, shape and colour, it is not easy to fasten on that one particular tree trunk which leads aright.

Suddenly the flankers reported seeing a Bolshevik about thirty yards to their left front. The column halted and the officer went forward to search the forest through his field-glasses, but there was not the sign of a soul. After this scare, however, the pace was slackened still more in order to reduce noise; yet the troops seemed incapable of moving silently. Even the snap of a twig seemed to sound like a pistol shot to straining and strained ears. Moreover, the nearer the column approached the enemy position the more the point and flankers saw men as trees, walking. At each alarm of " Hist! Bolo," the officer went forward to investigate. Each reconnaissance produced the same result—nothing but trees, trees and yet more trees, and never one on two legs. And each reconnaissance added to the delay, for the officer had to pick up his line before advancing again. The pace dropped from about five hundred yards an hour to barely three hundred, and the hours sped by. The forest was gradually becoming suffused with the rays of the rising sun; and still the column had far to go. But only space, not time, mattered on this venture. However, those behind, who had none of the anxiety and responsibility of leading and protecting the column, constantly urged the guide to move faster. In those days it was written in the little red books that the officer responsible for guiding a column on a compass march should be provided with a special escort whose duty it should be to protect him from the querulous and doubting questions of his superior officer.[14] Three times Captain Naylor came up to the head of the column and queried the direction of the guide and the distance traversed. Three times the guide replied that in his opinion the column was not yet on the flank and rear of the enemy.

At about 2 a.m. the column struck a path—narrow but well worn—which led in the right direction according to the guide's compass. Progress immediately became quicker and more silent. At this pace the guide reckoned that in half an hour it would be safe to wheel to the left and feel for the rear of the enemy's clearing. But once again Captain Naylor came forward to shake—albeit unwittingly—the fast-ebbing confidence of the guide, who diffidently suggested continuing for another half-hour. But Captain Naylor, over-ruling the suggestion, ordered Lieutenant Neville to turn left-handed and advance. Once off the path the noise increased considerably; surely the enemy could not fail to hear the ninety pairs of ammunition boots ploughing their way over and through the spalt brushwood and undergrowth. Gradually the forest thinned until at last daylight began to show between the trunks, betokening a clearing ahead.

Halting No. 1 Platoon, the officer took forward Serjeant Botley, Private Robbins and two men as scouts. Visibility increased considerably as the party advanced, but innumerable chips and twigs from felled trees made it impossible to move silently. Assuming that he was well in rear of the enemy's trenched position and that his chief concern was a reconnaissance with his right shoulder forward, the officer led the patrol more cautiously than ever, expecting at any moment to sight the enemy guns on his left front. " But when I was plumb in the middle of this clearing," he wrote, " I realized instinctively that my men were not following. I had a cold and lonely feeling. I looked round and saw them lying down on their bellies." Then it was that Serjeant Botley whispered "Bolos" and pointed to his right rear. As the scouts had seen mythical Bolsheviks all night, he ordered the patrol forward. " I had hardly uttered—when there was a cracking of whip-lashes all round me. In a split fraction of a second I must have turned about, for I just caught a glimpse of the machine gun which had fired at my back." With nothing worse than a wound in his arm and the cork removed from

---

[14] This useful instruction seems to have been omitted from *Infantry Training*, Vol. II, 1931, and *Field Service Regulations*, Vol. II.

his water-bottle, the officer made his swift way back to Captain Naylor, and reported what had occurred, but was unable to locate the exact position of the column or the enemy. One thing alone was certain and that was that it had not managed to elude the enemy's flank. Meanwhile the enemy was firing wildly into the forest with machine guns and rifles, and Captain Naylor, shouting at the top of his voice, could scarcely make himself heard above the echoing racket.

Eventually the platoons were deployed, bayonets were fixed and the whole line advanced. But so far from being on the flank of the Bolshevik position the raiders found themselves confronted with the seven-foot fence.

At this point Lance-Corporal Martin, with a Lewis-gun section of No. 2 Platoon, rushed forward and, resting his gun on the bottom rung of the fence, raked the enemy trenches at close range. Under this covering fire Captain Naylor and Serjeant Cleary rushed forward, scaled the fence and charged the machine gun which was still firing at them. Serjeant Cleary bayoneted one of the crew first and pressed his trigger afterwards, while Captain Naylor shot the last man of the gun's team through the head with his revolver. Following their gallant leaders, the troops swarmed over the fence and swept over the position. Unfortunately most of the garrison had fled before the attackers debouched from the forest and only one machine gun and eight dead Bolsheviks were found.[15] These were identified by Lieutenant Tamplin as belonging to the 156th Regiment.

Having mopped-up the position the raiders advanced six hundred yards up the Moscow road to the enemy's new position where Lieutenant Wakeford destroyed two blockhouses, while the raiders searched the surrounding forest for the guns without success. At 4 a.m. Captain Naylor withdrew his platoons by way of the river bank as arranged.

The Regiment's casualties were Lieutenant Neville, Lance-Corporal Lambourne and one other rank wounded.[16]

Once again the raid had not produced the results expected, but the difficulty of advancing through dense forest was further demonstrated, if that were necessary. Even with unlimited time at its disposal the column failed lamentably to avoid the enemy's flank.

There is little doubt but that the raiders were spotted during their approach march, but had the guide insisted on going deeper into the forest and continuing longer on his line, the raid must have succeeded in preventing the enemy's escape. However, the raiders hardly deserved the misfortune

---

[15] Later it was ascertained from deserters that on the night of the 2nd-3rd July two of the chief Bolsheviks of the 156th Regiment were killed, one being president of the regimental soviet (council).

[16] See Appendix XVIII.

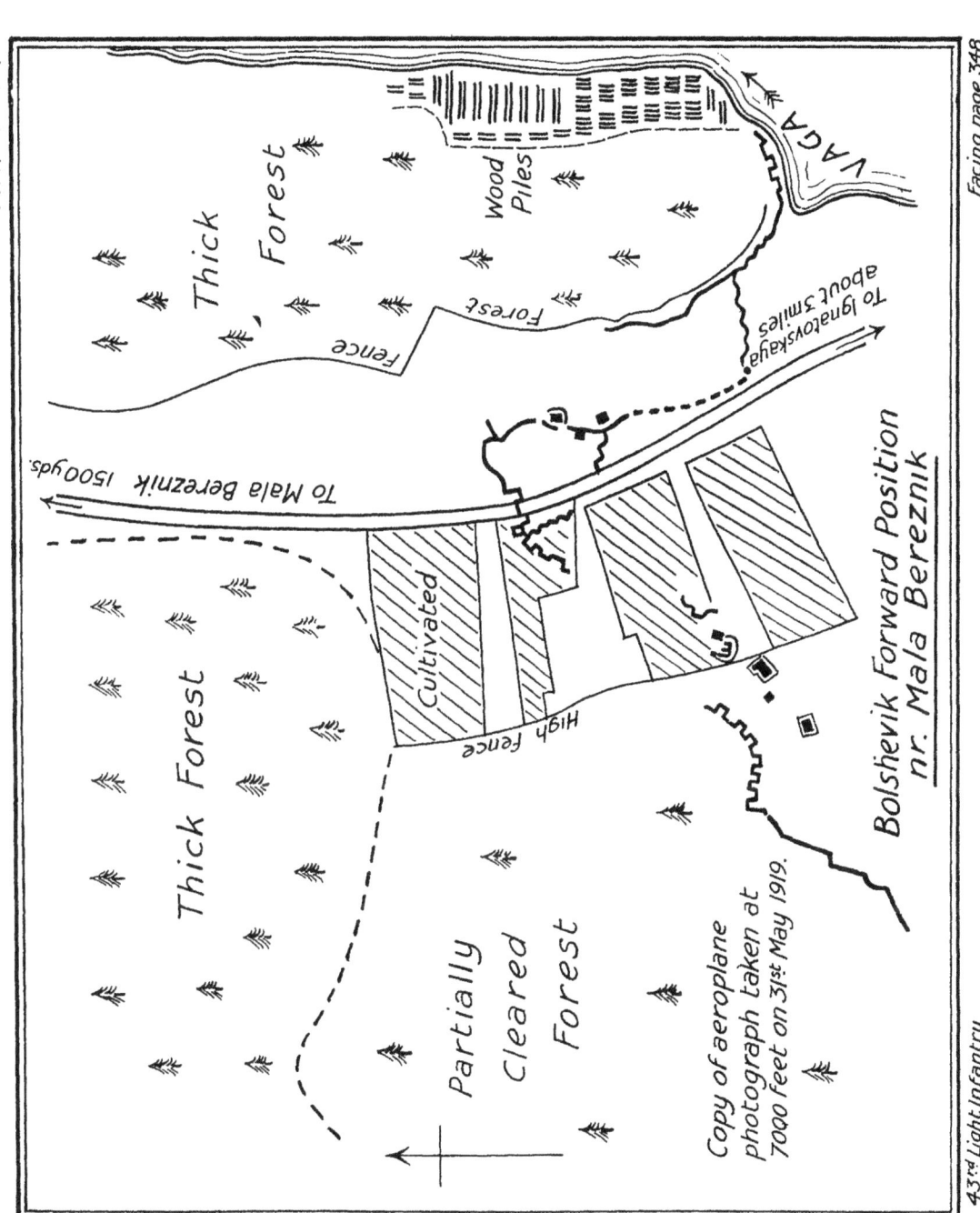

of finding only dead men in the forward position. Without a living Bolshevik to guide, the discovery of the gun position lay in Fortune's fickle favour.

Such success as the raid achieved was almost entirely due to the able and gallant leadership of Captain Naylor, who created order out of confusion under conditions of extreme difficulty. Without power to manœuvre, he managed to organize the attack of about ninety men strung out in file in the dense forest in an incredibly short space of time, and by sheer force of example led them forward. For this he was awarded a well-deserved bar to his *Military Cross*, and in the same *Gazette* 18556 Lance-Corporal Martin was awarded the *Meritorious Service Medal*.

CHAPTER XXX.

I.—THE MUTINY OF THE SLAVO-BRITISH LEGION.

DESCRIPTION OF THE POSITION—MUTINY OF THE SLAVO-BRITISH LEGION—A PRISONER RETURNS TO OUR LINES—THE BOLSHEVIK INTERNECINE BATTLE—LIFE AT NIJNI KITSA—FLIES, MOSQUITOES, CLEGS AND MONOTONY—RATIONS—HEALTH—MUTINIES ELSEWHERE—GENERAL SITUATION—PRESS CAMPAIGN AT HOME—GOVERNMENT DEFINES ITS POLICY—GENERAL IRONSIDE'S DIFFICULTIES—" D " COMPANY WITHDRAWN FROM VAGA COLUMN TO KONETZBOR—GENERAL HEADQUARTERS RETURN TO ARCHANGEL—VAGA COLUMN UNDER DVINA FORCE'S ORDERS.

(*See Maps facing pages 366 and 384, and on pages 338 and 376.*)

On the 4th July " A " Company took over the defences of Nijni Kitsa on the right bank from " B " Company, which went into rest with headquarters and two platoons at Seltso and two platoons at Koslovo.

Nijni Kitsa[1] was a wonderful natural fort standing on high ground and commanding all the approaches from the forest. The southern front of the perimeter, looking towards the Brown Patch, lay on top of a steep bluff at the bottom of which ran a purling stream wide enough to provide a natural obstacle, and well wired. On this front there was a field of fire of about fifteen hundred yards, but towards the eastern front it diminished where the forest encroached on the bluff, but here the stream still gave protection. On the north-eastern and rear fronts the ground was flat but open and well covered by machine guns. As a position it was almost impregnable without a very heavy bombardment, and even then the mutually supporting posts were scattered over such a wide area that the odds were against a bombardment, except by many more guns than the enemy possessed, doing any damage. Here for ten weeks " A " Company lived a life of undiluted monotony.

On the 8th July tidings of a serious mutiny of Russian troops on the Dvina came through to Seltso. Though it did not actually affect the Regiment on the Vaga where there was no Russian infantry, it put a completely different complexion upon the conduct of the whole campaign.

In England *The Times* announced on the 5th that M. Tschaykovski's Government would be able to maintain itself in the Archangel and Murmansk districts without assistance from the British before winter set in; and that if its hopes were realized there would be no British troops in North Russia

---

[1] See Map No. 26, p. 376.

1. Patrol of the transport section on the Chamovo Trail.
2. Koslovo Village.
3. Capt. Peck crossing the footbridge from Koslovo to Gunner Lines.
4. The Vaga River from Nijni Kitsa.
5. Group of Officers at Nijni Kitsa.

From left to right.—Lieutenant Booth; Lieutenant Lowndes; Second Lieutenant Sawyer; Lieutenant Neville; Lieutenant Giles; Lieutenant Hamilton; Lieutenant Burnett, Machine Gun Corps; Captain Naylor; Lieutenant Trewheler, King's Own Royal Regiment, interpreter.

by the end of the year. When, exactly twenty days later, *The Times* published an account of the mutiny of the Slavo-British Legion, public attention, sated with peace celebrations, peace marches, and peace treaties, was once again directed to the thorny situation in North Russia.

The Slavo-British Legion at the time of the mutiny was billeted between Topsa and Troitsa. There was not the slightest sign that a conspiracy was being hatched. Far from it. The Legion was expected to render a good account of itself; many of the men had actually fought against their former comrades so well that they had been decorated.

" Between 2 and 3 o'clock the firing began. The officers were resting in billets, but the Colonel—B. C. Wells—and Captain A. F. Burke were at Battalion headquarters. . . . Captain A. E. M. Finch, of the Seaforth Highlanders, was the first to be shot. The assassin fired at him through the window as he lay asleep in bed. . . . There were two other British officers in the billet with Captain Finch—Lieutenant G. W. Gosling, M.C., and Lieutenant Bland. They rushed out into the village street, only to be killed before they could get twenty yards away. The next victim was Lieutenant T. C. Griffiths, and then the mutineers attacked Captain D. B. Barr," who, " defenceless, made for the river. They fired volley after volley, and, with ten wounds, the young officer dived into the water and swam out to the monitor, five hundred yards away. No one shall say how he was able to perform the feat, for he was lacerated in two vital places. But he reached the boat, was taken on board, and conveyed the same morning to the hospital barge at Bereznik. He did not recover sufficiently to give any statement. . . . Eight or nine Russian officers were murdered before the mutineers were subdued. Nearly two hundred of the ex-Bolsheviks escaped into the woods, but cavalry went in pursuit and . . . thirty-five were captured. At one moment there was a danger of another Russian battalion being infected with the spirit of revolt. The ex-Bolos, after murdering their officers, ran towards a machine gun company, crying, ' We have killed the officers. You had better join us.' "[2]

Meanwhile General Grogan in Topsa, realizing that something terrible was happening, ran out in his pyjamas to the gun lines and, with the help of the C.R.A., fired a 4.5 howitzer into the howling mob of mutineers. This had the desired effect, for the mutineers immediately made tracks for, and dispersed into, the forest. Two companies of the 46th Royal Fusiliers hastily embarked at Osinova and took over the line at Troitsa, held by a skeleton force of sailors and marines which had been landed from the naval flotilla. " Eventually the line was consolidated, and fears of another outbreak were dispersed by the disarmament of all Russian troops."[3]

[2] *The Times*, 25th July, 1919.
[3] *Bolos and Barishniyas*, by Captain Singleton-Gates, p. 25.

The mutiny was a sad blow to General Ironside, who had believed in the sincerity of the Legion and in its capacity to form the nucleus of the Russian Army of the North. The loyal Russian officers, however, never believed in the scheme of turning Bolshevik prisoners to account. Their view was that the British, who came out professedly to help the loyal Russian Army, were greatly to be blamed for the mutiny: that the British had not tried to understand the Russian character, had been theatrical in their efforts to overcome Bolshevism, and the murder of five British officers by the mutineers was a natural result of moral weakness.[4] The difficulty in the formation of the Slavo-British Legion had been the supply of officers. There were very few officers of the old Tsarist Army available, and General Ironside had been forced to create officers from the shopkeeper class in Archangel. To supervise the training and to institute British methods of treatment of the men, British officers had been drafted into the Legion. But among the raw Russian officers were some of pronounced Bolshevik tendencies. These and any others so inclined were to be weaned from their political opinions, it was hoped, by the British system of fair dealing. The Russians did not understand British methods. From time immemorial they had been treated like cattle by those in authority; and they understood that treatment and no other. After the butchery the Russian officers voiced their opinions: " You blamed us for harshness, but that is the only way to deal with these people. These people do not understand kindness; and what they do not understand they suspect."[4] Accustomed to the flat of a scabbard across their cheeks if they were dirty on parade and to being knocked through the ranks for failing to look an inspecting officer in the eye, they considered the treatment meted out to them under the British code to be a direct sign of the pusillanimity of the officers; and that such men were certainly not fit to be officers. Like their ancestors, they became savages, lusting for blood. The Russian serjeant-major was foully done to death. Having cut his throat, the mutineers hacked off his arm with an axe when he put his hand up to close the gash. He was then dragged down to the river where they proceeded to castrate and disembowel him while still alive.

Part of the conspiracy luckily miscarried; the mutiny was to be the signal for the enemy to attack and destroy all the British and loyal Russians in the forward positions.

The outstanding result of this mutiny at the time was to make all Russians suspect. On the Vaga the only Russian troops were the gunners, who, time and again, had proved themselves staunchly loyal. But, with the mutiny, future propensities were apt to discount past services, and good and bad Russians were naturally tarred with the same brush. Should the gun-

[4] *The Times.*

ners suddenly mutiny, they might do incalculable damage, but their position, flanked by Koslovo and with Seltso in their rear, would soon be made very unpleasant. Therefore, on the Vaga, the Regiment felt comparatively secure.

On the 14th a corporal of the Royal Scots, attached to " C " Company, who had been captured in the raid on Ignatovskaya, came in to Scots Hill post. When questioned by Lieutenant Tamplin, the intelligence officer, he spun a specious yarn: after capture the prisoners had been taken to Kitsa whence he alone had been taken to the Bolshevik brigade headquarters at Shegovari. There he had been put on to work; and while the two Bolshevik officers who guarded him were absent he had slipped away and walked thirty versts along the river bank to Mala Bereznik. He produced photographs of himself sitting at a table spread with food and drink, and another arm-in-arm with the two officers. Tamplin soon perceived that he was prevaricating, and eventually extracted the true version. Since capture he had had only a small piece of bread and a little soup once a day; under this treatment the Bolsheviks prevailed on him to accept their terms of freedom which were that he should spread their propaganda in the Regiment. He was to tell the troops that everything that they had been told about the Bolsheviks was untrue; that the campaign was being conducted solely by the officers and senior non-commissioned officers who had a vested interest in it; that he was to incite the troops to hold soviets and issue their own orders; and that they should deal with their officers as the Slavo-British Legion had dealt with theirs, by murder. In actual fact the Bolsheviks had released him from their front line and had told him to carry on their evil work. He brought tidings of the other prisoners, who, he said, were being systematically starved.

On the 10th Lieutenant Denham, with thirty men of " D " Company, patrolled through the forest on the left bank, and found the enemy front line empty and dismantled. Continuing up the Moscow road for two hundred yards the patrol came under machine-gun and rifle fire from the direction of the river, and thereupon withdrew with one man wounded.

On the 16th two deserters[5] surrendered at Mala Bereznik and gave the information that the 6th Soviet Regiment was to relieve the 156th Regiment that night. The colonel therefore ordered a patrol action with artillery co-operation. At 10 p.m. when Lieutenant Denham left Scots Hill post the guns opened an intermittent bombardment on Ignatovskaya and the Moscow road. At 11 p.m. they switched on to the enemy advanced position. Under cover of the shell fire No. 16 Platoon then advanced through the forest,

[5] One deserter, once a platoon commander on the Dvina, had been an ardent Bolshevik until he was court-martialled and sentenced to fifteen years' hard labour because his platoon had run away. As all convicted criminals, both military and civilian, were automatically conscripted and as the families of convicts were also struck off rations, this man was completely disillusioned.

but, finding that it was too dark to observe the enemy's new position, Lieutenant Denham withdrew at 11.45 after firing a burst of rapid fire in the direction of the enemy. Thereafter ensued a battle royal. The Bolsheviks replied with guns, machine guns and rifles for over two hours. Firing was distinctly heard at Ignatovskaya and Kitsa long after " D " Company's patrol had returned to Mala Bereznik at 12.15 a.m. Later, on the 28th, it was gathered from a deserter that the bombardment of the advanced position caused the men of the 156th Regiment to scuttle back to Ignatovskaya, where the 6th Soviet Regiment met them with a hail of fire; not to be outdone, the 156th returned the fire; and altogether sixteen Bolsheviks were killed. After the internecine battle, it was given out that the British had attacked Ignatovskaya and had been repulsed with the loss of sixteen killed.

For " A " Company at Nijni Kitsa July was a dull month. Occasionally a Bolshevik patrol would open fire on the southern posts from the Brown Patch, and the reserve platoon from billets in the village would rush out and try to engage it, but never with any success.

On the 23rd " B " Company relieved " D " Company in Mala Bereznik and two platoons of " C " Company, under Captain Meade (43rd), took over Koslovo. A patrol of " B " Company under Lieutenant Clews went out at 11 p.m. on the 30th and, finding the enemy's position unoccupied, proceeded to dismantle the wire entanglements. While examining the trenches on the left of the road Lieutenant Clews saw a Bolshevik watching him from the bushes. Drawing a bead at a venture, he shot him; whereupon eight or nine Bolsheviks broke cover and doubled away; of these he shot two while the rest escaped into the forest. Soon after, the patrol reported that the enemy was working round the other flank, so Lieutenant Clews withdrew to Mala Bereznik.

From these records it will be seen that there was very little offensive action during July; but the Regiment was conducting an active defence. Though the troops had little fire to endure, the conditions on the Vaga were none too pleasant. The torrid heat continued throughout July with an occasional thunderstorm to lay the dust. The mosquitoes and " bees " continued to bite and buzz, and flies—like the flies in Mesopotamia—waxed abundantly in numbers. Added to these, sand-flies made their appearance to laugh at the meshes of a mosquito-net by night.

After the routine boat ceased to ply between Ust Vaga and Seltso owing to the low state of the water, rations and stores were brought up by convoys of hired droskies under civilian drivers. Strung out along the forest track, the small escort of ten men of the Regiment was unable to supervise and control the drivers who knew as little of English as the escort of Russian. The result was that at the halts the drivers invariably managed to pilfer and hide in the forest rations and stores—especially whisky—which they picked up on their return journey. Not once did rations arrive at Seltso complete during the time that they were conveyed by road.[6] On the 13th July the first and last consignment of fresh meat arrived. This Captain Mason buried as soon as volunteers from Headquarter Company had carried it ashore.

It was in July that the medical authorities, fearing an outbreak of scurvy, issued instructions for the artificial germination of tinned peas. A demonstration was given by Captain Mason and the quartermaster's storeman, Private Sadler. Representatives of all the companies were bidden to attend. With the instructions in his hand, Captain Mason read out:—

"A blanket is to be saturated thoroughly in water."

"Whose?" asked Captain Carr of the trench-mortar battery.

Silence.

"Lay out the saturated blanket in the sun and pour the contents of a tin of peas on one half of the blanket."

As if by numbers, Private Sadler decanted the shrapnel and spread out the "bullets."

"The unused half of the blanket is now folded over the peas, thus; and left for at least twenty-four hours. Only germinated peas are to be used for subsequent cooking."

Greatly impressed, the representatives dispersed to conduct *Organized Germination* within their own commands. The authorities proposed but the peas disposed. Having begged, borrowed or stolen blankets, the captains of companies attempted to carry out their instructions, but no amount of damp dalliance ever succeeded in arousing so much as a flicker of a flutter in the hearts of those obdurate Army peas. But though there was no germination there was likewise no scurvy.

Bread was another difficulty. Occasionally flour came up with rations. As there was no yeast, the Regiment was bidden to mix the flour with the froth of beer—when there was any beer to froth. This failed lamentably, and the little slabs of unleavened bread looked what they were—bricks, and fit only to be fired out of a gun.

Soon—all too soon—after the Regiment's arrival on the Vaga the "in lieus" made their appearance. Everything that was issued was in lieu of something that was not but should have been. Biscuits in lieu of bread, dates in lieu of jam, lard in lieu of margarine, etc. The men took the rations philosophically and with their usual good humour so long as there was a meal to be made off them. Later they were definitely neither good nor sufficient. Then the changes were rung by the practical-joke department: bully in lieu of Maconochie became Maconochie in lieu of bully, and so on.

[6] The Quartermaster often found cases of Maconochie deficient of a dozen or more tins, though the cases were outwardly intact.

The health of the troops was indifferent. Lack of exercise and recreation, continual front-line work and poor rations tended to lower their morale; and their bodies began to suffer from diarrhœa and boils. To counter these complaints fishing expeditions in search of fresh food were made in the only boat at Koslovo. It was found that a trench-mortar bomb dropped overboard in midstream caused havoc among the fish, and rendered sufficient fresh food for a breakfast. On one occasion the officers of " A " Company landed by this means a 20-lb. pike. Legitimate fishing never produced big enough catches to supply the mess.

On the 16th lateral communication between the right and left banks of the river was greatly improved by the completion of the foot-bridge between Koslovo and the gunner lines. This bridge—known as Wakeford's Bridge—was out of sight of the enemy lines in the elbow of the river, and was effectively commanded by a post on the bluff, supplied by the garrison of Koslovo.

II.—Political and Military Aspect in July.

It was not until the 25th July that the report on the mutiny of the Slavo-British Legion was published in England for political and military reasons. The reasons were not far to seek: the mutiny on the Dvina was followed by others; supposedly loyal Russian troops handed over Obozerskaya on the Railway front to the Bolsheviks; Russians mutinied and Onega fell into Bolshevik hands; and it was not until the situation was restored that the publication of the tidings was allowed. Of one thing there was no doubt. Bolshevism was in the ascendant. The situation elsewhere in Russia contributed to this rise in Bolshevik morale. The Esthonians and Finns had been checked in their advance on Petrograd, and Denikin's successes in the Crimea and South Russia where he had captured Kharkoff were discounted in the east by the retreat of Koltchak whose right wing had been pushed out of Perm, and whose centre was well east of Ekaterinburg by the end of the month.[7] There is no doubt but that Koltchak's failure caused the recrudescence of Bolshevism in the north; added to which the publication on the 5th July of the intended withdrawal of the British from Archangel forced Russians of all political persuasions to reconsider the potentialities. General Ironside's intended drive up the Dvina to Kotlas on the 15th had been frustrated by Koltchak's retreat and the scarcity of water in the river. What had the Russians to hope for from the White Guards? Denikin alone was successful, but he was hundreds of miles away and might not survive. It therefore behoved most of the Russians to start ingratiating themselves with the future rulers of the country lest retribution should overtake them unawares. In England the Press, at frequent intervals throughout July, urged

[7] See Map No. 20, p. 321.

the Government to declare its policy with regard to Russia. It was obvious, it said, that Germany was exploiting the Bolshevik revolution to her own ends; that the down-trodden people would appeal to Germany for help when they at last rose, as rise they must, against their tyrannical oppressors. Then would Germany step in, and by restoring order out of chaos gain the everlasting gratitude of the Russians. It was even said that many Germans were awaiting a mandate from the League of Nations for the rehabilitation of Russia.

When, therefore, the news of the mutinies was broadcast, the Press again took up the challenge. The expedition became the shuttlecock of party politics. There were those who clamoured for the immediate evacuation of North Russia while others pressed for reinforcements to be sent out at once to support the Relief Force, whose position was represented as being fraught with danger. *The Times* in a leading article said that the military situation in Northern Russia was worse than it was at the beginning of the year when the appeal was made for volunteers, and that there was a very serious danger of a first-class military disaster.[8] It pointed out that the disgrace of withdrawal would redound to the prestige of Bolshevism not only in Russia but in Asia, where signs were not wanting of Bolshevik intrigues in Afghanistan and Turkey; that the British could not withdraw without dishonour. " It has never yet been said with justice that we were false to our friends, and it must not be said now." Strong letters were written to the papers urging the immediate dispatch of winter clothing and a complete division of troops whilst yet there was time.

On the 30th the Government at last declared its policy. Mr. Winston Churchill, Secretary of State for War, stated that it had always been the intention of the Government to evacuate Archangel before another winter set in; that the Russian Provincial Government had been so informed; and that everything necessary for the safe extrication of the troops and those Russians whose lives depended on British protection had been ordered and was in process of preparation.

This declaration appeased the demagogues as much as it astounded the Russians. It so eased the consciences of the dockers that they permitted stores to be loaded for dispatch to Archangel,[9] but at the same time it doubled or trebled the difficulties of General Ironside's task. The Press at home discussed his movements, disclosed his intentions, and gave him good advice on how to conduct this complex campaign.

What had been suspected was confirmed: the Russians could expect no solid help from perfidious Albion who had used them to serve her ends, to

[8] July 25th 1919.
[9] The canteen in Archangel had been forced to close down in July because dockers refused to load stores bound for the troops fighting Bolsheviks.

contain the Germans in the last year of the war, and was now relegating them to their fate. Those Russians who wavered in their allegiance declared for Bolshevism, foreseeing the day of wrath to come. General Ironside was forced to abandon his original plan of establishing a sound position by means of Russian troops backed by British. Henceforth he could rely on British alone, and merely hope that those Russians still under arms would refrain from shooting him in the back.

With troops of doubtful loyalty under his command, his communications, always precarious, were rendered still more vulnerable; added to which the river was almost unnavigable in places owing to the low water and shifting sandbanks. Troops had to be withdrawn to guard the threatened spots. The 67th (Hampshire) Regiment was sent downstream to meet a threat towards Pinega; and on the 25th " D," the Royal Berkshire Company of the Regiment, was sent down to Archangel for an unknown destination,[10] its place being taken by the headquarters and two companies of the 3rd/4th North Russian Rifles.[11]

The Dvina front was now held by General Sadleir-Jackson's Brigade, consisting of the 45th and 46th Battalions The Royal Fusiliers, and one machine-gun battalion. It was with this force and the Vaga Column that General Ironside decided, like Sir John Moore, to strike the enemy hard and, under cover of the success, to hand over the line to the Russians and then withdraw. Captain Wyld, of the Regiment, then brigade major to General Sadleir-Jackson, came over from Kurgomin to Seltso to discuss the plan on the 26th. The Regiment was now under the immediate command of General Sadleir-Jackson, who had replaced General Grogan. The latter had been sent downstream to meet the Pinega threat; and General Headquarters had left Bereznik for Archangel.

---

[10] Headquarters and three platoons, " D " Company, were employed at Konetzbor on the Archangel–Onega road to guard the flank ; one platoon remained at Bereznik on guard duties, and later went to the Seletskoe front on the Emtsa River with three platoons of " C " Company under Captain Meade. See Map No. 21, p. 322.

[11] One platoon was attached to " A " Company in Nijni Kitsa. Captain Naylor promptly disarmed the men and used them to dig trenches.

CHAPTER XXXI.

I.—August on the Vaga.

Signs of offensive—Withdrawal of Russians from Vaga Column—Heavy kits sent downstream—The attack by Dvina Force—The Vaga Column ordered to co-operate—Weather breaks—Vaga Column's attack postponed and later cancelled—Patrolling—Two platoons of " C " Company withdrawn to Seletskoe—" A " Company takes over Koslovo in addition to Nijni Kitsa—Departure of the 60-pounder—Russian desertions—Withdrawal postponed—Plan of withdrawal—Captain Wyld's visit—General situation—Demonstrations on the Vaga Column—Bolsheviks bombard Mala Bereznik.

(*See Maps on pages* 322, 338 *and* 376, *and facing pages* 366 *and* 384.)

At the end of July Captain Naylor received a message from regimental headquarters intimating that information had been received of a projected enemy attack on Nijni Kitsa on the night of the 31st July/1st August. All that night " A " Company stood to arms ready to give the Bolsheviks a warm welcome, but nothing happened to dispel the monotony until the afternoon of the 1st, when shots were fired from the rye fields on to the forward face. But it proved to be a false alarm and the company, thankful for a small diversion, resumed the monotonous routine. Yet there were signs early in August of offensive action. Suddenly, on the 3rd, the ration of Russians was withdrawn from Nijni Kitsa to go, it was rumoured, to take part in an offensive on the Dvina front. " A " Company was not sorry to see the last of this consignment of allies of doubtful quality. Though Captain Naylor had segregated them in small parties every evening for work in the posts under supervision, it was always felt that the company harboured a potential scorpion in its breast. The two Russian officers, with close-cropped, bullet heads and sprouting beards, were a quiet couple who spoke no French so that communication was confined to dumb show. Unlike their countryman—one Cheryepanoff of the gunners—they drank no whisky and neither required nor expected a traditional Russian welcome. Cheryepanoff had, on a previous occasion, drunk a month's supply of " A " Company's whisky when he called in on the mess to borrow a candle. When eventually this gallant ally staggered out of the mess he was completely incapable of carrying out his instructions to observe a shoot. To him that was a matter of no consequence, for such was the Russian sense of duty.

Three days later suspicions were confirmed when six old and two brand-new 18-pounders and four 4.5 howitzers came up from Bereznik to reinforce the artillery, and the C.R.A. was ordered out to find an observation post on the Kitsa trail whence a forward observing officer could see Ignatovskaya and Maksimovskaya, as well as Kitsa. This entailed a trek of about three miles along the forest track, and then a wait for a couple of hours while the gunner officer, perched in a tree, registered the guns. Then a wearisome march back winding up the telephone lines.

On the 8th orders were received to pack heavy kits and kit-bags and send them down to Seltso whence they were to go back to Archangel. This done, the stage was set for the final offensive to cover the evacuation. The men of " A " Company, however, put a different interpretation on this activity, and shouts of " Roll on, the good ship *Czar*," were frequently heard when the kits were being stacked. The officers smelt brimstone, but knew nothing for certain; only that the taciturn captain was even more silent and solemn than usual. The usual rumour came up with rations that the Regiment would be clear of the Vaga by the 15th,[1] and on the truth of it C.Q.M.S. Lawrence offered to wager 200 roubles. Luckily for him no one took the bet.

Up to the 6th the weather had been superb, hot by day and considerably cooler by night; and the plague of mosquitoes and " bees " had noticeably abated, but early on the morning of the 10th, when a distant rumbling from the east betokened a heavy bombardment on the Dvina, the weather, stormy for the past few days, suddenly broke, and sheets of driven rain began to fall. At breakfast Captain Naylor warned the officers of " A " Company that the Vaga Column was to attack on the 13th, by which time a column of 2,500 men would be marching through the forest from the Dvina to take the Bolsheviks in rear at Shegovari; that two platoons from Nijni Kitsa and three platoons from Mala Bereznik were to co-operate with this movement by attacking Kitsa and Ignatovskaya respectively.

All day the rain, driven by a high wind, fell in dismal torrents, turning the dusty tracks into runnels of liquid, slimy mud, while in the dank forest the rain, broken by the interlocking branches, dripped incessantly and monotonously on to the undergrowth.

In the evening an encouraging message was received from the Dvina, three hundred prisoners and a gun having been captured. The following day the number of prisoners swelled to eight hundred with twelve guns; and on the 12th, Y day for the Vaga Column, the total reached 1,500 and more coming in to the cages. Late on the evening of the 10th, however, the Vaga Column's attack was postponed as the result of the foul weather, the tracks

---

[1] This was actually the day first appointed for the evacuation.

through the forest being no longer passable. On the 12th it was definitely cancelled and the troops had to resign themselves to wretched monotony once more.

Bereft of their kits and a change of clothing, the troops tried to fulfil their destiny by being patient and by checking the hourly rise in the river which would allow of traffic and perhaps better rations. Whereas patrolling by the reserve platoon had hitherto been hot work in the torrid heat, it now became a matter of wading through water. Every morning—just as dawn was breaking—a patrol under an officer of the reserve platoon went out. Crossing the stream at the foot of the bluff, the patrol would traverse the field of saturated grass and then dive into a belt of thickly treed undergrowth sodden with water; over another stream and, scrambling up a muddy path in single file, debouch on to the Brown Patch. Once in the open the patrol would extend so as to present a smaller target to any Bolsheviks who might be lurking with evil intent in any of the many hidden ravines with which the patch abounded. By this time soaked from head to foot, the patrol would wander on to the end of the clearing where the officer would leave a bundle of propaganda for the education of the misguided enemy and pick up a few copies of his. This exchange of propaganda was a regular routine, and by it " A " Company knew when the Bolsheviks last visited the place, yet never had the luck to meet them in the act. This done, the patrol would scour the clearing in an easterly direction, floundering knee-deep in bogs and swamps and splashing through pools of standing water; then, skirting the edge of the forest, make for the rye fields and so back to Nijni Kitsa by the Khutor[2] trail two or more hours later, a wet and bedraggled party.

The days of the midnight sun had now passed and the more normal nights from 9.15 p.m. to 2.30 a.m. required double sentries from 8.30 p.m. until the time to stand to arms at 2 a.m. Nothing ever happened by halves in North Russia: as the flush of spring had burst upon summer so autumn burst with a deluge of rain upon an early winter. Nights became cold in mid-August, hailing the first twinge of winter. Rain and yet more rain fell throughout the month interspersed with days of fitful sunshine and scudding clouds. The monotony became almost intolerable as the days dragged past without news of a move either forward or back.

On the 17th Captain Naylor resumed normal hours for meals and officers were detailed for duty in the perimeter throughout the night on four-hourly shifts.

On the 16th Lieutenant Tyrwhitt-Drake, with Lieutenant Trewheler and the regimental scouts, carried out a fine patrol. Entering the forest at Mala Bereznik, they advanced west on a compass bearing until they struck a wide

[2] See Map No. 22, p. 338. About 1,000 yards south of Nijni Kitsa.

fire-trace cut in the heart of the forest. Turning left-handed—that is, south—they marched about six miles before turning again. By this time they were well behind the enemy's lines, and eventually reached Khutor³ between Ignatovskaya and Maksimovskaya, where they captured a Bolshevik of the 156th Regiment. If only this fire-trace had been discovered earlier what different results would have attended the two raids in June and July!

It was on the 19th that the Regiment suffered a further reduction of its strength when Captain Meade, with two platoons (Nos. 9 and 11) of " C " Company from Koslovo, and No. 10 from Ust Vaga, was ordered to embark for the Seletskoe front, on the River Emtsa, to guard communications against attack from the Railway front. This left Ust Vaga under the protection of headquarters and No. 12 Platoon, " C " Company, a detachment of the Machine Gun Corps and a company of the 3rd/4th North Russian Rifles. To hold Koslovo No. 1 Platoon, of " A " Company (Lieutenant Neville and Second Lieutenant Holland), was detached from Nijni Kitsa and a platoon of Russians was sent up from Ust Vaga, all under the command of Captain L. R. Swinhoe, of " B " Company. This redistribution entailed continual front-line work for the three remaining platoons of " A " Company which could not now afford to hold one in reserve considering the length of perimeter to be manned. But this extra work was willingly borne, for, soon after, companies were notified that the evacuation would take place on the 1st. In preparation for this all reserve gun, small-arm and trench-mortar ammunition was sent down on the 20th, leaving the forward troops with the minimum compatible with safety.

Meanwhile Lieutenant Wakeford's sappers had been busy making rafts for the 60-pounder gun which was hauled out of its deep pit by a pair of diminutive ponies while the Russian gunners, in a fine pretence of pulling, leant on the drag ropes shouting and singing in unison. Could pandemonium have shifted that gun it would have rolled on to the raft of its own volition. Eventually at about 3 p.m. on the 22nd the old gun was dismantled and safely lashed on to the rafts, ready to be floated downstream to Bereznik.

These and other preparations for the evacuation of the front did not escape the notice of the Russians in the area. No sooner had the 60-pounder departed for other climes than a serjeant and ten men of the Russian artillery also departed and were no more seen. Probably they deserted to the Bolsheviks while the going was good.

By the 25th the river had risen sufficiently to allow the routine boat to reach Seltso with rations; and the following day Captain Wyld came over from the Dvina to bring the tidings that the evacuation was postponed until the 7th; and that the old orders would hold good. The plan of withdrawal

³ See Map No. 22.

had been issued to companies in detail, whereby the Vaga Column was to act as rear guard, embarking at Bereznik six hours after the last of the Dvina force. Thereafter the Regiment was to go straight through to Archangel and, having rejoined the brigade, was to hold the right of the perimeter astride the Onega road. Captain Wyld explained that the postponement was mainly due to the low state of the river and the shortage of tugs, which delayed the evacuation of stores and ammunition; and also to the vacillation of the Russian General Staff, which seemed incapable of deciding on a line of defence.

He brought first-hand information of the very successful attack on the 10th. Thanks to the atrocious weather, the enemy escaped certain annihilation, for the infantry, having got behind the enemy, found itself unsupported. Meanwhile the guns, cavalry and ration carts floundered axle-deep and up to the ponies' girths in glutinous mud for forty-eight hours. The Bolshevik fleet was caught by the infantry anchored in pools, unable to move forward or back, and quite ready to surrender. But when the artillery failed to appear, the enemy took heart to man the guns and did much damage. As so often in that other river war—in Mesopotamia—bad luck robbed the British of a decisive victory.

The postponement disappointed the troops. The weather was now cold as well as wet, and the spasmodic sunshine was rapidly losing its warmth. The interminable green of the forest was becoming tinged with the first soft shades of yellow where the silver birches and alders peeped through the serried pines and larches, and the starlit nights brought the first nip of frost. Now—once again—all was uncertainty, except the fact that the Vaga Column had very little ammunition in case of emergency.

On the 29th an attack to cover the withdrawal was made on the Railway front by Russians supported by a detachment of British, in which 350 Bolsheviks and all their guns were captured. To co-operate with it the Regiment demonstrated on both banks; the guns bombarded the enemy's forward position and communications, while a strong patrol from Mala Bereznik demonstrated with rifles and Lewis guns. On the right bank Lieutenant Sawyer's platoon went out to the Brown Patch in search of trouble, while Nos. 1 and 3 Platoons, bedight in the full panoply of war, marched down the hillside in single file to the little wooden church; then into dead ground and up the hill again under cover of the shacks, to complete the circle like so many cinema supers.

During the last ten days of the month Bolshevik activity noticeably increased, enemy patrols showing unwonted initiative in approaching Nijni Kitsa and Mala Bereznik. Then suddenly at about 1.15 p.m. on the 31st the Bolshevik guns started shelling Mala Bereznik; never before had they fired at midday. All the garrisons were galvanized by this phenomenal occurrence, but more amazing still was the fact that all the shells exploded. Hitherto the enemy had only shelled in the late afternoon and then an average of only one in seven used to explode, but this was quite a different affair. The bombardment increased in intensity, almost substantiating the recent rumour that German officers were in command of the enemy's guns. Moreover, their artillery had been heavily reinforced and it was estimated that one battery of field guns on the right bank and on the left bank two 4.2-inch guns, two 6-inch howitzers and one field-gun battery were in action, making a total of twelve pieces. The howitzers concentrated on Fort Garry and the Road posts, while the guns bombarded the wire in front of the Summer House and the Pimple posts. One thing was quite certain, namely, that the enemy's artillery had been brought up considerably closer than ever before. Without the 60-pounder the gunners could do little in retaliation. The heavier guns outranged the four 18-pounders and the absence of the old long gun which had always kept the Bolshevik artillery at a respectful distance was acutely felt. To find the position of the enemy's field guns was quite hopeless until an aeroplane from Bereznik flew over his lines late in the afternoon and dropped some bombs. The effect was miraculous and instantaneous. The bombardment ceased abruptly at 5.30 p.m. Despite of the weight and intensity of it, there were no casualties in " B " Company, and only one Russian gunner was wounded by shrapnel. But the damage to the wire in front of the Summer House and Pimple posts was considerable, and Captain Peck immediately detailed parties to mend it. This was not as easy as it might have been if most of the wire had not already been evacuated.

II.

By the end of August the situation had been adjusted on all the different fronts to meet the withdrawal, and, except at Onega, the Russians showed signs of more cohesion and loyalty. But their General Staff had not yet decided on the line to be held. First it was to be Morjegorskaya, north-west of Bereznik; then it was to be the present line on the Vaga and Troitsa on the Dvina; or again a perimeter round Archangel. This continued indecision naturally added to the difficulties of evacuation. Early in August the Press at home announced that General Sir Henry Rawlinson had been appointed commander-in-chief to co-ordinate the withdrawal, and was to sail at once with the 74th Highland Light Infantry as a special reinforcement in case of emergency.

CHAPTER XXXII.

September on the Vaga. The Enemy Attacks.[1]

Bolsheviks attack Mala Bereznik—"B" Company's counter-attack—Patrol actions—Communications cut—The garrison at Ust Vaga—Bolsheviks surround "C" Company at Ust Vaga—"C" Company's desperate fight—Major Northcote counter-attacks—Disperses Bolsheviks—Bolshevik plan frustrated—Reinforcements sent up——All Russians leave—Withdrawal postponed—Kits sent downstream—Bolsheviks bombard Mala Bereznik—Forest tracks trapped with bombs—Withdrawal again postponed—Frost—"C" Company reach Koslovo—Bolsheviks threaten Koslovo——Bombardment of Mala Bereznik—Enemy sighted from Nijni Kitsa—Bolsheviks surrender—The officer's story—Condition of his troops—Withdrawal ordered for the 15th—Cancelled—Reordered.

(See Maps on page 322, and facing pages 366 and 384.)

The night of the 31st August/1st September was strangely quiet after the long bombardment of Mala Bereznik. The air was crisp and the ground crackled underfoot. An arc of light spread across the northern sky from which shot tongues of dancing fire, piercingly bright. It was as if the world were crowned with a tiara of fire diamonds. The fiery facets flickered and flashed, darting among the needle-points of the pines; now fading, now flashing again from the same encompassing arc. Now that the mosquitoes and other plaguing insects had departed there was a stillness over the land that could almost be felt—a lull before a storm.

The morning of the 1st dawned crystal clear, silhouetting the deep, dark pines against a turquoise sky. All was quiet during the hour of standing to arms, and there was no sign to presage the immediate future. But at 9.15 a.m. out of the silence a bugle sounded at Mala Bereznik; then a roar of voices, closely followed by a shrieking salvo of shells and a barrage of machine-gun fire. A second later the answer came. The guns opened rapid fire on S.O.S. lines, and above the reverberating crashes of battle could be heard the unmistakable pop and blast of trench mortars, also firing rapid. The yelling mob of about four hundred Bolsheviks of the 156th Regiment were by this time out in the open making for the wire round the Pimple, Banya and Summer House posts. But their barrage was poor; and machine guns and Lewis guns accomplished what their own guns and our barrage had left undone. The roar faded out and the attack failed hopelessly.

[1] See Map No. 25, facing p. 366.

About half an hour later Summer House post reported that there were about two hundred Bolsheviks in the forest, " jabbering and arguing the toss."[2] Soon after, Captain Peck sent out Lieutenants Dibben and Clews with patrols to locate the enemy. Lieutenant Dibben found the enemy in the dead ground in front of the Pimple, digging in like rabbits. The patrol, charging, chased the enemy into the forest and took one man prisoner. Pursuing to the edge of the forest, Lieutenant Dibben spotted about two hundred of the enemy forming up for a second attack amid much shouting. Returning hastily to the trench-mortar battery, he gave the exact position of the enemy and waited for the bombs to do the rest. Fifteen rounds rapid fired straight into the enemy's demoralized mob produced the desired effect and the enemy dispersed to a safer distance. Lieutenant Clews from the Summer House found a line of twelve Bolsheviks killed by trench-mortar fire.

Meanwhile at about 9.30 a message from regimental headquarters was received at Koslovo ordering No. 1 Platoon to cross the river at once and remain at the gunner lines as a reserve to " B " Company in case of need. The message also intimated that all communication between Seltso and Ust Vaga had been cut and that a composite platoon from regimental headquarters under Lieutenant Tyrwhitt-Drake was on its way by road to Ust Vaga to find out what had happened.

In Koslovo the defences were handed over to the Russians and the detachment of sappers, and at 10 a.m. No. 1 Platoon marched down the bluff while the Russian allies, pointing to Mala Bereznik, shouted and laughed, " Plenty Bolo, plenty Bolo," in reply to which the platoon shouted back, " We'll give you plenty Bolo when we come back, don't you fear." After waiting about half an hour at the gunner lines for the telephone line to be opened to Mala Bereznik, the platoon was ordered forward to disperse the enemy forming up for another attack. But on arrival at Canadian Village Captain Peck was quite satisfied with the situation. The enemy showed no signs of resuming the offensive, and he had disposed of sixteen of them, killed, and taken two prisoners, at the expense of two men killed.

Elsewhere, however, the situation was far from secure, as the report from Seltso received at midday abundantly proved. Ust Vaga, the base of the Vaga Column, had all but been captured in the very early hours of the 1st.

The garrison consisted of headquarters and No. 12 Platoon, " C " Company, two sections of the Machine Gun Corps, details of the trench-mortar battery, Army Service Corps, Royal Army Medical Corps, and one company

---

[2] They were actually holding a soviet to decide whether they should resume the attack. In the Bolshevik army of those days a commander had to submit his plans and intentions to the commissars—elected by the men to represent their interests—for their approval before he could put them into operation. Consequently commanders and commissars very seldom agreed.

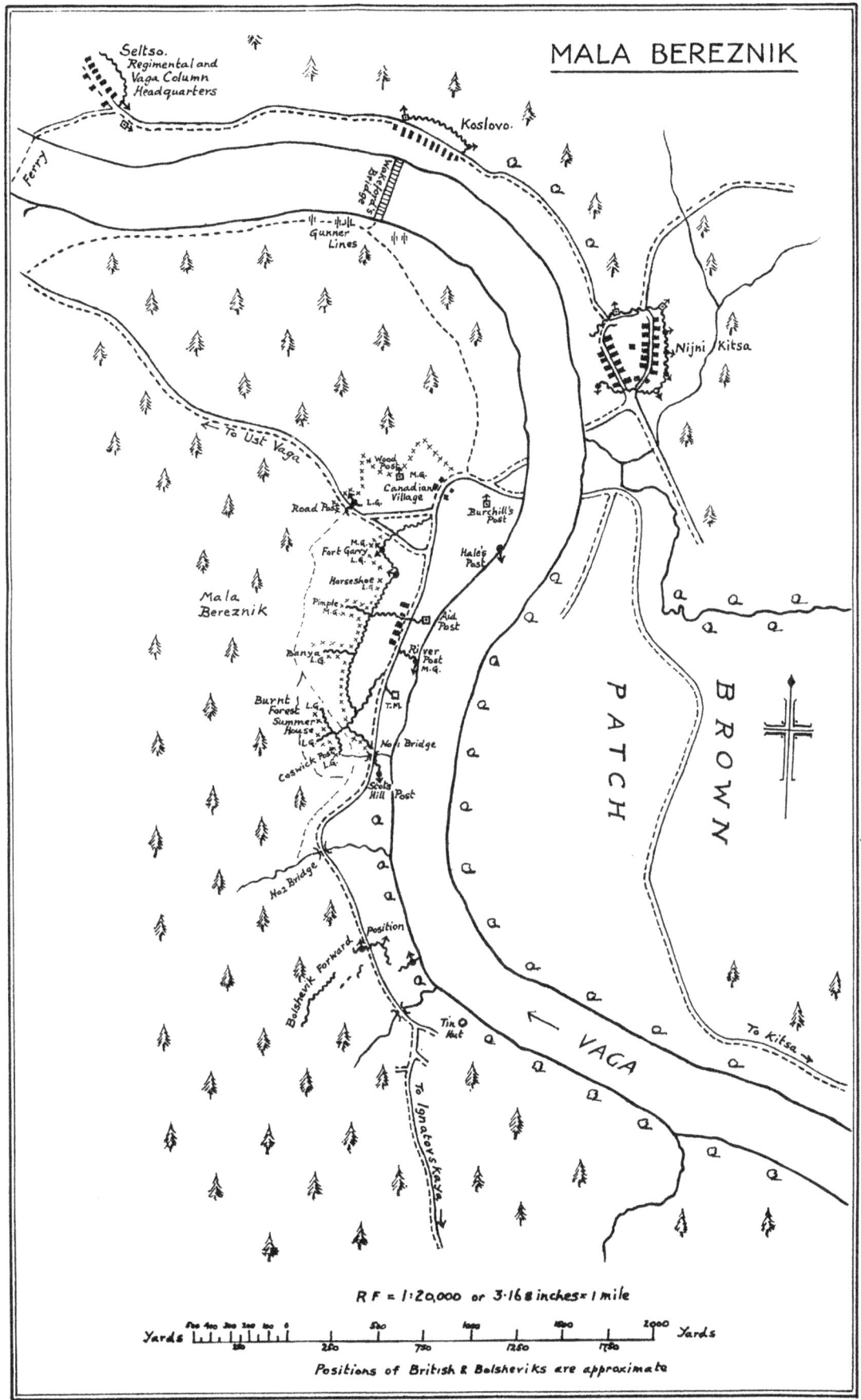

of the 3rd/4th North Russian Rifles, desertions from which had become a daily occurrence. The two southern blockhouses guarding the road from Mala Bereznik were held by the British machine-gun sections, and the rest of the perimeter, some five to six thousand yards in extent, was held by the Russians. In reserve Major Northcote, who commanded the garrison, kept his one and only British platoon concentrated in billets in the centre of the straggling village.

At about 2.30 a.m. on the 1st some civilians led in a column of about two hundred men of the 156th Bolshevik Regiment and a cavalry squadron under one Hadji Murad, a notorious cavalryman who styled himself the Red Eagle. This column had marched through the forest, cut the telephone line to Seltso, and then had been led quietly through the lines held by the Russians who afterwards reported that they had neither seen nor heard anything unusual. Having entered the defences along the river bank from the north, the enemy proceeded to attack the British machine-gun post from the rear, silently capturing one crew and killing the other.

Next, the civilian spies and traitors led the enemy to the shacks occupied by the British officers which had previously been marked by bunches of red rowan berries[3]; and these were quietly surrounded.

So far there had not been a sound to indicate the black treachery afoot, but the sentry of the quarter guard, noticing vague and shadowy movement of forms in the black depths of the night, darted indoors, bolted the rough timber door, and gave the alarm which saved the British garrison from a foul end. A moment later, a bomb, aimed at the window of " C " Company headquarters, exploded against the wall of the shack. Then the siege began by the enemy opening fire at the windows with rifles and machine guns and trying to force an entry up the ramp to the loft at the back of the shack.

Luckily there was plenty of ammunition at hand, and Major Northcote disposed of his handful of gallant men. Two old soldiers, taking up their position on each side of the ramp at the back of the shack, had some good snapshooting practice on live targets from behind excellent cover and held off the attackers successfully. With unerring aim and completely calm they felled any who dared to venture up the ramp.

Meanwhile in the officers' bedroom the windows were manned and a steady fire was maintained in retaliation. But whereas the Bolsheviks were firing wildly and indiscriminately, the garrison, bobbing up above the window-sill as in snapshooting, was able to keep up aimed fire which soon began to tell. The company serjeant-major, a marksman, quickly picked off some of the choicer Bolsheviks, who gradually began to retire.

[3] These had been noticed by officers and men of " C " Company some days before the attack, but no significance had been attached to them.

Now, the Red Eagle had omitted to cut the telephone lines connecting headquarters with the hospital and A.S.C., and thus Major Northcote was able to keep in touch and direct operations.

Directly the enemy retired to a safer distance, Major Northcote and Lieutenants Gibbons and Beck, clad in pyjamas and gum-boots, sallied out with the guard, turned out the men of the platoon—who had been left severely alone by the Bolsheviks—and led a counter-attack. First they drove off the enemy who had surrounded the hospital, which the medical officer, Captain Chandler, had been defending gallantly with a shot-gun for lack of a better weapon. Then Major Northcote set to work to clear the rest of the village with his one platoon.[4] The village being long and straggling, this was no easy task; and a party of very determined Bolsheviks held the blockhouses lately occupied by the British machine guns. One of these, situated on the river bank and in the open, gave great trouble, as it was in a matchless position to enfilade the men of " C " Company in all their attempts to clear the rest of the village.

In the first charge Lieutenant Beck had a revolver duel with the Red Eagle in the street. Though they both emptied their revolvers at each other, neither scored a hit.

It was now getting light, and Major Northcote realized that these two blockhouses would have to be systematically attacked before the situation could be restored. This was done under Lewis-gun covering fire, and the occupants were all killed without showing any signs of surrender.

By 6.30 a.m. the gallant handful of the Devonshire Regiment, long renowned for its fighting qualities, had completely cleared the village after four hours of intense and exciting fighting in which fourteen of the enemy were killed and eight captured.[5] An agent later reported that fifteen of the enemy's wounded were removed by the cavalry, making a total of thirty-seven. The garrison's British casualties were five killed, twelve wounded, and one missing; while the Russians had three men of No. 8 Company captured. These escaped later from a point about twelve miles out and managed to return to Ust Vaga.

The two machine guns whose crews had been surprised from the rear were later found in the forest abandoned by their captors in their flight.

As the result of this magnificent defence Major Northcote was awarded the *Distinguished Service Order* and Lieutenant Gibbons the *Military Cross*. The company serjeant-major received the *Distinguished Conduct Medal,* and eight men were awarded the *Military Medal*.

[4] The Russian troops disappeared into the forest when the action began and took no part in clearing the village.
[5] Seven of the prisoners were wounded.

The Bolshevik plan, as disclosed by the prisoners, was simple and only just failed. The capture of Ust Vaga was to have been the signal for an enveloping attack on Mala Bereznik. When this signal, expected at dawn, failed to materialize, Nos. 4, 6, 8 and 9 Companies of the 156th Bolshevik Regiment assaulted Mala Bereznik, only to be mown down by their own barrage and " B " Company's fire.

The prisoners also stated that it was known that the Vaga was very lightly held; and they had been told that the North Russian Rifles on both banks would mutiny on hearing the shout and bugle and would proceed to mop up the weak British garrisons from within while they attacked from without. Luckily the only Russians were on the other bank at Koslovo and Seltso. This abortive enemy attack brought one good thing in its train: it galvanized Dvina Force into recognizing the weakness of the Vaga Column. The colonel had not even one platoon in reserve wherewith to counter-attack without using Russian troops of doubtful loyalty to replace it in the line. Had the enemy shown more determination Ust Vaga would have been captured easily and Mala Bereznik cut off completely. Not only this. The rear of the Dvina Force would have been seriously threatened at the confluence of the two rivers.

The firing at Ust Vaga in the early morning had been heard at Bereznik though it had been inaudible at Seltso; and as soon as it was light an aeroplane went up to see what all the fuss was about. The pilot arrived in time to see a strange sight: a body of half-clothed officers and men fighting like tigers in the twilight. Having made his report, he flew up to Seltso to see what was happening there, and did some excellent work by spotting the enemy's new gun positions and by dropping bombs.

The night of the 1st/2nd was quiet, and on the 2nd two platoons of " B " Company, 46th Royal Fusiliers, arrived in the forward area. These were disposed as follows: one platoon at Mala Bereznik in relief of No. 1 Platoon, which returned to Koslovo; and one platoon at Koslovo in general reserve. Headquarters and the remaining two platoons reinforced " C " Company at Ust Vaga.

The same day definite information was received from Dvina Force that the Russians had decided to hold the line Pless—Chamovo—Mala Bereznik, and that the Regiment would hand over the line to the 3rd/4th North Russian Rifles. But on the 3rd they changed their minds again and all Russian troops were ordered to concentrate at Bereznik on the 4th, preparatory to taking up a line at Nikolskaya, about fifteen versts south of Emetskoe.

Accordingly No. 7 Company, North Russian Rifles, and the 1st Russian Field Battery with four British 18-pounders left by road at 5.30 p.m., leaving the Regiment's front without artillery of any kind. The same day also the two platoons of Royal Fusiliers were ordered to return to Ust Vaga in relief of Lieutenant Gibbons's platoon, which marched up to Koslovo.

On the 4th a staff officer arrived by the routine boat with orders for the evacuation of the front on the 7th; and the same day a section of 3-inch Russian field guns from Troitsa, manned by British gunners, arrived to cover the front. Not unnaturally the gunners found their weapons and ammunition strange, and all shooting was experimental. Moreover the ammunition was neither good nor sufficient. It became a matter of chance whether the shells ever reached their intended destination or exploded on arrival. On the first evening a practice shoot produced one premature which did no damage, but the following day a shell intended for the Tin Hut in the enemy's forward position fell in Canadian Village and wounded Lance-Corporal Newton, of " B " Company, much to Captain Peck's annoyance. His message to the gunners requesting them to refrain from further activities was couched in somewhat unparliamentary and caustic language.

On the 5th rations came up by convoy to supply the Regiment up to and including the 9th, to which day the withdrawal had been postponed; and the wireless set was dismantled and sent down to Ust Vaga by the returning convoy. The same evening the companies received orders to send down officers' valises, two blankets per man, all steel helmets, entrenching tools and handles at 6.30 a.m. on the 6th. Meanwhile a large ark was towed up to Koslovo where " A " Company and the platoon of " C " Company loaded their baggage. On the opposite bank a smaller barge took the kits of " B " Company, gunners and sappers. At 11 a.m. Lieutenant Dickenson, in charge of this weird flotilla, after loading the baggage from Seltso, set off to float down to Ust Vaga, which was reached at 4.30 p.m. The troops now had only one blanket per man for the cold, damp nights and days, and without a reserve of ammunition there was not an officer or man who felt at all secure.[6]

As if to test this very weakness the enemy started to bombard Mala Bereznik again at 9 a.m. as an obvious preliminary to another attack.[7] For over six hours shells fell all round Banya and the Pimple posts, doing considerable damage and cutting the wire, but only succeeded in wounding one man slightly. Once again there was an eager search all over the area for a spare coil of barbed wire to mend the gaps, but not a strand could be found, so thorough had been the evacuation of stores. All the night of the 7th/8th the garrisons of the forward villages practically stood to arms expecting an attack in the early hours of the 8th. But nothing untoward happened.

[6] Platoons had 1,000 rounds beyond what was carried on the man; and each machine gun had 4,000 rounds, or sixteen minutes' rapid fire.

[7] Later prisoners related that the 161st Regiment was ordered to attack, but had refused unconditionally to do so.

1. No. 4 Post, Nijni Kitsa, looking towards the Brown Patch.
2. Serjeant Bristow.
3. Mudborough Road, Nijni Kitsa.
4. Bolshevik Prisoners, captured 13th September 1919.
5. Going Downstream.

On the 8th the colonel issued clear and comprehensive orders for the withdrawal, in which he stated that the Vaga Column was to act as rear guard to the Dvina Force and cover its retirement; that the Vaga Column would evacuate its present positions on the morning of the 10th. Every conceivable contingency had been carefully thought out and provided for, and all ranks were detailed to special tasks. The afternoon was spent in trapping all the approaches to the several positions with surplus bombs. " A " Company, from Nijni Kitsa, laid trip wires across the rye fields, and the Chamovo and Khutor trails. At Koslovo it was not so easy to do this, as there was a very short field of fire, and at two points the forest encroached on the perimeter. But all the tracks were carefully trapped some distance within the forest and in the undergrowth nearest the platoon posts. These traps proved very efficacious later as signals of enemy movements, and were simple to make. The trip wires were laid about one foot above ground-level, and at frequent intervals hangers were dropped to which were attached Mills bombs by their rings so loosened that the slightest strain on the hangers would let the levers fly and fire the bombs.

All the 9th was spent in preparing for the immediate move and all arrangements were perfected. These included the mining of the corduroy bridges over streams and ravines and the best shacks in each village. As many as fifteen slabs of gun-cotton were placed in the stoves of each of five shacks in Nijni Kitsa and Koslovo and then covered over with ashes by Wakeford's sappers. In fact, it was almost dangerous to move about outside the immediate neighbourhood of the platoon posts. The day was quiet and a black, starlit night descended upon the Regiment, thankful at the thought that at last it was to move from this monotonous stagnation. All had been prepared; the convoy of seventy carts was waiting, and then a message came through postponing the move till further orders. It is almost impossible to describe the disappointment with which this news was received. For the sixth time the move had been postponed; the troops had been expecting and waiting for the end of the expedition which had long since lost its interest and even its usefulness. The nights were becoming bitterly cold with heavy ground frosts and an icy wind blowing from the north; and just when the Regiment required warm clothing it had been bereft of all but one blanket per man.

But there was nothing to be done about it now, except to hope that the heavy frosts which freeze the rivers would not catch the Regiment and bind it in their iron grips. So, heaving out the gun-cotton from the stoves in the billets, the troops off duty stoked up the fires and lay down on the hard floors, what time the bugs dropped off the ceiling, roused by the warmth of the stoves to seek their meat in due season. Outside an icy wind whistled round the eaves.

On the 10th rations came up to supply the Regiment up to and including the 15th, and on the 11th Major Northcote and headquarters, "C" Company, reached Koslovo. This party was full of rumours: that there were no more rations south of Archangel; that the Dvina Force was back in the old position at Pless; and that General Sadleir-Jackson was fully prepared to withdraw. Yet no tidings came through.

The 12th was quiet and uneventful; but at 2 a.m. on the 13th machine-gun and trench-mortar fire broke out at Mala Bereznik. In the cold, raw morning the whole column stood to arms. Nijni Kitsa reported that bomb traps had been exploding spasmodically throughout the night and that Bolsheviks had been seen as if making for Koslovo or Seltso. Mala Bereznik reported enemy prowling in the forest opposite the Pimple and Banya posts. Brimstone was in the air; and it only remained to guess where the attack was likely to come.

Everything pointed to the enemy making an attempt on Koslovo, which was the least defensible of all the villages. For four hours the troops stamped up and down in the icy blast without greatcoats, waiting for something to happen. At 6.30 a.m. the enemy artillery opened fire on Mala Bereznik with one battery of field guns, and kept up an intermittent bombardment until 4 p.m., during which Banya post was once again blown in, but only one man slightly wounded.

Soon after the shelling started Lieutenant Gibbons was ordered to cross over to Mala Bereznik with No. 12 Platoon to act as a reserve, leaving Koslovo to be defended by No. 1 Platoon and a few sappers and headquarters of "C" Company. All the morning the wires buzzed with reports to and from Seltso and still the expected attack never materialized. Then Hale's post on the left bank reported having seen the enemy moving towards Nijni Kitsa. This party was picked up and effective machine-gun fire opened on it with the result that three Bolsheviks were seen to fall. Midday came; the shelling continued; reports came in; nothing definite happened.

Soon after 4 p.m., however, when the shelling of Mala Bereznik ceased abruptly, the signallers at Koslovo reported that the line to Nijni Kitsa was "dis." As there had been no shelling on the right bank, this was strange. Almost immediately afterwards a Russian gunner officer appeared and said that he, too, could not get Nijni; and that he was going out with a linesman to mend the break. Half-way between the two villages, at a spot which could not be seen by the posts of either, the Russian found a Bolshevik sitting on the track with a white handkerchief tied to the muzzle of his rifle. Having mended the line, the officer took the prisoner on to Nijni Kitsa. The prisoner told Captain Naylor that there was a large party of Bolsheviks who wanted to surrender; and that his party had been detailed to attack Koslovo and another was waiting in the forest to attack Nijni. Captain

Naylor wired this news through to Koslovo at once, and the garrison once again stood to arms. For about an hour nothing happened, and then, at about 7 p.m., the machine-gun post on the rear face at Nijni spotted movement in the long grass and opened fire. Immediately a long line of Bolsheviks rose up waving white handkerchiefs, and came towards the wire.

These men belonged to the 161st Regiment—a new regiment in the Vaga area—and comprised one company, numbering 125 men, including a tall, good-looking officer.

The officer's story, as related to Lieutenant Trewheler, was interesting as giving evidence of Bolshevik military methods. The Vaga Column was to be attacked by two battalions on each bank, with one in reserve; the 161st Regiment, having refused to attack Mala Bereznik on the 7th, was in disgrace; but instead of receiving condign punishment was given another chance to regain its laurels by the capture of Koslovo and Nijni Kitsa, while two battalions attacked and captured Mala Bereznik. His company was to attack Koslovo which was reported to be held by blockhouses unprotected by wire; and for his attack he was assigned one machine gun which was to provide covering fire. Having captured Koslovo, he was to prevent reinforcements from reaching Nijni Kitsa, which was to be attacked simultaneously by four other companies of his regiment. Zero was to be at 4 p.m. on the 13th.

Before their departure, the Bolshevik commander encouraged the officers to succeed with the threat of instant death if they failed. On the 11th the Bolsheviks, having been issued with two days' meagre rations, set off through the sodden forest under the guidance of the scout officer, who alone knew the approaches to the two villages. But in the meantime these approaches had been trapped. The scout officer was the first to spring one and was killed. Thereafter no one knew the way. Wherever the demoralized and miserable troops went, bombs exploded, causing alarm and despondency as well as casualties. Without a guide the officer had nothing better to rely on than a map of the whole of Russia in Europe, on which the approximate position of Koslovo had been marked in pencil. The troops were so scared of springing bombs that he had the greatest difficulty in persuading them to move at all. Being a trusted officer, he had been allowed, as a great concession, to operate without a commissar to supervise his actions; and after forty-eight hours' wandering in the cold, damp forest he had little difficulty in prevailing upon his company to surrender. For this one object—to escape from the Bolsheviks—he had courted favour and played a double game.

Once again the Vaga Column was saved from an awkward predicament by the indetermination of the enemy. But, looking at the enemy as provided by the company of the 161st Regiment, it was easy to diagnose the cause of their failure. There was not a spark of intelligence in their faces as they huddled together in groups, wet, cold and hungry. Most of them were mere striplings of about sixteen, ill-fed, unwashed and fetid past description; and clad in a weird assortment of garments, even to quilted winter jackets and felt snow-boots. From such a mob, devoid of pride and training, resolution was not to be expected. They were, indeed, a pathetic sight.

After the surrender of the company the tension of the previous fifteen hours relaxed; and patrols from the villages reported no signs of further enemy concentrations. One such patrol from Nijni Kitsa reported twenty-six exploded traps, and found plenty of evidence of casualties.

The 14th dawned fine and quiet after a frosty night; and the morning was spent in expectation of orders to move. The situation looked rather precarious: there were only two days' rations and no reserves in the forward area, a minimum of ammunition and trench-mortar bombs, and only thirty rounds of shell per gun. At 2.30 p.m., however, the colonel called a conference at which he stated that the evacuation orders of the 10th were to apply to the 15th with one important exception, namely, that the Vaga Column would *not* act as rear guard to the Dvina Force as previously ordered. The Regiment was, in fact, to march straight from Ust Vaga to Bereznik and there embark, while the Dvina Force provided its own protection.

All was bustle and preparation in the forward area during the afternoon. Sappers laid mines under the bridges and set spring fuses; slabs of gun-cotton primed and fused, were concealed in the stoves of the best unoccupied shacks; ingenious traps were laid under the duckboards in the posts; and all correspondence of military value was collected ready for destruction in the morning. By nightfall nothing remained to be done except to go on the following morning from this God-forsaken area. But, sure enough, at 9.15 p.m. the usual message came through: " To-morrow's move will not take place unless further orders are received." Just one more playful postponement[8] had been expected this time, so that the disappointment was hardly so keen. It was a cold night in the posts: the north wind moaned and whistled in the trees; the ground was white and sparkling in the moonlight, and the stars shone like a myriad flashing diamonds. The grass and straw crackled and split underfoot, and men off duty huddled round braziers with the light of the flames playing and dancing on their faces and outstretched hands; the sentries, silent and impassive, stared into the black void, the everlasting forest.

At 11.30 p.m. a message came through ordering the evacuation on the morrow. No one believed it.

---

[8] These many postponements were due to a variety of causes : lack of transport to evacuate the stores on the Dvina ; scarcity of water in the river whereby two monitors, stuck on sandbanks, eventually had to be blown up ; Russian indecision on the line to be held, etc., with the result that the advantages gained by the offensive of 10th August were dissipated if not entirely lost, and the Bolsheviks, given the time necessary to recover from the thrust, followed up the gradual withdrawal of the British and increased the difficulties of evacuation by continual patrol actions.

CHAPTER XXXIII.

I.—The Withdrawal of the Vaga Column.

The 43rd evacuates positions—Ust Vaga handed over to Russians—The march to Bereznik—The 43rd embarks—The 43rd leaves Bereznik—Journey downstream—The 43rd reaches Archangel—Disembarks at Bakharitsa—Concentration of the 43rd—Surplus officers embark on the 25th—43rd on the 26th—Convoy sails on the 27th—Rough passage—Arrival at Liverpool—Reception—Disbandment—Rewards and decorations.

(See Maps on page 322, and facing pages 366 and 384.)

" Breakfast 5.15 a.m. At 5.30 carts came up from Seltso to take down Lewis gun boxes and cooking utensils." At 6.30 a.m. " C " Company headquarters and No. 12 Platoon marched out to take over Ust Vaga. " Then came the fun," wrote an officer. " We burnt every scrap of English literature, dropped tools, bombs and surplus ammunition into the wells and replaced the gun cotton in the stove of our bedroom, covering it carefully with cold ashes. Next, Wakeford arrived and set the bombs which were to explode seventy-five slabs of gun cotton if anyone trod on the corduroy bridge at the south end of the village—Koslovo."

At 8.15 on this frosty, sunny morning " A " Company marched through Koslovo by platoons, carefully avoiding the mined bridge, and down the cliff and over the bridge to the gunner lines. No. 1 Platoon was now rear guard on the right bank; and as soon as " A " Company cleared the bridge No. 1 Platoon crossed over, while the sappers hacked away the anchor ropes behind it. As the men stacked their packs on the carts opposite Seltso, pillars of smoke could be seen rising into the still, frosty air at Nijni and Koslovo where braziers and fires had been left burning.

Meanwhile Lieutenant Wakeford with his detachment of sappers marched off at 8.35 as advance guard. An hour later regimental headquarters and " A " Company moved into the forest from the ferry landing, and at 9.30 " B " Company, as rear guard, evacuated Mala Bereznik.

How different was that march from the one in June! Now the air was chill, the birches and undergrowth fulvous, and the track an inch deep in mud. But it was just as tedious and uninteresting until reaching the hamlet of Verchni-Konets, where some old women came out of the shacks and watched the column pass, howling and beating their breasts in paroxysms of

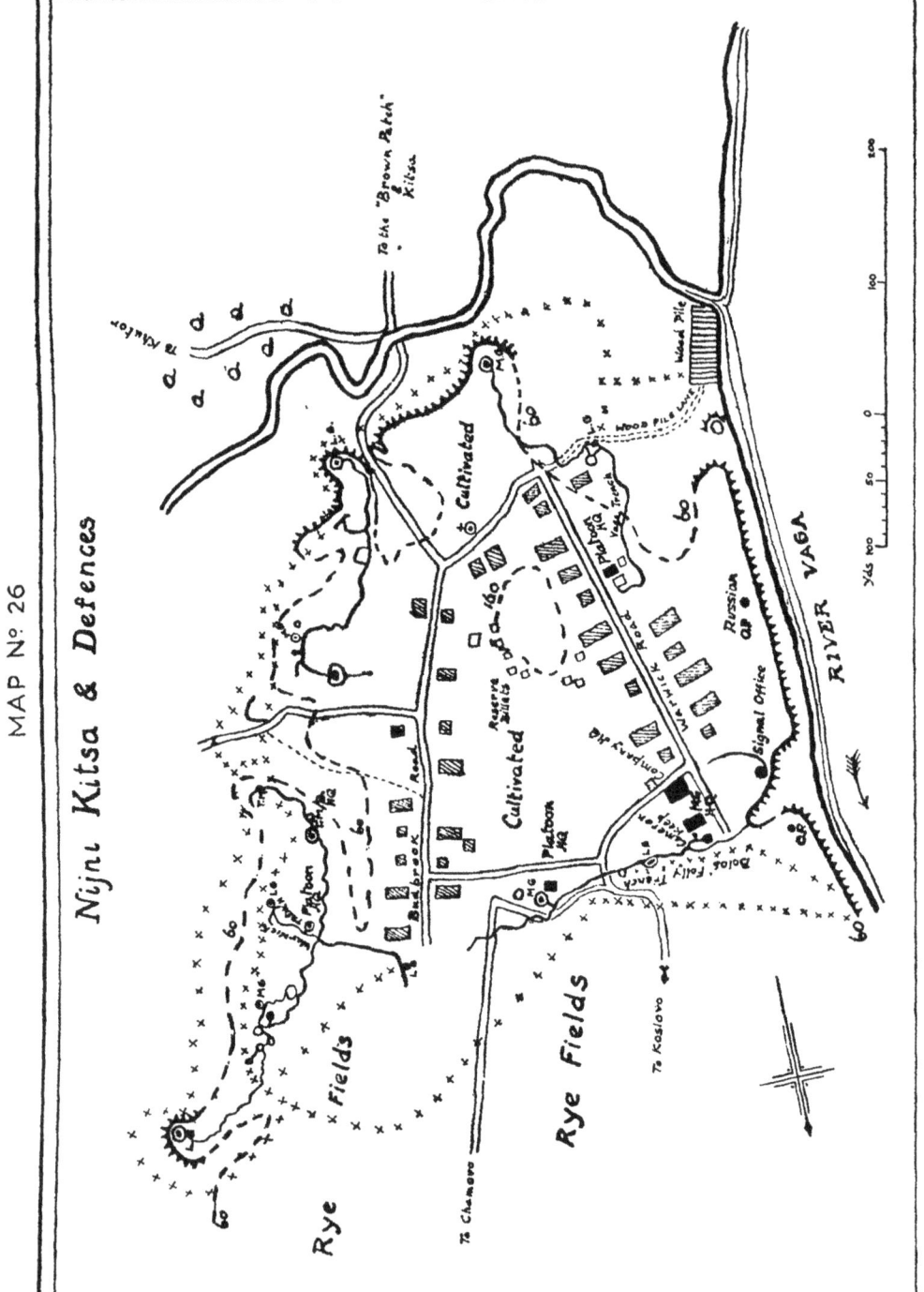

grief. Here a bridge was destroyed by the sappers after " B " Company had passed over.

On reaching Ust Vaga soon after midday " A " Company took over the defences from " B " Company, 46th Royal Fusiliers, which marched off to Bereznik. As soon as " B " Company arrived the sappers blew up the bridge over the stream at the south end of the village, and thereafter no civilians were allowed outside the perimeter. The night was quiet, but " sentries reported big explosions from the direction of our old lines, and we visualized great fat commissars being blown sky high on lighting the stoves or treading on the bridges. We were very tired, for this was the first march that anyone had done since the selfsame trek in June, and all realized the effect of stagnation."

Early the next day the defences of Ust Vaga were handed over to the Shenkursk Scouts, a body of volunteers who were to hold the village during the Regiment's retirement. They talked big of what they would do to any Bolshevik who approached the village, and, having drawn four machine guns and four Lewis guns, they slouched off to practise on the range and omitted to man the posts.

At 6.30 a.m. the main body, consisting of regimental headquarters, " B " Company, section of artillery, details of the Army Service Corps, and Intelligence party, resumed the march to Bereznik by the river road, as the short cut through the forest was reported impassable by wheeled traffic. " A " Company, the rear guard, left at 7 a.m. with No. 4 Platoon as escort to the carts, Nos. 1 and 2 main guard, and No. 3 rear party. As the company marched out of the dirty little village, sobbing old women keened and threw themselves down on the road rolling about in hysterical abandon, while the old men from behind their halos of hair watched their protectors depart in stolid and pitiful silence.

The march was extremely tedious and impeded by frequent checks to extricate the transport or guns from sucking morasses. At about 8 a.m. firing at Ust Vaga was plainly heard by the rear guard, and about half an hour later an agitated old civilian, carrying his boots to lend speed to his heels, came up with the rear party, shouting volubly, " Bolo, Ust Vaga; Bolo, Ust Vaga." Captain Watson—the chief intelligence officer of the column—questioned him; the Shenkursk Scouts had decamped to Bereznik by the forest track; the Bolsheviks had captured the village and were about to pursue. It seemed that a rear-guard action would be inevitable, but the Bolsheviks were content to follow at a safe distance without harassing the Regiment. On the column trudged through the slippery mud and in a fine, soaking drizzle interspersed with driven rain which rendered the track even more difficult for the little ponies of the transport. But at noon, after what seemed like an endless march, Bereznik hove in sight, and " B " Company embarked at once on board the ark *Ennessee*, followed by headquarters, " A " Company and trench-mortar battery.

At this point a most unfortunate thing happened for which the Regiment was in no way responsible. The Bolsheviks, following the Regiment, seized the point at the confluence of the two rivers and opened fire on the rearmost barges of the Dvina Force as they retired downstream, causing eleven casualties. As has been recorded, the Dvina Force in the final orders assumed responsibility for protecting its own withdrawal. Originally, it is true, the evacuation orders stated that the Vaga Column would be responsible for the confluence of the rivers and would not embark until six hours after the last vessel of the Dvina Force should have left Bereznik. But this important order was altered, and the commanding officer, on arrival at Bereznik, had no idea that the withdrawal of the Dvina Force was not completed.

To clear up the situation Lieutenant Sawyer's No. 2 Platoon, with a field gun, was hastily sent off to turn the enemy out. In drenching rain the party went back on its tracks, and later a platoon of Royal Marines was landed from a motor-boat to co-operate. An hour later a platoon of Royal Fusiliers relieved Lieutenant Sawyer's platoon, which returned at 5.30 p.m.

At 5.45 p.m. the barge was taken in tow and slipped downstream until 8.30 p.m., when the anchor was dropped. To be warm and dry, to have a clean change of clothing and a night in blankets or " flea-bags," free from bugs, was luxury compared to which a suite at the Savoy Hotel would have been mere squalor.

By midday the convoy reached Emetskoe, where the Emtsa bar practically blocked the channel and made navigation a matter of luck. It was here that the monitor *Glowworm* stuck for two months; the day after she floated off she blew up at Bereznik while trying to extinguish a fire on an ammunition barge. With much bumping and growling the old barge squeezed her amorphous bulk over the bar and then was moored to the bank to await the extrication of her less fortunate sisters, still stuck fast. For twenty-four hours the Navy used every device to shift the barges, but despite of all efforts two refused to be moved and had to be abandoned. In the evening the convoy slipped on downstream and halted for the night at Siskoe, where two Russian field guns were landed and handed over to the Russian authorities on the 19th.

All that day the two tugs strained into the teeth of a bitter wind which lashed the wide expanse of river into white horses and drove icy sleet before it. And as the convoy headed northward so the days grew perceptibly shorter, so that it was nearly time to anchor after passing Ust Pinega at 6 p.m.

That night the Regiment first saw the northern lights in all their panoply of beauty. Away in the north, like a fountain of fire, the waves of iridescent light welled up behind the jet needles of the pine tops, silhouetting each branch against the sky: like veils of rainbow silk, dancing, changing, flitting; now spreading across the sky in a fairy curtain, now vanishing to spring to life again in yet more vivid brilliance overhead, while, below, the great old river chortled alongside the barge and the chilly wind whispered in the tarpaulins.

At 5 a.m. on the 20th the old barge started on her last lap, and by midday the spires and towers of Archangel and the funnels and masts of shipping could be descried in the faint distance. But against the strong north wind and heavy sea the tugs could make but slow progress; and it was 5 p.m. before the convoy glided past the good ships *Czar* and *Czaritsa* on its way to Rikesika.[1] Soon after the barge had been tied up alongside a naval hospital ship, orders were received to go about and land at Bakharitsa, on the left bank opposite Archangel.

II.—Arrival at Archangel and Return to England.

On the morning of the 21st the Regiment landed in bitter, wet weather, and marched to quarters in huts, with headquarters in a good, weather-proof building. Here headquarters and three platoons of " D " Company had already arrived from the Onega road; and on the 23rd, when Captain Meade rejoined with three platoons of " C " Company and one platoon of " D " Company, the Regiment was once again concentrated.

At this point a short digression must be made to give an account of " D " Company's wanderings. As has been seen,[2] the widespread mutinies among the supposedly loyal Russian troops early in July so threatened his rear and flanks that General Ironside was fain to withdraw British troops from the front line to protect his communications by river and sea. It was to prevent the Onega mutineers from marching on Archangel that " D " Company was sent to Konetzbor.

On the 25th July " D " Company[3] left the Vaga Column and spent that night at Ust Vaga. The following day it marched to Bereznik, where one platoon was left to do guard duties while headquarters and the remaining three platoons embarked for Archangel, which was reached on the 31st without incident. On the 1st August the company re-embarked in a tug and, steaming north-west across the river behind the island, disembarked a few hours later at Rikesika. Before starting a doctor and an intelligence

---

[1] Across the river, north-west of Archangel.
[2] p. 356.
[3] p. 358.

party had been attached to the little expedition, and a Mr. Cox, a naval warrant officer, a man of boundless energy and resource who in course of time became the hub round which the wheel revolved. " It was he who organized and personally supervised the transport of all our supplies from Archangel; collected local transport and labour and despatched it on its way to Konetzbor; in the circumstances he achieved wonders entirely single-handed," wrote Lieutenant Colvill, who was one of the subalterns of the company and whose description is henceforth quoted.

" Having disembarked and collected sufficient carts, we set out to march to Konetzbor the same evening, a distance of about thirty versts. We reached our destination in the small hours of the morning somewhat weary, and billeted in the village on the ridge which was about a mile long and stood perhaps a hundred feet above the flat marshland and forest and was crossed at the northern end by the rough sandy road to Onega.

" On the way up we had left one platoon at Karoda Bridge, about nine miles down the track. This platoon sent out a further detachment of two sections to Amburtski Skit, a remote village some ten miles from the bridge through which passed an alternative track from the Onega direction towards Archangel. The only route to it from Karoda was a causeway of felled pine trees through deep swamp and forest.

" In course of time reconnaissance of the Konetzbor position was carried out from G.H.Q. and the detachment was considerably augmented until there were on the ridge ' D ' Company, less one platoon at Amburtski Skit and Karoda and one at Bereznik, one company of Russian engineers, one machine gun company, one mountain battery and one troop of cavalry improvised from Australian gunners or ex-gunners and other oddments under two subalterns of the 18th Hussars. There were various sappers; also one subaltern employed in surveying and mapping the whole area, who nearly expired from sheer exhaustion in the course of his labours in the swamp and forest.

" No advance against the position ever materialized; and the whole period was occupied in constructing defences which were very impressive, consisting of a system of blockhouses " commanding wide traces cut through the forest so as to produce interlocking fire. Each blockhouse contained a machine gun, and the wire aprons were constructed on the near side of the traces.

This position was duly handed over to the Russians before " D " Company withdrew to Archangel.

The five days in Bakharitsa were uneventful, being spent in fatigue work unloading barges and reloading on to transports and in trying to fit the men out with decent clothing. Many were almost in rags, uniform torn and dirty, boots in holes and puttees woefully ragged and frayed; but there was insufficient in store to fit them all out respectably for the homeward journey.

On the 25th Lieutenant Booth had a very lucky escape. On his way back from depositing a very big sum of money with the field cashier, the ferry launch was rammed by the tug *Roysterer* and sank in a few seconds in midstream. Lieutenant Booth, clad in a greatcoat and heavy boots, came to the surface and had to fight for his life with a Russian soldier who, unable to swim, clung round his neck. Luckily he was able to grasp the rudder of the *Roysterer* and there he remained until picked up by the repair ship, H.M.S. *Cyclops*. Meanwhile in Bakharitsa the adjutant was becoming anxious for the safety of the money as well as Lieutenant Booth, for Archangel and its precincts were not places in which to loiter alone too long in those days. However, having had his clothes dried by the hospitable Navy, he returned in the late afternoon none the worse for his experience.

The last days were days of hard work. Though thousands of pounds' worth of equipment, stores and ammunition were handed over to the Russian Army, there was much to be loaded for home; added to which, about fifty men of the Regiment were on guard duty day and night in conjunction with the Russian forces. So fearful were the Russian authorities of an outbreak of Bolshevism or sabotage that the guards had orders to fire at anyone after 8 p.m. Consequently shots were fired somewhat indiscriminately throughout the nights, but no casualties were ever reported.

On the 25th twenty-eight officers of the Regiment, together with their servants, embarked on board the *Braemar Castle,* as there was not room for all the officers to travel with their companies. The following day the Regiment, with three officers per company, went on board the *Czar* at 5.30 p.m., leaving " D " Company and the trench-mortar battery ashore to act as rear guard for the night.

The congestion aboard was such that the Regiment, over 700 strong, was allotted accommodation scarcely sufficient for 400; and consequently most of the men were compelled to sleep on deck; and for lack of space their kit-bags were stowed in the hold.

Meanwhile " D " Company took up positions surrounding the Bakharitsa compound; and an officer's guard was posted over the gangways of the *Czar*.

At 6 a.m. the *Czar* moved out into midstream opposite Archangel Priestan, and at 10.30 " D " Company embarked by tug. At 11.30 the *Manitou* passed downstream with the band of the 67th provocatively playing *Good-bye-ee, don't sigh-ee,* followed by the *Czaritsa* and other craft. Half an hour later the good ship *Czar* was tugged round and quietly slid downstream to the rendezvous. As a precaution the troops were ordered to remain between decks from 1 p.m. to 2 p.m., but there was no hostile demonstration; and gradually the towers and spires of Archangel faded into the distance.

Though there was none who was sorry to see the last of that weird land, yet there were many who could not refrain from wondering what vengeance awaited the inhabitants of the romantic town. The British convoy included about six thousand Russian refugees, but the area of British intervention must have contained many who had cause to curse the name of England. How many in that area actually succumbed to Bolshevik vengeance, to torture, starvation, slavery and sudden death will never be known; but it is safe to conjecture that more met their death by foul and ghastly methods than it is pleasant to contemplate.

From 4 p.m. to 7.30 p.m. the ships anchored off the bar at the mouth of the Dvina where the whole convoy assembled; and, led by the diminutive river craft and tugs under their own steam, headed north, one by one, into the bleak White Sea.

The first day out was calm. All day the *Czar* kept passing the river craft which were making heavy weather of the sea that they were never meant to withstand; and at 8 p.m., in an increasing sea, General Grogan was put off in a tug for Murmansk.

The men's accommodation was readjusted to their better comfort, and, moreover, just in time, for on the 29th the weather off the North Cape became very dirty. For twenty-four hours the ship plunged in a heavy sea through sleet and snow, taking it green with every pitch, and the situation on the men's decks became one that is better imagined than politely described.

It was a sorry company which paraded for the captain's inspection on the 30th, most of the men being forespent with exhaustion. During this storm many of the river craft foundered in the mountainous seas.

By the 2nd October the ship was passing the Shetland Isles once again, and the sea noticeably abated under the lee of the Hebrides. On the evening of the 3rd the lightships of Scotland and Ireland could be seen, and on the following morning the *Czar* steamed up the Mersey and anchored in midstream off Liverpool. From here the Regiment disembarked in tugs and was taken to the quay of Princes Dock where the Navy and Army Canteen Board and Red Cross provided tea, buns and chocolate for each man. It was then given out that the Regiment was to receive a civic welcome in contradiction of the prevalent rumour that it was to go on strike duty at once.[4] Headed by the band of the 45th Regiment (Sherwood Foresters), the Regiment marched through deserted streets to St. George's Hall, opposite

---

[4] The Regiment landed during the Railway Strike of 1919.

which it formed mass and received an address of welcome from the Lord Mayor and Corporation. Of public interest there was none, and what cheers the Regiment received came from a party of Foresters billeted in the Town Hall.

Thereafter the Regiment marched up to Knotty Ash Camp, receiving many hoots and jeers from the assembled strikers, and was lucky under the circumstances to escape bottles and other welcoming missiles.

On the 9th Major Crosse, D.S.O., of the 52nd, walked into the company lines to welcome the 43rd back to England, and was heartily welcomed in turn by his old subalterns.

The week in Liverpool was spent in the dispatch of the attached men to their depots or regiments. To their evident joy the men replaced their cap-badges, titles and even hackles, carefully preserved through many vicissitudes, and marched away from their foster-regiment.

Two days later, the 13th, headquarters and " A " Company,[5] 43rd, moved to a standing camp at North Ripon, where they were later joined by Major Whittall and the cadre from the Depot. During the next few days officers and men were sent on leave, and so ended the expedition to North Russia during which the Regiment suffered the following casualties:—[6]

1 Officer and 15 other ranks killed;
5 Officers and 41 other ranks wounded;
5 Other ranks missing.

Of these the following belonged to the 43rd:—

Killed.—Three other ranks.
Wounded.—Captain C. S. Baines, D.S.O., Lieutenants O. H. M. Sturges and J. E. H. Neville, M.C., and five other ranks.

Captain G. Naylor, M.C., was awarded a bar to the *Military Cross*, and Lieutenant H. E. F. Smyth the *Military Cross*; and 28750 Serjeant W. Warnock and 18566 Lance-Corporal C. Martin were awarded the *Meritorious Service Medal*.

Colonel W. Marriott-Dodington, C.M.G., and Lieutenant L. W. Giles, M.C., were mentioned in despatches.

And now my task is finished. Some may think that overmuch space has been devoted to the description of this curious campaign in which only an insignificant handful of the 43rd took part; and that little was achieved to warrant the grant of the battle honour " Archangel." The justification, if any be required, lies in the fact that it was really a unique campaign. Had the 43rd chanced to have been sent to the Dvina, there would have been more warlike actions to record; and, by the same token, had the

[5] See Appendix XVII. [6] See Appendix XVIII.

Bolsheviks in the last fortnight been induced to close with the defence, the two companies of the Regiment, outnumbered by ten to one, would have been faced with a fight for their very lives. Luck and the poor morale of the enemy saved the Regiment from an awkward situation.

The Peace Treaty was signed at the time when the 43rd was raiding the Bolshevik position at Ignatovskaya. The campaign was embodied in the German War and the troops were issued with the General Service and Victory Medals.

The campaign as the 43rd saw it was dull, very dull. Reduced to its elements, life is a matter of food and water, of which the former was neither good nor sufficient in the Vaga Column. But those who thought at all learned much of military value and were able to appreciate the difficulties of a river campaign, of forest fighting, and a withdrawal in the face of an enemy.

As is known, from the moment of the departure of the British, Bolshevism never looked back: Archangel fell before Christmas; and General Denikin in the south was gradually forced back and overwhelmed by the irresistible tide of madness; and, as it turned out, nothing that the British could have done would have availed aught against it. But it is curious that in North Russia to-day the Russians still curse what they call the *Intervention*. Had the scale of fortune been otherwise weighted there was and is no doubt but that a force or mission of British would have been required to rehabilitate Russia and prevent its exploitation by Germany; and for that purpose the North Russian Relief Force would have been ideally placed. But none of these things happened and the expedition was relegated to the limbo of unsuccessful adventures which have no memorial. It is to give it an honourable memorial that this story has been compiled at length and offered to the

43RD LIGHT INFANTRY.

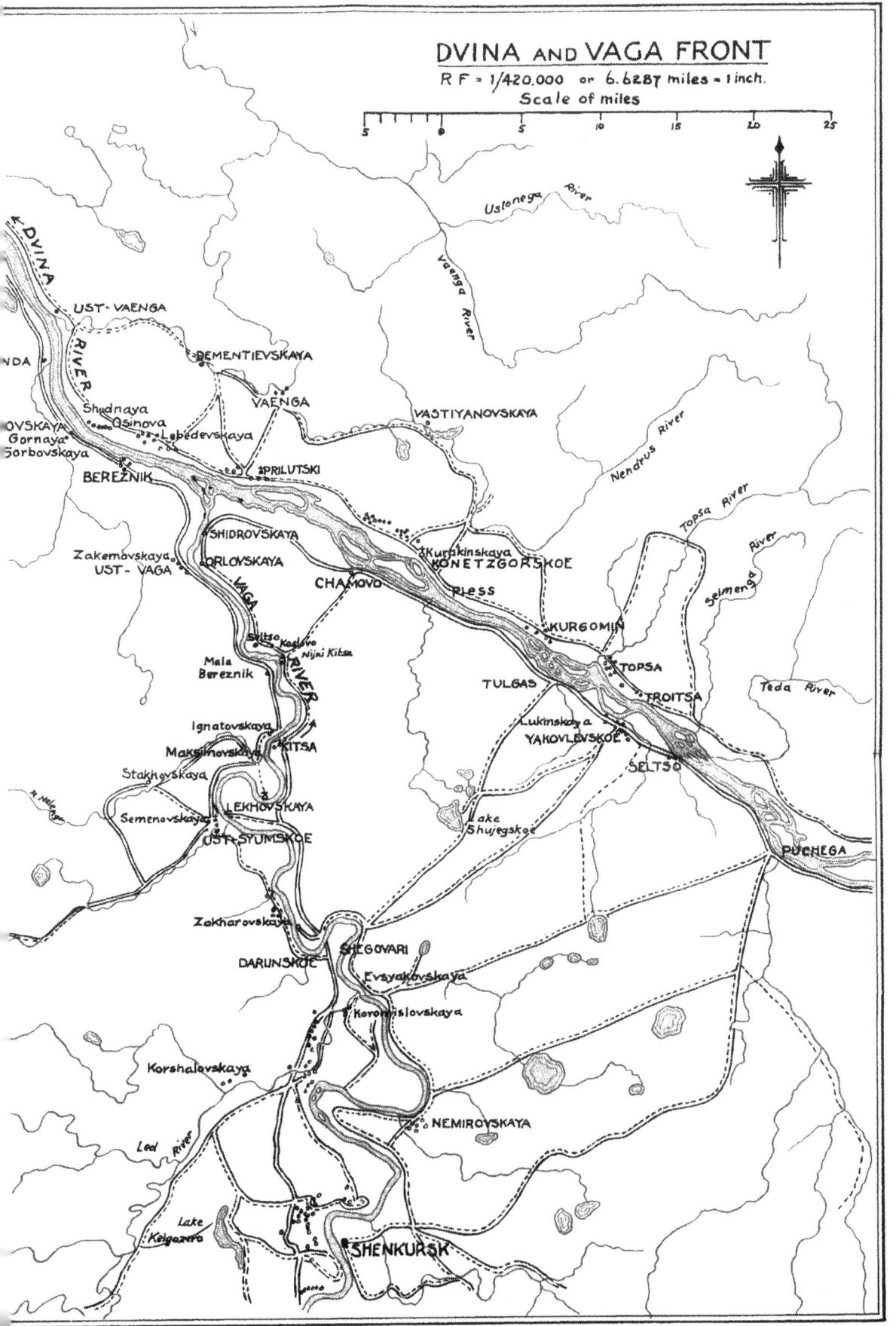

APPENDICES

APPENDIX I.[1]

Composition of Force "D" on the 1st December 1914.

Headquarters.
  General Officer Commanding: Lieutenant-General Sir A. A. Barrett, K.C.B., K.C.V.O., Indian Army.

General Staff Branch :—
  General Staff Officer, 1st Grade (Colonel R. N. Gamble, D.S.O., British Service).
  General Staff Officer, 2nd Grade.
  General Staff Officer, 3rd Grade.
  Two special service officers (attached).

Adjutant-General's and Quartermaster-General's Branches :—
  Deputy Assistant Adjutant General.
  Assistant Quartermaster-General.
  Deputy Assistant Adjutant and Quarter-Master General.

Attached :—
  Divisional Artillery Commander.
  Divisional Engineer Commander.
  Assistant Director of Medical Services.
  Deputy Assistant Director of Medical Services.
  Assistant Director of Supplies.
  Assistant Director of Transport.
  Deputy Assistant Director of Ordnance Services.
  Assistant Director of Veterinary Services.
  Deputy Judge Advocate General.
  Controller of Military Accounts and his assistants.
  Interpreter.
  Chaplain, Church of England.

Divisional Troops.

Cavalry :—
  33rd Queen Victoria's Own Light Cavalry.

Artillery :—
  Headquarters Divisional Artillery :
    Divisional Artillery Commander : Brigadier-General C. T. Robinson.
  10th Brigade, Royal Field Artillery.
    7th Battery, R.F.A.
    82nd Battery, R.F.A.
    63rd Battery, R.F.A.
    6th Ammunition Column, R.F.A.
  1st Indian Mountain Artillery Brigade.
    23rd Indian Mountain Battery.
    30th Indian Mountain Battery.

[1] *Official History*, Vol. I, p. 348.

Royal Engineers :—
  Headquarters, Divisional Engineers.
  No. 17 Company, 3rd Sappers and Miners.
  No. 22 Company, 3rd Sappers and Miners.
  No. 34 Divisional Signal Company.
  No. 3 Troop, Wireless Signal Squadron.

Pioneers :—
  48th Pioneers.

Infantry.

16th Indian Infantry Brigade (Brigadier-General W. S. Delamain, C.B., D.S.O., Indian Army) :—
  2nd Dorsetshire Regiment.
  20th Duke of Cambridge's Own Infantry (Brownlow's Punjabis).
  104th Wellesley's Rifles.
  117th Mahrattas.

17th Indian Infantry Brigade (Brigadier-General W. H. Dobbie, C.B., Indian Army) :—
  43rd Light Infantry.
  119th Infantry (The Mooltan Regiment).
  103rd Mahratta Light Infantry.
  22nd Punjabis.

18th Indian Infantry Brigade (Major-General C. I. Fry, Indian Army) :—
  2nd Norfolk Regiment.
  110th Mahratta Light Infantry.
  120th Rajputana Infantry.
  7th Duke of Cornwall's Own Rajputs.

Medical Services.

Assistant Director of Medical Services : Colonel P. Hehir, M.D., Indian Medical Service.
No. 16 British Field Ambulance.
No. 17 British Field Ambulance.
No. 125 Indian Field Ambulance.
No. 126 Indian Field Ambulance.
No. 127 Indian Field Ambulance.
No. 19 Combined Clearing Hospital.
No. 57 Indian Stationary Hospital.
No. 3 British General Hospital.
No. 9 Indian General Hospital.
No. 2 X-Ray Section.
Advanced Depot Medical Services.

NAVAL.

Senior Naval Officer : Captain A. Hayes-Sadler, R.N.

Armed Vessels.

H.M.S. *Espiègle* (Sloop), six 4-inch quick-firing and two 3-pounder guns and two maxims.
H.M.S. *Odin* (Sloop), four 4-inch quick-firing and two 3-pounder guns and two maxims.
H.M.S. *Lawrence* (Paddle Steamer, Royal Indian Marine), four 4-inch quick-firing and four 6-pounder guns.

Comet (Steam Yacht), one 3-pounder gun and three old Nordenfeldts.
Lewis Pelly (Small Steam Yacht), two 3-pounder Hotchkiss guns and one maxim.
Miner (Small River Steamer), one 12-pounder (8 cwt.) gun, one 3-pounder and one maxim.
Shaitan (Steam Tug), one 12-pounder (8 cwt.) gun and one maxim.
Sirdar-i-Naphte (Steam Tug), one 12-pounder (8 cwt.) gun and one maxim.
Mashona (Steam Tug), one 3-pounder gun.

H.M.S. *Ocean* (pre-Dreadnought), off bar of Shatt al Arab.

H.M.S. *Dalhousie* (Royal Indian Marine), four 6-pounder guns, off Bushire.

Unarmed Vessels.

Mejidieh, *Blosse Lynch* and *Malamir* of the Euphrates and Tigris Steam Navigation Company (Lynch Bros.).
Sumana, *Shihab* and *Shurur* of the Société de Transports Fluviaux.
The *Salimi* and six small launches taken up locally.

APPENDIX II.[1]

REORGANIZATION OF FORCE " D " AS ON THE 1ST APRIL 1915.

G.O.C. Force : General Sir John E. Nixon, K.C.B.

II INDIAN ARMY CORPS.

6th Cavalry Brigade :—
    " S " Battery, R.H.A.
    7th Lancers.
    16th Cavalry.

6th (Poona) Division.
    16th Infantry Brigade.
    17th Infantry Brigade.
    18th Infantry Brigade.

12th Indian Division.
    12th Infantry Brigade.
    30th Infantry Brigade.
    33rd Infantry Brigade.

Corps Troops :—
    Wireless Signal Troop.
    Bridging Train.
    Printing and Litho Sections.

6th Divisional Troops.

33rd Cavalry (less 2 squadrons).
10th Brigade, R.F.A. (18 guns).
Divisional Ammunition Column.
1st Indian Mountain Artillery Brigade (12 guns).
17th Field Company, Sappers and Miners.
22nd Field Company, Sappers and Miners.
34th Divisional Signal Company.
48th Pioneers.

12th Divisional Troops.

Two squadrons, 33rd Cavalry.
86th Heavy Battery, R.G.A. (4 guns).
104th Heavy Battery, R.G.A. (4 guns).
1st/5th Hampshire Howitzer Battery, R.F.A. (4 howitzers).
12th Field Company, Sappers and Miners.
Sirmur Imperial Service Company, Sappers and Miners.
12th Divisional Signal Company.

[1] *Official History*, Vol. I, p. 350.

APPENDICES

The composition of the infantry brigades of the 12th Division was:—

12th	...	2nd Queen's Own Royal West Kent Regiment, 4th Rajputs, 44th Merwara Infantry, 90th Punjabis.
30th	...	24th Punjabis, 76th Punjabis, 2nd/7th Gurkhas.
33rd	...	1st/4th Hampshire Regiment, 11th Rajputs, 66th Punjabis, 67th Punjabis.

COMMANDERS AND PRINCIPAL STAFF OFFICERS.

Army Corps Staff.

Senior General Staff Officer	Major-General G. V. Kemball.
General Staff Officer (1st Grade)	Major G. R. Cassells, 35th Sikhs.
General Staff Officer (1st Grade)	Major W. H. Beach, R.E.
D.A. and Q.M.G.	Brigadier-General W. G. Hamilton.
A.Q.M.G.	Colonel J. A. Douglas, C.M.G.
Deputy Director Army Signals	Major L. H. Queripel, R.A.
C.R.A.	Brigadier-General C. T. Robinson, R.A.
C.R.E.	Colonel J. P. Brewin, R.E.
I.G. Communications	Major-General K. S. Davison, C.B.
G.O.C. 6th (Poona) Division	Lieutenant-General Sir A. A. Barrett, K.C.B., K.C.V.O.
G.S.O.1 6th (Poona) Division	Colonel R. N. Gamble, D.S.O.
A.Q.M.G., 6th (Poona) Division	Colonel L. W. Shakespear.
G.O.C., 12th Indian Division	Major-General G. F. Gorringe, C.B., C.M.G., D.S.O.
G.S.O.1, 12th Indian Division	Major H. F. J. Browne, 5th Gurkhas.
A.Q.M.G., 12th Indian Division	Colonel C. E. Hendley.
G.O.C. 6th Cavalry Brigade	Brigadier-General H. Kennedy.
G.O.C. 16th Infantry Brigade	Brigadier-General W. S. Delamain, C.B., D.S.O.
G.O.C. 17th Infantry Brigade	Brigadier-General W. H. Dobbie, C.B.
G.O.C. 18th Infantry Brigade	Major-General C. I. Fry.
G.O.C. 12th Infantry Brigade	Brigadier-General K. E. Lean, C.B.
G.O.C. 30th Infantry Brigade	Major-General C. J. Melliss, V.C., C.B.
G.O.C. 33rd Infantry Brigade	Brigadier-General R. Wapshare.

APPENDIX III.[1]

COMPOSITION ON THE 14TH NOVEMBER 1915 OF MAJOR-GENERAL C. V. F. TOWNSHEND'S COLUMN ADVANCING ON BAGHDAD.

Cavalry :—
    Headquarters, 6th Cavalry Brigade.
    " S " Battery, R.H.A.
    7th Lancers (4 squadrons).
    16th Cavalry (3 squadrons).
    33rd Cavalry (3 squadrons).
    One squadron, 23rd Cavalry (Divisional Cavalry).
    Total : 11 squadrons and 6 guns.

Artillery :—
    10th Brigade, R.F.A. (63rd, 76th and 82nd Batteries).
    1st/5th Hampshire Howitzer Battery.
    86th Heavy Battery, R.G.A. (one section in barges).
    104th Heavy Battery, R.G.A. (less one section at Amara).
    One post gun, Volunteer Artillery Battery.
    Total : 29 guns (of which 3 guns were to be left with the garrison at Aziziya).

Infantry :—
    16th Brigade.
        2nd Dorsetshire Regiment.
        66th Punjabis.
        104th Rifles.
        117th Mahrattas.
    17th Brigade.
        43rd Light Infantry.
        22nd Punjabis.
        103rd Mahrattas.
        119th Infantry.
    18th Brigade.
        2nd Norfolk Regiment.
        7th Rajputs.
        110th Mahrattas.
        120th Infantry.
    30th Brigade.
        2nd/7th Gurkhas.
        24th Punjabis.
        76th Punjabis.

    Total : 16 battalions (of which half of the 24th Punjabis was to be left at Aziziya).

[1] *Official History*, Vol. II, p. 480.

Divisional Troops :—

>Maxim Battery.
>17th Field Company, Sappers and Miners.
>22nd Field Company, Sappers and Miners.
>Bridging Train.
>Searchlight Section.
>Divisional Ammunition Column.
>34th Divisional Signal Company.
>One brigade section, 12th Divisional Signal Company.
>>One section, Army Corps Signal Company.
>>One wagon wireless station.
>
>Two pack wireless stations.
>Field ambulances.
>Clearing hospitals (on the *Blosse Lynch* and *Mosul*).

Air Service :—

>Five aeroplanes, Royal Flying Corps.   Two more arrived on the 17th November.

APPENDIX IV.[1]

Order of Battle at Ctesiphon.

Column "A" (Major-General Delamain) :—
  16th Infantry Brigade.
    2nd Dorsetshire Regiment.
    104th Rifles.
  30th Composite Brigade.
    24th Punjabis (less half battalion in garrison at Aziziya).
    2nd/7th Gurkhas.
    66th Punjabis.
    117th Mahrattas.
  82nd Battery, R.F.A. (6 guns).
  1st/5th Hampshire Howitzer Battery (4 guns).
  Half 22nd Company, Sappers and Miners.

Column "B" (Brigadier-General Hamilton) :—
  18th Infantry Brigade.
    2nd Norfolk Regiment.
    7th Rajputs.
    110th Mahrattas.
    120th Infantry.
  63rd Battery, R.F.A. (6 guns).
  Half 22nd Company, Sappers and Miners.
  One pack wireless set.

Column "C" (Brigadier-General Hoghton) :—
  17th Infantry Brigade.
    43rd Light Infantry.
    22nd Punjabis.
    119th Infantry.
    103rd Mahrattas (less half battalion guarding shipping at Lajj).
  76th Battery, R.F.A. (6 guns).
  86th Heavy Battery, R.G.A. (2 guns).
  17th Company, Sappers and Miners.
  48th Pioneers.
  One squadron, 23rd Cavalry.
  One pack wireless set.

Flying Column (Major-General Melliss, V.C.) :—
  6th Cavalry Brigade.
    "S" Battery, R.H.A.
    7th Lancers.
    16th Cavalry.
    33rd Cavalry.
  Maxim Battery.
  Motor machine-gun section (two armoured cars and two lorries).
  76th Punjabis (equipped with sufficient A.T. carts to carry half the battalion).
  One pack wireless set.

[1] *Official History*, Vol. II, pp. 67-68.

APPENDIX V.

CASUALTIES AT CTESIPHON AND ON THE RETREAT FROM CTESIPHON, EXTRACTED FROM THE OFFICIAL LIST OF CASUALTIES INCURRED BY THE 43RD IN THE WAR.

8361	Private	Apps, Arthur, D.C.M.	k. in a.	1 Dec. 15
6011	Serjeant	Badby, Samuel	k. in a.	22 Nov. 15
8308	Private	Baker, Ernest Henry	k. in a.	22 Nov. 15
9747	Private	Baldwin, Harry	k. in a.	22 Nov. 15
9590	Lance-Corporal	Bartlett, Sidney	k. in a.	22 Nov. 15
	Serjeant	Bennett, 2nd/4thWiltshire Regt., "Q" Coy.	k. in a.	22 Nov. 15
9392	Lance-Corporal	Berry, Thomas William	k. in a.	22 Nov. 15
7977	Serjeant	Berry, William Frank	k. in a.	22 Nov. 15
8833	Private	Booth, Thomas Albert	k. in a.	22 Nov. 15
9120	Lance-Corporal	Bowers, Frank	k. in a.	22 Nov. 15
9135	Serjeant	Bricknell, Joseph	k. in a.	22 Nov. 15
8168	Private	Bull, Cervantes Harry	k. in a.	22 Nov. 15
7555	Private	Button, George Edward	k. in a.	22 Nov. 15
6072	Serjeant	Chadbone, Herbert	k. in a.	22 Nov. 15
7991	Private	Chambers, Joseph	k. in a.	22 Nov. 15
19589	Private	Chapman, Edmund	k. in a.	22 Nov. 15
9565	Private	Clack, Christopher Augustus	k. in a.	22 Nov. 15
8988	Lance-Serjeant	Collins, William	d. of w.	28 Nov. 15
20450	Private	Dunhill, Louis Overton Rhenous	k. in a.	22 Nov. 15
18572	Private	Ebury, John Richard	k. in a.	22 Nov. 15
9329	Private	Eden, Frederick	k. in a.	22 Nov. 15
6773	Serjeant	Gardiner, Robert	k. in a.	22 Nov. 15
9008	Private	Gibbard, Thomas	k. in a.	22 Nov. 15
8541	Lance-Corporal	Godwin, Alfred Charles	k. in a.	22 Nov. 15
8158	Private	Griffin, Charles	k. in a.	22 Nov. 15
8667	Private	Groom, John Robert	k. in a.	23 Nov. 15
8702	Lance-Corporal	Grover, Charles William	k. in a.	22 Nov. 15
8860	Private	Grover, William	k. in a.	22 Nov. 15
9447	Private	Harris, Percy Cooper	k. in a.	22 Nov. 15
9245	Lance-Corporal	Hawkins, John Frederick	k. in a.	22 Nov. 15
8890	Private	Hedges, Walter	k. in a.	22 Nov. 15
9316	Lance-Corporal	Heffer, Leonard	k. in a.	22 Nov. 15
	Serjeant	Heines, "Q" Coy.	k. in a.	22 Nov. 15
9290	Private	Horlock, Alfred	k. in a.	22 Nov. 15
8481	Private	Humphreys, Henry Daniel	k. in a.	22 Nov. 15
8290	Lance-Serjeant	Ives, William Henry	k. in a.	22 Nov. 15
5308	C.S.M.	Kemmis, Harry	k. in a.	22 Nov. 15
8427	Private	Kingsbury, William	k. in a.	22 Nov. 15
8558	Private	Kirby, Philip	k. in a.	22 Nov. 15
8738	Private	Lambert, Alfred Edward	d. of w.	4 Dec. 15
8629	Private	Liddell, Fred Baylis	k. in a.	22 Nov. 15

9226	Private	Lister, Frederick John	k. in a.	22 Nov. 15
9717	Private	Lovegrove, Horace Leonard	k. in a.	22 Nov. 15
8100	Private	Major, Henry	k. in a.	22 Nov. 15
8399	Serjeant	Marriott, Albert John	k. in a.	22 Nov. 15
18570	Private	Mason, Arthur Charles	d. of w.	4 Dec. 15
8211	Serjeant	Mathews, William James	k. in a.	22 Nov. 15
8304	Lance-Corporal	Mitchell, Thomas Edwin	k. in a.	22 Nov. 15
9690	Private	Mold, Arthur	k. in a.	22 Nov. 15
9076	Private	Payne, John Henry	k. in a.	22 Nov. 15
8953	Lance-Serjeant	Phillips, Reginald	k. in a.	22 Nov. 15
9649	Private	Pocock, George Henry	k. in a.	22 Nov. 15
9473	Private	Robinson, Frank	k. in a.	22 Nov. 15
8490	Lance-Corporal	Rutland, Joseph	k. in a.	22 Nov. 15
6449	C.S.M.	Shilcock, Henry Edward	k. in a.	22 Nov. 15
8663	Private	Simmonds, Albert Charles	k. in a.	22 Nov. 15
9198	Private	Simpson, Samuel Francis	k. in a.	22 Nov. 15
9280	Lance-Corporal	Sims, Fred	k. in a.	22 Nov. 15
9029	Private	Slade, William John	k. in a.	22 Nov. 15
9243	Private	Smith, Percy William	k. in a.	22 Nov. 15
9043	Lance-Serjeant	Smith, William	k. in a.	22 Nov. 15
8499	Private	Stallwood, Charlie	k. in a.	22 Nov. 15
9044	Private	Stockley, William Thomas	k. in a.	22 Nov. 15
7682	Corporal	Tatham, Ernest Thomas James	k. in a.	22 Nov. 15
8546	Private	Taylor, Henry	k. in a.	22 Nov. 15
9165	Private	Temple, John	d. of w.	3 Dec. 15
9767	Private	Terry, Edward Stephen	k. in a.	22 Nov. 15
8711	Private	Thomas, Arthur Leonard	d. of w.	5 Dec. 15
7790	Lance-Corporal	Thompson, Henry	d. of w.	28 Nov. 15
8200	Private	Walton, Claude Ernest	k. in a.	22 Nov. 15
8108	Private	Warner, Frederick George	d. of w.	10 Dec. 15
8995	Lance-Corporal	Webb, William James	d. of w.	23 Nov. 15
8834	Private	Wells, George Edward	k. in a.	22 Nov. 15
9519	Private	Western, Charles	k. in a.	22 Nov. 15
8991	Private	Wilkinson, Walter	k. in a.	22 Nov. 15
8353	Private	Williams, Charles Alfred	k. in a.	1 Dec. 15
9413	Private	Wood, Andrew	k. in a.	22 Nov. 15

APPENDIX VI.[1]

ORDER OF BATTLE OF THE FORCE, UNDER MAJOR-GENERAL C. V. F. TOWNSHEND, BESIEGED IN KUT.

Headquarters, 6th Division :—
   G.S.O.1 : Lieutenant-Colonel U. W. Evans, R.E.
   A.Q.M.G. : Lieutenant-Colonel W. W. Chitty.
16th Infantry Brigade (Major-General W. S. Delamain) :—
   2nd Dorsetshire Regiment (Major G. M. Herbert).
   66th Punjabis (Lieutenant-Colonel A. Moore).
   104th Rifles (Captain C. M. S. Manners).
   117th Mahrattas (Major McV. Crichton).
17th Infantry Brigade (Brigadier-General F. A. Hoghton) :—
   43rd Light Infantry (Lieutenant-Colonel E. A. E. Lethbridge, D.S.O.).
   22nd Punjabis (Captain A. O. Sutherland).
   103rd Mahrattas (Lieutenant-Colonel W. H. Brown).
   119th Infantry (Captain F. I. O. Brickman).
18th Infantry Brigade (Brigadier-General W. G. Hamilton) :—
   2nd Norfolk Regiment (Major F. C. Lodge).
   7th Rajputs (Lieutenant-Colonel H. O. Parr).
   110th Mahrattas (Major H. C. Hill).
   120th Infantry (Major P. F. Pocock).
30th Infantry Brigade (Major-General Sir Charles Melliss, V.C.) :—
   Half 2nd Queen's Own Royal West Kent Regiment (Major J. W. Nelson).
   One company, 1st/4th Hampshire Regiment (Major F. L. Footner).
   24th Punjabis (Lieutenant-Colonel H. A. V. Cummins).
   76th Punjabis (Captain E. Milford).
   2nd/7th Gurkhas (Lieutenant-Colonel W. B. Powell).
   Half 67th Punjabis (Major C. E. S. Cox).
Pioneers :—
   48th Pioneers (Colonel A. J. N. Harward).

Cavalry.

One squadron, 23rd Cavalry (Captain C. H. K. Kirkwood).
One squadron, 7th Lancers (Lieutenant F. T. Drake-Brockman).

Royal Engineers.
(Lieutenant-Colonel F. A. Wilson.)

Bridging Train (Captain E. W. C. Sandes).
17th Company, Sappers and Miners (Lieutenant K. B. S. Crawford).
22nd Company, Sappers and Miners (Lieutenant A. B. Matthews).
Sirmur Company, Imperial Service Sappers (Captain C. E. Colbeck).
Engineer Field Park (Captain H. W. Tomlinson).

[1] *Official History*, Vol. II, pp. 488-489.

Artillery.
(Brigadier-General G. B. Smith.)

10th Brigade, R.F.A. (Lieutenant-Colonel H. N. St. J. Maule):—
    63rd Battery (Major H. Broke Smith) ⎫
    76th Battery (Major O. S. Lloyd) ⎬ 18 guns
    82nd Battery (Major E. Corbould Warren) ⎭
1st/5th Hampshire Howitzer Battery (Major H. G. Thomson) ... 4 guns
86th Heavy Battery, R.G.A. (5-inch guns) (Lieutenant-Colonel M. H. Courtenay) ... 4 guns
One section, 104th Heavy Battery, R.G.A. (4-inch guns) (Major W. C. R. Farmar) ... 2 guns
Volunteer Artillery Battery (15-pounder) (Major A. J. Anderson) ... 4 guns
One spare 18-pounder gun ... 1 gun
One section, " S " Battery, R.H.A. (13-pounder guns) ... 2 guns
6th Divisional Ammunition Column (Captain E. T. Martin).

Miscellaneous.

Maxim Battery (six machine guns) (Captain C. H. Stockley).
Detachment, Army Signal Company (Major F. Booth).
34th Divisional Signal Company (Captain H. S. Cardew).
One brigade section, 12th Divisional Signal Company.
Wireless section (two wagon and one pack sets).
A few details, Royal Flying Corps (Captain S. C. Winfield-Smith).
Supply and Transport personnel, including details of the Jaipur Transport Corps and of the 13th, 21st, 26th and 30th Mule Corps (Lieutenant-Colonel A. S. R. Annesley).
No. 32 Field Post Office.
Three Chaplains—Rev. H. Spooner (Church of England).
        Rev. T. Mullen (Roman Catholic).
        Rev. A. Y. Wright (Wesleyan).

Medical Units.
(Colonel P. Hehir, I.M.S.)

No. 2 Field Ambulance.
No. 4 Field Ambulance.
No. 106 Field Ambulance.
Officers' Hospital.
No. 157 Indian Stationary Hospital.
No. 9 Indian General Hospital.
Half No. 3 British General Hospital.
One section, Veterinary Field Hospital (Captain H. Stephenson).

Naval Detachment.

H.M.S. *Sumana* (Gunboat, one 12-pounder and two 3-pounder guns)[2] (Lieutenant L. C. P. Tudway, R.N.).
Four steam launches.[3]
Two motor launches.
One 12-pounder gun intended for H.M.S. *Firefly*.[4]
Six barges.
Four 4.7-inch guns in horse-boats.

---

[2] These guns were mounted ashore in March 1916.
[3] Three were sunk on the destruction of the bridge on the 9th-10th December 1915.
[4] This was mounted ashore on the town river front at the beginning of January.

APPENDIX VII.[1]

REORGANIZATION OF TIGRIS CORPS, 15TH JANUARY 1916.

3RD DIVISION.
Major-General H. d'U. Keary.

7th Brigade :—
    1st/1st Gurkhas.   93rd Infantry.
    1st/9th Gurkhas.

9th Brigade :—
    1st/4th Hampshire Regiment (less one company).
    107th Pioneers.
    2nd Rajputs (less half battalion).
    62nd Punjabis.

28th Brigade :—
    2nd Leicestershire Regiment.   53rd Sikhs.
    51st Sikhs.   56th Rifles.

Divisional Troops :—
    One battery, 9th Brigade, R.F.A.
    61st Howitzer Battery.
    23rd Mountain Battery (less one section).
    Cavalry Brigade (less two squadrons).
    Administrative units.
    Field ambulances.

7TH DIVISION.
Major-General Sir George Younghusband.

19th Brigade :—
    72nd Highlanders.   92nd Punjabis.
    28th Punjabis.   125th Rifles.

21st Brigade :—
    73rd Royal Highlanders.   9th Bhopal Infantry.
    6th Jats.   41st Dogras.

35th Brigade :—
    1st/5th The Buffs.   37th Dogras.
    97th Infantry.   102nd Grenadiers.

[1] *Official History*, Vol. II, p. 257.

Divisional Troops :—

    9th Brigade, R.F.A. (less one battery).
    1st/1st Sussex Battery, R.F.A.
    72nd Heavy Battery, R.G.A.
    128th Pioneers.
    Two squadrons cavalry.
    Administrative units.
    Field ambulances.

Corps Troops :—

    13th Company, Sappers and Miners.
    Bridging Train.
    77th Battery, R.G.A.
    One section, 104th Heavy Battery, R.G.A.
    Air Service.

APPENDIX VIII.[1]

ORDER OF BATTLE AND DISTRIBUTION OF THE BRITISH FORCES IN MESOPOTAMIA ON THE 27TH FEBRUARY (EXCLUDING THE GARRISON OF KUT AL AMARA).

3RD DIVISION.
(Major-General H. d'U. Keary.)

7th Infantry Brigade (Major-General R. G. Egerton) :—
    1st Connaught Rangers (including drafts for the 2nd Royal West Kent Regiment).
    27th Punjabis.
    89th Punjabis.
    128th Pioneers.

8th Infantry Brigade (Lieutenant-Colonel F. P. S. Dunsford, 2nd Rajputs) :—
    1st Manchester Regiment.
    2nd Rajputs.
    47th Sikhs.
    59th Rifles.

9th Infantry Brigade (Brigadier-General L. W. Y. Campbell, 89th Punjabis) :—
    1st Highland Light Infantry.
    1st/1st Gurkhas.
    1st/9th Gurkhas.
    93rd Infantry.

4th Brigade, R.F.A. (7th, 14th, 66th Batteries).
20th Field Company, Sappers and Miners.
21st Field Company, Sappers and Miners.
34th Sikh Pioneers.
One squadron, 16th Cavalry.
No. 3 Divisional Signal Company.
Mobile Veterinary Section.

7TH DIVISION.
(Major-General Sir G. J. Younghusband.)

19th Infantry Brigade (Brigadier-General E. C. Peebles) :—
    Composite Highland battalion (2nd Black Watch and 1st Seaforth Highlanders).
    28th Punjabis.
    92nd Punjabis.
    125th Rifles.

[1] *Official History*, Vol. II, p. 510.

21st Infantry Brigade (Brigadier-General C. E. Norie) :—

    Composite English battalion (2nd Norfolk and 2nd Dorsetshire Regiments).
    6th Jats.
    9th Bhopal Infantry.
    Composite Mahratta battalion (drafts for Mahratta battalions in Kut).

28th Infantry Brigade (Major-General G. V. Kemball) :—

    2nd Leicestershire Regiment.
    2nd/43rd Light Infantry.
    51st Sikhs.
    53rd Sikhs.
    56th Rifles.

9th Brigade, R.F.A. (19th, 20th, 28th Batteries), 18 guns.
3rd Field Company, Sappers and Miners.
107th Pioneers.
One squadron, 16th Cavalry.
No. 7 Divisional Signal Company.
Mobile Veterinary Section.

Cavalry Brigade (Brigadier-General R. C. Stephen) :—

    14th Hussars.
    4th Cavalry.
    7th Lancers (three squadrons strong).
    33rd Cavalry (less one squadron).
    "S" Battery, R.H.A. (4 guns).

CORPS TROOPS.

35th Infantry Brigade (Brigadier-General G. B. H. Rice) :—

    Composite Territorial battalion (1st/5th The Buffs and 1st/4th Hampshire Regiment).
    Composite Dogra battalion (37th and 41st Dogras).
    97th Infantry.

36th Infantry Brigade (Brigadier-General G. Christian) :—

    1st/6th Devonshire Regiment.
    26th Punjabis.
    62nd Punjabis.
    82nd Punjabis.

12th Company, Sappers and Miners (less one section).
13th Company, Sappers and Miners.
Field Troop, Sappers and Miners.
13th Brigade, R.F.A. (2nd, 8th, 44th Batteries), 18 guns.
60th and 61st Howitzer Batteries (twelve 4.5-inch howitzers).
23rd Mountain Battery, less one section (four 10-pounder guns).
Home Counties Brigade, R.F.A. (less one battery) { 1/1st Sussex Battery; 1/3rd ,, ,, } =18 15-pounder guns.
One section 104th Heavy Battery, R.G.A. (two 4-inch guns).
7th Divisional Ammunition Column.

Signal Units :—

    Wireless, one wagon and two pack stations.
    No. 1 Army Corps Signal Company.
    No. 12 Divisional Signal Company (less two brigade sections).
    No. 33 Divisional Signal Company (two brigade sections).

Medical Units :—
- No. 18 Cavalry Field Ambulance (two sections).
- No. 131 Indian Cavalry Field Ambulance.
- No. 3 Combined Field Ambulance (two sections).
- No. 1 Field Ambulance (less headquarters).
- No. 20 Combined Field Ambulance.
- No. 7 British Field Ambulance.
- No. 8 British Field Ambulance.
- No. 19 British Field Ambulance.
- No. 20 British Field Ambulance.
- No. 21 Combined Field Ambulance.
- Nos. 111, 112, 113, 128, 129, 130 Indian Field Ambulances.
- No. 19 Combined Clearing Hospital.
- No. 4 Sanitary Section.

Various Administrative units :—

Air Service :
 One flight R.N.A.S. (only one aeroplane serviceable).
 "B" Flight, No. 30 Squadron, R.F.C. (three serviceable machines).

En route to join the Tigris Corps :—

37th Infantry Brigade (Brigadier-General F. J. Fowler) :—
 1st/4th Somerset Light Infantry.
 1st/2nd Gurkhas.

APPENDIX IX.

Casualties at the First Battle of Sannaiyat, 6th April 1916.

According to official returns the strength of the 2nd/43rd when it went into action was thirteen officers and two hundred and sixty-six non-commissioned officers and men. The official figures of casualties received from the base were :—

	Killed.	Wounded.	Missing.
Officers	5	8	—
Other ranks	51	170	14

Leaving 31 survivors.

According to the *Chronicle*, 1915-16, p. 175, Lieutenant Kinghorn brought back the survivors of the attack, numbering seventeen only. There were, presumably, fourteen other survivors at headquarters.

Those reported missing by the Adjutant-General's department on the 11th May were :—

Private Ashton.	Private Revell.
Private Birch.	Private Russell.
Private Bishop.	Private Spicer.
Private Bound.	Private Stark.
Private Edwards.	Private Todd.
Lance-Corporal Manning.	Private Wheeler.
Lance-Corporal Parker.	Private Williams, 2nd/4th Wiltshire Regiment.

All of whom, except Privates Bishop and Williams and Lance-Corporal Manning, appear in the official casualty list as killed in action. The names of the casualties have been compiled from the *Chronicle*, 1915-16, p. 175, and the official list. Some of the wounded may have died later either at sea or in India, but their names are now impossible to trace. Only those reported killed in action on the 6th and those who, from the date of their deaths, obviously died as the result of wounds received in this battle have been included. The lists and statistics do not pretend to accuracy, but they are a tolerable guide to the Regiment's losses in this disastrous action.

ROLL OF OFFICERS WHO WENT INTO ACTION.

Major L. J. Carter, commanding	Wounded.
Captain Hon. J. C. W. S. Foljambe, adjutant	Killed.
Lieutenant A. H. Seymour, 4th Duke of Cornwall's Light Infantry, machine gun officer	Survived.
Second Lieutenant A. H. Truman, bombing officer	Killed.
Captain S. F. Hammick, commanding "A" Company	Died of wounds.
Captain R. H. G. Tatton, commanding "B" Company	Wounded.
Lieutenant D. G. Firth, 5th Hampshire Regiment	Wounded.
Lieutenant E. C. Kinghorn, 4th Border Regiment	Survived.
Second Lieutenant H. D. H. Radford	Survived.
Second Lieutenant C. I. Widcombe	Killed.

APPENDICES

Second Lieutenant E. F. Coulthard	...	...	...	...	...	Killed.
Second Lieutenant A. H. Davis	...	...	...	...	...	Killed.
Second Lieutenant A. E. Gardner	...	...	...	...	...	Wounded.
Second Lieutenant C. H. Riley	...	...	...	...	...	Wounded.
Second Lieutenant H. T. C. Field	...	...	...	...	...	Wounded.
Second Lieutenant W. Rance	...	...	...	...	...	Survived.

SUMMARY OF CASUALTIES FROM OFFICIAL LIST.

	No. in Action.	Killed.	Died of Wounds.	Missing, believed Killed.	Missing.	Wounded.	Survived.
Officers, 2nd/43rd	13	5	1	—	—	4	3
Officers Extra-Regimentally Employed	3	—	—	—	—	2	1
Other Ranks	266	54	10	11	3	157	31
Total	282	59	11	11	3	163	35

KILLED IN ACTION AT SANNAIYAT.

			Formerly of
19535	Private	Barkuss, Harry Thomas	
8867	Lance-Corporal	Best, Joseph	
9255	Private	Bidmead, Arthur	
19785	Private	Bird, Frank	R. War. R.
21478	Private	Boulter, Percy Francis	Somerset L.I.
17597	Corporal	Buckingham, Reginald Sydney	
21881	Private	Burrows, Leonard James	R. Fus.
21590	Lance-Serjeant	Cantello, Ralph Cyril	Somerset L.I.
19681	Private	Capp, Edward	
21561	Private	Cook, Henry Stephen	Somerset L.I.
11478	Private	Cooper, Arthur Ernest	
21936	Private	Davey, Alfred George	R. Fus.
22010	Private	Davies, Daniel	R. Fus.
21593	Private	Davies, William John	Somerset L.I.
21476	Private	Davis, Walter	Somerset L.I.
18562	Private	Dyke, Christopher Handel	
11857	Private	Embra, Ernest	
21940	Lance-Corporal	Ford, Richard William	R. Fus.
26030	Private	Gilbert, Noel	
17990	Lance-Corporal	Goldsmith, Robert	
21846	Private	Gresty, Albert	
22012	Private	Harlow, William	R. Fus.
11937	Private	Hawkins, George Murray	
22003	Private	Holman, Alfred	R. Fus.
21927	Lance-Corporal	House, William Henry	R. Fus.
8992	Lance-Corporal	Inwood, Thomas	
12045	Private	Jenkins, George	
18057	Private	Lambert, Cyril	
8969	Private	Lawrence, James	
21578	Actg./Corporal	Legg, William Robert	Somerset L.I.
21983	Private	Lewis, Alfred	R. Fus.
16565	Private	Lloyd, Arthur	
16767	Private	Mann, Horace	

43RD LIGHT INFANTRY

Formerly of

12181	Private	Martin, Benjamin	
11069	Private	Maycock, Sydney	
21950	Private	Moring, Bernard	R. Fus.
21951	Private	Morley, Joseph	R. Fus.
14322	Private	Moss, Frederick William	
18846	Lance-Corporal	Oliver, Wallace	
21431	Private	Payne, William Henry	
9239	Lance-Corporal	Prince, William George	
19470	Private	Prue, Mark Edward	
21845	Private	Rawlins, William	R. Fus.
21955	Private	Rowley, Arthur	R. Fus.
19055	Private	Scraggs, Walter	
8741	Corporal	Searle, Harry Edward	
21959	Private	Seymour, George James	R. Fus.
21572	Lance-Corporal	Skuse, George Thomas	Somerset L.I.
18869	Private	Smith, Herbert Victor	
21515	Lance-Corporal	Vamplew, Ernest	Somerset L.I.
12513	Lance-Corporal	Vyse, William	
21480	Private	Williams, George	Somerset L.I.
8610	Private	Williams, Walter Eli	
21439	Private	Wimpenny, Joseph Tedbar	Somerset L.I.

DIED OF WOUNDS.

21445	Private	Davis, Henry	7/4/16	Somerset L.I.
17480	Lance-Corporal	Dover, Arthur	7/4/16	
21943	Private	Flux, Frank	12/4/16	R. Fus.
9920	Lance-Corporal	Jones, Charles	8/4/16	
19552	Private	King, Frederick	8/4/16	
21468	Private	Legg, John George	7/4/16	Somerset L.I.
7063	C.Q.M.S.	Miller, Robert Grattan	6/4/16	
18759	Private	Wade, Frederick	7/4/16	
17728	Private	Wagerfield, Arthur Thomas	9/4/16	
9932	Corporal	White, Joseph	7/4/16	

MISSING, REPORTED KILLED.

10069	Private	Ashton, Samuel	
18541	Private	Birch, John	
21442	Private	Bound, Thomas Samuel	Somerset L.I.
12170	Private	Edwards, Thomas William	
21928	Lance-Corporal	Parker, William George	R. Fus.
21954	Private	Revell, Alfred Charles	R. Fus.
21589	Private	Russell, Arthur Victor Newbury	
21530	Private	Spicer, Joseph	
21512	Private	Stark, Thomas	Somerset L.I.
9132	Private	Todd, Henry	
10590	Private	Wheeler, Walter William	

MISSING.

	Private	Bishop	
	Lance-Corporal	Manning	
	Private	Williams	2nd/4th Wilts Regt.

APPENDIX X.

CASUALTIES IN THE SIEGE OF KUT.

The following list of casualties has been compiled from the official list of soldiers who died in the war. The numbers do not tally with the figures given in General Townshend's book, page 356, because it has been impossible to differentiate between those who died or were killed in Kut; as the result of wounds or disease before the siege; as the result of the battle of Ctesiphon; or as the result of wounds or disease while serving with the 2nd/43rd in the relief operations.

General Townshend's reported casualties give a total of thirty-eight who died in action, of wounds and disease. Many of those below who died of disease were probably in base hospitals at the time. I can therefore lay no claim to accuracy. At this distance of time it is impossible to compile absolutely accurate lists.

KILLED IN ACTION.

18650	Private	Ashby, Archibald Frederick	29/12/15
9283	Private	Berry, William	26/12/15
8377	Private	Bovington, Alfred	7/1/16
7676	C.S.M.	Busby, Thomas Henry	7/1/16
8582	Private	Carter, Jess	19/12/15
9362	Private	Clamp, William	24/12/15
9015	Private	Evans, Alfred Samson	20/12/15
9158	Corporal	Hawkett, Horace Edward	20/12/15
19117	Private	Haynes, Joseph Harold	27/3/16
9705	Private	Moseley, Sidney	24/12/15
9273	Private	Parsloe, Sindo Ronto	27/12/15
9485	Private	Pratt, John	7/1/16
8848	Private	Rankin, William	24/12/15
9575	Private	Sharp, Ernest Arthur	24/12/15
9416	Lance-Corporal	Townsend, Frederick Henry James	29/12/15
	Serjeant	Woollard	

DIED OF WOUNDS.

6053	Private	Allum, Alfred Henry	1/1/16
9375	Private	Ayres, Ernest	23/3/16
9619	Lance-Corporal	Brunham, Harry	18/3/16
8864	Private	Budd, Albert George	2/1/16
8693	Private	Bunyan, John Henry	3/3/16
8454	Private	Campion, William James	13/12/15
8438	Private	Cannon, William	11/12/15
9529	Private	Crook, Charles Benjamin	18/3/16
8226	Private	Ealdon, Horace	17/12/15
8945	Private	Evans, Walter	31/12/15
8217	Private	Goodwin, James	13/12/15

8913	Private	Holloway, William	6/12/15
9651	Private	James, John Thomas	29/1/16
7829	Corporal	Parsons, Giles Jesse	9/1/16
9216	Private	Shepherd, Fred	10/12/15
8244	Private	Small, William	8/1/16
9605	Private	Stickley, Albert	8/12/15
9495	Private	Tims, Bertie	1/1/16
8324	Private	Tolley, John	3/4/16
8420	Private	Vinson, Arthur Benjamin	11/12/15

DIED OF DISEASE.

9395	Private	Benfield, John Albert	18/4/16
9241	Private	Edden, Arthur Clarence	14/1/16
9405	Private	Gage, Albert	16/4/16
9340	Private	Goddard, Reginald	23/4/16
8687	Private	Grace, Harry	12/2/16
6830	Serjeant	Grace, Henry, D.C.M.	21/4/16
8990	Private	Greenwood, John Thomas	27/2/16
8540	Private	Grey, Lawrence Percy, D.C.M.	16/4/16
8398	Private	Harris, Alfred Thomas	18/3/16
9334	Private	Larrett, Edward	18/1/16
9429	Private	Mills, George	12/4/16
8148	A./C.Q.M.S.	Robins, William Edward, D.C.M.	26/4/16
7930	Lance-Serjeant	Robinson, Charles	30/1/16
9115	Private	Russell, Stanley	5/1/16
9374	Private	Seymour, Albert	12/2/16
9731	Lance-Corporal	Shortman, Ephraim	31/3/16
8888	Private	Smith, Herbert James	27/4/16
9531	Private	Vernin, Jim	18/4/16
9691	Private	Walcroft, Arthur Joe	26/12/15
9261	Private	Whittington, Benjamin Arthur	25/4/16
9125	Private	Wilkinson, Charles	17/4/16

APPENDIX XI.

The Captivity.

The compilation of the statistics relating to the prisoners of war cannot possibly be completely accurate at this distance of time—1935. Moreover, it is doubtful whether an accurate list could ever have been produced. The difficulties of producing even such lists as these have been very great, entailing much patience on the part of those who have been worried for names and called upon to rack their memories for regimental numbers, initials and ultimate destiny of the prisoners.

These lists have been compiled as the result of exhaustive inquiries, in which Captain Roberts, M.C., and his staff at the Depot, ex-R.S.M. T. A. Love, D.C.M., the late ex-Serjeant W. Ward, D.C.M., and ex-Q.M.S. Burbidge, D.C.M., have rendered valuable help. It is almost entirely due to ex-R.S.M. Love and Lieutenant (now Major) Naylor, M.C., that most of the names of the prisoners have survived. The roll and ration books of the prisoners at Airan, kept by ex-R.S.M. Love, have been the keys to an otherwise closed past. But when, in September 1916, the camp at Airan was broken up and the prisoners were dispersed in Anatolia and Asia Minor, accurate information naturally disappears.

For the period of the journey into captivity reliance has been placed on Major Henley's diary in *Chronicles* for 1927 and 1928, and in the list compiled by Lieutenant Naylor during, and immediately after release from, captivity. This last, which can be seen in the regimental museum, has proved to be of great value, and is the authority for the fate of some of the prisoners during the journey from Shumran to Airan. The fate of many during that terrible march was as obscure immediately after the war as it is to-day; and it will never be known.

Another almost insurmountable difficulty has been the computation of the numbers of men of the Regiment, as opposed to attached men, who were taken prisoners in Kut. These statistics have mainly been concerned with the men of the 43rd, but it has been impossible to omit altogether the names of those who shared the vicissitudes of the 43rd by being on its strength. Indeed, it would be ungenerous to refuse those who served the Regiment so well.

The strength of the 43rd on the capitulation of Kut was " 385, including men in Kut hospital, and 77 attached from other regiments."[1]

The strength of the 43rd alone was therefore 308, according to R.S.M. Love's parade state; but the *Chronicle*, 1919-20, p. 53, gives the number of prisoners as 305, including 4 captured in 1915. Then again the marching strength of the 43rd on leaving Shumran was 253.[2] We know that probably 53 died at Shumran of enteritis and similar abdominal diseases[3]; that 58, unfit to march, were sent to Baghdad by steamer[1]; which leaves a difference of 21 men of the 43rd and attached who were presumably in hospital in Kut or exchanged from Kut during the truce.

Also, reservists employed in India before the war were called up and posted to the 43rd. Their names do not appear in the War Office official list of casualties, though, doubtless, they were reckoned as men of the 43rd in the parade states.

All things considered, it is surprising and fortunate that so much information survived the captivity. The Turks, in their ignorance of English, were suspicious of all literature, and robbed R.S.M. Love of his rolls of men under his charge with the greatest regularity.

Though perforce incomplete, these statistics are tolerably accurate, and serve to show the ghastly mortality among the rank and file of the 43rd.

[1] *Chronicle*, 1916-17, p. 103.
[2] *Ibid.*, 1916-17, p. 103; and 1928, p. 203.　　　[3] *Ibid.*, 1915-16, p. 132.

		Reservists and 43rd. attached.	Total.
Strength of rank and file, 29th April 1916		308 77	385
Died at Shumran	53		
In hospital	42		
Unfit to march	16		
Presumably exchanged or died in Kut ...	21		
	—		132
Marching-out state			253
Died in captivity		213 (?)	
Released in 1918		74	
Exchanged in 1916		18 1 officer and 5	310*
Unaccounted		75 (?)	75
			385

TRACED IN 1934-35.

Died in captivity	204	50 reservists 23 attached	277
Released or exchanged	68	7 attached	75
Possible survivors by release or exchange ...	23	7	30
			382

WARRANT OFFICERS, NON-COMMISSIONED OFFICERS, BUGLERS AND PRIVATES OF THE 43RD WHO DIED IN CAPTIVITY.

No.	Rank.	Name.	Coy.	Date of Death.	Presumed Place and Cause of Death.
8034	Serjeant	Adby, Richard James, D.C.M.	—	6 Oct. 1916	At Aleppo or Mamoura.
8379	Serjeant	Afflick, William	"S"	5 Sept. 1916	Probably at Afiun Qarahisar.
7265	Private	Ahern, James	"Q"	22 Nov. 1917	At Angora.
9001	Private	Alexander, Joseph	"S"	26 Aug. 1916	Of dysentery at Airan.
8681	L./Corporal	Anear, William Charles Arundel	"S"	1 Oct. 1916	Probably at Afiun Qarahisar.
9366	Private	Apted, Henry George	—	31 May 1916	At Shumran.
9184	Private	Archer, Thomas	—	31 July 1916	Not known.
8397	Serjeant	Armitt, Thomas William, D.C.M.	"R"	4 Nov. 1916	Of inflammation of intestines at Afiun Qarahisar.
9549	Private	Atkins, Frank Joseph	—	15 Aug. 1916	Not known.
9111	Private	Bailey, Henry George	—	31 May 1916	Probably at Baghdad.
9341	L./Serjeant	Baker, Herbert	"S"	2 Aug. 1916	At Baghche of dysentery.
8121	Serjeant	Baldock, George	"P"	19 Oct. 1916	Probably at Afiun Qarahisar of pneumonia.
9046	Corporal	Ballard, Sidney Nelson, D.C.M.	—	6 Sept. 1916	Probably at Damir Qapu.
9089	Corporal	Barfoot, Ernest Alfred	—	14 May 1916	Between Shumran and Baghdad.

* The officer, Lieutenant G. L. Heawood, is not included in this total.

APPENDICES

No.	Rank.	Name.	Coy.	Date of Death.	Presumed Place and Cause of Death.
9199	Private	Barnes, William	—	10 July 1916	At Baghche of cholera.
8181	Private	Bartlett, Albert John	—	31 Dec. 1916	—
8185	Serjeant	Bates, William Arthur	"S"	24 Sept. 1916	Probably at Afiun Qarahisar.
9105	Private	Baughan, Alfred Edward	—	16 Aug. 1916	At Baghche of beri-beri.
9449	L./Corporal	Baulch, Arthur	—	30 June 1916	Probably at Mosul.
8997	L./Corporal	Bonham, Albert	"P"	29 Jan. 1917	Probably at Angora.
8405	L./Corporal	Bradley, William George	"Q"	7 Oct. 1916	At Baghche of enteritis.
7628	Private	Breese, Matthew Ernest	—	30 June 1916	Not known.
8352	Private	Bridges, George Thomas	—	2 May 1916	At Shumran.
8228	Private	Brill, Ernest Charles	—	16 Aug. 1916	At Baghche of enteritis.
8371	Private	Brown, Charles	"S"	5 Sept. 1916	Not known.
9310	Private	Bullock, Edmund Augustus	—	9 July 1916	—
9367	Private	Bunce, Charles William	—	12 Jan. 1917	—
8472	Private	Burke, John	"P"	10 Sept. 1917	Probably at Konia.
9640	Private	Burt, William	—	12 July 1916	At Yarbashi.
9117	Private	Burton, William Joseph	"Q"	28 Mar. 1917	At Angora.
9556	Private	Bush, Henry William	—	12 Aug. 1916	At Airan of dysentery.
9681	Private	Carpenter, Bernard John	"Q"	30 Jan. 1917	—
8376	Private	Carter, Norman	—	10 May 1916	Between Shumran and Baghdad.
8759	Private	Casban, Leonard	"R"	1 April 1917	At Angora.
9096	Private	Champion, George	—	5 May 1916	At Shumran.
6162	L./Corporal	Charlett, John	—	28 Mar. 1917	At Angora.
9140	Private	Charlott, Bert	"Q"	30 Sept. 1916	At Tarsus.
9451	Private	Clark, Herbert Henry	—	20 July 1916	At Airan, of dysentery.
8930	Private	Clarke, George	—	4 June 1916	At Tikrit.
9193	L./Corporal	Clifford, Arthur	—	7 July 1916	At Emar Kasr.[5]
9459	Private	Cooper, George	"R"	27 Nov. 1916	—
8856	L./Corporal	Cousens, Henry	"P"	10 Dec. 1916	At Afiun Qarahisar of malaria.
8645	Private	Cox, Herbert Ralph	—	16 Aug. 1916	At Baghche of beri-beri and dysentery.
9183	Private	Cripps, Frederick Ralph	—	30 June 1916	Between Samarra and Ras al 'Ain.
9577	Private	Currell, Charles	—	30 June 1916	Between Samarra and Ras al 'Ain.
8657	Private	Cutler, Richard	"Q"	8 Dec. 1916	At Tarsus.
8227	Bandsman	Dart, William	—	11 Oct. 1916	At Angora.
8310	Private	Darvell, William	—	31 Aug. 1916	At Baghche.
5655	L./Corporal	Davis, George	"S"	24 Dec. 1916	At Afiun Qarahisar.
9099	Private	Day, Harry Thomas	—	3 May 1916	At Shumran.

[5] Kasr, west-north-west of Nisibin, is marked on the modern map.

43RD LIGHT INFANTRY

No.	Rank.	Name.	Coy.	Date of Death.	Presumed Place and Cause of Death.
9627	Private	Deane, Frederick	—	30 June 1916	Between Samarra and Ras al 'Ain.
8621	L./Corporal	Dickinson, Walter	—	15 Aug. 1916	At Baghche of heart failure.
7452	Corporal	Donohoe, William, D.C.M.	—	3 July 1916	Between Samarra and Ras al 'Ain.
6324	Serjeant	Doorey, Percy	—	31 July 1916	Between Samarra and Ras al 'Ain.
8969	Private	Drewett, Dick	—	7 Oct. 1916	—
9276	Private	Dunn, Harry	—	4 Aug. 1916	At Baghche of enteritis.
8543	Private	Duggan, James	—	14 June 1916	—
9644	Private	Eaton, William Thomas	—	16 July 1916	—
7984	Private	Eatwell, Thomas	—	11 June 1916	At Damir Qapu.
9466	Private	Eccleston, Albert Edward	—	4 May 1916	At Shumran.
8966	Private	Eden, Job	"S"	16 Oct. 1916	Invalided to Konia in September; probably died at Afiun Qarahisar.
9397	Private	Edkins, Charles	—	7 May 1916	At Shumran.
8597	Private	Edwards, James Ebenezer	—	22 June 1916	—
8931	Private	Estall, Ernest Algernon	—	8 May 1916	At Shumran.
8837	L./Corporal	Evans, Ernest Edward	—	31 July 1916	Between Samarra and Ras al 'Ain.
8654	Corporal	Evenett, Arthur, D.C.M.	—	31 July 1916	Between Samarra and Ras al 'Ain.
8318	Private	Faulkiner, Edward John	—	25 July 1916	At Baghche of beri-beri and dysentery.
6965	Private	Finnes, Frederick	"S"	8 Sept. 1916	At Mamoura.
9566	Private	Flux, Cecil Herbert	—	25 Aug. 1916	—
8919	Private	Franklin, Benjamin	—	10 June 1916	At Tikrit.
9181	Private	Frost, Sidney	—	31 May 1916	Between Samarra and Ras al 'Ain.
9014	Private	Fryer, Hugh	—	28 June 1916	—
8638	L./Corporal	Gardner, George Samuel	—	9 Oct. 1916	At Afiun Qarahisar.
8489	L./Corporal	Garland, Frederick	—	22 July 1916	At Angora.
8468	L./Corporal	Gaskin, Sidney	"P"	27 Sept. 1916	At Adana.
9245	L./Corporal	Gates, George	—	30 June 1916	Between Samarra and Ras al 'Ain.
8049	Serjeant	Gibbs, Richard Henry	—	7 Aug. 1916	At Dorak.[6]
9350	Private	Giles, Frank George	—	31 Dec. 1916	—
9476	Private	Giles, George Henry	—	31 Mar. 1917	—
8922	Private	Grant, Albert	—	31 Oct. 1916	—
8921	Private	Green, Albert	—	10 Nov. 1916	At Afiun Qarahisar.
9440	Private	Green, Leonard Isaac	—	3 May 1916	At Shumran.
9486	Private	Grover, James George	"R"	27 Sept. 1916	At Afiun Qarahisar of debility.
8212	L./Corporal	Gunter, Ivo	—	3 June 1916	—
8734	Private	Hames, Frederick George	—	18 Aug. 1916	At Entilli.[7]

[6] About 15 miles north of Tarsus.
[7] I have not been able to trace this place on modern maps of Turkey.

APPENDICES

No.	Rank.	Name.	Coy.	Date of Death.	Presumed Place and Cause of Death.
9628	Private	Hamley, Cecil	—	11 June 1916	Probably in Kut.
8668	Private	Harding, Edward Thomas	—	20 June 1916	On march to Ras al 'Ain.
8697	Private	Harding, William Thomas	"R"	24 Mar. 1917	At Angora.
9060	Private	Hardy, Harry Chowings	—	31 May 1916	Between Samarra and Ras al 'Ain.
8136	Private	Harman, Herbert	—	2 May 1916	At Shumran.
9358	Private	Harris, Edward Joseph	"R"	11 Aug. 1916	At Baghche of enteritis.
9457	Private	Harris, Reginald	—	9 May 1916	At Shumran.
9477	Private	Harris, Richard	—	6 Nov. 1916	At Afiun Qarahisar.
8128	Private	Hazell, William	"P"	24 Sept. 1916	At Konia.
8987	Private	Hicks, William, M.M.	—	18 June 1916	—
8538	Private	Higgins, George	—	2 May 1916	At Shumran.
9258	Private	Hodge, Albert (Formerly R. Berks. R.)	—	31 Dec. 1916	—
8120	L./Corporal	Hoggins, Ernest	"P"	8 Oct. 1916	At Tarsus.
9454	Private	Hopcraft, William George	—	29 July 1916	At Yarbashi.
9037	L./Corporal	Horwood, John, D.C.M.	"R"	3 Sept. 1916	At Airan of dysentery.
6896	Private	Horwood, William	"Q"	4 May 1916	At Shumran.
7990	Private	Howard, Walter Thomas	"P"	12 Aug. 1916	—
8434	Private	Howes, Alfred John Walter	—	7 May 1916	At Shumran.
8927	Private	Hunt, James	"S"	3 Nov. 1916	At Afiun Qarahisar of inflammation of the intestines.
9025	Private	Irons, Thomas George	—	8 May 1916	At Shumran of dysentery.
9373	L./Corporal	Irwin, John William Henry	—	31 Dec. 1916	—
9016	Private	Johnson, Ernest	"P"	29 Aug. 1916	At Baghche of enteritis.
9100	Private	Johnson, William	"R"	28 Feb. 1917	At Afiun Qarahisar of typhus.
8980	Private	Jones, William	—	31 July 1916	Between Samarra and Ras al 'Ain.
9436	Private	Joynes, Tom	—	30 June 1916	At Baghche of cholera.
9085	L./Corporal	Keen, Joseph Henry	—	6 Aug. 1916	At Airan of dysentery.
9438	Private	King, Harry Norman	—	8 June 1916	At Tikrit.
9204	Corporal	Lambert, Ernest	"R"	12 Oct. 1916	At Afiun Qarahisar of inflammation of the intestines.
9080	Private	Larner, William	—	6 May 1916	At Shumran.
9685	Private	Lay, Arthur	"P"	8 Nov. 1916	At Afiun Qarahisar of pneumonia.
8537	Corporal	Lee, Harry	—	31 July 1916	At Sharqat.
9049	Private	Luckett, Ernest Frederick	—	6-7 May 1916	At Shumran.
8583	Private	Marden, Albert William	"S"	1 Sept. 1916	At Airan of enteritis.

43RD LIGHT INFANTRY

No.	Rank.	Name.	Coy.	Date of Death.	Presumed Place and Cause of Death.
8105	Private	Matthews, William George	—	1 Oct. 1916	Between Samarra and Ras al 'Ain.
8443	Private	McGill, George	"P"	29 Aug. 1916	At Airan.
9124	Private	Meades, John	—	25 Sept. 1918	At Yarbashi.
9673	Private	Merritt, Edward George	"S"	30 June 1916	At Tikrit.
8677	Private	Metcalfe, Walter	—	30 June 1916	Between Samarra and Ras al 'Ain.
8459	Private	Miles, James	"Q"	1 May 1916	At Shumran.
9005	Private	Miles, Mark	—	30 Sept. 1916	—
9069	Private	Mobbs, Frederick Arthur	—	9 Aug. 1916	At Airan of dysentery.
8907	Private	Molloy, Edward	—	31 Aug. 1916	On march to Airan.
8369	Private	Mummery, Frederick	"S"	30 Nov. 1916	At Adana.
9664	Private	Nash, Robert James	—	25 Sept. 1916	—
9534	Private	Newell, Joseph	—	24 May 1917	—
9128	L./Serjeant	Olliff, Philip Joseph	—	14 July 1916	—
8383	Private	Painting, George Henry	"S"	21 Mar. 1917	At Angora.
9377	Private	Paske, Fred	—	7 May 1916	At Shumran.
9238	Private	Payne, Albert	"S"	6 May 1916	At Shumran.
9487	Private	Phillips, Jack	"Q"	30 Sept. 1916	At Afiun Qarahisar of malaria.
9208	Private	Pierce, George Hobbs	—	30 Aug. 1916	At Airan.
8346	Private	Pike, Harry	—	21 June 1916	—
8219	Private	Pollard, George	—	30 June 1916	At Yarbashi.
8368	Corporal	Powell, Albert Edward	—	1 Nov. 1916	At Afiun Qarahisar of dysentery.
9552	Private	Puddephatt, Arthur	—	30 Sept. 1916	—
6907	Serjeant	Pursglove, Albert Edward, D.C.M.	"R"	3 Feb. 1917	At Angora.
8797	L./Corporal	Quinton, Albert Edward	—	24 Nov. 1916	—
9020	L./Corporal	Rakestrow, William Gerald	"Q"	3 May 1916	At Shumran.
8107	Private	Rallison, Albert	"R"	27 Feb. 1917	At Angora.
8795	Private	Rattenbury, Charles Herbert	"S"	31 Oct. 1916	—
8573	Private	Rattledge, Ephraim	—	6-7 May 1916	At Shumran.
9421	L./Corporal	Read, Thomas Percy Owen	—	6 June 1916	At Mosul.
9654	L./Corporal	Redrup, Ernest	—	1 Nov. 1916	At Afiun Qarahisar of inflammation of the intestines.
8803	L./Corporal	Rees, Walter	"S"	23 Oct. 1916	At Tarsus.
8093	Serjeant	Richardson, Edward Richard	"P"	24 Sept. 1916	At Tarsus.
9471	L./Serjeant	Richardson, Herbert	—	4 July 1916	Between Samarra and Ras al 'Ain.
9387	Private	Rivers, Ernest William George	—	31 May, 1916	Between Samarra and Ras al 'Ain.
8171	Private	Rolfe, Alfred Thomas	"R"	30 Nov. 1916	At Angora.
8261	Private	Ross, Victor	"Q"	4 May 1916	At Shumran.

APPENDICES

No.	Rank.	Name.	Coy.	Date of Death.	Presumed Place and Cause of Death.
9023	Private	Rutland, Herbert	—	31 May 1916	Between Samarra and Ras al 'Ain.
9123	Private	Saunders, Charles	—	20 Mar. 1917	At Afiun Qarahisar.
8230	Private	Saunders, Frank	"R"	20 Feb. 1917	—
9053	Private	Saunders, Henry Jones	"R"	30 Sept. 1916	At Tarsus or Afiun Qarahisar.
8592	Private	Saxby, William Henry	—	14 July 1916	At Baghdad.
8639	Private	Shelverton, Henry William	—	9 July 1916	At Baghche of cholera.
9403	Private	Shillingford, Louis	"P"	31 Aug. 1916	At Konia of beri-beri.
9306	Private	Shillum, Charles	—	16 June 1916	—
8600	Private	Simpson, John	—	30 June 1916	Between Samarra and Ras al 'Ain.
9686	Private	Smith, Ernest Thomas	—	31 Dec. 1916	—
8057	Serjeant	Smith, Frederick, D.C.M.	—	15 Aug. 1916	At Yarbashi.
9695	Private	Smith, Leonard	"R"	28 Jan. 1916	At Angora.
9475	Private	Smith, Thomas	—	30 Nov. 1916	—
8055	Private	Spiers, Stephen	—	31 May 1916	At Samarra.
8920	Private	Standage, Arthur	—	6 May 1916	At Shumran.
8729	L./Serjeant	Staples, George William	"Q"	12 Oct. 1916	At Angora.
9506	Private	Symonds, James Alfred	—	30 June 1916	Between Samarra and Ras al 'Ain.
7740	Bugler	Taylor, Arthur Heath	—	—	Known to have died between Samarra and Ras al 'Ain. Erroneously reported killed in action on 31 Dec. 1916.
9489	Private	Taylor, Mark	—	31 July 1916	—
9000	Private	Todd, Augustus	—	22 July 1916	Between Samarra and Ras al 'Ain.
9579	Private	Tott, Frederick Selby	—	6 May 1916	At Shumran.
9223	Private	Trinder, William	—	30 Sept. 1916	At Adana.
9391	Private	Tuffrey, Trevor Sidney	—	31 July 1916	—
8643	Private	Tyler, John	"R"	1 Oct. 1916	At Afiun Qarahisar.
5235	C.Q.M.S.	Voller, Thomas	—	31 July 1916	At Mamoura.
9058	Private	Walder, Herbert William John	—	30 June 1916	At Sharqat.
8311	Private	Walker, Albert James	—	12 Feb. 1916	At Angora.
8507	Private	Walker, Henry	—	3 May 1916	At Shumran.
9574	Private	Wallis, Alfred John	—	30 June 1916	—
9367	Private	Ward, Ernest Walter	—	7 Aug. 1916	At Airan of dysentery.
9321	Private	Wavell, Percy	—	8 May 1916	At Shumran.
8737	Private	Webb, Alexandra	"R"	3 Nov. 1916	—
9670	Private	Webb, William Albert	—	29 May 1916	—
8169	Private	Westall, Jesse	—	29 April 1916	—
6467	O.R.Q.M.S.	White, Frederick Ernest	—	21 July 1916	At Mamoura of beri-beri.

No.	Rank.	Name.	Coy.	Date of Death.	Presumed Place and Cause of Death.
9250	Private	White, Wallace George	—	1 May 1916	At Shumran.
9163	Private	Wilkins, Horace Cecil …	—	25 June 1916	Between Samarra and Ras al 'Ain.
9302	L./Corporal	Williams, Harold George	"P"	12 May 1916	Between Shumran and Baghdad.
8513	L./Corporal	Williams, Harold …	—	31 Dec. 1916	Between Samarra and Ras al 'Ain.
8918	Corporal	Wilmott, Frank Llewellyn	—	21 June 1916	At Emar Kasr.
8210	Private	Wilson, George … …	—	30 Sept. 1916	Between Samarra and Ras al 'Ain.
9564	Private	Winfield, Bertram George	—	15 July 1916	—
9191	Private	Winfield, Ernest Frank	—	31 Aug. 1916	At Mosul.
9560	Private	Witney, James William	"S"	4 Nov. 1916	—
9394	L./Corporal	Woodage, Heber William	—	21 Oct. 1916	At Afiun Qarahisar of dysentery.
8944	L./Corporal	Woodbridge, Aubrey …	—	5 Nov. 1916	At Afiun Qarahisar of inflammation of the intestines.
9215	Private	Woodward, George Payne	"R"	19 Oct. 1916	At Afiun Qarahisar.
9077	Private	Worley, Edmund James	"S"	31 Aug. 1916	At Airan of dysentery.
9309	Private	York, Thomas … …	"Q"	22 Sept. 1916	Between Samarra and Ras al 'Ain.
8954	Private	Young, Alfred … …	—	9 July 1916	—

RESERVISTS OR ATTACHED MEN WHO DIED OR ARE PRESUMED TO HAVE DIED IN CAPTIVITY.

No.	Rank.	Name.	Coy.	Date of Death.	Presumed Place and Cause of Death.
2056	Private	Aklyt, C. H. … …	—	7 Oct. 1916	At Afiun Qarahisar of typhus.
—	—	Blowfield, — … …	—	—	—
11522	Private	Brown, T. … …	—	28 Jan. 1917	At Afiun Qarahisar of kidney complaint.
—	—	Bryant, — … …	—	—	—
—	Private	Burton, Joseph … …	"Q"	1917	At Angora.
—	C.S.M.	Butcher, — … …	—	—	—
8536	Private	Cardinal, G. … …	—	9 Oct. 1916	At Afiun Qarahisar of dysentery.
—	Private	Cherry (Border Regt.) …	—	Jan. 1917	At Yozgad.
10277	L./Corporal	Chitty, Charles (R. Fus.)	—	Sept. 1916	At Afiun Qarahisar.
12412	Private	Cook, J. (R. Fus.) …	—	3 May 1916	At Shumran.
9918	Private	Cowie, Alexander (Gordons)	"S"	Sept. 1916	At Yarbashi.
—	—	Cumming, — … …	—	—	—
—	Corporal	Dawson, — … …	—	Dec. 1916	At Afiun Qarahisar.

APPENDICES

No.	Rank.	Name.	Coy.	Date of Death.	Presumed Place and Cause of Death.
845	Private	Devaney, P.	—	—	—
—	—	Dickson (or Dixon)	—	—	—
8664	Private	Dobbs, T. H. (1st/Foresters)	"R"	11 Nov. 1917	At Adabazar.[8]
9151	Private	Dossin, —	—	24 Oct. 1916	At Afiun Qarahisar of dysentery.
8618	Private	Etienne, —	—	1 Oct. 1916	At Afiun Qarahisar of pneumonia.
—	—	Fawcett, —	—	—	—
9486	L./Corporal	Fisher, E. A. (4th/Worcesters)	"S"	6 Sept. 1916	At Airan.
12546	Corporal	Gates, G. (R. Fus.)	"P"	—	—
8853	Private	Goring, H. (W. Riding Regt.)	—	3 May 1916	At Shumran.
—	Private	Hamilton, William	"R"	—	—
—	—	Haslett, —	—	—	—
—	—	Henry, —	—	—	—
8085	Private	Hill, J. W. (K.S.L.I.)	"P"	—	At Adana.
—	—	Hitchcock, —	—	—	—
8849	Private	Hoskins, A. J. (W. Riding Regt.)	—	—	—
8899	Corporal	Jepson, A. (Worcester Regt.)	—	7 July 1916	At Emar Kasr.
9910	Private	Kerr, J. G. (1st/Foresters)	"R"	—	—
7899	Private	Kirkoff, William (2nd/R. W. Fus.)	"S"	1 Sept. 1916	At Airan of dysentery.
—	Private	Lacey (Manchester Regt.)	—	Aug. 1916	At Ahmed Pasha Chiftlik.
7315	Private	Leach, E. G. H.	"Q"	—	—
—	—	Lloyd, —	—	—	—
9274	Private	Mackintosh, A. (Seaforths)	—	July 1916	At Mamoura.
9550	Private	McGlade, H. (K.O.S.B.)	—	3 May 1916	At Shumran.
8366	Private	McLaren, H. G. (K.S.L.I.)	—	June 1916	Between Samarra and Ras al 'Ain.
9611	Private	Miller, G. (Welsh Regt.)	—	—	—
9851	Private	Nicholls (Liverpool Regt.)	—	June 1916	Between Samarra and Ras al 'Ain.
—	—	Owers, —	—	—	—
—	Q.M.S.	Packer, H. J. (A.O.C.)	—	July 1916	At Baghche.
—	—	Petit, —	—	—	—
—	Private	Riley, —	—	27 Mar. 1917	At Yozgad.
10247	Private	Rowbottom, J. (Liverpool Regt.)	—	June 1916	At Dorak.
—	Private	Rutherford, —	—	—	—
9274	L./Corporal	Shooter, W. (Manchester Regt.)	—	June 1916	Between Samarra and Ras al 'Ain.
—	—	Southern, —	—	—	—
10497	Corporal	Trine, G. (H.L.I.)	"Q"	14 Sept. 1916	At Adabazar.
9094	Private	Waller, —	"R"	—	—
—	—	Walters, —	—	—	—

[8] In Asia Minor, east of Ismid.

43RD LIGHT INFANTRY

ATTACHED.

2ND/5TH SOMERSET LIGHT INFANTRY.

No.	Rank.	Name.	Coy.	Date of Death.	Presumed Place and Cause of Death.
—	Private	Adams, Albert	—	18 June 1916	—
1377	Private	Adams, Arthur	—	Sept. or Oct. 1916	—
2839	Private	Morgan, Reginald	"R"	9 Oct. 1916	At Afiun Qarahisar.
1812	Private	Pipe, Norman	"R"	—	—
2800	Private	Turner, Robert	—	12 Aug. 1916	At Baghche of enteritis.
3185	Corporal	Simpson, A.	—	15 July 1916	At Yarbashi of dysentery.

1ST/4TH BORDER REGIMENT.

No.	Rank.	Name.	Coy.	Date of Death.	Presumed Place and Cause of Death.
—	—	Coates, —	—	Sept. 1916	At Angora.
2097	Private	Gardiner, J.	—	June 1916	Between Samarra and Ras al 'Ain.
1810	Private	Parkes, —	—	Dec. 1916	At Angora.
1366	Private	Strickland, —	—	—	Between Samarra and Ras al 'Ain.
—	Private	Taylor, Frederick	"Q"	24 Aug. 1916	At Airan.
847	Private	Taylor, Robert	"S"	24 Aug. 1916	At Airan.
1242	Private	Wilson, E.	—	—	No trace.

2ND/4TH BORDER REGIMENT.

No.	Rank.	Name.	Coy.	Date of Death.	Presumed Place and Cause of Death.
1753	Private	Bond, Harry	"P"	—	No trace.
2471	Private	Jackson, Samuel	"P"	—	No trace.
2271	Private	Parmley, —	—	—	No trace.
2295	Private	Thomas, —	—	—	No trace.

2ND/4TH WILTSHIRE REGIMENT.

No.	Rank.	Name.	Coy.	Date of Death.	Presumed Place and Cause of Death.
2962	Private	Archer, W. H.	—	3 May 1916	At Shumran.
2653	Private	Baker, William A.	"Q"	—	Probably at Adana.
3186	L./Corporal	Barnes, Joseph	"Q"	—	Probably at Afiun Qarahisar.
2787	Private	Brown, Percy	"Q"	6 Dec. 1916	At Afiun Qarahisar of dysentery.
2862	Private	Froome, W. A.	—	5 May 1916	At Shumran.
3136	Private	Hopgood, —	—	9 May 1916	At Shumran.

43RD LIGHT INFANTRY: KNOWN SURVIVORS OF CAPTIVITY.

No.	Rank.	Name.	Coy.	
—	Private	Algar, —	—	Exchanged from Baghdad.
5766	C.Q.M.S.	Arlett, H., D.C.M.	"P"	—
6414	Private	Barlow, Albert	"Q"	—
9422	L./Corporal	Beck, Walter	"R"	—
8480	Private	Bennett, Douglas W.	"S"	Late Cook-Serjeant at the Depot.
8191	Bugler	Berry, Charles	"P"	—
—	Private	Brotherton, —	"S"	Servant to Lieutenant Naylor.
—	Private	Bunce, —	—	Exchanged from Baghdad.

APPENDICES

No.	Rank.	Name.	Coy.	
5487	Q.M.S.	Burbidge, J. W., D.C.M.	"S"	—
—	L./Corporal	Carter, V. A.	"P"	—
8387	Private	Chatten, William	"P"	—
9637	Private	Claridge, H.	—	Exchanged from Baghdad.
9680	Private	Collins, J. A. E.	—	—
16140	L./Corporal	Compton, R. W.	—	—
—	—	Cowley, —	—	—
—	—	Cox, J. W.	—	—
8591	Private	Day, F.	—	Exchanged from Baghdad.
—	Private	Draper, D.C.M.	—	—
—	Private	Edmunds, —	—	Exchanged from Baghdad.
—	—	Ellis, —	—	—
—	Private	Finch, W. S.	—	Servant to Major Henley.
—	—	Gardiner, G. E.	—	—
—	Bugler	Grantham, —	—	—
—	—	Harrod, —	—	Exchanged from Baghdad.
9725	Private	Haynes, C.	"R"	Exchanged from Baghdad.
9196	L./Corporal	Hellin, Joseph	"P"	—
—	—	Hirons, G.	—	—
—	—	Hoskins, W.	—	—
—	—	House, —	—	Since died.
—	—	Howe, J. H.	—	—
—	Private	Hunt, —	—	—
—	—	Jackson, —	—	Exchanged from Baghdad.
—	Corporal	Jones, —	—	Took his discharge in India.
7363	Bugler	Kennard, Harry Joseph	"S"	Late Bugle-Major, 43rd.
8428	Private	Lambert, Aaron	"R"	—
—	C.Q.M.S.	Lawrence, —	—	—
5574	R.S.M.	Love, Thomas Albert, D.C.M.	"P"	—
9315	Private	Mahon, Edward	"Q"	—
9336	Private	Martin, Philip William	—	Exchanged from Baghdad, and erroneously reported died.
—	—	Miles, H.	—	Exchanged from Baghdad.
9143	Private	Miller, P. R., D.C.M.	—	—
—	L./Corporal	Mumford, —	—	Exchanged from Baghdad.
—	Serjeant	Munn, A. C.	—	Exchanged from Baghdad.
—	—	Neale, —	—	Exchanged from Baghdad.
8812	L./Corporal	Nestor, —	—	Escaped from Baghdad.
—	—	Nutt, —	—	Exchanged from Baghdad.
8478	Private	Oakes, A.	—	Exchanged from Baghdad.
—	—	Orchard, —	—	Exchanged from Baghdad.
8996	Bugler	Paice, Arthur	"Q"	—
8330	Private	Parfett, Frederick	"S"	—
—	—	Parsons, —	—	—
—	L./Corporal	Ponting, F. G.	—	Servant to Major Henley.
9130	Private	Prior, J.	—	—
9448	Private	Risby, W. J.	"R"	Exchanged from Baghdad.
—	Private	Sadler, R.	—	Late Quartermaster's Storeman.
—	—	Saker, —	—	Servant to Major Julius, brigade-major, 17th Brigade.
—	—	Small, —	—	—
8484	Private	Stokes, Charles W.	"P"	—
—	—	Sutton, —	—	—
8395	L./Corporal	Swift, T.	—	—

43RD LIGHT INFANTRY

No.	Rank.	Name.	Coy.	
8757	L./Corporal	Swift, William, D.C.M.	"S"	Servant to Colonel Lethbridge.
8493	Serjeant	Thompson, S.	"P"	Exchanged from Baghdad.
—	Private	Twynham, —	—	—
—	Corporal	Upstone, —, D.C.M.	—	—
6334	Serjeant	Ward, William, D.C.M.	"Q"	—
—	—	Waters, —	—	Exchanged from Baghdad.
—	Private	Whitefoot, —	—	Servant to Captain Startin, R.A.M.C.
—	—	Young, A.	—	—

POSSIBLE SURVIVORS OF THE 43RD.

No.	Rank	Name	Coy.	
6078	Private	Byrne, John	"R"	—
—	Private	Clarke, —	—	Servant to Major Davy.
8401	Corporal	Clements, Joseph	—	—
9277	Private	Cross, Edward	"S"	—
8257	Private	Dickens, David	"Q"	—
9601	Private	Dut(f)field, H.	—	—
9530	Private	Duggan, Thomas	"Q"	—
—	Private	Eades, —	—	—
8929	L./Corporal	Farrant, William	"Q"	—
8455	Private	Gaskin, William	"S"	—
9541	Corporal	Johnson, Hector	"Q"	—
9474	Private	Jones, J.	—	—
—	Private	Kew, —	—	—
9160	Private	May, Sydney	"R"	—
9189	Private	Mills, Alfred	"S"	—
9197	Private	Ryma(i)ll, Ernest	"R"	—
9633	Private	Tappin(g), George	"Q"	Wounded, 9th May 1915.
9013	Private	Titchener, Charles	"Q"	—
9547	Private	Turley, F.	—	—
8685	Private	Watson, James	"Q"	—
9205	Private	Watts, Hubert	"P"	—
7878	Private	White, Thomas	"Q"	—
8572	Private	Willis, George	"Q"	—

SURVIVORS OF ATTACHED.

No.	Rank	Name	Coy.	
—	—	Bulman, —	—	Exchanged from Baghdad.
1465	Private	Carruther, George	—	1st/4th Border Regiment.
—	—	Follows, —	—	Exchanged from Baghdad.
—	—	Hawkins, —	—	2nd/5th Somerset Light Infantry.
—	—	Sanderson, —	—	Exchanged from Baghdad.
—	L./Corporal	Shopland, S. J.	—	2nd/5th Somerset Light Infantry. Exchanged from Baghdad.
3278	Private	Styles, Cyril	—	2nd/4th Wiltshire Regiment.

RESERVISTS: PROBABLE AND KNOWN SURVIVORS.

No.	Rank	Name	Coy.	
605	Private	Brown, Robert	"Q"	Rifle Brigade.
1662	L./Corporal	Chapman, Stanley	"P"	Rifle Brigade.
7712	Private	Dewey, George	"S"	4th/60th Rifles.
1935	L./Corporal	Hillman, —	—	Manchester Regiment.
7479	Corporal	McMullen, Wilfred	"Q"	1st South Lancashire Regiment.
9687	Private	Wright, Charles	"R"	1st King's Own Scottish Borderers.
8682	Private	Wright, F. T.	"Q"	Royal Sussex Regiment.

APPENDICES

APPENDIX XII.[1]

ORDER OF BATTLE AT KHAN BAGHDADI, 26TH MARCH 1918.

15TH DIVISION.
(Major-General Sir H. T. Brooking, K.C.B.)

11th Cavalry Brigade (Brigadier-General R. A. Cassels) :—
  7th Hussars.
  Guides Cavalry.
  23rd Cavalry.
  25th Machine Gun Squadron.
  " W " Battery, R.H.A.—6 guns.
  " W " Battery Ammunition Column.
  No. 5 Field Troop, Sappers and Miners.
  11th Cavalry Brigade Signal Troop.
  11th Cavalry Brigade Supply and Transport Company.
  No. 152 Cavalry Combined Field Ambulance.
  Detachment, No. 30 Sanitary Section.
  No. 8 Mobile Veterinary Section.
  " M " Anti-aircraft Section.
  Headquarters and two sections, 15th Machine Gun Squadron ⎫ Attached.
  One Pack Station, 1st Wireless Squadron ⎭

Divisional Cavalry :—
  " D " Squadron, 1st/1st Hertfordshire Yeomanry.
  10th Lancers, less two squadrons.

Artillery.

215th Brigade, R.F.A. (1086th, 816th, 524th Batteries) ... ... 22 guns.
222nd Brigade, R.F.A. (375th, 1070th, 1072nd, 77th Batteries) ... 22 guns.
395th Siege Battery, R.G.A. ... ... 4 howitzers.
No. 118 Anti-aircraft Section.
Independent Ammunition Column.
Nos. 8, 13, 14 (less one section) Light Armoured Motor Batteries.

Infantry.

12th Infantry Brigade (Brigadier-General F. P. S. Dunsford) :—
  1st/5th The Queen's Royal Regiment.
  2nd/39th Garwhalis.
  1st/43rd Erinpura Regiment.
  90th Punjabis.
  No. 128 Machine Gun Company.
  12th Light Trench Mortar Battery.
  12th Small Arm Ammunition Section.
  12th Brigade Supply and Transport Company.

[1] *Official History*, Vol. IV, p. 373.

42nd Infantry Brigade (Brigadier-General F. G. Lucas) :—
    1st/4th Dorsetshire Regiment.
    1st/5th Gurkhas.
    2nd/5th Gurkhas.
    2nd/6th Gurkhas.
    No. 130 Machine Gun Company.
    42nd Light Trench Mortar Battery.
    42nd Small Arm Ammunition Section.
    42nd Brigade Supply and Transport Company.

50th Infantry Brigade (Brigadier-General A. W. Andrew) :—
    43rd Light Infantry.
    6th Jats.
    24th Punjabis.
    1st/97th Infantry.
    No. 256 Machine Gun Company.
    50th Light Trench Mortar Battery.
    50th Small Arm Ammunition Section.
    50th Brigade Supply and Transport Company.

ATTACHED.

1st/7th Gurkhas.

Engineers and Pioneers :—
    448th, 450th, 451st Field Companies, R.E.
    48th Pioneers.
    19th Company, Sappers and Miners   } Attached.
    Detachment, No. 1 Mobile Bridging Train

15th Divisional Signal Company.
No. 275 Machine Gun Company.
No. 34 Ordnance Mobile Workshop.
15th Divisional Troops Supply and Transport Company.
Nos. 23, 34, 105, 108 Combined Field Ambulances.
No. 16 Sanitary Section.
No. 6 Mobile Veterinary Section.

Two flights, 30th Squadron, R.F.C.
No. 52 Kite Balloon Section.
No. 8 Litho Section.
Two pack stations, 1st Wireless Signal Squadron.
No. 1 Combined Field Ambulance.
No. 27 Casualty Clearing Station.
No. 12 Mobile X-ray Unit.
No. 33 Motor Ambulance Convoy.
No. 40 Motor Ambulance Convoy, less ten cars.
No. 1 Mechanical Transport Column.
No. 1013 Mechanical Transport Column.
No. 1016 Mechanical Transport Column.

APPENDIX XIII.

Roll of Officers Commanding the 43rd Light Infantry, 1914-1919.

Lieutenant-Colonel and Brevet Colonel Ernest Astley Edmund Lethbridge, C.M.G., D.S.O., from inception of operations up to 29th April 1916.

Major Lindsay James Carter, D.S.O., 2nd/43rd from its formation in January 1916 up to 6th April 1916.

Major Hon. William Reginald Shute Barrington:—
2nd/43rd from 6th April 1916 to 29th April 1916.
43rd from 30th April 1916 to 27th July 1916.

Captain Geoffrey Wrench Titherington : 28th July 1916 to 14th August 1916.

Major R. H. Crake, King's Own Scottish Borderers : 14th August 1916 to 5th October 1916.

Lieutenant-Colonel Ladislas Herbert Richard Pope-Hennessy, D.S.O. : 5th October 1916 to 14th March 1917.

Captain George Edward Whittall, M.C. : 14th March 1917 to 22nd March 1917.

Major and Brevet Lieutenant-Colonel Francis Harry Stapleton : 22nd March 1917 to 21st July 1917.

Captain and Brevet Major (Acting Lieutenant-Colonel) George Edward Whittall, M.C. : 21st July 1917 to 12th April 1919.

Colonel Wilfred Marriott-Dodington, C.M.G. : end of March 1919 to 21st December 1919.

APPENDIX XIV.

Records of Services of Officers of the 43rd Light Infantry

Name	Battalion	Second Lieutenant	Lieutenant	Captain	Major	Lieut.-Colonel	Remarks
ADAMS, H. C.	3rd	14.5.1915	...	...	...	...	Joined 2nd/43rd, 20th April 1916; marched with a platoon of "A" Company from Sahiliya to Ana to attend the Durbar, 3rd November 1918.
ANDERSON, F. E.	9th	12.7.1915	15.11.1916	...	...	...	Joined 43rd, 11th October 1916; regimental sniping officer, 31st December 1916; to Kut for duty on light railway, 13th May 1917; finally employed as Deputy Assistant Director of Railways, Baghdad; temporary captain, 23rd October 1917.
ANDREWS, P. J.	Bucks.	29.8.1917	...	...	...	...	Joined 43rd from India, 26th April 1918; returned to India for transfer to Indian Army, 27th September 1918.
BACON, W. G.	Bucks.	26.9.1916	...	...	...	...	Joined 43rd from India, 6th June, 1918; demobilized, 26th December 1918.
BAINES, Cuthbert Savile	52nd and 43rd	14.5.1910	8.10.1913	18.10.1915	...	...	Embarked with the 52nd, 13th August 1914; "B" Company present in the following operations—Mons, 23rd August–5th September, 1914; Marne, 1914, 7th–10th September; Aisne, 1914, 12th–15th September; Ypres, 1914, 9th October–22nd November; Langemarck, 1914, 21st–24th October; Gheluvelt, 29th–31st October; Nonne Bosschen Wood, 11th November; wounded and invalided to England; awarded the Distinguished Service Order, 1st January 1915; rejoined the 52nd, 24th March 1915; present at Aubers, 9th May; Festubert, 1915, 15th–25th May; wounded in the attack at Richebourg, 16th May; invalided to England; staff captain, Ministry of Munitions, 18th August 1915; temporary major, 2nd/6th Royal Warwickshire Regiment; rejoined 52nd as senior major, August 1916; present in the operations on the Ancre, 1916 (Beaumont Hamel), 13th–18th November; Bapaume, 1917, 17th March; Arras, 1917, 9th April–4th May; Vimy, 1917, 9th–14th April; Scarpe, 1917, 9th–14th April, 23rd–24th April, 3rd–4th May; Arleux, 28th–29th April; to the command of the 2nd/7th King's Liverpool Regiment (temporary lieutenant-colonel), September 1917; despatches; bar to the Distinguished Service Order; joined the 43rd, April 1919; to North Russia in command of "A" Company, May 1919; severely wounded in the raid on Ignatovskaya, 26th–27th June.
BANKS, Cyril Marshall	9th	12.7.1915	1.7.1917	...	...	...	Enlisted 4th September 1914; 12th Gloucestershire Regiment; attached 2nd/5th The Buffs, August 1915–August 1916; joined 9th Battalion of the Regiment, August 1916; to Mesopotamia, December 1916; attached 8th Welch Regiment; present at the second battle of Kut al Amara, February 1917; pursuit to Baghdad; hospital, sick, May 1917; joined 43rd, July 1917; present at Khan Baghdadi, 26th March 1918; "C" Company; commanded amalgamated company, 24th January 1919; demobilized, August 1919.
BARRINGTON, Hon. William Reginald Shute	3rd	...	...	6.1.1897	...	...	To Mesopotamia, with draft of 300 men, December 1915; joined 2nd/43rd 12th February 1916; second in command present at the attack on the Dujaila Redoubt, 8th March; commanded 2nd/43rd and 43rd after Major Carter was wounded, 6th April 1916; to hospital, 27th July–16th September; second in command to Lieutenant-Colonel Crake, 16th September–5th October; commanded "A" Company, 5th October–22nd February 1917; to India on duty, 22nd February 1917.

APPENDICES

Name	Bn		Date		Notes
†BICKNELL, Herman Kentigern	3rd	...	30.7.1916	...	Lieutenant, 11th York and Lancaster Regiment, 18th March 1915; transferred to 3rd Battalion as captain; joined 43rd and posted to "D" Company, 22nd January 1917; to Maqil to relieve Second Lieutenant Grosvenor as assistant provost marshal, 29th March 1917; died at Baghdad of heat-stroke, 24th July 1917.
BLEEZE, Henry William	9th	4.10.1915	1.7.1917	20.7.1917	Joined the ranks of the 16th London Regiment (Queen's Westminster Rifles), 6th August 1914; to France, 31st October; present at the second battle of Ypres; first and second battles of Hooge; returned for commission, 26th September 1915; bombing officer, 9th Battalion, 10th May 1916; instructor, school of bombing, Clapham, 18th July; to Mesopotamia, 7th September; joined 43rd at Amara, 11th October; "C" Company, No. 11 Platoon; appointed bombing officer; to hospital with sand-fly fever, 23rd August–3rd September 1917; command of "C" Company vice Terry, 11th December; present at Khan Baghdadi, 25th–26th March 1918; despatches; instructor, divisional platoon commanders' school, 5th May; instructor, infantry school, Baghdad, 10th November; despatches, 7th February 1919; command of the 43rd after departure of cadre; joined 1st/5th The Buffs with demobilizable men of 43rd, 10th March; acting major, 20th March; commandant, 17th Divisional Lewis gun school, 1st June.
BOOTH, Philip	52nd and 43rd	24.11.1915	1.1.1917	1.2.1923	Joined the 52nd from the 3rd Battalion, 20th September 1916; "C" Company; present in the operations on the Ancre, 1916 (Beaumont Hamel); at Bapaume, 1917, 17th March; Arras, 1917, 9th April–4th May; Vimy, 1917, 9th–14th April; Scarpe, 1917, 23rd–24th April, 3rd–4th May; Arleux, 28th–29th April; Cambrai, 1917, 20th November–3rd December; attached to headquarters, 5th Infantry Brigade, December 1917–May 1918; took part in the operations at St. Quentin, 21st–23rd March 1918; Bapaume, 1918, 24th–25th March; Somme, 1918, 21st March–5th April; appointed regimental musketry officer, May 1918; later transport officer; present with the 52nd in the operations, Somme, 1918, 21st August–3rd September; Albert, 1918, 21st–23rd August; Hindenburg Line, 12th September–9th October; Havrincourt, 12th September; Canal du Nord, 27th September–1st October; Cambrai, 1918, 8th–9th October; Selle, 17th–25th October; reverted to musketry officer, 30th November; to Germany with the 52nd; joined the 43rd, April 1919; "A" Company; to North Russia in command of No. 4 Platoon, May 1919; present in the raid on Ignatovskaya, 26th–27th June; on return in November, posted to 52nd.
†BROOKE, Richard Reginald Maude	43rd	9.12.1899	12.12.1901	28.12.1908	Born 4th February 1878; gazetted from the Militia and posted to the 43rd at Aldershot, under orders for South Africa; embarked with the Mounted Infantry Company, and served with it for the greater part of the South African War; operations in the Orange Free State, February–May 1900, including actions at Vet River (5th and 6th May) and Zand River; operations in the Transvaal, west of Pretoria, July–29th November 1900; operations in Orange River Colony (May–November 1900), including actions at Ladybrand (2nd–9th September) and Bothaville; operations in Cape Colony, south of Orange River, 1899–1900; operations in the Transvaal, December–July 1901 and October 1901–31st May 1902; operations in Orange River Colony, July 1901–October 1901 and January–March 1902. Queen's medal with three clasps; King's medal with two clasps. Returned to England with the 43rd; transferred to the 52nd in India, January 1903, with which he returned to England in November 1903. Served at the Depot, December 1908–1912; adjutant, 2nd Volunteer Battalion of the Regiment (afterwards 4th Battalion, T.F.); rejoined 52nd, April 1912; posted to 43rd in India, July 1912; sailed with the 43rd for Mesopotamia as second captain of "P" Company, November 1914; succeeded to the command of "R" Company when Captain Stapleton was appointed D.A.Q.M.G., 6th Division. He was killed in action in the Qurna Regatta, 31st May 1915, whilst leading "R" Company in the attack on Norfolk Hill. He was mentioned in despatches after his death.

43RD LIGHT INFANTRY

Name	Battalion	Second Lieutenant	Lieutenant	Captain	Major	Lieut.-Colonel	Remarks
†Brown, Fred	43rd	7.11.1914	...	...	...	...	Promoted from lance-corporal, 14th Hussars; embarked with the 43rd for Mesopotamia as subaltern in "S" Company; present at the Qurna *Regatta*, 31st May 1915; battle of Es Sinn or Kut al Amara, 28th September 1915; at the battle of Ctesiphon, 22nd November 1915, he acted as galloper to Brigadier-General Hoghton, commanding the 17th Brigade, and had a horse shot under him; rejoined the 43rd at V.P. on the 23rd November; retreat to Kut; in the siege of Kut he commanded "P" Company; killed by a sniper's bullet, 10th December 1915; despatches.
Brown, James Raitt	9th	18.11.1915	1.7.1917	...	...	...	Joined 43rd, 6th October 1916; posted to "B" Company; to hospital with enteric, November 1917; rejoined September 1918; mentioned in despatches, London Gazette, 27th August 1918.
Carter, Lindsay James	43rd	4.1.1893 (52nd)	1.3.1896	27.2.1900	23.6.1913 (43rd)	...	Joined the 52nd at Bareilly and served in the Indian Frontier Campaign, 1897-1898. In this campaign he showed himself to be a fine soldier, full of energy and quite fearless. He carried a wounded man away on his back under a hot fire from the best shots in the world. The man was killed while he was being carried, but with no injury to his rescuer. Returned to England with the 52nd in 1903; adjutant, 3rd York and Lancaster Regiment, 1904-1907; joined the 43rd in Burma in 1909; went on service with the 43rd to Mesopotamia, November 1914, in command of "Q" Company; invalided to India, May, 1915; returned January 1916; to command the 2nd/43rd, composed of drafts and details for the 43rd besieged in Kut. He commanded in the attack on the Dujaila Redoubt, 8th March, and in the disastrous attempt to force the Sannaiyat position on 6th April 1916, when the 2nd/43rd was completely wiped out except for seventeen other ranks and one officer; he was severely wounded in the arm. He received the Distinguished Service Order and, what probably pleased him more, a letter of thanks from General Kemball for the gallantry and tenacity shown by the Regiment. To North Russia with the 43rd as senior major; retired in January 1920, after 27 years of service. Died at Kempsey, Worcestershire, 16th September 1925. He was born on the 2nd August 1872, and was the eldest son of James Colebrooke Carter, late 43rd Light Infantry. He was educated at Wellington College and R.M.C., Sandhurst. See *Chronicle*, 1925, p. 232.
Colvill, David Chaigneau	52nd and 43rd	27.10.1916	27.4.1918	...	...	...	Joined the 52nd from the 3rd Battalion, 30th August 1917; "A" Company; present in the operations at Cambrai, 1917, 20th November-3rd December; St. Quentin, 21st-23rd March 1918; Bapaume, 1918, 24th-25th March, 31st August-3rd September; Somme, 1918, 21st March-5th April, 21st August-3rd September; Albert, 1918, 21st-23rd August; attack on and capture of Sapignies, 25th August; gassed, 9th September; invalided to England; awarded the Military Cross; joined the 43rd, April 1919; "D" Company; to North Russia, May 1919; present in raid on Bolsheviks, 2nd-3rd July; to the Onega front, August; posted to 43rd on return, November 1919.
†Coulthard, E. F.	9th	13.5.15	...	...	...	...	To Mesopotamia with draft of 350 men for the 97th Regiment, December 1915; attached Connaught Rangers, 12th February 1916; joined 2nd/43rd, 29th February; present at the attack on Dujaila Redoubt, 8th March; killed at Sannaiyat, 6th April 1916.
†Courtis, John Harold	43rd	6.2.1909	27.11.1912	10.6.15	...	...	Went on service with the 43rd, November 1914, as machine gun officer; present at the Qurna *Regatta*, 31st May 1915; appointed brigade machine gun officer, August 1915; commanded the 17th Brigade machine guns at Es Sinn and Ctesiphon; was mortally wounded when the 43rd made the flank march to attack Water Redoubt. He was the son of Sir John Courtis of Llandaff; was born 25th July, 1888, and was educated at Repton and Sandhurst.

APPENDICES

Name	Battalion	Date	Date	Notes
†DANCEY, George	43rd	...	29.12.1916	Promoted quartermaster from acting regimental serjeant-major; present with the 2nd/43rd in the operations for the relief of Kut; awarded the Distinguished Conduct Medal; present at Khan Baghdadi, 25th-26th March 1918; awarded the Military Cross. Appointed quartermaster, April 1919; to North Russia, May 1919; died, 2nd June 1919.
DAVENPORT, C. T.	3rd	29.5.1915	6.9.1916	To Mesopotamia with draft of 350 men for the 97th Regiment, December 1915; attached Connaught Rangers, 12th February 1916; joined 2nd/43rd, 12th February; present at the attack on the Dujaila Redoubt, 8th March; contracted dysentery and was invalided to England at the end of June 1916.
†DAVENPORT, Frank Maturin	43rd	6.2.1909	20.11.1912	Went on service with the 43rd, November 1914, as a subaltern of "Q" Company, which he commanded at the battle of Es Sinn or Kut al Amara; killed at the battle of Ctesiphon, 22nd November 1915. He was the only son of Alfred Davenport, and was born 30th August, 1888; educated at Rugby and Sandhurst.
†DAVIS, Anthony Hugh	3rd	11.6.1915	...	The youngest son of the late Lawrence Davis of Twyford; educated at Cheltenham; joined the Public Schools Battalion on the outbreak of war; joined the 2nd/43rd, March 1916; killed at the first battle of Sannaiyat, 6th April 1916, aged 31.
DODINGTON, Wilfred Marriott-	52nd and 43rd	19.10.1892	16.11.1895	Joined the 52nd from the Militia; present at the operations on the North-West Frontier of India, 1897-98; Mohmand; medal with clasp; Tirah; operations in the Bara Valley, 7th-14th December 1897; clasp; adjutant, 1900-04; passed staff college, 1905; G.S.O. 2nd Grade, South-East Coast Defences, 16th July 1912; special appointment, 3rd July 1915; G.S.O. 2nd Grade, 4th October 1915; despatches (Dardanelles); brevet of lieutenant-colonel, 1st January 1916; brigadier-general commanding 161st Brigade in Egypt, Sinai, etc., June 1916-April 1918; despatches; brevet of colonel, 1st January 1918; command of 192nd Brigade in Norfolk, April 1918; Companion of St. Michael and St. George; to command of 43rd, April 1919; to North Russia; present in the raid on Ignatovskaya, 26th-27th June; retired, 21st December 1919; died at Tiverton, 23rd April 1931. He was the son of Lieutenant-Colonel Thomas Marriott-Dodington of Horsington, Somerset, and was educated at Wellington College. See *Chronicle*, 1931, p. 277.
DRAKE, Thomas Tyrwhitt-	52nd and 43rd	14.7.1915	15.11.1916	Joined the 52nd from the 3rd Battalion, 5th October 1915; "B" Company; present in the operations on the Somme, 1916, 1st July-18th July; at Delville Wood, 15th July-3rd September; on the Ancre, 1916 (Beaumont-Hamel), 13th-18th November; awarded the Military Cross, 1st January 1917; grenade officer; present in the operations at Bapaume, 1917, 17th March; Arras, 1917, 9th April-4th May; Vimy, 1917, 9th-14th April; Scarpe, 1917, 23rd-24th April, 3rd-4th May; Arleux, 28th-29th April; awarded bar to Military Cross, 22nd September; present at Cambrai, 20th November-3rd December; St. Quentin, 1918, 21st-23rd March 1918; Bapaume, 1918, 24th-25th March, 31st August-3rd September; Somme, 1918, 21st March-5th April, 21st August-3rd September; Albert, 1918, 21st-23rd August, including attack on and capture of Sapignies; scout officer; Hindenburg Line, 12th September-9th October; command of "A" Company; Havrincourt, 12th September; Canal du Nord, 27th September-1st October; Cambrai, 1918, 8th-9th October; Selle, 17th-25th October; awarded second bar to Military Cross, October 1918; to Germany with the 52nd in Army of Occupation; joined the 43rd, April 1919; scout officer; to North Russia; present in the raid on Ignatovskaya, 26th-27th June; raid on Bolshevik forward position, 2nd-3rd July; reposted to the 52nd on return, November 1919.

427

Name	Battalion	Second Lieutenant	Lieutenant	Captain	Major	Lieut.-Colonel	Remarks
EAGLE, Harold S.	52nd and 43rd	26.2.1915	17.2.1916	23.2.1923	...	...	Joined the 3rd Battalion; served with the 7th Battalion in Salonika; wounded in the attack on Horseshoe Hill, August 1916; invalided to England; joined the 52nd 19th February 1917; "B" Company; regular commission as lieutenant, 1st January 1917; present at Bapaume, 1917, 17th March; Arras, 1917, 9th April–4th May; Vimy, 1917, 9th–14th April; Scarpe, 1917, 9th–14th April, 23rd–24th April, 3rd–4th May; Arleux, 28th–29th April; wounded; Cambrai, 1917, 20th November–3rd December; transferred to "D" Company; present at St. Quentin, 21st–23rd March 1918; Bapaume, 1918, 24th–25th March, 31st August–3rd September; acting captain commanding "D" Company, 12th April; present at Somme, 1918, 21st March–5th April, 21st August–3rd September; Albert, 1918, 21st–23rd August, including capture of Sapignies, 25th August; Hindenburg Line, 12th September–9th October; Havrincourt, 12th September; Canal du Nord, 27th September–1st October; Cambrai, 1918, 8th–9th October; Selle, 17th–25th October; to Germany with the 52nd in the Army of Occupation; joined the 43rd, April 1919; transport officer; to North Russia; posted to 52nd on return, November 1919.
FENWICK, J. S.	5th	22.8.1914	30.7.1916 (43rd)	...	...	...	Joined the 2nd/43rd, 26th June 1917; appointed to the Indian Army on probation, 15th March 1918; present at Khan Baghdadi, 25th–26th March, in command of No. 13 Platoon; rejoined 43rd, 1920; resigned the same year.
FIELD, H. T. C.	9th	12.5.1915	30.7.1916 (43rd)	1.1.1917	...	...	To Mesopotamia with draft of 300 men, December 1915; joined 2nd/43rd, 12th February 1916; present at the attack on the Dujaila Redoubt, 8th March; wounded at Sannaiyat, 6th April, when bombing officer to the 28th Brigade; invalided to India; rejoined at Amara, 27th June; command of "C" Company, 23rd August–23rd October; command of "B" Company 23rd–28th October, when Captain Wheelwright assumed command; to hospital, 11th December–3rd January 1917; command of "B" Company from Captain Wheelwright, 3rd January; present at Khan Baghdadi, 25th–26th March 1918; despatches, 15th April 1918.
FITZGERALD, Calvert	52nd and 43rd	8.5.1901 (52nd)	14.4.1905 (52nd)	8.5.1911 (3rd)	25.9.1917 (43rd)	...	Retired from the 52nd, 4th May 1910; rejoined 52nd 29th December 1914; "C" Company, Captain Southey, August 1915; joined 43rd, 25th January 1917; employed with machine gun section; machine gun officer in succession to Captain Southey, August 1915; joined 43rd, 25th January 1917; temporary machine gun officer; command of "A" Company vice Major Barrington, 22nd February 1917; second in command, 29th September; present at Khan Baghdadi, 25th–26th March 1918; demobilized 24th January 1919.
†FOLJAMBE, Hon. Josceline Charles William Saville	43rd	...	20.5.1908	14.3.1914	...	...	The third son of the 1st Earl of Liverpool; educated at Eton; gazetted second lieutenant, Northumberland Fusiliers, 18th January 1902; lieutenant, 15th December 1905; transferred to the 43rd, 20th May 1908; appointed adjutant, 43rd, 6th May 1913; present as adjutant at the Qurna Regatta, 31st May 1915; battles of Es Sinn and Ctesiphon, where he was wounded; rejoined from India and appointed adjutant, 2nd/43rd, February 1916; present at the attack on Dujaila Redoubt, 8th March; killed at Sannaiyat, 6th April 1916; mentioned in despatches three times; brevet of major, 17th April 1916.

APPENDICES

Name	Bn				Notes
†FORREST, Charles Evelyn	43rd	1.12.1897	25.10.1898	22.2.1903	1.9.1915	Born 21st August 1876; the son of the late John Forrest of Grymsdyke, Buckinghamshire; gazetted from the Militia; served in the South African War, 1899–1902, being employed with the Mounted Infantry; slightly wounded; operations in the Orange Free State, February–May 1900, including actions at Vet River, 5th and 6th May, and Zand River; operations in the Transvaal in May and June, 1900, including the action near Johannesburg; operations in Cape Colony, south of the Orange River, 1899–1900; operations in the Transvaal in May–July 1901 and October 1901–21st May 1902; operations in the Orange River Colony, July–October 1901; despatches, *London Gazette*, 10th September 1901; Queen's medal with three clasps; King's medal with two clasps; Distinguished Service Order; adjutant of a Territorial Force battalion, 1910–11; was serving with the 43rd in India on the outbreak of war; in command of "S" Company; served continuously throughout the operations on the Tigris, battles of Es Sinn and Ctesiphon, where he was killed in the assault on Water Redoubt. He was a good all-round sportsman, a good shot, a keen and bold rider to hounds, and played polo for the 43rd in India.
GARDNER, A. E. ...	3rd	3.5.1915	...	6.9.1916		To Mesopotamia with draft of 300 men, December 1915; joined 2nd/43rd, 12th February 1916; present at the attack on Dujaila Redoubt, 8th March; wounded at Sannaiyat, 6th April; invalided to England.
GARRARD, G. F. ...	9th	12.5.1915	...	30.7.1916		To Mesopotamia with draft of 300 men, December 1915; joined 2nd/43rd, 12th February 1916; present at the attack on Dujaila Redoubt, 8th March; invalided sick to India, March 1916.
GILES, Leslie William	52nd and 43rd	24.11.1915	...	1.1.1917		Joined the 52nd from the 3rd Battalion, 20th September 1916; "B" Company; present in the operations on the Somme, 1916, November; Ancre, 1916, 13th–18th November (Beaumont-Hamel); awarded the Military Cross; Bapaume, 1917, 17th March; acting captain commanding "B" Company, April; present in the operations at Arras, 1917, 9th April–4th May; Vimy, 1917, 9th–14th April; Scarpe, 1917, 9th–14th April, 23rd–24th April, 3rd–4th May; Arleux, 28th–29th April; Cambrai, 1917, 20th November–3rd December; to England on duty, 8th February–10th July, 1918; present at Bapaume, 1918, 31st August–3rd September; Somme, 1918, 21st August–3rd September; Albert, 1918, 21st–23rd August, including capture of Sapignies; Hindenburg Line, 12th September–9th October; Havrincourt, 1918, 12th September; Canal du Nord, 27th September–1st October; Cambrai, 1918, 8th–9th October; Selle, 17th–25th October; bar to Military Cross; to Germany with the 52nd in the Army of Occupation; posted to the 43rd, April 1919; "A" Company; to North Russia in command of No. 3 Platoon; took part in the raid on Ignatovskaya, 26th–27th June; mentioned in despatches; posted to 52nd on return, November 1919.
†GRIFFIN, Sydney James	3rd	23.4.1915	...	6.9.1916		To Mesopotamia with draft of 300 men, December 1915; joined 2nd/43rd, 12th February 1916; present at the attack on Dujaila Redoubt, 8th March; command of "A" Company, 4th August–5th October; to hospital, 12th December–2nd February 1917; platoon commander, "C" Company; died of wounds received at the battle of Khan Baghdadi, 26th March 1918, when in command of No. 4 Platoon, aged 22. He was the son of M. J. Griffin, 32 Juxon Street, Oxford.
GROSVENOR, G. R. ...	9th	14.4.1915	...	1.7.1917		To Mesopotamia with draft of 300 men, December 1915; joined 2nd/43rd, 12th February 1916; present at the attack on Dujaila Redoubt, 8th March; relieved Lieutenant Murphy as assistant provost marshal at Maqil; temporary captain, 23rd December 1916; joined Stokes Mortar battery at Amara on relief by Captain Bicknell, 28th March 1917.
HAMILTON, Anthony Baldwin	...	27.10.1916	...	27.4.1918		Joined the 7th Battalion on Salonika front, July 1917; assistant transport officer; posted "A" Company; took part in the advance into Bulgaria in the autumn of 1918; to the 43rd, April 1919; to North Russia; Lewis gun officer.

43RD LIGHT INFANTRY

Name	Battalion	Second Lieutenant	Lieutenant	Captain	Major	Lieut.-Colonel	Remarks
†HAMMICK, Stephen Frederick	52nd and 43rd	24.1.1894	5.6.1897	11.12.1900	...	...	Retired to the Reserve of Officers, 2nd November 1909; served in the South African War, 1899-1902; relief of Kimberley; operations in the Orange Free State, February-May 1900, including Paardeberg, 17th-26th February; slightly wounded; operations in the Orange River Colony, May-November 1900; operations in the Transvaal, March-July, 1901 and October 1901-21st May 1902; operations in the Orange River Colony, December 1900-March 1901 and July 1901-March 1902; employed with Mounted Infantry; Queen's medal with three clasps; King's medal with two clasps; rejoined on the outbreak of war and served with the 52nd in France, 30th November 1914-16th May 1915; wounded at Richebourg and invalided to England; with draft for the 43rd in Mesopotamia, December 1915; joined the 2nd/43rd, February 1916; posted to "A" Company; present at the attack on Dujaila Redoubt, 8th March; mortally wounded in the attack on Sannaiyat, 6th April 1916; died at Basra, 18th April 1916. He was the only son of Colonel Sir St. Vincent Hammick, Bart., late 43rd Light Infantry, and was born on the 2nd February 1871. He was educated at Marlborough and Brasenose College, Oxford.
HARDIE, F. M.	43rd	15.9.1915	11.12.1916	...	...	...	Joined the 43rd, 28th June 1916; invalided to India, 27th August 1917.
HARMAN, R. M.	52nd and 43rd	29.5.1918	...	...	...	...	Joined the 52nd, 30th December 1918; "D" Company; posted to 43rd, April 1919; to North Russia; "B" Company (Royal Warwickshire Regiment).
HENLEY, Cornish Frederick	43rd	4.5.1898	23.10.1899	3.10.1904	1.9.1915	...	Served in the South African War, 1899-1902; relief of Kimberley; operations in the Orange Free State, February-May 1900, including operations at Paardeberg, 17th-26th February; actions at Poplar Grove and Driefontein; operations in the Orange River Colony, May-November 1900; operations in the Transvaal, April-July 1901 and October 1901-May 1902; operations in the Orange River Colony, December 1900-April 1901 and July 1901-March 1902; Queen's medal with four clasps; King's medal with two clasps; went on service with 43rd to Mesopotamia in command of "P" Company; wounded at the Qurna *Regatta*; invalided to India; rejoined the 43rd at Kut al Amara after the retreat from Ctesiphon; took part in the defence of Kut al Amara and was wounded, December 1915; prisoner; mentioned in despatches.
HILL, T. A.	4th	21.7.1916	21.1.1918	...	...	...	Joined from India, 26th April 1918.
HOLLAND, Francis Cuyler	...	21.12.1917	21.6.1919	...	...	...	Joined the 52nd from the 3rd Battalion, 17th October 1918; "D" Company; took part in the operations on the Selle, 17th-25th October; to Germany with the 52nd in Army of Occupation; posted to the 43rd, April 1919; to North Russia as supernumerary; did duty with "A" Company; posted to 52nd on return; resigned his commission, March 1922; died 28th December 1928; See *Chronicle*, 1929, p. 227.
HOLT, Edward	...	4.7.1916	10.12.1916	...	...	...	Gazetted second lieutenant, 5th Battalion Royal Warwickshire Regiment, 25th November 1914; temporary captain, 16th July 1916; gazetted to the Regiment as above; Military Cross; joined the 43rd, April 1919; to North Russia in command of No. 1 Platoon; invalided, 12th June 1919.

Name	43rd	Date 1	Date 2	Date 3	Notes
HORAN, Keith	43rd	5.2.1913	17.9.1914	14.12.1915	Went on service with the 43rd, November 1914; "P" Company; present at the Qurna *Regatta*, 31st May 1915; invalided to India on account of ill-health, 13th June 1915, and later to England; adjutant, Indian Volunteers, 23rd May 1916.
HUGGARD, G. C.	3rd 43rd	18.4.1915 4.1.1917	6.9.1916	...	Joined 2nd/43rd, February 1916.; present at the attack on Dujaila Redoubt, 8th March; invalided to India on account of ill-health, March 1916; rejoined from India, 4th November 1916; posted to "D" Company; joined Stokes mortar battery on formation at Amara, 28th March 1917; seconded to Royal Air Force.
†HYDE, Arthur Clarendon	43rd	...	24.2.1898	16.12.1908	Gazetted second lieutenant, West India Regiment, 25th July 1891; lieutenant, 19th July 1893; transferred to the Regiment, 22nd February 1908; aide-de-camp to the Governor and Commander-in-Chief, Bermuda, 1900-02; adjutant of Militia, 1907-08; present at the operations in Sierra Leone, 1898-99; Kareen Expedition medal with clasp; went on service with the 43rd, November 1914, as senior major; present at the Qurna *Regatta*; commanded the 43rd at the battle of Es Sinn in the absence of Lieutenant-Colonel Lethbridge, on sick leave in India; mentioned in despatches; killed in action in the opening stage of the battle of Ctesiphon, 22nd November 1915.
IVEY, Thomas E.	43rd	...	22.9.1903	1.7.1917	Quartermaster of the 43rd on mobilization; present at the Qurna *Regatta*; battles of Es Sinn and Ctesiphon; besieged in Kut al Amara, December 1915–April 1916; prisoner of war. Died, 23rd October 1919.
JOYCE, Herbert Conway	9th	2.11.1915	1.7.1917	...	Joined from India, 27th July 1917; invalided to India, 25th August 1917; rejoined from the base, 24th March 1918; present at the battle of Khan Baghdadi, 25th-26th March, in command of No. 3 Platoon, in command of demonstration platoon, Baghdad, 27th June 1918; demobilized, 26th December 1918.
†KEARSLEY, John Steuart	43rd	10.12.1913	8.1.1915	...	Gazetted from Special Reserve; temporary lieutenant, 14th November 1914; went on service with the 43rd; "R" Company; was present at the Qurna *Regatta*, battle of Es Sinn, and was killed at the battle of Ctesiphon in the attack on Water Redoubt. He was the youngest son of Major and Mrs. Kearsley of 116 Eaton Square, and was born on the 25th July 1892.
LETHBRIDGE, Ernest Astley Edmund	43rd	...	10.10.1885	27.9.1893	2.9.1904 23.10.1913 Adjutant, Militia, 1894-96; served in the South African War, 1899-1902; relief of Kimberley; operations in the Orange Free State, February-May 1900, including operations at Paardeberg, 17th-26th February; actions at Poplar Grove and Driefontein; operations in Orange River Colony, May-November, 1900; Operations in Orange River Colony, December 1900-May 1902; despatches, 8th February and 10th September 1901; Queen's medal with three clasps; King's medal with two clasps; Distinguished Service Order; in command of the 43rd on the outbreak of war; commanded at the Qurna *Regatta*, 31st May 1915; invalided to India from Amara, sick, July 1915; rejoined at Aziziya, November 1915; commanded at Ctesiphon; in the retreat to Kut al Amara, and defence of Kut al Amara, December 1915-April 1916; prisoner of war; despatches twice; brevet of colonel; Companion of the Order of St. Michael and St. George; French Croix de Guerre (with palms).
LETHBRIDGE, Duncan John Legh	43rd	1.5.1917	1.11.1918	...	Joined the 43rd, 8th November 1918; returned to England with the cadre, 22nd February 1919; rejoined 43rd after leave, April 1919; to North Russia, May; signalling officer; resigned his commission, June 1921.

Name	Battalion	Second Lieutenant	Lieutenant	Captain	Major	Lieut.-Colonel	Remarks
LOVEROCK, R. C.	43rd	7.11.1914	18.8.1915	1.1.1917	...	...	Promoted second lieutenant from colour-serjeant, Durham Light Infantry; went on service with the 43rd; "Q" Company; appointed assistant military landing officer, Basra, 20th July 1915; temporary captain, 6th October 1915; Distinguished Service Order, 17th September 1917.
LOWNDES, Frederick Charles Louis Aloysius	52nd and 43rd	7.4.1916	7.10.1917	...	...	...	Joined the 52nd from the 3rd Battalion, 20th September 1916; "A" Company; took part in the operations on the Ancre, 1916 (Beaumont Hamel), 13th-18th November; rejoined, 9th June 1917; "A" Company; attached 5th Brigade and 2nd Divisional Headquarters; took part in the operations at Cambrai, 1917, 20th November-3rd December; St. Quentin, 21st-23rd March 1918; Bapaume, 1918, 24th-25th March; Somme, 1918, 21st March-5th April; wounded while serving with 2nd Divisional Composite Battalion, April 1918; rejoined 52nd, 11th October; took part in the operations on the Selle, 17th-25th October; to Germany with the 52nd in the Army of Occupation; posted to the 43rd, April 1919; to North Russia as supernumerary; took over No. 3 Platoon from Lieutenant Giles, 27th June; resigned his commission, September 1924.
MASON, Alfred Ernest	43rd	7.11.1914	10.6.1915	1.1.1917	...	...	Promoted second lieutenant from regimental serjeant-major; employed at the Depot, India, 1st March 1915-23rd October 1915; present at the battle of Ctesiphon in charge of Brigade Reserve Ammunition Column; retreat to Kut al Amara; acting adjutant during the siege; despatches; prisoner of war. Rejoined the 43rd from prisoner of war, March 1919; messing officer; to North Russia; appointed quartermaster on death of Lieutenant Dancey, 3rd June 1919; died, 10th January 1928, when quartermaster of the Depot. See *Chronicle*, 1928, p. 206.
MEADE, John Windham	52nd and 43rd	1.10.1914	10.6.1915	1.1.1917	...	...	Joined the 52nd, 28th May 1915; "C" Company; wounded at Givenchy, 9th July 1915; invalided to England; to Mesopotamia with draft of 350 men for the 97th Regiment, December 1915; attached to Connaught Rangers, 12th February 1916; joined 2nd/43rd, 29th February; present at the attack on the Dujaila Redoubt, 8th March; wounded, 9th April; invalided to England; rejoined the 43rd with draft of 90 men, 22nd June 1917; to hospital, 26th July; command of "D" Company, 2nd August; present at Khan Baghdadi, 25th-26th March 1918; command of 43rd, 24th January 1919; brought cadre from Hit to Basra, February; returned to England, April 1919. To North Russia, supernumerary; attached to "C" Company (Devonshire Regiment); detached with Nos. 9, 10 and 11 Platoons and one platoon of "D" Company to the Seletskoe front to guard the right flank and communications from a Bolshevik threat down the Emtsa River, 19th August; rejoined at Archangel, 23rd September.
MILFORD, T. R.	3rd	11.6.1915	1.7.1917	...	...	...	Joined the 2nd/43rd, 20th April 1916; invalided to India; rejoined, 6th November 1916; appointed signalling officer, 18th November 1916; present at Khan Baghdadi, 25th-26th March 1918: transferred to Royal Air Force, Egypt, 25th September 1918.
MORLAND, Walter Edward Thomson	43rd	18.1.1902	11.8.1905	22.1.1914	18.1.1917	...	Served in the South African War, 1899-1902; operations in the Orange River Colony, April-May 1902; Queen's medal with three clasps; employed with King's African Rifles (4th Uganda Battalion), 1908-11; Somaliland, 1908-10; medal with clasp; went on service with the 43rd from India, November 1914; appointed brigade *bellum* officer, Qurna, May 1915; present at Qurna *Regatta*; battles of Es Sinn and Ctesiphon on General Townshend's staff; retreat to, and defence of, Kut al Amara; aide-de-camp to General Townshend and imprisoned with him; despatches; Distinguished Service Order; Military Cross.

APPENDICES

Name	Bn	Date 1	Date 2	Date 3	Notes
MUNDEY, Stanley Cyril Beresford	43rd	9.6.1909	17.4.1913	10.6.1915	Gazetted from Special Reserve; remained in India in command of Depot 17th November 1914–17th May 1915; attached as observer to Royal Flying Corps, 9th September 1915; present at the battles of Es Sinn and Ctesiphon; besieged in Kut al Amara; despatches; prisoner of war at Yozgad.
MURPHY, D.	43rd	7.11.1914	27.10.1915	1.10.1917	Promoted second lieutenant from lance-corporal, Yorkshire Regiment; "P" Company; went on service with the 43rd, November 1914; present at the Qurna *Regatta* and battle of Es Sinn; wounded at Ctesiphon, 22nd November 1915; invalided to India; rejoined and posted to "A" Company, 10th January 1917; to Amara on formation of Stokes mortar battery, 28th March 1917; returned to England with the cadre, April 1919.
MURRAY, C. H.	43rd	8.9.1917	...	...	Promoted from lance-serjeant; command of Rest Camp, Falluja; joined Dunsterforce, 11th January 1918, and served with it until 17th January 1919; returned to England with the cadre, April 1919.
NAYLOR, George	43rd	7.11.1914	27.9.1915	1.1.1917	Promoted from serjeant, Somerset Light Infantry; "S" Company; present at the Qurna *Regatta*, Es Sinn and Ctesiphon (in charge of salvage section); besieged in Kut; in command of "S" Company; wounded, 24th December 1915; despatches; awarded the Military Cross; prisoner of war at Kastamuni. Rejoined from prisoner of war, April 1919; to North Russia; present in the raid on Ignatovskaya in command of right half of "A" Company; succeeded to the command of "A" Company after Captain Baines was wounded, 27th June; commanded raid on Bolshevik forward position, 2nd–3rd July; awarded bar to Military Cross; posted to 43rd on return, November 1919.
NEVILLE, James Edmund Henderson	52nd and 43rd	26.1.1916	1.1.1917	...	Joined the 52nd from the 3rd Battalion, 18th December 1916; "B" Company; took part in the operations at Bapaume, 1917, 17th March; Arras, 1917, 9th April–4th May; Scarpe, 1917, 23rd–24th April, 3rd–4th May; Arleux, 28th–29th April; Cambrai, 1917, 20th November–3rd December; St. Quentin, 21st–23rd March 1918; Bapaume, 1918, 24th–25th March; Somme, 1918, 21st March–5th April, 21st August–3rd September; Albert, 1918, 21st–23rd August; awarded the Military Cross, 1st January 1918; wounded in the attack on and capture of Sapignies, 25th August 1918; invalided to England; joined the 43rd, March 1919; "A" Company; to North Russia; took part in the raid on Ignatovskaya, 26th–27th June; wounded in raid on Bolshevik forward position, 2nd–3rd July; posted to 43rd on return, November 1919.
NORTHCOTE, Dudley Stafford	9th 3rd	27.11.1914	...	1.7.1917	Served with the 6th Battalion in France; wounded and invalided to England; joined the 43rd, 14th June 1917; "A" Company; present at Khan Baghdadi, 25th–26th March 1918, in command of No. 2 Platoon; adjutant, Armenian refugees relief centre, Baquba, October 1918.
PARKINSON, Edward Baldrey	9th	22.4.1915	1.7.1917	...	To Mesopotamia with draft of 350 men for the 97th Regiment, December 1915; attached to Connaught Rangers, 12th February 1916; joined 2nd/43rd, 29th February; appointed transport officer in succession to Second Lieutenant Wilmot; present at the attack on the Dujaila Redoubt, 8th March; present at Khan Baghdadi, 25th–26th March 1918; temporary captain; despatches; demobilized January 1919. He was never sick during nearly three years' service in Mesopotamia.

Name	Battalion	Second Lieutenant	Lieutenant	Captain	Major	Lieut.-Colonel	Remarks
POPE - HENNESSY, Ladislas Herbert Richard	43rd	...	5.2.1898	11.9.1902	25.10.1913	...	Gazetted second lieutenant, Welch Regiment, 28th September 1895; transferred to the Regiment, 9th October 1895; brevet of major, 26th March 1906; temporary lieutenant-colonel commanding battalion, King's African Rifles, 15th April 1906; employed with West African Frontier Force, 1898-99; employed in British East Africa Protectorate, 1899-1907; staff officer to Inspector General, King's African Rifles, 1907-08; special service, Somaliland, 1908-09; brigade-major, 1st West Riding Infantry Brigade, T.F., 12th May 1913; War service: West Africa, 1897-98; employed in hinterland; medal with clasp; British East Africa, 1901; operations against Ogaden Somalis in Jubaland; medal with clasp; East Africa, 1905; operations in Sotik (in command); despatches; Distinguished Service Order; Nandi, 1905-06; despatches; brevet of major; clasp; Somaliland, 1908-09; despatches; clasp; interpreter, 2nd class, in French, January 1912; passed staff college; general staff officer, 3rd grade, 15th March 1915; general staff officer, 2nd grade, 15th July 1915; special appointment, Ministry of Munitions, 18th January 1916; general staff officer, 2nd grade, 41st Division, 21st March 1916–1st July 1916; acting lieutenant-colonel, commanding 43rd, 5th October 1916–14th March 1917; general staff officer, 1st grade, 3rd (Lahore) Division (temporary lieutenant-colonel), 19th March 1917; despatches twice; Chevalier of the Legion of Honour; brigadier-general, general staff, 1st (Indian) Army Corps (temporary brigadier-general), 5th September 1917; despatches; brevet of lieutenant-colonel, 1st January 1918; colonel, 1st January 1919; command of 52nd, 14th November 1919.
POWELL, James Jervoise	43rd	30.12.1908	24.7.1911	10.6.1915	...	...	Went on service with the 43rd, November 1914; "S" Company and regimental signalling officer; appointed signalling officer to the 17th Brigade, 31st May 1915; present at the Qurna *Regatta*; severely wounded at Es Sinn; mentioned in despatches; invalided to England; joined 3rd Battalion, August 1916; appointed to command of company of gentlemen cadets, Royal Military College, Sandhurst, November 1916; acting major, May 1918; joined the 52nd, September 1918; senior major; present at Rumilly, 1st October 1918; temporary command of the 17th Royal Fusiliers, 3rd November 1918; rejoined December and marched with the 52nd into Germany, 9th December 1918.
RADFORD, Herbert Daniel Hardcastle	3rd	30.12.1914	17.2.1916	...	...	...	Served with the 1st The Buffs in France, 1915; wounded, 21st July; invalided; joined 2nd/43rd, 28th March 1916; present at the first attack on Sannaiyat, 6th April, and survived; invalided sick to India, June 1916; rejoined and posted to Stokes mortar battery at Amara, 28th March 1917; to India to join Royal Flying Corps, March 1918; sick with pneumonia at Bombay; returned to Mesopotamia for demobilization.
RANCE, William	3rd	20.5.1915	6.9.1916	...	...	...	Served with the 19th Royal Fusiliers from 4th September 1914; to Mesopotamia, December 1915; joined 2nd/43rd, 12th February 1916; "A" Company; present at the attack on the Dujaila Redoubt, 8th March; present at Sannaiyat, 6th April, as orderly officer to Major-General Kemball, commanding 28th Brigade, and survived; to hospital with enteric; rejoined, 18th May 1917; appointed staff officer to Aziziya Mobile Column; rejoined 43rd, 18th November; "B" Company; acting captain and administrative commandant, Madhij, 12th February 1918; rejoined, 24th April; demobilized, 24th January 1919.
REYNARDSON, Henry Thomas Birch	43rd	19.1.1912	25.7.1914	25.11.1915	...	...	"R" Company; went on service with the 43rd, November 1914, as machine gun officer; in charge of regimental *bellums*, April-May 1915; present at the Qurna *Regatta* and battle of Es Sinn; severely wounded at the battle of Ctesiphon; invalided to England; author of *Mesopotamia* and a valuable diary of the campaign up to December 1915.

APPENDICES

RIDDLE, A. E. S.	3rd	30.3.1915	6.9.1916	...	Joined the 52nd, August 1915; "C" Company; wounded 7th/8th September 1915; joined the 2nd/43rd, 26th April 1916; invalided to India, July 1916; rejoined, 10th March 1917; "D" Company; to hospital; rejoined, 17th July; "B" Company; present at Khan Baghdadi, 25th-26th March 1918; transferred to Salonika with 224 surplus personnel, 26th November 1918.
RILEY, C. H.	3rd	19.5.1915	6.9.1916	...	To Mesopotamia with draft for 97th Regiment, December 1915; attached to Connaught Rangers, 12th February 1916; joined 2nd/43rd, 29th February; present at the attack on the Dujaila Redoubt, 8th March; wounded in the attack on Sannaiyat, 6th April; invalided to England.
ROBERTS, B. F.	3rd	26.6.1915	1.7.1917	...	Joined the 2nd/43rd, March 1916; machine gun officer, 31st December 1916; present at Khan Baghdadi, 25th-26th March 1918; command of "C" Company, 5th May 1918; demobilized, 26th December 1918.
ROCK, Leonard Joseph	3rd	17.6.1915	1.7.1917	...	Joined the 43rd, 19th June 1916; "C" Company; hospital, 19th July-29th September; joined Dunsterforce, 11th January 1918; rejoined the 43rd, 9th December 1918; demobilized, 16th January 1919.
SAWYER, Charles Anthony	43rd	21.8.1918	21.2.1920	...	Joined the 43rd at Aldershot, March 1919; to North Russia, assuming command of No. 2 Platoon, 27th June; posted to the 43rd on return, November 1919; killed in a motor accident, 20th February 1924. See *Chronicle*, 1924, p. 220.
SHAW, A. J.	5th	5.12.1915	1.7.1917	...	Joined from India, 15th October 1917; appointed divisional gas officer at Ramadi, 26th November 1917; acting captain, 28th November 1917.
SHEPHERD, J. G.	2nd/4th	15.5.1915	1.7.1917	...	Joined from India, 8th November 1917; present at Khan Baghdadi, 25th-26th March 1918, in command of No. 7 Platoon.
†SIMPSON, Rupert Victor	43rd	20.1.1900	15.3.1902	28.12.1908	1.9.1915	The seventh son of the late C. H. Simpson of Ackworth and Rugby; born on the 16th February 1880; educated at Eton and Sandhurst; went on active service in South African War, 1899-1902; operations in the Orange River Colony, May-November 1900, December 1900-January 1902; Queen's medal with three clasps; King's medal with two clasps; appointed adjutant, 43rd, 1910-13; accompanied the 43rd to Mesopotamia, November 1914; present at the Qurna *Regatta*, and was killed leading his company at the battle of Es Sinn, 28th September 1915.
SMITH, H. V.	6th 5th 43rd	5.2.1915 5.10.1915 5.2.1915	... ...	... ...	Temporary captain, 26th October 1915; joined the 43rd from Basra, 24th March 1918; command of demonstration platoon, Baghdad, 26th July-4th August 1918.
SMYTH, Herbert Edward Fitzroy	43rd	16.6.1915	27.10.1916	...	Joined 2nd/43rd, 28th February 1916; present at the attack on Dujaila Redoubt, 8th March; "B" Company, No. 6 Platoon; command of "A" Company, 7th April-19th May; to hospital with jaundice and malaria; rejoined, 6th November; acting staff captain, 50th Brigade, 28th November 1917; rejoined 31st January 1918; acting captain, 13th February; adjutant, Ramadi Area, 28th February; present at Khan Baghdadi, 25th-26th March, in command of No. 6 Platoon; acting adjutant *vice* Titherington, 12th July; to England with cadre. Appointed adjutant *vice* Captain and Brevet Major G. W. Titherington, April 1919; to North Russia; took part in the raid on Ignatovskaya, 26th-27th June; awarded Military Cross; resigned appointment of adjutant, July 1920.

43RD LIGHT INFANTRY

Name	Battalion	Second Lieutenant	Lieutenant	Captain	Major	Lieut.-Colonel	Remarks
STAPLETON, Francis Harry	43rd	3.2.1897	5.3.1898	11.9.1902	1.9.1915	21.12.1919	Went on service with the 43rd, South African War, 1899-1902; wounded; staff captain (intelligence), 1900-02; relief of Kimberley; operations in Orange Free State, February-May 1900; operations in Orange River Colony, April-May 1902; operations in Cape Colony, December 1900-April 1902; despatches; Queen's medal with three clasps; King's medal with two clasps; adjutant, 22nd March 1902-21st March 1905; adjutant, Militia, 1906-09; passed staff college; went on service with the 43rd, November 1914, commanding "R" Company; D.A.Q.M.G., 6th Division, 24th April 1915; despatches; invalided, 7th August 1915; returned to Mesopotamia, 10th December 1915, and joined General Aylmer's staff; brevet of lieutenant-colonel, 3rd June 1916; commanded 43rd, 22nd March 1917-21st July 1917; appointed general staff officer, 1st grade; A.A.Q.M.G., 17th Division, 25th September 1917; Companion of the Order of St. Michael and St. George; Serbian Order of the White Eagle with Swords.
STEPHENS, Rupert	43rd	6.6.1903	23.10.1905	14.3.1914	6.1.1918	...	Aide-de-camp to H.E. The Viceroy of India, 18th October 1912, until the war broke out; rejoined the 43rd and went on service to Mesopotamia as second captain of "R" Company; present at the Qurna *Regatta*; invalided to India, August; A.D.C. to the Commander-in-Chief in India, September 1915; embarked at Bombay to rejoin, November 1915; to hospital, Basra, sick, December 1915; camp commandant, Maqil, January 1916; commandant, Maqil-Kurmat-Ali area (D.A.A.G. and temporary major), April to August 1916; despatches; invalided to India with paratyphoid, August 1916; commandant, British Combined Depot, Bangalore, October 1916; to France, November 1916; posted to 1st/1st Buckinghamshire Battalion of the Regiment, January 1917; commandant, 48th Divisional School, February 1917; senior major, 1st/4th Gloucestershire Regiment, April 1917; command of same, May 1917; to command of 1st/4th Oxfordshire and Buckinghamshire Light Infantry, June 1917; acting lieutenant-colonel.
STURGES, Octavius Hugh Mansfield	52nd and 43rd	11.8.1915	11.12.1916	...	...	...	Joined the 52nd from the 3rd Battalion, 20th September 1916; "B" Company; took part in the operations on the Ancre, 1916, 13th-18th November (Beaumont-Hamel); wounded and invalided to England; rejoined 16th May 1918; to Senior Officers' School, Aldershot, August 1918; rejoined, 5th November 1918; to Germany with the 52nd in the Army of Occupation; joined the 43rd, April 1919; to North Russia in command of No. 2 Platoon; took part in the raid on Ignatovskaya, 26th-27th June; severely wounded; invalided to England; resigned his commission, 28th October 1920.
TATTON, Robert Henry Grenville	3rd	21.5.1904	12.9.1906	10.10.1914	...	...	Served in France with the Duke of Cornwall's Light Infantry, and was wounded; joined the 2nd/43rd, February 1916; commanded "B" Company; present at the attack on Dujaila Redoubt, 8th March; wounded at Sannaiyat, 6th April 1916; invalided to England.
TERRY, William Edward Cecil	43rd	4.5.1907	4.5.1910	10.6.1915	...	...	Staff captain, 5th Infantry Brigade, 5th August 1914; general staff officer, 3rd grade, 2nd May 1915; wounded in the battle of the Aisne, and invalided to England; general staff officer, 3rd grade (operations), XI Army Corps, 5th November 1915; staff captain, "H.Q." Advanced Base, Lines of Communication, 31st January 1916; joined 43rd, 5th October 1916; command of "C" Company; hospital, 1st-24th October 1916; to staff, 15th Division, 28th November 1917; command of "B" Company, 43rd, 2nd January 1918; D.A.Q.M.G., Hillah-Hindiya District, 13th February 1918; transferred to Home Establishment, November 1918.

APPENDICES

Name	Battalion				Remarks
THOMPSON, A. L.	9th	25.9.1915	1.7.1917	...	Saw service in France as private in the London Rifle Brigade; joined 43rd, 22nd June 1917; present at Khan Baghdadi, 25th–26th March 1918; "C" Company; escorted Nazim Bey, commander of the 50th Turkish Division, to Baghdad; transferred to 7th Battalion at Salonika, 26th November 1918.
TITHERINGTON, Geoffrey Wrench	43rd 52nd	2.9.1913	8.1.1915	2.3.1916	Joined the 52nd from Oxford University, 8th October 1914; "C" Company and temporary lieutenant, 15th November 1914; Aisne, Flanders, North of France; wounded at Richebourg, 15th–16th May 1915; invalided to England; joined 2nd/43rd, 20th April 1916; appointed adjutant, 2nd May 1916, after Captain Foljambe was killed; present at Khan Baghdadi, 25th–26th March 1918; despatches, 15th April 1918; brevet of major, 3rd June 1918.
TOMPKINS, A. L.	5th	7.10.1915	1.7.1917	...	Previous service in France with a regular battalion of the Northamptonshire Regiment; joined the 43rd from England, 14th June 1917; assistant signalling officer, 28th January 1918.
TRENGROUSE, Wilfred Trevenan	43rd	24.4.1918	24.10.1919	...	Joined the 43rd, April 1919; to North Russia with 238th Light Trench Mortar Battery; posted to 43rd on return, November 1919.
†TRUMAN, Alfred Holloway	3rd	4.5.1915	...	...	To Mesopotamia with draft for the 97th Regiment, December 1915; attached to Connaught Rangers, 12th February 1916; joined 2nd/43rd, 29th February; present at the attack on Dujaila Redoubt, 8th March; appointed bombing officer; killed at the first attack on Sannaiyat, 6th April 1916.
WARREN, Richard Courtenay	52nd and 43rd	16.8.1916	16.2.1918	...	Joined the 52nd from the 3rd Battalion, 1st January 1917; "A" Company; took part in the operations at Bapaume, 1917, 17th March; Vimy, 1917, 9th–14th April; Scarpe, 1917, 9th April–4th May; Arleux, 28th–29th April; awarded the Military Cross for a daylight patrol in the Canal Right sector at La Bassée when he destroyed with mobile charges a German sap-head, 15th September 1917; took part in the operations at Cambrai, 1917, 20th November–3rd December; invalided to England with blood poisoning, January 1918; rejoined 18th July 1918; "B" Company; took part in the operations on the Somme, 1918, 21st August–3rd September; Albert, 1918, 21st–23rd August; wounded in the attack on Sapignies, 25th August; awarded bar to Military Cross for an attack on a machine-gun post when he killed or dispersed the enemy holding up the advance; joined the 43rd, April 1919; to North Russia as assistant adjutant; posted to 43rd on return, November 1919. He was murdered by Sinn Feiners on the 28th June 1921. See *Chronicle*, 1921, p. 203.
WATTS, Langton Roper	3rd	11.6.1915	1.7.1917	...	Joined 43rd, 19th June 1916; hospital, 22nd December–30th March 1917; present at Khan Baghdadi, 25th–26th March 1918; No. 1 Platoon; attached to Somerset Light Infantry, 1919; assistant adjutant, British convalescent camp, and staff captain, Deolali, 1920–23.
WHEELWRIGHT, T. H.	6th Wilts. 1st Garr'n.	28.11.1914	15.2.1915 15.7.1916	25.2.1918	Joined 43rd, 28th October 1916; command of "B" Company; relieved Captain Fitzgerald at Basra, 7th January 1917; deputy assistant adjutant-general, 15th April 1917.

43RD LIGHT INFANTRY

Name	Battalion	Second Lieutenant	Lieutenant	Captain	Major	Lieut.-Colonel	Remarks
Whittall, George Edward	43rd	24.1.1906	11.12.1908	8.1.1915	...	...	Went on service with the 43rd, "R" Company, and transport officer; appointed military landing officer, Basra, 9th February 1915; embarkation staff officer, D.A.Q.M.G., 12th May 1915; rejoined the 43rd, command of "D" Company, 31st December 1916; Military Cross, 22nd December 1916; acting senior major, 28th February 1917; post commandant, Imam al Mansur, 20th March 1917; brevet of major, 3rd June 1917; to command of Mobile Column and Defence Troops, Aziziya, 8th July, 1917; command of 43rd from Brevet Lieutenant-Colonel Stapleton, 21st July 1917; acting lieutenant-colonel, 25th September 1917; commanded at Khan Baghdadi, 25th-26th March 1918; mentioned in despatches six times; brought the cadre back to England, April 1918.
†Widcombe, Charles Ingleton	3rd	17.4.1915	...	...	...	...	Commissioned from the Public Schools Battalion; to Mesopotamia with draft for the 97th Regiment, December 1915; attached to Connaught Rangers, 12th February 1916; joined 2nd/43rd, 29th February; present at the attack on the Dujaila Redoubt, 8th March; killed in the first attack on Sannaiyat, 6th April 1916. He was the only son of Mr. and Mrs. Harris Widcombe of Datchet, and was educated at the Imperial Service College, Windsor.
Williams, Tudor Price	3rd	16.12.1914	17.2.1916	...	...	...	Joined the Royal Naval Division as seaman, October 1914; joined the 43rd, 26th April 1916; command of "A" Company vice Smyth to hospital, 19th May; to hospital with paratyphoid, 4th August; invalided to India; rejoined 7th July 1917; present at Khan Baghdadi, 25th-26th March 1918; "D" Company, No. 16 Platoon; to Baghdad under civil commissioner, 29th March-18th April 1918; appointed to education department, 23rd April; invalided to England and demobilized, February 1919.
Wilmot, Douglas Alfred Theodore	9th	12.5.1915	30.7.1916	...	...	...	Previous service with Artists Rifles in France; to Mesopotamia with draft of 300 men, December 1915; joined 2nd/43rd, 12th February 1916; transport officer until succeeded by Parkinson; present at the attack on Dujaila Redoubt, 8th March; present at Khan Baghdadi, 25th-26th March 1918; adjutant, embarkation camp, Basra, 21st August; acting captain; served with a provisional battalion at Quetta during the Afghan War, 1919; medal; he was never sick during three years' active service.
Wooding, W. W.	43rd 52nd "C" Company.	9.11.1914 for service in France; joined 2nd/43rd, February 1917	25.11.1915	1.1.1917	...	...	Promoted from the ranks of the 52nd for service in France; joined 2nd/43rd, February 1916; acting quartermaster; relieved by G. Dancey; "C" Company.
†Wynter, Francis Constantine William	43rd	18.5.1911	22.3.1914	27.10.1915	...	...	Went on service with the 43rd, "S" Company, censor at Basra, 7th December 1914-12th May 1915; present at battle of Es Sinn; killed at battle of Ctesiphon, 22nd November 1915. He was the youngest son of the late P. H. M. Wynter of The Hays, Ramsden, Oxfordshire, and was educated at Harrow and Hertford College, Oxford.

APPENDIX XV.

RECORDS OF SERVICES OF OFFICERS ATTACHED TO THE 43RD LIGHT INFANTRY.

NAME	BATTALION	SECOND LIEUTENANT	LIEUTENANT	CAPTAIN	MAJOR	LIEUT.-COLONEL	REMARKS
ANDERSON, —	R.A.M.C.	...	...	...	...	...	Medical officer to the 2nd/43rd on formation; present at the attack on the Dujaila Redoubt, 8th March 1916; at the battle of Sannaiyat, 6th April; despatches; posted to field ambulance, May 1916.
BURRELL, Henry Norman	60th Rifles	7.4.1915	1.7.1917	...	...	...	Joined the 43rd from India, 26th January 1918; present at Khan Baghdadi, 25th-26th March; "C" Company.
BUTCHER, Herbert Charles	2nd/5th Hampshire Regt.	11.12.1914	1.7.1917	...	...	...	Joined the details of the 43rd at Ali Gharbi, December 1915; present at the attack on the Dujaila Redoubt, 8th March 1916; "B" Company; to hospital, 23rd October; invalided to England; employed Ministry of Munitions.
CRAKE, Ralph Hamilton	K.O.S.B.	...	...	...	10.11.1908	11.5.1916	Seconded to Indian Volunteers on outbreak of war; joined and assumed command of 43rd, 14th August 1916, from Captain Titherington; acting lieutenant-colonel; second in command to Lieutenant-Colonel Pope-Hennessy, 5th October; transferred to command of 8th Cheshire Regiment, 13th Division, 28th February 1917.
DE SELINCOURT, L.	2nd/7th Hampshire Regt.	3.11.1914	...	...	...	...	Joined the details of the 43rd at Ali Gharbi, December 1915; present at the attack on Dujaila Redoubt, 8th March 1916; severely wounded, 16th March; invalided to India.
ELLIOTT, C. E.	1st/7th Hampshire Regt.	...	2.12.1913	...	...	...	Joined the details of the 43rd, at Ali Gharbi, December 1915; wounded, 21st February 1916; invalided.
FIRTH, D. G.	1st/5th Hampshire Regt.	...	12.6.1914	...	...	...	Joined the details of the 43rd at Ali Gharbi, December 1915; present at the attack on the Dujaila Redoubt, 8th March 1916; wounded at Sannaiyat, 6th April; invalided.
GILCHRIST, W.	1st/4th D.C.L.I.	...	3.12.1913	...	...	...	Joined the details of the Regiment at Ali Gharbi, December 1915.
HAZELL, A. J.	76th Regt.	7.11.1914	...	...	...	...	"Q" Company from 16th December 1914; present at the battle of Es Sinn; wounded at Ctesiphon; invalided.

43RD LIGHT INFANTRY

Name	Battalion	Second Lieutenant	Lieutenant	Captain	Major	Lieut.-Colonel	Remarks
HEAWOOD, G. L.	4th Wilts. Regt.	...	12.12.1914	...	...	...	"P" Company from 28th August 1915; present at the battles of Es Sinn, 28th September, and Ctesiphon, 22nd November; commanded "Q" Company on the retreat to Kut and during the siege; prisoner of war; subsequently exchanged from Baghdad.
†HIND, Henry Basil Lindesay	3rd Somerset L.I.	...	24.9.1914	...	...	...	"Q" Company, from 17th June 1915; present at the battle of Es Sinn, 28th September; killed at Ctesiphon, 22nd November.
KINGHORN, E. C.	2nd/4th Border Regt.	...	30.7.1915	...	...	...	Joined the details of the Regiment at Ali Gharbi, December 1915; present at the attack on the Dujaila Redoubt, 8th March 1916; present at the attack on Sannaiyat, 6th April, and brought the remnants of the 43rd, seventeen men in all, out of the line that evening; command of "D" Company, 23rd August; handed over to Whittall, February 1917; acting captain, 20th March; command of "C" Company vice Terry, sick, 1st October-26th November; reverted to second lieutenant and transferred to Royal Flying Corps at Falluja as observer, 29th January 1918.
MELDON, W. W.	4th Durham L.I.	...	...	12.8.1914	11.1.1918	...	"R" Company from 17th June 1915; wounded at the battle of Es Sinn, 28th September; invalided.
MELLOR, John Serrocold Paget	2nd/5th Somerset L.I.	22.8.1914	21.11.1914	...	...	...	"R" Company from 28th September 1915; present at the battle of Ctesiphon, 22nd November; commanded "R" Company in the retreat to Kut and the siege; wounded in the wrist in the gallant defence of the Fort, 24th December; prisoner of war.
MOLONY, J. T.	1st/4th Dorset Regt.	3.4.1915	1.7.1917	...	...	...	Joined from India, 10th December 1918.
MURRAY, K. R.	4th Wilts. Regt.	...	12.12.1914	...	...	...	Joined the 43rd details at Ali Gharbi, December 1915; invalided on account of ill-health, March 1916.
PRICE, Alfred	107th Regt.	7.11.1914	6.11.1915	17.9.1918	...	...	"P" Company from 16th December 1914; present at Qurna *Regatta*, 31st May 1915; employed British infantry base depot, Amara, September 1915; rejoined, 4th April 1917; "A" Company; command of "D" Company, 13th May; acting captain in command of "A" Company, 26th August; present at Khan Baghdadi, 25th-26th March 1918.

APPENDICES

SEYMOUR, A. H.	...	4th D.C.L.I.	29.8.1914	1.6.1916	1.6.1916	Joined the 2nd/43rd, February 1916; present at the attack on the Dujaila Redoubt, 8th March; machine gun officer after Lieutenant Staley was killed; present at, and survived, the battle of Sannaiyat, 6th April; brigade machine gun officer; invalided with enteric, May 1916.
SMITH, James Ord Pender	...	R.A.M.C.	...	...	...	Joined the 43rd as medical officer, 1st January 1918; wounded at Khan Baghdadi; Iraq medal.
†STALEY, F. C.	...	5th Somerset L.I.	3.1.1913	22.8.1914	...	Joined the 43rd details at Ali Gharbi, December 1915; machine gun officer on formation of the 2nd/43rd; killed in the attack on the Dujaila Redoubt, 8th March 1916.
STARTIN, James	...	R.A.M.C.	...	...	...	Medical officer of the 43rd on mobilization; present at the Qurna *Regatta*, 31st May 1915; battle of Es Sinn, 28th September; battle of Ctesiphon, 22nd November; retreat to Kut; siege of Kut; despatches; Military Cross; prisoner of war.
STEELE, L. V.	...	60th Rifles	7.7.1916	7.1.1918	...	Joined 43rd, 26th June 1917; present at Khan Baghdadi, 25th–26th March 1918; "D" Company; transferred to Salonika, 26th November.
VINE, E. G.	...	10th D.C.L.I.	5.12.1915	1.7.1917	...	Joined 43rd, 8th November 1917; present at Khan Baghdadi, 25th–26th March 1918; "D" Company.
WEBBER, Sydney Littleton	...	46th L.I.	...	31.12.1914	...	"P" Company from 17th June 1915; present at the battle of Es Sinn, 28th September; wounded at Ctesiphon, 22nd November; invalided.
WELLS, Percy George	...	2nd/8th Regt.	19.11.1915	1.12.1916	...	Joined 43rd, 28th August 1916; "D" Company; transferred to "A" Company, 23rd December; to hospital, 11th February 1917; on rejoining transferred to Royal Flying Corps, Egypt.
WILSON, A. P.	...	4th Border Regt.	27.9.1914	...	...	"S" Company from 28th August 1915; present at Es Sinn, 28th September; wounded at Ctesiphon; invalided.
WILSON, S.	...	1st/4th Somerset L.I.	9.6.1914	...	...	Joined the details of the 43rd at Ali Gharbi, December 1915; present at the attack on the Dujaila Redoubt, 8th March 1916.

APPENDIX XVI.

SUMMARY OF OFFICER CASUALTIES IN MESOPOTAMIA

FORTY-THIRD

Killed	15
Died of wounds	1
Died of disease	1
Wounded	11
	28

ATTACHED

Killed	2
Wounded	8
	10
Total	38

APPENDIX XVII.

Order of Battle, "A" Company, North Russia.

Captain C. S. Baines, D.S.O., commanding;
  severely wounded 26/6/19 at Ignatovskaya.
Captain G. Naylor, M.C., second-in-command;
  to command 26/6/19.

C.S.M. Henderson.

C.Q.M.S. Lawrence.

No. 1 Platoon:

Lieutenant E. Holt, M.C.;
  invalided 12/6/19.
Lieutenant J. E. H. Neville, M.C.;
  to command from 12/6/19. Wounded 2/7/19.
Lieutenant A. B. Hamilton;
  from 2/7/19 to 5/8/19.
Second Lieutenant F. C. Holland;
  supernumerary.

Serjeant W. Warnock;
  to Police at Bereznik.
Serjeant Jones;
  to Police at Bereznik.
Serjeant Botley.

Serjeant Overton;
  supernumerary.

No. 2 Platoon:

Lieutenant O. H. M. Sturges;
  wounded 26/6/19 at Mala Bereznik.
Second Lieutenant C. A. Sawyer;
  to command 27/6/19.

Serjeant Bristow.

Serjeant Henry;
  officers' mess serjeant.

No. 3 Platoon:

Lieutenant L. W. Giles, M.C.;
  second-in-command of company from 27/6/19.
Lieutenant F. C. L. A. Lowndes, M.C.;
  to command 27/6/19.

Serjeant White;
  killed at Ignatovskaya.
Serjeant Hunt.

No. 4 Platoon:

Lieutenant P. Booth.

Serjeant Bailey.

APPENDIX XVIII.

Casualties of the Vaga Column.

43rd LIGHT INFANTRY.

9950	Private	Colwell, L.	Wounded	27/6/19	—
28170	Private	Edwards, S. J.	Wounded	3/7/19	—
9968	Private	Fidler, A.	Wounded	27/6/19	—
19134	Bugler	Hobbins, H.	Wounded	27/6/19	—
265498	Lance-Corporal	Lambourne, W.	Wounded	3/7/19	—
18356	Private	Pimm, N.	Killed	1/9/19	Attd. T.M.B.
44923	Private	Stroud, W.	Wounded	27/6/19	—
9615	Serjeant	White, J. H., M.M.	Killed	27/6/19	—

Attached to " A " Company.

62944	Lance-Corporal	Cross, N. B.	Wounded	27/6/19	60th Rifles.
69205	Private	Dunne, H.	Wounded	9/6/19	60th Rifles.
114560	Lance-Corporal	Harvey, P.	Wounded	27/6/19	Durham L.I.
41668	Private	Henry, F.	Killed	27/6/19	R. West Kent Regt.
53504	Private	Longley, E.	Wounded	27/6/19	K.O.Y.L.I.
41246	Private	Love, M.	Wounded	27/6/19	R. West Kent Regt.
10886	Lance-Corporal	Marsh, A.	Wounded	27/6/19	R. West Kent Regt.
1179	Private	Maynard, H.	Wounded	27/6/19	R. West Kent Regt.
9906	Private	Robinson, A.	Killed	27/6/19	R. West Kent Regt.
41576	Private	Ross, G.	Wounded	27/6/19	H.L.I.

" B " (OR ROYAL WARWICKSHIRE REGIMENT) COMPANY.

24249	Private	Clifton, J.	Wounded	27/6/19	—
41398	Private	Jenkins, E. T.	Wounded	23/6/19	—
60503	Private	Ladds, A.	Wounded	7/9/19	—
50268	Lance-Corporal	Newton, H.	Wounded	5/9/19	—
60917	Private	Phillips, H.	Killed	1/9/19	—
60227	Private	Ponting, D.	Killed	1/9/19	—
60211	Private	Southam, J.	Wounded	27/6/19	—
11716	Serjeant	Wilkes, G.	Died of wounds	1/9/19	—

" C " (OR DEVONSHIRE REGIMENT) COMPANY.

52124	Private	Churchward, J.	Wounded	27/6/19	—
061	Private	Carter	Prisoner	27/6/19	—
022	Private	Clements, J.	Wounded—prisoner	27/6/19	—
32453	Private	Eccleston, E.	Wounded	27/6/19	—
37845	Private	Heard, G.	Wounded	1/9/19	—

APPENDICES 445

17669	Serjeant	Herbert, P.	Killed	27/9/19	—
024	Private	Ingram, T.	Wounded	1/9/19	—
34459	Private	Mitchell, T.	Wounded	1/9/19	—
8637	Lance-Corporal	Moody, H.	Wounded	1/9/19	—
81265	Private	Page, W. B.	Wounded	1/9/19	—
742633	Private	Pine, W. H.	Wounded	1/9/19	—
046	Corporal	Stevens	Wounded	27/6/19	—
79022	Private	Sylvester, E.	Wounded—prisoner	27/6/19	—
036	Private	Welch, W. W.	Killed	27/6/19	—

"D" (OR ROYAL BERKSHIRE REGIMENT) COMPANY.

18189	Lance-Corporal	Cooper, J.	Wounded	1/9/19	—
11767	Lance-Corporal	Gasson, A.	Wounded	10/7/19	—

Attached to "B," "C" and "D" Companies.

52124	Private	Gowrie, W.	Wounded	27/6/19	Royal Scots.
19577	Private	McLeod, J.	Wounded	1/9/19	Royal Scots.
53125	Private	Stuart, J.	Wounded	27/6/19	Royal Scots.
47302	Private	Walker, H.	Missing	27/6/19	Royal Scots.
10963	Private	Whalley, J.	Wounded	27/6/19	King's Own.
35699	Corporal	Ferries	Wounded	27/6/19	R. Scots Fus.
55296	Private	Peek, A.	Wounded	27/6/19	Cheshire Regt.
22738	Private	Nelson, J.	Died of wounds	1/9/19	K.O.S.B.
32709	Private	Underwood, F.	Wounded—prisoner	27/6/19	K.O.S.B.
20022	Private	Baker, D.	Wounded	1/9/19	Gloster Regt.
10349	Corporal	Mitchell, T.	Wounded	1/9/19	H.L.I.
57514	Private	Black	Wounded	27/6/19	R.N. Devon Hussars.
49181	Private	Gough, E.	Wounded	27/6/19	R.N. Devon Hussars.

8TH BATTALION MACHINE GUN CORPS.

20562	Private	Connelly	Wounded	27/6/19	—
19909	Private	Conner	Missing	1/9/19	—
5176	Private	Fisher, W.	Killed	1/9/19	—
48734	Private	Mann	Wounded	27/6/19	—
48141	Private	McMillan	Wounded	27/6/19	—
17540	Corporal	Spiers, M.	Wounded	1/9/19	—
87167	Private	Tugwell	Wounded	27/6/19	—

ROYAL ENGINEERS.

55296	Sapper	Beach	Wounded	27/6/19	—

ROYAL ARMY SERVICE CORPS.

51964	Corporal	Almond, G. H.	Killed	1/9/19	—
20327	C.S.M.	Foggo, G.	Wounded	1/9/19	—

ROYAL ARMY MEDICAL CORPS.

220102	Private	Myatt, H.	Wounded	1/9/19	—

43RD LIGHT INFANTRY

ENEMY CASUALTIES (KNOWN).

Date.	Killed.	Wounded.	Deserters.	Prisoners.	
13/6/19	—	—	—	1	
16/6/19	8	—	—	—	
17/6/19	—	—	1	—	
26-27/6/19	3	1	1	17	2 M.Gs.
3/7/19	8	—	—	—	1 M.G.
5/7/19	—	—	1	—	
15/7/19	—	—	2	—	
20/7/19	—	—	1	—	
28/7/19	—	—	1	—	
30/7/19	3	—	—	—	
16/8/19	—	—	—	1	
1/9/19	30	—	—	10	
13/9/19	2	—	3	122	
14/9/19	—	—	—	1	
	54	1	10	152	Total 217

ENEMY CASUALTIES (FROM DESERTERS AND PRISONERS).
(Additional to foregoing.)

26-27/6/19	...	60
16/7/19	...	30
16/8/19	...	⎫
18/8/19	...	⎪
21/8/19	...	⎬ 140 by bombardment.
23/8/19	...	⎪
28/8/19	...	⎭
1/9/19	...	15 to 20 wounded at Ust Vaga.
		30 to 40 wounded at Mala Bereznik.
13/9/19	...	10 at Mala Bereznik and Nijni Kitsa.
		Total 250 to 300

INDEX

INDEX

ABADAN, 10, 11, 15-24, 27, 38.
Abdul Hassan, 251, 275.
Abu Aran, 32, 55, 56-57, 61, 62.
Abu Jisra, 273.
Abu Rumman, 184, 193.
Adams, 2/Lieut. H. C., 203, 299, Appendix xiv.
Adana, 233, 235.
Adby, 8034 Serjt. R. J., D.C.M., 221, Appendix xi.
Afghanistan, 6, 7, 10, 11, 72, 132, 259, 272, 282, 357.
Afiun Qarahisar, 235, 243, 248.
Ahmed Bey, 281.
Ahmednagar, 13-14, 22.
Ahwaz, 33-39, 43, 47, 49-50.
Airan, prisoners sent to, 234, 235, 237.
Aircraft, British, 29, 39, 57, 77, 103, 122, 123, 155, 194, 212, 286, 287-296, 335, 337, 364, 369. See *Royal Flying Corps*.
Aircraft, Turkish, 286.
Ajaimi, Muntafik Shaikh, 21, 29, 33, 37.
Akaika Channel, 69.
Al Hasa (Arab State), 8.
Al Huwair, 53-54, 56, 57.
Aldershot, 301-302, 308.
Aleppo, 27, 242, 245, 280.
Ali Gharbi, 68, 74-75, 132, 133, 137, 143, 146, 148, 161, 162, 261.
Ali Ibn Husain, 49.
Ali Sharqi, 74.
Allawi, 43.
Allen, 20107 Pte. A., 254.
Allenby, General Sir E. H. H., G.C.M.G., K.C.B., 298.
Alus, 294-295.
Amanus Mountains, 233, 243, 245, 277.
Amara, 27, 30, 33, 35, 48, 49, 54, 62-64, 63, 68, 72, 144, 146, 161, 165, 184, 253-256, 257, 258, 259, 260, 261, 272, 301.
Amburtski Skit, 380.
Ammunition, 5, 135, 138, 149, 284, 362, 363.
Ana, 288, 294-295, 297, 299.
Anderson, Major A. J., 140, 141.
Anderson, Lieut. F. E., 256, 264, 265, 266, Appendix xiv.
Anderson, Lieut., R.A.M.C., 177, 192, 200, Appendix xv.
Andrew, Brig.-Gen. A. W., C.M.G., 284, 289-296.
Andrews, 2/Lieut. P. J., 298, Appendix xiv.
Anglo-Persian Oilfields, 3, 5, 11, 34, 35, 36, 44, 47, 48, 50, 70, 73, 134, 259-260.

Angora, 235, 243, 245, 248.
Apps, 8361 Pte., D.C.M., 221, Appendix v.
Aqaba, 14, 27.
Arabia, 10.
Arabistan, 30, 35, 38.
Archangel, 306, 314, 316, 318, 319, 324, 335, 350, 352, 356-358, 360, 363, 372, 379, 380, 382, 383, 384.
Archangel Priestan, 381.
Arlett, 5766 Serjt. H., D.C.M., 36, 51, 65, 114, 221, Appendix xi.
Armenians, 245, 285.
Armistice, Bulgarian, 298.
Armistice, Turkish, 298.
Armistice, German, 299.
Armitt, 8397 Serjt. T. W., D.C.M., 61, 222, 225, Appendix xi.
Army Corps, I Indian, 259, 273, 283, 288, 298.
Army Corps, II Indian, Appendix ii.
Army Corps, III Indian, 259, 261, 268-271, 273-274, 281-282, 288.
Army Corps, Tigris, 191, 251, 257, 259, Appendices vii, viii.
Army Corps, IV Turkish, 27.
Army Corps, XII Turkish, 9, 27.
Army Corps, XIII Turkish, 9, 10, 127, 272-274.
Army Corps, XVIII Turkish, 271, 273, 274.
Army in India, 4-5, 279.
Artillery, 5, Appendices i, iii, iv, vi, vii, viii, xii.
Artillery, Batteries of. See *Batteries*.
Artillery Brigade, 9th, 178, 197.
Artillery Brigade, 10th, 20, 77.
Artillery Brigade, 66th, 184.
Artillery Brigade, 215th, 285, 286.
Artillery Brigade, First Home Counties, 132.
Artillery Brigade, 1st Indian Mountain, 14.
Artillery, Bolshevik, 331.
Artillery, Russian, 331, 336, 337, 352, 360, 362.
Artillery, Turkish, 142.
Ashhurst, Miss Audrey, 237-238.
Atab, 261, 262, 270, 275.
Ataba Marsh, 78, 82, 149.
Austin, Brig.-Gen. H. H., 262.
Austria-Hungary, 304, 307.
Aylmer, Lieut.-Gen. Sir Fenton J., V.C., K.C.B., 145-146, 148-149, 151-157, 162, 163, 165, 167, 172, 176, 177, 179, 180, 181, 182, 185, 187.
Aziziya, 94, 95, 100, 121, 124, 227, 237, 270, 271, 276, 280, 281.

BABYLON, 299.
Badajoz, 194, 195, 196, 197, 198, 199.
Baghche, 233, 234, 237.
Baghdad, 1, 2, 12, 16–17, 27, 35, 44, 72–73, 95–98, 132, 165, 228, 237, 239, 244, 251, 259, 271, 272, 273–274, 275, 277–278, 285, 301.
Baghdadiya, 101.
Bahrein, 11, 15.
Baines, Capt. C. S., ix, 311, 327, 329, 331, 336–342, 343, 383, Appendices xiv, xvii.
Bait Isa, 176, 202, 213, 251.
Bakharitsa, 325, 379–381.
Bakhtiaris, 34.
Balad Station, 274.
Balad Ruz, 281.
Baldwin, Lieut. H. E., 312.
Balkan Wars, 2, 7, 9.
Ballard, 9046 Cpl. S. N., D.C.M., 89, 171, 222, Appendix xi.
Baluchistan, 11.
Bani Lam, 8, 33, 38, 46, 72.
Bani Turuf, 33, 38, 49.
Banks, Capt. C. M., viii, 289, 299, Appendix xiv.
Baquba, 273, 275, 277.
Baratoff, General, 165, 251, 259.
Barbukh Creek, 27, 63.
Barjisiya Wood, 45.
Barfoot, 9089 Serjt. E. A., 227, 244, Appendix xi.
Barford, Cpl., 87.
Barlow, 6414 Serjt. A., 221, Appendix xi.
Barr, Capt. D. B., 351.
Barrett, Lieut.-Gen. Sir A. A., K.C.B., K.C.V.O., 20–21, 27, 29, 31–32, 33, 34, 35, 38, 39, 43, 44.
Barrington, Hon. W. R. S., 147, 160–162, 168, 177, 192, 200, 254, 264, Appendices xiii, xiv.
Barrow, General Sir E. G., G.C.B., 11.
Basra, 5, 8, 10, 12, 15, 17, 20, 21, 27, 30, 33–34, 35, 121, 132, 144, 159, 165, 177, 182, 252, 258, 260, 272, 278, 301.
Basra (river steamer), 270.
Basra, *Vali* of, 10, 11, 25.
Basra *Vilayet*, 44, 48, 49, 69, 72, 259.
Battery, R.H.A., "S," 35, 38, 44, 94, 118.
Battery, R.H.A., "W," 294.
Battery, R.F.A., 8th, 178.
Battery, R.F.A., 61st (Howitzer), 178.
Battery, R.F.A., 63rd, 20, 31, 44, 80, 81, 101, 105–106, 136.
Battery, R.F.A., 76th, 20, 25, 31, 44, 82–86, 105–106, 108–120.
Battery, R.F.A., 82nd, 20, 24, 68, 82–86, 105–106, 118.
Battery, R.F.A., 2/105th, 262.
Battery, R.F.A., 1088th, 296.
Battery, R.G.A., 86th, 33, 57, 77, 105–106, 108–120.
Battery, R.G.A., 104th, 33, 57, 77.
Battery, T.F., 1/5th Hampshire Howitzer, 39, 44, 48, 57, 77, 82–86, 105–106.
Battery, Light Armoured Motor. See under *Light*.
Battery, Light Trench Mortar. See under *Trench Mortar Battery*.
Battery, Maxim. See *Maxim*.
Battery, 55th Mountain, 336.
Battery, 23rd Indian Mountain, 14, 44, 151–153.
Battery, 30th Indian Mountain, 14, 25, 31, 56, 57, 58–62.
Battery, Volunteer Artillery, 137, 139–141, 230.
Battery, 1st Russian Field, 331, 336, 337, 352, 360, 362, 369.
Battles. See *Baghdad, Ctesiphon, Dujaila, Es Sinn, Hanna, Khan Baghdadi, Kut al Amara, Nasiriya, Qurna, Ramadi, Sannaiyat, Shaiba, Shaikh Saad, Umm at Tubul, Wadi*.
Bawi, 271.
Bawi (tribe), 36, 49, 73.
Beck, Lieut. M. G., 312, 368–369.
Bellum brigade, 51, 52.
Bereznik, 324, 326, 327, 335, 344, 351, 358, 360, 363, 364, 369, 374, 377–378, 379, 380.
Berville, 220.
Bhisti Rustum, Jemadar, 225.
Bicknell, Capt. H. K., 267, 280, Appendix xiv.
Bieberstein, Baron Marschall von, 2.
Bisaitin, 68.
Bishop, Pte., 285.
Bland, Lieut., 351.
Bleeze, Capt. H. W., viii, 256, 264, 266, 289, 292, 293, 299, Appendix xiv.
Blosse Lynch, 27, 29, 64, 101, 102, 120.
Boddington, Pte., 285.
Bolsheviks, 282, 285, 304–308, 306, 316–317, 320, 363–364. See *Regiments*.
Booth, Major F., 170.
Booth, Lieut. P., ix, 311, 328, 337, 381, Appendices xiv, xvii.
Boswell, 17402 Pte., 254.
Botley, Serjt., 347.
Bovington, C.S.M., 301–302.
Bozanti, 243.
Braemar Castle, H.M.T., 381.
Brazier, 8993 Pte. A. E., 88.
Breslau, 10, 11, 12.
Brest-Litovsk, 282, 304, 316.
Brigades. See *Artillery, Cavalry, Infantry, Light Armoured Motor*.
Brinkman, Pte., viii.
Brissell, Mr., 229.
Bristow, Serjt., 330, 337, 345.
Broad Wadi, 285, 286.
Brooke, Capt. R. R. M., 23, 48, 51–52, 58–60, 65, 90, Appendix xiv.
Brooking, Major-Gen. Sir H. T., K.C.B., 257, 280, 281, 285, 286, 288–296, 299.
Brown, 2/Lieut. F., 14, 24, 70, 117, 130, 138, 221, Appendix xiv.
Brown, Lieut. J. R., 256, 264, 266, 280, 299, Appendix xiv.
Brown, Lieut.-Colonel W. H., 137, 217.
Brown, 21163 Pte., 254.
Browne, Lieut. E. S., R.F.A., 342.
Brusa, 243, 248.
Brusiloff, General, 318.
Bughaila, 227, 239, 268–269.

INDEX

Bulbul, 63.
Bulgaria, 298.
Bull, 9136 Serjt. M. M., viii, 286, 301–302.
Burbidge, 5487 Q.M.S. J. W., D.C.M., ix, 138, 221, 225, 237, Appendix xi.
Burgoyne, General John, 237.
Burhanieh, 224, 239.
Burke, Capt. A. F., 351.
Burke, 8472 Pte., 244, Appendix xi.
Burrell, Lieut. H. N., 289, 298, Appendix xv.
Burton, 21835 L./Cpl., 254.
Bushire, 43.
Bustan, 104, 107, 108, 122, 123.
Butcher, Lieut. H. C., 147, 168, 177, Appendix xv
Butcher, C.S.M., 229, 230.
Butler, Pte., 60.
Butterfly, H.M.S., 149, 270.
Byng, Admiral, 279.

CAMP TIGRIS, Qurna, 26, 40.
Candler, Edmund, 196–198, 201.
Caporetto, 283.
Care Committee, Regimental, 236, 237–238.
Carr, Capt. J. L., 312, 355.
Carter, Major L. J., D.S.O., 23, 58, 71, 160, 167, 168, 169, 177, 192, 195, 197, 198–199, 221, 222, 311, 329, 331, Appendices ix, xiii, xiv.
Carter, 8376 Pte. N., 227, 244, Appendix xi.
Cassels, Brig.-Gen. R. A., C.B., D.S.O., 294.
Casualties, 32, 39, 45, 70, 110, 111, 112, 114, 115, 131, 138, 141, 153, 156, 173–174, 182, 193, 205, 220, 252, 259, 296.
Casualties, 43rd's, 32, 46, 54, 55, 60, 61, 66–67, 76, 84, 88, 95, 111, 112, 114, 115, 127, 139, 141, 169, 181, 197, 198, 208, 220, 225, 235, 253, 254–255, 276, 280, 285, 293, 296, 330, 342, 343, 368, 383, Appendices v, ix, x, xi, xvi, xviii.
Casualties, Bolshevik, 343, 348, Appendix xviii.
Casualties, Turkish, 32, 45, 60, 61, 64, 70, 116, 119, 123, 141, 153, 293–296.
Cavalry British, 7th Hussars, 294, 301.
Cavalry, British, 14th Hussars, 124.
Cavalry, British, 1/1st Hertfordshire Yeomanry, 286.
Cavalry, Indian, 7th Hariana Lancers, 35, 77, 81, 125, 151–153, Appendix vi.
Cavalry, Indian, 10th Lancers, 256, 261, 262, 264, 276, 280, 286, 296.
Cavalry, Indian, 16th Cavalry, 38, 77, 81.
Cavalry, Indian, 23rd Cavalry (Frontier Force), 294, Appendix vi.
Cavalry, Indian, 33rd Light Cavalry, 20, 31, 34, 38.
Cavalry, Indian, Guides Cavalry (Frontier Force), 294.
Cavalry Brigade, 6th Indian, 38, 44, 47, 49, 76–77, 101, 105–106, 120, 122, 123, 124, 125, 136, 146, 149, 151–153, 155, 169, 178–181, 251, Appendices ii, iii, iv, viii.
Cavalry Brigade, 11th Indian, 288, 290–296, 298, Appendix xii.
Cavalry Division, Indian, 259, 263, 268–271.
Cavalry, Turkish, Iraq Brigade, 112.

Cave, Cpl., 89.
Chahela Mounds, 79, 251.
Chamberlain, Austen, 49.
Chamovo, 334, 369, 371.
Chandler, Capt. F. C., M.C., R.A.M.C., 311, 368–369.
Cheryepanoff, Lieut., 359.
Chitral, 166, 207.
Christian, Brig.-Gen. G., D.S.O., 178, 179.
Churchill, Winston, 357.
Cleary, Serjt., 348.
Clery's Post, 79, 81.
Clews, 2/Lieut. J., D.C.M., 354, 366.
Clifford, Capt., R.A.M.C., 229.
Climo, Colonel S. H., D.S.O., 55, 65, 66, 112.
Clio, H.M.S., 57, 60–63.
Cobbe, Lieut.-Gen. Sir A. S., V.C., K.C.B., D.S.O., 257, 273–274.
Colvill, Lieut. D. C., M.C., ix, 312, 344–349, 380, Appendix xiv.
Comet, H.M.S., 57–64, 76, 101, 125, 127.
Communications, Line of. See *Tigris Line of Communication Defences*.
Company, "A," 2/43rd, 167, 179.
Company, "B," 2/43rd, 167.
Company, "P," 43rd, 23, 31–32, 37, 55, 58–62, 68, 83–88, 93, 108–120, 127, 136, 138, 140, 141, 170, 189, 225.
Company, "Q," 43rd, 23, 31–32, 37, 47, 55, 58–62, 76, 83–88, 93–94, 108–120, 123, 127, 136, 138, 140, 141, 170, 172, 185, 188, 189, 225.
Company, "R," 43rd, 23, 31–32, 37, 55, 58–62, 83, 88, 93–94, 108–120, 127, 136, 139–141, 170, 189, 225.
Company, "S," 43rd, 23, 31–32, 37, 47, 52–53, 55, 58–62, 76, 83–88, 93, 108–120, 127, 136, 137, 138, 140, 141, 170, 189, 214, 225.
Compton, 16140 L./Cpl. R. W., 222.
Constantinople, 241, 243.
Cookson, Lieut.-Comdr., R.N., 54.
Corunna, 237, 324.
Coulthard, 2/Lieut. E. F., 147, 169, 178, 192, 197, Appendices ix, xiv.
Courtis, Capt. J. H., 22, 23, 46, 52, 65, 68, 70, 74, 86–87, 106, 115, Appendix xiv.
Cowley, 8041 Serjt. (later R.S.M.) A. H., 65, 299.
Cox, Sir P., 30, 207.
Cox, Warrant Officer, R.N., 380.
Crake, Lieut.-Colonel R. H. (K.O.S.B.), 255, 256, 262–263, 264, 266, Appendices xiii, xiv.
Cranefly, H.M.S., 149.
Creagh, General Sir G. O'Moore, V.C., G.C.B., G.C.S.I., 6.
Crewe, Lord, 11, 48–49.
Crimea, 304, 356.
Crofton's Post, 203.
Crosse, Major R. B., D.S.O., 52nd, 383.
Crowborough, 310.
Ctesiphon, 44, 101–120, 123, 145, 165, 166, 168, 187, 199, 209, 212, 228, 239, 271, 293, 343, Appendices iv, v.
Cuyler, Lieut.-Colonel Sir C., Bart., 237.
Cyclops, H.M.S., 381.

Czar, H.M.T., 311, 360, 379, 381, 382.
Czaritsa, H.M.T., 378, 381.
Czechoslovakia, 307, 308.

DAGHISTANI, 68.
Dahra Bend, 268.
Damir Qapu, 242, 247.
Dancey, Lieut. G., M.C., D.C.M., 168, 264, 266, 288, 290, 294, 298, 311, 324, Appendix xiv.
Dardanelles, 11, 73, 133.
Darley, Lieut.-Colonel, 79, 263.
Davenport, Lieut. C. T., 147, 169, 178, 192, 201, 208, 254, Appendix xiv.
Davenport, Capt. F. M., 23, 45, 53–54, 62, 71, 81, 84, 107, 109, 115, Appendix xiv.
Davidson, Brig.-Gen. S. R., 273.
Davies, 21565 Serjt. E., 299.
Davies, Major-Gen. H. R., C.B., viii.
Davies, Mrs. H. R., 237–238.
Davis, 2/Lieut. A. H., 177, 185, 192, 197, Appendices ix, xiv.
Davison, Major-Gen. K. S., C.B., 33.
Day, 9099 Pte. H. T., 222, Appendix xi.
de Selincourt, 2/Lieut., 147, 168, 177, 184, Appendix xv.
de Vitré, Lieut. E. C. Denis, 312.
Dean, 9479 L./Cpl. A., 299.
Delamain, Major-Gen. W. S., C.B., D.S.O., 11, 14–15, 20, 37, 38, 54, 68, 74, 81–88, 92, 105–106, 109–120, 122, 223, 224, 226, 228, 239, 243.
Denham, Lieut. A. S., M.M., 312, 353–354.
Denikin, General, 308, 320, 356, 384.
Despatches. See *Honours and Awards*.
Devanney, 845 Pte. P., 222, Appendix xi.
Dhibban, 285, 301.
Dibben, Lieut. W. L., M.C., 312, 366.
Dickenson, 2/Lieut. E. B., 312, 370.
Diltawa, 273.
Distinguished Conduct Medal. See *Honours and Awards*.
Distinguished Service Order. See *Honours and Awards*.
Division, British, 13th, 160, 183, 184, 191, 192–193, 194, 200, 201, 202, 208, 209, 259, 261, 269–271, 273.
Division, Indian, 3rd, 5, 145, 169–170, 178, 180, 181, 182, 191, 193, 199, 202, 251, 259, 268, 283, Appendix vii.
Division, Indian, 6th, 11, 13, 14, 54, 73, 75, 76–80, 99–100, 101, 108–120, 123, 126–127, 138, 139–141, 162–166, 171, 185–190, 202–220, 224, 276. See also *Force "D" and Battles, Appendices ii, iii, vi, and 16th, 17th and 18th Indian Infantry Brigades*.
Division, Indian, 7th, 7, 132, 143, 146, 148, 149, 151–153, 155–156, 157–159, 169, 182, 183, 191, 193–201, 203–204, 257, 259, 268–271, 274, 283, Appendix vii.
Division, Indian, 12th, 73. See *Force "D," Appendix ii*.
Division, Indian, 14th, 257, 259, 261, 269–271.
Division, Indian, 15th, 257, 280, 285, 289–296, Appendix xii.

Division, Indian, 17th, 279, 281, 298.
Division, Indian, 18th, 279, 283.
Division, Turkish, 35th, 27, 33, 37, 74, 103–118, 127, 146.
Division, Turkish, 36th, 27.
Division, Turkish, 37th, 9, 74.
Division, Turkish, 38th, 9, 33, 74, 103–118, 127, 146.
Division, Turkish, 45th, 103–118, 125–126, 146.
Division, Turkish, 50th, 285, 287–288, 289–296.
Division, Turkish, 51st, 103–118, 119, 125–126, 146.
Division, Turkish, 52nd, 146.
Dixon, 8037 Cpl. A., D.C.M., 88, 90.
Diyala River, 104–105, 117, 122, 271, 273–274.
Djavid, Pasha, 27.
Djemal Pasha, 10.
Dobbie, Brig.-Gen. W. H., C.B., 27, 55.
Dodington, Colonel W. Marriott-, C.M.G., 308, 311, 331, 335–336, 341–342, 344, 353, 371, 374, 383, Appendices xiii, xiv.
Dolabia, 230.
Donaghan, Colonel, R.A.M.C., 60.
Donohoe, 7452 L./Cpl. W. E., D.C.M., 90, 222, Appendix xi.
Donoughmore, Lord, 278.
Dragonfly, H.M.S., 149.
Drake, Lieut. T. Tyrwhitt, M.C., 308, 311, 314, 329, 346, 361–362, 366, Appendix xiv.
Draper, 8347 Pte. G. F., D.C.M., 90, Appendix xi.
Dredge, 9528 Cpl., 286.
Duff, General Sir B., G.C.B., K.C.S.I., K.C.V.O., C.I.E., 44, 97, 144, 216, 257.
Dujaila Redoubt, 176, 177–178, 179–180, 181, 182, 187, 188, 251, 262–263, 265, 276.
Dundonald, Lord, 64.
Dunlop, Lieut.-Colonel H. H., 50, 68.
Dunsterforce, 282, 285, 298.
Dunsterville, Major-Gen. L. C., C.B., 282.
Dvina Force, 324, 334, 336, 360–361, 363, 369, 372, 374, 378.
Dvina, River, 314, 316, 320, 323, 324, 334, 335, 382, 383.
Dyer, Colonel, 318.

EAGLE, Lieut. H. S., 311, 334, Appendix xiv.
Eden, Mrs. A. J. F., 237–238.
Egerton, Major-Gen. Sir R. G., C.B., 257.
Egypt, 10, 14, 144–145, 307.
Ekaterinburg, 356.
Elizabeth, Queen, 316.
Ellenga, H.M.T., 301.
Elliott, Lieut. C. E., 147, 168, 169, Appendix xv.
Emetskoe, 326, 378.
Emtsa River, 323, 358, 362, 378.
Engineers, Royal. See *Royal Engineers*.
Ennessee, 377.
Enver Pasha, 216, 235, 241, 277.
Erzerum, 9.
Eskichehir, 243.
Espiègle, H.M.S., 19, 25, 27, 31–32, 38, 45, 51–52, 56–63.

INDEX

Es Sinn, 77–78, 82–90, 92, 93, 149, 165, 167, 170, 176, 183, 185, 187, 212, 257, 261, 264, 275, 276.
Euphrates, 16.
Euphrates Blockade Force, 43, 46.
Evans, 9015 Pte. A. S., 222.
Evans, Brig.-Gen. U. W., C.B., C.M.G., 243.
Evenett, 8654 L./Cpl. A., 222, Appendix xi.
Evsyakovskaya, 334.
Ezra's Tomb, 17, 27, 29, 33, 63, 161, 260.

FAIL, 76.
Falkenhayn, General von, 277, 281.
Fallahiya, 170, 176, 193, 194, 252.
Falluja, 16, 278, 279, 281, 284, 288.
Fane, Major-Gen. Sir V. B., K.C.I.E., C.B., 274.
Fao, 15, 19, 24.
Farrant, 8929 L./Cpl. W. J., 90, Appendix xi.
Fenwick, Lieut. J. S., 289, Appendix xiv.
Field, Capt. H. T. C., 147, 168, 178, 192, 197, 254, 255, 267, 289, 299, Appendices ix, xiv.
Finch, Capt. A. E. M., 351.
Finch, Pte. W. S., 239, Appendix xi.
Finland, 304, 356.
Firefly, H.M.S., 101, 125, 127, 128, 270.
Firman, Lieut. H. O. B., R.N., 205.
Firth, Lieut. D. G., 147, 168, 177, 192, 197, Appendices ix, xv.
Fitzgerald, Major C., viii, 267, 288, 292, 294, 297, Appendix xiv.
Foljambe, Capt. and Brevet-Major Hon. J. C. W. S., 23, 70, 76, 89, 90, 99, 106, 109, 110, 115, 168, 177, 192, 197, 199, 221, 222, Appendices ix, xiv.
Force " D," 11, 15, 47. See *6th and 12th Indian Divisions, Appendices i, ii.*
Ford, Pte., 169.
Forrest, Major C. E., D.S.O., 24, 58, 70, 107, 109, 111, 115, Appendix xiv.
Fort, in Kut al Amara, 134, 136, 137, 138–141, 142, 162–166, 189, 209, 214, 217.
Fort Frazer, Qurna, 37, 40, 41, 48.
Fort Fry, Qurna, 40, 41.
Fort Lanyan, Qurna, 41.
Fort Peebles, Qurna, 37, 40, 41, 52.
Fort Snipe, Qurna, 40, 41, 45, 48, 56.
Fort Winsloe, Qurna, 40, 41, 45.
Fortescue, Sir John, 220.
Fortifications. See *Dujaila, Redoubts, Vital Point, Water Redoubt.*
Fowke, Lieut.-Gen. Thomas, 279.
Frazer, Lieut -Colonel G. S., 24.
Fry, Major-Gen. C. I., C.B., 20, 21, 25, 44, 45, 74, 79, 81–88.
Fuhaima, 295.
Fulaifila, 69, 260.

Gadfly, H.M.S., 270.
Gardiner, L./Cpl., 54.
Gardner, Lieut. A. E., 147, 168, 178, 192, 197, Appendices ix, xiv.
Garland, George, 14.
Garrard, Lieut. G. F., 147, 168, 178, Appendix xiv.
George V, King-Emperor, 172.

Georgia, 285.
Germany, 1, 10, 13, 43, 276, 283, 303–308, 357.
Ghabishiya, 43, 46.
Ghadir, 38, 43.
Gibbons, Lieut. H., M.C., 312, 368–369, 370, 372.
Gibbs, 8049 Serjt. R. H., 128, 230, Appendix xi.
Gibson, Cpl., 280.
Gilchrist, Capt. W. F. C., 140, 142–143, 170, 214, 217.
Gilchrist, Lieut. W., 147, 168, Appendix xv.
Giles, Lieut. L. W., M.C., ix, 311, 328, 331, 337, 341, 344, Appendices xiv, xvii.
Glowworm, H.M.S., 378.
Goeben, 10–11, 12.
Golding, Pte., D.C.M., 199, 250.
Goltz, General von der, 2, 9.
Gorringe, Lieut.-Gen. Sir G. F., K.C.B., C.M.G., D.S.O., 49, 53, 69–70, 73, 145, 160, 169, 172, 182, 183, 191, 193, 198, 201, 202, 204, 214, 216, 251, 257.
Gosling, Lieut. G. W., 351.
Grace, 6830 Serjt. H., D.C.M., 90, 91.
Green, Pte., 326.
Green, 9075 Serjt. J., M.M., 293, 299.
Grey, 8540 Pte. L. P., D.C.M., 222.
Grier, Brig.-Gen. H. D., C.B., 243.
Griffin, Lieut. S. J., 147, 168, 178, 192, 201, 208, 267, 289, 291–292, 293, Appendix xiv.
Griffiths, Lieut. T. C., 351.
Grogan, Brig.-Gen. G. W. St. G., V.C., C.B., C.M.G., D.S.O., 311, 314, 351, 358, 382.
Grosvenor, Lieut. G. R., 147, 168, 178, 192, 201, 261, Appendix xiv.
Guadeloupe, 220.
Gun Hill (Qurna), 40, 45, 55, 56, 61.
Gunter, 8212 L./Cpl. Ivo, 247, Appendix xi.

HADITHA, 287, 294–295, 296, 297.
Hadji Murad, 367–369.
Haffa, Shaikh of, 51.
Halla, 31.
Hamam Ali, 247.
Hamilton, Lieut. A. B., 311, Appendices xiv, xvii.
Hamilton, Lord George, 278.
Hamilton, Brig.-Gen. W. G., C.B., D.S.O., 105–106, 109–116, 243.
Hammar Lake, 16, 29, 47, 257.
Hammick, Capt. S. F., 147, 160, 167, 168, 177, 183, 192, 197, 199, 222, Appendices ix, xiv.
Hanna, 155, 156, 157–158, 162, 163, 168, 169, 170, 176, 177, 183, 184, 185, 191-193, 208.
Harba, 274.
Harbourne, 2/Lieut. H. G., 312.
Hardie, Lieut. F. M., 254, 264, 266, Appendix xiv.
Harding, 8668 Pte. E. T., 230, Appendix xi.
Hardinge of Penshurst, Lord, 11, 35, 97, 98, 132, 133.
Harman, 2/Lieut. R. M., 312, Appendix xiv.
Harper, 6742 Bugler F. G., 88.
Harvey, 8687 Pte. J. H., 222.
Harward, Colonel A. J. N., 114.
Hassaiwa, 273.

Hassan Begli, 233, 243, 245.
Havre, 301.
Hazell, 2/Lieut. A. J., 71, 107, 115, Appendix xv.
Headdon, C.S.M., 301–302.
Heawood, Lieut. G. L., 106, 117, 128–129, 130, 140, 142, 170, 188, 189, 219, 224, 239. Appendix xv.
Hehir, Colonel P., I.M.S., 228.
Henley, Major C. F., viii, 23, 58, 60, 62, 65, 71, 90, 129, 130, 136, 138, 163, 224, 225, 239, 244, 245, 246, 248, Appendix xiv.
Hennessy, Lieut.-Colonel L. H. R. Pope-. See *Pope-Hennessy*.
Hicks, 8987 Pte. W., 222, Appendix xi.
Hight, Lieut. P. H., 312.
Hilla, 16, 299.
Hinaidi, 281, 284.
Hind, Lieut. H. B. L., 71, 107, 111, 115, Appendix xv.
Hindenburg, Marshal von, 305.
Hit, 277, 285, 286–287, 298, 299, 301–302.
Hodgson, C.S.M., 301–302.
Hoghton, Brig.-Gen. F. A., 74, 82–88, 105–106, 109–120, 212.
Holberton, Lieut. J. C., 312.
Holland, Lieut. F. C., 312, 362, Appendices xiv, xvii.
Holt, Lieut. E., M.C., 311, 327, 328, Appendices xiv, xvii.
Honours and Awards, 65, 90–91, 114, 199, 221–222, 250, 286, 293, 297, 299, 344, 349, 368, 383.
Hor Abdulla, 15.
Hor Bahmanshir, 15.
Horan, Capt. K., 23, 58, 66, 71, Appendix xiv.
Horse Shoe Marsh, 78, 81, 84–85, 92.
Horwood, 9037 L./Cpl. J., D.C.M., 90, 91, Appendix xi.
Huggard, Lieut. G. C., 147, 168, 178, 264, 267, Appendix xiv.
Hughes, 2/Lieut. N. L., 312, 341, 342.
Hunt, Serjt., 331, 341.
Hunter, 28315 Pte., 286.
Hussey, 8777 Pte. F. J., 90.
Hyde, Major A. C., 23, 31, 37, 59, 70, 79, 90, 106, 108, 109, 115, Appendix xiv.

IBN RASCHID, Shaikh of Hail, 8.
Ibn Saud, Emir of Nejd, 8, 10, 17.
Ignatovskaya, 335–344, 345, 353, 354, 360, 362, 384.
Illa, 49.
Imam al Mansur, 260, 262, 263, 264, 275.
Imam Mahdi, 270.
India, 7, 10, 11, 72, 132, 144–145.
India, The Army in. See under *Army*.
Infantry, 38th British Brigade, 193.
Infantry, 39th British Brigade, 193.
Infantry, 40th British Brigade, 193, 198.
Infantry, 238th Special British Brigade, 311, 324.
Infantry, Sadleir-Jackson's, 358.
Infantry, 7th Indian Brigade, 145, 178, 279, Appendices vii, viii.
Infantry, 8th Indian Brigade, 145, 178, 180, Appendix viii.
Infantry, 9th Indian Brigade, 145, 151–153, 155–156, 178, 180, Appendices vii, viii.
Infantry, 12th Indian Brigade, 33, 35, 37, 69, 257, 286, 288–296, Appendices ii, xii.
Infantry, 16th Indian Brigade, 11, 14, 15, 19–20, 38, 44–45, 58–64, 74, 76–80, 93, 94, 105–106, 118, 123–124, 125–127, 134, 219, Appendices i, ii, iii, iv, vi.
Infantry, 17th Indian Brigade, 14, 31–32, 41, 51, 54–57, 58–62, 63–64, 74, 76–80, 82–86, 93, 94, 105–106, 107–120, 122, 124, 125–129, 134, 212, 217, Appendices i, ii, iii, iv, vi.
Infantry, 18th Indian Brigade, 14, 20, 25, 44–45 74, 77–80, 85–86, 92, 94, 101, 105–106, 112, 118, 123–124, 125–127, 134, 219, Appendices i, ii, iii, iv, vi.
Infantry, 19th Indian Brigade, 146, 148, 151–153, 155–156, 193–199, 203–204, 252, 253, 269, Appendices vii, viii.
Infantry, 21st Indian Brigade, 146, 151–153, 155–156, 169, 183, 184, 193, 203–204, 269, Appendices vii, viii.
Infantry, 28th Indian Brigade, 143, 146, 148, 151–153, 155–156, 168, 169, 178, 180, 193–199, 203–204, 250, 251, 252, 253, Appendices vii, viii.
Infantry, 30th Indian Brigade, 39, 44, 47, 69–70, 73, 78, 80, 105–106, 112, 124, 125, 127, 135, 219, Appendices ii, iii, iv, vi.
Infantry, 33rd Indian Brigade, 39, 43–44, Appendix ii.
Infantry, 34th Indian Brigade, 132, 133, 148, 257.
Infantry, 35th Indian Brigade, 132, 133, 146, 148, 151–153, 155–156, 178, 203–204, 257, 271, Appendices vii, viii.
Infantry, 36th Indian Brigade, 133, 148, 169, 178, 180, 203–204, 251, 257, Appendix viii.
Infantry, 37th Indian Brigade, 160, 178, 180, 257, Appendix viii.
Infantry, 41st Indian Brigade, 160.
Infantry, 42nd Indian Brigade, 160, 257, 281, 285, 286, 288–296, Appendix xii.
Infantry, 50th Indian Brigade, 279, 281, 284, 285, 286, 288–296, Appendix xii.
Iremonger, Pte., 60.
Ironside, Major-Gen. Sir Edmund, K.C.B., 305, 314, 317, 319, 324, 335, 352, 356, 357–358, 379.
Islahiya, 232, 233, 237, 242, 245, 247–248.
Italy, 2, 7, 9, 260, 283, 305.
Ivan the Terrible, 316.
Ivey, Major T. E., 23, 57, 67, 70, 106, 117, 130, 217, 221, 224, 239, 246–248, Appendix xiv.

JABAL HAMRIN, 273, 274, 282, 287.
Jackson, Pte., 53.
Jackson, Brig.-Gen. Sadleir-, 358, 372.
Jahalah Canal, Amara, 65, 68.
Jehad, 3, 11, 30, 34, 35, 43.
Jones, Rev. Ishmael, 312.

INDEX

Joyce, Lieut. H. C., 289, Appendix xiv.
Julius, Major, 133.
Julnar, H.M.S., 121, 205, 214–215, 223.
Jumaisa, 101.

KARADA, 281.
Karbala, 285.
Karkha, River, 38, 49.
Karroda Bridge, 380.
Karun, River, 15, 16, 36, 134.
Kastamuni, 239, 245, 248.
Kearsley, Lieut. J. S., 24, 41, 51, 60, 66, 70, 107, 111, 115, Appendix xiv.
Keary, Major-Gen. H. D'U., C.B., D.S.O., 177, 178, 202.
Keeling, 23425 Pte., 255.
Keen, Serjt., 301–302.
Keinch, 7884 L./Cpl. J., 88.
Kemball, Major-Gen. G. V., C.B., D.S.O., 54, 151–153, 156, 178, 179–181, 192, 194–199.
Kerensky, 303.
Kermanshah, 165.
Khafajiya, 49, 68.
Khalil Pasha, 215–216, 223, 230, 260, 271.
Khamisiya, 47.
Khan Abu Rayan, 285, 286.
Khan Baghdadi, 286, 287, 288, 289–297, 299, Appendix xii.
Khaniqin, 251, 273–274.
Kharkoff, 356.
Kharnina, 240.
Khudaira bend, 261, 263, 268.
Khutor (Ignatovskaya), 362.
Khutor (next Nijni Kitsa), 361, 371.
Kidd, 793 Serjt. J., D.C.M., 90, 91.
Kifri, 274.
King, Lieut. H. J., ix, 312.
Kinghorn, Lieut. E. C., 147, 168, 177, 192, 197, 198, 200, 254, 255, 261, 264, 267, Appendices ix, xv.
Kitchener of Khartum, Lord, 11, 251.
Kitsa, 330, 335–337, 354, 360.
Klaus, Herr, 234.
Knotty Ash, 383.
Kochhisar, 230, 242.
Kola, River, 305, 313.
Koltchak, Admiral, 308, 320, [324, 334–335, 356.
Konetzbor, 358, 379–380.
Konia, 235, 243.
Koslovo, 329, 350, 353, 354, 356, 362, 366, 369, 370, 371, 372–373, 375.
Kotlas, 323, 324, 335, 356.
Kubaish, 69.
Kulek, 243.
Kumait, 69, 73.
Kurdistan, 7, 16.
Kurgomin, 358.
Kurmat Ali, 16, 38, 43, 160.
Kut al Amara, 44, 69, 72, 73–80, 82–88, 100, 121, 124, 132–133, 134–143, 162–166, 167, 171, 185–190, 205–220, 251, 260, 263, 268–269, 277, 301, Appendices vi, x.

Kutuniya, 99, 101, 124.
Kuwait, 7, 10, 15, 21.

LACY, 18551 L./Cpl., 254.
Ladysmith, 174–175.
Lajj, 102, 117, 118, 120, 121, 122, 123, 124, 239, 271, 343.
Lake, Lieut.-Gen. Sir P. H. N., K.C.B., K.C.M.G., 96, 157, 159–160, 167, 182–183, 201, 204, 205–208, 215, 216, 219, 250, 251, 257, 258.
Lambourne, 265498 L./Cpl. W., 348.
Lambourne, Pte., 169.
Lawrence, C.Q.M.S., 360.
Lawrence, H.M.S., 10, 25, 57, 58–63.
Leach, 7315 Pte. E. G. H., 222, Appendix xi.
Lenin, 304.
Lethbridge, Lieut. D. J. L., 301–302, 311, Appendix xiv.
Lethbridge, Colonel E. A. E., C.M.G., D.S.O., viii, 14, 22, 23, 30, 31, 33, 52, 57, 59, 61, 65, 66, 71, 90, 97, 99, 106, 108, 109, 110, 111, 112, 114, 115, 117, 118, 123, 130, 140, 142, 174, 212, 217, 221, 222, 224, 235–236, 239–244, 246, 248, 249, Appendices xiii, xiv.
Lewis Pelly, 25, 47.
Light Armoured Motor Battery, 8th, 288–296.
Light Armoured Motor Battery, 13th, 288–296.
Light Armoured Motor Battery, 14th, 288–296.
Light Armoured Motor Brigade, 288–296.
Little, 8460 Pte. H., 88.
Liverpool, 382, 383.
Lockhead, 2857 Pte., 254.
Lot's Mounds, 262.
Love, 5574 R.S.M. T. A., D.C.M., ix, 110, 114, 118, 221, 222, 225, 226, 227, 230, 231, 233–234, 236, 237, Appendix xi.
Loverock, Capt. R. C., D.S.O., 14, 23, 71, Appendix xiv.
Lowndes, Lieut. F. C. L. A., M.C., 311, 344, Appendices xiv, xvii.
Lucas, Brig.-Gen. F. G., D.S.O., 285, 290.
Ludendorff, General, 304.
Lynch, Capt., 8.
Lyttelton, General Sir N., 278.

MAADEN, 245.
Macdonald, Major A. G., D.S.O., 312.
Machine Gun Corps, 8th Battalion, 308, 342, 362, 367–369.
Machine Gun Squadron, 15th, 294.
Machine Gun Company, 256th, 284, 296.
Machine Gun Company, 275th, 288.
MacLeod, Lieut.-Colonel Charles, 195.
MacMunn, Lieut.-Gen. Sir G., K.C.B., K.C.S.I., D.S.O., 256, 258.
Madhij, 285, 288.
Mahsoudi, 51, 101.
Maidan-i-Naftun, 3, 27.
Maksimovskaya, 335–337, 360, 362.
Mala Bereznik, 327–329, 335, 336–337, 341–342, 344, 345–349, 361–362, 363–364, 365–366, 368–369, 370–371, 372, 373, 375.
Malamir, H.M.S., 47.

Mallet, Sir L., G.C.M.G., C.B., 10.
Mamoura, 232, 233, 235, 237, 243.
Mandali, 281.
Manitou, H.M.T., 381.
Mantis, H.M.S., 269, 270.
Maqasis, 176, 177, 187, 205, 214, 251.
Maqil, 24, 26, 27, 145, 255, 258.
Mara, 273.
Marid, 38.
Marmariss, 9, 63.
Marshall, Lieut.-Gen. Sir W. R., K.C.B., 274, 282, 285, 286, 298, 299.
Martin, 18556 L./Cpl., 348, 349, 383.
Mason, Capt. A. E., 14, 23, 35, 106, 117, 130, 142, 163, 222, 224, 240, 308, 311, 324, 327, 331, 355, Appendix xiv.
Mason's Mounds, 184.
Matthews, Lieut. A. B., R.E., 81, 108.
Maude, Lieut.-Gen. Sir F. S., K.C.B., C.M.G., D.S.O., 193, 257, 258–260, 261, 263, 268–269, 270–271, 272–274, 279–280, 281–282.
Maunder, 2/Lieut. W., M.C., 312, 342.
Maxim Battery, 105–106, 118, 137.
McKay, Lieut. W. S., 312.
Meade, Capt. J. W., ix, 147, 169, 177, 192, 201, 208, 289, 297, 301–302, 311, 331, 354, 358, 362, 379, Appendix xiv.
Medical, 50, 67, 89–90, 116, 120–121, 148, 149, 173, 252, 255, 258, 272–273, 343, Appendices i, iii, vi, viii, xii.
Medina, Shaikh of, 51.
Mejidieh, H.M.S., 31.
Meldon, Major W. W., 71, 84, 88, Appendix xv.
Melliss, Major-Gen. Sir C. J., V.C., K.C.B., 45, 105–106, 125, 127, 223, 228, 229, 230, 231, 232, 233.
Mellor, Lieut. Sir J. S. P., Bart., viii, 107, 111, 112, 113, 114, 117, 118, 130, 138–139, 140, 141, 224, 240, 244, Appendix xv.
Meritorious Service Medal. See *Honours and Awards*.
Merritt, 9673 Pte. E. G., 222, 247, Appendix xi.
Mersina, 235.
Mesopotamia, 7, 8–9, 16–18.
Mesopotamia Commission, 257, 278–279.
Miles, Pte., 87.
Milford, Lieut. T. R., 203, 264, 266, 288, 298, Appendix xiv.
Military Cross. See *Honours and Awards*.
Military Medal. See *Honours and Awards*.
Miller, General E., 314, 316–317.
Miller, 9143 Pte. P. R., D.C.M., 221, Appendix xi.
Mills, Pte., 87.
Miner, H.M.S., 25, 31, 32, 57, 60–62.
Mirage, 20, 79, 80.
Mohammerah, Shaikh of, 7, 10, 11, 15, 17, 20, 21, 24, 34, 36, 39.
Monro, General Sir C. C., G.C.M.G., K.C.B., 257, 259, 260.
Moore, Sir John, K.B., 282, 324, 358.
Morjegorskaya, 364.

Morland, Major W. E. T., D.S.O., M.C., viii, 23, 28, 36, 41, 52, 54, 58, 65, 71, 90, 102, 108, 163, 190, 215, 216, 217, 221, 222, 224, 239, Appendix xiv.
Mortars. See *Trench Mortar Battery*.
Mosul, 63, 76, 101–102, 120.
Mosul, 229, 230, 231, 237, 241, 244, 247, 248, 272, 279, 298.
Moth, H.M.S., 270.
Moulding, 2/Lieut. J., 312.
Mousley, Capt. E. O., 228, 231, 232.
Mudelil, 260.
Mundey, Capt. S. C. B., 70, 219, 222, 223, 224, 240, Appendix xiv.
Munn, Serjt. A. C., 129, 173, 219, 225, 229.
Muntafik, 8, 27.
Murmansk, 304, 305, 306, 313, 316, 324, 350, 382.
Murphy, Capt. D., 14, 23, 70, 106, 115, 267, 301–302, Appendix xiv.
Murray, General Sir A., 302, 310.
Murray, 2/Lieut. C. H., 285, 301–302, Appendix xiv.
Murray, Lieut. K. R., 147, 168, 178, Appendix xv.
Musaiyib, 16.
Musandaq, 151.
Mushahida, 273.
Muzaffari, 43.
Muzaibila, 27, 55, 61, 62.
Muzaira'a, 25, 29, 31, 32, 35, 36, 37, 57.

NAHR AL KALEK, 270.
Nahr Umar, 278.
Nasiriya, 27, 30, 35, 38, 43, 47, 49, 69, 70, 72, 182, 257.
Navy. See *Royal Navy*.
Naylor, Capt. G., M.C., viii, ix, 14, 24, 47, 70, 107, 116, 117, 119, 130, 137, 138, 140, 163, 170, 171, 190, 212–213, 214, 221, 222, 224, 239, 246–248, 308, 311, 336–342, 344, 345, 349, 358, 359, 360, 361, 372–373, 383, Appendices xiv, xvii.
Nazim Bey, 217, 287, 296.
Neale, 8732 Pte. J. W., 90, Appendix xi.
Neville, Lieut. J. E. H., M.C., 308, 311, 336, 339, 346, 347, 348, 362, 383, Appendices xiv, xvii.
Newton, L./Cpl., 370.
Nicholas II, Tsar of Russia, 303–304.
Nicholls, Pte., 280.
Nijni Kitsa, 329, 330, 334, 336, 344, 350, 354, 359, 361, 363–364, 371, 372, 373, 374, 375.
Nisibin, 230, 231, 232, 237, 242, 244, 247, 248.
Nixon, General Sir J., K.C.B., K.C.V.O., 44, 46, 47, 48–49, 53, 54, 65, 67, 69, 72–80, 93, 94, 95, 97, 102, 107, 121, 132, 133, 144–145, 148, 157, 205–208.
Norfolk Hill, 40, 45, 54–62.
North-West Frontier, 6, 47, 68, 260, 272, 282, 298.
Northcote, Major A. F., D.S.O., 312, 341–342, 367–369, 372.
Northcote, Lieut. D. S., ix, 289, Appendix xiv.

INDEX

Nuhairat, 48, 57, 58.
Nukhaila, 37, 38, 43, 46.
Nukhailat, 77, 79, 80, 81, 176.
Nukhta, 273, 284.
Nunn, Capt., C.M.G., D.S.O., R.N., 124, 216, 217, 270.
Nur-ud-Din, 78, 80, 108–119, 122, 125, 215.

OBOZERSKAYA, 356.
Observation Post, Qurna, 40, 46.
Odessa, 15, 304.
Odin, H.M.S., 10, 11, 19, 25, 46, 51, 52, 57, 58–63.
Officers, 14, Appendices xiv, xv, xvi.
Olliff, Cpl., 89.
Omaiya, 261.
One Tower Hill, 40, 45, 46, 54–62.
One Tree Hill, 45, 54–62.
Onega, 356, 363, 364, 379–380.
Ora, 77, 162.
Osinova, 326, 351.

P 1. (Paddler No. 1), 74.
P 2., 57, 63, 76, 93.
P 3., 54, 74.
P 5., 121.
P 32., 280.
P 35., 281.
P 52., 261.
Packer, Armourer Q.M.S., 227.
Paines, 2/Lieut. F. W., 312.
Palestine, 280, 281, 283, 298.
Pan-Islamic Movement, 2, 7.
Pan-Turanian Movement, 2, 282.
Parker, Capt. O. M., 312.
Parkes, 9166 L./Cpl., D.C.M., 39, 90.
Parkinson, Lieut. E. B., 147, 169, 178, 192, 201, 261, 264, 266, 288, 291, 298, Appendix xiv.
Parr, Lieut.-Colonel H. O., 224, 239.
Parsley, Lieut., 133.
Pear Drop Bend, 54.
Peck, Capt. A. J., 312, 364, 366, 370.
Perm, 356.
Perry, Lieut. M. H. C., 312.
Persia, 7, 10, 30, 72–73, 132, 165, 259, 272, 277, 280, 282, 298.
Persian Gulf, 2, 5, 8, 15, 43.
Petrograd, 304, 313, 324, 356.
Phillips, Pte., 280.
Pinega, River, 323, 358.
Pioneer, 270.
Pioneers. See under *Regiments*.
Pipe-Line. See *Anglo-Persian Oilfields*.
Pless, 369, 372.
Plevna, 166.
Policy, 27, 30, 34–35, 44, 48–49, 72–73, 95–98, 133, 257–260, 356–358.
Ponting, Serjt. F. G., viii, 239, Appendix xi.
Pools of Siloam, 178.
Pope-Hennessy, Lieut.-Colonel L. H. R., C.B., D.S.O., viii, 256, 264, 266, 276, Appendices xiii, xiv.
Port Said, 301.

Posante. See *Bozanti*.
Powell, Capt. J. J., viii, 24, 35, 41, 61, 63, 65, 71, 87–89, 90, Appendix xiv.
Pozanti. See *Bozanti*.
Price, Capt. A., 68, 71, 289, 290, 291, 297, Appendix xv.
Prinkipo, 240.
Prior, Serjt., 301–302.
Prisoners, Officers, 239–244, 245.
Prisoners, Rank and File, 224, 225, 226, 227, 228, 229–232, 233, 234, 235, 236, 246–248, 249, Appendix xi.
Puchega, 334.
Pursglove, 6907 Serjt. A. E., D.C.M., 59, 65, 89, 222, Appendix xi.
Purvey, 28150 Pte., 286.
Pusht-i-Kuh, Vali of, 36.

QALA SALIH, 17, 63, 64, 161, 260.
Qala Shadi, 128, 269, 270.
Qasr-i-Shirin, 273.
Qurna, 16, 21, 24–25, 26, 28, 29, 30–31, 33, 35, 36, 40–41, 43, 45–46, 51–63, 134, 161, 257, 260, 278.
Qusaiba, 106.

RADCLIFFE, Major F. W., 19.
Raddatz, General, 274.
Radford, Lieut. H. D. H., 177, 185, 198, 200, 201, 208, 254, Appendices ix, xiv.
Railway Front, 320, 335, 356–357, 363.
Railways, 257, 260, 262, 270, 272, 275, 277–278.
Rakestrow, 9020 L./Cpl. W. G., 222, Appendix xi.
Ramadi, 280, 281, 285, 301.
Rance, Lieut. J. E. W., 312.
Rance, Lieut. W., viii, 147, 168, 178, 192, 197, 198, 298, Appendices ix, xiv.
Rankin, 8848 Pte. R. W., 222.
Ras al 'Ain, 230, 231, 232, 237, 242, 243, 244, 247.
Rawlinson, General Sir H., 311, 364.
Read, 9421 L./Cpl. T. P. O., 244, Appendix xi.
Redoubt "A," Kut, 137, 138, 185, 189.
Redoubt "B," Kut, 134, 163, 170, 171, 172, 185, 188, 189.
Regatta, The Qurna, 56–57, 58–62.
Regiment, British, 2/10th Royal Scots, 328.
Regiment, British, 1/5th The Queens, 288.
Regiment, British, 1/5th The Buffs, 271, 301.
Regiment, British, Royal Warwickshire, 309, 312, 329, 335–336, 350, 354, 363–364, 365–366, 370–371, 375.
Regiment, British, 45th Royal Fusiliers, 358.
Regiment, British, 46th Royal Fusiliers, 351, 358, 369, 370, 377.
Regiment, British, 2nd Norfolk, 14, 20, 25, 31–32, 34, 64, 141, 170, 183, 209, 224, 262, 264, 269–271, 276, 301.
Regiment, British, Devonshire, 309, 312, 332, 335–336, 341–342, 354, 358, 362, 366–369, 372, 379.
Regiment, British, 1/6th Devonshire, 261.

Regiment, British, 1/4th Somerset Light Infantry, 74.
Regiment, British, 2nd Leicestershire, 143, 183, 194–199, 252.
Regiment, British, 1/4th Border, 74.
Regiment, British, 2/4th Border, 74.
Regiment, British, 2nd Hampshire, 308, 358, 381.
Regiment, British, 1/4th Hampshire, 39, 51, 153, 209.
Regiment, British, 2/7th Hampshire, 281.
Regiment, British, 2nd Dorsetshire, 14, 19, 76, 80, 82–86, 112–114, 209, 261, 276.
Regiment, British, 1/4th Dorsetshire, 22, 281, 292.
Regiment, British, 2nd Black Watch, 151, 194, 253, 271.
Regiment, British, 43rd Light Infantry, 13, 14, 22, 23, 24, 26, 27, 29, 31–37, 40–41, 45–46, 48, 51–71, 74–90, 93–95, 99, 101–102, 107–121, 123–131, 134–143, 146–147, 160, 162–166, 170–175, 185–190, 208–220, 223–249, 252–256, 260–267, 275–277, 280, 281, 284–287, 289–302, 308–314, 317, 324–328, 330–332, 335–337, 339–349, 355, 358–363, 365–377, 379, 381–384, Appendix xvii.
Regiment, British, 2/43rd Light Infantry, 160–162, 167–169, 177–181, 183, 184, 192, 194–200, 202–204, 208. See 43rd.
Regiment, British, 52nd Light Infantry, 14, 309.
Regiment, British, 1st Sherwood Foresters, 382–383.
Regiment, British, 6th Loyal, 271.
Regiment, British, Royal Berkshire, 309, 312, 325, 331, 344, 353–354, 358, 379–381.
Regiment, British, Royal Marines, 351.
Regiment, British, 2nd Royal West Kent, 33, 37, 68, 124, 160, 162, 209.
Regiment, British, 2/4th Wiltshire, 74.
Regiment, British, 1st Manchester, 180.
Regiment, British, 2nd Highland Light Infantry, 364.
Regiment, British, 1st Seaforth Highlanders, 149, 194, 269.
Regiment, British, 1st Connaught Rangers, 162.
Regiment, British (Composite Battalion), "Norsets," Norfolk and Dorsetshire Regts., 169.
Regiment, British (Composite Battalion), Highland (Black Watch and Seaforths), 194, 203, 252, 253.
Regiment, British (Provisional Battalion), 153, 155–156, 159.
Regiment, Indian, 2nd Q.V.O. Rajput Light Infantry, 159.
Regiment, Indian, 4th Prince Albert Victor's Rajputs, 33, 36, 261.
Regiment, Indian, 6th Jat Light Infantry, 151, 284, 289–296.
Regiment, Indian, 7th Duke of Connaught's Own Rajputs, 14, 20, 25, 27, 31–33, 34, 35, 44, 113.
Regiment, Indian, 9th Bhopal, 151.
Regiment, Indian, 11th Rajputs, 39.
Regiment, Indian, 20th Duke of Cambridge's Own Infantry (Brownlow's Punjabis), 14, 19, 34, 80, 82–87, 269.
Regiment, Indian, 22nd Punjabis, 14, 31–33, 37, 56–63, 74, 82–87, 108–120, 127, 137, 139, 185.
Regiment, Indian, 24th Punjabis, 44, 117, 284, 289–296.
Regiment, Indian, 26th Punjabis, 179.
Regiment, Indian, 34th Sikh Pioneers, 178.
Regiment, Indian, 2/39th Garwhal Rifles, 288.
Regiment, Indian, 41st Dogras, 151.
Regiment, Indian, 44th Merwara Infantry, 33.
Regiment, Indian, 48th Pioneers, 20, 44–45, 78, 81, 105–106, 108–120, 141, 290, 296.
Regiment, Indian, 51st Sikhs (Frontier Force), 143, 183, 194–199.
Regiment, Indian, 53rd Sikhs (Frontier Force), 143, 194–199.
Regiment, Indian, 56th Punjabi Rifles (Frontier Force), 143, 151–153, 194–199.
Regiment, Indian, 66th Punjabis, 39, 116.
Regiment, Indian, 67th Punjabis, 39, 68, 80, 137, 138, 170.
Regiment, Indian, 76th Punjabis, 44, 105–106, 118.
Regiment, Indian, 90th Punjabis, 33, 37, 286.
Regiment, Indian, 92nd Punjabis, 153, 203, 269.
Regiment, Indian, 96th Berar Infantry, 261.
Regiment, Indian, 1/97th Deccan Infantry, 284, 286, 289–296.
Regiment, Indian, 103rd Mahratta Light Infantry, 14, 27, 31–33, 37, 41, 54, 56–63, 67, 79, 82–86, 127, 137, 139–140, 141.
Regiment, Indian, 104th Wellesley's Rifles, 14, 25, 45, 82–87, 116.
Regiment, Indian, 107th Pioneers, 144, 153.
Regiment, Indian, 110th Mahratta Light Infantry, 14, 20, 25, 115.
Regiment, Indian, 117th Mahrattas, 14, 19, 38, 82–86, 116.
Regiment, Indian, 119th Infantry (The Mooltan Regiment), 14, 31–33, 41, 54–64, 75, 79, 82–85, 108–120, 137, 139, 140.
Regiment, Indian, 2/119th Infantry (The Mooltan Regiment), 256, 263.
Regiment, Indian, 120th Rajputana Infantry, 14, 20, 25.
Regiment, Indian, 128th Pioneers, 151–153.
Regiment, Indian, 130th Baluchistan Infantry, 14.
Regiment, Indian, 2/5th Gurkha Rifles (Frontier Force), 292.
Regiment, Indian, 1/6th Gurkha Rifles, 276.
Regiment, Indian, 2/6th Gurkha Rifles, 292.
Regiment, Indian, 2/7th Gurkha Rifles, 44, 80, 116, 117, 256.
Regiment, Indian, 1/8th Gurkha Rifles, 269.
Regiment, Indian, 9th Gurkha Rifles, 254.
Regiment, Bolshevik, 6th Soviet, 331, 353, 354.
Regiment, Bolshevik, 156th, 348, 353, 354, 362, 365–369.
Regiment, Bolshevik, 161st, 370, 373.

Regiment, Russian (White), 3/4th North Russian Rifles, 358, 359, 362, 367–369.
Regiment, Slavo-British Legion, 1st Battalion, 318, 337, 351–353, 356–357.
Regiment, Turkish, 43rd, 141.
Regiment, Turkish, 114th, 9.
Regiment, Turkish, 169th, 293.
Reilly, Major H. L., R.F.C., 103.
Reynardson, Capt. H. T. Birch, viii, 24, 34, 36, 51–53, 58, 70, 86–87, 93, 106, 115, 119, Appendix xiv.
Rice, 8765 Pte. C., 254.
Rice, Brig.-Gen. G. B. H., 151.
Richardson, 8093 Serjt., 225, Appendix xi.
Riddle, Lieut. A. E. S., 254, 285, 289, Appendix xiv.
Rikesika, 379.
Riley, Lieut. C. H., 147, 169, 178, 192, Appendices ix, xiv.
Ripon, North, 383.
Robbins, Pte., 347.
Roberts, Lieut. B. F., 177, 185, 192, 261, 264–266, 288, 298, Appendix xiv.
Roberts, Capt. F. M., M.C., ix.
Robertson, General Sir W. R., G.C.B., K.C.V.O., D.S.O. (C.I.G.S.), 258–260, 263.
Robins, 8148 C.Q.M.S. W. E., D.C.M., 222.
Robinson, Brig.-Gen. C. T., 38.
Rock, Lieut. L. J., viii, 254, 264, 267, 285, Appendix xiv.
Rosher, Lieut.-Colonel H. L., 19, 38.
Rout, 8335 Pte. J. A., 88.
Royal Engineers, Appendices i, vi, vii, viii, xii.
Royal Flying Corps, 57, 77, 79, 82–88, 103, 257, Appendices viii, xii. See also *Aircraft*.
Royal Navy, 25–26, 209, 305, 320, 351 Appendices i, vi.
Roysterer, H.M. Tug, 381.
Ruck, 21452 Pte., 184.
Rumailan Kabir, 230, 242.
Rumania, 260, 283, 307.
Russia, 1–2, 165, 260, 272, 274, 279, 282, 303–308, 357.
Russia, North, 302, 303–308, 314–317, 319–326, 334–335, 357, 363, 364, 369, 374, 384.
Ruta, 27, 29, 31–34, 53, 55, 56, 62.
Rutland, Pte., 60.
Rybot, Major N. V. L., D.S.O., ix.

SABORNAYA QUAY, 314, 318, 324.
Sadiya, 277.
Sadler, Pte., 355, Appendix xi.
Sahil, 21, 33.
Sahiliya, 285–290, 296–298.
Saihan, 20.
Sakhlawiya Canal, 273.
Sakrikiya, 27.
Salimi, 43, 51–52.
Salonika, 248, 298.
Samarra, 17, 229, 230, 239, 244, 246, 274, 278, 282.
Samawa, 259.
Sandes, Major E. W. C., R.E., 170.

Sannaiyat, 77–78, 169, 176, 177, 183, 193–200, 202, 214, 250, 252, 263, 268–269, 293, Appendix ix.
Sanniya, 20.
Sappers and Miners, 3rd, 12th Company, 44, 144, 178.
Sappers and Miners, 3rd, 13th Company, 132, 155–156, 159.
Sappers and Miners, 3rd, 17th Company, 20, 24–25, 31, 77, 81.
Sappers and Miners, 3rd, 22nd Company, 14, 77, 82–86, 112.
Sappers and Miners, Sirmur, 137, 170, 185.
Saratoga, 224, 237.
Savitch, General, 318.
Sawyer, 2/Lieut. C. A., 308, 311, 344–348, 363, 378, Appendices xiv, xvii.
Saxby, 8592 Pte. W. H., 222, Appendix xi.
Scriven, 29038 Pte. W., 254.
Seager, C. S., ix.
Sedgefly, H.M.S., 280.
Seletskoe, 358, 362.
Seltso, 329, 331–333, 343, 345, 350, 353–355, 358, 360, 362, 366, 367, 369, 370, 372, 375.
Senna Canal, 178, 181, 182.
Serbia, 260.
Seymour, Capt. A. H., 147, 168, 177, 192, 198, 200, 201, 253, Appendices ix, xv.
Shahraban, 273, 279.
Shaiba, 24, 34, 35, 37, 38, 43–46, 134, 165, 248.
Shaikh Saad, 74, 76–77, 148–149, 151–153, 155, 161–163, 184, 191, 251, 253, 257, 260–262, 270, 275, 276.
Shaitan, H.M.S., 25, 57, 62–64, 101.
Shakeshaft, Capt. A. J., 216, 217, 228, 229, 231.
Shamshamiya, 19.
Sharqat, 229, 237, 241, 244, 247, 248.
Shatt al Adhaim, 273, 274.
Shatt al Arab, 8, 10–12, 16.
Shatt al Hai, 27, 38, 69, 72, 134, 137, 167, 176, 179, 185, 259–261, 263, 268–269.
Shaw, Abraham, 14.
Shegovari, 334, 353, 360.
Shepherd, Lieut. J. G., 289, 298, Appendix xiv.
Sherlock, Armourer Staff-Serjt., 285.
Shiaba, 227, 233.
Shilcock, 5787 C.S.M. T. J., 60, 65.
Shiraz, 43.
Shrapnel Hill, 55, 61, 62.
Shukri Bey, 280, 287.
Shumran, 129, 148, 167, 187, 219, 223–226, 237, 239, 244, 263, 268–270, 275.
Shushan, 43, 53, 57–62, 101.
Shwaiyib River, 25, 30, 35, 37, 41.
Sikkim, 250.
Simpson, Major R. V., 24, 58, 62, 68, 70, 88, Appendix xiv.
Sindiya, 273.
Singleton, Lieut. M., R.N., 63.
Sinn. See *Es Sinn*.
Sinn Abtar Redoubt, 176, 179, 251.
Siskoe, 378.
Slattery, Lieut. S. C. P., 326.

Smith, C.S.M., 169.
Smith, 8057 L./Sergt. F., D.C.M., 222, Appendix xi.
Smith, Lieut. H. V., 298, Appendix xiv.
Smith, 21883 Pte., 254.
Smyth, Lieut. H. E. F., M.C., viii, ix, 177, 178, 192, 250, 251, 264, 266, 289, 297, 298, 301–302, 311, 383, Appendix xiv.
Somme, 260.
Souhanets, 326.
Spackman, Lieut., I.M.S., 244.
Spencer, Pte. A. V., 275.
Spooner, Rev. H., 119, 232.
Staley, Lieut. F. C., 147, 168, 178, 181, Appendix xv.
Stapleton, Lieut.-Colonel F. H., C.M.G., viii, 24, 48, 65, 71, 221, 276, 280, Appendices xiii, xiv.
Startin, Capt. J., M.C., R.A.M.C., 24, 47, 71, 89, 106, 117, 130, 190, 221, 222, 224, Appendix xv.
Steele, Lieut. L. V., 289, Appendix xv.
Stephens, Major R., viii, 24, 29, 35, 59–62, 66, 71, Appendix xiv.
Stevens, Pte., 89.
Stevens, 7478 Serjt. E. W., 65.
Stokes, 8484 Pte. C., 222, Appendix xi.
Sturge, Pte., 201.
Sturges, Lieut. O. H. M., 311, 328, 336, 339, 342, 343, 383, Appendices xiv, xvii.
Subhi Bey, 25.
Suez Canal, 5, 301.
Sulaiman Askari Bey, 29, 32, 33, 45, 248.
Sumaika, 277.
Sumana, H.M.S., 43, 51, 57, 62–64, 101, 128, 134–136, 214, 270.
Sunaidij, 240, 241.
Suq ash Shuyukh, 47, 69.
Suwada Marsh, 77–78, 79, 84–87.
Suwaikiya Marsh, 71, 81, 149, 155–157, 169, 172, 193, 196, 198, 202–203.
Swift, 8395 Serjt. T., D.C.M., 222, 239, 345, Appendix xi.
Swinhoe, Capt. L. R., 312, 362.
Sylvester, Serjt., 301–302.

Tahiti, S.S., 301.
Tamplin, Lieut., R.F.A., 346, 348, 353.
Tappin, 9633 Pte. G., 54, Appendix xi.
Taranto, 248, 301.
Tarantula, H.M.S., 270.
Tarsus, 235, 243.
Tatton, Capt. R. H. G., 147, 162, 167–169, 177, 183, 192, 197, Appendices ix, xiv.
Taurus Mountains, 235, 277.
Taylor, 7740 Pte. A. H., 230, Appendix xi.
Tehran, 34.
Tel Ermin, 244, 247.
Terry, Capt. W. E. C., 256, 261, 264, 267, Appendix xiv.
Thompson, Lieut. A. L., 289, 298, Appendix xiv.
Thongwa, H.M.T., 23, 24.
Thorny Nala, 182, 184.
Tigris, 16–17.

Tigris Line of Communication Defences, 260–261, 270, 275, 276.
Tikrit, 229, 237, 240, 241, 244, 246–248, 282, 285.
Times, The, 344, 350–351, 357.
Titherington, Capt. and Brevet-Major G. W., 203, 208, 250, 254, 255, 264, 266, 288, 297, 299, 308, Appendices xiii, xiv.
Tompkins, Lieut. A. L., 298, Appendix xiv.
Topsa, 351.
Townshend, Major-Gen. Sir C. V. F., K.C.B., D.S.O., 48, 53, 54, 61–64, 66, 73–80, 88, 96–99, 101, 102, 105–117, 121–126, 128–143, 146, 157, 159, 163, 165–166, 172, 185–188, 201, 205, 207–212, 215, 216, 219, 223, 224, 239, 278.
Transport, Land, 44, 47, 75, 77, 100, 101, 144, 148, 179, 181, 257, 260, 334.
Transport, River, 21, 28, 34–35, 38, 39, 44, 47, 67, 76, 89, 97, 100, 144–145, 148, 149, 182, 183, 257, 258, 260, 278, 323, 325, 354, 362, 374.
Trench Mortar Battery, 239th Light, 312, 326, 336, 366, 372, 381.
Trengrouse, 2/Lieut. W. T., 308, 312, Appendix xiv.
Trewheler, 2/Lieut. N., 312, 319, 331, 361–362, 373.
Trine, 10497 Cpl. G., H.L.I., 222, Appendix xi.
Tripoli, 9.
Troitsa, 351, 364, 370.
Trotsky, 304.
Truman, 2/Lieut. A. H., 147, 169, 178, 192, 197, Appendices ix, xiv.
Tschaykovski, M., 350.
Turco-Italian War, 2.
Turkey, 1–3, 8–12, 30, 226–249, 280, 298, 307, 357.
Turkish Army, 8–12, 33, 35, 37–38, 55–56, 74, 77–78, 100, 103, 136–172, 176, 191, 285, 287–296, 298.
Turner, Pte., 53.
Twin Canals, 182, 257, 260, 262, 276.

UKRAINIA, 304, 307.
Umm al Baram Marsh, 176.
Umm at Tubul, 124, 125–127, 130, 131, 239, 280.
Umm Qasr, 15.
Upstone, Cpl., D.C.M., 87, 90, 119, Appendix xi.
Uqbah, 285.
Ust Pinega, 325, 378.
Ust Vaga, 327–329, 331, 335, 344, 354, 362–363, 366–370, 374–377, 379.

VAGA COLUMN, 327, 331, 334, 352–353, 360, 361, 369, 371, 373, 374, 379, 384, Appendix xviii.
Vaga River, 323, 324, 326, 328–329, 334, 354, 361.
Verchni-Konets, 375.
Verdun, 172, 260.
Viatka, 320, 324, 335.
Vigo, 237.
Vine, Lieut. E. G., 289, 298, Appendix xv.
Vital Point, 104, 106, 109, 110, 114, 115.
Vogt, 234.
Voller, 5235 C.Q.M.S. T., 225, 232, 247–248, Appendix xi.

INDEX

Vologda, 335.
V.P. See *Vital Point*.

WADHAM, 2/Lieut. J. W., 312.
Wadi, 155–156, 162, 177, 180–181, 183, 184, 187, 250, 251.
Wadi Brooking, 291–297.
Wadi Haqlan, 295.
Wadi Hauran, 294–296.
Wadi Khanana, 241.
Wakeford, Lieut., R.E., 346, 348, 356, 362, 371, 375.
Wallace, Capt., 114.
War Committee, 259–260.
Ward, 6334 Serjt. W., D.C.M., 221, 225, 237, Appendix xi.
Warnock, Serjt., 344, 383.
Warren, Lieut. R. C., M.C., 308, 311, 324, Appendix xiv.
Water Redoubt, 110–112, 114, 116, 118, 119.
Watson, Capt., R.F.A., 377.
Watts, Lieut. L. R., 254, 289, Appendix xiv.
Webb, 21997 Pte., 254.
Webber, Lieut. S. L., 71, 106, 115, Appendix xv.
Wells, Lieut.-Colonel B. C., 351.
Wells, Lieut. P. G., 264, 267, Appendix xv.
Wells, Pte., 67.
Westropp, Lieut. L. H. M., 312.
Wheelwright, Major T. H., 264, Appendix xiv.
White, 6467 O.R.Q.M.S. F. E., 225, 232, Appendix xi.
White, 9615 Serjt. J. H., M.M., 341, 342, Appendix xviii.
White Sea, 313–314, 323, 382.
Whittall, Capt. and Brevet-Major G. E., M.C., viii, 23, 34, 65, 71, 221, 258, 266, 267, 277, 280, 288–297, 299, 301–302, 383, Appendices xiii, xiv.

Widcombe, 2/Lieut. C. I., 147, 169, 178, 192, 197, Appendices ix, xiv.
Wilcox, 2/Lieut. M. A., 312.
Wilks, 8903 Pte. H., 254.
Williams, 9302 L./Cpl. H. G., 227, Appendix xi.
Williams, Lieut. T. P., viii, 250–254, 289, Appendix xiv.
Willingdon, Lady, 26
Wilmot, Lieut. D. A. T., ix, 147, 168, 177, 261, 264, 266, 289, Appendix xiv.
Wilson, Sir Arnold, 197.
Wilson, 2/Lieut. A. P., 107, 115, Appendix xv.
Wilson, Mrs. C. M., O.B.E., 237.
Wilson, 8210 Pte. G., 230, Appendix xi.
Wilson, 2/Lieut. S., 147, 168, 178, 192, Appendix xv.
Wooding, Capt. W. W., 147, 168, 264, 267, Appendix xiv.
Woolpress Village, 134, 261, 268.
Wright, 8985 L./Serjt. J., 88.
Wyld, Capt. J. W. G., 358, 362–363.
Wynter, Capt. F. C. W., 24, 70, 106, 112–115, Appendix xiv.

YAKASUB, 134. See *Woolpress Village*.
Yakovlevskoe, 334.
Yilderim, 277, 281.
Young, L./Cpl., 244.
Young, Serjt., 301–302.
Younghusband, Major-Gen. Sir G. J., K.C.M.G., K.C.I.E., C.B., 143, 148, 149, 151–153, 155–156, 177, 193–200, 203, 257.
Yozgad, 245–246, 249.
Yudenitch, General, 308.

ZOR, 99, 101–102, 124, 228, 271, 276.
Zubair, 43, 159.

www.ingramcontent.com/pod-product-compliance
Lightning Source LLC
Chambersburg PA
CBHW080720300426
44114CB00019B/2431